BRITANNIA

To B. W. T. Handford who first encouraged my interest in
Ancient History and Archaeology

BRITANNIA

A History of Roman Britain

Sheppard Frere

Routledge & Kegan Paul
London, Henley and Boston

First published in 1967
This revised edition published in 1978
by Routledge & Kegan Paul Ltd
39 Store Street
London WC1E 7DD,
Broadway House
Newtown Road
Henley-on-Thames
Oxon RG9 1EN and
9 Park Street
Boston, Mass. 02108, USA
Set in Intertype Lectura
Printed in Great Britain by
Lowe & Brydone Printers Limited,
Thetford, Norfolk

ISBN 0 7100 8916 3

CONTENTS

LIST OF PLATES

6

7

LIST OF TEXT-FIGURES

PREFACE

The advances made during the last twenty-five years in our knowledge of the history and archaeology of Roman Britain can be best illustrated by the extent to which R. G. Collingwood's great summary of the subject in *Roman Britain and the English Settlements* (1936) is now out of date. But the inspiration of his book when it appeared will not be forgotten by those who read it at the time, and there is no doubt of the value of a general summary of existing knowledge, if only as a spur to advance.

The present book is one of a series, by various authors, on the Provinces of the Roman Empire. Here I have tried to present the history of Roman Britain, using the available literary and epigraphic sources, and the results of archaeological research. I have not attempted to describe the archaeology of Roman Britain as such, and in those chapters which deal with the towns and countryside and the economics and religion of the province I have confined myself of set purpose to a selective historical interpretation rather than a general description of all available remains.

No one who sets out to write a book of this size on such a subject can well avoid making great use of the thoughts and works of other scholars in the field, some of which have become adopted imperceptibly into my own thoughts through constant reading, lecturing or discussion; and it may be that not all have been adequately acknowledged in footnotes or in the bibliography. This I hope will be taken by those concerned as a compliment. In particular, of course, I owe much to the earlier writings of Haverfield, Collingwood and Sagot, and much also to the published works of my friends and colleagues Mr A. L. F. Rivet, Professor E. Birley and the late Sir Ian Richmond. Professor Birley and Sir Ian Richmond have very kindly answered one or two questions which have arisen during the writing of the book, and I have also had help on particular topics from Mrs M. A. Cotton, Lady (Aileen) Fox, Mrs K. Hartley, Miss A. S. Robertson, Mrs A. Ravetz, Mr R. P. Wright, Dr J. C. Mann, Dr J. Wilkes, Mr J. S. Wacher, Dr J. P. C. Kent, Mr F. H. Thompson, Mr C. E. Stevens, Dr J. Morris, Mr H. C. Bowen, Dr G. Webster, Dr I. M. Stead and Professor W. G. Hoskins, all of whom I desire to thank. Above all, I owe much to the friendly criticism and suggestions of Mr B. R. Hartley, who has kindly read the whole book in its first typescript, to its great advantage. In most cases I have taken his advice, and always on questions of chronology, but he is not responsible for errors which may be due to my holding to my own opinion where we disagreed.

The great corpus of Romano-British inscribed stones, *The Roman Inscriptions of Britain*, Vol. 1, by R. G. Collingwood and R. P. Wright, appeared too late for me to use it while writing, but I have revised all references to inscriptions mentioned in the text, to give the *RIB* numbers, in the belief that this will now be standard practice. References to Dio's Roman History are to the text in the Loeb edition, and those to *Panegyrici Latini* are to the Oxford Text of Sir Roger Mynors. Reference by footnote is normally made to works specifically mentioned in the text: a wider selection of modern sources will be found in the bibliography at the end. I have often referred to general works from which primary references may be obtained, for otherwise the bibliography would have extended to inordinate length. Because Otto Seeck's edition of the *Notitia Dignitatum* was reprinted in 1962, I have not thought it necessary to print the British lists of the Notitia.

This book was written during 1964 and 1965 while I held a post at the Institute of Archaeology at London University. I have taken account of a few publications of later date. I have to thank Mr H. M. Stewart for much help with the maps, most of which are entirely drawn by him, and Miss H. Fuller for her careful typing and retyping of the text. I am also very grateful to Dr J. K. St Joseph, Mr Arnold Baker and Mr B. W. Cunliffe for providing photographs and to Lt-Col M. A. Lloyd for his drawing of the Verulamium inscription.

S. S. FRERE

January 1966

PREFACE TO SECOND EDITION

The resetting of this book for a paper-back edition has enabled me to undertake some revision. The archaeology of Roman Britain is a rapidly expanding subject. During the seven years which have elapsed since its first appearance, there have been important new discoveries as the result of excavation, field-work and aerial photography, some of which have changed historical perspectives or have thrown new or more detailed light upon questions discussed in the first edition; and there have also been numerous works of synthesis or discussion as well as publications of basic evidence, such as Mr B. R. Hartley's 'The Roman occupation of Scotland: the evidence of samian ware' in *Britannia* iii (1972), which have compelled radical reconsideration of opinions formerly held. I have tried to include as much of the new evidence as is relevant to the main themes of the book, within the limits of what can properly be called revision, but without attempting to rewrite the whole work. There are other fields, such as the Iron Age, or the fifth to seventh centuries, where comparable advances in knowledge or revolutions in outlook – and indeed in method – are being achieved, which would have involved a considerable lengthening of treatment. This has not been attempted: I have confined myself, in the main, in these sections of the book, to the correction of mistakes. The periods which precede or follow Roman Britain deserve their own books and are receiving full-scale treatment at other hands, as in B. W. Cunliffe's *Iron Age Communities in Britain* (1974), Leslie Alcock's *Arthur's Britain* (1971), J. N. L. Myres' *Anglo-Saxon pottery, the Settlement of England* and John Morris' *The Age of Arthur* (1973).

Thanks must be expressed to Professor P. A. Brunt, Mr A. R. Burn, Professor B. W. Cunliffe, Mr J. P. Gillam, Dr W. H. Manning and many other friends who have helped me to eradicate mistakes in the text or to include new information, and to Mrs M. Cox for re-drawing the maps.

S. S. FRERE

January 1974

ROMAN BRITAIN

■ Inchtuthil
CALEDONIAN
CONFEDERACY
■ Carpow

◎ Coloniae or Municipia
● Civitas capitals
○ Other towns
■ Fortresses
Civitas boundaries approximate only.

Roman Miles
0   50   100

COAL

VOTADINI

DAMNONII

SELGOVAE

NOVANTAE

IRON

COAL
Corbridge
Carlisle
TEXTOVERDI
CARVETII
LEAD
Kirkby Thore

Anglesey
COPPER

LEAD
COPPER
DECEANGLI
CANGANI

ORDOVICES

DEMETAE

GOLD

Carmarthen

SILURES
IRON

Isca Venta Silurum
COAL

Kenchester

LEAD

DUMNONII

TIN

TIN

B
R
I
G
A
N
T
E
S

CABRANTOVICES

JET
Catterick
Isurium
Brigantum
YORKSHIRE
POTTERIES
LEAD
York PARISI
Brough
Petuaria

SETANTII

COAL
Wilderspool
Buxton
Deva Salinae
DERBYSHIRE
POTTERIES
POTTERY
LEAD
COAL
QUERNS
Templeborough
Lincoln
Horncastle

CORNOVII

LEAD
POTTERY
COPPER
Viroconium
Cornoviorum
Wall Mancetter
LEAD

CORITANI

SALT
Margidunum
Ancaster
IRON
STONE
Ratae
Corianorum
Durobrivae
Great Casterton
POTTERY
SALT
SALT

ICENI
Caister
Venta
Icenorum

POTTERY

Salinae
Alcester
DOBUNNI
Towcester
Godmanchester
Irchester
Cambridge
Great
Chesterford
Braughing
CATUVELLAUNI
Verulamium
TRINOVANTES
POTTERY
Camulodunum
OYSTERS
Caesaromagus

IRON
Glevum
Corinium
Dobunnorum
Alchester
OXFORD
POTTERIES
Dorchester
POTTERY
SALT

Cunetio
Calleva Atrebatum
ATREBATES
Londinium

STONE
Bath
Sandy Lodge
BELGAE
LEAD
NEW FOREST
POTTERIES
FARNHAM
POTTERIES
Venta
Belgarum
REGNENSES
IRON
IRON

CANTIACI
STONE Durovernum
Cantiacorum
Richborough
Dover
Lympne

Ilchester
Lindinis
DUROTRIGES
Dorchester
Durnovaria
PURBECK MARBLE
SHALE
Isca
Dumnoniorum

Bitterne, Clausentum
Novomagus
Regnensium
Isle of
Wight

Boulogne

I

The background:
the earliest British Iron Age

The civilisation of Roman Britain was a synthesis of things Roman and Celtic. Though it owed an incalculable debt to introductions from abroad and its preponderating element was imported from the civilisation of the Mediterranean, this civilisation took root in a Celtic land and enjoyed a native contribution: 'Romano-British' is a term not wholly synonymous with 'Roman'. Britain formed part of the Roman Empire for close on 400 years, a not inconsiderable slice of her total recorded history; and during this time there was ample opportunity for interaction and development. But a study of Roman Britain sees not only the processes of time at work; there were the powerful influences of geographical environment, as well as previous regional differences in the inheritance of the inhabitants, to modify and colour the history of the province. In this chapter and the next we must examine this environment and these differences, so that a picture can be formed of the British contribution to the synthesis.

The insularity of Britain has always been a factor, and in recent centuries an important factor, in her history. The complete security from invasion which she has enjoyed for 900 years, however, has been due to the existence of a strong central government and to the conscious development of naval and military policies impossible without centralisation. In more primitive times the existence of the Channel meant that, though settlement from overseas was possible, it rarely took the form of a full folk-migration, owing to difficulties of transport; invaders came and conquered, but their numbers were usually small enough to be gradually absorbed. Episodes such as the Roman conquest have been rare, partly for the reason stated and partly because the inhabitants of the opposite coasts for the most part lived in a disorganised barbarism almost as completely un-centralised.

Britain, lying as she does off the coast of north-west Europe, is accessible from various directions, and in different periods of history each direction in turn has achieved significance. Due west was Ireland, wealthy enough for trade but too small to be the source of more than raids, and facing a mountainous and on the whole in-hospitable shore. Due east the wide and stormy North Sea provided security until the appearance of more sea-worthy shipping in the late Roman period. The narrow waters of the English Channel give com-paratively easy access from similar lowland country on the plains of northern France; and it was from the coastlands stretching round from the Rhine delta to Brittany that most of the early settlers came. But a fourth route is available to maritime initiative from the western estuaries of France, from north-west Spain and ultimately indeed from the Mediterranean itself through the straits of Gibraltar; this leads to the south-western parts of Britain and both sides of the Irish Sea. This route was of great significance for the famous pre-historic tin trade of Cornwall, and enabled south-western Britain, and Ireland too, to maintain a tenuous contact with Mediterranean civilisation in the centuries following the fall of Rome. The travels of the Celtic Saints at that epoch match those of the neolithic settlers over the same waters 3,000 years earlier.

With access so easy to adequately equipped settlers from so many directions, it is not surprising to find that the human pattern of Iron Age Britain provides much variety. But the character of the Island itself offers very different environments in its various parts, such as would accentuate or foster differences, both in settlement pattern and in methods of livelihood. With primitive equipment and without a highly organised and centralised society, it was impossible for early settlers to do more than acquiesce in the facts of physical environ-ment. These were controlled by the influence which the geology of the country, in association with climate, exerted on vegetation. Even the highly organised Romans could do no more than modify these in-fluences. Indeed, their effect is still apparent today.

The geography of Britain shows a broad division into highland and lowland zones; the former, in the west and north, being an area of old hard rocks rising into moderate mountain chains up to 2,000 feet high or more, and for the most part barren and inhospitable owing to heavy rainfall and the leaching of the soil; the latter, in the east and south, consisting of more recent, less upstanding geological formations, softer and more readily weathered, and bearing more fertile soils. This broad distinction is of profound importance in itself, and is accentuated by the fact that much of the highland zone extends northwards into areas where inclement climate is an additional handicap to agriculture. In detail, of course, there is much variation. The highland zone is not a unity like the lowland, for Dumnonia is small and separated from Wales by the Bristol Channel, and Wales from the North by the Cheshire gap, a westward extension of the Midland Plain. In the highland zone pockets of lower, more fertile ground exist on which agricultural settlements can grow. But even where these areas were fully settled they were often cut off by inhospitable hills which prevented easy communications or mature political growth. In the lowland zone also the pattern was complex; comparatively large areas of light well-drained subsoil, such as gravel, chalk or limestone, are separated by belts of heavy clay which in primitive conditions were so heavily afforested that they formed barriers to intercommunication. Trackways developed along the ridges of well-drained hill-ranges, such as the famous Icknield Way, or the 'Pilgrims' Way' along the North Downs, or the 'Jurassic route' along the Cotswolds and through Northamptonshire up to Lincolnshire. Few rivers in Britain can compare with the rivers of Gaul for facilities offered to transport, but the role of the Thames in this respect should not be forgotten. It was one of the most outstanding contributions of Rome in Britain that she broke through the successive belts of forest with her new main roads (pl. 10a), and for the first time knit together the various habitable belts in one unified transport network, which for the most part radiated from London. Another was the construction of new towns on sites whose selection in most cases has been justified by the verdict of posterity. In the Iron Age nucleated settlement was conditioned for the most part by primitive considerations, such as the position of chieftains' strongholds or the existence of good agricultural soil. Only towards the close of the pre-Roman period did recent settlers, the Belgae, begin to develop large settlements on lower ground at river-crossings, which hint at the growth of trade. Such sites as Canterbury or Colchester illustrate this process, but the large settlements concerned were hardly to be described as towns. To Rome we owe the choice of such sites as London, York, Gloucester, Lincoln or Exeter where large modern towns still thrive, while sites like Reading or Shrewsbury or Norwich are but little removed from the position originally selected.

Evidence of Iron Age agriculture is well attested in south-east Britain, and as far north and west as the Jurassic belt; but beyond the Gloucester–Lincoln line a different economy seems to have been practised, that of pastoralism eked out by garden cultivation. Julius Caesar, though he did not penetrate within 100 miles of such people, was well informed when he wrote: 'The people of the interior for the most part do not sow corn but live on milk and meat, and dress in skins'. The wealth of such people, like that of the patriarchs of the Old Testament, was reckoned in cattle and sheep. Very large areas were required for pasturage, so that tribal lands might be very wide yet not heavily populated, and the people themselves may have been semi-nomadic, as they accompanied their flocks and herds in search of fresh pasture, and in the seasonal alternation from summer to winter grazing-grounds. It is evident that the control of such people posed a novel problem to the Roman authorities completely different from that of the settled agricultural peoples of the south. The former were more mobile, not tied to landed property or to valuable permanent homes, and probably they were physically tougher in war. Moreover, to move forward sufficient forces into such territory involved logistic complications over the supply of corn for the troops; it now had to be brought great distances from the growing-grounds. It is not surprising to find that a determined effort was made in the early years of the Roman occupation to limit the province to the lowland zone, at first with a frontier based on the Fosse Way, and, when that proved impossible, with another based on the line of the Severn; and that the intractable problem of the occupation of the rest was solved by a power able to develop transport facilities, including water transport, and willing to encourage the extension of intensive agriculture into areas which had not previously known it.

Yet advance into the highland zone was inevitable, not only because of the intransigent character of the inhabitants, whose immemorial custom it was to supplement their livelihood with booty or tribute exacted from the settled farmlands of their neighbours, but also because the mineral wealth of Britain lay very largely in the mountains. Of metals, only iron was to be found in the lowland zone, in the rich clay deposits of the Weald of Kent and Sussex and in the limestone of Northampton and Lincolnshire; lead from which silver could be won was present only in Somerset and copper in east Cheshire, though these last deposits were curiously neglected in the Roman period. Larger lead fields were to be sought in North Wales, Derbyshire or Yorkshire; copper in Wales and Anglesey; gold in Wales, tin in Cornwall and iron in the Forest of Dean. Apart from these minerals and others (like coal) of more restricted exploitation, the wealth of Britain lay in its corn lands, which produced an exportable surplus, in the leather and woollen products of its herds and flocks, and in its overflowing manpower, which Rome could put to good use in her armies on other frontiers. The value of Britain to the Empire, though not undisputed at the time,[1] is shown by the maintenance there for almost four centuries of a garrison amounting to a tenth part of the entire imperial army.

The general historical effect of Britain's geographical character is that the lowland zone, being nearer the continent and easier to overrun, has been the frequent recipient of new cultures which its agricultural wealth enabled to flourish; whereas the highland zone beyond lies farther from the source of new cultures, and by its very nature has been unable to receive them unmodified. These results are very apparent in the period of the Roman occupation of Britain, in which a flourishing Romano-British civilisation took root in the lowlands, while the highland zone was almost continuously a zone of military occupation held down by force, in which little spontaneous civilising development took place among the natives. But this is only the generalised pattern, for in detail quite large areas within the highland zone are, as we have seen, lowland in character, and some of them had always been accessible to the influence of the sea routes: in these areas, if military fluctuation allowed, civilisation of a sort could take root. Such areas are the plain of Glamorgan, parts of Yorkshire, the valley of the Eden and some of lowland Scotland. On the other hand, the conservative character of the north and west, with its ability to resist intrusion, had the effect of enabling traditions of Romano-British civilisation to survive there, if only faintly, long after the collapse of Roman Britain itself. And these traditions could be nurtured by contacts, via the western sea-ways, with surviving centres in Gaul and in the Mediterranean basin itself.

The relatively small numbers to which invading or migrating bands were confined by the difficulties of crossing the sea, and the consequent survival in Britain of older strains of culture unsubmerged, had the effect of giving the British Iron Age a strongly insular character. Though some originality can be seen in the development of its art or, on a lower plane, of special weaving appliances, it is insularity which is strikingly demonstrated in such mundane features as the ubiquitous employment of round rather than rectangular houses: for the round house is an insular feature continuously employed from the Bronze Age, while on the Continent rectangular houses were in fashion.[2] Because of this insularity, the cultures of the British Iron Age, though they derive from continental cultures, do not strictly correspond in detail. There is much overlapping. The use of continental cultural descriptions is thus apt to be misleading, nor, of course, can we yet discern or use the names of actual tribes; and an insular terminology has accordingly been evolved. In the British Iron Age three principal cultural groupings have been recognised, and classified as Iron A, Iron B and Iron C. These cultures had their histories, but the terms A, B and C are cultural not chronological; the A culture, though the first to start, could overlap or outlast in some areas the development of B or C cultures in others, and Iron B and Iron C will be found to continue in adjacent regions side by side. The chronology of the Iron Age is best dealt with by division into Periods as follows: Period I 650–350; Period II 350–150; Period III 150–the Roman Conquest. As could be anticipated, the growth of knowledge has shown the cultural pattern to be complex, but regional differences can be classified by geographical and numerical qualifications, such as Southern First A or South-Western Third B. Such a system of classification requires an intellectual effort to master it, but granted the complexity of the pattern, this effort of memory is less than that required if purely cultural labels derived from type sites, such as the 'All Cannings Cross' or 'Hunsbury' cultures, were to be used instead, since the former system contains its own clues. In recent years, it is true, some have expressed the wish to resume the use of cultural labels in accordance with the normal practice in Prehistory; but as yet no general system of that kind has been fully stated or agreed, such as could be used with any clarity as an alternative to that set out in this and the following chapters. Here it will not be necessary to survey the Iron Age cultures of Britain in detail from the beginning: rather an attempt will be made to give a general outline as a background for the more detailed survey of Britain on the eve of the Roman conquest which is offered in Chapters 2 and 4.

Iron A

The expansion of European societies and the migrations of peoples had already resulted in the movement of groups into Britain during the Late Bronze Age and the forging of strong cultural links with the continent. This process was still continuing as the knowledge of iron-working became diffused: the innovations now introduced were further examples of contacts which had been intermittently maintained for 500 years, and the settlers who brought the first iron-using cultures to these islands were but following in the footsteps of their kindred. Knowledge of the new metal, however, was to prove a great advance: for iron is much more widespread than copper or tin, and thus in time metallic tools became available more cheaply and to a wider section of society.

The earliest users of iron reached Britain probably quite late in the seventh century BC. Already at that date men had been coming individually and in small groups to penetrate the eastern coasts; and in South Wales, too, finds near Cardiff and at Llyn Fawr in Glamorgan show penetration, perhaps in search of iron deposits. The type of sword (Hallstatt C) currently used by warriors on the mainland of Europe was introduced here and soon copied locally, and these British copies are themselves found on the continent: before long, however, for whatever reason, the use of swords was discontinued. By the end of the sixth century workshops had been established here which were manufacturing a specifically British kind of dagger; they were to continue producing for two centuries. Thus indigenous peoples were quick to take advantage of the new technology. The culture of these early adventurers and settlers was the continental Hallstatt culture, the first to have the use of iron in Europe. This began to be superseded in parts of western Europe by the culture known as La Tène about the middle of the fifth century; and later settlers of this early phase of our Iron Age were already being affected to greater or lesser extent by La Tène developments. These developments did not, of course, appear everywhere on the Continent at once, and people living in the extreme north-western fringes might remain unaffected, or only partially affected, for some time. Iron A, therefore, is a Hallstatt and La Tène amalgam. Exact dating of settlement sites in this phase, and indeed generally in Iron Age Britain, is a matter of some difficulty, owing to the extreme scarcity of datable metal objects – cauldrons, daggers, brooches, swan-necked pins or swords – in association with the plentiful finds of pottery. Pottery-making was a domestic industry and was subject to a natural conservatism, whereas styles in metal objects tended to change more rapidly, and the objects themselves were often either imported or made by craftsmen in touch with continental developments. It is our misfortune that objects of metal are usually found by themselves, unassociated with pottery. Nevertheless, an outline chronology is provided by the former, and there is sufficient development in the pottery sequence, aided by occasional associations, to allow some measure of equation.

In east Yorkshire a settlement at Staple Howe of Iron A produced association with Hallstatt C razors of the late sixth century, and another settlement at Scarborough was probably about as early. The earliest pottery at All Cannings Cross and other early sites in Wessex shows close similarity to pottery of even earlier type (Hallstatt B) from sites in eastern France, as does some from the Thames basin with Urnfield pottery farther north. At Fengate near Peterborough an iron pin with bronze disc-head of north German type dates from the fifth century at the latest.

These and other examples show that settlers were arriving in the late sixth and fifth centuries, bringing a late Hallstatt culture with them, and regional differences in their equipment show that they were coming from various parts of north-west Europe. From the later part of the fifth century and into the fourth, subsequent arrivals were bringing possessions that show the influence of the early La Tène culture now spreading from eastern France. Sites connected with such people are those at Long Wittenham in Berkshire and Chinnor in Buckinghamshire; while at West Harling in Norfolk the apparent difficulty caused by the association of pottery showing undoubted La Tène influence with pottery of distinctly earlier character is lessened once it is realised that they are the waste from two successive huts. In the dagger series there are parallel close contacts with developing continental practice. None of these settlers arrived in large groups; all were adventurers or refugees. They were all, however, both culturally and racially akin, and their influence spreading out over southern Britain created a culture which is essentially uniform, and which is classified as Iron A.

It was a culture based on agriculture. Though the swords and daggers skilfully produced by specialist craftsmen hint at the existence of rich patrons among the chieftains, the great bulk of the population were peasant farmers of no outstanding wealth. Settlements were mainly undefended, and consisted either of simple farmsteads working small estates of up to seventy or one hundred acres or else of larger village-groupings standing in bigger areas of fields. These fields are of the Celtic type, small square or oblong areas only a few hundred feet in dimension (pl. 10b), whose shape and size suggest the use of a light and primitive form of ox-drawn plough, and they represent an agricultural tradition which had already been implanted for a thousand years in parts of Britain. They survive today mainly on the chalk downs, demarcated by lynchets – the banks which accumulate as the soil is slowly ploughed or weathered to the lower edges of the cultivated area. Aerial photography suggests that formerly such farms extended over flatter areas of light soil, for instance the gravel spreads of the major English rivers such as those of the middle Thames, the Warwickshire Avon or of the rivers round the Fens, where subsequent cultivation has removed all surface traces.

At harvest time the seed-corn was separated from the rest and carefully preserved in small square or oblong granaries. The food-corn was first parched, to make it crisp and to prevent germination, and then stored in deep pits lined, no doubt, with basketry or leather. When required, the grains were ground on simple saddle-querns. The pottery was hand-made, without a wheel, probably mainly at home, but there is evidence also for specialist potters trading wares over long distances. The cooking vessels were very crudely made; their shapes are either rounded in the Hallstatt tradition or angular in imitation of shouldered bronze buckets; the finger-tip decoration on the angle is reminiscent of the rivets on the latter, and the red colour-coat resulting from the application of a haematite slip was also intended to recall the sheen of bronze. Finer vessels, often beautifully made and expertly polished, were used for cups and dishes, but these, also, in the details of their shape and decoration usually recall bronze prototypes. The bronzes themselves, however, were expensive, and probably rare except in chieftains' houses; in any case their value as scrap-metal when worn out has usually precluded their survival. Spinning and weaving were other industries carried on in the home with simple equipment. The houses were circular, but some were large and possessed elaborate timber-framing. Cows and sheep as well as pigs and goats supplemented the economy and so did hunting; but basically it was an agrarian landscape. The crops sown were barley, rye or beans and early forms of wheat; an important development by this period was the use of spelt, which being a hardier plant enabled winter sowing to supplement the spring-sown crops. This introduction not only lessened the labour to be undertaken in the spring but involved a further innovation in farming practice, since it became necessary to stall the herds to obtain manure; random dunging by herds cropping the stubble in the winter was only possible in spring-sown fields. That cattle-ranching on a larger scale also played a part in Iron A is suggested by areas of downland with no traces of ancient ploughing, where linear ditches suggest the boundaries of grazing areas. This picture of Iron A farming is necessarily generalised, being built up from evidence mainly from the chalklands of the south. That there were regional differences is suggested by the almost total absence of storage pits from early sites in East Anglia and in the south-west.

Little Woodbury is the classic site of a Wessex farmstead of Iron A. Here a palisaded farmyard of more than three acres contained two successive circular houses, the earlier and larger being fifty feet in diameter. Little evidence survived for the nature of the upper structure of the huts, apart from the plan of the timber framework: they were probably walled in clay or terre pisée between the framework, which is the traditional local manner. The renewal of post-holes in the house and in subsidiary structures such as drying racks and granaries pointed to long life, and it was noticed that throughout the lifetime of the farm certain areas in the yard tended to be associated with certain activities.

As well as the structures already mentioned, there were frequent storage pits, and also a large area riddled by successive bench-like hollows thought to be a working area where at successive harvests winnowing was carried out by hand. All these features seem to be characteristic of Iron A farmsteads on the chalk.

In Devon and Cornwall the sites at Kestor and Bodrifty, though of Iron A, reveal a slightly different pattern. The circular huts are mainly from twenty to thirty feet in diameter, and though they have a timber framework, revealed by a ring of post-holes, the main outer wall consists of a double wall of boulders filled in with rubble. At Kestor twenty-seven huts are loosely scattered along the sides of a ridge, in the vicinity of a larger hut set in a walled yard; they stand among the lynchets and field walls of a contemporary field system. At Bodrifty about a dozen similar huts stand mainly within a walled enclosure of three acres, and many others are scattered in the vicinity. At neither site were any storage pits discovered; thus, though corn-growing is attested at both sites, it is possible that cattle-rearing played a more important part in the economy in the south-west than it did in Wessex.

The hill-forts of Iron A are no longer to be regarded as examples of defensive methods newly introduced; they are developments of types which had been current in Britain for at least 400 years; since 1000 BC defences on this side of the Channel had developed parallel with those in adjacent areas on the continent. More or less well-dated examples of Bronze Age hill-forts are now known at Dinorben (ninth century), Ivinghoe Beacon (eight-seventh century), and elsewhere, such as at Crickley Hill. Continental ramparts of the Hallstatt period are primitive copies of Mediterranean urban walls; their essential characteristic is that the rampart core is enclosed front and back by dry stone revetment walls, producing a stout vertical rampart behind the ditch. Timber framing is usually employed, taking the form of spaced vertical timbers recessed front and back in the face of the walling, and tied to each other transversely through the body of the rampart. In Britain this type of fortification is found, but there are insular differences, possibly connected with the absence of suitable material for dry stone walling in most of the areas of primary settlement. Instead, after the ditch, perhaps eight feet deep and twice as wide, had been dug, the produce was often piled up behind a timber fence. In this way an almost vertical wall-face was created, the front consisting either of continuous vertical logs set in a foundation trench, or (more usually) of horizontal ones held back by spaced uprights. Normally this revetment is tied back to a parallel row of verticals behind, though these are not always so numerous as the front row. Occasionally, when suitable stone could be found, drystone walling was employed between the posts in the continental manner, as in the outwork or barbican which was added to the original entrance at Maiden Castle; elsewhere it is possible that rough dry walling in unsuitable materials such as chalk or flint nodules was sometimes attempted. In Cornwall the promontory fort of Maen Castle, near Lands End, had a thick wall of granite blocks packed in soil, for here suitable rock was available. At the gates tree trunks large enough to carry a rampart-walk over the gate were often set up, and the gate itself is often slightly set back within the incurving ends of the rampart. The arrangement in these early examples is not sufficiently pronounced to be styled an inturned entrance,[3] but it is definite enough. Such a timber-revetted type of fortification would be effective for about fifteen or twenty years, until the timbers rotted; then it collapsed unless repaired. Its character suggests the primitive nature of warfare in the earlier centuries of the Iron Age with no weapons but spears or daggers and a few slings, and no engines of war to effect a breach.

The primary area of Iron A in Britain lies south and east of a line from Scarborough to Gloucester. But beyond that line in the west the sea routes had led to scattered settlements on the coast of Wales, as at Dinas Powys in Glamorgan, at Caldy Island, or at Castell Odo on the northern peninsula, and possibly also farther round still, in Cheshire and Shropshire. At most sites, however, the scarcity of pottery which accompanies the pastoral way of life makes definition difficult. Along the east coast the sea routes led to eastern Scotland, but here also the pattern of settlement is still very imperfectly known. The agricultural basis of the culture was hard to establish in the adverse conditions of the north, and finds of datable objects are once again very rare. But Scotland had had its contacts with the Continent in the Late Bronze Age, and examples of timber-laced ramparts in Scotland have been shown to go back to the sixth or seventh centuries. In addition to finds of metal-work, round houses similar in design to the homesteads of Iron A in south Britain are known, and in two cases these are undefended, excavation in both producing 'flat-rimmed' pottery which is clearly akin to the Late Hallstatt types current farther south. There are also settlements surrounded by palisade-enclosures very reminiscent of sites like Staple Howe, and these are often found to precede and underlie the ramparts of hill-forts subsequently erected on the site. At Jarlshof in Shetland there is a well-explored settlement of this date which

25

gives an interesting picture of the adaptations to environment forced on the new arrivals to the far north.

In many parts of Britain, then, evidence exists for elements of new culture introduced by fresh arrivals. The previous inhabitants, however, were not exterminated or driven out. Side by side with the settlers, whom they far outnumbered, they lived on, accepting, adapting, intermingling. In this way Iron A, and subsequently B and C as well, attained their insular specifically British character; for the native element made a considerable contribution to each.

1. Appian (*Roman History*, preface §5), writing in the second century, says that the Romans hold the most important half of Britain, but do not need the rest of it; for even the part they do occupy is not profitable to them.

2. In recent years many rectangular building-plans have been recognised in Britain, some of which may have been houses; but they are still relatively uncommon and appear in the main to be a feature of the earlier centuries of the Iron Age.

3. True inturns, with the gate set far back in a narrow passage, formed by turning the rampart-ends inwards through a right angle, were a later development.

Iron B and Iron C in Britain

A number of the hill-forts in Britain can now be seen to originate in the period before 500 BC, but many were still being constructed during the century following 400. This may be partly due to the growing pressures induced by expanding population, but it is also undoubtedly true that the years around 300 saw a renewal of migration from the Continent. What Celtic migration was like can be gathered from accounts of the earlier Celtic invasion of Italy culminating in the sack of Rome about 390, or the slightly later invasions of Greece and Asia Minor about 279; but in the case of Britain there was the Channel to cross, and this as usual prevented mass migration. Nevertheless, the arrival of chieftains and of warrior bands can be deduced from the considerable changes which now took place. New methods of fortification appear; the ancient Hallstatt type of vertical wall passes out of use. And not only do new types of pottery begin to be seen and new methods of finishing its surface, but La Tène art-styles, applied to the decoration of metal-work and even of pottery, are introduced and quickly take root. At the same time the workshops which supplied the earlier British daggers go out of production; a new style of dagger with anthropoid hilt is introduced; and long swords make their appearance for the first time for three centuries. Though much of the new metal-work and many of the new swords seem to have been made in Britain itself, and might therefore be represented as native developments, this explanation does not explain their genesis or cover the other changes: the comparatively sudden appearance of new styles of metal-work at this date seems best explained by the arrival of new craftsmen following in the wake of new patrons. Such new arrivals need not, and probably were not, large in numbers; they are much more likely to have consisted for the most part of comparatively small yet powerful war-bands under princely leaders, whose power both politically and culturally was out of all proportion to their numbers. This power may have been based on a new weapon of war – the chariot – itself an aristocratic accoutrement in the main, and one able to support the wide influence of the few. The use of chariots at this date in the south may perhaps be inferred from bridle bits now appearing for the first time, and is supported by the existence of certain linear earthworks, as in the Chilterns, which appear to be designed to prevent it. A century or so later chariots were still found in burials in East Yorkshire, although chariot burials on the Continent had long gone out of fashion. They are, it is true, not yet widely attested from Britain south of the Humber, but rich burials of any kind are so excessively rare that this is not in itself an insuperable difficulty. The Yorkshire group of settlers maintained their own traditions in conditions of relative cultural isolation.

This period of change and new introductions marks the appearance of Iron B, which is essentially a La Tène culture. From the new arrivals (First B) the influence of the new styles became widespread as they were adopted by the original inhabitants. This leavening of the older culture is known as Second B, and it took on varying characteristics in the different regions. The regionalism just mentioned may mark the growth of tribes or groups of tribes; but there was to be much more migration from across the Channel before more than a few of the historically attested tribes of the eve of the Roman conquest can be recognised. These regional groups of Iron Second B developed at various dates from the late third century and through the second. Moreover, the culture as a whole was socially stratified as well as regionally diversified. We know little at present of the dwellings of the rich, but parts of their equipment for parade, warfare or domestic furnishing are better attested, and have been much studied, most brilliantly perhaps by Sir Cyril Fox.[1] Their wide distribution gives a certain unity to the diversity seen in the peasant groupings. This unity was facilitated by intercourse along the Jurassic ridge between the Bristol Channel and the Humber, and by trade routes following the Thames Valley. At first metal was scarce, especially bronze: we find ponies' bits or parts of chariots made of iron and thinly sheathed in bronze; not until the first century BC were such things produced wholly in cast bronze. It was from the ports of the Bristol Channel that supplies of bronze were made available – so the distribution suggests – and some of the principal workshops of Iron B are thought to have been in this region. Contact was maintained with the Continent, for new swords and scabbards of La Tène II type appear, but they also soon develop distinctively insular characteristics and were made in British workshops. Some of this acquaintance with new continental features may have resulted from contact with the earliest groups of invaders of Iron C.

The La Tène culture of the Continent had developed a highly original art. Though based on classical forms such as the tendril or palmette and on eastern animal patterns, it translated these forms into abstract, non-representational figures, delighting in curving patterns, asymmetrical yet balanced, or in flowing interlocking scrolls; these could be emphasised by rounded relief or by elaborate hatching in the flat. This art was transplanted to Britain in Iron B, and there took on new life with original features. Sword-scabbards, horse-trappings, the metal parts of chariots, shields, tankards and even brooches or domestic pottery, all could be decorated with bewildering, skilfully drawn patterns in the La Tène style. Apart from the pottery, which does show regional variations reflecting the local peasant traditions of its makers, the principal examples of this art are found on expensive pieces of metal equipment which illustrate the background of patronage. Certain schools of craftsmen have been recognised, though not exactly located; but the distribution of objects transcends the tribe or individual region. Products of mastercraftsmen travelled freely and probably so did the smiths themselves; debris from the workshop of a travelling bronzesmith has been found at Gussage All Saints in Dorset.[2] Perhaps the most surprising area of finds is Dumfriesshire in south-west Scotland. Here, it is clear, Second B chieftains had settled by the end of the third century, probably from Yorkshire, though possibly by the western sea-ways; and here they maintained themselves, as later finds of metal-work show, down to the first century AD. A traditional connection between this region and Yorkshire accords well with later historical situations, both in the time of Venutius (p. 119) and in the second century AD. The Stainmore Pass affords a connecting route of high antiquity and easy access.

Thus, elements which reflect aristocratic culture are widely diffused: the regional differences are largely a matter of pottery, which reflects the cultural divisions of the common people. Southern Second

B was perhaps the earliest. Pottery jars in black polished wares develop with new round-shouldered forms, and other shapes next appear which seem to copy wooden bowls. Rather restrained and simple curvilinear decoration is frequently applied to these vessels. Fresh forms of bronze brooch begin to spread. Eastern Second B is best illustrated in east Yorkshire, where the remains clearly exhibit a La Tène aristocracy ruling over a native population far less receptive of new influences than most. There are features, such as their rectangular ditched burial-enclosures as well as imported metal-work and Mediterranean coral to decorate their brooches, which link them directly with the Continent. Further down the Jurassic belt the decorated pottery of Hunsbury is a classic example of Second B pottery at its most developed. Though highly decorated, it employs distinctively different art-forms from the pottery of Glastonbury.

In Gloucestershire and beyond there was a pottery development parallel with that in the southern region with slight differences in shape.[3] Crouched inhumation-burials appear to be typical.

The Cornish peninsula had long been in commercial contact with the Continent over the sale of tin, as the recorded visit of Pytheas of Marseilles about 320 BC reminds us.[4] Diodorus, in a famous passage which is derived probably from Pytheas, tells us of the inhabitants of *Belerium* (Lands End) who worked the tin and carried it to *Ictis* (St Michael's Mount): there it was bought by merchants who took it to Gaul, and ultimately after a journey of about thirty days they brought their wares by pack-horse to the mouth of the Rhone. It seems clear that this trade was flourishing before the beginning of the third century; there is a wide scatter of Greek coins in southern Britain (some at least of which are likely to be evidence of trade), and brooches of Iberian pattern suggest even earlier contact with Spain. In the second century intercourse continued, as is shown by the hoard of coins from Paul: these are coins of north Italian type, datable to the second half of the second century, and they illustrate at once the far end of the trade route and also the absence in Cornwall, or indeed the whole south-west, of nearer coinages. This, as we shall see, has a chronological bearing on the date of foreign settlement.

The first contact between the south-west and the La Tène culture of Brittany was peaceful, being brought about by the intercourse of traders; and it should date to the third century. During the second century intercourse continued, and now a South-Western distinctive local culture can be recognised.[5] Breton-type pottery occurs in Cornwall, and cliff-castles – a form of hill-fort occupying a sea-girt promontory – such as are well known in southern Brittany, are found here too. These cliff-castles are usually defended by multiple ramparts to provide a defence in depth; and this feature, together with the step sometimes provided on the back of the rampart – another Breton feature – shows that the sling was the weapon in common use. Thus, there was close contact between the two regions, and we may suspect that some cliff-castles, such as Gurnard's Head and Sennen, were defended trading stations from about 200. Decorated pottery of an elaborate kind, with Breton affinities, can be dated almost as early at Castle Dore; this is a small multiple-enclosure fort of a local south-western type, where accordingly we may recognise the development of a native culture.

Somewhat later, beginning perhaps soon after 125, we find considerable signs of increasing contact with Normandy; the type-sites are the Rumps and St Mawgan in Pyder, where there are defended settlements with much pottery copying shapes current across the Channel. But the absence of local coinage in Cornwall carries the implication that these movements occurred before the Armorican coinage had developed in the homeland.[6]

It may have been from Cornwall that the idea of multiple ramparts spread to other areas in the south-west and west, for there was undoubtedly contact by coast-wise trade. But in these other regions they are constructed on quite a different scale, and may well be an independent local development born of internecine strife. Yet sling warfare was certainly employed in some, as was proved at Maiden Castle, and Armorican merchants were certainly active on the coasts of Dorset and Hampshire. The cross-channel trade reached its climax in the half century before Caesar's Gallic War, as is shown by the scatter of Armorican coins along the coast and by the settlement at Hengistbury Head.[7] This site was also in trade-contact with Italy at this time, as the many finds of amphorae of Dressel form 1 A show.[8] Breton influences can be seen in the internal rim-grooves and counter-sunk handles of its pottery; other pots seem to copy bronze bowls. The weaving equipment underwent modification, and multivallation spread among the hill forts. Here once again a date of c. 125 is suggested for the formative phase of this culture, for other-

31

wise Armorican silver coinage would have been transplanted to Dorset. During the first half of the first century, the inhabitants had begun using iron currency bars as a means of exchange and of hoarding wealth. These bars are sword-shaped; their distribution suggests a dispersion along the Jurassic way, where examples in Northamptonshire and Lincolnshire may, however, have been made locally. Another form of bar, spit-shaped, and slighter in form and weight, seems to have been made around the lower Severn valley. If these various forms of bar were used as primitive currency, they soon yielded before the spread of coinage proper from the south-east. For as it was, Dorset was overrun by Belgic chieftains with a different coinage tradition (see p. 35) perhaps about 80–70 BC; but these soon changed from a gold to a silver standard under the influence of cross-channel trade.

It may have been the stimulus of this same Breton trade, fertilising a stock made more artistic by contact with the craftsmen of the metal workshops, that at length contributed to the development (c. 100 BC) of another group in the Bristol Channel area.[9] The typesite is Glastonbury, a crannog village, difficult of access in the marshes of Somerset. Here a well-sheltered harbour gave access to a trackway leading to the metalliferous Mendips, and a large and long-lived settlement developed. It is chiefly remarkable for the highly decorated pottery of its later phases. Pottery of a similar type is widely distributed, though in small quantities, in Somerset, Devon and Cornwall, where, as we have seen, it had developed under Breton influence. It is probably simplest to attribute the origin of Glastonbury and Meare to traders coming up from Devon and Cornwall in the later second century.

The rich trade with the tribes of Armorica which for so long had exercised a powerful influence on south-western Britain came to an end with Caesar's conquest of Brittany in 56. The navy of the Veneti was destroyed and the tin-trade was disrupted. This had important economic consequences (p. 56).

A further group can be identified in western Britain.[10] These settlers had contacts with Northern Spain (an area which had had earlier connections with south-west Britain) via the western sea-route; they pushed up the Bristol Channel and settled in western Gloucestershire and Herefordshire. Their characteristic stamped pottery is found also, though sparsely, in Cornwall. They, too, seem to have been interested in metallurgy, for they obtained control of the iron-producing area of the Forest of Dean. In south-eastern Britain another group represented by a distinctive type of pottery is found in Surrey and Sussex (another iron-producing district), and sporadically round the Thames estuary.[11] Its origins are uncertain.

The hill-forts also must be reckoned to reflect the aristocratic element in society, and the various types current in Iron B very often transcend the boundaries of the peasant cultures. Down to about 400 they had continued to multiply, but thereafter a tendency can be seen for power to become concentrated in fewer but more powerfully defended strongholds. Second B, as we have seen, represented a tranformation of Iron A, and the hill-forts show no great variation save that the ramparts when reconstructed are in simple dump construction: that is, they rely not on a vertical wall as did the Hallstatt type, but on a continuous glacis from ditch bottom to rampart top. Some hill-forts were greatly enlarged, but at Maiden Castle, where this was done at a date reckoned as *c.* 200 BC, the culture had not yet been seriously affected by Second B. In west Devon, Cornwall, west Somerset and south Wales a local variety known as multiple-enclosure forts is found, whose distribution points to the use of the sea-routes and whose form to the herding of cattle; in Cornwall they are not found in the same area as the cliff-castles. In east Devon, Dorset, western Hampshire and east Somerset the hill-forts are defended by close-set bivallate or multiple ramparts often of enormous size and strength; from this region they extend up the Jurassic belt as far as Northamptonshire and also along the Welsh Marches. This spread of multivallation in the south-west reaches a climax in Third B. In south-eastern Britain univallate hill-forts of simple dump construction were still being built by Second B folk, and at a later stage some of these were refortified with partial bivallation, probably against intruders from Belgic Gaul. In all this development there is a tendency for greater attention to be paid to entrances, where the gates are often set well back in a long narrow passage framed by inturns of the ramparts. Such a move could be introduced at the old hill-fort at the Trundle in Sussex in its latest phase, even though no other steps were then taken to elaborate the defences. In rocky areas, especially in the west, stone revetments are found on the face and sometimes even within the rampart; elsewhere dry stone walls of great strength are employed. Horizontal transverse timber lacing is also a method sometimes used to solidify the rampart.

Hill-forts are not uncommon anywhere save in eastern Britain and the Pennine area, but it is true to say that the vast majority of those in England concentrate in Wessex with its adjoining areas and in the Welsh Marches. Sometimes, as in Sussex and parts of Wessex, it is possible to see that one large hill-fort dominates a natural region and might therefore be considered as a communal defensive centre; but despite these signs of greater centralisation of power, the proliferation of hill-forts in general suggests an 'anarchy', a period of increasing baronial lawlessness, when each chieftain with his retainers was compelled to fortify because of the uncontrolled aggressiveness of the others. This might be due to growing land-shortage in Wessex or to successive waves of refugees from Western Third B, Belgic and then Roman expansion in the Marches.

Iron C

Meanwhile in Eastern Britain a new series of incursions was beginning, which after a period of turmoil were to mould her peoples into the tribes known when history first throws light on the situation. These are the invasions, attested by Caesar, of the Belgae, tribes who inhabited the area soon to become Gallia Belgica between the Seine, the Marne and the Rhine. These Belgae were culturally quite distinct from the tribes of Armorica whose activities affected the south-west; both their coins and their pottery and even their fortifications are easily distinguished. Formerly it was thought that they came in two main migrations, but Mr D. F. Allen's reappraisal of the coinage has demonstrated a much more complicated and realistic pattern. The earliest coins are continental. They do not indicate the presence of traders, for they are not found in the wealthier areas of Iron B such as east Yorkshire or Gloucestershire, but only in the regions of known Belgic settlement. Indeed, before the production of small change in silver and copper later in the period, high-value gold coins do not represent a money-economy, but rather an ostentatious method of storing wealth and of rewarding service. Like the subsequent groups of gold coins of similar continental origin which in due course gave rise to native issues, they must represent the arrival of chieftains and war-bands. A true trading pattern is seen rather in the distribution

34

of Armorican silver coins in Britain, which is almost entirely coastal.

The coins can be arranged in a chronological series of groups on the evidence not only of design and typology but also of decreasing weight and specific gravity; these groups have been called Gallo-Belgic A-F. The distribution points to a complex series of movements into south-eastern and eastern Britain: it does not correspond with what we know of the position of later tribes or kingdoms, but represents an altogether earlier formative phase of raiding and migration by bands of adventurers. In the end successive bands succeeded in bringing over quite large parties of settlers, sufficient not merely to impose a new aristocracy but to supplant the culture of the peasant population.

The date of the earliest arrivals is difficult to fix with any precision. Owing to the earliest phases being those of movement and conquest, there is an absence of settlement material, and the relevant burials have not been found. The newcomers are represented at present only by their coins. The earliest of these [12] can be dated well before 100 BC, and possibly almost as early as 150. This would place them well back in La Tène II, whereas the developed culture of Iron C is associated with features of La Tène III. They should be accompanied by altogether earlier cultural characteristics, and it is likely that some at least of the La Tène II swords in Britain, many of which have been found in just the appropriate areas, should be assigned to them.

The third coin-series was the first imported coinage to be copied in Britain itself;[13] already on these the design, originally modelled on the gold coinage of Philip II of Macedon, had seriously deteriorated from the standard of Gallo-Belgic A. Of the copies, British A are found in Sussex, Surrey, Hampshire and southern Oxfordshire, and later were themselves copied by British B, whose distribution extends through western Hampshire into Dorset; there the two types gave rise to the tribal coinage of the Durotriges. As a worn coin of British B was found in the Le Catillon hoard, buried in Jersey at the time of Caesar's Gallic wars, and as the same hoard showed that ordinary Durotrigan silver coins were already in circulation, it is evident that British B must go back at least to c. 70 BC, and British A earlier still; while for Gallo-Belgic C, which gave rise to both, a date of c. 100 BC is entirely reasonable. The arrival of settlers or refugees from the Continent continued. A very numerous Gallo-Belgic coinage [14] appears to date from about the time of Caesar's Gallic wars; it may represent a comparatively large-scale movement of refugees from his conquest. Caesar himself [15] mentions the flight hither of leaders of the Bellovaci in 57, and later alludes to intervention from Britain in the Gallic wars.[16] Last of all the continental coin-series to reach Britain is one which must have been brought over after Caesar's wars, as is shown by the extreme scarcity of the actual imported pieces (for Caesar suppressed the issue of gold in Gaul); rare though they are, however, they gave rise to a numerous native coinage, British Q, which later shows itself to be connected with the name of Commius. This man, too, appears in the pages of Caesar, first as friend and then as bitter foe; and his subsequent flight to Britain, probably in 50, is recorded by Frontinus (p. 56).

The coins of Gallo-Belgic F and British Q have on the reverse a horse with a triple tail. The coins of Commius and the earliest coins of his son, Tincommius, kings of the Atrebates, are practically identical with these, save for the added names. The triple-tailed horse seems to be the badge of the Atrebatic kingdom, and the distribution of the coins, uninscribed as well as inscribed, gives us an approximate picture of the extent of Commius' realm. But the triple-tailed horse appears also on a second group of coins (British R) which can be associated with the historical Dobunni: the reverse of these is closely similar to, and clearly derived from, British Q, while the obverse carries a badge resembling a palm-branch. It seems obvious that the early rulers of the Dobunni were Belgic, and that they arrived from Commius' kingdom. But while the later coins of the southern dynasty, from Tincommius onwards, diverged into much more classical designs, those of the Dobunni stayed obstinately conservative: the original design remained intact until Boduocus about AD 43 placed his name BODVOC on the obverse in place of the palm.

Other derivatives of Gallo-Belgic C, termed British H and British I, were circulating in Lincolnshire and the Midlands, in the area later known to belong to the Coritani; here too we can be sure that Belgic chieftains had conquered the Iron B population, and Belgic pottery is known from a number of sites in Lincolnshire. The later inscribed coins of the Coritani bear double names such as ESUP-ASU, VOLISIOS-DUMNOCOVEROS, or VOLISIOS-DUMNOVELLAU, which, as Mr D. F. Allen has suggested, may indicate a dual magistracy: we might see here the results of the fusion of the two groups represented by British H and I into one single tribe. In Norfolk and Suffolk also the early coinage of the Iceni is in part derived from Gallo-Belgic C, and in part from British L; here, too, we should recognise a Belgic royal house ruling over earlier groups, though there is little Belgic material culture among the Icenian peasants themselves until the eve of the Roman conquest. The Trinovantes also must be considered to be at least partly Belgic, for Gallo-Belgic A coins are found in their territory; and though they appear to have resisted later attempts at conquest, they did at last succumb to the users of Gallo-Belgic E. In 54 BC they were being attacked by Cassivellaunus from their western flank; but this fact does not prove them non-Belgic, for in this early phase of settlement conflicting chieftains were warring for living room: there was no united army of conquest.

The picture of Britain that emerges from a study of the coins and other archaeological material is that in Kent, Hertfordshire and Buckinghamshire, and in eastern Hampshire, West Sussex and Berkshire successive Belgic migrations had produced a large body of settlers: beyond these regions conquering chieftains had asserted their authority over subject populations, but actual settlement by Belgic peasants was thin. In these areas the conquerors could be absorbed by the conquered. The Durotriges had been conquered thus; but their close mercantile connections with the tribes of Brittany, who used silver coins, caused them to abandon the gold standard and themselves change over to a silver coinage. As we have seen, this had already happened by Caesar's time, and after his wars these connections were disrupted. The other Belgic rulers later issued silver and copper coins, but only as small change for their continuing gold currencies. Their appearance, however, from about 20 BC meant the emergence of a true money-economy.

By the time that settlement and burial material of the Belgae become frequent enough to be recognised, they have entered the La Tène III phase. Their culture differed in several respects from that of Iron B. In the first place they cremated their dead; cremation cemeteries mark the areas of full settlement. Those at Aylesford and Swarling in Kent are recognised as type sites. The poor had their ashes placed in an urn which was sometimes accompanied by subsidiary vessels containing a viaticum. The wealthy were often buried in elaborate richly furnished tombs, sometimes surmounted by a barrow. Many of the more elaborate tombs, especially in the area of the Trinovantes, date from the decades after 50 BC, and are often accompanied by Italian wine-amphorae (in one tomb with a total capacity of over twenty gallons) and other provision for feasting, such as spits, fire-dogs and vessels of pottery or even of silver. One earlier tomb at Aylesford contained imported bronze vessels of Italian origin.

Their pottery was made on the potter's wheel. The application of rotary motion to this device, and to querns or hand-mills for domestic corn-grinding, was an invention of which knowledge was now spreading in Gaul; and it is occasionally found in the south-west also, especially on imported pottery. The use of the potter's wheel in Iron C was a step towards the professionalisation of the pottery industry. Much of the pottery was probably now made by specialists instead of domestically in the home: probably, then, by men rather than by women. The pedestal urn, which had had a long history in Gaul, was one of the types now introduced, and it was much used for burials, even after it had begun to disappear from the household range. Bead-rim vessels, often heavily combed, were another new type, based ultimately on metallic prototypes; and in the first century AD many new forms modelled on the platters and precious-metal cups of the classical world appear.

Hill-fort building was not much undertaken by the Belgae in Britain. Their own oppida are much larger than the normal hill-fort and do not seek out the hill-tops. In the early phase of settlement in the south-east, indeed, or in the areas where a Belgic ruling caste was holding a down a conquered people, pre-existing hill-forts are re-used and even refortified, as at Bigbury in Kent or Maiden Castle in Dorset. But Wheathampstead, which also dates to this phase but was a creation of the Belgae themselves, is double the size of Maiden Castle and lies not on a hill-top but beside the marshy flood-plain of the River Lea. Caesar speaks of a stronghold in Kent hidden in the woods and possessing strong natural and artificial defences, and of Cassivellaunus' oppidum he writes that it was defended by woods and marshes, and large enough to contain many men and cattle. 'The Britons call it an oppidum,' he goes on, 'when they have fortified thickly wooded spots with a rampart and ditch, as a place to retire to in order to avoid the attacks of their enemies.' Later Belgic oppida, like Camulodunum, Bagendon or Selsey, constructed in more settled times by more powerful rulers, occupied far larger areas defended partly by natural features, partly by banks and ditches. The dykes of Camulodunum enclose twelve square miles, though much of this area was no doubt devoted to pasture or market gardens.

Belgic settlement thus began the exploitation of heavier soils in valley bottoms or in the widespread loam-lands of eastern Britain. Their ability to do this was no doubt due to the greater availability of iron tools, such as axes for clearing the vegetation. It used to be thought that they introduced a heavier plough, equipped with coulter, whose use facilitated the exploitation of such soils. But the evidence for this idea does not stand up to examination. Only three of the so-called coulters are known; and they differ fundamentally in shape and weight from the undoubted coulters of Roman Britain; moreover, the latter seem themselves to be a development only of the later Roman period. The Belgic 'coulters' were probably bill-hooks, and with this recognition the case for a heavy Belgic plough collapses. Nevertheless, the Belgae were assiduous farmers, and aerial photography has supplemented the evidence of excavation for the widespread distribution of the small farms of this period. Corn storage was now for the most part carried out in large pottery vessels – another benefit of improved pottery – and the use of storage pits diminishes, though it does not entirely disappear.

The Belgae greatly stimulated the metal industries of Britain. Iron became much more plentiful in supply, and so did bronze. Exploitation of the iron field of the Weald was greatly expanded, if indeed it did not now for the first time begin; and metal was probably traded from the Forest of Dean and other iron-fields such as Northamptonshire. The skilful craftsmanship of the Belgic blacksmith can be seen in the surviving fire-dogs, the Welwyn amphora-stand, or in the slave-chains with elaborate neck-shackles which enabled captives to be controlled on the estate or for the foreign slave-market. The Belgic leaders, like the chieftains of Iron B, continued to patronise the bronze-smiths of Britain, and much of the fine late La Tène art of Britain is of Iron C. There were several innovations. The staved wooden vessels from Aylesford and Marlborough, decorated with bronze bands bearing repoussé decoration, are likely to have been imports, but they had their influence over here. On them and on other bucket mounts of a humbler sort we see a much more realistic portrayal of animal and human figures. Further examples of staved

vessels are to be found in the tankards, which were a Belgic introduction, though the type later spread westwards among other tribes.
Many bronzes are decorated with studs of red enamel *en cabochon*,
recalling the coral studs used in earlier times for the same effect;
subsequently, areas of red enamel in champlevé technique are found
decorating bronzes usually connected with pony harness. Outstanding works of art such as the Battersea shield or the Waterloo helmet
illustrate the rich panoply of Belgic warrior leaders, just as the
plainer scabbards of La Tène III type point to that of the ordinary
warrior. The famous gold torcs from the Snettisham treasure, whatever the explanation of their find-spot, illustrate the wealth and the
magnificent craftsmanship at the disposal of royal princes or
Druidical high priests in this Belgic society as do those from Ipswich.
On a lower plane, many of the coin-designs illustrate aspects of life
and art, ranging from quintessential horses, boars, or wolves, through
martial equipment like the carnyx (the war-trumpet with animal
mouth) to horse- or footmen armed with a variety of weapons: some
illustrate peaceful aspects of life, such as dress, smithing or music.

After about 30 BC great changes can be seen to affect the character
of Iron C. In the first place political stability began to take the place
of conflict, as the long settlement phase drew to a close. Following
the lead of Commius, other kings began to inscribe their names and
titles on coins, and in this way something of the political history
of the period can for the first time be discerned: this will be described in Chapter 4. Secondly, this political stability in Britain,
leading on to more settled and unified government over far wider
territories than previously, coincided with the new stability introduced into the affairs of Rome by Augustus. There could not fail to
develop an intercourse with the Roman Empire, which manifested
itself on the political as well as on the economic plane. By the opening of the first century AD we have plentiful evidence of ever-increas-
ing trade, while Roman imports give a new precision to
archaeological dating, as well as illustrating the growing wealth of
Britain.

1. *A Find of the Early Iron Age from Llyn Cerrig Bach, Anglesey*
(Cardiff, 1946); *Pattern and Purpose* (Cardiff, 1958).
   2. *Antiquity* xlvii (1973), 109 ff.

3. This is classified as Western Second B.

4. Much earlier contacts, in the sixth century, are recorded in Avienus, *Ora Maritima*. Fifth- and fourth-century Greek pots are known from two sites in Cornwall and from elsewhere in Britain. See A. Fox, *South West England* (London, 1964), p. 116.

5. South-Western Second B.

6. It is possible that some of the makers of cordoned pottery were refugees from Caesar's conquest of the Armorican peninsula in 56, but if these came in any number the absence of coining is striking. The site at St Mawgan itself seems to belong to a later phase, but this does not invalidate the date here suggested for the beginning of the migration.

7. In Dorset the variant culture produced by this intercourse is called Southern Third B.

8. D. P. S. Peacock, in M. Jesson and D. Hill, *The Iron Age and its Hill-forts* (1971), p. 173.

9. South-Western Third B.

10. It is classified as Western Third B.

11. South-Eastern Third B.

12. Gallo-Belgic A and B.

13. Gallo-Belgic C.

14. Gallo-Belgic E.

15. *B.G.*, ii, 14.

16. *Ibid.*, iv, 20.

3
Caesar's Expeditions

In the previous chapters we have traced the prehistory of Britain in the Iron Age down to the time when contact was established with the world of Rome. Mediterranean civilisation had developed on the foundation of the city state, and this was still the essential local unit; but above it had sprouted the grandiose visions of world empire which the west inherited from Alexander. Under the Roman Republic the Senatorial Government had tried to limit their expansion to the Mediterranean sea-board, despite the pressure of the mercantile class for wider opportunities of exploitation. But in the first century BC the government was fast losing, if it had not already lost, control, and power was falling more and more into the hands of powerful dynasts, such as Sulla, Pompey and Caesar, who commanded large armies and controlled influential political organisations. By the time that Britain passed fully under Roman rule the process was complete, and the Augustan Empire had been established. To such a state world-rule was part of its philosophical inheritance; it did not have to be justified, but might be limited by temporary considerations of empirical convenience.

In 58 BC Caesar had undertaken the governorship of the provinces of Illyricum and of Cisalpine and Transalpine Gaul. The latter was Provence, the hinterland of the Rhone mouth and the coastlands which guarded the route to Spain. In the years that followed he became involved in defending and extending Roman interests in Gaul beyond the boundaries of this province. Having dealt with the attempted migration of the Helvetii and the dangerous nuisance of Ariovistus and his Germans in 58, he was drawn on to intervene the following year in Belgic Gaul. He had become convinced that Roman control was necessary for the defence of the Rhine against renewed German penetration, and seems at first to have intended a protectorate over Gaul itself, leaving the inhabitants very largely to manage their own affairs under governments friendly to himself. But this protectorate became less and less possible as the pattern of resistance followed by intervention recurred. In 57 he defeated the Belgic confederation of tribes in north-west Gaul, and also received the surrender of the maritime tribes of Normandy and Brittany.

He could not have been operating in this region for long before becoming aware of the influence exerted by Britain on Gallic affairs. The tribes of Armorica were in close commercial contact with the south-west of Britain, which was the source of considerable mineral wealth. When Armorica revolted in 56, military assistance was received from Britain; and in Belgic Gaul also he found that there were close political and military contacts with tribes across the Channel. Within living memory Divitiacus, king of the Suessiones (round Soissons), had ruled in Britain as well.[1] Malcontents could escape the Romans by flight across the sea, as happened in 57 when chieftains of the Bellovaci had fled thither.[2] There were, therefore, sound military reasons for intervention in addition to considerations of economic gain; nor must we under-estimate the prestige which would accrue from a successful intervention in Britain. For at that time it was still regarded as a mysterious isle, only vaguely known to the classical world: it lay beyond the Ocean, which the popular outlook still regarded as bounding the habitable world.

There are good reasons for suggesting that Caesar had planned a British expedition for 56, the year before he actually came; but because his plans came to naught they received scant publicity from Caesar himself. In that year the ocean-going fleet of the Veneti was to hand, its pilots long experienced in the Channel routes leading to the south-west. In 57 Publius Crassus had been operating in Brittany with one legion, and later wintered near the mouth of the Loire: it is very probably he to whom Strabo[3] is referring when he tells us of a visit to the Cassiterides or tin islands (probably the Scillies) by a Roman of this name, which resulted in increased geographical knowledge. This sounds very like a reconnaissance of the western route. Moreover, elsewhere Strabo[4] gives as one of the motives for the Venetic rebellion of 56 the fear that an invasion of Britain would interrupt their commerce. Invasion, then, was certainly in the air at this time, though, as we have seen, not yet mentioned in Caesar's own Commentaries. In the winter of 57 large forces were stationed in

43

western as well as in Belgic Gaul, where they would be conveniently available for embarkation. But in the event, the rebellion in 56 of the Armorican tribes and the necessity of destroying the Venetic fleet nullified these plans, and the plan which succeeded them involved an invasion of the Belgic south-east of Britain in 55. In late 56, therefore, we find Caesar hastening to subdue the Morini and Menapii, who controlled the Channel coasts in the neighbourhood of the Straits of Dover. In fact, however, the invasion of 55 was delayed, partly owing to the difficulty of bringing these tribes to battle and more seriously owing to a new, large-scale invasion of Germans from across the Rhine. Much of the summer of 55 was taken up with these matters and with a short demonstration in strength beyond the Rhine; it was not until August that he was free to turn his attention to Britain.

There were not sufficient transports available for more than a small force, but neither was there time for more than a reconnaissance. This Caesar determined to attempt. He tells us that from Gallic merchants he had been unable to obtain much information of military value, but he had received offers of surrender from a number of British tribes once his plans had become known. The political situation in Britain was as fluid as had been that in Celtic Gaul and tribes under attack from their neighbours were glad to obtain Roman support. Plainly there were immediate advantages in retaining the initiative and in going to see for himself: and behind these reasons lay the deeper personal motives only discernible from a study of the Roman political scene. Mr C. E. Stevens has shown[5] that the legality of an invasion of Britain, however strategically desirable, was doubtful, or at best uncertain. The penalties for a governor illegally acting outside his province were heavy, and Caesar had powerful political enemies eager to bring him down. A small, short expedition would test public opinion in Rome; and if this were unfavourable the exploit could be represented as a mere punitive excursion similar to the one already made across the Rhine. In the event the verdict was overwhelmingly favourable, and the Senate even voted a thanksgiving of twenty days, five longer than that given in 57 for the subjection of Gaul itself. Part of the enthusiasm was undoubtedly fired by the achievement of campaigning beyond Oceanus and thus opening a new field to Roman endeavour. The way was clear for the conquest of Britain, and the necessary time was available as well. For early in 56

44

had occurred the conference of Luca, as a result of which he had obtained a five-year prolongation of his command. With Gaul apparently pacified, this left six campaigning seasons available for over-running Britain, amply sufficient for the reduction of the lowland zone.

On 26 August, therefore, Caesar crossed the Channel, intending only a limited stay. He assigned two legions, the Tenth and Seventh, and about 500 cavalry to the task, but the cavalry did not arrive owing to contrary winds. The approach of the season of equinoctial gales in late September meant that he had less than a month for action before return would become imperative. Though, as we have seen, he had other motives, the immediate purpose of such a short and limited expedition must have been reconnaissance for the larger invasion planned for 54. Much of the original intelligence collected will have related to Wessex and the south-west, and his more recent enquiries had told him nothing of the size of Britain, or the character of its interior, or the fighting qualities of its inhabitants. The confused state of military information about the south-east is shown by his use of Commius as an envoy. This Atrebatic chieftain had the reputation of possessing much influence in the south-east, but in fact was arrested as soon as he landed. The Atrebatic settlers lay farther west.

Commius had been sent over with the returning ambassadors from those British tribes who had offered hostages and obedience. His orders were to visit as many tribes as possible and persuade them to make their peace. Caesar had also sent ahead a trusted tribune, C. Volusenus, with a single warship to carry out a naval survey of the coast and discover a landing place. This officer was away five days, and will certainly have explored the coast from Hythe to Sandwich. The curious fact is his failure to discover the harbour of Richborough, which was so successfully used a century later. Whatever its cause, this failure had profound effects on the campaign both this year and next, for on both occasions Caesar had to land on an open beach, and on both occasions his transports were gravely damaged by storms.

Perhaps Volusenus did not go as far north as Richborough, or perhaps he did not care to explore too closely inside coastal inlets in a single ship. We have no evidence to suggest coastal changes in the century between Caesar and Claudius, though this part of the coast

45

has, of course, changed profoundly in the period between Caesar and the present day; it is certainly curious that, even if Richborough was missed by Volusenus, it was not discovered by patrols after the landing. Another possibility is that the harbour of Richborough was not as splendid as its modern reputation; but there must have existed some sort of inlet at the mouth of the Stour, even if it was not large enough to accommodate the whole fleet, and Caesar does not appear to have known of its existence. This was undoubtedly the penalty paid for the absence of the cavalry. Short of actual archaeological identification of Caesarian earthworks, no better indentification of the landing-place is likely to be available than that offered by Rice Holmes's masterly and very full examination of the evidence. The point of departure was Portus Itius, convincingly identified with the later Gesoriacum, the harbour of Boulogne. Eighteen transports had been held up by contrary winds eight miles farther up the coast at Ambleteuse, and these were assigned to the cavalry; but they missed the tide and next day were blown back by contrary winds.

Caesar himself with the two legions – about 10,000 men – set sail at midnight, and by nine the next morning was off Dover, where he saw the formidable cliffs lined with defenders, and realised the impossibility of landing thereabouts. He lay at anchor till three o'clock, to await the slower-moving transports, and employed the time in briefing his officers. When the rest of the fleet arrived he moved northwards and ran the ships ashore in the neighbourhood of Walmer and Deal. The Britons had followed along the coast, and were there to oppose the landing. The shelving beach compelled the soldiers to jump down into deep water, and the heavily armed legionaries were at a disadvantage; but Caesar was able to use the lighter warships with their artillery and complements of slingers and archers on the left flank, and he also manned smaller boats with reinforcements under orders to support any bodies of troops seen to be in difficulties. The eagle-bearer of the Tenth legion bravely leapt into the water, and the soldiers plucked up heart to follow him. Eventually a foot-hold was gained on the beach, and a determined charge put the enemy to flight. It was now that the lack of cavalry made itself felt, for the rout could not be made final. Nevertheless, the mercurial temperament of the Britons at once compelled them to seek terms; they handed over Commius, surrendered some hostages and promised more. They also dismissed their levies, and

46

soon a trickle of distant chieftains began to appear, to ask for peace.

Four days later the cavalry transports were sighted: but before they could make land they were scattered by a storm and with difficulty returned to the Continent. The same storm coincided with a full moon and an exceptionally high tide. The beached warships were badly damaged and the transports which had been riding at anchor were soon in grave difficulties. Some were lost, the rest found to be unusable.

This disaster turned the tables. The Britons took fresh hope and began to slink away to raise their forces once again: the Romans were without means of retreat or of supply. But Caesar was equal to the emergency. Forage parties were organised, and the rest of the army, working with great energy, repaired all but twelve ships, using the material from these to patch the rest. While this was going on the Seventh legion, whose turn it was to forage, was ambushed by a British force consisting largely of chariots and cavalry. It was saved by the sharp eyes of the cohorts on guard duty at the camp who observed an unusual cloud of dust in the direction taken by the legion. Caesar hastened to the rescue and drove off the enemy, but once again his lack of cavalry prevented effective pursuit. Nevertheless, his success produced a further offer of British hostages, and taking advantage of this success, such as it was, Caesar set sail that night with his whole force and returned to Gaul.

The first British expedition had not enjoyed the success intended. The non-arrival of the cavalry and the naval disaster had ignominiously pinned him to the coast of Kent, and more determined leadership on the part of the British might have placed him in considerable jeopardy. From a different point of view, however, his success had been spectacular. The fact that the Ocean had been crossed and surrenders made by the barbarians of Britain was what appealed to Rome and resulted in the unprecedented grant of a *supplicatio* lasting twenty days. And Caesar himself had learnt the character of British fighters; had encountered war-chariots for the first time and had seen how to deal with them; had found that an invading army could seize sufficient corn in Britain for its needs; and had discovered what seemed a suitable landing place for next year's campaign. The risks which are inseparable from success in war had been faced, and the balance in the end was satisfactory.

In 54 operations were on a much larger scale. As many as 600 transports had been constructed to a special design during the winter, as well as twenty-eight warships; including last year's ships and some privateers, over 800 vessels were to cross the Channel in one fleet. The new transports were lower in the beam than usual, for ease of loading and beaching, and rather wider than normal to carry more cargo, and they were all fitted with oars as well as sail. Caesar had assembled a large army at Boulogne: five of his eight legions and 2,000 cavalry were chosen to accompany him. There were thus many more animals as well as men to transport, and for a full-scale expedition a heavy baggage train was required. Labienus was left with the remaining three legions and 2,000 cavalry to keep the peace in Gaul, and to see to the proper supply of corn and the security of the ports.

Owing to various delays the expedition did not finally set sail till the beginning of July; on 29 August Caesar wrote to Cicero that he was shortly going to re-embark his forces, and the evacuation was probably completed by about the middle of September. Caesar thus spent just over two months in Britain, and during that time, despite a second serious naval disaster, he defeated and imposed terms on the Belgic confederacy which opposed him. No one could have done more: many ancient generals would have achieved less. In fact, his success is closely parallel, in its scale and in the time taken, with that of Aulus Plautius a century later; and the latter's task was simplified by the centralisation of Belgic power which had occurred in the meanwhile.

The expedition sailed at nightfall about 6 July, and in the morning Britain was seen on the left. The wind had dropped at midnight, and the fleet was drifting with the tide up Channel. Then the tide turned, oars were got out and a landfall made at a point chosen as best for the purpose the previous year. These facts make it certain that the landing took place in the area between Deal and Sandwich. It was unopposed. As he soon learnt from prisoners, the Britons had been alarmed by the unprecedented size of the fleet and had retired to high ground inland. Everyone was on land by midday and a camp was built. As soon as he had discovered the whereabouts of the enemy he decided on a bold stroke. A night march would bring him to the Stour crossing, which they were massing to defend twelve miles away, before he was expected. He left ten cohorts and 300 cavalry under Q. Atrius to guard the camp. The beach was open and gentle, and he took the risk of leaving the ships at anchor instead of consuming valuable time hauling them up to security.

In the early morning he reached the Stour and easily drove the Britons from the crossing. The principal ford lay at the future site of Canterbury. No settlement yet existed on this site, but a hill-fort lay on the heights above at Bigbury, 1½ miles beyond the ford. This must be the place in the woods with strong natural and artificial fortifications previously prepared for inter-tribal war, which Caesar describes, and to which the defeated Britons retired. His night march had paid its dividend.

The entrances to the earthwork were blocked with felled trees, and from the edges of the wood the Britons sallied out in small groups and impeded the advance. However, the Seventh legion formed a dense column with shields locked over their heads, and captured the hill-fort by assault across a causeway made by filling the ditch with earth and faggots. Caesar never had the same trouble over British hill-forts as he encountered in Gaul: it would have been a different story, perhaps, if his plans to invade the south-west had come to anything.

The capture of Bigbury terminated that day's fighting: pursuit was postponed, for a camp had to be constructed. This camp has still to be located. It must occupy some 150 acres, perhaps at Harbledown. The next day he had just despatched three columns of mixed cavalry and infantry in the pursuit – already he had mastered the tactics necessary to cope with British chariots – when messengers arrived from Q. Atrius with the news that disastrous damage had been suffered by the fleet in a storm the night before: almost all the ships had been driven on shore. He recalled the battle-groups which were not yet quite out of sight, ordered a retreat to the coast, and himself went on ahead to assess the damage. Forty ships proved to be a total loss, but an inspection showed that the rest might be repaired. This was a serious set-back. The damage itself was the least of his worries: precious time had to be wasted hauling up every-thing beyond the reach of the waves and in constructing a strong landward fortification. Messengers were sent to Labienus for crafts-men from the Continent, and with orders for the legions there to start constructing ships. By working night as well as day the task of beaching and fortification was completed in ten days: the repair of the surviving ships would, of course, take longer.

The beaching of 760 ships was an enormous task, and enormous, too, must have been the area to be included in the new ramparts. It is easy to see why on first landing he had not delayed his march until such a task had been undertaken; and it is important to remember that, even if he had done so, the thirty-six hours or so available before the onset of the storm would not have sufficed to avert more than a very small part of the disaster. The real fault lay in not having discovered a suitable harbour. If Richborough was too small, or for any reason now unknown to us unsuitable, a landing somewhere in the Thames mouth might have been wiser, though it would have meant a longer voyage and one into unknown waters. This difficulty over suitable harbourage may have been one of the factors which influenced Plautius a century later to cross in three divisions.

We may conclude that Caesar's judgement of the risks was not at fault. Speed – the famous *Caesariana celeritas* – was ever the secret of his success. The ten days' delay now enabled the Britons to do what he had hoped to prevent. Submerging their differences, they chose Cassivellaunus as supreme commander. Cassivellaunus, 'the first British historical personality', ruled beyond the Thames: though Caesar does not say so, it is probable that he was king of the Catuvellauni, who are later vouched for in the Hertfordshire–Buckinghamshire–Cambridgeshire area north of the Thames. Their area of settlement at this stage was probably neither so widespread nor so well defined, but Cassivellaunus was undoubtedly a distinguished war-lord. Under his command a much larger confederate army drawn from all sources was awaiting Caesar in the neighbourhood of the Stour crossing. This time there was no set battle. British cavalry and charioteers kept up a running fight with the Roman cavalry, but were unable to prevail, unless they could cut off groups which pursued too far. They were aided by their knowledge of the surrounding woods: later in the day, when the Roman camp was being constructed, they unexpectedly appeared in a fierce attack on the troops on guard and succeeded in eluding two cohorts sent to cut them off.

The Romans had not encountered chariot-warfare in Gaul, and at first found it hard to adapt themselves to it. Chariots had a complement of one warrior and one driver. They were drawn by two ponies, but although certain classical authors, confusing them with Persian chariots, credit them with axle-scythes, such things are neither

50

mentioned by Caesar nor attested by archaeology. Their tactics were to drive swiftly over the battlefield, hurling javelins and creating confusion and panic with their dashing horses and the noise of the wheels. If they could get among the cavalry the warrior dismounted to fight, and the charioteer retired to be at hand to aid a speedy retreat. The chariot gave the fighter the mobility and speed of cavalry, without preventing him exhibiting the virtues of infantry as well. Daily practice gave great skill in manoeuvring at speed over rough ground. The warrior would even dash out along the pole and stand on the yoke while travelling at full gallop. The secret of the chariot was its resilient wheel made of a one-piece felloe – an invention, it seems, of the Celts. The Roman legionaries, weighed down with heavy armour, could not pursue when the enemy gave ground, nor did they dare to leave the close formation in which they had been taught to fight. The Roman cavalry could master the chariots, but when enticed too far from the supporting legions by simulated flight, they in turn failed before the dismounted warriors. Ancient cavalry was poorly mounted, and they had no stirrups. The correct tactics to employ against the chariots, as Caesar soon learned, was to keep cavalry and infantry in touch and acting in concert. After that they caused no further trouble.

The next day the opportunity came for a decisive Roman victory. The Britons attempted to repeat their success of the previous year against a detachment on foraging duty. But this time the column, commanded by C. Trebonius, consisted not only of three legions but the whole of the cavalry. The Romans were able to turn the tables, and flight became a rout as the Roman cavalry, emboldened by the support of the legions, kept up the pursuit. This failure took the heart out of the Britons: the allies melted away and no further pitched battle took place. Cassivellaunus was left as the objective, and Caesar now pressed on towards the Thames, which formed the southern borders of his kingdom. The river was fordable, Caesar says, at one point only, and there only with difficulty. This crossing had been protected with stakes on the bank and others under water, but the passage was forced – the legionaries up to their necks in water as they waded over – and the Romans were across.

The identification of this ford has been confused by the natural eagerness of antiquaries to place it at spots such as Brentford or Walton where stakes have been recorded. In fact, however, these points are all too far upstream for probability, and the remains in question would be more easily explained as fish-weirs or pile-dwellings.[6] The Claudian army in AD 43 found a ford at London,[7] and it is hard to see how Caesar could have missed it; and as shortly afterwards he found himself in Trinovantian territory (Essex), this strengthens the case for London. There is not the least need for the stakes to have survived; indeed, it is hard to see how they could have, even had they been allowed to obstruct the crossing after the war.

Cassivellaunus now pinned his faith on guerrilla tactics. The country north of the Thames was much more thickly wooded than Kent, but it was his home ground, and his people knew all the tracks. Dismissing his infantry, he retained only 4,000 chariots. With these he kept up worrying skirmishes and cleared the Roman route of inhabitants and cattle alike. Caesar was compelled to keep his cavalry near the column for fear of ambushes, and his policy of devastation was in consequence much restricted. However, he still had one card up his sleeve.

Mandubracius, a prince of the Trinovantes, had fled to Caesar in Gaul when his father, their king, had been killed by Cassivellaunus. The Trinovantes now sent envoys to Caesar offering surrender, and asking for the young prince to succeed his father as king. They sent hostages and grain, and for their part were protected from devastation by Roman troops as well as from attack by Cassivellaunus. When this became known, other tribes (otherwise unknown to us) – the Cenimagni, Segontiaci, Ancalites, Bibroci and Cassi – joined them in surrender. Cassivellaunus in this way paid for his previous aggressive policy, and Caesar learnt from his new allies the whereabouts of Cassivellaunus' oppidum. This was quite close, but its secret had been preserved through the effectiveness of Cassivellaunus' scorched-earth policy.

If this oppidum was Wheathampstead it lay on the west bank of the River Lea. Caesar remarks on the strength of its defences, but he attacked it on two sides and soon broke in, capturing large numbers of cattle – no doubt those previously swept from his path – and killing or taking prisoner many Britons. The strategic skill of Cassivellaunus and his powers of leadership are mostly clearly seen now in the closing stages of the campaign. With Caesar already at his gates, he had sent orders to the four kings who ruled in Kent to attack the naval camp: and despite the black appearance of his prospects these orders were obeyed. It was a shrewd blow aimed where it could damage Caesar most dangerously. But the attack did not succeed: the Britons were easily routed by the garrison, and when the news reached Cassivellaunus he determined to give in. This he did, using the mediation of Commius.

This last fact probably means that Caesar had taken the initiative in offering acceptable terms. He had every reason to do so for, as he himself makes clear, it would have been easy for his enemy to prolong opposition until the end of the campaigning season. Moreover, it is likely that disturbing news had come from Labienus, sufficiently unsettling to cause him to alter his original intention of wintering in Britain. It may have been in connection with this news and change of plan that he paid a visit to the coast about 5 August. He does not record this himself, but we learn of it from a letter of Cicero's. The visit must have been snatched in mid-campaign, as a short consideration of dates will show. The landing had taken place about 6 or 7 July. The wreck and ten days' reconstruction take us to about 19 July before the campaign can have been restarted. Trebonius' victory will have occurred about 21 July. The march to the Thames and beyond can hardly have been over in little more than a fortnight; and if it was, there is a long unexplained delay thereafter, for as we have seen Caesar had still not yet evacuated Britain by 29 August. The visit to the coast can hardly have been connected with the attack on the naval camp, for this cannot have occurred so early, since it is associated with the closing events of the campaign. The visit in fact seems to have taken place while the army was safely in Essex, and the motive was probably the necessity for urgent and rapid communication with the Continent. Caesar himself tells us that one of his reasons for deciding to winter in Gaul was the danger of sudden uprisings there, and it was known that the harvest that year had been poor.

Both sides were thus interested in coming to terms, and these were quickly agreed. Hostages were given, an annual tribute was fixed, and the security of the Trinovantes from aggression was arranged. The army now returned to the coast, where the fleet lay repaired. Owing to the number of prisoners and shortage of vessels, Caesar decided to evacuate in two stages; but few of the empty vessels were able in the event to return to Britain because of contrary winds, and after a long wait he crowded everyone into the ships he had and on a calm night sailed for Gaul.

1. *B.G.*, ii, 4.
2. *Ibid.*, ii, 14.
3. *Ibid.*, iii, 5, 11.
4. *Ibid.*, iv, 4, i.
5. *Antiquity*, xxi (1947), 3–9.
6. Bede, for instance (*H.E.*, i, 2), says the stakes were still visible in his day, as thick as a man's thigh and sheathed in lead. This sounds more like the piles of a Romano-British bridge. He does not give the position.
7. Changes in the relative level of land and sea in post-Roman times have resulted in the tides reaching far higher up the Thames than they did in Caesar's day. Recent work has suggested the likelihood that there was a ford near Tilbury. If so, and if it was the one used by Caesar, it would bring him more easily to the territory of the Trinovantes; and it might throw light on the location of Cassivallaunus' territory, which, we are told, adjoined the river. I am grateful to Mr W. Rodwell for knowledge of the ford.

4
Caesar to Claudius

Caesar had come and gone. The future denied him the opportunity of ever returning, but this failure to complete his work in Britain was only to be certified by the passage of time. A century and a half later the historian Tacitus summed up the situation as it then appeared to him by saying that Caesar had revealed rather than bequeathed Britain to Rome; and Claudius could go so far as to claim to be the first Roman to reduce the barbarians beyond the Ocean to obedience. Thus, subsequent generations came to overlook what had been achieved. But to contemporaries, and for more than a generation after the expedition, the picture was probably different. Mr C. E. Stevens has pointed out that in his description of the conditions of surrender Caesar employs legal and technical terms such as *dedito* and *vectigal*, which specifically indicate the first steps in forming a province out of conquered territory.[1] The final steps, as it turned out, were never taken; but for some time to come the possibility of taking them remained, and there are indications in contemporary writers that this fact was recognised down to 40 BC and even later. However, treaties had been made and tribute imposed, and hostages taken to secure obedience. It is often carelessly stated that the tribute was never paid; but there is no evidence for this, and it is most unlikely. The treaties with Cassivellaunus and the Trinovantes would have been binding so long as the rulers concerned survived: only when they died would a new situation develop. Cassivellaunus is unlikely to have broken his agreements while Caesar lived, and for Mandubracius and the Trinovantes, whose submission had altered the whole course of the campaign by leading the wavering tribes into alliance with Rome, strict compliance with Roman requirements was even more necessary in their own interests. Some reflection of the fruits of Roman friendship can be seen in the large number of Italian wine-amphorae which now begin to appear in the tombs of the Trinovantian nobility.

Thus, for Britain a new era had opened. The Roman empire now reached the Channel, and its menace or its friendship were ever-present political choices; for what had been done once could be done again. The old-established trade-routes had been disrupted; tin for the time being was no longer exported to Armorica from the South-West and meanwhile the development of Spanish tin-production captured the market; for more than a generation there is little sign, except in Essex, of cross-channel contacts between the Belgic South-East and Roman Gaul. Instead, it has been suggested that new contacts were sought across the North Sea. There is, however, little evidence of this at present, and indeed south-eastern Britain had few exports which were likely to find a market in barbarian Europe.[2]

In one other respect the situation was altered. Commius had been a friend of Caesar, as we have seen, and had been generously rewarded for his services; but after the British expeditions he took the side of Vercingetorix in the great Gallic rebellion, and played a prominent part in the resistance. Labienus had attempted to have him assassinated, but he escaped with a severe head-wound; a second attempt to kill him failed, and when he finally submitted it was on condition that he should never again have to meet a Roman. Shortly after this, probably in 50 BC, he seems to have made his escape to Britain, for Frontinus recounts the strategem whereby he eluded pursuit by spreading sail although the rising tide had not yet floated his ships: the Romans, thinking him afloat, abandoned the chase. In Britain coins bearing the name of Commius derive from the uninscribed British Q series, which is otherwise identical and presumably represents the earliest issues of the group over which he eventually attained supremacy. The distribution suggests an entry in the Chichester area and the establishment of a kingdom south of the middle Thames. He will have been joined by many refugees from Gaul; but, as we have seen, he already possessed connections among the earlier settlers in these parts. His successors, Tincommius, Eppillus and Verica, each describes himself as *Commi filius*. This introduces a certain chronological difficulty, since Commius was active in 54 BC and Verica still alive in AD 43; but it is probably better to accept this than to imagine that the Commius of the coins is not the historical Commius or that *Commi F.* on the coins means other than what it says.

The establishment of this southern kingdom of Belgae was to have far-reaching results. Though Belgic settlers in its area were probably not as numerous as north of the Thames or in Kent, and its subjects largely consisted of native peoples ruled over by a Belgic aristocracy, it did result in the spread of Belgic civilisation over much of southern Britain which had escaped the earlier migrations. Even in the early days its existence circumscribed the expansion of the Catuvellauni, who were already debarred from expansion eastwards. Later on, by an ironical development of events, it became closely associated with Rome in Augustus' policy of creating a balance of power in Britain; but this was not until after Commius' death, when his son Tincommius was king. As we shall see, this new policy of the son of the man who had vowed never to set eyes on another Roman was not to meet the unqualified approval of his followers.

The political history of the period is largely to be inferred from a study of the coins. In the northern area Cassivellaunus did not inscribe coins, and it is not even possible to be sure what coins he issued. The choice seems to lie between Gallo-Belgic E, which have too wide a distribution to be ascribed solely to him but might be the coins of a confederation, and British L, which are thought to be too late in date. The first Catuvellaunian king to issue inscribed coins was Tasciovanus, who is not otherwise attested in history. He probably began his reign *c.* 20 BC, and might perhaps have been Cassivellaunus' grandson. By now the capital was at *Verulamium* (Prae Wood), as the mint-marks show. His earliest coins derive from British L, though later in the reign more sophisticated designs appear.

Among the early issues is a very scarce type bearing the mint-mark of *Camulodunum* – Colchester. This was the capital of the Trinovantes, and these coins show that Tasciovanus had resumed expansion eastwards. This was contrary to Caesar's arrangements, but not necessarily in breach of them unless the treaty had been renewed. However, even if Cassivellaunus' successors had not felt bound to renew their agreement, the Trinovantes would surely have felt a compulsion to remain under Roman protection. This attack on them, then, may have involved an appeal to Rome, and in any case cannot have been pleasing to the government of Augustus, since it

57

would bring a hostile power to the coast. A Roman defeat on the Rhine in 17 BC may have emboldened Tasciovanus to take this step, but the presence of Augustus himself in Gaul in 16 almost certainly caused him to withdraw. For this must be the meaning of the scarcity of the issue, and the dates fit the position of these coins in the sequence of Tasciovanus' issues.

Tincommius succeeded his father perhaps about 25–20 BC. His earlier issues closely resemble those of his father, but later in his reign completely new types suddenly appear which not only closely resemble Roman coin-types but are also so well made that they are certainly the work of Roman die-cutters. This suggests a technical mission, which, as G. C. Boon has said,[3] is hardly likely to have been confined to mint-improvement. Later kings of his line boasted the title REX on their coins, which strongly supports the idea that they had entered into treaty-relationships with Rome, and had been granted this title of recognition, which was not British. Tincommius himself did not enjoy this distinction, but it seems very probable nevertheless that he entered some sort of agreement with Augustus, for later on we find him a refugee and suppliant in Rome. The date of such an agreement is again probably *c.* 16 BC, for now, or shortly after, Roman imports and pottery begin to appear at *Calleva* his capital, and one of the coin types copied is an Augustan issue of between 15 and 12 BC. If so, we can begin to see the establishment of a new Roman policy towards Britain. Earlier in his reign Augustus seems to have kept open the possibility of a reoccupation of the island. In 34 and again in 28 and 27 BC military expeditions were planned, but were postponed owing to more pressing commitments; and for some years after this the idea of intervention was kept alive in the works of court poets. The motive may have been, as Dio once suggests, to complete the work of Caesar, but the occasions for a demonstration may also have been the need to re-establish the treaties with new rulers: and in 27, Dio tells us, the Britons would not come to terms. Later in the reign, however, we hear no more of intervention, and indeed a changed relationship with Britain is reflected in an ode of Horace published in 13 BC, though written perhaps two years earlier.

By giving support to Tincommius, Augustus probably intended to effect a balance of power between the two chief Belgic kingdoms of Britain, which would make reoccupation unnecessary. This, indeed, had already been delayed so long that it could not have been achieved without a full-scale expedition. If such was his intention, it seems to have been successful, at least for most of his reign. Tincommius, it is true, was eventually expelled and fled to Rome some time before AD 7; but the expulsion seems to have been the result of domestic intrigue rather than Catuvellaunian aggression, for he was succeeded by his brother Eppillus. Augustus therefore did not attempt to restore Tincommius; instead, with greater realism, Eppillus was granted recognition as *Rex*, and Verica after him. Eppillus had only a short reign at *Calleva*, to judge by the rarity of his coins with this mint-mark. He seems to have been soon ousted by his younger brother Verica, and thereafter gained himself a principality in Kent. Verica was certainly ruling during the reign of Tiberius, since some of his coins copy Tiberian types, and without doubt he is to be recognised as the Berikos of Dio's Greek text, who fled to Claudius on the eve of 43. Roman influence in the southern kingdom is reflected not only in the frequent copying of Roman coin-types, and the occasional presence of Roman die-cutters, but also by the symbol of the vine-leaf on certain coins of Verica, which indicated the prominence attached to Roman trade connections.

In the northern kingdom Tasciovanus continued to rule down to about AD 5–10. Under him the Catuvellauni, though prevented from overrunning the Trinovantes, continued to expand. The kingdom stretched from Northamptonshire to the Thames, and may even have included part of Kent west of the Medway. Some of his coins bear the title RIGONUS, which appears to be the Celtic counterpart of Rex, and hint thus at a war of propaganda which is more obviously reflected in the ear of barley appearing on the coins of Cunobelin, his son; for this barley not only advertises the agricultural wealth on which the kingdom's prosperity rested but also, perhaps, opposes the idea of British beer to the luxurious imports of wine suggested by Verica's vine-leaf. This was only propaganda, for in fact large quantities of wine reached the tables of Catuvellaunian nobles, as the surviving amphorae attest.

In Essex the earliest inscribed coins bear the name of Addedomaros, who was an approximate contemporary of Tasciovanus. The distribution and character of his coins show that he maintained himself against his western enemies; but in the end he was supplanted, or succeeded, by Dubnovellaunus, who had been the first king to inscribe coins in Kent. It now seems probable that it was Addedomaros who was buried in the Lexden tumulus at Colchester. It is likely that Dubnovellaunus had been driven from Kent by Eppillus, some time about AD 1, whether or not he already possessed territory north of the estuary. Dubnovellaunus then ruled at *Camulodunum*, but not for long. His name appears in Augustus' *Res Gestae* along with that of Tincommius, and this probably means that he had been driven out before AD 7; it probably also implies that, like Tincommius, he had had previous dealings with Augustus. He was supplanted at *Camulodunum* by Cunobelin, son of Tasciovanus; and from this date onwards the Trinovantes were finally submerged in the new Catuvellaunian empire.

Cunobelin was the greatest of the Belgic kings, and he had a long reign of almost forty years, during which he gained control of most of south-eastern Britain. Suetonius could call him *Britannorum rex*. It is evident that his seizure of *Camulodunum* and conquest of the Trinovantes was contrary to Roman policy as so far traced, but nevertheless it was successfully accomplished. If the conquest of the Trinovantes occurred in AD 9 or soon after, taking advantage of Roman weakness created by Varus' disastrous defeat and loss of three legions in the German forests that year, it is possible that Cunobelin was acting in pure defiance of Augustus. On the other hand, Augustus had already been ruling nearly forty years, and it is not unlikely that he had altered his ideas about Britain, where in any case the supplanting of the Trinovantian king Addedomaros by Dubnovellaunus of Kent had already confused the Caesarian position.

Now the geographer Strabo, writing soon after Augustus' death and giving reasons for non-intervention in Britain, states that certain British rulers had obtained Augustus' friendship by embassies and courtesies, and had set up offerings on the Capitol, thus making the island virtually Roman.[4] This certainly cannot refer to the fugitive princes Tincommius and Dubnovellaunus, who came in person, and could have no claim to set up offerings in the Capitol; nor could their presence in any way suggest that Roman control in Britain had been advanced, but rather the reverse. The passage records submissions or alliances from Britain itself. And as this not inconsiderable diplomatic success is unrecorded by Augustus himself in his *Res Gestae*, it is probable that it occurred after AD 7, when that document is thought to have been last revised. One of the kings is likely to have been Verica who received, as we have seen, recognition as *Rex*. Another may well have been Cunobelin himself, who certainly at one period issued bronze coins bearing the title *Rex*, and whose new capital at *Camulodunum* has been found to be so full of products imported from the Roman empire. Cunobelin has often been considered as anti-Roman in policy, but there is no real support for this view in the first half of his reign; and while he no doubt pursued an independent path, he was probably sufficiently realistic to see the advantages of a timely gesture whereby the consequences of his march to the coast might be averted. Another friendly gesture occurred in AD 16, when some ship-loads of Roman soldiers belonging to Germanicus' army were wrecked on the British coast and were returned to the Continent. On the Roman side, alliance with both British kingdoms would have obvious advantages. It would end the dangers of being involved in support of the less powerful Atrebates, and would open wide commercial possibilities north of the Thames. As Strabo put it, there was now no political reason to intervene, and Rome received much profit from import and export dues without having to finance an occupying army. The exports of Britain, he tells us, were corn, cattle, gold, silver, iron, hides, slaves and hounds; while ivory ornaments, amber and glass and other manufactured trinkets were imported in return. To the list of British products pearls should be added: Caesar had dedicated a breastplate studded with them in the temple of Venus Genetrix.

Under Tiberius relations with Britain remained static. Cunobelin overran east Kent and expanded his kingdom also beyond the upper Thames north of the Kennet. Nor was the southern kingdom to remain unmolested. Epaticcus, another son of Tasciovanus, is seen by the distribution of his coins to have been creating a kingdom for himself in the northern part of Verica's territory, and it is probable from the coins and pottery types found there that *Calleva* itself fell to him about AD 25. Cunobelin's power by this time was so paramount that these events cannot have taken place without his consent.

This encroachment on the Atrebatic kingdom could not have been achieved without protest at Rome from the victims, but the government of Tiberius was set against foreign adventure, and considered itself bound by Augustus' testament that the empire should be contained within existing bounds. Moreover, if Cunobelin himself was a Roman ally, as we have suggested, the situation may not have seemed so dangerous: it could be represented as a mere internal struggle of little interest outside Britain. The fact remains, however, that Verica's territory was gradually reduced to little more than the west Sussex coastal plain, and even this was lost by AD 42 or 43 when Verica fled to the Court of Claudius. While Cunobelin lived there seemed little cause for action, but when he died in 40 or 41, the situation seriously and quickly deteriorated, as we shall see, with the succession of his sons Caratacus and Togodumnus, two young men with no sense of restraint or of diplomatic moderation.

This, then, is the probable political history of the period. The evidence on which it is based is numismatic and archaeological. The coins of Commius whose find-spots are known are too few for their distribution to show where the focus of the kingdom lay in his day. *Calleva*, the Belgic site at Silchester, first appears by name as the mint-mark of Eppillus' coins, but it is probable from the archaeological finds that it was already the capital of Tincommius. Lying in the heaths and forests of the Berkshire–Hampshire border, it misses the opportunities that a site on the Thames would have given. A southern capital and mint probably also existed near Chichester. Coin finds are numerous in the vicinity, and the Chichester Dykes are probably best understood as its outer perimeter, perhaps dating from the last years of Verica.

Whether or no Wheathampstead had been the original nucleus of the Catuvellauni, their capital had been established at *Verulamium* by the start of Tasciovanus' reign and here also a mint was in operation. The site, lying above the valley of the Ver, enjoyed better communications north-westwards and westwards than had Wheathampstead. Not much is known of the site itself, but its defences have been traced over an extent of three-quarters of a mile along the valley crest. The bank and ditch in question were of very moderate strength, and formed probably little more than the boundary of the inner nucleus of a much wider and more sprawling settlement. Scattered traces of occupation, and the debris of the mint itself, are now known in the valley below beneath the later Roman city and outside it to the south; fragments of much stronger dykes are known to the north and beyond the river to the east, and these perhaps are all that are left of the real perimeter. Such enclosure dykes, as those of *Camulodunum* show, might delimit a very wide area within which settlement was sporadic, the remainder being devoted to pasture and tillage or market gardens. The inner defences of Prae Wood itself were strengthened at a date which is probably the eve of the Claudian conquest.

More is known of *Camulodunum*. Here on the plateau between the Roman River and the Colne twelve square miles of land are demarcated by powerful rectilinear dykes, and within this area an inner nucleus, defended by the Sheepen dyke, proved to be the capital of Cunobelin. But *Camulodunum* itself is attested before the date of his accession, and it is probable that the earlier nucleus lay at Gosbeck's Farm, south-west of Sheepen, where some curving dykes of contour type seem to pre-date the rectilinear ones. Here, then, around a sacred site – the shrine and hill, no doubt, of Camulos, the war god – lay the original *Camulodunum*, capital of Addedomaros and the Trinovantes. The site was well chosen. It has a gravel subsoil, and lies within easy reach of the estuaries and harbours of the coast, while the upper waters of the rivers give easy access across their watersheds to the chalk country beyond. It is protected by the convergence of the two valleys and by the added defences of the dykes. Enclosing the large area they do, these suggest a different tactic from that of the older hill-forts, and it has been thought that the dyke was the Belgic answer to the threat of chariotry. Against chariots these earthworks were an effective obstacle, but in undertaking their laborious construction Cunobelin was committing the common error of preparing for the last war rather than the next. The dykes of *Camulodunum* were destined to meet an army and a method of attack against which they had not been designed.

Camulodunum had fallen to the Catuvellauni, as we have seen, about AD 5–10. This drive to the east was full of significance for their later history, since in effect it converted them from an inland power, hemmed in by the isolation of marshes and forests, to a maritime one able to develop and exploit new commerce with the freshly established markets and production centres of the Roman Rhineland. It thus assured the continued ascendancy and wealth of the Catuvellaunian royal house and ensured that the advantages of continental trade should not become the prerogatives of the princes of Kent and Sussex. Of the Sheepen site itself little could be recovered by excavation owing to the thoroughness of later destruction there. The habitations were for the most part small huts of prehistoric character. Industry is attested by the working of bronze

63

and iron, and by the manufacture of pottery. Trade is indicated by the large quantities of imported amphorae once containing wine and oil, and of imported plates and drinking vessels whose presence in such large numbers points to a revolution in manners, such specialised vessels being earlier quite unknown. The amphorae are in the main Italian, but there are some examples from Spain; the table-services are either in Arretine ware from Italy or in a variety of Gallo-Belgic wares from Northern Gaul and the Rhineland. Some of these vessels – but only imported ones – are inscribed with owners' marks, suggesting that literacy was beginning to spread among the wealthier classes who could afford the better wares. The local potters, who felt it necessary to imitate the potters' stamped signatures seen on imported plates and cups, rarely achieved more than a series of illiterate strokes.

Another large Belgic oppidum lay at Canterbury on both sides of the Stour. Nothing is known of its defences, but huts and drainage gullies have been found over a wide area, and the place was probably important enough to be the capital of some of the Kentish princes. The huts are circular or subrectangular, and sometimes recessed some two feet into the ground. Crudely baked slabs of clay were used for the hearths, the first tiles to be made in Britain, and plentiful oysters attest the growth of a trade which was to become highly organised in the subsequent period. A unique silver coin inscribed VODENOS is among the finds: this prince seems to have ruled about the beginning of the first century AD. But Kent was not a unified kingdom: another large oppidum, which possessed a mint, lay beneath Rochester. Both sites are low-lying or valley sites, and illustrate the changes of settlement-pattern introduced by the Belgae.

Beyond the metropolitan area of Belgic settlement lay other tribes, whose use of coin and further features of Iron C show that, if not wholly Belgic in ethnic character, they were at any rate ruled by Belgic princely families. This indeed was largely the case also in the southern kingdom. It was a state of affairs brought about by the confused Belgic migrations described in Chapter 2. In East Anglia north of the Trinovantes lay the Iceni. Their inscribed coins, which about AD 30 succeeded an uninscribed gold and silver series, give the following sequence of royal names. The first is CANS DVRO, which may perhaps be a dual name indicating magistrates: there follow ANTED, ECEN, AESU and SAENV, the first being the only king to issue gold

64

coins as well as silver: the others issued silver only. Gold was, of course, less useful for ordinary commerce than silver, and the growing use of coinage for everyday commerce is shown by the numerous silver and bronze issues of Tasciovanus and Cunobelin: early coinages solely in gold were probably mainly used for princely bounties. It is also probable, however, that gold was increasingly difficult to obtain for the Iceni; if indeed they are to be recognised as the Cenimagni who surrendered to Caesar, much of their gold may have drained away over the years in tribute to Rome. The main nucleus of the tribe occupied south-west Norfolk and north-west Suffolk, and hostility towards the Catuvellauni must have developed as the frontiers of Tasciovanus approached their borders. Under Cunobelin actual encroachment took place, to judge by the aristocratic burial of Catuvellaunian type from Snailwell, and perhaps that at Elvedon too. Another concentration of population existed in the Norwich area, and as we shall see in the next chapter was perhaps not always under the same ruler as the other. The main body of the peasantry seem to have been poor and backward, but the treasure of Snettisham and other finds of rich decorated metal-work show that the aristocracy and priesthood were wealthy. Many of the surviving examples of horse- or chariot-equipment date from the last days of Icenian independence about AD 60, when the territory had already been penetrated by artistic and commercial influences of a Romano-Belgic kind from Colchester, but it is clear that the aristocracy they represent had enjoyed a long prosperity, which Iron B chieftains had helped to found.

Farther north-east in Lincolnshire, Leicestershire, Nottingham and Rutland and northern Northamptonshire lay the Coritani. Belgic pottery is known in this area, especially from Dragonby near Scunthorpe and Thorpe near Newark; from Old Sleaford, the site of a mint, where this pottery was associated with decorated wares of the Iron B tradition, as it was also at Ancaster; and from at least one brine-boiling establishment on the Lincolnshire coast. Belgic bronze brooches are known from Dragonby and South Ferriby. Similar pottery, perhaps of slightly later date, is known from Leicester itself, but it is not yet certain how far, if at all, its presence there is connected with a Roman military base at the site. The coins themselves are, as we have seen (p. 36), derived from Gallo-Belgic originals through British H and I; and since in the subsequent inscribed series we find coins bearing a double name, it can be suggested that the tribe was ruled by dual magistrates. If such existed, they must have held office for several years each, since there are not enough names to cover the period if they were annually changed. In any case, it seems likely that the arrangement commemorated the fusion of two originally separate groups. The coins in question were once thought to be Brigantian, but their distribution makes attribution to the Coritani unquestionably correct. Both gold and silver were minted. This tribe also had a common boundary in Northamptonshire with the expanding empire of Cunobelin, and is likely to have been hostile to him. They occupied a territory which was rich both in iron and in horse-pastures, and they controlled the north-eastern half of the ancient trade route known as the Jurassic way.

The south-western half of this route lay in the territory of the Dobunni. We have seen that the earliest uninscribed coins, British R, existing in this area are closely connected with those of British Q and the coins of Commius. They reflect an intrusion into south Gloucestershire by a Belgic group from Commius' realm some time between 30 and 20 BC, and this means that the Dobunni, too, were a partly Belgic tribe, though in their case the rest of the population (Western Second and Third B) were far more culturally advanced than was the case among the Coritani or Iceni. Objects such as the Birdlip mirror which are the products of the earlier group demonstrate the advanced nature of their culture.

The history of the Dobunni from this time on is one of gradual expansion south-westwards into Somerset as far as the Mendips, and north-eastwards farther into Gloucestershire, where the oppidum of Bagendon was founded; and thence as far afield as Worcestershire and western Oxfordshire. Vivid traces of this process can be seen in the massacres at Worlebury and Bredon Hill. At or shortly after this time the coins become inscribed, perhaps c. AD 20. The abbreviated names of kings appear in the following sequence: Anted, Eisu, Catti and Comux; last of all come Corio and Bodvoc. The last four names, to judge by the distribution of their coins, ruled over parts of the kingdom only, Catti and Comux being succeeded by Corio and Boduocus (as his full name may have been) respectively. It is a significant fact that all these kings and their unnamed predecessors continued to mint the traditional triple-tailed horse on their coins and were quite uninfluenced by the Roman types of Tincommius and his successors. Only Boduocus showed any originality, and the significance of the good Roman lettering of his coins will be discussed in Chapter 5. It seems probable that the Dobunni refused to follow the lead of Tincommius in adapting himself to Roman policy, preferring to maintain the attitude traditional among refugees from Gaul. Excavations at Bagendon, one of their chief oppida and mints, showed that the site had been established perhaps about AD 15, and that already by this date commercial relations with the Catuvellauni had begun; for not only is there at Bagendon much pottery of Catuvellaunian type – and the defences of the oppidum are also inspired from there – but also the many imported vessels can hardly be derived from any other source. It is true that a trade-route was maintained with the Durotrigan harbour at Poole, but there is no suggestion that this port saw the introduction of luxury pottery from the Continent. If during Cunobelin's reign this peaceful intercourse was allowed to develop across his western border it seems likely that Cunobelin received corresponding commercial advantages – the import of iron and copper and tin – which outweighed the desirability of conquest in this direction. Indeed, as well as raw materials, we may consider the likelihood of trade in actual manufactures from western workshops and the hiring of master-craftsmen trained therein.

South of the Dobunni lay the Durotriges, in Dorset and the southern parts of Wiltshire and Somerset. Here again we seem to have a Belgic aristocracy ruling over a tribe which was basically of Iron B. In Chapter 2 we saw the development of trade with Brittany and the introduction or local development of multivallation in the hill-forts. The coins, however, are derived from the Belgic British B coinage, and the evidence of the Le Catillon hoard shows that this intrusion of a Belgic ruling caste had occurred well before the time of Caesar's Gallic War; but under the influence of Armorican trade the original gold standard had been converted to a silver currency. The Gallic wars for a time disrupted trade connections with the Continent, and thereafter the Durotrigan coinage began a process of degeneration both in metal-standard and in execution. It was never inscribed. The new culture which accompanied the coins introduced several changes in the way of life as well as new pot-forms; the burial-rite however, remained inhumation, and this suggests that the new Belgic leaders were not very numerous. At Maiden Castle the main rampart was refortified with a timber palisade and storage-pits were no longer used. The pottery is still basically for the most part of Iron B type, but now often made on the wheel; the influence of Armorican pottery is also apparent; but there are some new types of obvious Belgic character. Some of these, as for instance the tazza or pedestalled cup, show links with the Catuvellauni and are probably to be explained by trade contacts; for the reality of trade with the Catuvellauni is demonstrated by fine lathe-turned urns of Kimmeridge shale which are not infrequently met with in chieftains' graves in Cambridgeshire and Essex.

The Durotriges possessed several very sizeable and well-defended oppida, among them Hod Hill, Hambledon, South Cadbury Castle and Maiden Castle; and on the edge of their territory an important fortified post lay at Hengistbury Head, which has some claim to be the Dunium of Ptolemy's Geography. Many other powerful hill-forts continued to be occupied down to the Roman conquest, and this suggests that after the decline of Durotrigan prosperity consequent on the Gallic Wars, the normal process of political unification was halted, and that the tribe continued in political anarchy under a large number of rival nobles, each in his stronghold. A tradition of hostility to Rome survived until AD 43: it had not been mitigated as elsewhere by the nearer threat of Catuvellaunian domination, nor had it been mollified by the undoubted trade in wine which amphora-fragments attest.

East and north-east of Durotrigan territory the area of Salisbury Plain has produced evidence of Belgic occupation. Coins of British Q stretch across north Wiltshire, and the coins of Commius and his sons reach westwards to the Swindon neighbourhood; but in the region south of this the Belgic occupants used no coins. This must mean that they were or became independent of Atrebatic rule,[5] and the fact is reflected in the creation here, later on, of the Roman *civitas* of the Belgae. This is an ethnic not a tribal title and implies that this civitas was an agglomeration of petty groups. The multivallate hill-forts, however, extend eastwards across this area as far as the Test; they suggest resistance by Iron B groups to expansion from the primary Belgic area east of this river, an expansion which is vouched for at several of them, where Belgic occupation and sometimes even refortification succeed the Iron B phases at these camps.

Beyond the outer ring of Belgic or partly Belgic kingdoms and tribes lay other groups with earlier cultural traditions. In south Somerset, Devon and Cornwall the origins of the Dumnonii can be traced to the South-Western Second B culture, though they were reinforced especially in Cornwall by Breton immigrants, some of whom may have arrived as refugees as late as Caesar's conquest of Armorica. The burial-rite is crouched inhumation in a stone cist. Trade in metals was still active both along the south coast and especially up the Bristol Channel to the ports of the Dobunni. In Devon, west of the Exe, the siting and planning of settlements point to stock-herding as one of the principal activities, but east of the river the land becomes more suitable to arable. Here the type of hill-fort is different and multivallates occur. It seems certain that this land was a zone of contention between the Durotriges and the Dumnonii, and that the former were successfully expanding into it. Quite soon the south Somerset plain had been overrun, since many of the Duro-trigan coins found there are of early type: evidence of penetration towards Exeter is provided at Hembury, where the earlier Dum-nonian hill-fort was taken over and reconstructed by people using Durotrigan pottery. The occurrence of this pottery at Exeter itself, however, is likely to be due to introduction by the Roman army and its camp-followers. The lake-villages of Glastonbury and Meare give us the most intimate glimpse of Dumnonian culture owing to the survival there of such rich finds; these included the skilled wooden products of carpenters and lathe-turners, the workshop debris of bronze-smiths and enamellers, and a wide variety of iron tools. Other finds illustrated trade in Cornish tin, local lead from the Mendips, Dorset shale from Kimmeridge and spit-shaped iron currency-bars from the Forest of Dean.

Across the Bristol Channel lies South Wales. Here the plain and hills of Glamorgan formed the homelands of the Silures, whose eastern boundary was no doubt the Wye, since beyond it Dobunnic coins circulated. Northwards they will have extended to the upper Wye valley and perhaps beyond. They thus lay westwards of the distribution both of Western Second and Third B sites, and were probably in the main aboriginal descendants of the Bronze Age and earliest Iron A settlers of the region; occasional discoveries of decorated metal-work, however, point to the presence of wealthy leaders with a taste for the culture of Iron B. Some of these finds may be the product of trade, but others were certainly made locally, perhaps by itinerant craftsmen. Occasional elements also of Iron C culture, such as pottery and brooches, appear on Silurian sites; but these were probably introduced by the followers of Caratacus after AD 43, and do not point to pre-Roman Belgic penetration, as the absence of a coinage shows.

Much of Silurian territory is high barren plateau, poorly drained and boggy. The slopes of the hill-land were densely wooded, and so were the valley floors. The strength of the tribe, to judge by the distribution of defended settlements, lay on the coastal plain and in the valleys of the Wye and upper Usk. Almost certainly they were largely pastoral by occupation, and their territory contains similar multiple-enclosure earthworks to those of the Dumnonii, which are thought to have been designed for herding. The people themselves were described by Tacitus as swarthy and curly-haired, which made him think them of Iberian stock.

The Pembroke peninsula and adjacent areas were the home of the Demetae. The elevation of the land here is lower, the hills more rounded and the earth more fertile. It is possible that the Demetae were exposed to Silurian aggression, for the scarcity of Roman military establishments in their territory suggests that they became philo-Roman. On the other hand, large hill-forts are rare in their territory; instead there are numerous small defended enclosures of very doubtful defensive value, and these do not afford a picture of a people under heavy pressure.

The core of the Ordovices lay in north-west Wales, in Caernarvonshire and Merionethshire, another mountainous and difficult district. It is possible that they were a confederacy of tribes rather than a single people, for Anglesey was certainly within their overlordship, and so presumably was much of central Wales.[6] They, too, will have been largely pastoral, deriving agricultural produce from Anglesey and the Lleyn peninsula, just as the Silures derived theirs from the coastal plain behind them.

The fourth tribe known from Wales was the Deceangli, who inhabited Flintshire and Denbighshire, an area rich in copper and lead. This tribe and its south-eastern neighbour the Cornovii lay astride the route northwards up the Welsh Marches, whose use by invaders and refugees is graphically illustrated in the numerous great hill-forts of the region, which often show many periods of refortification. The proliferation of hill-forts here and among the Silures probably points to a lack of political coherence, such as was suggested for the Duro-triges also. The Cornovii occupied the land between the estuary of the Dee and the headwaters of the Trent and Severn. Much of this area was lowland forest; the core of the tribe lay in the more open lands of southern and western Shropshire. There are indications that the Cornovii were friendly towards the Romans, and this may mean that they were under pressure from the Ordovices. Roman forts, in-deed, long occupied parts of their territory, but these may have been as much for protection as for control. On the other hand, locally independent chieftains may not all have been trustworthy.

North of the Cornovii and Coritani lay the Brigantes. These Tacitus describes as numerically the largest tribe in Britain, while Ptolemy states that they stretched from sea to sea. Their precise southern boundary is uncertain, but is usually thought to run from the Mersey to the Humber, curving southwards to include the Peak district of Derbyshire; for Coritanian coins hardly extend in this direction be-yond the vale of Trent except for three hoards in southern Yorkshire, which are clearly out of context and deposited by refugees. The north-eastern limits of the tribe lay on the Tyne as epigraphic, literary and archaeological evidence converge to show: here Hadrian's frontier of Britain virtually coincided with the tribal boundary. But north-westwards of this Brigantian land probably ex-tended beyond the Roman wall to include the fertile basins of the Lyne, Esk and Annan. East Yorkshire, however, was excluded. This was the territory of the Parisi, whose ancestors had introduced the Eastern B culture to this area long before. The Parisi maintained their independence and may even have been developing commercial relations with the middlemen of *Camulodunum* or directly with the Roman continent.

The Brigantes, however, were far less sophisticated. Despite the presence of areas of fertility, little trace of pre-Roman agriculture is known in their territory: the economy was based on flocks and herds. Julius Caesar had described their way of life when he wrote, 'the people of the interior for the most part do not grow corn but live on milk and meat and dress in skins', though the same description might apply to the peoples of Wales. Much of the vast area attributed to this tribe is barren mountain moorland or bog. The centres of popu-lation were separated by these hills, and themselves lay in favourable valleys or plains of lighter soil: some fifteen such major concentra-

71

tions can be recognised.[7] The scattered nature of the grouping no doubt then as now gave rise to regionalism, but the absence of agriculture inhibited the development of powerful independent principalities. Instead a single kingdom had emerged, whether by consent or conquest, but its power was shaky. However, the primitive nature of Brigantian economy should not blind us to their military power, or to the wealth enjoyed by the nobility, which is reflected for us in the metal-work, for instance, of the Stanwick hoard. The known finds, however, are almost all of late date, and they suggest that the prosperity of the Brigantian kingdom was related to its status as a Roman client power, and even that the unification of the territory was a fairly recent one. One surprising feature of the whole region is the great scarcity of hill-forts, and some of these were probably erected after AD 43. Their shortage is very likely to be explained by the relatively primitive and semi-nomadic culture of the inhabitants, but among the few are some of the most impressively inaccessible in Britain, such as Ingleborough, Mam Tor and Carrock Fell. That at Almondbury near Huddersfield – which has been suggested for the site of Queen Cartimandua's headquarters – is multivallate and may have continued to be occupied at a relatively late date under Iron B influence coming via the Marches. The picture of the Brigantes that emerges is of a primitive and pastoral though numerous population ruled by Iron B chieftains, many of whose families may have themselves been recent arrivals; and of political centralisation only in process of achievement by AD 43.

Beyond the northern boundary of the Brigantes lowland Scotland held four tribes. The Votadini occupied the eastern lowlands and the coast north of the Tyne, with the Selgovae in the central region to their west. North of the Solway, Dumfriesshire and Galloway were in the territory of the Novantae, north of whom lay the Damnonii embracing the Clyde valley. Beyond the Forth–Clyde isthmus, in the area later to become the homeland of the Picts, Ptolemy gives us the names of eleven tribes, of whom little can be said individually except that the most northerly of them, the Cornavii, and the Damnonii, too, have names which recall those of tribes in southern Britain and may be offshoots from them; but the Cornavii may take their name simply from the headland of Caithness.

The territory of most of these tribes is characterised by numerous hill-forts, and in this respect they differ from the Brigantes. The presence of so many fortifications suggests a rather more advanced culture, with greater agricultural resources. Many of the hill-forts have timber-laced ramparts and some of them are now known to have been built at the very beginning of the Iron Age or even earlier. The character of the local rock often led to a curious but unintentional result when fire was applied to the timbers; the stones fused and the ramparts became in large part vitrified. Vitrified forts, of course, are not, as was once thought, a special category; vitrification could happen anywhere, at any period, if the geology were suitable. Some hill-forts in Scotland have a long history of occupation. Objects found, such as ring-headed pins and La Tène Ic brooches, show that the material culture had much in common with that of southern Britain, though pottery is in general more rare: possibly containers of wood or leather were used instead. Later fortifications, as in the south, no longer employed timber-framing; instead, increasing use was made of stone walls and – where the rocks allowed – of ditches. Iron B features appear in the metalwork and perhaps suggest some immigration from the south, and refugees from Roman rule may also be expected. It is noteworthy that Professor K. H. Jackson's study of the linguistic problems of the origin of the Picts has led him to a similar conclusion.[8] The differences in dialect between the Iron Age inhabitants of Scotland north of the Forth and those of the rest of Britain would be accounted for if the former spoke a Hallstatt dialect, while the language of the latter had undergone change from new arrivals in Iron B and C.

North of the Great Glen and extending thickly through the Orkneys and Shetlands, a completely different type of fortification is dominant – the brochs. These defended homesteads – the apogee of the hedgehog principle – indicate a way of life based on the family rather than on any wider unit, the families concerned being occupied with primitive farming and fishing, and perhaps with piracy. The mutually exclusive distribution of brochs and hill-forts suggests both that the brochs developed later than the hill-forts and that their occupants were opposed. Mutual plundering and slaving raids would compel both to maintain fortifications, but the social and geographical organisation of the broch-builders was such as to compel individual rather than group protection. Internecine strife between the two peoples is the context of the 'submission' of the Orkneys to Claudius in AD 43, though in fact the gesture was premature, for

Roman arms did not arrive to suppress the hill-fort people until another forty years had passed.

Though hill-forts with timber-laced ramparts were the earliest type of hill-fort to reach Scotland (succeeding the palisaded enclosures mentioned on p. 25), other types followed in due course, including multivallates. South of the Forth–Clyde isthmus great numbers of hill-forts exist, especially in the country of the Votadini and Selgovae, though these hill-forts are usually small in size. The Votadini, whose western border was roughly the line of Dere Street and the upper Tyne valley, had a large oppidum at Traprain Law, which became of considerable importance in the later Roman period. The Selgovae had an important oppidum on Eildon Hill North, which had attained an area of thirty-nine acres when it was destroyed in 79, but showed two previous lines of successively enlarged fortifications. This indicates the long history of Iron Age development in this part of Scotland; but the co-existence of great numbers of smaller fortresses points to general insecurity, and shows that tribal cohesion and centralised control had not proceeded very far. The Selgovae were perhaps the more powerful tribe of the two, and their hostile pressure on the Votadini may have caused that tribe to turn early to Rome for support. The former, however, for long retained an unremitting enmity towards Rome, which carefully planned military occupation could usually control but not abate.

This, then, was the state of Britain on the eve of the Roman conquest. That conquest itself was the work of Claudius in 43, but only because the attempted invasion of Gaius in 40 had ended in fiasco. Tiberius had died in 37. Gaius, his youthful successor, quickly became perverted by power, and the record of his reign is hopelessly confused by the hatred and ridicule of its historians. In 39 the emperor left hurriedly for Germany to suppress a conspiracy; but he had already planned a military expedition across the Rhine for that year. The troops, however, proved poorly disciplined and out of training, and while he was restoring the situation his attention was directed to Britain by the arrival of Adminius, a son of Cunobelin, who had been exiled by his father. This prince, it appears, too easily persuaded Gaius that Britain was ripe for plucking, but when the army was assembled at Boulogne a mutiny broke out. Three years later the legions certainly showed reluctance to embark for a land which lay outside the circle of the civilised world, and that the same reluctance was encountered by Gaius seems both likely enough and the best explanation of the garbled accounts which are all we have for guidance. The expedition was abandoned, and its sole memorial was the great lighthouse which Gaius had caused to be erected at Boulogne.

Gaius was murdered in 41, and it fell to Claudius, his uncle and successor, to revive the British project. There were sound reasons both of a personal and political kind for this, whatever we may think of Gaius' motives. In the first place, Claudius himself, though the son of Drusus and brother of Germanicus, both of them distinguished generals, had led a sheltered life owing to physical deformity. He had been despised by his family and allowed little part in public affairs. He possessed, however, his share of the pride for which the Claudii were famous, and he now felt particular need for military success in order to establish himself in the regard of the army to whose loyalty to his family he owed his throne. The personal motive behind the conquest must not be underrated: world rule was part of the psychological inheritance of the Caesars, its consummation merely attending on convenience. Moreover, if foreign conquest was to be undertaken there were good reasons to choose Britain for its object. In the first place much of the necessary staff-preparation must already have been completed for Gaius. Then in Britain the situation required action. Cunobelin had recently died, leaving his kingdom divided between Togodumnus and Caratacus. These young men were headstrong and ambitious, and they began a programme of aggression and enlargement. It is probable that they overran the Dobunni; this in itself would not affect their relations with Rome, but when they overran the remnants of the Atrebatic kingdom and expelled Verica the situation was different. Verica was a Roman ally; his arrival in Rome presented more than an excuse for intervention: failure to take action now would be damaging to Roman prestige already tarnished by the failure of Gaius. The Augustan precedent of recognising the alternative successor could not be followed, since the kingdom itself had ceased to exist. Moreover, the flight of Verica was followed by an impudent demand for his extradition; and when it was not complied with disturbances broke out. Whether Sir Ian Richmond was right in suggesting that these disturbances took the form of raids on the Gallic coast, or whether they were riots which threatened the lives of Roman merchants in Britain, there is little evidence to decide;[9] but in either event the long summer of peaceful relations with Britain was over.

Gaius had raised two new legions,[10] and this meant that the Rhine garrison, to which they had been added, was dangerously powerful, the careful balancing of the strength of army-groups being one of the secrets of successful imperial statecraft. Even if two legions were to be used to strengthen the defences of the British-facing coast, they would still be in Gaul. The safer, as well as the bolder, course would be to deal with Britain by placing the necessary forces in the island itself, where they would form a separate army-group beyond the sea, and where their supplies could be charged to the new province. Moreover, there was now available more exact knowledge than Caesar had had of the mineral wealth of Britain, the *pretium victoriae* as Tacitus put it,[11] and the vast manpower of the island would be a useful asset – a sort of invisible export balancing the costs of occupation – for conscription overseas. Thus, the new province might be expected, in the long run, to pay for itself.

One further point is relevant. Britain had the reputation of being the home of Druidism; but in Gaul Augustus, Tiberius and Claudius all took steps to stamp out the savage rites associated with this priesthood. While H. Last was no doubt correct [12] in stressing that this aspect of Roman policy was based on cultural rather than political motives, one cannot doubt that one of its results was to imbue surviving Druids with hostility, and it is a fact that in Britain this priesthood did nourish the opposition. Suppression of Druidism in Gaul can never have been completely successful with Britain unsubdued, and for its conquest therefore the existence of Druidism on the island may have formed a subsidiary motive.

1. *Antiquity*, xxi (1947), 3–9; *Aspects of Archaeology in Britain and beyond*, ed. W. F. Grimes (London, 1951), 332–44.

2. There are two British coins from Denmark and one from Belgium. The Belgic bronze bowl from Poland (*Antiq. Journ.*, xliii (1963), 27–37), should not be forgotten.

3. G. C. Boon, *Roman Silchester* (London, 1957), p. 219, note. 28.

4. Strabo, iv, 5, 3.

5. It has been suggested that the inhabitants of Salisbury Plain, like the Dobunni, rejected the Romanising policy of Tincommius.

6. The name of one component, the Gangani of the Lleyn peninsula, has been preserved by Ptolemy.

7. The names of five of these groups or *pagi* can be recovered: the Gabrantovices in north Yorkshire (perhaps really part of the Parisi), the Setantii in Lancashire (the Fylde), the Textoverdi in the upper valley of the (south) Tyne, the Lopocares round Corbridge and the Carvetii in the upper Eden valley. The last became an independent civitas in the third century (p. 214). The Corionotatae (*RIB*, 1142) were probably a sept of the Selgovae.

8. K. H. Jackson, in Chapter vi, *The Problem of the Picts* (ed. F. T. Wainwright, Edinburgh, 1955).

9. I. A. Richmond, *Roman Britain* (London, 1955 and 1963), 18. *Britanniam . . . tumultuantem ob non redditos transfugas* is the phrase Suetonius (*Divus Claudius* 17) uses: it supports the latter view.

10. For arguments that it was Gaius, not Claudius, who raised xv Primigenia and xxii Primigenia see Balsdon, *JRS*, xxiv (1934), 13–16.

11. *Agricola*, 12.

12. *JRS* xxix (1949), 1–5.

5
The Claudian Conquest: the rebellion of Boudicca and its aftermath

In AD 43 the conquest of Britain was begun. An army of four legions with auxiliary troops, amounting in all to about 40,000 men, had been assembled at Boulogne. The legions were the II Augusta, IX Hispana, XIV Gemina and XX Valeria, and the general was Aulus Plautius, hitherto governor of Pannonia. Legio IX had accompanied him from his province, but the other three were drafted from the Rhine garrison, Legio II from Strasbourg, Legio XIV from Mainz (both in Upper Germany), and Legio XX from Neuss.[1] The sailing was delayed by a mutiny, since the soldiers affected the superstition that the Ocean, part of which separated them from Britain, marked the boundary of the proper world of mankind: beyond it lay unknown hazards. It was not until Narcissus, one of Claudius' freedmen ministers, had been sent from Rome to address them that they returned to their senses, influenced not by any words of his but by the ludicrous humiliation of seeing an ex-slave on the general's tribunal. Their sense of humour exerted itself, and with cries of 'Io Saturnalia' – a reference to the festival when slaves assumed their masters' clothes – the angry tension was released, and embarkation followed at once. But by now time had been wasted; it may already have been past the end of April.

Dio, who is our only considerable source for these events, says that the expedition sailed in three divisions so as not to be hindered in landing, but was driven back on its course; we are left to judge whether three separate landings took place or whether after diversionary movements the army re-united at a single landfall. Excava-

78

tions at Richborough have revealed an early Claudian defensive beach-head perimeter which is clearly the scene of the main and probably the only landing. Otherwise the possibilities resolve themselves into two alternative theories. Some, struck by the pattern of the roads in east Kent, have suggested landings at Dover and Lympne, from which converging movements would unite at Canterbury. In favour of this theory is the probable inability of Richborough to house the vast invasion fleet; warned by Caesar's naval disasters, Plautius may have determined to get as many of his ships as possible into the safety of harbours. Against this, however, it can be said that hitherto no evidence has been found of early military activity at either Dover or Lympne; that the roads can hardly have been built at the time of the advance, and that after it only one supply-port, Richborough, would be required; and that excavations at Canterbury have given no indication of the large military base which would seem to be thus indicated there. The other theory recalls that one of the reasons for the expedition was the restoration of Verica, and so suggests a landing in West Sussex. Against this can be urged the folly of committing a force sufficiently large to be useful to a landing so far away that it could play no part in the decisive phases of the campaign. No sensible general would so divide his army initially; for the objective could be more easily attained by applying decisive force in the decisive place. Furthermore, the detachment which is attested as operating along the south coast a year later is *Legio* ii, and this is known to have been in Kent in 43.

At Richborough, then, the army landed. The site was well chosen, for it has a sheltered harbour and occupies a slight rise in the surrounding flats: at this time it was not yet an island, despite frequent assertions. In the late Roman and early Saxon periods land-subsidence led to this result, but no general bent on a victorious invasion would be so timid as to land on an island, from which he would then have all the trouble of relanding on the mainland.

Unlike Caesar, Plautius did not have to face an opposed disembarkation. The Britons, misled by news of the mutiny, were expecting another fiasco, and at first Plautius had difficulty in finding an enemy to fight. However, in two skirmishes somewhere in east Kent both Caratacus and Togodumnus were successively routed, and they then retired to the line of the Medway, presumably to gather stronger forces. Disunity of this sort was often a factor in Celtic defeat. Soon

79

after this, part of the Dobunni surrendered, no doubt the half of the tribe ruled by Boduocus. 'Bodunni', indeed, is the name here given us by the text of Dio, but no such tribe is known, and in any case the surrender of part only of some small local tribe in east Kent would seem too insignificant to mention. The emendation to 'Dobunni' gives us a known tribe, the surrender of part of which would be a political gain of noteworthy magnitude; but it does not involve the supposition of a Roman expeditionary force operating in Gloucestershire, as has sometimes been thought, for the surrender could have been made either by embassy or in the field itself. Moreover, such action by Boduocus at this time is plausible. He himself is known from coins whose Roman lettering distinguishes them from all their predecessors; his tribe had enjoyed friendship and trade with the Catuvellauni in Cunobelin's time, as the distribution of coins and other objects shows. But this amicable intercourse had ceased with Cunobelin's death and the more domineering policy of his sons (Dio states that the tribe was now under Catuvellaunian control). A timely surrender to the winning side was clearly to his interest.[2]

The Roman forces were still east of the Medway when this occurred, and Plautius built a fort before advancing farther: at a guess this may have been placed near Harbledown to overlook the crossing of the Stour at Canterbury, where a large Belgic settlement existed. The Britons meanwhile had massed to oppose the crossing of the Medway, and thither Plautius now arrived to fight what was to be the decisive battle of the campaign. There was no bridge, so some Celtic or German auxiliaries who were trained to swim in full equipment were first sent over; and when these had caused considerable confusion by attacking the chariot-horses more troops, including the Second legion under its legate Vespasian, followed under the overall command of Flavius Sabinus. Even so, the result hung doubtful and the battle was renewed next day, an unusual event in ancient warfare. At last victory was achieved by an attack led by Hosidius Geta.

Where did this battle take place? Though Dio does not name the river, it can hardly not be the Medway. The Roman army had to advance along existing tracks, for its own supply-roads came later. The best known ancient track westwards from Canterbury is the so-called Pilgrims' Way, and this has been suggested as the route used by Plautius, leading to a battle at the Medway crossing at Aylesford. However, more recently the existence has been demonstrated of a Belgic settlement under Rochester, important enough to have possessed a mint; and it can hardly be doubted either that trackways connected it with Canterbury or that it presented in itself an important military objective. Furthermore, in 1957 a hoard of thirty-four Roman gold coins, the latest being issues of Claudius of AD 41, was found at Bredgar near Sittingbourne. This sum is too small to represent a subsidy to some native prince, but it is too large to be the savings of an ordinary legionary soldier: moreover, the coins show progressive decrease in wear from the earliest to the latest, which suggests that they represent a cross-section of the currency such as might be obtained from the sale of property or repayment of a debt. Such a large sum (three months' pay of a centurion) was probably the property of an officer, concealed before some skirmish, and it reinforces the view that the army passed north of the Downs by the route later laid out as Watling Street. Thus, we can picture the battle taking place near Rochester, and the width of the river there is more consistent with the recorded difficulty of crossing than it is at Aylesford. When the army moved forward once more a fort must have been left to guard the Medway-crossing: it is certain that no fort exists at Aylesford, but there is a suitable site for one beneath Rochester Castle.

The Britons now fell back on the Thames near London 'near where the river flows out into the ocean and at high tide forms a pool'. The Romans found the fords hard to discover, but auxiliary troops once more swam across, and others found or built a bridge upstream,[3] perhaps near Westminster. The marshy valley of the Lea, however, and the thickly wooded country near it presented difficulties. The Romans suffered losses in skirmishes, and though Togodumnus was killed in one of these, British resistance was strengthened rather than weakened by his loss.

So far the campaign had followed that of Caesar fairly closely, except that the main battle had taken place at the Medway rather than in east Kent. But there is no need to suppose that Plautius was taken by surprise at the Medway (not finding it in his Caesar), as R. G. Collingwood suggested, or that his staff were so poorly provided with military intelligence that they were reduced to leaning heavily on Caesar's memoirs as a hand-book. South-eastern Britain had been increasingly penetrated by Roman merchants since Augustus, and there had been much political intercourse as well. We need not doubt that the Roman Staff was perfectly acquainted with the geography and other features of the area in which the army had to operate.

Claudius himself was naturally anxious to be present in person at a decisive moment in the campaign, and Plautius had instructions to send for him if a check occurred. At this point, therefore, the advance was halted and the army retired behind the Thames to await the Emperor. If, in fact, the decisive battle had already been won, at least he could enter *Camulodunum* as a conqueror. It was now about the beginning of July, and Claudius will have arrived about the middle of August – bringing with him detachments of the Praetorian Guard, probably under their prefect, Rufrius Pollio, and possibly vexillations from other legions;[4] he also brought elephants, though more from determination to conquer in style than for their practical use, frightening though they would appear.

There was still time to capture *Camulodunum* and level its inner defences, but Claudius remained no longer than sixteen days in Britain; leaving orders with Plautius to continue the campaign, he departed probably about the beginning of September to cross the Channel before the equinoctial gales began. He travelled back slowly through Gaul, and arrived in Rome after an absence of six months early in 44, when he celebrated the triumph which the Senate had voted him. While at *Camulodunum* he had received the surrender of numerous tribes, some already conquered, others anxious to join the winning side. The former were disarmed; the others received treaties which regulated their relations with the Roman governor. The Senate voted Claudius and his legates permission to negotiate binding agreements without reference back, and to this power are probably due some distinctly original arrangements.

On the inscription of his triumphal arch dedicated in 51 he claims to be the first to have reduced barbarian tribes beyond the Ocean to Roman obedience (thus tacitly forgetting Caesar's achievements) and records the surrender of eleven British kings. One of these was probably Caratacus whose capture in 51 came just in time for inclusion; another might possibly be some chieftain from the Orkneys who was curious enough or hopeful enough to send an embassy, for Eutropius records the addition of these islands by Claudius to the empire.[5] The identity of some of the others will be discussed shortly.

Claudius had left the government of the Empire in the hands of a trusted colleague, Lucius Vitellius, with whom he had shared the consulship in the first six months of 43, and was naturally accompanied to Britain by a high-ranking staff. Among consulars known to have been here in addition to Plautius the commander were M. Licinius Crassus Frugi (later to be executed), A. Didius Gallus, Servius Sulpicius Galba, D. Valerius Asiaticus, Cn. Sentius Saturninus and probably M. Vinicius. Saturninus may have played some active part in affairs, since he is singled out by Eutropius [6] as responsible, with Plautius, for the conquest, and it has been suggested that it was he who was plenipotentiary in the restoration of Verica's kingdom. Didius Gallus, later to return to Britain as governor, seems to have been in command of the cavalry in Britain for a short while before being despatched to Moesia. Among senior holders of praetorian rank were T. Flavius Sabinus, Vespasian's elder brother, and Hosidius Geta, both of whom were promoted to the consulship in c. 45, no doubt for the distinguished part they played in the Medway battle. The latter may be the general who distinguished himself in Mauretania the year before.[7] Both of these were on Plautius' own staff. There was also T. Plautius Silvanus Aelianus,[8] who being related to Aulus Plautius was also probably on his staff. Vespasian himself, of comparatively junior praetorian standing, was legate of Legio II Augusta:[9] the names of the other legionary legates are not recorded. Of lower rank were C. Stertinius Xenophon, Claudius' doctor, and Ti. Claudius Balbillus, both serving as praefecti fabrum, and P. Graecinius Laco, procurator of Gaul. Claudius also brought his two sons-in-law, L. Junius Silanus Torquatus and Cn. Pompeius Magnus (son of M. Licinius Crassus Frugi). All these senators were awarded triumphal ornaments; nevertheless, the care which Claudius took to leave the empire in safe hands during his absence suggests that some of them may have been brought to keep them under his own eye. Saturninus had been consul in 41 when Gaius was murdered, and had advocated a restoration of the republic. Asiaticus was suspected of aiming at the throne on the same occasion. Galba was very well connected and did in fact become Emperor in 68; Silanus and Pompey and the latter's father, too, were executed or driven to suicide later in Claudius' own reign, and so was Vinicius.

The further stages of the military campaign were assisted by the political alignments already existing in Britain as the result of previous Roman policy and the expansionist activities of Cunobelin and his sons. The southern dynasty had had a long tradition of friendship with Rome, and now the leaders of other tribes were anxious to become allies, partly from motives of self-preservation and partly because they, too, were hostile to the house of Cunobelin. The best known of these princes are Cogidubnus, who succeeded to the realm of Verica, Prasutagus of the Iceni and Cartimandua of the Brigantes. A fourth, as we have seen, was very probably Boduocus.

The origins of Cogidubnus are not clear, but that he ruled at Chichester is testified by the undated dedication of a temple to Neptune and Minerva found there in the eighteenth century; on this he calls himself Tiberius Claudius Cogidubnus, thus emphasising the Roman citizenship given him by the Emperor over any royal descent he may have enjoyed in his own right. He also proclaims the titles of *Rex* and *Legatus Augusti in Britannia*.[10] Tacitus [11] tells us that he survived loyal to within living memory, which in the context must mean into the seventies; and he also tells us that this loyalty had been rewarded by the addition of further *civitates* to his kingdom; but we are not told when he became king. Verica had lived long enough to seek refuge with Claudius and to provide a pretext for invasion, as we have seen; and it is perhaps simplest to suppose that Verica was restored in 43, to be succeeded soon afterwards by a much younger and more energetic kinsman. Julio-Claudian policy was normally against the perpetuation, without good reason, of client-kingdoms by succession, but in this case there were special circumstances – the old age of Verica, the evident philo-Romanism of Cogidubnus (who had himself perhaps been an exile in Rome) and the political obligation inherent in having supported Verica's cause.

Prasutagus presents a difficulty in that though he is known to have died in AD 60, the date of his accession is obscure. Client-kings did not usually retain the right of coinage, and no coins of Prasutagus are known. But one coin hoard found in 1960 near Lakenheath included issues of Claudius in association with three native coins bearing the legend SVBIDASTO round a head modelled on a Roman prototype: it seems likely that at least one ruler of the Iceni, not Prasutagus, issued coins after 43. Furthermore, a native coin-mould was found at Needham, Norfolk, in association with pottery of Claudian date. The easiest explanation is that Prasutagus himself did not succeed till *c.* 47 (or else previously ruled only a part of the tribe) and after that date entered into closer relations with Rome. Mr D. F. Allen has indeed suggested that Antedius continued to rule over part of the tribe until this date (and so could qualify as one of the *xi reges* who surrendered to Claudius), and that the ECEN coins were those of Prasutagus after 47, issued on behalf of the confederacy of Iceni.[12] But there is a clear contrast between the successful and ambitious romanising efforts of Cogidubnus and those of Prasutagus, who did indeed open his territory to the activities of merchants and financiers, but has left no such solid achievements as temples or inscriptions or the creation of urban life.

Cartimandua has been seen as a Belgic princess, but this was a deduction from the coinage once thought to be Brigantian but now correctly attributed to the Coritani. She is first mentioned in 51, and her actions show that she had by then entered into treaty-relationship with Rome. How much earlier this had taken place is not certain, but surely at latest in 47, when the Roman frontier marched with hers. On the whole, it is likely that she already ruled the Brigantes in 43 and had made her peace with Claudius then, and is one of the *xi reges*. We are hampered by the loss of Tacitus' account of the conquest period, but the assumption is implicit in his later statement that Venutius, Cartimandua's husband, in the governorship of Didius Gallus had long been loyal and had even been protected by Roman arms. This can only refer back to the events of 48, when Ostorius had intervened in Brigantia, which he was under no obligation to do unless there was a treaty already in existence. Cartimandua will have calculated that alliance would strengthen her position at home, as indeed was the case.

Boduocus is known to us only from his coins, which come at the end of a sequence of issues of Dobunnic rulers; and a study of their distribution and related dating evidence shows that perhaps just before AD 43 this tribe was divided. Boduocus' coins, with the good Roman lettering of his name replacing the traditional Dobunnic emblem on the obverse, circulated in Gloucestershire, while the more conservative coins of Corio . . . circulated both north and south of this principality. As already explained, it is very likely that it is to Boduocus the historian Dio is referring when he describes the surrender of a part of the 'Bodunni', which can be taken as a textual corruption of Dobunni; and if so Boduocus will be another of the *xi reges* to have been awarded a treaty; though in his case mutual interest soon demanded that his territory should be garrisoned against the raids mounted by Caratacus from South Wales.[13] As neither Corio's nor Boduocus' coins seem to appear much before 43, they must both be allowed reigns after that date: but when Corio . . . at length made his surrender his kingdom was suppressed and was made part of the composite *civitas Belgarum* (p. 68).

The names of the other five kings who made their peace are lost to us, but it is likely enough that both the Coritani, who had been under pressure from Cunobelin, and possibly also, now or later, the Cornovii, were also among those who made their submission. Thus, once the power of the Catuvellaunian kingdom and its subsidiaries had been broken – as happened in the first year – the progress of the campaign was simplified. There remained no enemy of outstanding power this side of Severn or Trent. Small expeditionary forces consisting of single legions and their auxiliaries, or even of vexillations, were sufficient to fan outwards over the lowland zone putting down such opposition as still resisted, strengthening and supporting friendly régimes, and establishing lines of communication. The immediate flanks were in safe hands, East Anglia under Prasutagus or his predecessor, and Sussex and Hampshire under Verica and Cogidubnus.

The whole army had advanced on Colchester. Now Legio IX was pushed forward round the Fens towards the Trent and Humber, and Ermine Street was garrisoned by forts a day's march apart. In the absence of careful excavation, military remains in this part of Britain cannot always be safely distributed between the conquest campaigns and those undertaken against Boudicca. But a conquest-period fort lay at Chelmsford, and another later reduced in size and then strengthened during the alarm of AD 60, is known at Great Casterton; another fort not yet explored exists at Water Newton, and others can be assumed with greater or less assurance at Ancaster, Godmanchester and Cambridge (Fig. 2, p. 88). A large marching camp have been seen from the air at Home near Newark and at Ancaster.

The fortress of Legio IX was eventually established at Lincoln, where tombstones, of two soldiers lacking cognomina, have been taken to show occupation before 60. Other datable material indicative of the Claudian period is at present so rare at Lincoln as to suggest that the fortress was not founded before the governorship of Didius Gallus (52–57) and maybe later.[14] The aerial photography of Dr J. K. St Joseph has discovered two fortresses of about thirty acres, the one at Longthorpe near Peterborough, the other at Newton-on-Trent, due west of Lincoln. Fortresses of this size are not sufficiently large for a whole legion, but would be adequate for part of one possibly brigaded with some auxiliary cavalry. Other comparable fortresses are now known in other parts of Britain and will be mentioned later; they reinforce the deduction that columns or battle-groups of less than full legionary size were commonly employed on a permanent footing. In the case of Legio IX, it seems very probable that it was divided into three vexillations, and that these were given independent winter-quarters in the early years, the legion being reunited at Lincoln only when the strategic situation had altered.[15] This new situation might be the preoccupation of Didius Gallus with Brigantia or the regrouping of Paullinus after Boudicca's rebellion.[16] Even then the small size of the new fortress – $41\frac{1}{2}$ acres as against 46 acres at Gloucester, 49 acres at Caerleon and $52\frac{1}{4}$ acres at Inchtuthil – may suggest that a vexillation was still expected to be permanently outposted.[17]

A reserve force probably consisting of part of Legio XX and some auxiliaries was kept at Colchester. The fortress occupied part of the site of the later *colonia* and its garrison is attested by two well-known tomb-stones, one of M. Favonius Facilis, a centurion in the Twentieth, the other of Longinus Sdapeze son of Matycus, a *duplicarius* in an auxiliary cavalry regiment, the First Ala of Thracians. These, both being serving soldiers, probably died before the garrison left in 49; and the condition of their tomb-stones suggests that these were overthrown by Boudiccan rebels in AD 60.[18] What was probably a military supply depot of this date at the mouth of the Colne was unfortunately destroyed virtually without record in gravel-workings at Fingringhoe. Here supplies of men and equipment could be landed directly from the Rhine mouth, and hence supplies collected at *Camulodunum* could be shipped coastwise, for instance to the Witham.

Little is known yet of the activities of Legio XIV, which must have advanced over the Midlands; but though the initial advances in all cases will have made use of native trackways, road-building, if only in a preliminary way, must soon have followed; and just as the Ermine Street shows the way to Lincoln, so the Watling Street can

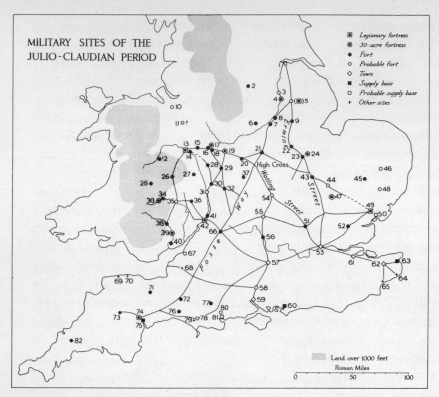

2　Military sites of the Julio-Claudian period

1 Winteringham	20 Mancetter	38 Abergavenny
2 Templeborough	21 Leicester	39 Usk
3 Littleborough	22 Great Casterton	40 Coed-y-caerau
4 Newton-on-Trent	23 Water Newton	41 Kingsholm
5 Lincoln	24 Longthorpe	42 Gloucester
6 Broxtowe	25 Nantmel	43 Godmanchester
7 Margidunum	26 Leintwardine	44 Cambridge
8 Thorpe by Newark	(Jay Lane)	45 Ixworth
9 Ancaster	27 Cleobury Mortimer	(Pakenham)
10 Chester	28 Greensforge	46 Scole
11 Whitchurch	29 Metchley	47 Great Chesterford
12 Caersws	30 Droitwich	48 Coddenham
13 Wroxeter	31 Worcester	49 Colchester
14 Leighton	32 Alcester	50 Fingringhoe
15 Red Hill	33 Clyro	51 Verulamium
16 Stretton Mill	34 Clifford	52 Chelmsford
17 Kinvaston	35 Kenchester	53 London
18 Eaton House	36 Cannon Frome	54 Towcester
19 Wall	37 The Lunt, Baginton	55 Alchester

88

be taken to indicate the track of the Fourteenth; and the first alignment of this road goes only as far as the Fosse Way at High Cross,
south-west of Leicester. So far we know little of military posts along
its course, except at *Verulamium*, but sites like Dunstable, Towcester or Whilton Lodge are spaced at appropriate intervals, and
forts might be expected at them. Leicester itself is a likely place for
a fortress for part at least of the legion.

The progress of Legio II is better known since its legate Vespasian
later became Emperor, and Suetonius' Life records that in thirty
battles he reduced two very powerful tribes, over twenty hill-forts
and the Isle of Wight – a campaign which probably lasted three to
four years. Excavations at Fishbourne near Chichester have revealed
military store-buildings at the head of Chichester harbour, and this
site in friendly territory would be a suitable base for mounting an
attack on the Isle of Wight. Later, as the advance moved on into
Dorset beyond Southampton Water, Fishbourne would be out of
touch, but early samian has appropriately been found at Hamworthy
on Poole Harbour, where perhaps an advance base was established,
and another early military site has been found near Wimborne.
Naval activity would in any case be required for the conquest of
Wight, and sea-borne supplies carried to suitable harbours along
the south coast would ease the problems of transport. The twenty
oppida can be safely placed in Durotrigan and neighbouring territory, where actual traces of fighting are known at three of them.
At Hod Hill a barrage of *ballista* bullets illustrates the capture of
the hill-fort, and even more dramatic evidence was discovered at the
excavation of the war-cemetery at Maiden Castle. Here skulls with
sword-cuts, and even a spinal column deeply pierced by a Roman
iron arrowhead, were found among the burials of the casualties. The
great defences of Maiden Castle are among the most impressive

known in Britain; but at neither hill-fort is there any trace of siege-works, of rampart-breaches or of causeways filling ditches. The gates were well defended and skilfully protected by earthwork, but they were of wood. The hill-forts themselves were not designed to face the long-range fire-power of Roman field artillery. Once the defenders had been driven from the ramparts by *ballista*-fire the gates yielded to burning as happened at South Cadbury. To capture hill-forts became a routine; the only difficulty lay in their number, not their strength. If the Durotriges were one of the two powerful tribes encountered by Vespasian the other was probably the Dumnonii. Both have many hill-forts, and both, in fact, put up so stout a resistance that their territory had to be extensively garrisoned for a generation. Conquest-period forts are known at Hod Hill, near Blandford (pl. 1a), and at Waddon Hill, near Bridport; another has been destroyed at Ham Hill, near Ilchester, to judge by the relics found in quarrying; and undated forts are known also at Wiveliscombe, Somerset, and at North Tawton, Devon. Beyond Exeter the occupation of Cornwall was postponed, for a fort at Nanstallon near Bodmin seems to have a Neronian origin; other supporting forts remain to be found. If Hod Hill is typical the garrisons of some of these were mixed, consisting of a vexillation of legionaries brigaded with auxiliaries; and in effect Legio II, despite heavy fighting, would have been bogged down in this area by the reduction of its man-power, withdrawn in static garrison duties. The legionary head-quarters and base at first may have been established at Wimborne or at Dorchester, Dorset, where legionary equipment, early samian ware and the behaviour of the main road all hint at such a con-clusion as a possibility; but a fortress must soon have been estab-lished farther forward at Exeter; alternatively, this legion, like the Ninth, may have been divided. Unfortunately the point is not yet certain. Ptolemy, the second-century geographer, used first-century sources for his description of Britain, but for legionary dispositions he seems to have used an independent and more recent list. He knows, for instance, that Legio VI is at York (where it did not arrive before the reign of Hadrian) and Legio XX at Chester. Legio II he places at *Isca Dumnoniorum* (Exeter), and this has usually been held to be a mistake for Silurian Isca (its fortress at Caerleon after 75). Confusion there certainly has been; but it would be easier to explain if it were founded on fact. A military origin for Exeter in this period is vouched for by early Claudian samian and by an unusual quantity of early coins, and recent excavations have revealed barracks and other military buildings as well as a very large bath-house; the latter can only be explained by the presence of the legion. Furthermore, excavation below the yard of the later town baths revealed part of a timber-framed building whose presence there at the very least implies a radical change of plan in the layout of the city, but is probably best seen as a military building earlier than the civil town: its plan can be interpreted either as part of the centurion's end of a normal barracks or as a building in the *canabae* outside the fortress. Elsewhere in Exeter early buildings were demolished in the period 65–70, which is just the time when Legio II is likely to have moved to Gloucester, leaving the area free for the foundation of the town (p. 109). Such a fortress at Exeter at this date may have been much smaller than full legionary size, and this may account for the *praefectus castrorum* being in charge of it in AD 60.

In 47 Plautius' term of office came to an end, and he returned full of honour to Rome to celebrate an ovation, the last recipient of this honour in history. His tenure of Britain had been mostly occupied with the military and political exigencies. Legionary vexillations had been established in permanent quarters near the limits of the advance. Colchester was still the main base, with at least the headquarters of a legion there, but another important centre for supplies had been established at Richborough. A network of auxiliary forts guarded the lines of communication and the zone of the frontier itself; for by 47 most of the lowland zone of Britain had been overrun and a frontier had been constructed based on the Fosse Way. This remarkable road runs from Exeter to Lincoln, whence its line is continued north to the Humber by the Ermine Street. Along and in advance of this connecting route forts are known or suspected,[19] and the road itself shows by its engineering and design – never deviating more than six miles from the direct alignment – that its conception was both unitary and military. Collingwood, who first recognised it as a military *limes*,[20] connected it with the next governor, Ostorius Scapula, and with the famous emendation of a corrupt sentence in Tacitus' Annals – *cunctaque cis Trisantonam et Sabrinam fluvios cohibere parat.*[21] But Webster has more recently shown [22] that this connection is not consistent with the military situation confronting Scapula. It is too complete to be considered merely a temporary stage of consolidation, nor would we expect such a stage in mid-campaign or between one governorship and the next. As the basis of a *limes*, it marks the intended limits of the first Claudian province, and it follows that imperial policy at first envisaged occupation only of the lowland zone. This makes sense. For though much of Britain's mineral wealth lay beyond the area thus defined, protectorates beyond the frontier could be expected to take it into account, while the position of the frontier itself at the northern limit of the native arable was convenient to the commissariat. The history of the next two centuries was to illustrate the difficulties of attempting to control the semi-nomadic economy of the sturdy pastoral tribes beyond, while ever deeper involvement would call for radical overhaul of the food-supply.

Wales and Brigantia

However, this early frontier was not to last: the tribes of Wales and even the nominally allied Brigantes would not let well alone. P. Ostorius Scapula, the succeeding governor, arrived to find the frontier in flames. Caratacus, Cunobelin's surviving heir, had fled to Wales, and his commanding personality was able to rouse both Silures and Ordovices to aggression. Late in 47, attempting to take advantage of the new governor's arrival after the close of the campaigning season and his lack of local knowledge, one or other of these tribes – we are not told which – raided 'allied' territory. This must mean either the kingdoms of Boduocus and Corio . . . or the territory of the Cornovii. Ostorius, however, drove them out, and by the next year he had assessed the situation and was ready with planned action. The frontier left by Plautius was already out of date in its middle sector, since here it made no contact with the real centre of anti-Roman activity in the north-west, the Ordovices of North Wales. Between lay the Cornovii, themselves a possible source of trouble, but more probably an allied tribe who were sharing the brunt with their southern neighbours the Dobunni. Ostorius made preparations to advance beyond the province into the gap between the headwaters of Trent and Severn. But first he must secure his rear. Plautius had established the province and had defined its boundary. Now tribes within it, whether allied or not, were to be disarmed. This measure amounted to an application of the *Lex Julia de vi publica* [23] which forbad the possession of arms except for hunting or self-defence on a journey; indeed, it may have been a somewhat arbitrary extension of its terms, since conquered territory had already been disarmed by Claudius, and allied tribes were bound by treaty rather than by Roman law. These treaties were arbitrarily altered, for Ostorius now distinguished between *civitates foederatae* within the province and the other *socii* beyond it; but the Iceni, who had never been overrun but had voluntarily entered Rome's alliance, resisted, and were joined by neighbouring tribes. They took up arms and concentrated at a spot defended by a rampart with narrow entrance so that cavalry should not break in. But Ostorius moved swiftly up with auxiliary forces only, and using his dismounted cavalry to augment his infantry, took the place by storm. In the battle the governor's son distinguished himself. The site of these operations has not been identified. The 'neighbouring tribes' would seem to indicate at least the Coritani, so the rallying point can hardly be one of the north Norfolk hill-forts; it is more likely to be found in the Cambridge or Peterborough region. A possible site is Stonea Camp, where remains of this date have been found. A study of the distribution of Icenian remains, particularly their coinage, suggests that the tribe had more than one focus; it is quite possible that it was the westerly group, ruled perhaps by 'Subidasto', who joined with its neighbours in this adventure, and that Prasutagus was ruler of one of the other groups which did not join in, and that as reward he had his territory extended. It is hard to see otherwise how he could have survived rebellion, or have been allowed to succeed a rebellious father.

With his rear thus made safe. Ostorius early in 48 advanced towards the Cheshire gap. With fine strategical insight he had quickly realised its significance: penetration here would divide the tribes of Wales and the Marches from those of the Pennines, and so would limit the objectives of subsequent operations in the west by cutting off the enemy from the possibilities of either reinforcement or retreat. More particularly, his choice of objective would seem to indicate the source of aggression the year before. We have already seen that the tribes in the hills were in any case more mobile than their lowland-zone contemporaries, but now their numbers were swelled by considerable groups of dissidents fired by desperation and with a wider vision of resistance: these would pass from tribe to tribe, inflaming aggression as they went. A successful campaign was in full swing and was already overrunning the Deceangli of Flintshire when disturbances broke out in Brigantia.

The federal character of the Brigantes made close control by Cartimandua difficult, and some of the western groups in the tribe had close connections with the Marches: for this area had long been a corridor for migration from the south, or of northward retreat before successive conquests by Western Third B peoples, princes of the Belgic Dobunni, and the Roman army itself. The reaction of these groups to Ostorius' thrust was beyond the power of Cartimandua to control, and opposition to her policy may have been fanned by the Druids of Anglesey, who saw themselves soon to be isolated from their sources of support in Brigantia [24] and doomed to extinction.

Ostorius wisely broke off his campaign when to continue would be to arouse the north as well as the west. The value of the flank-protection afforded by Cartimandua's régime was still pre-eminent: the queen received military support and the governor turned his attention to the Silures on his left front. Yet the failure to close the trap in 48 had its foreseen results in 51, when Caratacus moved into North Wales and later escaped to Brigantia. Meanwhile, however, the land between Upper Trent and Severn was held, and it seems likely that large vexillations of Legio xiv were stationed in new fortresses at Wall and Kinvaston and probably Metchley.

About twenty miles east of Wroxeter a very large fort has been found at Kinvaston near Penkridge. Originally it enclosed twenty-six acres, but in a later occupation was reduced to eighteen acres. Both forts are much larger than the size required for even the largest auxiliary unit, but too small for a complete legion. Like Longthorpe and Newton-upon-Trent, they probably represent the winter-quarters of a battle-group, a vexillation of legionaries with perhaps some auxiliaries, and the most likely time for the arrival of such a formation in this area is Ostorius' campaign of 48; but a trial trench did produce a sherd of samian pottery which falls best in Nero's reign, and which perhaps indicates the period of the second occupation. A second large fort of sixteen acres is known at Metchley, where once again a smaller fort later took its place, though this time of normal size; while at Wall the known extent of military occupation of this date implies a comparable or larger size.

The Silures in south-east Wales, guided at first by Caratacus' brilliant leadership, were to prove themselves the toughest and most successful opponents which the Roman army was to encounter in these islands, and herein they were assisted by the character of the terrain. This is for the most part broken and well wooded and very difficult to penetrate: ambuscades are easy. Before mounting a campaign Ostorius had to regroup his army. The Roman frontier was protected by a network of auxiliary forts whose garrisons, normally 500 strong, were adequate for police work but powerless against well-conceived raids in strength, and in the campaigning season many of their effectives might be away on active service. Legio XIV had been newly advanced, as we have seen is probable, to the Wall-Penkridge area; and Watling Street was now extended westwards to the Severn bank at Wroxeter, close to which an auxiliary fort is now known, and there is a tombstone of a cavalryman from a part-mounted cohort of Thracians to testify to the garrison.

Wroxeter itself is a superb site with a wide prospect up the Severn Valley into the very heart of central Wales, and was later to become a legionary fortress. Other forts to hold the line of the road were probably now established at Stretton Mill near Penkridge and at Red Hill, while at Leighton a very large fort seen from the air probably also pre-dates the arrival of legionaries at Wroxeter. Legio II was still fully stretched in the occupation of the south-west, with headquarters perhaps at Exeter and Dorchester, and Legio IX was equally stretched in the north-east behind the Trent. The remaining legion, XX, was still based at Colchester, though no doubt detachments from it had been used on campaign, This legion was the obvious choice now that the time had come to concentrate against South Wales. A fortress was built near Gloucester in 49, the site being well chosen – the lowest possible place for a bridge, and so sited as to outflank the ford in the Arlingham bend of the Severn lower down. That the troops placed there were, in fact, from the Twentieth is suggested by a tombstone of a member of that legion found at the site.[25] To maintain security after it had gone, permission was obtained to found a *colonia* at Colchester. Here, therefore, veteran legionaries, newly discharged, were settled with grants of land; and for a time at any rate, while vigour lasted, they would form an effective military substitute in case of need. The official title of the colony, Colonia Victricensis, may even suggest that the veterans were those of Legio XX Valeria Victrix; but the title more probably commemorated the British victory of Claudius, and the title Victrix may not have been awarded to the legion, as it certainly was not in the case of the Fourteenth, till after the part it played against Boudicca.[26]

At Gloucester the legionary fortress whose site was later taken over by the colonia is now known to date from c. 67, and was built for Legio II Augusta. The fortress of Legio xx probably lay nearby at Kingsholm, where much military equipment has been found. Kingsholm is the goal of the original road-system here and, as we have seen, may previously have been occupied by an auxiliary fort, the garrison of which is attested by the tombstone of Rufus Sita, cavalryman in the sixth part-mounted cohort of Thracians. The fort will have been part of the original garrisoning of Boduocus' kingdom against the early raids of Caratacus, and perhaps a foundation of Plautius. There would be no necessity for this regiment to remain once the legion had come.

It was not sufficient to thrust forward these two legions. The fortresses had to be connected by lateral roads with each other, and more roads built for communication in the triangular salient thus advanced west of the Fosse; and suitable routes for these roads had first to be surveyed. Forts had to be provided to protect the roads.[27] Military roads run from Penkridge and Wall to Metchley, and thence to Gloucester. Another road from Wroxeter to Gloucester keeps east of the Severn with forts at Greensforge, Droitwich and probably Worcester. A third road far forward of this takes the Church Stretton gap (pl. 2) and runs past Leintwardine, where a pre-Flavian fort exists, then back to Gloucester through Hereford. Other roads between the two are partly known, and the existence of a fort at Cleobury Mortimer far from any known route illustrates the gaps in present knowledge. Probably the Leintwardine route marks the end rather than the beginning of the campaign, and is more probably the work of Didius Gallus, the next governor.

All these preparations took time, and that they were more widespread still is suggested by the discovery that the small fortlet at Old Burrow over 1,000 feet above the Bristol Channel on the edge of Exmoor was constructed at this time. It watches shipping in the estuary and seems designed as the eyes of a fleet; this hints at the widespread character of Silurian raids. Caratacus was seriously alarmed by the turn events had taken. He foresaw the slow penetration of Siluria from Gloucester and its gradual encirclement from Wroxeter up the Severn Valley. To anticipate this, and to throw the Roman offensive off balance he decided to remove its objective to a more distant sphere, and therefore transferred resistance in 51 to the territory of the Ordovices. The heart of their country was Snowdonia, an almost inpenetrable fastness, but not well suited to the presence of large forces, and easily cut off from retreat. He decided to mass his forces in an impregnable position among steep hills, a river in front and the easier approaches defended by piled stones, and there teach the Romans a lesson. Tacitus' description of this site does not make its identification obvious, but Dr St Joseph has suggested a position just west of Caersws,[28] which is plausible, and where remains of earthworks strengthen its claim. Here after some struggle the Romans broke in. The battle was lost and Caratacus' wife, children and brothers captured; but he himself, undaunted, took horse for Brigantia, where he could hope to raise his standard once more and rally anti-Roman elements. For Cartimandua, the danger was serious. If Caratacus succeeded, her rule was over. Moreover, she was bound by her alliance and by bonds of gratitude. Caratacus was arrested and handed over a prisoner: he was sent to Rome, and there made a dignified public spectacle.[29]

But in Britain the struggle continued. The Silures kept up their resistance unflagging. Roman attempts were made to penetrate the difficult territory west and north-west of Gloucester; here, once the upper Wye valley is reached near Hereford, a choice of routes is offered, either due west up the Wye or south-west via Monmouth towards Usk. Tacitus tells us of a legionary force under the senior staff officer, the *praefectus castrorum*, which was attempting to build forts in Silurian territory, but which nearly suffered disaster in a surprise attack. Help arrived just in time, but not before this officer and eight centurions had been killed. At Clyro in the upper Wye valley there is a large fort of 25½ acres, resembling in size those already discussed at Kinvaston, Longthorpe and Newton-upon-Trent. It has not yet yielded decisive evidence, but it is reasonable to suggest that Clyro was the scene of this event; its size is suitable for the accommodation of some twenty legionary centuries and perhaps two auxiliary cavalry regiments. But only 2½ miles away another very large fort of sixteen acres has recently been discovered at Clifford: it lies in a less good position and may therefore pre-date Clyro, and

97

it offers an obvious alternative venue. At Usk itself, on the other line of penetration, military remains are of a slightly later date.

Guerrilla warfare continued inconclusively. But in 52 Ostorius Scapula died, worn out by the struggle and his lack of success. Before his successor Didius Gallus could arrive a legion itself – perhaps the Twentieth – had been defeated, and the situation further deteriorated with widespread Silurian raids.

The governorship of Ostorius was a period of progress. The original aim of Claudius, to hold the lowland zone with a buffer of friendly protectorates beyond, was seen to be impracticable, and further advances were made to the limit of the mountains. The menace of Caratacus was removed; but even this did not lead to the establishment of a peaceful frontier in the Marches, and the military problem of Wales was to tax imperial patience for a generation yet. Ostorius showed himself a skilful general with a fine grasp of strategic and tactical possibilities, and with a slow patience shown in his determination never to move rashly or without due preparation and consolidation of existing gains. He was great enough to accept a check when a more headstrong man might have stirred up a hornets' nest, as in 48, when he rated the security of his northern flank in Brigantia above the possession of the Cheshire gap. His choice of Kingsholm for a fortress stood for twenty years.

Internally also there was advance. The province was consolidated by enforcing a distinction between *civitates foederatae* within the frontier and the allied states beyond it. The former, as in Gaul, became independent only in name and for internal politics; they were no longer allowed to bear arms. By degrees their local independence was to be still further reduced, as one by one they were absorbed on the death of existing rulers. It was probably about this date that Boduocus ceased to issue coins. Britain began to take on the aspect of a normal province, and as part of this process Ostorius took the first steps to foster Romanisation of civilian life. The *colonia* at Colchester, indeed, had a dual purpose, military as well as civil: *subsidium adversus rebelles et imbuendis sociis ad officia legum:* it was both a garrison and a school of the Roman way of life. Here, too, was introduced the provincial centre of the Imperial Cult, which had a parallel purpose. Romanisation worked at first through towns, and this was a beginning. But Ostorius did more than this, for to his rule must also be ascribed the foundation of *Verulamium* as a municipium probably of 'Latin' citizens.[30] Thus both the model of a full Roman community and the hope of achieving local self-government in native communities were laid before the eyes of Britons, sufficient progress in this field for the moment. London, however, must already have been rapidly growing as a port, and it is possible that some of the native *civitates peregrinae*,[31] for instance in Kent and Hertfordshire, had also been begun; certainly Cogidubnus was making parallel progress in his allotted area. Tacitus' reference to his loyalty, and also to the presence of allied troops in the fight with the Iceni in 48, may go far to explain the augmentation of his kingdom and his unique distinction of being both client king and imperial legate. The latter term implies membership of the Senate, which in precisely this year Claudius, taking the opportunity of the census then being held, had extended to certain Gallic notables: it also probably implies praetorian status.[32] Much of the rest of the province was still under direct military rule administered through local garrison commanders; but in Somerset a beginning had been made, under legionary control, of exploiting the Mendip lead.[33]

Ostorius' successor was Aulus Didius Gallus (52–7). He had been consul in 36, and had (it seems) accompanied Claudius to Britain as general of cavalry, later campaigning in the Crimea and rising to the proconsulate of Asia; he was by now both distinguished and very senior.[34] On arrival he found, as we have seen, that the position in Britain had already gone from bad to worse since Ostorius' death: the Silures had defeated a legion, and were now raiding far and wide. Didius seems to have contained them, but he did not press on with the advance. Tacitus scornfully records that he merely acted on the defensive; but in doing this we may be sure that Didius was acting on instructions from the Emperor, whose representative he was. Provincial legates were carefully selected with an eye to what was to be required of them, and will have received careful briefing on appointment; and throughout their tenure they were in close touch with Rome. Claudius, in other words, in his last years was still convinced of the correctness of his original policy of holding lowland Britain only; he was anxious to avoid the conquest of Wales and ordered a disengagement on this front. We are not told how Didius solved the difficult problem of expelling the raiding Silures from the province and then keeping them out, without a repetition of the costly campaigning of Ostorius. The answer is one for archaeology to give, for it must lie in a really efficient frontier system of roads and forts. Indeed, the one good mark this governor receives from Tacitus is for having pushed forward certain forts. Perhaps the Church Stretton–Leintwardine road is his construction rather than that of Ostorius, and the early foundation of Usk may be due to him. The first fort there is at least fourteen acres in size, but it is unnecessarily low-lying, and in Roman times was liable to flood; this would suggest that one of its functions was as a supply port at the base of a road. A few sherds of about this date are known from Abergavenny, and if the road through it from Usk to Kenchester, there joining the Leintwardine road, could be attributed to Didius it would suit the known situation and have the effect of debarring the Silures from the more low-lying parts of their eastern border-lands. Another fort recently identified at Coed-y-caerau nearer the mouth of the River Usk may belong to the same system, for it seems too close to Caerleon to be contemporary. The fortress at Clyro may also be the work of Didius.

The fortress at Wroxeter used to be attributed to the foundation of Ostorius, but sufficient datable material from the site is now available to make it virtually certain that its foundation was not so early. It was perhaps Didius who brought together the detachments of Legio XIV once more and advanced the whole legion to Wroxeter. Such a move might well account for his greater ability to check the Silures, and would firmly anchor the northern end of the Leintwardine–Church Stretton road. But alternatively, and more probably on present evidence, the movement may have been initiated by Veranius and the fortress completed by Suetonius Paullinus.[35] That the fortress existed by AD 60 is suggested by the progress of Paullinus' campaign in North Wales, and is more certainly shown by datable pottery as well as by the tomb-stones of two soldiers of Legio XIV who lack cognomina – an early characteristic – and on which the title Martia Victrix is not given to the legion. That this fortress was ever a double legionary fortress is a mistaken inference from the presence of a tomb-stone of a soldier of Legio XX; but this man was a *beneficiarius* detached from normal duty to serve on the governor's staff.[36]

At any rate, by vigilance and good management Didius brought the Welsh front under control. The scene now shifted to Brigantia.

It was probably Cartimandua's act of surrendering Caratacus which led to a breach with her husband Venutius; on him Caratacus' mantle, as leader of resistance, now fell. Tacitus' chronology is confused. At first the discord was internal, and Cartimandua held her own by laying hands on Venutius' relatives. Then the struggle grew more intense, and Didius despatched auxiliary forces to her aid, which for a time restored the situation: the first fort at Templeborough may mark the station of one of these. Later a legion under its legate Caesius Nasica (no doubt Legio IX) had to intervene more massively. The struggle seems to have lasted most of Didius' time, that is down to 57. But Venutius – 'pre-eminent in military skill' [37] – needed no further lessons that nothing could be successfully achieved while Roman forces were free to intervene. He bided his time even in 61, but was quick to seize it in 69.

Didius Gallus was succeeded, probably in 57, by Q. Veranius. His choice as the first governor under Nero's administration is interesting, for he was in the prime of life; born c. AD 12, he had held the consulship in 49 and had a great military reputation won some ten to fifteen years earlier in Asia Minor against hill-tribes comparable to the Silures. Suetonius (§ 18) mentions in passing, though without giving any indication of date, that Nero had thought of evacuating Britain, but desisted for fear of belittling Claudius' achievements. If Nero's decision was the result of an appraisal at the outset of his reign the decision will have been made by 57, for the despatch to Britain of a man like Veranius, and Suetonius Paullinus after him, shows that by then he had determined on conquest. Another possible, and perhaps more likely, moment for doubt about holding Britain would be on first hearing the shattering news of Boudicca's rebellion. Certainly the surrender of a province which already contained a Roman colony, and on which so much blood and money had been spent, can hardly have been contemplated save for the most pressing reasons. Mere caprice or the chance reading of Veranius' will can have had nothing to do with it. A possible incentive for considering the matter early in the reign may have been affairs in the East, where Armenia had been lost and the Romans at first were almost powerless to take counter-measures owing to the total demoralisation of their troops. In these circumstances the transfer of the powerful Army of Britain to reinforce more vital interests may have been momentarily conceivable, but in the event unnecessary.

By 57, at any rate, Nero had decided that Claudius' policy in Britain was too expensive, and that the proper course was to complete the conquest of Wales. We know nothing of Veranius' activities there, except that, when he died within his first year of office, he stated in his will that if he had had a full three years he would have completed the task. That he achieved much in a brief time is indicated by subsequent events. Suetonius Paullinus, his successor (after two years' successful campaigning in which he put the finishing touches to Veranius' work), is found invading Anglesey. A campaign so far away and the employment there of part of Legio xx (if this is a justifiable inference from its presence in his column shortly afterwards) would be quite inconceivable while Silurian vigour remained untamed. Veranius must have penetrated Siluria, and Suetonius completed its defeat. Nothing more is heard of the Silures for seventeen years, but the full occupation of their territory was prevented by the outbreak of rebellion in East Anglia.

Archaeologically there is not yet much to show. Seven marching camps of legionary or larger size are known in South Wales, indicating campaigns as far west as Neath or Llandovery, but temporary camps are notoriously difficult to date, and some at least may date from the campaigns of Frontinus in 74. At Nantmel an earthwork which is likely to be a Roman fort lies far too close to Castell Collen to be part of the regular fort-system in Wales initiated by Frontinus, and may turn out to be a fort established in an earlier campaign.

For at least thirteen years (47–60) there had been almost unceasing military activity on the Welsh frontier, but by 58 a breakthrough had been achieved. Paullinus finished the resistance in South Wales and in 60 was attacking Anglesey. This island had a double importance both as a Druidical stronghold of nationalism and as a granary of the Ordovices. The end of Welsh ability to resist was clearly within sight when the outbreak of Boudicca's rebellion brought last-minute reprieve, and postponed final occupation for fifteen years. Yet long and successful though the resistance of the Welsh tribes appears, we must not forget that at first, during Claudius' life-time, his governors were not primarily bent on the conquest of Wales but on the establishment of a satisfactory frontier along its borders. Once this policy had been reversed, as it was in 57, the three-year estimate of Veranius was not wide of the mark.

At present little can be said of the civilian side of the administration of either Didius or Veranius. Didius in particular had both opportunity and inclination for administration, but the details elude us. There was much building to be undertaken at Colchester; existing roads laid out for an immediate military purpose needed more solid reconstruction, and the road system itself called for augmentation; there are hints of early growth in towns like London, Canterbury and Silchester; interesting wooden buildings of this period were taking the place of the abandoned depot at Fishbourne, and the export of Mendip lead is attested.[38] Britons, too, were clearly being conscripted for service in the army; a British unit is mentioned in a diploma, or discharge certificate, of the year 80 granting Roman citizenship after twenty-five years' service. As the army developed its widespread network of forts in the frontier regions, the problem of supply will have become more complex. The development of the great supply base at Richborough during this period with its massive warehouses illustrates the steps taken, but other similar store-centres remain to be found. Possibilities exist at Topsham near Exeter and Sea Mills near Bristol.

The Rebellion of Boudicca

C. Suetonius Paullinus, like his predecessor, had a great military reputation, for early in Claudius' reign he had learnt in Mauretania the wisdom of swift advance over the mountains to the enemy's sources of corn-supply: this was the strategy we see him operating in Britain. But after his consulship (c. 43) he had been unemployed – as far as is known – until sent to Britain on the death of Veranius, probably early in 58. After two years of successful operations, during which, as we have seen, he must have dealt finally with the Silures, we find him in 60 mounting an offensive against Anglesey.[39] Probably 58 sufficed for the Silures, since 59 would be required for overrunning the Deceangli in preparation for the campaign against Anglesey. This island lies far along the coast of North Wales, and to attack it would have been impossible without security in the south. But once this had been achieved, the island became an important objective. Not only was Anglesey rich in copper ores but it was also the granary of the Ordovices and the sustainer of their resistance; in addition, it was full of political refugees, and was also an important Druidical centre (perhaps even their headquarters). This priesthood

103

had been forbidden in Gaul by Tiberius and Claudius because of its savage rites. The Romans were tolerant of most native cults, but the human sacrifice practised by the Druids put them beyond the pale. A chance find of objects, made during the construction of an aerodrome on Anglesey in 1942 at Llyn Cerrig Bach, and brilliantly studied by Sir Cyril Fox, has been shown to represent offerings at a Druidical shrine, and illustrates the wide connections with all parts of Britain enjoyed by the cult. The offerings, accumulated from pilgrims for more than two centuries, had been either individually consigned to the spirit of the waters or more probably concealed at the time of the Roman attack.

Suetonius had prepared a fleet of flat-bottomed transports: the obvious base for this work is the estuary of the Dee, and there is reason to suppose that an auxiliary fort had occupied the site of Chester before the foundation of the legionary fortress some fifteen years later. At the Menai Straits the invading army was faced by a horrifying multitude on the farther shore. Black-clad females, long-haired and brandishing torches, mingled with the men, resembling Furies; and beyond stood the Druids with potent magic calling down curses with uplifted arms. For a moment the Roman forces hesitated, as well they might; but then they recovered and surged forward, the infantry in boats, the cavalry swimming. The rabble was cut down; the sacred groves, red with the blood of Roman prisoners, were destroyed; and a fort was constructed for a Roman garrison.

But at this moment terrible news was brought of the rebellion of Boudicca. Prasutagus, king of the Iceni, famed for his wealth, had died. With his death his treaty lapsed; and as he had no son, the kingdom was due to be incorporated in the Roman province. If he had hoped, by naming Nero as part-heir, to preserve the kingdom to his daughters – and this is not certain – such measures could have no effect on Roman policy, which favoured the gradual suppression of client-kingdoms in Britain. Slaves from the procuratorial office arrived to take over the property, and centurions from the governor's staff to reduce the kingdom to provincial status. With the governor himself campaigning far away, control was lax and outrages took place. Boudicca herself, the widow of Prasutagus, was flogged and her daughters violated. The nobility of the Iceni were given rough treatment and arrests were made. This harsh brutality sparked off the rebellion, but it was nurtured on grievances more widely spread. The

Trinovantes had suffered much from the insulting arrogance of the colonists at Colchester, who treated their lands as *agri captivi* and helped themselves at will to more than their allotted plots, evicting the rightful owners. There could be no security or peaceful growth under such conditions, but justice could not be obtained from the military arm, who turned a blind eye to abuse, in secret hope of similar licence when their turn should come. Excavation at *Camulodunum* has revealed the harsh conditions under which the natives lived as they quarried and made tiles for the new colonia. The leaders of other tribes were oppressed partly by the exactions of Roman money-lenders, to whom they had to have recourse for the capital expenditure required of them in the expensive processes of Romanisation — new towns, country houses in the Roman style, education in the new civilisation — and in particular in the costly service of the newly introduced Imperial Cult. This had been organised at *Camulodunum* with the new colony, and it was intended as a focus of loyalty. At first probably centred on an altar to Rome and Augustus on the Gallic model, the cult was now being extended by the addition of a large and expensive temple to the deified emperor Claudius. To serve the cult there must have been set up a provincial council, to which each *civitas* sent delegates, and the annual priesthood of the province was filled by election from these. In the early days there were too few candidates eligible for office, since not many *civitates* had yet been organised; and accordingly, the expense fell heavily on too few shoulders. Many felt themselves facing ruin, and would once again apply to the money-lenders. Chief among these, according to Dio, was Seneca the philosopher, Nero's tutor, who had been calling in the vast sums he had lent. Finally, Decianus Catus, the procurator of the province, himself had been trying to exact the subsidies that Claudius had paid to friendly Britons, on the ground that they were loans. Thus, when the moment came, the Iceni were not left to resort to arms alone.

Colchester was the first objective of the rebels. Here the colonists had been lulled by the false reassurances of secret sympathisers with the Icenian cause. The town was still open and undefended, and no emergency rampart was built, nor were the non-combatants evacuated. The colony was now eleven years old, and the original veterans were well past the flower of vigour; no help could come from Paullinus in Anglesey, and the procurator, apparently already operating from London, when appealed to could despatch barely 200 men. These were of little avail against the large horde of tribesmen which now appeared before the town and settled in an armed camp on the ancient site of Cunobelin's oppidum near by. The Roman town of half-timbered houses was burnt with no time to salvage the contents of shops, and a last stand in the stone temple was overwhelmed in two days.

News of the uprising had reached Petillius Cerialis, legate of Legio ix; but as he hurried south to the rescue he was ambushed, his infantry was massacred, and he himself had to gallop back with his cavalry to the security of his fortress. This was a grave set-back to the Roman cause, but the losses cannot have been as heavy as Tacitus implies. A legion consisted of some 5,000 infantry, but after the rebellion the legionary reinforcements sent over to make up the losses amounted to only 2,000 men, so it appears that Cerialis had only a vexillation of his legion to hand in the emergency. Indeed, it is very likely that the Ninth was still brigaded in two or more fortresses, and that Cerialis set out with part of the legion from Longthorpe. Meanwhile Decianus Catus the procurator withdrew to Gaul, leaving southern Britain leaderless.

Paullinus, however, was equal to the emergency. His infantry, consisting of Legio xiv and part of xx with their auxiliaries, would take at least two weeks to cover the 250 miles to London from Anglesey: with his cavalry he pushed ahead of them down Watling Street through unknown risks to the defence of London. Legio ix was now immobilised, but orders were sent to summon Legio ii (from Exeter?). The legate of this legion was absent, and the commander for the moment was Poenius Postumus, the *praefectus castrorum*. He disobeyed his orders and refused to march: the sudden responsibility was too great. The distance, the uncertainty and possibly the dispersed state of the legion were cumulatively too difficult.[40] Thus, when Suetonius Paullinus reached London he realised there were too few troops to defend it. There was no alternative but to withdraw. London would have to be sacrificed. Those who could march came with him: the rest remained to die. At *Verulamium* the scene was re-enacted, and both cities fell to Boudicca. Excavation at each has revealed the burnt debris of her destruction, and Tacitus quotes the official figure of 70,000 slain, citizens and allies, at the three sacked towns. The Britons, he says, had no thought of taking prisoners but only of slaughter, the gibbet, the fire and the cross.

When the governor rejoined his column he found that, with auxiliaries gathered from the nearest forts, he had some 10,000 men. These were all too few to meet a horde reckoned even with exaggeration at twenty-three times that number. Yet everything from instinct and policy to growing shortage of supplies bade him fight soon. He chose a site protected on its flanks and rear by woods and hills, with an open plain in front, and there he met Boudicca. Where this spot was it is now impossible to say: reasonable guesses have placed it close to Watling Street, north-west of Towcester or near Mancetter, south-east of Atherstone.

Roman discipline and superior armament prevailed after a long struggle, and the retreating British were entangled in their own wagon-lager drawn up behind their lines as a grandstand for their women. It was said that 80,000 British fell, for the loss of only 400 Roman slain. When news of the victory reached him Poenius Postumus knew what must be done: he fell on his sword.

The province had been gloriously recovered, but Paullinus was unbendingly stern towards the rebellious. Legio xiv, which had borne the brunt, received the titles Martia Victrix, and Legio xx may also have received the title Victrix.[41]

Reinforcements – 2,000 legionaries, eight auxiliary infantry and two auxiliary cavalry units – were sent from the Rhine. The whole army was concentrated against the rebel tribes, whose territory was thoroughly laid waste. Boudicca by now was dead. The new auxiliaries were brigaded together in new winter-quarters; a likely site for this has been identified at Great Chesterford. Other forts were built in East Anglia at Chelmsford, Coddenham and Pakenham near Ixworth, and perhaps at Scole. To free forces for these new duties forts farther west were abandoned, as at Waddon Hill, or else were redesigned for a new unit, as at Cirencester. At the latter traces of at least two different forts have been found partly superimposed, and we have the tomb-stones of two troopers from different cavalry-units, Dannicus of the Ala Indiana and Sextus Valerius Genialis of the Ala i Thracum. But the military grip was tightened on territory far wider than that of the Iceni. A new fort is known at Baginton near Coventry; existing forts were maintained at Great Casterton and Dorchester-on-Thames. It is clear that Paullinus' thoughts ran primarily upon repression and punishment: military forts mean military government. His ravages were to impoverish East Anglia for a generation.

Operations thus continued into 61, but now new hope dawned for the British. The new procurator sent out to succeed Decianus Catus was named C. Julius Alpinus Classicianus. This man took a statesman's view of the situation and was not afraid either to oppose the governor or to report to Rome adversely upon the fiscal effects of his policies: what was now required, he submitted, was a new man with a new policy. Nero despatched Polyclitus, one of his trusted freedmen, to hold an enquiry; and though in his report faces were saved, opportunity was taken shortly afterwards to recall Paullinus on the pretext of the loss of some ships. He was superseded by Petronius Turpilianus, who had just laid down the consulship (61), but he did not retire in disgrace. Five years later he was given the honour of a second consulship, and we find him playing the part of a senior marshal on Otho's side in the civil war of 69.

Classicianus died in office and was buried in London, and his tombstone, now reassembled in the British Museum, gives us interesting information about his background. His name and tribe both suggest that he was of provincial origin, probably from the country round Trier, and that his father or grandfather had obtained Roman citizenship at the latest from Augustus: the grant might even have been made by Caesar earlier still: one from Gaius to Classicianus himself – the only other possibility – is unlikely. His wife was Julia Pacata, daughter of Indus. Julius Indus was a well-known man in his time, from the same part of Gaul, who had taken the Roman side in the rebellion of Florus in AD 21; a cavalry regiment raised by him, the Ala Indiana, later formed part of the garrison of Britain. The new procurator was thus a member of the new provincial aristocracy of service now emerging to take increasing share in imperial administration. What Romanisation in a barbarian province should involve was within his family experience, and these ideals he was applying in Britain. His outlook was wider than that of Paullinus: though Tacitus denigrates his motives, he had the greater wisdom; and, as Collingwood affirmed, he was the real hero of the story 'who stood up to Suetonius in his hour of victory as the champion of the British people'. His tomb is a precious historical possession.

P. Petronius Turpilianus had been consul in the first part of 61; he governed Britain till 63. Under him the war was ended, and his mild administration, though it won no praise from Tacitus, suited the requirements of the situation. His successor was M. Trebellius Maximus, consul in 56, who had just served on a commission to revise the census lists and tax assessments of Gaul. This experience was doubtless one of the factors in his choice for Britain, for what was still required was a period of peaceful rule and tactful settlement. His governorship was successful, for he remained in office until 69; and the continuity of administration thus effected, together with the liberal policies of Classicianus, did much to heal old wounds. Security indeed was so assured that in 66 the most famous legion of the British garrison, Legio xiv, was withdrawn for service in the East. This left the Wroxeter fortress empty, which with Wales unconquered was dangerous; and it must have occasioned a reorganisation of the line of battle. When Agricola was legate of Legio xx he and his legion took a major part in the campaigns of Cerialis in the north; and this suggests that Legio xx had taken over the Wroxeter fortress after the departure of Legio xiv. This would necessitate moving Legio ii Augusta to take the place of the Twentieth at Gloucester; but part of it was probably outposted immediately at Usk,[42] and in any event after only a few years the legion moved forward in 74 to take up what was to prove its permanent home at Caerleon in the heart of Siluria. Exeter then will have ceased to be held by a legion in 67, and the site soon developed as the capital of the Dumnonii.[43]

Despite Tacitus' hints that Romanisation was proceeding, archaeology has little to tell of the governorships of Turpilianus or Maximus. On the frontier the forward policy of Nero's early years was perforce abandoned for a while, but the situation did not remain entirely static. Although in the north Cartimandua's kingdom continued to provide security, in the west preparations were eventually put in hand for further action. The occupation of Cornwall may have been effected c. 61 – a task of limited difficulty.[44] The continued watch on the Silures is illustrated by the new fortlet at Martinhoe which now replaced in more permanent form the fortlet at Old Burrow, with the same function of watching for landings from across the Bristol Channel. But on the Welsh border recent discoveries have shown that active preparations for a major campaign were in hand. In addition to the new fortress at Gloucester itself, an even larger base (of fifty-one acres) now replaced the earlier fort at Usk. Part of it was a supply base, but its size suggests the concentration of a very considerable advance force. The disappointed anticipation of booty, to which abandonment of these preparations during the Civil War would give rise, gives point to Roscius Coelius' complaint that the legions were 'despoiled and impoverished',[45] and to Tacitus' comment [46] on the resulting mutiny: 'accustomed to campaigns, the troops ran riot in time of peace'.

Within the province the work of reconstruction must have been begun with the refoundation of the colony at Colchester and with the rebirth of London. By 60 London had already become an important mercantile centre, and its early development as a great port and supply base is illustrated by the main roads which radiate from London rather than from Colchester. The fact that Classicianus died and was buried at London supports the view that already in his day primacy of administration was passing to it, and what we know of his predecessor suggests that even earlier the procurator had his office there. But when Boudicca rose, London had not yet achieved self-governing status as a colony or *municipium*: it was a growing *vicus* not yet stabilised, but with a very large population. Status we can assume came soon, but we have no facts. How quickly reconstruction advanced at Colchester or London we do not know, but at both there was incentive, Roman prestige at the former, at the latter mercantile activity. The curious fact is that at *Verulamium*, the third of the sacked towns, where we do possess some facts, it is certain that reconstruction was very much delayed; the centre of that city was not rebuilt for fifteen years or more.[47] It will have been in these years that the future emperor Titus served in Britain as a military tribune and won a high reputation for energy and integrity: Suetonius (*Titus* § 4) remarks upon the number of statues and busts with inscriptions to him which were to be seen in Britain.

In 68 the Roman world came to the edge of disaster. A rising in Gaul against Nero's misrule drove him to suicide, and a struggle for power began – the Year of the Four Emperors. Conflicting Army-groups put forward rival candidates for the purple, and though the Army of Britain did not actually intervene with its own candidate, vexillations were sent from all three legions to support Vitellius; the Fourteenth was supporting Otho. This reduction in strength meant the postponement of the projected Welsh campaign, and the troops were discontented at the loss of opportunity for booty; Maximus' character was not sufficiently military to impose discipline by force of personality or by exercise. Outright mutiny broke out from which the governor escaped with his life but without prestige; the leader of the opposition was Roscius Coelius, legate of Legio xx, whose sedition became so successful as to drive Trebellius to quit his province and take refuge with Vitellius. He was not restored: Vitellius in 69 despatched Vettius Bolanus to succeed him.

The rule of the three governors who succeeded Suetonius Paullinus put Britain on her feet once more and restored her self-respect. The credit must go principally to Trebellius Maximus. There was never a repetition of Boudicca's rebellion; indeed, we find British regiments serving ten years later in Agricola's army. It was these governors who laid the essential foundations for the great advances in all fields in the Flavian period. But a policy favourable to the province could be unpopular with the army; it was Trebellius' misfortune that the outbreak of civil war made control of his troops almost impossible.

1. We have no list of the auxiliary troops concerned, but the following regiments are attested in Britain before AD 70 and so were probably part of the expeditionary force; but it must be remembered that eight infantry cohorts and two alae of cavalry were sent as reinforcements from the Rhine in 61.

Ala 1 Thracum (Colchester); Ala Indiana and Ala Thracum (Cirencester); Cohors vi Thracum (Gloucester); another Cohort of Thracians (probably ii or i) (Wroxeter). Dio, lxii, 12, 3 mentions archers. Tacitus, *Histories*, i, 59, ii, 66, mentions eight cohorts of Batavians who were attached to Legio xiv. It would be tempting to equate these with the eight cohorts sent to reinforce Paullinus in 61, but to do so would not allow them sufficient time to acquire their great reputation in Britain. More probably they were the 'Celts' whom Dio (lx, 20, 2) describes as swimming both Medway and Thames in full equipment, a habit easily acquired in their home districts, and one repeated at the Po in 69 (Tacitus, *Histories*, ii, 17). The Thracian regiments also perhaps came in 43, but 46 or 47 is a more likely date, for in 46 Thrace became a province. Though it did not become a province till that year, Tacitus (*Annals*, iv, 46) tells us that as early as 26 there was a rebellion in Thrace against Roman conscription: thus, though Longinus at Colchester had served fifteen years (*RIB*, 201), he can still have been buried before AD 49. The Ala Indiana could have formed half the thousand cavalry sent in 61; it left Britain again *c.* 69 for Lower Germany.

2. The matter is fully discussed by Professor C. F. C. Hawkes in E. M. Clifford, *Bagendon, A Belgic oppidum* (1961).

3. It is not clear whether Dio is referring to an existing bridge (*pontem* in his source) or to pontoons (*pontes*) constructed for the purpose. For an alternative site for the crossing, see p. 54, n. 7.

4. *CIL*, xiii, 5093, mentions a tribune of Legio iv, who was recalled to the colours for the British expedition. For the Praetorian Guard in Britain see *CIL*, xi, 395, and for Rufrius Pollio, Dio, lx, 23.

5. Eutropius, vii, xiii 2–3. *Brittanis intulit bellum, quam nullus Romanorum post C. Caesarem attigerat, eaque devicta per Cn. Sentium et A. Plautium, inlustres ac nobiles viros, triumphum celebrem egit. Quasdam insulas etiam ultra Brittanias in oceano positas imperio Romano addidit, quae appellantur Orchades.* . . . If Vespasian was sent by Claudius on a return mission to the north it might explain poetic references to his 'conquest' of Thule and Caledonian groves, which as Professor Momigliano has shown (*JRS*, xl (1950), 41–2), refer to this period of his career, and also Suetonius' reference to his achievements under Claudius' own command: for Claudius had left Britain before his south-coast campaign began. See p. 73 for the situation in the north.

6. See previous footnote.

7. Or he may be his brother: see *PIR sub nomine* and Syme, *American Journal of Philology*, 77 (1956), 270.

8. *CIL*, xiv, 3608. . . . *legatus et comes Claudii Caesaris in Britannia.*

9. Tacitus, *Histories*, iii, 44. *CIL*, iii, 6809, gives us the name of the senior staff-officer of this legion, P. Anicius Maximus, *praefecto castrorum Leg. II in Britannia . . . donato ab. imp. donis militaribus ob expeditionem honorato corona murali et hasta pura ob bellum Britannia.*

10. *RIB*, 91. The significance of the latter title is discussed on p. 99 and n. 32 below.

11. *Agricola*, 14.

12. *Britannia*, i (1970), 16.

13. Early forts for auxiliaries lay at Cirencester and probably at Kingsholm, near Gloucester.

14. This suggestion cannot be regarded as a certainty owing to the small amount of material from early levels; but it conforms with what evidence there is.

15. In spite of the tomb-stones, the account of Cerialis' defeat in 60 suggests very strongly that the legion was still divided at that date and not yet at Lincoln; for not only was he probably operating with less than a full legion, but Longthorpe might seem a fortress more suitable to the geographical context (see p. 106).

16. The consistent absence of Claudian finds from excavation in the fortress and its defences almost compels a date after his reign for its foundation. But the Fosse Way and Ermine Street, roads which converge on Lincoln and presuppose a military post there, were certainly built by 47. This difficulty can be overcome by assuming the presence of an original auxiliary fort at Lincoln, perhaps under the castle, where exacavation has never taken place (cf. *RIB* 266). Finds at the east gate of the fortress support this by proving that the site was occupied before the fortress gate was built (*Archaeologia* civ (1973), 144), and excavations at Longthorpe have confirmed the presence there of legionaries and cavalry, and suggest that the site was given up soon after 60 (*Britannia* v (1974)).

17. This suggestion, if accepted, itself supports a comparatively late date for Lincoln. The fortress was held by the Ninth till 71. If the fortress was built in 47 for most of the legion, there is ample time before 71, and opportunity in the various subsequent regroupings, for the remaining detachment to have returned and for the fortress to have been enlarged to a convenient size; whereas if the fortress dates from soon after 60 the detached vexillation need never have returned until the advance to York. The York fortress is of fifty acres.

18. There is also a pre-Flavian *mortarium* from Colchester inscribed before firing with the words, IVSTI SVPERI; this implies a military potting establishment.

19. The spacing of the sites at Broxtowe, Mancetter, Alcester, Gloucester and Sea Mills at a uniform distance apart and at a uniform distance beyond the Fosse is systematic and significant. A fort at Littleborough would complete the system by guarding the lowest crossing of the Trent.

20. *JRS*, xiv, 252–6.

21. 'He made preparations to occupy everything this side of Trent and Severn.'

22. *Arch. Journ.*, cxv, 49 ff, following a suggestion of T. Davies Pryce, *Antiq. Journ.*, xviii (1938), 29 ff.

23. *Digest*, xlviii, vi, 1.

24. Sir Cyril Fox, *A Find of the Early Iron Age from Llyn Cerrig Bach, Anglesey* (1946), 62, Fig. 34.

25. *RIB*, 122, found at Wotton, just outside Gloucester.

26. Alternatively, *Colonia Victricensis* may commemorate the refounding of an original *Colonia Claudia*, after its destruction by Boudicca, with new drafts from both these legions.

27. An interesting indication of troop movements at about this time is given by the reduction of the existing fort at Great Casterton; the reduced accommodation implies a change of garrison and a smaller unit.

28. *Antiquity*, xxxv (1961), 270–1.

29. It was in Rome he asked the famous question: 'Why do you, with all these great possessions, still covet our poor huts?'

30. See pp. 231 f., 450.

31. See pp. 231–3 for this term.

32. Claudius had previously (AD 41) given consular rank to Agrippa I and praetorian rank to Herod of Chalcis (Dio lx, 2–3). But an alternative suggestion which is attractive is that Cogidubnus owed his promotion as legatus to long-standing friendship with Vespasian and outstanding support to him in 69 (B. W. Cunliffe, *Excavations at Fishbourne, 1961–1969* (1971), 13 f.).

33. For the growth of the lead industry see p. 321 ff. below.

34. *American Journal of Philology*, 69 (1948), 218–22; *Hesperia*, x (1941), 239–41; *L'Année Epigraphique*, 1949, 11.

35. A similar foundation-date for Clyro is very possible.

36. *RIB*, 293.

37. Tacitus, *Annals*, xii, 40.

38. See p. 321 ff. for the development of this industry.

39. Tacitus dates the event to 61, but Sir Ronald Syme (*Tacitus*, ii, 765) has shown the difficulty of assigning all the recorded events to this single year, and suggests that the outbreak of Boudicca's rebellion, and hence the North Wales campaign, belong to the year before.

40. If the fire which destroyed part of Winchester at this time was caused by hostile unrest south of the Thames, this may have been an additional factor in his decision. That there was rebellion even nearer at hand has been suggested by recent excavations at South Cadbury.

41. The title is not certainly attested before this date, e.g. the Wroxeter tombstone, which could be earlier than 60, lacks it (*RIB*, 293).

42. The new Gloucester fortress enclosed only $43\frac{1}{4}$ acres.

43. Legio XIV was sent back to Britain by Vitellius in 69, but next year was sent to help crush the revolt of Civilis in Lower Germany; it did not return to Britain, nor do we know where it was stationed during its short stay in 69–70. The fort at Cirencester seems to have been evacuated about now, probably as part of the same reorganisation.

44. The fort at Nanstallon was occupied at this date, as the samian shows; excavations by Lady Fox have shown that its initial construction fell within the decade 55–65 (*Britannia*, iii (1972), 56–111).

45. Tacitus, *Hist.*, i, 60.

46. Tacitus, *Agricola*, 16.

47. See pp. 134, 282.

6

The Flavian Period

The crisis of the Empire in 69 ended with the victory of Vespasian. The new Flavian dynasty, two of whose emperors had seen service in Britain, was now to inaugurate a new era in the province with far-reaching advances both in the military sphere and in that of cultural development. Roman control was established over Wales, and in the North conquest was to embrace almost the whole island before the necessity of moving troops to more pressing fields of war compelled curtailment. The military advance was the work of three governors of distinguished military ability, Petillius Cerialis (71–4), Julius Frontinus (74–8) and Julius Agricola (78–84). At least two of these, the first and third, had been chosen for their previous knowledge of the province. The logic of strategy would advise the elimination of Wales, because of its dangerous position on the flank, before advancing far into Brigantia; but in fact this logical order was inverted by the force of inherited events. It was in the governorship of Vettius Bolanus (68–71) that the situation in the north had begun to crumble, and the events of 69 must be scrutinised more closely if the situation is to be understood.

The rise and fall of Galba and Otho had not directly affected Britain or the loyalties of the British garrison. Only Legio XIV, already withdrawn from the province in 67, had become involved on Otho's side; the three legions still in Britain took no part until Vitellius marched against Otho, when 8,000 legionaries were summoned thence to support him. Vitellius sent Vettius Bolanus to succeed Trebellius Maximus as governor, and after his victory over Otho at Bedriacum in April 69 he sent the Fourteenth back to Britain. Here it remained until the next year, when it left to share in the suppression of the rebellion of Civilis in the Rhineland, being thereafter posted to Mainz. Bolanus, therefore, faced a difficult situation.

His legions were of divided loyalty, and three of them were at half strength. A further demand, this time for auxiliaries, from Vitellius met with an evasive reply, for not only was Vitellius' future becoming increasingly uncertain as Vespasian's fortunes rose but the military situation in Britain itself was growing steadily more serious. Discipline had disappeared in the last year of Maximus, and Bolanus lacked the means of restoring it. He had seen service in the East under Corbulo in 62, and had held the consulship in 66: according to Tacitus he was an honourable if easy-going man, and popular, though lacking authority. In the circumstances of the moment even a martinet might doubt what steps to take. But Bolanus was not left in idleness.

Since the days of Claudius the Brigantian client kingdom under Queen Cartimandua had protected the northern flank of the province and had made unnecessary a massive deployment of force in that quarter. It stretched from sea to sea and blocked the entire north. The arrangement was worth some effort to preserve, and earlier governors had been sensitive of the need. But the kingdom lacked basic stability (pp. 71, 94), and was further weakened by dynastic strife. Cartimandua's internal troubles began when she had surrendered Caratacus in 51. Venutius, her husband, had assumed the leadership of the anti-Roman elements in Brigantia, but by 57 a series of checks from Roman troops had taught him that he must bide his time. Even in 60 he was not ready to intervene, or Cartimandua was strong enough to stop him. Since then the situation had further deteriorated. Thinking to undermine his power by winning over his supporters, the queen had divorced him, taking as new consort his squire Vellocatus, who was, of course, of noble birth and aristocratic connections. But her calculations were at fault. Venutius' strategic insight told him that now was the chance he had so long awaited. The Roman world was dissolving in civil war. The British legions were weakened and divided. In Brigantia rebellious elements were ready to strengthen his hand, and he had powerful allies in the north.[1] He made war on his wife, and drove her to appeal for Roman aid.

Bolanus had to act, but the extent of his power to do so, and of his success, is uncertain. Tacitus tells us that a force of auxiliary infantry and cavalry was despatched, which after some indecisive fights succeeded only in rescuing Cartimandua. This suggests that

116

Bolanus could not afford to use his legions, depleted as they were and still undisciplined; he was unable to defeat Venutius or restore the client-kingdom. 'The throne was left to Venutius: the war to us.' The poet Statius, on the other hand, paints a rather different picture in a poem in honour of Bolanus' son: he mentions the establishment of forts and the winning of a breastplate from a British king. One important step worth taking would be to garrison the Parisi, who were more Romanised than the Brigantes, and may have feared them, and whose conquest by Venutius would lose him an important position on the flank. Perhaps to Bolanus should be ascribed the early fort at Brough-on-Humber and what may be a fortress of the 30-acre type already discussed (for a legionary vexillation or group of auxiliary regiments organised as a battle-group) at Malton. Whatever his successes, Bolanus failed to quell Venutius. This failure meant that an actively hostile power now faced the northern frontier of the province; and when Petillius Cerialis arrived in 71 to take over from Bolanus this was the situation with which he was instructed to deal urgently. The breakdown of the Brigantian alliance had far-reaching consequences. If it could have achieved stability Rome would have been saved long years of war, and once Wales had been subdued and tamed, the costly garrison of Britain might have been reduced. The logical alternative was to attempt the conquest of the whole island, after which the same results might flow. But the character of the hill-men, strengthened and embittered by contingents of refugees from farther south filled with the spirit of resistance, proved in the end too unrelentingly hostile, and the military effort beyond what Rome could conveniently afford. The break with Brigantia was a turning-point of history matched only by the retreat from Scotland a generation later: from this time onward Rome was committed to keeping very large forces in Britain for an indefinite period. But this was a burden for the future: for the present the empire was still in a phase of confident expansion, and such forebodings were far from the thoughts of those who framed Flavian policy.

Q. Petillius Cerialis was a friend and relative of Vespasian, and to this he owed his advance. He was a man of dashing, even headstrong, character, and with a flair for action rather than patient consolidation. He had been legate of Legio IX during the Boudiccan rebellion, when his rashness had resulted in serious defeat. His first consulship was held in 70, and he was sent at once to the Rhine to deal with the rebellion of Civilis. The following year he was sent on to Britain, bringing with him Legio II Adiutrix to replace the Fourteenth and to restore the garrison of Britain to four legions. This legion was newly raised and not yet experienced. It was placed in the fortress of Lincoln, while Cerialis honoured his old Legion IX, formerly in garrison there, by using them as the spear-head of his advance. A new fortress was built at York for this legion: it appears to be of full size (50 acres), but was not at first constructed in any great strength, for the ramparts were rebuilt only some ten years later. Nevertheless, the choice of York showed brilliant topographical insight, and no doubt was the result of previous acquaintance with the area: York held the keys of Brigantia and has remained the military centre of northern England ever since.

The extent of Cerialis' activities is hard to make out in detail. Tacitus merely tells us that after a number of battles, some of them bloody, he conquered much of Brigantia and overran more of it. Elsewhere he mentions that Agricola, now legate of Legio XX, was given a share in the work, and this, as we have seen, implies that his legion was now at Wroxeter. The difficulty of tracing the footsteps of Cerialis in detail is due to his neglect of fort-building. At Brough and Malton military establishments were held at this date, Brough being a normal fort and Malton something much larger. These are usually taken to be foundations of Cerialis, but it has been suggested above that Bolanus may have been responsible.[2]

At any rate, whether or not the Parisi were being invaded for the first time, it was wise to approach the Vale of York from the east, for here there was good dry ground all the way, and the Humber crossing presented the only difficulty; the alternative route from the south involved skirting round many miles of very marshy ground, with the danger of Brigantian flank attacks from the hills driving the columns back against the marsh.[3] The fortress of York can more certainly be attributed to Cerialis, since the authority of Tacitus is against the moving of a legion by Bolanus; and once York was founded as a legionary fortress, a large base at Malton loses much of its point. It was, however, continuously occupied until c. AD 79, when a smaller but still very large fort (8½ acres) of normal pattern replaced it. But in all the rest of Brigantian territory the known forts go back no earlier than Agricola's governorship, wherever excavation has tested the matter. Only at Carlisle is there a suggestion of anything pre-Agricolan: it is possible therefore that a base was created here to make contact with the sea after an advance from York. That such an encirclement was the plan of campaign is suggested by the results of excavation at Stanwick and by the existence of pre-Agricolan marching camps in the Stainmore pass.

At Stanwick a 17-acre hill-fort of the normal type appears to have been constructed in the early fifties – just about the time of Venutius' first breach with Cartimandua – and there were two subsequent enlargements which converted the site from a hill-fort into a vast perimeter defended by massive dykes. The first enlargement enclosed 130 acres, mainly of level pasturage, and care was taken to include a water supply: the second increased the area to 730 acres. The first enlargement could be dated c. AD 50–70; the second was subsequent but did not yield closely datable evidence, save that it had not been quite completed when it was destroyed.

Stanwick occupies a strategic position near Scotch Corner, where the Roman road across Stainmore diverges from that running north to Corbridge. These roads follow routes of high antiquity, and the position is well chosen for summoning aid both from the north-east and the north-west. The site lies beyond the immediate range of Roman troops operating from the old province, and thus in every way suits the context of Venutius' struggle with Cartimandua and with Rome, which its archaeological dating suggests. The place may have been originally chosen and built by Venutius in the governorship of Didius, and the first enlargement fits in with his actions in the governorship of Bolanus, as does the third with that of Cerealis, whose rapid advance found it still under construction. The purpose was to mass and defend a large body of tribesmen and especially their herds; the dykes recall those of *Camulodunum*, the most advanced fortifications known to native Britons. But advanced though they were by British standards, they could not hope to stand up to legionary attack, while the very size of the perimeter made it impossible to defend. The excavators found that though some of the contemporary pottery was of local Brigantian home-made type, much of it was of superior wares imported from the south of Britain or beyond, which demonstrates the dependence of even anti-Roman persons outside the province on luxuries brought in from the Roman market.

At Stanwick, then, we may place Venutius' last stand. At the summit of the Stainmore pass beyond lies the marching-camp of Rey Cross (20 acres) of legionary size, and with especially massive ramparts because of the impossibility of ditch-digging in the rock. Its relationship with the Roman road (which cannot be thought later than Agricola's governorship) shows the camp to be earlier, and the details of its castrametation also point to this conclusion, being old-fashioned by Agricolan standards. Two other marching camps of the same series are known beyond it, a day's march apart, at Crackenthorpe and Plumpton Head. They point the path of a legion advancing towards Carlisle: the campaign of Cerialis seems the earliest context for this.

When Cerialis was recalled to hold a second consulship early in 74 the Brigantes were battered and leaderless; but no steps seem to have been taken as yet to police the territory adequately, or to incorporate it formally in the province. This process was not put in hand for six years. Instead, the conquest of Wales was first undertaken.

Sextus Julius Frontinus, who succeeded Cerialis, had been praetor in 70, and had played a distinguished part in the suppression of the Gallic rebellion. The date of his consulship is uncertain, but it was probably held in 73. Frontinus became an eminent elder statesman in later life: remaining unemployed during most of the tyranny of Domitian, he was put in charge of the aqueducts of Rome by Nerva, and composed a manual on the subject which tells us much about his conscientious and reforming administration. He received a second consulship in 98 and a third in 100. Another of his books was *Stratagems*, but this throws less light on Britain than might have been hoped.

His first task was to conquer the Silures. Nothing is recorded of this tribe since 57, but by now a new generation of warriors was growing up, and any lessons taught by Veranius or Paullinus were passing into oblivion. It may well be that the reason for breaking off the Brigantian settlement so abruptly was that the Silures were already on the move. Of the details of Frontinus' campaigns we know nothing, but from the apparent ease with which the Roman army this time swept over South Wales, we may suppose landings on the plain of Glamorgan rather than another attempt to breach the natural land defences of Siluria. Certainly new forts are found at harbours all along the South Welsh coast – at Cardiff, Neath and Carmarthen – and Legio II Augusta was now placed in a new fortress at Caerleon near the mouth of the Usk. From these positions valleys lead conveniently into the interior: the Towy valley in particular running north-eastwards from Carmarthen, and the Usk valley leading inland from Caerleon and curving westwards to Brecon, both offer easy routes and between them almost cut off the larger part of Silurian territory. Brecon itself is another key point from which valleys radiate. In all these valleys roads were built and forts placed a day's march apart. Thus, a net-work was constructed which cordoned off each separate block of hills: unauthorised movement on any scale became impossible. Naturally these forts could not be placed in isolated positions before a crushing victory had been won; the first stage of the conquest must have been the search for, and destruction of, the main war-bands of the tribe, and it is to this stage that we must ascribe the marching-camps. In contrast to the forts, these lie on the high plateaux: only there was rapid open movement possible to a large body of troops. A total of seven marching-camps is known at present in South Wales. Two successively at Y Pigwn (37 and 25 acres) and one at Arosfa Gareg (45 acres), both near Llandovery, and one at Ystradfellte (21 acres) mark routes skirting or penetrating the Brecon Beacons; three others near Neath (61 acres), Aberdare (16 acres) and Pontypridd (37 acres) represent troops operating in the Glamorgan uplands. None of these are dated, but some at least will belong to this campaign. The differences in size between these camps, even making allowance for irregular ground, are striking. It is impossible to trace the march of a particular force as could be done in the Stainmore pass; and clearly many others remain as yet undiscovered. The camp near Neath is particularly noteworthy for its size. A camp of 61 acres would theoretically hold three legions. This one occupies partly broken ground, but even so a very large force indeed was involved. Several others are of larger than legionary size.

The fuller account which Tacitus doubtless wrote of Frontinus' work in Britain in his *Histories* is unfortunately lost. All we possess is a summary sentence in the *Agricola*. This mentions only the Silures as objects of his conquest, but no weight can be put on this limitation. They were by far the most famous people in Wales, and in this thumb-nail sketch serve only to indicate that Frontinus was not fighting the same enemy as Cerialis. There is no doubt that the

Ordovices were also overrun by Frontinus. At first Legio xx from Wroxeter probably joined in the Silurian campaign by advancing into central Wales by the Severn valley. But before the end of his term of office Frontinus had almost certainly begun the construction of the fortress of Chester for Legio ii Adiutrix, though water-pipes were still being installed there in the early months of 79. The threat to the Ordovices of a fortress in this position is obvious. The Deceangli in between had probably been subjected since 60; lead pigs from mines in their territory are dated as early as 74. But the Ordovices were more than threatened. Garrisons were being installed in their country, for they destroyed one of these – a cavalry regiment – shortly before Agricola's arrival. Yet the conquest was not quite complete when Frontinus left, for Agricola rounded it off in his first year with the capture of Anglesey. To find garrisons for at least twenty new auxiliary forts must have meant a radical reorganisation of troop-positions in southern Britain. The forts in the Dumnonian peninsula at least will have been abandoned now. The bearing of this on the development of local self-government will be discussed shortly (p. 134); evidence, too, is beginning to accrue, for instance at *Verulamium*, of Frontinus' interest in the growth of towns.

Gnaeus Julius Agricola is the most famous of the governors of Britain, because of the biography written by his son-in-law Tacitus. Were it not for this, our knowledge would be dark indeed, for only three inscriptions of this governor have so far come to light.[4] Nevertheless, the *Agricola* is an early work of Tacitus and does not represent his mature view; this, unfortunately, is lost to us in the missing portions of his *Histories*. The biography is partisan: it tends to ignore or play down the achievements of its hero's predecessors in order to focus attention on his own. To perceive this is one thing, but to remedy it quite another, where evidence is short. Agricola served in Britain as military tribune on the staff of Suetonius Paullinus, and had probably been present on the earlier Anglesey expedition. Eight years later, after his praetorship, he was sent back to Britain by the government of Vespasian to take over from Roscius Coelius command of Legio xx, whose discipline and loyalty were both in question. Under Bolanus there were no opportunities for distinction, but under Cerialis Agricola was given field experience, at first in command of his legion, later of larger forces. He earned good reports, and on return to Rome was promoted patrician. After governing Aquitania he was elected to the consulship. The date of this is not exactly known, but was probably late in 77; and immediately after it he was appointed to Britain. Here he will have arrived half-way through the summer of 78; it is probable that Frontinus had already left, for no campaign was in progress and the army was relaxed. But the Ordovices had just destroyed an *ala* stationed in their territory, and since Agricola already knew the ground, he was able swiftly to mount a punitive expedition which cut to pieces almost the entire tribe. He thus no doubt averted the development of a much more serious situation the next year, and his action illustrates the wisdom of the Flavian choice of 'specialist' governors who already knew the province. No stranger would have dared to plunge into this difficult country so late in the season. He then went on to capture Anglesey by a *coup de main*, not bothering to wait for transports but making his auxiliaries swim beside their horses. This sounds like the Batavi again.

The conquest of Wales having been thus consolidated, he was able to turn his attention to the north. Here the Brigantes had been beaten by Cerialis five years before, but the task of occupying their territory had been left incomplete. It is possible that Vespasian now had in mind only the reduction of Brigantia, but he died in June 79 while the first campaign was still in progress; and if so Agricola had no difficulty in getting Titus' permission to go farther. A strong case could be made for overrunning the Selgovae and Novantae also, the tribes from whom Venutius had derived support.

Tracing the course of Agricola's six campaigns in the north has always been a matter of considerable difficulty, owing to the scarcity of topographical information given us by Tacitus. His account can, however, be supplemented by the evidence of archaeological discovery and especially of aerial photography, both of which have yielded a rich harvest. In 79 the advance northwards was begun. The only indications of its direction and extent given by Tacitus are the statement that Agricola himself chose the sites of camps and himself reconnoitred estuaries and forests, and the information that the following year's campaign ended at the Tay. Though personal reconnaissance of estuaries and forests is a stock attribute of good generals in Roman literature, it does suggest the western rather than the eastern side of the Pennines; and there is, in fact, no evidence that Cerialis had ever overrun this difficult area. The plan of campaign

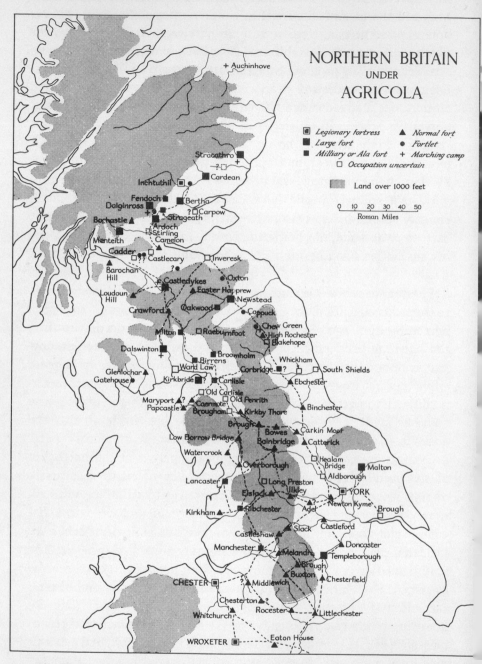

NORTHERN BRITAIN
UNDER
AGRICOLA

+ Auchinhove

▣ *Legionary fortress*   ▲ *Normal fort*
■ *Large fort*   ● *Fortlet*
■ *Milliary or Ala fort*   + *Marching camp*
        ☐ *Occupation uncertain*

░ *Land over 1000 feet*

0 10 20 30 40 50
    Roman Miles

Stracathro
?? +
Cardean

Inchtuthil ▣ ●

Fendoch ■
Dalginross   Bertha
+   ?☐ Carpow
Borcastle ▲   Strageath
Ardoch
Stirling
Menteith   Camelon
Cadder ▲
?? Castlecary   Inveresk ☐
Barochan   ?
Hill   ● Oxton
Castledykes   ●
Loudoun   Easter Happrew
Hill   Newstead
Crawford ▲   Oakwood   Coppuck ●
Milton   Chew Green ●
Raeburnfoot ☐   High Rochester
Dalswinton   Blakehope ☐
+   Broomholm   Whickham
Birrens   ■?☐ South Shields
Glenlochar ▲   Ward Law ☐   Corbridge
Gatehouse   Kirkbride ☐?   Carlisle   Ebchester ▲
Old Carlisle ☐
Maryport ▲?   Old Penrith ☐
Papcastle   Caermote   Kirkby Thore ☐   Binchester ▲
Brougham   Brough ▲   Carkin Moor ▲
Low Borrow Bridge ▲   Bowes   Catterick ▲
Bainbridge   Healam ☐
Watercrook ▲   Bridge
Overborough ▲   Aldborough   Malton ■
Lancaster ●   Long Preston ☐   York
Elslack ▲   Ilkley   ▣ YORK
Kirkham ▲   Ribchester ▲   Adel ▲?   Newton Kyme ▲
Castleshaw   Slack   Brough ☐
Manchester ■   ▲Melandra   Castleford ▲
Brough   Doncaster ▲
Buxton ▲   Templeborough ■
CHESTER ▣   ? Middlewich   Chesterfield ●
Chesterton ?   Rocester ▲   Littlechester ▲
Whitchurch
WROXETER ▣   Eaton House ▲

3 The forts of Agricola in the north.

124

may have involved two parallel columns, one marching north from York and the other from Chester, contact being made from time to time across the passes. This is a deduction from the road system which Agricola soon established (Fig. 3), no doubt on lines now explored, and it is one which suits the geography of north Britain. The roads were necessary to link the forts which, as we shall see, he established as he advanced.[5] No doubt Agricola himself led the western column, giving the place of honour to his own division, Legio xx.[6] The tactics were terrorising raids followed by offers of reasonable terms. In this way he won over many peoples who had till then maintained their independence, and he stationed garrisons in their territories. Traces of this campaign can perhaps be seen in the slighted ramparts of the native strongholds on Ingleborough and Carrock Fell, if indeed these particular hill-forts had not fallen previously to Cerialis. The Tyne–Solway isthmus was perhaps the limit of the first campaign and, as we have seen (p. 71), this line was approximately the northern boundary of the old Brigantian kingdom.

The next year, 80, however, saw the advance continued, and this time new tribes were encountered; for by the end of it devastation had been carried to the Tay estuary.[7] Despite bad weather, enemy resistance was beaten down, and once more forts were constructed so that garrisons could winter in conquered territory. As a result of this reconnaissance to the Tay, the advantages of the Forth–Clyde isthmus as the site of a fortified frontier were appreciated: next year, 81, forts were established on this line, and the troops were also employed in consolidating the gains already made. This would be the moment for more thorough road-building than had been possible so far, and for a more thorough disposition of forts at strategic points.

The exact character of the boundary established at the isthmus by Agricola is uncertain. It used to be supposed that his forts lay beneath those of the later *limes* on this line known as the Antonine Wall; but an absence of Flavian pottery from the majority of these sites compels a reconsideration of this view, nor are the sites of the independent forts of the Agricolan system necessarily the best for forts attached to a linear barrier. At Bar Hill and Croy Hill fortlets underlie the Antonine Forts; these could conceivably be Agricolan, granted that they were occupied for too short a period for broken pottery to accumulate (AD 81–3); but it has been suggested that they

125

represent a preliminary phase of the Antonine arrangements, like the fortlet at Duntocher.[8] One Agricolan fort lies at Camelon, about two miles north of the Wall; two others may have lain near but not precisely at the Antonine Wall forts of Castlecary and Cadder; another may have existed near Mumrills.[9]

It seems probable that the emperor Titus had decided, on the basis of Agricola's reports, to limit conquest to southern Scotland. Not only did the northern isthmus provide a conveniently short line for the frontier but, as we have seen (p. 73), it was also to some extent a linguistic and cultural boundary. All to its south could be described as Britons, whereas the Caledonian tribes to its north were of different stock. Tacitus mentions that they had reddish hair and large limbs, which made him think them akin to the Germans. The northern lands could be looked on as almost a different island.[10]

Of the two main Roman roads through southern Scotland, one runs north from Carlisle up Annandale; once over the watershed, this road divides, one branch going to the Clyde valley, the other to Inveresk on the Forth. The other main road runs up from Corbridge over the Cheviots to Newstead and on to Inveresk. Both are heavily garrisoned with forts. The eastern road is approximately on the western border of the Votadini, and the effect of both roads is to cordon off the Selgovae from their neighbours. This effect is heightened by at least two other cross-roads which cut through Selgovian territory. The whole system pivots on the large fort of Newstead, which lies in the valley below the slighted oppidum of the Selgovae on Eildon Hill North (p. 74). In contrast to the treatment of the Selgovae, Traprain Law, perhaps even at this time the principal oppidum of the Votadini, has produced Roman pottery of Flavian date: evidently it was allowed to continue. And the territory of the Votadini contains remarkably few Roman forts. This tribe in later times was traditionally friendly to Rome, and it is likely that this tradition goes back to their first contact with the Roman army. Other tribes – the Brigantes or Selgovae – whose experience of it was bitter, remained unrelenting in their hostility for over a century. We may deduce that the Selgovae and the Novantae were the chief foes in the Lowlands, and that Agricola came to some arrangement with the Votadini. Such a state of affairs would be typical both of Celtic reaction to Rome and of Roman statecraft: Tacitus remarks that alliances between two or three tribes were rare in Britain. The Selgovae were a powerful and formidable enemy; but it is probable that they were bewildered by the speed of the Roman advance, and we have seen (p. 74) that the numerous small hill-forts in their territory imply a lack of political centralisation which may have proved disastrous when the moment of crisis so swiftly arrived. The moment passed and the Selgovae found themselves cut off from their neighbours and from each other, and subject to military rule.

The turn of the Novantae came next year, in 82. The great promontory of south-west Scotland lies on the flank of that part of the Lowlands already conquered. The Novantae, who occupied its southern portion, had been isolated from the Selgovae by the cordon of the Annandale road. But their hostility presented a continuing menace not only to that road with its garrisons but also to the Cumberland coast across the Solway. The reduction of this flank, then, could be postponed as a temporary expedient, but not permanently neglected, difficult though much of the country is. In 82 Agricola crossed the estuary at the head of a sea-borne invasion. This method of attack had a twofold advantage: not only will it have been unexpected by the Novantae but by it his columns will have been enabled to march with the lie of the land instead of across it, since all the river valleys on the south coast run north and south. In the course of this campaign the army encountered tribes hitherto unknown – presumably groups in Ayrshire, for the Novantae themselves must have been well known.

Until recently archaeology had little to show in this area, and there are still many sites to be discovered. A Roman road runs westwards from Castledykes down the Irvine valley past a fort at Loudoun Hill, and making, no doubt, for a harbour near the river's mouth. As a result of aerial photography in the dry summer of 1949, later confirmed by excavation, Agricolan forts are now known at Dalswinton (pl. 1b) and Glenlochar in the Nith and Dee valleys; and west of the latter a fortlet of Flavian date, possibly Agricolan, has been discovered at Gatehouse of Fleet. Clearly a road connected these sites too, penetrating the southern borders of the Novantae, and probably making for a port near Stranraer. We can assume that there was a north–south link road along the west coast. Agricola's army certainly reached the south-western extremity of Galloway which faces Ireland, and the general was of the opinion that that island could easily be conquered. He had received a fugitive Irish prince, who would be useful if it came to the point; and he had found that information on Irish harbours and approaches was to be had from merchants who traded there. It was his estimation, surely optimistic, that one legion and a few auxiliaries would suffice for the work. However, if he made recommendations to Rome on these lines, they were turned down. Titus had died in September 81, and the new emperor Domitian, impressed perhaps with the speed and success of Agricola's campaigns, seems to have decided that if further military advances were to be made, it would be more realistic to complete the conquest of Britain. He accordingly reversed the decision to stand on the Forth–Clyde line. This must be the meaning of Tacitus' obscure remark on the subject of this frontier, that here, still short of the limits of the island, a halting-place was found – 'if the valour of our armies and the glory of the Roman name had allowed it'. It was necessary to his purpose to avoid giving Domitian the credit for allowing his hero the advance which led to his great victory. At the same time Domitian himself was about to embark on an important war in Germany in 83, and called for vexillations from all four British legions.[11] If Agricola could advance without these troops he was free to do so.

In 83 accordingly the advance northwards was resumed, but this time geography imposed a different plan of action. The hitherto successful advance in two columns each side of the central spine of hills was no longer possible, as a glance at the map of the Highlands will show. This was already known to Agricola from naval reconnaissance. Plutarch tells us how at Delphi in 83–4 he met a Greek schoolmaster from Tarsus, named Demetrius, recently returned from Britain, who had taken part in the exploration of the western islands. This reconnaissance took place perhaps in 82. There are echoes of an eye-witness, too, in Tacitus' description of the wide domain of the sea in Caledonian latitudes, 'which is not limited to the coast as elsewhere, but penetrates sinuously deep inland, mingling with mountain ranges as though in its own element.' Two alternatives were left. One was to penetrate the Highland massif itself, which Agricola was too good a general to attempt before the enemy had been broken; the second was to advance with his entire force up the eastern plains, which encircle the Highlands on two sides. A successful battle after that might bring the whole land within his grasp. Northwards of Inverness lay the country of the broch-builders (p. 73). These may well have been friendly to Rome because of hostility to the Caledonian hill-fort builders and, if so, presented no serious military problem.

The drawback to such a march lay in the insecurity engendered by a single lengthening life-line. The long supply route marked by the road running north from Stirling to Stracathro was easily vulnerable to surprise attack issuing from the mouths of Highland glens beside its path. Agricola took steps to deal with this grave problem, and nothing shows his qualities as a commander more convincingly. The tactical problem was solved by placing a fort to block the exit from each glen:[12] the strategic difficulty was solved by increasing use of waterborne transport. But the fleet had a further purpose also. Its appearance in the north gravely disturbed the consciousness of security which the remoter Caledonians had hitherto enjoyed; a series of landings far behind the lines might stimulate the enemy to abandon the wise strategy of guerrilla warfare and risk the crushing defeat which alone could end the war.

News of his intentions had already reached the Caledonians, or perhaps the early naval explorations had warned them of their danger, for a confederacy had been formed which was already massing large forces. A Roman fort was attacked, and Agricola learnt that the enemy was approaching in several columns. He therefore divided his own army into three divisions, and the camp of one of these, Legio IX, was attacked. This legion was below strength, as we have seen; but Agricola himself came up in time with relief, and the enemy was put to rout, only to escape into the marshes and woods. After this the advance was maintained with renewed confidence, and may have reached the neighbourhood of Aberdeen if the reference to frequent meetings with the fleet has any meaning. Summer ended, however, indecisively. It will have been in this year that the decision was reached to place a legion – probably Legio XX – in a new fortress at Inchtuthil on the Tay. This fortress guarded the main exit from the Highlands through the Tay gorge at Dunkeld, and formed the hub of Agricola's system for the occupation of the north. A short distance north of it runs the Cleaven Dyke, an obvious Roman boundary guarded by a watch-tower. This does not extend far enough to mark an actual frontier. It probably defined the territorium of the legion, a provision area under strict military control.

In 84 it remained to force a battle, and this was at last achieved by sending the fleet ahead to raid and burn, so that the enemy's

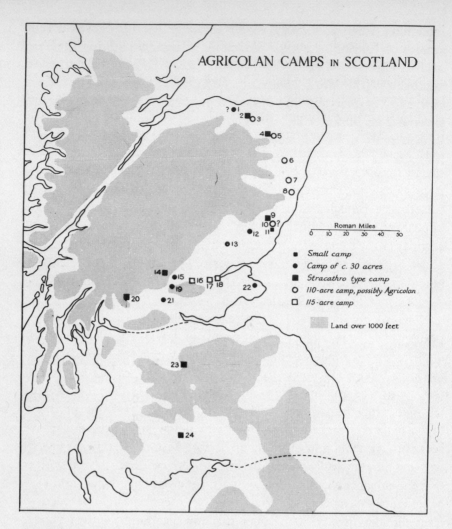

AGRICOLAN CAMPS IN SCOTLAND

Roman Miles
0 10 20 30 40 50

■ Small camp
● Camp of c. 30 acres
■ Stracathro type camp
○ 110-acre camp, possibly Agricolan
□ 115-acre camp

Land over 1000 feet

4 Agricolan marching camps in Scotland

1 Bellie
2 Auchinhove
3 Muiryfold (Pass of Grange)
4 Glenmailen (Ythan Wells)
5 Glenmailen (Ythan Wells)
6 Kintore
7 Normandykes

8 Raedykes
9 Stracathro
10 Logie (?)
11 Dun (Montrose Basin)
12 Finavon
13 Cardean
14 Dalginross
15 Dornock

16 Dunning
17 Abernethy
18 Carpow
19 Ardoch
20 Menteith
21 Dunblane
22 Bonnytown
23 Castledykes
24 Dalswinton

remaining areas of supply lost all security. The result was a full-scale mobilisation of all the remaining Caledonian states. They are said to have raised more than 30,000 men, who awaited Agricola's approach at the Mons Graupius. The exact position of this famous battle is still uncertain, but it should be sought in the approaches to Inverness at some point where the natural features enabled the Roman route to be foreseen. A line of Roman marching-camps running up the eastern side of Scotland has long been known, and in recent years aerial photography has filled in some of the gaps; but it has also added complications. It can now be said that they represent more than one campaign (Figs. 4, 8, p. 202). One series of camps is of great size, c. 130 acres. Camps of this area are sufficiently large for a force of 30,000 men, or three legions and an equal number of auxiliaries. One of these camps can be shown to be later than a permanently established signal station near Ardoch: it is probable that they represent the campaigns of Severus. A second series of camps, 63 acres in size, closely resembles the 130-acre series in shape and proportion and also appear to be of early third-century date (p. 200 f.). In addition there are three, or perhaps four, other groups. One, represented by squarish camps of c. 115 acres at Dunning and Abernethy, is taken to have been built on Agricola's march to the Tay in 80. A second group has areas in the region of 30 acres, and the third, though varying considerably in acreage, has a distinctive type of *clavicula* at the gates (the 'Stracathro type'). There are good grounds for assigning both of these series also to Agricola's forces, and some at any rate of them to the year 83 when his army was marching in three divisions. A fourth group may be indicated by four camps in the far north which are of c. 110 acres; it is not yet certain whether these represent the final stages (with depleted forces) of Severus' campaign, or whether they are to be connected with Agricola's last campaign in 84. Certainly the absence of evidence for a concentration of his forces before Mons Graupius has hitherto been an embarrassment; but further camps of this size must be found to the south before the group can be attributed to Agricola with any certainty. Be this as it may, at the furthest site of all to the north-west yet discovered, a camp of Stracathro type at least 30 acres in extent has been identified from the air at Auchinhove near the pass of Grange. The site of Mons Graupius should be looked for beyond this camp.

The Caledonians had many leaders, one of the chief of whom was Calgacus, into whose mouth Tacitus puts a speech of great imagination. In the battle which followed, Agricola stationed his legions in front of the Roman camp, but behind his line of battle, which consisted entirely of auxiliary troops. He placed 8,000 infantry (some twelve or sixteen regiments which included formations enrolled in southern Britain) in the centre, and 3,000 cavalry (five or six alae) on the flanks. The legions stood in reserve, and in fact were not employed. The Roman line lacked superiority of position, for the Caledonian forces could be seen rank on rank up the slope behind their chariotry, and Agricola had to extend his line for fear of being surrounded. His problem was to get the Caledonians off the higher ground, and this he achieved by allowing his centre to fight itself to a standstill on the slope: once the enemy, attracted by this sight and contemptuous of the small number of men fighting, had moved down in hopes of sweeping round the Roman rear, he routed them with four fresh cavalry regiments held in reserve for this purpose. Ten thousand Caledonians were said to have perished for the loss of only 360 Roman troops.

The victory had been gained late in the season. There was no time for further campaigning. Agricola led his army into the lands of the Boresti and there took hostages (presumably from all the defeated tribes). The Boresti are otherwise unknown, but their name has been connected with Forres in Moray. The fleet was ordered to sail round the north of Britain, and thus established that it was an island; on this voyage, too, they explored the Orkneys and received their surrender. On land Agricola slowly returned to winter-quarters farther south. When the news of the victory reached Rome, Domitian awarded him triumphal ornaments, and arranged for his recall. Agricola had been in Britain more than six years, an unusually long term for the Governor of this province: the routine exploitation of victory could be left in accordance with precedent to his successor.

It remains to sum up Agricola's achievements. There is no doubt that on the military side he had a distinguished record in Britain.[13] In six years he had almost doubled the area under Roman control, granted that Cerialis had done the hard work in Brigantia. He had an eye for country, and his fort-sites were well chosen: many remained occupied for centuries. Moreover, he was an innovator in fort-design. Again, and unlike most Roman generals, he had a masterly appreciation of the role of sea-power in extended military operations and was notably successful in his use of the fleet both for aggression and for supply. In both these aspects of strategy he may have built on the experience of Frontinus, whose fort-system in Wales was equally well planned and who may have similarly used his fleet. Nevertheless, the military problems of Scotland were not identical with those of Wales, and Agricola's instinct never faltered there. The rapidity and sheer competence of the reconnaissance which found the way for his columns and the key positions for his forts must command respect; and when the policy of cordoning the hills foundered on the geography north of the Forth Agricola was not at a loss. In the final battle, too, he used new tactics. The conception of a decisive battle fought by auxiliaries only, with the legions looking on, had never been successfully attempted before. It is true that in 70 Cerialis at the battle of Vetera had placed his legions in the second line, but in this muddled battle they were soon engaged in heavy fighting, and there is no indication that the general had planned otherwise. The battle of Mons Graupius was a notable advance on this. Tacitus tells us that the idea was to save *Roman* manpower; but that is a propaganda point which tells only part of the truth. The auxiliaries themselves were potential Romans, who received citizenship on discharge. They were, however, more expendable; yet the real significance of these tactics, as Professor Richmond pointed out,[14] is that provincials – even Britons – were now able to play a major part in Imperial defence. Already leading provincials had risen to high rank in the administration (p. 108); but now the rank and file had shown their reliability. The provinces were on the way to partnership in Empire.

In his civilian administration Agricola was imaginative. Born in Narbonensis of provincial Roman stock, he lacked the arrogance of the true Roman aristocrat and was able to sympathise with the difficulties of provincials. In his very first winter in Britain he checked various administrative abuses, small perhaps in themselves, but cumulatively leading to hatred of Rome. The *annona*, or corn tribute, which had to be delivered by the provincials to the military authorities, was a case in point. The Britons, says Tacitus, submit to taxation cheerfully, provided there is no abuse. But the arrangements for the annona had fallen into the hands of profiteers who would compel delivery to far distant forts instead of conveniently adjacent ones if their price was not met, and there were even cases known where Britons had had to buy back from Roman granaries at greatly inflated prices in order to meet their obligations. All this was stopped.

In his second winter we are told that he embarked on a more ambitious programme of education and of romanisation. 'With private encouragement and public aid he pressed forward the construction of temples, forums and town-houses, praising those who were keen, censuring those who were not. Thus, competition for his favour was as effective as compulsion. The sons of leading men were educated in the liberal arts, and he stated his opinion that the natural ability of the Britons was superior to the studied industry of the Gauls. The result was that refusal to learn Latin was replaced by a desire to excel in it. In the same way Roman dress came into fashion and the toga was everywhere seen.'

The educational part of the policy is illustrated by the story of Demetrius of Tarsus, already quoted. The presence of a Greek teacher in Britain just at this time can hardly be either coincidental or unique. The growth of literacy is illustrated by late first-century business documents found in London, and that it went deeper is suggested by the fact that just at this time literate potters' stamps begin to appear on local pottery. As for the urbanising policy, an illustration came to light at *Verulamium* in 1955 with the discovery of the forum inscription bearing Agricola's name, and dated to the winter of this very year, 79. The policy itself must have taken several years to implement,[15] and the *Verulamium* forum had probably been begun under Frontinus; but the dedication of the new forum of a municipium doubtless involved the governor's presence, and it may have been this event which fixed the date in Agricola's, and thus in Tacitus', mind.[16] The reference to forums in the account of the new policy implies, indeed, that the reforms went further, for the forum with basilica was an integral part of the physical trappings of local self-government. But in truth the extension of self-government by the establishment of new areas of local administration, or *civitates,* was an essential preliminary to Agricola's northern campaigns. Though the number of pre-Flavian forts yet discovered in southern Britain is small (fig. 2, p. 88), it is already clear that many of them lay in places like Exeter, Cirencester, Chelmsford or Dorchester-on-Thames which subsequently became civilian towns. This must surely mean that much of southern Britain down to the Flavian period was under

134

one form or another of military rule (p. 235). But Agricola's campaigns into Scotland involved the construction of over sixty new forts as winter-quarters of auxiliary troops. These forces had all moved forward from original bases farther south. Thus the necessities of the military situation compelled new arrangements for the control of this region. Self-governing civitates were accordingly established in areas which were ripe for the step after forty years of supervision. Once again, this process had probably been begun by Frontinus, who required troops for the occupation of Wales, and who may have established at least the Dumnonii as a civitas. Elsewhere, however, forts continued to be occupied down to Agricola's time, for instance at Great Casterton among the Coritani, and Dorchester-on-Thames among the Catuvellauni. The extent of Agricola's work in this field remains to be established as excavation produces more exact information about the date of the evacuation of forts. But meanwhile we may note the evidence already accruing of a Flavian date for the construction of the forum at Cirencester in addition to those at Exeter and London. The forums at Silchester and Winchester may be a few years later, perhaps about 100, while the establishment of a capital for the Iceni at Caistor by Norwich is usually placed about 70: the troops holding this territory may have been moved by Cerialis or Frontinus. It was probably in connection with this big programme of civic development, coupled with the governor's pre-occupation with military affairs, that we begin to find provincial law-officers – legati iuridici – appointed to Britain (pages 224–5).

At present Agricola's most striking mark on Roman Britain remains his system of roads and forts devised for control of the north (fig. 3, p. 124). In the lands up to the Tyne–Solway line at least forty forts were held, of which all but seven were new foundations:[17] in lowland Scotland there were at least a further twenty forts or fortlets, and north of the Forth another nine or ten in addition to the legionary fortress. The construction of over sixty forts was a major work in itself, but the organisation of supply for this large and scattered force called for administrative genius. Not least it called for the survey and construction of a minimum of 1,300 miles of road. The map of this road-system shows how the blocks of hill-land are penetrated and surrounded, so that patrols could prevent unauthorised movement and quickly reach the sources of trouble. Beyond the northern isthmus the discovery by aerial photography of the fort at Stracathro shows that the whole of Strathmore was permanently occupied right up to the point where the mountains approach the sea at Stonehaven.

Many of these forts shows signs of originality. Some, like Newstead, Castledykes, Bochastle, Oakwood or Milton, display novel experimentation in the plan of ditch systems or ramparts, designed to strengthen the gate. Some, like Malton, Newstead or Dalswinton (pl. Ib), are of large size, designed for the occupation of a composite force. Others again, like Chew Green, Cappuck, Oxton or Gatehouse of Fleet, are of very small size, designed for the reception of part of a unit only. It is noteworthy that the majority of these small forts are in Scotland, which suggests that as the area of conquered territory extended northwards, shortage of manpower began to be felt. In north-west Wales the fort at Pen Llystyn was replaced about this time by a fortlet occupying less than a quarter of the original area. In the second century, when more facts are available, we know the names of some sixty-five auxiliary regiments in Britain: the real total may have been slightly, but not much, larger. Agricola's army may have been rather more numerous than this, since auxiliaries were probably later withdrawn both by Domitian (to accompany Legio II Adiutrix to Moesia) and by Trajan; but there is no reason to think that it can have exceeded the ninety auxiliary regiments required to hold the known forts, and even this total is surprisingly large.[18] Clearly he had reached the limits of his resources despite the subdivision of certain units between fortlets. It would have been impossible for him to exploit his victory and occupy the coastal plain round to Inverness, let alone garrison the Highlands, without substantial reinforcements. These he might hope to obtain from the emperor who had authorised the advance north of the Forth in 83; but if so, his hopes were disappointed. Thus, an impasse had been reached at the time of his recall, full of possibilities for misunderstanding between the general and his Emperor.

Agricola, then, had been a great and energetic governor, but his tenure of Britain was the climax of his career. He had hopes of the command in Syria, but it was not forthcoming, nor was he given a command in the Danube wars; and later the Emperor made it clear that he was not to put in for the proconsulship of Africa or Asia, two offices regarded as the crowning honour of a senatorial career. Part of the reason for this, no doubt, was the limitations of Agricola's experience: his whole military life had been lived in Britain, and it may be the Britons were still underestimated as enemies. This, however, in itself is not sufficient to account for his eclipse. Part of the cause may lie in Agricola's own character, which had always been subservient to those above him, part perhaps in his lack of powerful connections. Nor must we discount the reason given by Tacitus – the jealous and suspicious nature of Domitian himself: very soon steps had to be taken which made it impossible any longer to hold even the land already occupied north of the Forth, and the rift between the two became complete.

These steps were necessitated by events on the Danube, where in 85 there occurred a serious invasion of Dacians; the invaders were expelled, but when in 86 a punitive expedition crossed the river it was disastrously defeated and its general killed. A second expedition had to be prepared and larger forces assembled. The year 87 was spent in preparation, and in 88 a great victory was won on Dacian soil. Legio II Adiutrix is known to have arrived in Moesia by 92,[19] and it may have been withdrawn from Britain to form part of the new army late in 86 or, more likely, in 87. Thus, more vital Roman interests compelled the reduction of the garrison of Britain, and this in turn meant that insufficient troops remained to encompass the occupation of Scotland. Legio II Adiutrix had been stationed at Chester since about 77; with its departure a vital gap opened in the legionary dispositions in Britain which could only be filled by withdrawing the legion (probably Legio xx) at Inchtuthil. Excavation has shown that the fortress at Inchtuthil had not been completely finished when dismantling began; and a coin minted perhaps in 87 shows that occupation continued at least till that date. With Legio xx at Chester, the fortress at Wroxeter, hitherto kept in working order though without garrison, was finally demolished and its site made over to the civitas of the Cornovii for the construction of their capital.[20]

The problems connected with the total evacuation of Scotland will be discussed in the next chapter. Here we need only to note that it took place in more than one stage, and that on the accession of Trajan all lowland Scotland south of the Isthmus was still held – though with fewer forts. When Tacitus, therefore, summing up the events of Roman history between AD 68 and the death of Domitian in 96, states *perdomita Britannia et statim missa* – the conquest of Britain was completed and then let slip – his epigram is not to be taken too seriously; and yet in a sense it is true. For Agricola had won the victory which should have enabled the occupation of all Caledonian territory; he left the province to his successor quiet and safely held;[21] but by removing a legion and still more by refusing auxiliary reinforcements, Domitian let slip the opportunity of following up the victory. It was inevitable in the wider interests of Rome at that moment. Nevertheless, if Domitian was the Emperor who had authorised the invasion of Scotland north of the isthmus in the first place, his action in preventing the consummation of the conquest must have appeared particularly arbitrary to Agricola and his circle. It was, too a decision of destiny. Subsequent generals might campaign as far afield, but never again was there to recur the opportunity to unify the whole island in one province.

1. When Tacitus says he summoned help from outside the words must indicate the tribes of southern Scotland, all other directions being ineligible.

2. The question is not one which can be decided without further evidence. We do not even know whether Cerialis arrived in Britain in time to utilise the campaigning season of 71; if he did so, the conquest of East Yorkshire might usefully be attributed to the first of his three campaigns. But we do not know whether the Parisi resisted Roman occupation or welcomed it as a protection from Brigantian aggression; but the fewness of the forts in their territory supports other scanty evidence that they were friendly to Rome. In this case their occupation would not require a major campaign and could therefore be within Bolanus' power. If the first fortress at York was of full size there remains the question what forces held the fortress at Malton, if founded by Cerialis; it would fit well with Bolanus, as a fortress for a mixed battle-group of normal type. As for Cerialis, even when Venutius had been crushed, there still remained the fifteen or more septs of the Brigantes (p. 71f.) to overrun against bitter opposition – task enough, surely, for three campaigns.

3. The indecisive nature of the fighting attributed by Tacitus to Bolanus might be accounted for by the hazards of this latter route.

4. Two at Chester, already mentioned, on lead water-mains, and the other from the Forum at *Verulamium* (pp. 134 and 232 (fig. 9)).

5. *civitates . . . praesidiis castellisque circumdatae* is the Tacitean summary of the operation (*Ag.* 20), giving pride of place to the forts rather than the roads; no doubt the latter were at first mere tracks,

later to be improved, but in fact the two elements were mutually indispensable, and the policing system now laid down remained in force for the rest of the Roman period.

6. Legio IX was still commanded at this time by C. Caristanius Fronto (*ILS*, 9485). In later years Agricola's own winter headquarters were at York, to judge by Demetrius'·dedication there to the gods of the governor's residence (*ILS*, 8861). His other dedication to Ocean and Tethys makes his identification with Plutarch's Demetrius (p. 109) certain. See R.C.H.M., *Roman York* (1962), p. 133; *RIB*, 662–3.

7. There is nowadays general agreement that whether Tacitus wrote *usque ad Tanaum* (*aestuario nomen est*) or *usque ad Taum*, the estuary of the Tay is meant. See *JRS*, xxxiv (1944), 39; R. Syme, *Tacitus* (Oxford, 1958), p. 122.

8. K. A. Steer, *JRS*, l (1960), 88–90. At Bar Hill hazel roots had time to grow in the disused ditches of the fortlet before the Antonine Fort was built; unless, indeed, they were later roots which had worked their way down.

9. Sir George Macdonald's statements about the presence of Flavian pottery on certain Antonine Wall sites are inaccurate. See B. R. Hartley, *Britannia*, iii (1972), 6 ff.

10. *Summotis velut in aliam insulam hostibus* (Tacitus, *Agricola*, 23).

11. *ILS*, 1025 and 9200.

12. These forts, of course, had a strategic purpose too: that of containing the Highland tribes, whose territory could not be overrun until a victory had been won elsewhere.

13. Only the thoughts of an Irish expedition suggest doubts of his judgment; but this is not to be taken too seriously, perhaps; and certainly no detailed planning can have been completed.

14. *JRS*, xxxiv (1944), 43.

15. Suetonius' remark (already quoted, page 110) about the number of statues of and dedications to Titus which were to be seen in Britain is probably relevant here.

16. Fig. 10, p. 232.

17. On fig. 3, thirty-five forts are shown as certain; in addition, Agricolan occupation at Aldborough, Brougham, Greta Bridge, Kirkbride and Old Penrith can be assumed with reasonable sureness.

18. At least twenty Flavian forts are known in Wales in addition to those in northern Britain.

19. *ILS*, 2719.

20. This paragraph represents what may be termed the orthodox view of events. But in some ways it would be more congruous with what little evidence we have to suppose that Legio II Adiutrix remained in Britain (at Chester) until 89 or 90. In that case the withdrawal from northern Scotland, *c*. AD 87, will have been a policy decision based on the lack of auxiliary troops needed to complete the occupation of Scotland and not on lack of legionaries. Agricola's

existing arrangements there were precarious indeed unless completed, for his purpose was to contain the mountains and grip firmly the sources of enemy supply in Mar and Cawdor. The lack of sufficient auxiliaries to encompass this would be sufficient reason to write off the half-completed occupation north of the Forth. Legio II Adiutrix will have returned to Chester and Legio xx to Wroxeter. There are two tombstones of the former legion from Lincoln, covering the period 71–7, but no less than nine from Chester, covering the period from 77 to its withdrawal. This by itself means little, for the circumstances of discovery were different; but we may draw attention also to the following points. The Wroxeter fortress had been unoccupied since 83, and will have required some rebuilding. Three periods of timber military buildings have in fact been observed there: the third is difficult to account for save on the supposition that there was rebuilding here after the return from Scotland. The unfinished late-first-century bath-building at Wroxeter (p. 277), recognised by its excavator as of legionary construction, would now fall into place as the bath-house of the projected new fortress. The building opposite it may even have been begun as the principia, and the unfinished state of both will be due to the transfer of Legio xx to Chester about 90: the failure to complete them is very hard otherwise to explain. The withdrawal of Legio II Adiutrix will be seen as the result rather than the cause of the loss of Scotland. An inscription (*ILS*, 9193) records a centurion of this legion who was decorated in the Dacian war (at the latest in 89). Either, then, the legion had moved in time to take part in this campaign or, perhaps more likely, this centurion was serving in the vexillation which had left Britain in 83 and had been transferred to Moesia ahead of the main body.

21. It was probably Agricola who erected the Great Monument at Richborough, which is best interpreted as a triumphal trophy, marking the conquest of all Britain, at the gateway to the island.

7

The retreat from Scotland: Hadrian's frontier

The period of some forty years after the recall of Agricola is darkened by the absence of any historical source; it has to be conned with the aid of archaeological discovery assisted by occasional inscriptions. The references of Juvenal to the storming of Brigantian hill-forts, and to a British king Arviragus who is evidently hostile, do not help much,[1] and may even relate to Agricola's campaigns, in which it is considered possible that Juvenal himself took part. The identity of Agricola's successor is not known for certain, nor are any steps identifiable which he may have taken to begin the consolidation of northern Scotland. The reason, as we have seen, is doubtless that there were no auxiliary troops to spare.[2] Suetonius records that Domitian put to death one governor of Britain, Sallustius Lucullus, for naming a new lance after himself. This story may disguise the possibility that he was suspected of tampering with the loyalty of the provincial army. Lucullus may or may not have been Agricola's immediate successor; but the most likely date for his execution is 89, and the most likely reason is that he was thought to be involved in the conspiracy of Saturninus, legate of Upper Germany, which was suppressed that spring. No further governors under Domitian are known except a certain Nepos, mentioned as recently governor in a diploma of 98; he has been identified as P. Metilius Nepos, consul in 91; and was probably appointed before Domitian's murder in 96. This man was succeeded by T. Avidius Quietus, who had been consul in 93. Avidius was a man of taste and cultivation; he was a member of Pliny's circle and was acquainted with Plutarch. Years earlier he had been a friend of Thrasea Paetus, put to death by Nero in 66. He was thus by now in middle age, and perhaps owed his province to the friendship of Nerva. He will have held Britain from 97 or 98 till perhaps 100 or 101. His successor was probably L. Neratius Marcellus, consul in 95, who was certainly governor in January 103, as another diploma informs us. Neratius, too, was a friend of Pliny. He was probably in Britain by 101, for a letter of Pliny, usually dated to that year, mentions a military tribunate which the writer had obtained from Neratius for Suetonius the historian. But the latter did not take up the appointment; he wrote Pliny a charming letter asking if it could be transferred to his relative Caesennius Silvanus. No other Trajanic governor of Britain is known except perhaps M. Appius Bradua, who is described on an inscription as holding this office under Hadrian, but who may have been appointed in the last years of Trajan and overlapped with the next reign. He is sometimes identified with the M. Atilius Bradua who was consul in 108, and he may have held Britain from 115 to 118.[3]

A Trajanic legate of Legio xx is known from an inscription at Chester. He was Titus Pomponius Mamilianus Rufus Antistianus Funisulanus Vettonianus, who subsequently became consul in 121.

The army of Britain was reduced before 92 by the removal of Legio ii Adiutrix to the Danube, and Professor E. Birley has shown that some auxiliary regiments, notably three Batavian units, probably accompanied it.[4] The immediate effect of this was to make it impossible to hold Agricola's conquests in the far north; when the decision was reached, perhaps as early as 87, to abandon Inchtuthil[5] and move back Legio xx to Chester or Wroxeter it became evident that the Clyde–Forth isthmus would have to be the frontier. Many forts south of this line in lowland Scotland were extensively reconstructed, though others were probably abandoned, as for instance Castledykes, Oakwood and Easter Happrew. North of it no fort except Ardoch is known to have been retained, and even at Ardoch the evidence is doubtful.[6] Beyond Ardoch there has been all too little excavation of forts; but at Fendoch and Cardean there is only one period as there is at Inchtuthil itself; and Strageath, though reoccupied in Antonine times, also shows only one Flavian period.

South of the Isthmus there were drastic changes. At Newstead, which now became a key position, the exceptionally large Agricolan fort (10·6 acres) was entirely remodelled, and a much larger fort (14·3 acres) was put in its place. Not only was the new fort of greater size; its defences were of greatly increased strength. The rampart was 45 feet thick now instead of 23 feet, and this implies a height of about 28 feet instead of the previous 15. That the date of this reconstruction was not later than about 90 was suggested by the presence of two coins of AD 86 in mint condition, which were incorporated in the filled-in ditch of the first fort. To judge by the relics, the garrison of this exceptional fort was a vexillation of legionary infantry and an *ala* of auxiliary cavalry. It was thus equipped both for striking at a distance and for heavy fighting closer at hand. This altogether unusual state of affairs emphasises the importance which its strategic position, behind the front line and at the heart of Selgovian territory, gave to Newstead in the new scheme of defence.

In South-west Scotland a comparable importance attached to Dalswinton (pl. 1b). Here also Agricola had installed a large fort (8·59 acres), of sufficient size to hold two part-mounted cohorts; and here again the late Domitianic fort was made much larger (10·29 acres), to hold perhaps two cavalry regiments. Elsewhere extensive alterations, sometimes involving changes of garrison, took place. At Milton the fort was reconstructed. At Glenlochar a new fort was built (probably for a *cohors milliaria equitata*) on a fresh site altogether, and the same thing happened at Birrens. At Broomholm the existing rampart was strengthened, as it was also at High Rochester and at the fortlet of Cappuck. Thus, the Lowlands of Scotland were the scene of tremendous activity at this time: it is clear that the Roman grip on the Selgovae and Novantae was greatly intensified, though with some economy of forces.

The occupation lasted long enough for the natives to become acquainted with Roman goods. Coins and pottery and other objects of trade began to circulate on native sites away from the forts, and the weight of their distribution appears to coincide with the area under Roman control.[7] But before the processes of Romanisation could proceed far, that control was removed. The forts were held until the turn of the century, but not long after 105 a serious setback – perhaps a disaster – occurred. Excavations at Newstead, Dalswinton, Glenlochar, Cappuck, Oakwood, High Rochester and Corbridge have shown that these forts perished by fire. Now fire alone is not proof of enemy destruction, for the Romans themselves often burnt what was not worth salvaging when they evacuated a fort.[8] But Corbridge is too far south to have been intentionally evacuated, and at Newstead were found human bones and immense quantities of equipment, including damaged armour, showing that there at least the destruction of the fort was due to hostile action. Yet it is inconceivable that the Romans should have been driven from Scotland by superior force and should have accepted the situation. It is more reasonable to suppose, though we have no certain information, that Trajan's Dacian wars, the first in 101–2, the second in 105–6, had called for reinforcements from the army of Britain. This in turn might well evoke a decision to retire from southern Scotland: such a decision was needed, for future experience was to demonstrate the truth that with only three legions in Britain it was impossible to hold permanently the lands north of the Tyne–Solway isthmus. The attacks on Newstead and Corbridge will have been the work of a new generation of Selgovians taking advantage of a moment of confusion. Not all the other burnt forts, however, were necessarily destroyed by them. Indeed, this is unlikely, since a serious outbreak would surely have called for serious counter-measures, and probably a temporary reoccupation. The retreat from southern Scotland under Trajan is, then, best regarded as a planned withdrawal decided upon after a review of manpower, and as a result of the need for more men on the Danube; and not as a retreat enforced by a victorious rising of the north.[9] There were local disturbances or attacks, as at Newstead or Corbridge, once the decision became known; but the majority of burnt forts may have been burnt by their retiring garrisons. We must remember that the timber buildings had been standing some fifteen to seventeen years, more than half the limit of their useful life: the timbers would not be worth salvaging.

The date of the withdrawal is indicated by the occurrence of a few sherds of samian pottery at Newstead and Dalswinton which are definitely later than 100, and by the discovery in the burnt debris at Corbridge of a coin-hoard in which the latest coin was minted in 98, while a coin of 103 was found in the rampart of the fort which replaced the one destroyed and another of the same date in a post-trench in the new fort. A date of about 105 would suit these events on the evidence so far available.

Where the new Trajanic frontier was now placed it is not yet completely agreed, but all the evidence suggests that it lay on the line of the Stanegate, Agricola's road across the Tyne–Solway isthmus. The alternative to this would be the Cheviot Hills, which strike

144

farther north-east, where the present Border runs. But the fort of High Rochester, south of these hills, appears to have been burnt at this time and was not reconstructed till Antonine times; whereas on the Stanegate the Agricolan forts at Carlisle, Corbridge and possibly Whickham together with a late Domitianic one at Chesterholm were supplemented by new ones at Old Church Brampton, Nether Denton, probably Carvoran and perhaps at Castlesteads and Newbrough, while the intervals between these forts were each occupied by a fortlet. Those so far known lie at High Crosby, Castle Hill Boothby, Throp and Haltwhistle Burn. The exact dating of these additions is in dispute, some authorities holding that they date only from the beginning of Hadrian's reign; but the fortlets in particular have no place in the earliest scheme for Hadrian's Wall and mark a time when the Stanegate itself was the frontier. It was so, indeed, in the earliest years of Hadrian, before the Wall was built, but the situation then was merely a continuation of that existing in the second half of Trajan's reign: moreover, there were signs that the occupation of the Haltwhistle fortlet had not been brief. North of the Stanegate free-standing signal stations earlier than Hadrian's Wall exist at Pike Hill and Walltown Crags; it is not clear whether these are Trajanic or additions to the system made in the earliest years of Hadrian.

The main outline of events is thus dimly discernible, but the details and personalities are lost to us. That there was heavy fighting in Britain both in Domitian's reign and in Trajan's is certain. Professor Birley has shown how the Second Cohort of Asturians, which had been in Germany as late as 89, had arrived in Britain by 105 on the evidence of diplomas.[10] This movement in itself implies reinforcement of the army in Britain.[11] But, furthermore, Birley has called attention to the gravestone of C. Julius Karus, tribune of Legio III Cyrenaica at Alexandria, who died while outposted to Cyrene on a recruiting expedition. In his previous appointment Karus had been prefect of these Asturians, and had won outstanding decorations in a British war. This war, as Birley has shown, must be later than 89, when the regiment was still in Germany, and earlier than 128, when Legio III left Alexandria; he suggested that it was probably during the reign of Trajan and before 115 when the Jewish rebellion in Cyrene broke out. In fact, it may well have been earlier than 100, for two milestones erected in that year on the Cyrene-Apollonia road record construction undertaken by recruits levied in

145

Cyrenaica [12] – perhaps these whom Karus was sent to raise. Birley has also called attention to another regiment of the British garrison, Cohors I Cugernorum, recorded under that name in 103; by 122 it had received the titles Cohors I Ulpia Traiana Cugernorum Civium Romanorum. These were battle honours awarded by Trajan. Some of this fighting may have taken place in Wales, where the first fort at Forden Gaer was burnt about AD 90 and a new fort at Caer Llugwy was built about the same time.

There was also consolidation. All three legionary fortresses were about thirty years old, and their timbers would need renewing. In fact, we have evidence from inscriptions that all three were beginning to be reconstructed in stone, an investment which shows that no further movement was foreseen. A building at Caerleon bearing a large stone inscription was dedicated in 100; a fragment of a similar inscription, probably from a gate, at Chester dates to after 102; and a gate at York is dated 107/8.[13] The date of the Caerleon stone shows that this programme had no direct connection with the retreat from Scotland. The fort at Hardknott in the Lake District was built now, as the pottery shows, though there is also an inscription of the next reign; this fort supplements that at Ambleside, which was not founded before 90 at the earliest. A stone inscription, perhaps from the headquarters building, dedicated to Trajan, has been found at Lancaster, and the fort at Templeborough seems to have been rebuilt in stone at this time. In Wales a new fort was built at Gelligaer, and there is a fragmentary stone inscription, probably Trajanic, from Castell Collen, indicating a partial rebuilding in stone there too. The fort at Forden Gaer may also have been reconstructed in this reign. Part of the same programme, perhaps, was the erection of a fort at London just north-west of the inhabited area. It was eleven acres in size and was surrounded by a stone wall with earth rampart behind. The precise date of its foundation is uncertain, but is thought to be about 100. Its purpose was no doubt partly to accommodate the governor's guard, but the existence of numerous legionary gravestones from London suggests also that here was Army headquarters (p. 227).

Another form of consolidation which occurred about this time was the foundations of two more *coloniae*, the first at Lincoln and the second at Gloucester. The foundation date of *Lindum colonia* was probably late in Domitian's reign, about 90; the evidence – an inscription from Mainz – only defines it as Flavian, but the site was a fortress until 77, and only after Agricola's campaigns would there be suitable opportunity for discharging veterans. The date of *Glevum colonia* is defined by an inscription at Rome as occurring in Nerva's reign (96–8).[14] Both these colonies occupied the sites of previous fortresses – land, in other words, which was already imperial property, which suggests that the government was anxious not to repeat the mistakes which had marred the foundation of *Camulodunum*. Their foundation strengthened the civilising influences at work in the province, by providing further examples of Roman communities in being, both in friendly territory, but the one not far from Brigantia and the other close to the Silures.

Hadrian

The Emperor Trajan died in August 117. The event marked the termination of an era, for the period of uninhibited expansion was over. Never again was Rome able to indulge her taste for world-conquest. The emperors who succeeded Trajan were to be concerned rather with consolidating existing gains, with finding safe boundaries and with keeping the barbarians out. Defence rather than attack became the objective, and if there were from time to time advances, these were made only with the intention of finding shorter or more reliable frontier lines or for other sound defensive reasons. In Britain the new era had been born some little time prematurely; for the reign of Trajan, so glorious in the military sphere elsewhere, in Britain had witnessed retreat. But it was Hadrian, his successor, who gave up Trajan's Mesopotamian conquests on the ground that what could not be held must be liberated; and who devoted his life to the construction of efficient permanent boundary lines in many parts of the empire.

At the moment when Hadrian became emperor there was war in Britain once more. We are told no details, but the words of Hadrian's biographer, 'the Britons could no longer be held under Roman control', suggests that a rebellion, no doubt in the north, was at any rate part of the trouble. The short re-occupation of the fort at Brough on Humber about this time may have some connection with it.

The Brigantes, however, always possessed a close connection with the Selgovae and Novantae of southern Scotland: it is rarely that

147

we find trouble with the one without the involvement of the other group; nor did ancient writers clearly distinguish between them. When in the sequel we find Hadrian constructing a wall to separate the Brigantes from their northern allies we can feel confident that the war did indeed involve them both. Whatever the details of the insurrection, it was suppressed in 118, as a reference to Hadrian's second consulship shows us on an inscription from Jarrow; this once adorned some great monument which was erected a few years later near the east end of Hadrian's Wall to commemorate the victory and the completion of the frontier. And the following year, 119, saw the issue of commemorative coins.

This victory was the work of Q. Pompeius Falco, consul probably in 108 and thereafter governor of Lower Moesia, who governed Britain from 118 to 122. In the latter year Hadrian himself, who had begun a tour of inspection of the Western provinces in 121, arrived in Britain where 'he instituted many reforms and was the first to build a wall 80 miles long to separate the barbarians from the Romans'.[15] He appointed A. Platorius Nepos as governor in 122 to carry out his policy. Nepos, who had been consul in 119, after which he governed Lower Germany, was a close friend of Hadrian at this time and possibly a kinsman, though later the friendship was broken. It is likely that he accompanied the emperor to Britain, and probably also brought over Legio VI Victrix with him; for this legion had previously been stationed at Vetera in Lower Germany, and is recorded in Britain early in his governorship (p. 160). The length of his term of office is not certain, but he probably remained till 125. The name of his successor is not directly attested; there is a governor whose name cannot be clearly read, who set up an inscription at Bewcastle not later than 128. This man was perhaps succeeded by M. Appius Bradua (p. 142), for whom the dates 128–31 may be suggested. From about 131, however, the governor was Sex. Julius Severus, consul in 127, a man with a high military reputation and a distinguished record, who like Falco had come to Britain from the governorship of Moesia, and who about 134 was transferred from Britain to suppress the rebellion of Judaea. His successor was P. Mummius Sisenna, who had been consul rather late in life in 133, and who was certainly in Britain early in 135, where his son [16] was serving as legate of Legio VI.

This is the bare skeleton of known facts concerning Britain in

148

Hadrian's reign, during which there is one major achievement to be described: and one still mysterious event to be placed in a suitable context. The achievement is, of course, Hadrian's Wall, one of the most remarkable constructions of any Emperor at any time. The mystery is the disappearance of Legio ix from recorded history (p. 160).

The idea of a linear frontier was a recent development in Roman planning. The early Empire had depended for its frontiers on rivers or deserts or fortified zones. The word *limes*, used for a frontier, had the primary meaning of path, and came to be used of a military road. In the time of Augustus or Tiberius such a *limes* could be roads running directly into hostile territory; but by the later first century it was normally conceived of as a transverse road such as the Stanegate, carrying military installations such as forts or signal towers. Under Domitian, however, a beginning had been made in Upper Germany of strengthening the frontier with an actual fence. Hadrian in Germany developed this idea and constructed a continuous wooden palisade supported by the usual look-out and signal stations, and by forts moved up close behind its line. Such fences had little military value in themselves, but they did define the frontier, prevent small-scale crossings by unauthorised persons and channel travellers to the supervised entry-places. Moreover, the whole conception, abandoning defence in depth as it did, showed that no large-scale warfare was envisaged. The garrison could deploy forwards in case of need through gaps in the fence.

In Britain affairs were different and a much stronger barrier was constructed in stone, supported, moreover, by a system of forts and roads running back to the legionary fortresses at York and Chester. Though Hadrian's biographer, writing in the fourth century, described the wall as dividing Romans from barbarians, at the time it was constructed it served to divide the unruly Selgovae from the equally unruly Brigantes: it could rely on no peaceful hinterland. While one of its purposes was to define the frontier of the province and debar raids from the north, and in the long run to provide peaceful conditions for economic development in the region behind it, another was quite certainly to prevent that joint planning between northerners and Brigantians which had been a fruitful source of trouble in the past. Brigantian territory was still occupied, but of necessity the forts had to be considerably thinned out in order to

149

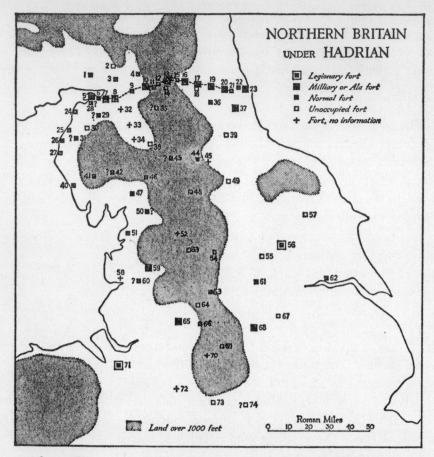

NORTHERN BRITAIN
UNDER HADRIAN

☒ Legionary fort
▨ Milliary or Ala fort
◼ Normal fort
◻ Unoccupied fort
+ Fort, no information

Land over 1000 feet

Roman Miles
0 10 20 30 40 50

5   The military occupation of the north under Hadrian (pp. 151, 182). *Note:* ? beside a fort indicates that its occupation is not entirely certain.

1 Birrens	14 Chesterholm	27 Moresby
2 Broomholm	15 Carrawburgh	28 Kirkbride
3 Netherby	16 Chesters	29 Old Carlisle
4 Bewcastle	17 Haltonchesters	30 Caermote
5 Bowness	18 Corbridge	31 Papcastle
6 Drumburgh	19 Rudchester	32 Wreay
7 Burgh by Sands	20 Benwell	33 Old Penrith
8 Stanwix	21 Newcastle	34 Brougham
9 Castlesteads	22 Wallsend	35 Whitley Castle
10 Birdoswald	23 South Shields	36 Ebchester
11 Carvoran	24 Beckfoot	37 Chester-le-Street
12 Great Chesters	25 Maryport	38 Kirkby Thore
13 Housesteads	26 Burrow Walls	39 Binchester

40 Ravenglass	52 Long Preston	64 Castleshaw
41 Hardknott	53 Ilkley	65 Manchester
42 Ambleside	54 Adel	66 Melandra Castle
43 Brough under Stainmore	55 Newton Kyme	67 Doncaster
44 Bowes	56 York	68 Templeborough
45 Greta Bridge	57 Malton	69 Brough on Noe (Derbyshire)
46 Low Borrow Bridge	58 Kirkham	70 Buxton
47 Watercrook	59 Ribchester	71 Chester
48 Bainbridge	60 Walton-le-Dale	72 Chesterton
49 Catterick	61 Castleford	73 Rocester
50 Overborough	62 Brough on Humber	74 Little Chester
51 Lancaster	63 Slack	

find garrisons to man the Wall (fig. 5). Thus an experiment was made: the military supervision of the Brigantes was considerably reduced, in the hopes that they might, if left to themselves, become more contented, less rebellious; and instead, the main strength of the occupying forces was used to man the Solway–Tyne isthmus.

Excavation on the line of the Wall has shown that the earliest plan for the system gravely underestimated the opposition it would arouse. A series of improvements was quickly put in hand. The Hadrianic frontier today consists of six elements. There is first the continuous wall fronted by a large ditch. Secondly, there are the milecastles, which are fortlets evenly spaced along the wall, a Roman mile apart; thirdly, the turrets, small towers, evenly spaced, two between two milecastles. The north gates of the latter carried towers corresponding with the turrets. The fourth element is the garrison forts; the fifth is the earthwork long known as the Vallum, but consisting of a wide ditch flanked some distance each side by a mound.[17] Lastly, there is the military way, the later road behind the wall. The mutual relationships, both chronological and topographical, of all these elements is complicated, and the true position has only been discovered painstakingly by excavation within the last half-century.

The earliest plan was to strengthen the Stanegate frontier with a ditch and wall provided with milecastles and turrets. The Stanegate itself with its forts lies in the valleys of the Eden, Irthing and Tyne; the barrier was placed on the north crest of the valleys, where in the central sector the basalt outcrop of the Whin Sill (pl. 4), provides an impressive ridge with craggy precipitous northern slopes.

It thus gained a good outlook northwards, where possible: only in its western part, in the region of Carlisle, does the ground fail to provide command. As originally planned the barrier ran from New-castle to Carlisle and on along the southern shore of the Solway to Bowness beyond the lowest ford of the estuary, a distance of seventy-six Roman miles. From Newcastle to the crossing of the Irthing there was to be a wall of stone ten feet thick, with a parapet walk some fifteen feet above ground: the parapet itself would give the northern face a height of some twenty feet. West of Irthing, however, it was found that there were no convenient supplies of limestone for the large quantity of mortar needed; and the wall in this sector, rather under half its length, was accordingly built of turf, twenty feet wide at the base and with an estimated height of some twelve feet to parapet walk. This turf wall could have been put up in six months, but to build the same length in stone would have added at least two years to the programme; thus the Turf Wall was in some sense a stop-gap, and its replacement in stone at leisure was in fact begun before the end of Hadrian's reign. Nevertheless turf-work was a normal method of fortification and implies no diminution of effectiveness.

At every Roman mile (1,620 yards) a fortlet was provided (c. 0·08 acre) for the patrolling garrison. These were of turf and timber in the turf-wall sector, but of stone elsewhere. They contained sometimes a pair of small barracks, but more usually only one, sufficient accommodation for eight or thirty men. Wide gateways, of massive build, pierced their north and south walls so that the troops approaching from the Stanegate might rapidly deploy from behind the screen offered by the wall itself. Here, too, civilian traffic could be scrutinised.

Though the accommodation remains constant, the milecastles fall into three types when details of their planning and of the design of their gateways are studied; these three types can be related to the three legions II, VI and XX which have left epigraphic records of their building activity. The turrets likewise fall into three types: they consist of stone towers [18] fourteen feet square internally and about 540 yards apart – a third of a Roman mile – recessed in the body of the wall. Their purpose was clearly for observation and signalling.

The building of all this, and possibly the hewing of the ditch, was the work of the British legions.[19] They were each allotted sectors, starting from Newcastle, *Pons Aelius*, where a new bridge was built over the Tyne. These sectors where identifiable were short, consisting usually of only about five miles or a little more. Within them one group of working parties laid the foundation of the wall and built the milecastles and turrets at their measured positions: the other cohorts built the wall itself on the foundation laid. Within each legionary length inscribed stones once marked each end of the lengths built by each century, cohort and, finally, by the legion itself.

Not unnaturally the parties laying the foundations and building the structures gradually drew ahead of the others, especially as they were permitted for the time being to omit the foundation here and there on the crags of the central sector. It was at the moment when the foundation builders had reached the Irthing and the ten-foot wall itself had reached the north Tyne that a change of specification was introduced for the wall, and a new plan was made under which forts were to be added to the wall itself, to house the fighting garrisons hitherto left on the Stanegate to the rear. Under the new specification the wall was to be only eight Roman feet thick; this is known today as the Narrow Wall. It was also now decided to extend the wall at its east end by another four miles (thus giving the barrier a total length of eighty miles), taking it to Wallsend, beyond which infiltration across the widening estuary of the Tyne would be more difficult: this extension consists of the Narrow Wall, and as the broad foundation is missing in this sector, the length is clearly an after-thought. The Wallsend fort is of one build with the Narrow Wall. An extension of the Narrow Wall was also made for five miles westwards from the Irthing to replace the turf wall here. The replacement took a different line from its predecessor for part of this sector, and this has enabled the Turf Wall and its structures to be studied in isolation. This extension took the stone wall to the limits of available limestone; but its construction is probably to be related to a change of garrison at Birdoswald. This fort had perhaps been planned to house a cavalry regiment, and so projected through the Wall to have three gates north of it; but it was actually garrisoned by infantry. These did not require three gates north of the wall, and the opportunity was taken to provide more space round the fort (which has a steep drop behind it) by shifting the wall to join the

153

fort's northern corners. The rebuilding in stone was then extended as far as limestone was available. Possibly plans to carry it further were interrupted by the decision to move forward into Scotland in 139.

It is not known for certain what the reason was for changing from broad to narrow wall, or whether it involved reducing the height as well as the width of the barrier. The narrow wall was normally built on the front edge of the broad foundation, and there was an offset where it joined the milecastles and turrets which had already been built to the width of the broad foundation, and which had short spurs or wing walls added on either side to take the broad wall when it should eventually arrive. The core of the broad wall has been found in some sectors to be constructed of stones set in clay or rubble instead of cement. Such a form of construction might account for its 2:3 proportions, and experience might show that such a core was liable to movement on steep hills; it has been suggested that this instability was the reason for the decision to change to the narrow-gauge wall with its concrete core. Unfortunately it is not certain whether the broad wall always originally possessed a stone and clay core. In some sectors, by contrast, a concrete core has been observed which may be original, though it might also be accounted for by rebuilding later. The narrow wall used less material and could be built more quickly. Bede, writing in the eighth century, described the narrow wall as eight feet thick and twelve feet high: it is not, indeed, absolutely certain that it was standing to its full height when he saw it, but his words seem definite and authoritative. Though the turrets and milecastles of the central sector had already been built to the height of the broad wall, it would be an easy matter to adapt them to the narrow wall, if it was of lower elevation, with three or four steps. It may well be thought likely that in addition to considerations such as these, the decision to change to the narrow gauge was part of the further decision to move the garrisons up to the wall. For once the forts had been added to the wall, the Vallum was constructed to the south of the line; and this additional barrier, together with the nearby presence of the garrison, would justify some economy in the height of the wall itself. And, after all, the reduction in height to twelve feet, if genuine, merely equalised the height of the stone wall with that of the turf wall farther west.

That the forts were a secondary addition to the wall system is shown by the fact that at Chesters, Housesteads and Great Chesters milecastles or turrets attached to the broad foundation underlie the forts; at Birdoswald the turf wall with its ditch and a turret underlie the fort, while at Halton the wall-ditch (and no doubt the broad foundation also, though this has not been found, lying as it does beneath the modern road) runs below the fort. Nevertheless, the fort at Halton, though secondary, still produced an inscription of Platorius Nepos, and another comes from Benwell. It is clear from this that the moving up of the garrison was an early alteration to the plans. The date of the change to the narrow gauge is not so directly attested; but, as we have seen, it can best be explained as part of the same new policy. In the central sector, however, where the character of the country gave greater immunity, at least one section of the narrow wall was not finished till 128 at the earliest; for at Great Chesters the narrow wall is of one build with the fort, which has produced an inscription thus dated.

There had only been seven forts on the Stanegate frontier, with perhaps another two east of Corbridge; under the new arrangements eleven forts were added to the wall,[20] the Stanegate ones being, of course, evacuated. All the new forts were for large garrisons, either alae 500 strong or milliary cohorts: the plan seems to have been [21] to place 4,000 infantry in the centre and 2,000 cavalry on either flank, leaving the bridgehead at Newcastle to be held by the 500 infantry already there. Later this scheme was slightly modified by placing smaller forts at Castlesteads, Carvoran, Great Chesters and Carrawburgh, thus reducing the gaps between the infantry forts in the centre, though leaving the same total of 4,500 infantry, and by adding a fort for 500 infantry at Wallsend at the east and Drumburgh at the west. The total garrison of the Wall forts, now sixteen in number, was thus 9,500 men.

Once the forts were in position, or at any rate once their positions had been fixed, the Vallum – or *Fossatum* – was constructed (pl. 3). This was a formidable ditch normally twenty feet wide and as much as ten feet deep, with a flat bottom eight feet in breadth, though somewhat less wide and deep where cut through rock. On each side of the ditch there is a berm of thirty feet flanked by turf-revetted mounds twenty feet wide and originally some six feet high. The effect thus created was of a boundary consisting of a ditch, impassable or very difficult to pass on foot, occupying the centre of a strip eighty feet wide defined by banks.[22] Earlier theories regarded it as the original Hadrianic frontier, but its behaviour in swerving to avoid the sites of forts shows that it was planned later than these, while the fact that it swerves to avoid a short-term turf wall milecastle in the Birdoswald sector where the narrow wall, later but still Hadrianic, takes a more northerly course with its own milecastles, proves that the difference in time is not great. The Vallum is crossed by original causeways only at forts and some of the milecastles. At the former the causeways were revetted in stone, and stone gateways have been found which were controlled from the north. At the milecastles there are gaps in the north mound but not in the south, and the berm of the ditch, lightly metalled where necessary, seems to have formed a trackway which could be patrolled, and along which supplies might reach the milecastles. Indeed, until the construction later in the century of the military way, as the Roman road is called which runs just behind the wall, this trackway was the only means of supplying the milecastles. It has therefore been suggested that the trackway is earlier than the Vallum itself, which was so constructed as to incorporate it. This would account for the regular, well-engineered course taken by the Vallum, with its straight stretches and easy gradients closely resembling those of a Roman road; though it must be admitted that the earthwork is laid out on the same principles, even in sectors where it is too distant from the Wall to have had any connection with a patrol track. This close relationship of the fort and milecastle garrisons with the Vallum disproves R. G. Collingwood's theory that the Vallum was a civil frontier manned by the procurator's staff. It clearly belongs to the military, and it is noteworthy what care was taken to make it continuous. There exist one or two places where the rock was so difficult to cut that the Wall-ditch was allowed to be left incomplete; but no rock was too hard for the Vallum. Moreover, at White Moss, where the waterlogged condition of the ground made it impossible to cut a normal ditch, the Vallum was built up like a canal and thus carried forward, as it was also at the crossing of the Poltross burn. That the Vallum should be continuous and complete was evidently felt to be important, expensive addition though it was to the system. What was its purpose? It was not a strictly military defensive system, for the ditch is not of military shape, nor are the symmetrical banks defensive; furthermore, the Vallum takes no account of commanding ground. Rather it is a barrier and line of demarcation defining the rear of the Wall-zone, and preventing entry except at fixed points. Unauthorised intruders would find it hard to explain themselves; military stores would be safer; and all attempts at contact between Brigantians and their friends in the north were made very much more difficult.[23]

But the fact that the Vallum was necessary at all suggests that quite a considerable and unsettled population lived near the rear of the wall, just as the removal of the fighting garrison to the wall itself shows that hostile pressure from the north was increasing in intensity; aerial photography and field-work are beginning to show us where and how this native population lived. It was to divide these two foes that the wall was built. The eastern half of the wall does appear to coincide approximately with the boundary of Brigantia (p. 71), but in the western half the line may have cut across a salient of Brigantian territory in order to make contact with the southern shore of the Solway. It was just this sector, too, which lacked commanding views northward; and in consequence three outpost forts were maintained north of the Wall, at Birrens, Netherby and Bewcastle. These not only provided early warning of hostile movements but also maintained Roman control over the outlying parts of Brigantia. Netherby and Bewcastle, and almost certainly Birrens,[24] have produced Hadrianic inscriptions; the wording of these (except the Bewcastle example, which is too fragmentary) implies that they were in existence by 128.

The eastern flank of the wall was protected by the deep estuary of the Tyne, and by the cavalry fort at South Shields, which overlooked the mouth of the river, where no doubt a detachment of the fleet was stationed. The configuration of the coast here offered no threat. It was different at the west end, where, though the wall continues to a point below where the Solway is fordable, the coast of Cumberland continues vulnerable beyond it to crossings by boat from the opposite coast. Along this coast, therefore, the wall system was continued for another thirty-five miles. The curtain wall itself could be replaced by the shore, but a system of mile-fortlets and signal towers exactly comparable to those on the wall extends probably to St Bees Head; and reinforcing them are four forts, the first at Beckfoot ($2\frac{1}{2}$ acres), the next at Maryport (5.2 acres), the third at Burrow Walls ($2\frac{3}{4}$ acres) and the last at Moresby ($3\frac{1}{2}$ acres). The latter at least was constructed in or after 128.[25] These four forts are supported farther inland by others at Papcastle and Old Carlisle (pl. 6a), the latter cavalry.[26] At some later date which is not quite certain the rest of the turf wall, with its turf-built forts and milecastles, was rebuilt in stone. In this reconstruction the Wall was designed to be nine feet thick, and it is known as the Intermediate Wall. This replacement was undertaken either at the very end of Hadrian's reign or more probably about twenty years later. It will be discussed when the work of the governors Julius Verus and Calpurnius Agricola is considered (pp. 182 and 192, n. 21).

It is evident that the construction of this great system took a considerable period to complete, and was much more complicated than had at first been planned. The main features of its final form had already begun to appear before the end of Platorius Nepos' governorship, but the coastal system was still being built in or after 128, as was the fort at Great Chesters. The fort of Carrawburgh has yielded part of an inscription of Julius Severus, governor about 130–3, which, of course, might be the date of Great Chesters too. At Carvoran the fort was being constructed even later, for the same commandant whose name appears on building records in the fort wall dedicated an altar for the health of L. Aelius Caesar, Hadrian's adopted heir, who assumed this title in 136. Carvoran is thus likely to be the work of the governor P. Mummius Sisenna. A building inscription of Julius Severus at the fort of Bowes in the Stainmore pass suggests further troop concentrations under this governor.

All this reinforces the conclusion that the building of Hadrian's Wall was much resented. Indeed, it must have interfered with traditional movement from pasturage to pasturage, quite apart from the political division which it was its purpose to enforce. For the intention of the wall itself was certainly political rather than primarily military. It was not designed as a fighting platform to be defended like a city-wall; it has few of the characteristics of such a scheme, nor were the garrisons equipped or trained for this sort of warfare. The wall was there to control movement and to give an elevated platform for observation sufficiently high to protect the sentries from molestation. The size and hostility of the adjacent populations on both sides thus made it necessary to provide a rather more powerful barrier than that constructed in Germany. Forts were then provided on the line of the wall because of increasing hostile pressure, in order that Roman reaction could be more immediate, and experience evidently soon led to further strengthening of the centre and of the west coast. But the planning of the forts and the size of the milecastle gateways, no less than the heavy provision of cavalry, demonstrates clearly that the military aspect of the wall was to act as a fortified base from which to sally out in force, and against which it would be possible to roll up enemy bands after their retreat had been cut off. The wall itself provided cover from behind which surprise sallies could be directed through whichever gates were convenient, if things came to this; but normally, of course, the army would expect to meet the enemy in the open, well beyond the Wall. Yet the absence of outpost forts in this period, except in the west, does seem to indicate that under Hadrian military planning did not envisage so extended a surveillance of the barbaricum as later experience showed to be necessary, and that therefore the Wall had a tactical function.

The forts, as we have seen, were garrisoned by auxiliary regiments of cavalry and infantry. It remains to consider how the milecastles were held. There is no direct evidence how the necessary 1,000–1,500 men were found. It is usually believed that they were a patrolling garrison of lower-grade soldiers belonging to the *numeri* recently introduced into the Roman army. These were territorial formations recruited from warlike frontier tribes, who possessed lower status and privileges than the *auxilia*. Against this view is the fact that no inscriptions attest the presence of numeri in Britain before the third century, and then only in forts. In forts also they are found on the German frontier, where they could be subjected to closer discipline. An alternative view would be that the milecastles were manned by detachments from the auxiliary regiments in garrison. Against this theory, however, there are powerful arguments: first, that the detachment of a couple of centuries from each regiment on the wall would detract from their serviceability, and since many were cavalry, the scheme would be extravagant. A more serious obstacle is the fact that the milecastles were planned and built before the forts were there to provide the suggested detachments. The probability, therefore, is that two or three cohorts of auxiliaries were spread out in vexillations along the wall to undertake this duty. In favour of this view is the probable Hadrianic altar at Milecastle 19, set up by a vexillation of the first cohort of Vardulli, and recording the erection of a shrine near by.[27] This regiment is not yet attested elsewhere in Hadrian's reign, and the nearest forts, from which otherwise the vexillation might be thought to have come for some special duty, such as repairs, are cavalry forts. This evidence is not, of course, conclusive, and the problem must remain insoluble until further evidence appears.

The western sector of the wall was the most dangerous, as we have seen, both on account of the nature of the ground and because of the hostile population beyond it. It is not surprising to find, then, that at Stanwix near Carlisle was stationed the Ala Petriana, the only milliary Ala in Britain. Such regiments are always found in the post of danger, and the prefect of this Ala was the senior officer of the whole wall garrison. Here, then, lay Command headquarters, conveniently near the centre of the line, and it has been shown that a signalling system existed along the road from Carlisle to York, which would enable the prefect at Stanwix to communicate with the legionary legate at York in a matter of minutes (p. 449).

The second topic remaining to be discussed is the disappearance of Legio IX. This legion is last attested on the York inscription of 107/8; later, its place in the York fortress was taken by Legio VI Victrix. The latter reached Britain from Lower Germany [28] in time to build the fort at Halton on the wall under Platorius Nepos, and it was probably brought over by Nepos himself in 122, for he had been governor of Lower Germany until transferred to the British command.[29] In support of an early arrival, it has been pointed out that the two large altars, both dedicated by Legio VI, the one to Ocean and the other to Neptune, and both found in the River Tyne at Newcastle, were probably consecrated at the opening of the new bridge at *Pons Aelius*, and this bridge must have been one of the earliest wall-works to be constructed. The most obvious reason for bringing in Legio VI is to replace Legio IX; and as the Ninth is not recorded, for instance, either as having taken part in Trajan's Parthian wars, or among the numerous inscriptions of the builders of Hadrian's Wall, its disappearance has usually been considered to have been due to defeat or disgrace in the warfare reported in Britain at Hadrian's accession. If it had merely suffered very heavy casualties in battle its numbers would have been made up by drafts from elsewhere or by new recruitment. Its complete disappearance would mean either total annihilation or cashiering. Annihilation is unlikely, since the names of several survivors are known; cashiering would take place after a disgraceful defeat involving, for instance, the loss of the Eagle.

Yet there are grounds for doubting whether Legio IX was lost as early as 117–18. Professor Birley has shown that the recorded careers of some of the survivors are hardly consistent with its disappearance as early as this:[30] they would be even more unduly retarded than might be expected. We have next, no knowledge of the date when Legio VI was first stationed at York: it would be difficult to prove that it was before 130. The absence of building records on Hadrian's Wall could possibly be explained if Legio IX had worked in the turf-wall sector, where the building records were in timber: the only one of these to have partially survived does not include the name of the Legion responsible.[31] The transfer of Legio VI would in this case be explained by the large scale of the work, and the requirement of large numbers of legionary craftsmen.[32]

Then, again, the destruction of a legion in battle would have called for the despatch of immediate reinforcements, We have two inscriptions [33] which record such reinforcements, which included 1,000 legionaries each from Legio VII Gemina (from Spain) and VIII Augusta and XXII Primigenia (both from Germany), under the senior centurion of Legio III Augusta (from Africa); but once again a date of about 130 would suit the careers of the men involved better than a date of about 118.[34] Finally, we have the remark of the orator Fronto writing soon after 161 to the emperor Lucius Verus, when he alludes to heavy losses in the reign of his grandfather Hadrian at the hands of Jews and Britons. Fronto is clearly referring to legionary losses: Legio XXII Deiotariana is believed to have been annihilated in the Jewish war, and the British reference can be taken as referring to the loss of the Ninth, which the order of words suggests is contemporary or later – or at least not fifteen years earlier.

The disappearance of Legio IX thus presents a difficult problem. The scattered threads of evidence all suggest serious fighting in Britain about 130, and this would suit the appointment of Julius Severus to the British command about that year, since he was one of the foremost generals of the day.[35] Sisenna, on the other hand, was undistinguished, and unlikely to be sent to a province still seriously disturbed.[36] But there remains also the probability that the legion was withdrawn from Britain at some date between 108 and 126 and that it perished unrecorded later on, either in Judaea in 132–5 or later still. Evidence which might support such a view is the discovery of a tile-stamp and a mortarium-stamp of Legio ix at Nijmegen in Holland. This site had been the fortress of Legio x Gemina until about 104, after which it seems to have been held by a mixed force of auxiliary troops. Legio ix may have replaced this force at Nijmegen about 121, or even as late as 126, and may have remained there for a few years before being sent to the east; and this seems a reasonable solution. It is difficult to see how such stamps could be explained by the mere passage of vexillations of the legion, for instance, in 83; for troops on active service do not settle down to make tiles and pottery, and in any case the troops concerned were then brigaded with soldiers from other legions. These finds certainly suggest that the Ninth may have been stationed at Nijmegen for a short time at some period after 108, the latest date known for its presence at York, and perhaps from about 126. Further evidence is needed before more can be said.

1. For Arviragus, iv, 127; for Brigantes, xiv, 196.
2. The idea, sometimes advanced, that the forts north of the Forth were built not by Agricola but by his successor has no basis in common sense, and ignores strategic necessities.
3. As Professor Birley has suggested. On the other hand, if he governed Germany first, as the inscription (*ILS*, 8824a) implies, also under Hadrian, his tenure of Britain must have come later on, perhaps in the years 128–31 (see p. 148).
4. *Roman Britain and the Roman Army* (1953), 21. A vexillation of British auxiliaries – including part of the Ala Tampiana – is known to have been sent to Pannonia at this time (*ILS*, 2515).
5. Inchtuthil, Sir Ian Richmond told me, has produced five coins in demolition contexts; four of these are of 86 and one perhaps of 87, and all were in mint condition when dropped. Moreover, construction was still unfinished when the order came to evacuate, and this must reduce our estimate of the life of these coins before loss.
6. B. R. Hartley, *Britannia*, iii (1972), 14.
7. See map prepared by Miss A. S. Robertson in Richmond, *Roman and Native in North Britain* (1958), p. 72, and her map of first-century coins in *PSAS*, xciv (1960–61), 182.
8. Not all excavators record whether nails found in the burnt

debris are bent by extraction with the claw-hammer; but this is an important criterion of intentional demolition.

9. The appearance of British numerii in Upper Germany about this time suggests that the tribes were weakened by conscription (see p. 175 and note 7).

10. *Roman Britain and the Roman Army* (1953), 22–4.

11. The auxiliary vexillation sent to Pannonia from Britain by Domitian (p. 162, note 4) can be shown to have returned here sometime between 101–2 and 122 (J. E. Bogaers, 'Die Besatzungstruppen des Legionslagers von Nijmegen im 2 Jahrhundert n. Chr.', Studien zu den Militärgrenzen Roms (1967), pp. 54 ff.: see also *Numaga*, xii (1965), pp. 10 ff.

12. For one of these see *Papers of the Brit. School at Rome*, xviii (1950), 87; for the other *L'Année Epigraphique*, 1957, 133.

13. Caerleon, *RIB*, 330; Chester, *ibid.* 464; York, *ibid.* 665

14. For Lincoln *CIL*, xiii, 6679, and discussion in *Arch. Journ.*, ciii, 29 and 64; for Gloucester CIL, vi, 3346=*ILS*, 2365, and discussion in *ibid.*, 70.

15. S.H.A., *Vita Hadriani*, 11. One of the results of his reforming zeal, no doubt, is to be seen in the Wroxeter forum inscription (p. 277).

16. This was P. Mummius Sisenna Rutilianus, whose credulous superstition was ridiculed by Lucian in *Alexander the False Prophet*.

17. *Fossatum* would be a better description, as Professor I. A. Richmond remarked, *History*, xliv (No. 150) (February 1959), 6.

18. Even in the turf wall the turrets are of stone.

19. Some small part was taken, too, by detachments from the fleet. Well over a million cubic yards of stone had to be quarried for the wall.

20. A small bridge-head fort of about 2.5 acres probably already existed at Newcastle (*Pons Aelius*) and made the twelfth.

21. There is, in fact, insufficient evidence for certainty about the nature of the Hadrianic garrisons, and the suggested scheme has been contested (*AA*[4] xlvii (1969), pp. 15 ff.). In the absence of inscriptions naming garrisons of this period we need more details of barrack accommodation if types of garrison are to be identified.

22. The whole barrier is one *actus* wide (pl. 3).

23. A re-examination of the dating evidence at the native settlement at Milking Gap, which lies between the Wall and the Vallum, has led Mr J. P. Gillam to suggest that the Brigantian owner was ' expelled from the military zone when the Vallum was built. *Roman and Native in North Britain* (ed. I. A. Richmond), 62–3. In recent years plough-marks proving earlier cultivation of the soil have been found beneath the forts of Rudchester, Haltonchesters and Carrawburgh.

24 Bewcastle, *RIB*, 995; Netherby, *RIB*, 974; Birrens, Birley, *T. Dumfries and Gal. Ant. Soc.*, xxxviii (1961), 142–3.

25. *RIB*, 801.

26. The *ala Augusta* was the garrison later in the century.

27. *Archaeologia Aeliana* [4], ix, 205; *RIB*, 1421.

28. *ILS*, 1100.

29. But there is nothing to show that it did not arrive as early as 119.

30. *Roman Britain and the Roman Army* (1953), pp. 26–30; and his more recent paper in R. M. (Butler (ed.), *Soldier and Civilian in Roman Yorkshire* (1971), pp. 71–80.

31. Nevertheless, there are varieties of turret-type in the Turf Wall which make it unlikely that only one legion was responsible.

32. It would be necessary to find a fourth legionary fortress: possibly Legio ix moved to Carlisle and Legio vi took its place at York.

33. *ILS*, 2726, 2735.

34. A soldier of the Eighth, Junius Dubitatus, lost his shield in the Tyne: its metal boss is now in the British Museum (*CIL*, vii, 495; B. M. Guide: *Antiquities of Roman Britain* (1951), fig. 35). Another inscription recording the presence of this legion comes from Brougham or Kirkby Thore (*RIB*, 782). Legio xxii was once thought to be recorded at Corbridge (*Ephemeris Epigraphica*, vii, 988), but this reading is not supported by *RIB*, 1130; an inscription from Scotland (*RIB*, 2216) set up by a vexillation of this legion can hardly, in view of its find-spot, be related to the reign of Hadrian, A tile of Legio xxii is recorded from Gloucestershire (Baddeley, *A Cotteswold Shrine*, 5), but it is certainly a modern importation.

35. The civil settlement at Walton-le-Dale, Lancs., which no doubt belongs to a fort not yet found, was destroyed by fire about this time. *Trans. Historic Soc. of Lancs. and Cheshire*, 109 (1957), 1–46.

36. The fact that the Ala Tampiana was transferred to Noricum before 138 is additional evidence that the crisis was over in Britain.

8
The Antonine Wall and the frontier in the second century

On the death of Hadrian in July 138 the succession passed to Antoninus Pius (138–61). The change of emperor initiated a swift change of frontier policy in Britain. The wall of Hadrian was abandoned, and after the reconquest of the Lowlands a new barrier, built of turf, was drawn across the Scottish isthmus. The new governor, responsible for executing the new policy, was Q. Lollius Urbicus. These events are recorded only in a single sentence in Capitolinus' biography of Pius.[1] 'Through his legates he carried on many wars; for he conquered the Britons through Lollius Urbicus the governor, and, after driving back the barbarians, built another wall, of turf.' An inscription at Corbridge shows that Lollius Urbicus was putting in hand construction in preparation for the campaign as early as 139, and coins of Antoninus Pius show that the necessary victory had been gained by late in 142 or early in 143. Thus the decision was immediate.

Lollius Urbicus, a native, it seems, of Roman Africa, had shown sufficient promise as a young man to ensure rapid promotion in the emperor's service. He had enjoyed a distinguished career under Hadrian, serving on his staff in the Jewish rebellion of 132–5; later he had held the consulship, perhaps in 135, and then had governed Lower Germany. He must have been selected for the British command as one of the earliest acts of Antoninus Pius, and remained governor until perhaps 144; his successor, attested on a diploma of 146, was Cn. Papirius Aelianus.[2]

Corbridge had been the site of one of Agricola's forts; the five-acre fort which succeeded it, however, on a new site some little distance off, belonged to the Stanegate rather than to Hadrian's Wall, and the garrison had been moved away when that wall was built. Now the fort was regarrisoned and re-equipped. The earlier military phases of Corbridge's history always reflect events in Scotland rather than those on the nearer frontier. The large inscription of 139 and another of 140 show that important building was in progress during those years; and about this time also we find inscriptions recording rebuilding at the forts of Risingham and High Rochester, the latter mentioning Urbicus by name. Further inscriptions mentioning him come from the Antonine Wall itself at Balmuildy, and the wall has, of course, also produced numerous distance-slabs dedicated to Antoninus Pius and recording the lengths constructed by various legionary units. As this wall is built of turf, its identity with the work referred to by Capitolinus is certain. Though not so far illustrated by such accurately dated inscriptions, Antonine rebuilding can be shown to have taken place during this reign at the Flavian fort-sites of Newstead, Crawford, Castledykes, Glenlochar and Loudoun Hill; and new forts were built in new positions at Lanchester, Bothwell-haugh, Inveresk, Cramond and Carzield. In addition, fortlets were built at or near previously occupied sites at Cappuck, Chew Green, Lyne and Raeburnfoot, and on fresh sites at Birrenswark, Fairholm, Dalmakethar, Milton, Redshaw Burn, Wandel, Barburgh Mill and Durisdeer and perhaps Castle Greg. Thus, the military grip on the Lowlands was reasserted almost as strongly as in Flavian times, but the much greater use now made of fortlets rather than full forts is noteworthy, and will be discussed shortly (pp. 170, 185).

The Antonine Wall itself is thirty-seven miles long, running from the fort at Old Kilpatrick on the Clyde to Bridgeness on the Forth, ending a short distance west of the fort of Carriden. For much of its length, the barrier has excellent command of the ground, with wide prospects to the north. In front was a broad ditch, normally up to forty feet wide and twelve feet deep. The Wall itself, or *Vallum* as some of the inscriptions name it, rested on a foundation of stones usually fourteen feet wide, sometimes pierced by culverts. This kept the base drained, and prevented spreading. The wall itself was built of turf sods and can be calculated to have stood about nine feet high, with a rampart-walk six feet wide on its summit: a wooden breast-work would give the front of the wall an elevation of about four-teen feet. Thus, it uses not quite two-thirds the volume of turf in a given stretch that the Turf Wall of Hadrian uses; and the ditch is proportionately larger than Hadrian's, which makes possible these economies in the scale of rampart provided.[3]

The other elements of the frontier consisted of forts, fortlets, signal platforms and the Military Way. There were also outpost forts at each end. Along the line of the wall fourteen forts are known, and the spacing suggests that originally there were eighteen (or nineteen if one existed at Bridgeness). Except for Bar Hill, all these forts are attached to the rear face of the Wall. Notable peculiarities are their variation in size and their close spacing. They lie about 2 miles apart (instead of 5–7 miles as on Hadrian's Wall). The fort at Mumrills is 7·1 acres in size, amply sufficient for a cohort 1,000 strong, part-mounted; Old Kilpatrick (4·7 acres), Balmuildy (4·3 acres), Castlecary (3·99 acres), Bar Hill (3·6 acres) and Cadder (3·2 acres) were large enough for cohorts 500 strong, and the first two may have held larger garrisons. But the other forts whose areas are known are much smaller: Bearsden (2·7 acres), Westerwood (2·34 acres), Croy Hill (2·4 acres), Rough Castle (1·55 acres) and Duntocher (0·64 acres) can only have held vexillations from larger units, despite the fact that Rough Castle has produced an inscription of Cohors VI Nerviorum, a unit the whole of which it certainly could not contain. Moreover, Castlecary has produced inscriptions of two milliary cohorts; Mumrills, on the other hand, has yielded inscriptions not of a unit of the size expected but of an ala 500 strong (Ala I Tungrorum) and of a cohort of the same strength (Cohors II Thracum); nor is there much reason to suppose that these were present in garrison together.

In recent years two additional fortlets (0·23 acres) have been discovered by air-photography at Wilderness Plantation and Glasgow Bridge. These are only slightly larger than the milecastles on Hadrian's Wall, and they match a third at Watling Lodge which was destroyed in 1894.[4] It is possible that a regular series of 'interval fortlets' remains to be discovered; but those so far known occupy the middle of extra-long gaps between forts, and therefore quite probably do not form part of a regular series.

Nevertheless, as Mr J. P. Gillam has observed, there are indications that the Antonine Wall-system, like Hadrian's, suffered change during construction. The large forts with the exception of Cadder are structurally earlier than the wall (Bar Hill, being detached, offers no evidence); the reverse is true of all the small ones except

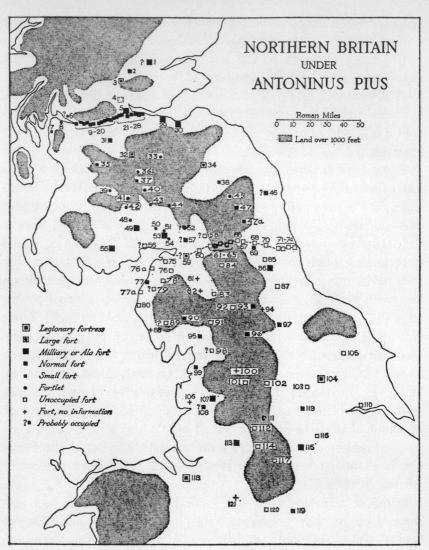

6 The military occupation of the north under Antoninus Pius (pp. 166, 175, 185).

Forts in Northern Britain under Antoninus Pius

NOTE (a) *The forts of Hadrian's Wall were under care and mainten-*
ance in this period.
   (b) *The symbol 'Large Fort' means one over 7 acres.*

1	Bertha	44	Raeburnfoot	84	Whitley Castle
2	Strageath	45	Chew Green	85	Ebchester
3	Ardoch	46	Learchild	86	Lanchester
4	Stirling	47	High Rochester	87	Binchester
5	Camelon	47a	Risingham	88	Ravenglass
6	Dumbarton (?)	48	Barburgh Mill	89	Hardknott Castle
7	Outerwards	49	Carzield	90	Ambleside
8	Lurg Moor	50	Fairholm	91	Low Borrow
9	Whitemoss	51	Birrenswark		Bridge
10	Old Kilpatrick	52	Broomholm	92	Brough under
11	Duntocher	53	Birrens		Stainmore
12	Castle Hill	54	Broadlee	93	Bowes
13	Bearsden	55	Glenlochar	94	Greta Bridge
14	Balmuildy	56	Ward Law	95	Watercrook
15	Cadder	57	Netherby	96	Bainbridge
16	Kirkintilloch	58	Bewcastle	97	Brompton on
17	Auchendavy	59	Stanwix		Swale
18	Bar Hill	60	Castlesteads	98	Overborough
19	Croy Hill	61	Birdoswald	99	Lancaster
20	Westerwood	62	Carvoran	100	Long Preston
21	Castlecary	63	Great Chesters	101	Elslack
22	Seabegs	64	Chesterholm	102	Ilkley
23	Rough Castle	65	Housesteads	103	Newton Kyme
24	Falkirk	66	Carrawburgh	104	York
25	Mumrills	67	Chesters	105	Malton
26	Inveravon	68	Haltonchesters	106	Kirkham
27	Kinneil	69	Corbridge	107	Ribchester
28	Carriden	70	Rudchester	108	Walton-le-Dale
29	Cramond	71	Benwell	109	Castleford
30	Inveresk	72	Newcastle	110	Brough on
31	Bothwellhaugh	73	Wallsend		Humber
32	Castledykes	74	South Shields	111	Slack
33	Lyne	75	Kirkbride	112	Castleshaw
34	Newstead	76	Old Carlisle	113	Manchester
35	Loudoun Hill	76a	Beckfoot	114	Melandra Castle
36	Wandel	77	Maryport	115	Templeborough
37	Crawford	77a	Burrow Walls	116	Doncaster
38	Cappuck	78	Caermote	117	Brough on Noe
39	Kirkconnel	79	Papcastle		(Derbyshire)
40	Redshaw Burn	80	Moresby	118	Chester
41	Durisdeer	81	Old Penrith	119	Little Chester
42	Carronbridge	82	Brougham	120	Rocester
43	Milton	83	Kirkby Thore	121	Chesterton

Duntocher. Thus the original scheme may have been for a system resembling Hadrian's Wall in spacing of garrisons, here *c.* eight miles apart; but a closer grouping of garrisons in additional small forts may have been decided upon before many interval (milecastle-type) fortlets had been supplied.

It can be seen that the same shortage of men which is suggested by the numerous fortlets in southern Scotland may have compelled economies and simplification in the garrison of the Wall itself. The posts were filled by dividing units where necessary, but the forts were placed closer together for better supervision of the frontier and so that they could be easily reinforced. It is very unlikely that the patrolling and fighting garrisons were organised separately, as they may have been on the southern wall.

No turrets have so far come to light, but if timber signalling towers had been provided it would be almost impossible now to locate them. There are, however, a number of beacon-emplacements attached to the back of the Wall. These are not regularly disposed the length of the Wall for lateral signalling: two are known each side of Rough Castle, and two on the west slope of Croy Hill. This distribution suggests that their purpose was connected with long-distance signals linking the outposts on the north-east with the rearward fighting units.

Close behind the wall ran the Military Way, the road connecting the forts; it passed through most of these as their *via principalis*, but by-pass loops were also provided for long-distance traffic. Most of the forts possessed annexes, the purpose of which may originally have been to provide for the safety of baggage trains and stores, but undoubtedly they came to be used by civilian traders and camp-followers, and an inscription from Carriden set up by the *vikani consistentes Veluniate* prove the establishment of at least one regular *vicus*, or community with local self-government.

It has sometimes been suggested that though the Antonine Wall was less than half as long as the Wall of Hadrian, this advantage was counter-balanced by gross tactical weakness on the flanks, which rest on estuaries easily crossed by boat. This view is a misconception. A road left the western terminal at Old Kilpatrick to run beyond the wall along the north bank of the Clyde: it probably led to a harbour at Dumbarton, above which the river was not then navigable. A harbour beyond the protection of the wall implies strength not weakness, quite apart from the possibility of naval patrols. Nor was the left shore of the estuary left unprotected: a large fort recently discovered at Whitemoss (Bishopton) probably held cavalry and controlled the lowest ford, while farther west two fortlets at Lurg Moor (0·42 acres) and Outerwards (0·12 acres) kept watch over the estuary. These are remnants of a once more complete system of surveillance of this western flank.

It was the eastern end of the wall, however, which faced the larger concentration of population and the route from the north; and here the Romans boldly grasped the problem and its solution. Forts indeed guarded the southern shore of the Forth at Carriden, Cramond and Inveresk; but in addition Agricola's road north of the wall was seized and reoccupied by outpost garrisons in the forts at Camelon, Ardoch (pl. 5b), Strageath and Bertha. This garrisoning of Strath Allan and Strath Earn was not as full and intensive as that undertaken by Agricola, and it suggests a protectorate rather than an occupation. Certainly Roman objects were widely circulating on non-military sites in this area in the second century, and almost as far north as Aberdeen. Whatever the precise political arrangements, it is evident that no hostile movement could develop in this quarter unperceived.

Like Hadrian's Wall, the Antonine Vallum was constructed by legionaries; this is made quite certain by the inscriptions on the distance-slabs. What is uncertain is whether the ditch was dug by the legionaries or by native forced labour; no doubt, however, legionary labour was mainly reserved for the more skilled tasks. The forts also appear to have been built by legionaries, but probably not by the parties building the wall. In some cases the forts were clearly planned, and in many cases actually built, before the adjacent parts of the Antonine Wall; and this is especially obvious at the western end. Here the forts of Castlecary and Balmuildy have stone ramparts which pre-date the wall, and at Old Kilpatrick the fort ramparts, this time of turf, were obviously originally free-standing, since their northern corners are rounded. It can thus be deduced that the Antonine Wall was begun from its east end, but that forts at the western end were installed almost immediately, without waiting for the Wall's arrival. This conclusion was further confirmed by excavation at Duntocher in 1948–51, where it was discovered that first a fortlet and then a fort had been constructed on the site before the arrival of the Vallum. Indeed, the fortlet at Duntocher very probably belongs to a preliminary stage in the seizure of the isthmus, before the details of the wall had been planned at all, for it matches similar fortlets found below the forts at Bar Hill and Croy Hill. These were thought by Macdonald to be Agricolan, but the total absence of Flavian pottery from these sites throws doubt on his conclusion (p. 125f.). What may be another comparable fortlet has been observed from the air at Mumrills.

Distance-slabs recorded work by all three legions. All the stones of Legio VI and all but one of Legio XX were set up by legionary vexillations rather than by the legion itself, while the stones of Legio II do not record vexillations. This has led to the suggestion that the whole of Legio II was working on the Wall but that the other two legions supplied detachments only, perhaps as few as 1,000 men from each. However, if that were so one would expect the distances built by Legio II to be at least twice and probably three or four times longer than those constructed by the others. But this is not what we find; the figures in most instances agree with each other very closely. There is other evidence to suggest that in fact each legion was divided into two working parties; we may suppose that the greater part of all three legions was present, the difference in inscription-styles being left to the officers concerned. Duplicate stones were set up at each end of the lengths built by each party, but no sub-units such as cohorts and centuries left records as they did on Hadrian's Wall.

There is one peculiarity of the stones: those found between Bridgeness and Castlehill, that is to say over more than eight-ninths of the total distance starting from the east end, record the distances in *passus*, Roman paces of five feet. These distances are on average 5,357·5 yards or 3·2 Roman miles: a more realistic figure is in fact rather longer (3·66 Roman miles), since one very short length reduces the average. On the other hand, west of Castlehill the distances are recorded in feet, and average 1,233·5 yards, or only 0·74 Roman miles. It is clear, too, that great care was taken to divide up this stretch of wall equally between the various legions. When the distances allotted to the two working parties of each legion are added together the result shows that to Legio II was assigned 7,411 feet, to Legio VI 7,381 feet and to Legio XX 7,411 feet! The reason for this change of building-length is not recorded. It is most likely to be due to an assessment of the topography, for here and here alone the Wall approaches close to unfavourable ground. The Kilpatrick Hills might have been considered as presenting a danger which could be met by closing up the working parties, so that in effect all three legions were concentrated in this four-mile sector during its construction. Concern with the security of this end of the wall had already been shown by the Roman command when they caused the forts here to be built in advance of the arrival of the Wall.[4a] It cut right through the territory of the Damnonii, and must have aroused opposition.

In recent years aerial photography by Dr J. K. St Joseph has added to knowledge of the frontier by the discovery of fourteen marching camps near the line of the Wall. Some nine at least of these, by their uniform size of just over five acres, and to some extent by their uniform spacing, suggest the housing of the construction parties.

The historian may feel some surprise in relation to the Antonine Wall, first, that it was built when it was, and secondly, that it was built at all. He requires an explanation for the sudden replacement of the Hadrianic system so recently, so expensively and so laboriously brought to perfection. He needs to know whether the prevailing use of turf and timber on this frontier carries the implication that it was regarded as a temporary expedient. The co-existence of two alternative, or parallel, frontier systems introduces a certain fluctuation into the affairs of the second century which he cannot yet chart in accurate detail.

Why was the frontier moved? There is little direct evidence. A passage in the contemporary Greek writer Pausanias has been thought to refer to these events.[5] 'Antoninus Pius never willingly made war; but when the Moors took up arms against Rome he drove them out of all their territory. . . . Also he deprived the Brigantes in Britain of most of their land because they too had begun aggression on the district of Genunia whose inhabitants are subject to Rome.' The statement is not of much value as it stands, since it is clear that Pausanias imagined the Brigantes to be outside the province, whereas they had been within it for more than sixty years; nor do we know where Genunia lay. Two explanations have been offered. The first has been argued by Birley. During this reign only in 139–40 could even a fraction of the Brigantes be thought of as outside the province, and their attack on Genunia must have taken place then, since otherwise the advance into Scotland would have been aggression, which Pausanias denies that Pius ever committed. This explanation lays emphasis on Antoninus Pius' pacific reputation. An alternative view sees in this passage a reference to the Brigantian rebellion of 154, and emphasises the deprivation of Brigantian territory. For only in the aftermath of this rebellion does a context for this appear with the re-occupation of the Pennine Forts and re-imposition of military government, and even perhaps the foundation of the colony of York (p. 213). It must be owned that neither explanation quite covers all the facts. The Gordian knot may be cut by allowing that the term Brigantes is not used by Pausanias with the same precision as it has hitherto been used in this book. If by Brigantes he can be permitted to mean 'the Brigantes and their friends in the north', or even 'the inhabitants of northern Britain', the passage acquires sense and the context becomes clear, the governorship of Urbicus.[6]

Whether or not that is what Pausanias meant, disturbances in southern Scotland were clearly the cause of the Roman advance. There the Votadini can be thought of as a philo-Roman tribe (p. 126). Their neighbours the Selgovae were not. It is possible, indeed, that fear of the Selgovae was the motive which led the former into treaty relationship with Rome. (Such a relationship is an assumption, but not one without support.) All was in their favour so long as Rome held southern Scotland, but the new frontier of Hadrian excluded them. No doubt paper arrangements were made for their security in any treaties which followed Hadrian's victory of 118; but the fact remained that the heart of their lands lay beyond effective aid from the garrisons of Hadrian's Wall. An attack on some sub-division of the Votadini by the Selgovae is the most reasonable explanation of Pausanias' statement. Hadrian's Wall, in other words, impregnable defensive barrier though it was, had been put in the wrong place for intervention farther north: it lay out of effective contact with the Lowland tribes. Rome still needed to influence events in this area, and if her influence was not accepted peaceably there was no alternative to reconquest.

The reconquest of Lowland Scotland, then, was directed primarily at the control of the Selgovae and perhaps also of the Novantae. But as Capitolinus stated in the sentence already quoted (p. 165), the Turf Wall of Pius was not built until the barbarians had been driven back. This phrase recalls that of Tacitus describing Agricola's Forth–Clyde frontier, and must mean that irreconcilable warriors from these tribes retired beyond the isthmus; this movement was to have serious repercussions in later years. Nevertheless, the military strength of the tribesmen who remained could be greatly abated by

Roman conscription. Legally they were *dediticii*: they had surrendered unconditionally. Many of their young men may have been transported to the upper German frontier and then drafted into *numeri* in the Roman army. *Numeri Brittonum*, of which at least ten are known, are first attested there by inscriptions in 145, and this fitted well with the theory that the numeri in question had been raised after the re-conquest of southern Scotland. But recently Dr Baatz [7] has shown that British numeri were in Upper Germany from considerably earlier: the first of them may have been enlisted shortly before the withdrawal from Scotland under Trajan if not earlier still. But though these discoveries upset the neatness of the old equation, there is no need to doubt that drafts were required from time to time by existing numeri, or indeed that conscripted Lowlanders would have been in demand almost everywhere on the Roman frontiers to reinforce these or other units. Those that remained soon began to trade with Roman merchants: it is not a case of wholesale depopulation.

At first, then, all went favourably for Rome. Once again Newstead occupied a key position in the scheme: the new fort, 14·7 acres in extent and now provided with a stone wall, contained as garrison two cohorts of Legio xx and a regiment of auxiliary cavalry, the Ala Augusta Vocontiorum. The auxiliary regiments which had been stationed on Hadrian's Wall were redeployed, some of them being moved up to the new wall, and Hadrian's frontier was thrown open, though garrisons still guarded the Cumberland coast. The Hadrianic Vallum was formally breached by throwing in earth from the two mounds every forty-five yards to form causeways across the ditch, and their gates were removed from the milecastles, thus allowing free access across the old military zone. The Wall-forts themselves, however, seem in most cases to have been maintained perhaps on a care-and-maintenance basis; at Benwell, Halton, Chesters, Housesteads and Great Chesters we have inscriptions which suggest the presence of legionaries at this date, no doubt skeleton detachments posted for that purpose. That at Housesteads was certainly in garrison.[8]

To maintain this greatly extended occupation more forts were evacuated in the Pennines [9] (fig. 6), and it is possible that some of the Welsh garrisons were reduced by detachments; but recent work by Miss G. Simpson has shown that the older theories of massive disengagement in Wales to find troops for northern Britain are untenable. Despite troop-shortages, however, soldiers could be spared for the Moorish campaign of 145–7; an inscription recently published from Rome records Sextus Flavius Quietus, chief centurion of Legio xx *misso cum exercitu* on this expedition. Likewise half the milliary Second Cohort of Tungrians was present in Raetia in 147, but was back in Britain ten years later.

To the second century, and probably mainly to this period in it, belongs the beginning of a change in the habitation-pattern in the eastern lowlands. Here the hill-forts are found to have gone out of use; settlements and individual farmsteads now appear on open sites, built circular-fashion of thick rubble walls faced each side with stone. Sometimes these are found overlying the abandoned ramparts of hill-forts; often there are signs of an expanding population. Their distribution is principally Votadinian, but seems to extend into the eastern boundaries of the Selgovae. This is clearly due to the impact of Rome, and the suppression of the old warlike way of life. That the Votadini were especially philo-Roman is indicated by the number of Roman objects of second-century date found at Traprain Law, their capital.

The first Antonine occupation of Scotland ended abruptly with destruction. The date of this can be fixed by indications of serious trouble in Britain between 154 and 158 given by coins and inscriptions and confirmed by troop movements. First, coins of Pius minted in 154–5 show a reverse-type of Britannia subdued. These suggest that war or rebellion had been put down by 155. That the trouble was suppressed only at the cost of heavy legionary casualties is indicated by an inscription dredged from the Tyne at Newcastle which records the arrival of reinforcements for all three British legions from the armies of both German provinces under the governor Cn. Julius Verus.

Verus was another example of the careful selection and quick promotion of *viri militares* in the imperial service. He had been legate of Legio xxx Ulpia in Lower Germany, and after holding the consulship – perhaps in 151 [10] – became Governor of Lower Germany. He may well have brought the legionary vexillations with him, and the date should not be later than 155. The troops had evidently just landed at Newcastle and had not yet been distributed. Verus was still in Britain in 158, as a building-inscription at Birrens tells us, and the scene of his activities is suggested by these two inscriptions and another at Brough in Derbyshire. This distribution – with which he associated the sentence of Pausanias already quoted – led Haverfield in 1904 to suggest that the trouble was not an invasion from the north, but a rebellion of the Brigantes in the Pennines; and this suggestion is amply borne out by the re-occupation of forts in the Pennines seen on fig. 7 (p. 183) and dated to this and the following governorships. It may even be supported by the fact that the fort at Lancaster was burnt at this time. Why else was this heavy re-occupation necessary?

It remains to consider, however, in what way a Brigantian revolt could involve the loss of the Antonine Wall. If there had been an invasion from the north which resulted in the destruction of the wall with all its forts and the loss of almost all the forts in the Scottish lowlands as well, it is strange that we hear no echo of the disaster in our written sources, scanty though these are. Even if Pausanias is referring to events at this date rather than 139–40, he mentions only the Brigantes. The explanation must be that a serious rebellion in the Pennines would necessitate the concentration of all available Roman forces on that region: and a large part of that concentration would have to be drawn from Scotland. The forts of the Antonine Wall and of the region to the south of it were, then, evacuated by the Romans and burnt to prevent them being of use to the enemy. It is very likely, indeed, that action by the Brigantian rebels was concerted with some of the tribesmen of southern Scotland. There was nothing to prevent such consultation now that Hadrian's barrier was open, and that something of the sort happened at Newstead is plain from the recovery of human bones and equipment from pits of this period there, though not in such quantity as in the previous rising. The siege-camps at Birrenswark, too, if used in real war and not just for training, would suggest the same thing, for they probably date to this period (pl. 5a). The fort of Birrens is also known to have been destroyed; its debris yielded a newly minted coin of 154.

The Roman reaction, then, was to retire from Scotland in order to crush the rebellion, for there was no strategic reserve of troops which could be called upon for such a purpose. The processes of rebellion and pacification, however, were prolonged into the next reign, for as late as 163 there was a threat of war in Britain, and Calpurnius Agricola was despatched to suppress it.[11] Inscriptions show that Calpurnius Agricola, too, was constructing forts in northern England. Moreover, in 1911 excavations at Corbridge unearthed a bronze jug containing a hoard of 160 Roman gold coins closing with an issue minted in 159–60. The hoard must have been buried in some emergency at Corbridge in 160–2 and not recovered.

It is clear that the crisis was acute and prolonged, and this view is reinforced by what is known of the calibre of the governors sent to deal with it. Verus, himself a man of outstanding ability, was succeeded in 158 or early 159 by a man whose name is incompletely recorded (. . . anus Lon(gus) or Lon(ginus)),[12] but early in 161 his place was taken by M. Statius Priscus Licinius Italicus. This man had had a remarkable career, starting with service as an equestrian officer and a decoration from Hadrian in the Jewish rebellion. After serving as a procurator in southern Gaul he was promoted to the Senate, commanded two legions in succession and governed Dacia in 157–8; he held the consulship (*consul ordinarius*) in 159, after which he governed Upper Moesia in 160–1, and came from there to Britain.[13] His rapid promotions point to ability, and it is evident that his appointment to Britain was due to the need of a first-class general. After him came Sextus Calpurnius Agricola, about whose previous career little is known; he had been consul in 158 or 159 and was appointed to Britain perhaps late in 162, or early 163; he was certainly here in 163–4 as is proved by a Corbridge inscription,[14] and perhaps remained till 166.

Excavation has shown that on Hadrian's Wall at about this period the milecastle gateways were rehung with gates, and in most cases the Vallum-crossings, inserted about 140, were removed. This implies that this Wall was being re-commissioned, and the date is probably given us by an inscription,[15] now lost, which records repairs to the face of the wall itself by Legio vi in 158. This reconstitution of Hadrian's barrier is known as that wall's period Ib, and it is further illustrated by changes of auxiliary garrison. Not all the garrisons of all the forts are yet known, of course. But Benwell, held by a cavalry regiment, as the stables show, in the reign of Hadrian, and apparently occupied by legionaries under Pius, was now – or later in the Antonine period – converted to house the milliary Cohors i Vangionum Equitata. Chesters had the same history, the Antonine garrison being the quingenary Cohors i Dalmatarum Equitata. At Carrawburgh Cohors i Aquitanorum Equitata was succeeded by

Cohors 1 Cugernorum; similar changes can be traced at other forts. At Carvoran the First Cohort of Hamian Archers, a Syrian regiment, returned to the fort which they had held under Hadrian, having occupied Bar Hill from 144 to 155. It is noteworthy that in this reorganisation no attempt was made to follow the Hadrianic pattern of garrisons; few of the cavalry forts regained their cavalry, and at least one of them, Chesters, though capable of housing a milliary cohort of infantry, was given a garrison little more than half this size. This suggests that the tactical problem was different.

It has usually been considered unlikely that the two walls were held simultaneously, and more probable that, if Period Ib on Hadrian's Wall started under Julius Verus or Calpurnius Agricola, the second occupation of the forts in Scotland and on the Antonine Wall was a later phenomenon. That Birrens had been rebuilt in 158 had long been known, but Birrens was an outpost of Hadrian's Wall, and its reconstruction might be no more than the beginning of Period Ib there. In 1947 Professor Richmond was able to show that the second Antonine occupation of Newstead must have followed fairly closely on the destruction of the first Antonine fort there, and more recently the same has been found at Crawford. Since Newstead and Crawford are too far north to have any connection with the phases of Hadrian's Wall, it began to seem as if southern Scotland as a whole was soon reoccupied. This view was reinforced by the knowledge that Corbridge was being reorganised by Calpurnius Agricola as a supply base. But the difficulty preventing a firm conclusion lay in the lack of dating evidence on the Antonine Wall itself. The excavations on this wall had in the main taken place in the first quarter of this century, and their records lack the scientific precision required to solve a chronological point of this sort. Sir George Macdonald had been of the opinion that the forts of the Antonine Wall had been twice destroyed and twice rebuilt, but the dates of the three occupations thus suggested could only be established on general grounds. Dr K. A. Steer has made an important advance with the convincing demonstration [16] that the second occupation of the Antonine Wall began before the death of Pius in 161. The original masonry of its fort buildings is usually so well constructed as to imply legionary work, and this inference is supported at some forts, including Castlecary, by the discovery of actual legionary building inscriptions. But the forts of Castlecary and Rough Castle have also produced auxiliary building records: these must consequently go with the rebuilding of the second period, which is notably inferior in quality. But these two auxiliary building records are dedicated to Antoninus Pius, and must have been erected before his death. At Bar Hill the case is even plainer. Here we have records of two regiments in garrison, Cohors I Hamiorum Sagittariorum, the Syrian Archers, and Cohors I Baetasiorum. It was the latter who erected the building inscription in honour of Pius, and this stone, together with a large altar also inscribed by them, was found among much broken stonework and debris filling the well of the headquarters building. Clearly this debris was the product of the final destruction of the fort at the end of the second occupation (for otherwise the well would have been cleared out); and the inscription shows that this occupation began before 161. To clinch the demonstration, some iron arrowheads, presumably left behind by the Archers, were found in the mud at the bottom of the well beneath all the later debris.

In the first edition of this book it was suggested that both walls were held in parallel from c. 160 to 180 and thereafter Hadrian's Wall alone until 196. The military burden imposed by this task was admittedly very great and it was shown that unless economies had been arranged by manning forts at less than full strength, or alternatively unless there were differences in the dates of occupation of individual forts within the period — differences which at the time were impossible to demonstrate — there would have been a shortfall of c. 9,000 men in the forces available. In 1972, however, Mr B. R. Hartley published the dating-evidence provided by samian ware for the military occupations in northern England and Scotland [17] and was able to prove conclusively that the second Antonine hold on Scotland was exceedingly brief, and that forts there were not held concurrently with those in northern England for more than a very short time. Solutions to some of the problems of the later second century are now in sight.

During the rebellion in southern Scotland and the Pennines the Roman army, as we have seen, pulled back temporarily, and Hadrian's frontier was recommissioned to bar communication with the north, though its forts may have continued to be held by small legionary vexillations. The rebuilding of Birrens in 158, as we have seen (p. 179), has uncertain relevance for the reoccupation of southern Scotland as a whole; but by the following year at the latest the Roman army was back on the Antonine Wall and in the outposts beyond it. Behind it southern Scotland, too, was reoccupied, though with some changes in garrison. The fortlet at Lyne was replaced by a full-sized fort; Carzield and Loudoun Hill were not reoccupied and several fortlets, e.g. Barburgh Mill, were also left empty. The Antonine Wall itself seems to have been held with fewer troops. Newstead was still the key position and was now held by a milliary ala instead of by the mixed force of legionaries and cavalry previously in garrison.[18]

The second Antonine occupation of Scotland was of short duration, for it did not bring peace; presumably there were not enough troops to make the system work by policing in force the whole of the huge and geographically difficult area between the Peak and the Forth. The excavators of both Lyne and Crawford have noted evidence suggesting that the occupation of these forts was brief, and at Glenlochar the small quantity of late Antonine pottery found reinforces this conclusion. Mr Hartley, too, has shown that, save at two forts soon to be mentioned, there is an entire absence of samian in the Scottish forts datable after c. 165.

In 163 Calpurnius Agricola was sent as governor in face of the threat of war; he rebuilt a number of forts in northern England,[19] and it was probably therefore he who decided to withdraw Roman troops once more from Scotland in order to find the men for a firmer grip on more vital territory nearer home:[20] the outbreak of trouble on the continent prevented the possibility of reinforcement from the Rhine armies. Alternatively, perhaps, it was the next governor, in 169 (see p. 186). Whatever the precise date, this time Newstead was retained; by means of its powerful cavalry garrison Roman supervision could be widely exercised. Cappuck, too, seems to have been held, which suggests that, in addition to the nearer system of outpost forts in the west, a much more extended series was maintained on the east, serviced by Dere Street. The failure of the original Hadrianic frontier had stemmed from its distance from the sources of hostility: shortage of forces compelled Calpurnius Agricola to re-establish that frontier, but his arrangements were a bold attempt to remedy its defects and at the same time to afford support to the friendly Votadini. These external arrangements explain the different order of battle now found on the Wall (p. 178f.). The re-occupation of Hadrian's Wall, however, involved replacing the Turf Wall of its western sector with a new stone wall: no doubt this turf wall had

181

deteriorated since 140, and its replacement was thought to be ultimately more economical than extensive repairs. The new wall was built to an intermediate gauge of nine Roman feet; it incorporated the stone turrets of the turf wall but was provided with new stone mile-castles.[21]

The process of evacuating the Brigantian hill-lands had been begun under Hadrian (fig. 5, p. 150), who retained a cordon of forts on their south and west flanks. In his reign about 9,500 men had held the forts on the Wall, with another 1,500–2,000 men in the mile-castles; a further forty or so mile-fortlets lined the Cumberland coast (say 1,000 men). West of a line from Ribchester to Brough-under-Stainmore and Whitley Castle eighteen forts were certainly or probably still held, accounting for 9,000 men; east of this line there were only 1,500 men in Durham and north Yorkshire at three forts, while the south edge of the Pennines was held by four or five forts (2,500 men) with an outlying fort at Brough on Humber. The distribution shows that it was the Lancashire–Cumbrian region about which the Romans were most apprehensive, whether from external or internal hostility. Northern England as a whole was held by a total of 26,000 men.

This number is well within the limits indicated by other evidence. First, there is the information given by diplomas. These certificates, engraved on bronze, granting Roman citizenship and legal marriage rights, were issued to auxiliary soldiers on discharge after serving twenty-five or more years with the colours; each individual received his diploma, but as the discharges took place in batches, each document contains a list of all the regiments in the provincial army due to discharge men on the same occasion. In this way they provide valuable information concerning the identity of the auxiliary regiments in each province, and if sufficient diplomas exist, it is possible to construct an army list which must be almost complete. For the army of Britain there are diplomas or parts of them for the years 98, 103, 105, 122, 124, 135, 146 and 159; and in consequence the names are known of 14 alae (1 of them milliary), 6 milliary cohorts and 38 cohorts 500 strong, which served in Britain during this period. In addition, a further milliary cohort and 6 quingenary cohorts can be supplied from epigraphic evidence, making a total of 65 regiments, or 36,500 men.[22]

It is perhaps unlikely that any very large number of auxiliary

NORTHERN BRITAIN
IN THE
SECOND ANTONINE
PERIOD. 158 - c. 165

Roman Miles
0 10 20 30 40 50

▨ Land over 1000 feet

◨ Legionary fortress
■ Milliary or Ala fort
▪ Normal fort
• Fortlet
□ Unoccupied fort
+ Fort, no information

7 The military occupation of the north under Marcus Aurelius.
Note:? beside a fort means that it was only probably occupied
(or unoccupied) as indicated.

1 Bertha	8 Duntocher	15 Bar Hill
2 Strageath	9 Castle Hill	16 Croy Hill
3 Ardoch	10 Bearsden	17 Westerwood
4 Camelon	11 Balmuildy	18 Castlecary
5 Stirling	12 Cadder	19 Seabegs
6 Whitemoss	13 Kirkintilloch	20 Rough Castle
7 Old Kilpatrick	14 Auchendavy	21 Falkirk

183

22 Mumrills	57 Carvoran	90 Greta Bridge
23 Inveravon	58 Great Chesters	91 Ravenglass
24 Kinneil	59 Chesterholm	92 Hardknott Castle
25 Carriden	60 Housesteads	93 Ambleside
26 Cramond	61 Carrawburgh	94 Low Borrow
27 Inveresk	62 Chesters	Bridge
28 Bothwellhaugh	63 Haltonchesters	95 Watercrook
29 Lurg Moor	64 Rudchester	96 Bainbridge
30 Outerwards	65 Benwell	97 Catterick
31 Loudoun Hill	66 Newcastle	98 Overborough
32 Castledykes	67 Wallsend	99 Malton
33 Lyne	68 South Shields	100 Lancaster
34 Newstead	69 Corbridge	101 Long Preston
35 Crawford	70 Kirkbride	102 Elslack
36 Durisdeer	71 Beckfoot	103 Ilkley
37 Milton	72 Maryport	104 Newton Kyme
38 Raeburnfoot	73 Burrow Walls	105 York
39 Cappuck	74 Moresby	106 Kirkham
40 Chew Green	75 Old Carlisle	107 Walton-le-Dale
41 Learchild	76 Caermote	108 Ribchester
42 High Rochester	77 Papcastle	109 Castleford
43 Risingham	78 Wreay	110 Slack
44 Carzield	79 Old Penrith	111 Castleshaw
45 Broomholm	80 Brougham	112 Manchester
46 Birrens	81 Kirkby Thore	113 Melandra Castle
47 Glenlochar	82 Whitley Castle	114 Templeborough
48 Ward Law	83 Ebchester	115 Doncaster
49 Netherby	84 Lanchester	116 Brough on Noe
50 Bewcastle	85 Chester-le-Street	(Derbyshire)
51 Bowness	86 Binchester	117 Buxton
52 Drumburgh	87 Brough under	118 Chester
53 Burgh by Sands	Stainmore	119 Chesterton
54 Stanwix	88 Maiden Castle	120 Rocester
55 Castlesteads	89 Bowes	121 Little Chester
56 Birdoswald		

regiments remains unknown in this period, but a further check can be obtained from the number of forts established on a permanent basis by Agricola or retained in use during his governorship. As we have seen (p. 135f.), these amounted to at least 20 in Wales, at least 57 and perhaps 73 in Northern Britain, together with 8 small forts holding perhaps half a cohort each. A conservative estimate suggests that Agricola disposed of about 90 auxiliary regiments, c. 50,000 men. In the time of Hadrian the army of Britain had been reduced by a legion, and the auxiliary troops may well have been reduced too, though perhaps not in proportion. We may guess that some 75 regiments remained, or about 42,500 men.

With 26,000 men in the north in Hadrian's reign, there thus remain some 16,500 to be accounted for. The northern garrison might be larger, seeing that 7 forts are marked as giving no information (fig. 5, p. 150), and Wales and its borders at this date had a garrison of at least 9,500 men in at least 14 forts; 8 forts in Wales yield no information, 3 were evacuated [23] and 1 reduced in size.[24]

Under Antoninus Pius the region south of Hadrian's Wall was held now by only 14 forts containing 8,000 men. North of Hadrian's Wall the lowlands were held by 17 forts (9,550 men) and 14 fortlets (700 men); the Antonine Wall had 18 forts (c. 6,500 men), and beyond it the outpost forts may have accounted for 2,500 men. Thus, the total number of auxiliaries in northern Britain was about 27,250 and of these only 33 per cent were facing an external enemy. In Wales it is likely that Gelligaer and Penydarren and probably Tomen y Mur were evacuated, leaving at least 11 forts with 7,500 men. This total of 34,750 men is still well within the limits of forces available and was achieved by skilful dispositions and the use of fortlets when possible.

In the second Antonine period, 158–63, with Scotland occupied, there is evidence of greater strain on manpower. In the Pennines about 26 forts (21,300 men) may have been held, though it is difficult to be sure in this short period; Hadrian's Wall was probably still held by small parties of legionaries, irrelevant to the present context. In lowland Scotland there were 14 forts (9,200 men) and perhaps 5 fortlets (500 men). On the Antonine Wall the garrison was now perhaps 6,250 (Bearsden was unoccupied), and beyond it were 4 outpost forts (2,500 men). Thus in northern Britain as a whole there were 30,750 auxiliaries and this total could be achieved without unduly reducing the garrison of Wales (reckoned as still 7,500 men). But this total in the north is only 2,500 more than the total in the previous period, which had proved insufficient to prevent rebellion. It is not hard to understand the pressures which led Calpurnius Agricola to abandon Scotland.

In the third Antonine period, in the reign of Marcus Aurelius, we find accordingly the garrison of northern England strengthened. In the Pennines 30 (perhaps 33) forts (with 14,300 men) and 16 on Hadrian's Wall (now with 10,000 men) contained the Brigantes with

24,300 men. North of the Wall 6 forts were held (3,750 men). In Wales, too, there were at least 14 forts (9,500 men) in occupation at this time. The total of some 37,550 auxiliaries is still, however, about 5,000 below the potential of troops available as reckoned on p. 185. The figures as a whole testify to the large native populations in lowland Scotland and in Brigantia, which are not easy otherwise to estimate.

Events after the governorship of Calpurnius Agricola are ill-recorded. There are hints of renewed trouble in Britain in 169, but we know nothing of its nature or of the steps taken unless, indeed, this was the moment when Scotland was given up.[25] Possibly, however, it was a revolt in Wales, as might be suggested by the burning of the Wroxeter forum and adjacent parts of the town about this time. At Worcester too the debris of a conflagration has been found. But it is not always certain that fires represent enemy action: Roman forts, as we have seen, were sometimes demolished and the unwanted debris burnt by the retiring garrison; and in towns which were still largely half-timbered chance fires would spread disastrously, fanned by the wind. London had been ravaged by fire in Hadrian's reign, but there is nothing to suggest that it was not an act of God, as later in 1666. A large part of *Verulamium* had been destroyed in a conflagration about 155, and though this date is more suggestive, we cannot show that it was not coincidence. Nevertheless, unrest or rebellion in Wales would seem to be suggested by certain troop-movements. The second forts at Leintwardine and at Walltown in the Marches may belong to this period, and forts were rebuilt also in Wales about this time at Forden, Coelbren and Caernarvon. The empty fort at Gelligaer seems to have been reoccupied for a short period in the second half of the century, perhaps at this time.

In 175 Britain was reinforced by 5,500 Sarmatian cavalry. At first sight this might suggest preparations to deal with rebellion or reconquest, but in fact the circumstances were peculiar. Marcus Aurelius had been fighting on the Danube and had planned to exterminate the troublesome Iazyges, but an outbreak of rebellion in Syria compelled him to make hurried terms; under these the tribe agreed to keep well away from the Roman frontier and to furnish 8,000 cavalry. The larger half of these was sent immediately to Britain, but we cannot tell how far the reason was the military needs of the province and how far the wish to keep the Sarmatians out of harm's way and unable to escape. Nevertheless, the reinforcement must have been very welcome, though we know nothing of how it was used. The horsemen were probably formed into *numeri*, for in the next century a Numerus of Sarmatians was in garrison at Ribchester. Archaeological evidence of Sarmatians has been found also at Chesters on Hadrian's Wall, but otherwise there is no trace. This suggests that the bulk of the force did not remain in Britain long: they may not have returned after the expedition of Albinus in 196.

Q. Antistius Adventus is the next governor of Britain to be recorded: he was probably in the province from about 175 to about 178, and once again a man with a distinguished military record was chosen. He had served in the Parthian War of Verus, held the consulship probably in 166 or 167, and had governed Lower Germany. His successor was probably the (?) Caerellius whose career is recorded on an altar at Mainz.[26] These men maintained the *status quo*; but not long after the death of Marcus in 180 a serious crisis arose. Dio tells us that the greatest war in Commodus' reign occurred in Britain, when the tribes crossed the wall that separated them from the Roman garrison and slew a general (possibly the governor is meant) at the head of his forces. In great alarm Commodus sent Ulpius Marcellus against them, who inflicted terrible damage.[27] Though the exact date of this invasion is not recorded, it can be shown that Ulpius Marcellus was sent to Britain in the summer of 180.[28] By 184 a victory had been won, since in that year commemorative coins were issued and Commodus assumed the title of Britannicus; but the war was continued longer, since similar coins were issued in 185. A hoard of silver coins terminating with an issue of 186–7 found at Briglands in Kinross-shire may imply that operations continued to that date, but it may equally represent the savings of some wealthy native or trader who still had access to recent currency.

Though Dio does not specify which Wall was stormed, it is now impossible to believe that it was the Antonine Wall as stated in the first edition of this book, since the evidence, as we have seen, is against that wall having been in commission after *c.* 163–6. The Wall which was crossed, accordingly, was Hadrian's, and it is possible that the scene of the attack may be localised near Dere Street. Signs of burning and destruction have been noted at Rudchester, Haltonchesters and at Corbridge, which could conceivably be associated with this episode; they would, however, suit a context in 197–8 even better (p. 217, n. 3). On the Antonine Wall Macdonald considered that there was sufficient evidence to suggest a short third period of occupation, a rebuilding after the rebellion; but similar evidence has not appeared in recent excavations, and it is very doubtful whether the indications mean more than that preliminary preparations had been put in hand.[29]

It seems clear that Ulpius Marcellus carried out a series of punitive expeditions [30] and then withdrew once more to Hadrian's Wall. If he had planned to rebuild the Antonine Wall, he abandoned the attempt before work had proceeded far.[31] He probably also withdrew the troops occupying Newstead and other forts beyond the Wall on Dere Street. The evidence at Newstead is ceramic,[32] but we also have the evidence of a Severan inscription at Risingham,[33] which records the rebuilding about 205–8 of the fort gateway and walls 'which had collapsed through age'; it is sometimes thought that this was a euphemism for enemy destruction, but it is simpler to take it literally (p. 384) as evidence of abandonment. Moreover, two inscriptions from Benwell suggest that there was some reorganisation on the Wall itself.[34]

Such a withdrawal after a victorious campaign would have been accompanied by appropriate treaty arrangements with native states, all the more so if Roman garrisons were removed from their territories. It was surely now, as a result of these arrangements, that the confederacy of the Maeatae came into being. In the time of Severus we found Scotland divided between two great confederacies into which the individual tribes had merged themselves. The Maeatae lived 'close to the Wall which divides the island into two parts', and the Caledonii 'beyond them'.[35] It is sometimes argued that the wall referred to was the Antonine Wall; but this does not suit the context in Dio's narrative who, writing of events in 208, must mean Hadrian's Wall, recently reconditioned by Severus. The Selgovae, then – though not the Votadini, who already had their own treaty with Rome – had become part of the Maeatae, but the evidence of place-names shows that this confederacy included land north of the Forth which in Antonine times had been under Roman protection. We know also that in 197 the Caledonians 'had broken their undertakings'.[36] This is suggestive evidence for the work of Marcellus, who will have imposed those undertakings on the Caledonii [37] as well as forming a separate confederacy to counterbalance them in lands more easily supervised by Rome. The price paid for the friendship of this new Maeatic confederacy was withdrawal of direct control by Roman garrisons. Such a policy was fully consistent with the new policy which Commodus had already initiated on the Danube in order to bring Marcus' long wars in that region to a close. There, in return for the surrender of prisoners and deserters and the supply of 13,000 native troops, the renunciation of inter-tribal warfare and the control of assembly, the occupying armies were withdrawn and Roman subsidies were paid. It was a policy which was to be resumed in Britain with great success by Caracalla.

It had been necessary to build the Antonine Wall in order to enforce Rome's will on the refractory tribes of southern Scotland, for the Hadrianic frontier had proved too remote for active intervention. But now, forty years later, direct rule had done its work. Under Commodus a new phase opened in which Roman influence was accepted in the Lowlands in return for local autonomy, and the tribes could accordingly be used as a buffer between Hadrian's Wall and the North. The new policy was rightly conceived once its prerequisites had been achieved, and as re-established by Caracalla was to ensure almost a century of peace. But its smooth initial development was first to be interrupted in the years 196–211 by events and temptations which could hardly have been foreseen. Moreover, the third-century scheme included careful provision for Roman supervision, which the present scheme under Commodus neglected to provide.

Whether the achievement of such a result within a limited time had been the purpose of Antoninus Pius when he built his frontier in turf and timber cannot be asserted, for it by no means follows that turf-work was regarded as less permanent than stone. Roman policy was empirical, and the Antonine Wall was built in the most up-to-date techniques of Roman field-engineering, and was designed to last indefinitely.

L. Ulpius Marcellus was a stern unlikable man, of austere self-righteous character, famous for his ability to do without sleep and luxurious living, and not above play-acting to increase this reputation. Despite his victories, his governorship ended with mutiny among his forces, and he narrowly escaped execution at the hands of Commodus. The causes of unrest in the army are doubtful. Possibly the new policy in Scotland was not properly understood: possibly no donative had been given as a reward of victory; possibly the governor's heavy hand proved intolerable. At any rate the legions attempted to set up an emperor of their own, a legate named Priscus. Another cause of discontent was the fact that Perennis, Commodus' praetorian prefect, had appointed men of equestrian rank to command the legions in place of their senatorial legates, whether in reaction to the attempted elevation of Priscus or in furtherance of his own designs on the throne. His action can be illustrated by an inscription convincingly assigned to this period by Pflaum, which records the appointment of L. Artorius Castus when praefectus castrorum at York to command two British legions in an expedition sent to suppress a rebellion in Brittany.[38] The appointment of equestrian prefects to command legions became normal practice later, in the third century, but public opinion was not yet ready for the step. The displaced legates were able to win sympathy in Rome, and the British army itself sent a mutinous delegation of 1,500 to Rome to publish its grievances. These troops happened to encounter Commodus near the city, and were able to encompass the downfall of Perennis.

After this Commodus appointed P. Helvius Pertinax to Britain in 185. This man, destined on the assassination of Commodus to become emperor for three months in 193, was of lowly birth but had risen by influence and merit through the normal career of an equestrian official, during which he had served as military tribune in Britain. Later as a Senator he had shown conspicuous military ability and had held the consulship in 174 or 175. Pertinax, like Marcellus, was a disciplinarian, and his qualities were severely tested in the mutinies he had inherited from his predecessor; in one outbreak he was offered the throne, in another he almost lost his life at the hands of a legion. Despite this he had the situation in hand within a year, if coins of 186 with the legend CONCORDIA MILITUM can be taken to refer to this. Shortly afterwards, perhaps in 187, Pertinax resigned on the grounds of his unpopularity with the army. The name of his successor is unknown, but probably in 191 the governorship passed to D. Clodius Albinus, who was certainly in Britain when Commodus was assassinated on the last day of 192.

1. S. H. A., *Vita Ant. Pii*, 5, 4.

2. After him we know no governors until Julius Verus, but it should be noted (*Acta Antiqua*, ix (1961), 199) that two men, P. Cluvius Maximus and T. Flavius Longinus, had careers which suggest they may have governed Britain during this period.

3. Nevertheless, about 850 acres of turf – about 1⅓ square miles – had to be cut for the rampart, corresponding to a band 63 yards wide right across the isthmus.

4. What is possibly a fourth can be seen at Rough Castle.

4a. For another, highly ingenious, theory accounting for the change in measurement, which, however, rests on too many imponderables, see Sir George Macdonald, *The Roman Wall in Scotland*[2] (Oxford 1934), pp. 393–400.

5. Pausanias viii, 43, 4.

6. Juvenal's talk of *Brigantian hill-forts* (xiv, 196) is equally loose, for Brigantia is one of the few areas where hill-forts are notably rare (p. 72).

7. D. Baatz, *Kastell Hesselbach* (Limesforschungen xii (1973), pp. 70 ff.

8. *RIB*, 1583, an altar bearing a dedication to Jupiter, Cocidius, and the Genius of the Place by *Milites Legionis II Augustae agentes in praesidio*. This lacks a date, but its context is provided by the others.

9. On present evidence these included Ebchester, Melandra, Slack, perhaps Lancaster, and probably the fortlet at Castleshaw.

10. As suggested by Birley. Degrassi proposes him for 154, but this scarcely leaves room for the Lower German command, even if he left for Britain in emergency. For his career see *ILS*, 1057, 8974.

11. Capitolinus, S.H.A., *Marcus*, 8, 7: *imminebat etiam Britannicum bellum . . . et adversus Britannos quidem Calpurnius Agricola missus est.*

12. *CIL*, xvi, 130. Better readings are probably . . . *annus Len* (*tulus*) or . . . *anus leg* (*atus*).

13. His career is outlined in *ILS*, 1092.

14. *JRS*, xxxiv (1944), 87, No. 4; *AA*[4], xxi (1943), 245, *RIB*, 1149.

15. *RIB*, 1389.

16. *Archaeologia Aeliana*[4], xlii (1964), 1–39.

17. *Britannia*, iii (1972), pp. 1–55.

18. The garrison was presumably the *Ala Petriana milliaria* which normally occupied Stanwix when Hadrian's Wall was in use. The move is not attested by inscriptions but the plan of the fort at this date seems to make it certain.

19. Calpurnius Agricola is mentioned on inscriptions at Corbridge and Carvoran, Ribchester, Chesterholm and Hardknott Castle; and there is a contemporary inscription from Ilkley (dated between 161 and 169). Of these the stones from Carvoran and Ilkley are altars

not building-records, but testify to occupation. The rest of the forts on fig. 7 (p. 183) are inserted on the map on the evidence of pottery. The heavy reoccupation of the Pennines can be appreciated by a comparison of the map with fig. 6 (p. 168), the map of forts occupied under Pius. It will be understood that the evidence on which figs. 3–7 are based is of very varying quality, and no fidelity is claimed for them in detail.

20. See p. 185.

21. The date of the Intermediate Wall, though not completely certain, is usually taken to be as stated in the text; the less likely alternative is that it was built at the very end of Hadrian's reign.

22. I have used a list of regiments compiled by Professor Birley which he kindly made available to me; the list is so nearly the same as that printed by Grace Simpson, *Britons and the Roman Army* (London, 1964), pp. 181–2, that I have not thought it necessary to print a list here.

23. Castell Collen, Trawscoed and Coelbren.

24. Tomen y Mur.

25. S.H.A., *Marcus*, xxii, 1: *imminebat et Parthicum et Britannicum bellum.*

26. *CIL*, xiii, 6806.

27. Dio, lxxiii, 8. Another governor of the same name, perhaps his grandson, is recorded in Lower Britain forty years later (p. 206).

28. *RIB*, 1329.

29. The evidence has been re-examined in detail by Steer (*AA* [4] xlii (1964), 29–39): apart from one or two repairs which might have taken place during the second occupation, the structural evidence is consistent with levelling and tidying up either in the course of evacuation or preparatory to rebuilding.

30. An inscription from Carlisle (*RIB* 946) and dated by Rostovtzeff to the reign of Commodus (*JRS* xiii (1923) 96), refers to the 'rout of a huge multitude of barbarians'.

31. There are two altars from the Antonine Wall which must be later in date than 165. The first (*RIB*, 2148), found just outside the fort of Castlecary, was set up by men of Legio vi who described themselves as *cives Italici et Norici*; Dr J. C. Mann (*Hermes* 91 (1963), 487), has shown that they are likely to be transfers from Legio ii Italica which was first raised in Italy in 165 and then served in Noricum from 171. A vexillation might have been spared to help in Britain after the conclusion of the Marcomannic Wars in 180; it cannot be as late as Severus, by whose time all the original Italians will have been discharged. The second altar was found in the fort ditch at Old Kilpatrick (*Britannia*, i (1970), 310), and was set up by *Cohors i Baetasiorum* under the supervision of a centurion of Legio i Italica (which was stationed in Lower Moesia). One possible context for the presence of this centurion in Britain is the campaigns of

Severus, for Severus relied heavily on vexillations from the Rhine and Danube legions; but there is really no indication, in archaeology or in probability, that Severus was intending to rebuild the Antonine Wall at that time (p. 201). The Baetasii were at Bar Hill in 159–63 and at Maryport later. Their presence at Old Kilpatrick, together with the centurion from Moesia, is best explained in the context of Ulpius Marcellus, whose date is close enough to 200 to cover the supposed 'early third-century character' of this altar. He too could have been reinforced with continental legionary vexillations now that the Marcomannic war was over. Both altars imply the presence of troops on at least a semi-permanent footing and thus are to be associated with the Antonine Wall third period rather than with mere passage on campaign.

There are also on record two coins, possibly of Commodus, one from Bar Hill and the other from Kirkintilloch (but they are of doubtful significance); and there is a third, better attested, of c. 174, from Mumrills.

32. *Britannia*, iii (1972), 53.

33. *RIB* 1234 (=*ILS* 2618): *portam cum muris vetustate dilapsis*.

34. The temple of Antenociticus (which seems to have been finally destroyed in 197) contained two late Antonine altars, one dedicated by the milliary Cohors I Vangionum, the other by Tineius Longus, prefect of cavalry (see *RIB* 1328–9). Longus was at Benwell in 180, so presumably the Vangiones arrived as the result of troop movements by Ulpius Marcellus.

35. Dio, lxxvii, 12.

36. Dio, lxxvi, 9, p. 216.

37. But it is worth noting that there are no marching camps yet known north of the Forth which can be assigned to an Antonine context.

38. H. G. Pflaum, *Les Carrières Procuratoriennes Equestres sous le Haut-empire romain* (Paris, 1960), I, 535; *CIL*, iii, 1919, 8513, 12813; *ILS*, 2770 (uncorrected). The removal of these two legions could hardly have been contemplated until a genuine settlement had been achieved in the north.

9
Severus and the third century

The assassination of Commodus, which was soon followed by that of Pertinax,[1] left open the succession to the Empire; for the provincial armies would not accept the sale of the throne to Didius Julianus by the praetorian guard which then followed. Clodius Albinus, governor of Britain, was one of the claimants, whose noble birth and constitutional reputation gained him senatorial support. There were two other provincial governors who had their armies' backing. Pescennius Niger in Syria controlled nine legions; nevertheless, he suffered the twin disadvantages of long distance from Rome and an army weaker than that which sustained his chief rival. L. Septimius Severus in Pannonia was supported by the powerful legions of the Danube and soon by those of the Rhine also – sixteen in all – and he was able to march on Rome without delay.

Clodius Albinus had the support only of three legions in Britain and one in Spain. He was given the title of Caesar by Severus, with implied right of succession, before the latter marched against Niger; and with easy-going blindness he remained content with this, whether because of the relative weakness of his forces or because of a genuine hope that the arrangement would preserve peace. But after the fall of Niger early in 194 it became evident that Severus had no intention of respecting the claim of Albinus, and a breach was soon inevitable. He was worried by the partiality shown by the senate for Albinus, and sent messengers to kill him. Escaping this danger, Albinus began his preparations;[2] he had himself proclaimed Augustus in 196, and in the autumn of that year he crossed to Gaul with as large an army as he could raise in Britain, and with the support of the garrison of Tarraconensis, Legio VII Gemina. No doubt he hoped to win over the legions of the Rhine; but though he defeated Lupus, legate of Severus, the legions did not come over. His only immediate accession of strength was the Thirteenth Urban Cohort stationed at Lyon, but control of important Gaulish recruiting grounds was now in his hands. The decisive clash took place near Lyon in February 197; Dio gives the numbers involved as 150,000 on each side: and after a hard-fought battle Albinus was defeated and killed himself. Severus exacted heavy punishment, including confiscations of estates, from all who had supported Albinus. This had serious consequences, for instance, to the wine-trade between Spain and Britain (p. 330), and its effects may conceivably be recognisable at certain villa-sites in Britain, for example, Lullingstone (p. 312). Indeed, in 197 Sextus Varius Marcellus, a relative of the emperor by marriage and a Syrian by birth, was despatched as Procurator to Britain; the reason behind this exceptional appointment of an oriental was no doubt to ensure that supporters of Albinus should be hunted out by an officer of un-impeachable devotion to the new ruler's interests.

The military balance between Albinus' legions and those of the Danube army was so adverse that it is clear he must have stripped Britain of every available auxiliary, the security of the frontier (it might be thought) being the only restraining consideration. But in reality the bulk of the forces holding Hadrian's Wall and its vicinity were removed, for the fort of Old Carlisle is the only one in all northern Britain which is known to have retained as garrison in the third century the same regiment which had served that duty in the second. At all the others of which we have record the garrison was different under Severus, and this must be due to extensive re-organisation after the movements and casualties of the expedition and to the fact that a decade passed before restoration could be undertaken.

But if Albinus hoped that existing treaties would hold the Maeatae to their duty and keep the frontier safe, he was miscal-culating the strength of temptation, and forgetting how recent were the agreements by contrast with the long tradition of hostility. Be-hind the Maeatae the Caledonians were active, and in front of them the Brigantian hill-men almost certainly broke out. In Wales also there are signs of rebellion and the destruction of forts. The result of all this was that on the recovery of Britain the government of Severus was faced throughout the military zone with the need to expel the enemy and to restore its military installations. A number of forts on Hadrian's Wall and in the Pennines had been violently destroyed.[3] Others needed repairs, and almost all received a change of garrison. It is not always easy to decide whether particular examples of damage or repair were necessitated by hostile wrecking or by the processes of natural decay. The Severan reconstruction of the frontier involved the rationalisation of the turret system, in which a large number were suppressed as well as some of the milecastles. Without special evidence, it would be unreasonable to attribute the demolition of these to the enemy; in others ash from hearths may have been mistaken by early investigators for proof of arson. Nevertheless there remain many signs that Hadrian's Wall had been extensively damaged. In at least three forts destruction by fire has been noted, and at the majority of excavated forts there are indications of demolition and reconstruction, as there are also at many milecastles and turrets. The efforts of someone to lever over the north gate of Milecastle 37 near Housesteads can still be seen and dated to this time, and at other milecastles damage to, or demolition of, gate-piers has been recorded.[4] At the forts of Housesteads and Birdoswald patches due to rebuilding can still be seen in the fort walls; elsewhere the Wall itself has been rebuilt from its foundation over many hundred yards at a time. All this work seems rather too much for natural decay alone to have caused in only forty-five years, and some of the phenomena are best explained as unhurried wanton damage by people who had no respect for government property and who were motivated by hatred of the Wall and all it stood for. But when reconstruction was put in hand it was naturally extended to other structures where repairs were required. The Wall and its forts, after all, formed a unitary system, and this is the justification for what are called Wall-periods; restorations are more likely in such a system to be widely undertaken along it rather than as unconnected individual programmes at particular forts: rebuilding necessitated by damage in one area might well trigger off a series of less urgent repairs elsewhere.

Much of this destruction must have been the work of local bands of hillmen; forts like Bainbridge and Ilkley lie too far within the hills to be the prey of invaders from beyond the wall, who if they penetrated so far South will have been in search of richer booty. In fact, however, there is little or no evidence for extensive raiding and destruction in the richer parts of northern England. Neither Catterick nor Aldborough appear to have been destroyed at this time, and it is no longer believed that the fortress of York suffered damage.[5] The destruction seems confined to the installations connected with local military control.

But the Maeatae had certainly penetrated into the province and were sustaining the resistance.[6] Virius Lupus was sent by Severus to recover Britain; and, fearing that the Caledonians were about to aid the Maeatae in breach of their agreements, and unable to obtain the forces he required from Severus, he was compelled to pay the latter a large subsidy for their withdrawal, gaining a few prisoners of war in exchange.[7] This was an application of the principle Divide and Rule: Roman policy was perforce to reconquer piecemeal. There are inscriptions recording restoration by Lupus at Brough under Stainmore (dated 197), and at Ilkley and Bowes in the same or early the following year, and an undated one also at Corbridge. The Severan inscription from Ribchester may also very probably belong to this governorship; its date is not earlier than 198. Evidently a methodical restoration of the Pennine forts was under way.[8]

The earliest records of restoration on Hadrian's Wall, on the other hand, date from 205 or later. Fairly clearly there was hard fighting to be undertaken against the Brigantian uplanders, which may have lasted almost a decade. The fort at Bainbridge has produced two inscriptions, one of 205 recording barrack-building under C. Valerius Pudens, and one of his successor L. Alfenus Senecio apparently mentioning work on the annexe wall. Bainbridge is admittedly a remote site in upper Wensleydale, and its rebuilding may have been postponed. On the other hand, the fort at Bowes in Stainmore, whose bath-building had been restored by Lupus, has also produced a building inscription of Senecio, as has that at Greta Bridge. This supports the suggestion that action against the Brigantian hill-men was prolonged;[9] renewed outbreaks may have been precipitated by the restoration of the Wall barrier.

Even so the eight years' failure to reconstitute Hadrian's Wall is curious, since the barrier would have served to cut off the rebels from help in Scotland. Though conceivably due to prolonged and fierce warfare in the Pennines, this failure is much better explained if Lupus and his successors had been instructed to punish the Maeatae by once more taking them under direct rule — in effect to reoccupy Scotland. Such a task, on top of present difficulties in the

197

Pennines, might well account for the long struggle, especially if the returning Roman forces were seriously depleted. And it might even provide an acceptable context for preparations to rebuild the Antonine Wall (that wall's so-called 'third period' [10]) which were noted earlier (p. 188), as well as the Severan samian noted at Newstead by Hartley. Any such attempt, however, was abandoned by 205, when we find Alfenus Senecio reconstructing the Hadrianic frontier.

Virius Lupus remained governor perhaps until 201 or 202. The date of his consulship is not known, but he was probably legate of one of the German provinces in 196, for he is certainly to be identified with the Lupus defeated by Albinus in that year. In 202 there seems to have been an interregnum, for this is the most likely date for M. Antius Crescens Calpurnianus, who was acting governor while holding office as Iuridicus Britanniae.[11] C. Valerius Pudens will have taken over from him in late 202 or 203, and was in Britain certainly until 205. After holding the command of Lower Pannonia he had been consul probably in 194 and then had governed Lower Germany before holding office in Britain. He was succeeded perhaps in 206 by L. Alfenus Senecio: the date of Senecio's consulship is not known, but he seems to have been governor of Syria [12] in 200. The date of his tenure of Britain is given by the inscription set up between 205 and the end of 207 [13] at Risingham, an outpost fort north of the Wall.

It was in Senecio's governorship that restoration of Hadrian's Wall began, to judge by the inscriptions. We find him restoring the granaries at Birdoswald and probably at Corbridge, and other buildings at Chesters and Housesteads. At Benwell, as already mentioned, his name occurs on a dedication to Victory and Dio, too, writing of 206 alludes to victories in Britain.[14] An inscription on the rock-face of a quarry just behind the Wall near Brampton records legionary work there in 207. Finally, at Risingham Senecio restored a gate and the fort-walls in 205–7. There are also a number of undated inscriptions from the Wall recording work undertaken by civitates in southern Britain – two mentioning the civitas Dumnoniorum, one the civitas Catuvellaunorum, two the Durotriges Lendinienses and one obscurely referring to a civitas Bricic.[15] It is certain that the civitates took no part in the original building of the wall under Hadrian, and that these inscriptions record a subsequent repair. But whether they should be ascribed to the Severan or Constantian reconstructions – or even to 369 – is not at all clear. They are usually taken to date to the time of Severus.[16]

By the end of 207, at any rate, the military re-occupation of the frontier, its hinterland and its outposts was complete. But there still remained the task of punishing the tribes of central Scotland and of restoring Roman hegemony in the Lowlands. Senecio lacked the forces necessary for such an enterprise, and according to Herodian [17] the governor wrote to Severus reporting the military situation as still serious, and asking either for reinforcements or for an imperial expedition led by Severus himself. The latter suggestion was taken up eagerly, for Severus was still ambitious for personal military re-nown, and was anxious to remove his sons from the temptations of court life in Rome. Despite physical infirmity, which necessitated his travelling in a litter, he made rapid preparations, and in 208 arrived with large reinforcements, including legionary vexillations from the Continent,[18] and new levies raised in Gaul and Britain, and accompanied by the empress Julia Domna, his two sons Caracalla and Geta, Papinian the praetorian prefect, Castor one of his confidential freedmen and a staff of high-ranking senators. Imperial headquarters were set up at York, and peaceful overtures from Scotland brushed aside. The campaigns were to be under the direction of Severus and his elder son; Geta, the younger, was put in charge of the province in the rear.

The accounts of the campaigns which have come down to us in the writings of Herodian and Dio are meagre in content and hostile in outlook, nor is their confusion at present greatly illuminated by archaeological evidence. According to the historians, the first objective was the Caledonians, and this campaign we may assign to the years 208–9. It resulted in a cession of territory by the Caledonians. The next year (210) saw a revolt of the Maeatae, against whom Severus could not campaign in person owing to illness, but sent Caracalla instead. Victory, however, did not end the war, for the Caledonians prepared to take a further part, and Severus was making ready for a personally conducted expedition when he died at York on 4 February 211. The whole impression given is of ineffective counter-marching and of inability to bring the Caledonian guerrilla fighters to action.

Archaeology can point to military building at Corbridge, including two granaries [19] and the great unfinished store-building known as

199

site xi. This has been variously interpreted by Professor Birley as an unfinished headquarters building for a projected legionary fortress, and as the forum of a projected civitas; but the evidence is still in favour of its being a courtyard store-building comparable to those which exist at *Vindonissa*, *Novaesium*, *Carnuntum* and *Lambaesis*. If supplies were originally ordered to be assembled at Corbridge for an orthodox penetration up Dere Street into Maeatian territory it would seem that the plan was soon changed; for other evidence suggests that instead an amphibious expedition was substituted with objectives much farther north. An inscription from Rome, assigned on reasonable ground to this period by Pflaum, suggestively records the combination of the fleets of Germany, Moesia and Pannonia under one command with the Classis Britannica.[20] At South Shields a second supply base was built, for the fort there contains an unusually large number of granaries of this date – at least twenty instead of the normal two – sufficient, it can be calculated, to house three months' rations for 40,000 men. It has also yielded a collection of numerous lead seals, many of them bearing the heads of Severus and his sons and the inscription AVGG; these indicate the arrival of baggage and stores in bulk no later than 209. These supplies were assembled on the south side of the Tyne Estuary, which has no direct land communications northwards, but which gives ready access to the harbour. Likewise in Scotland the only forts hitherto showing Severan occupation are Cramond on the south shore of the Forth, and Carpow on the south shore of the estuary of the Tay. It is significant that with the possible exception of Newstead no forts in the Lowlands were re-occupied, though some marching camps in this area may be Severan, dating from the campaign of 210, and of course the bulk of the army proceeded by land towards the territory of the Caledonii in 208–9. Cramond was a fort of six acres; but Carpow was a much larger fortress, apparently about thirty-two acres in area, and probably intended for part of Legio VI, many of whose tile-stamps have been found there. The placing of a large legionary force at Carpow may be the context of the cession of territory by the Caledonians, though it is probable that the lands of the Votadini were enlarged at their expense also (p. 208f.). As well as these two permanent posts, there are marching camps in north-east Scotland which are likely to be Severan, though precise dating evidence is not yet available. These are the 63-acre and 130-acre camps noted

200

earlier (p. 131), together with the four 165-acre camps leading north from Newstead which seems to have been the marshalling point of the land-forces. The 63-acre camps are earlier (but not much earlier) than the 130-acre series, and both types are closely associated in details of castrametation and often on the ground also. We may assign the smaller camps to the campaign of 208 and the 130-acre ones (large enough for three legions and an equal number of auxilliaries) to the year 209. Virtually the complete campaign of 208 can thus be traced from the crossing of the Forth near Stirling to that of the Tay at Carpow; then northwards, east of the Sidlaw hills, to the North Esk river at Keithock and back down Strathmore; it ravaged much of the fertile heartland of the Caledonii. The second campaign traverses Strathmore and penetrates beyond the North Esk at least as far as Kair House; the slightly smaller camps beyond this are perhaps unconnected (p. 131).

This distribution of forts – and camps – allows us to form certain conclusions about Severus' purpose. It is evident from his neglect to garrison the Lowlands that he was not intending a permanent occupation of Scotland. Rather we may feel confident that he wished to remain as mobile as possible and to retain the maximum intitiative for strikes deep into Caledonia from a few permanent bases on the east coast. We may also suppose that the Maeatae in the Lowlands were not at first regarded as a serious problem, for otherwise it would have been impossible to by-pass them as he did.

There is also numismatic evidence bearing on the war. Coins of 208 record the *Profectio Augustorum*, and there are also two remarkable issues of the same or the following year portraying two different bridges. The issue of Severus shows what looks like a permanent bridge with towers at either end; that of Caracalla is a bridge of boats with the legend *Traiectus*. Coins of 209 also portray Neptune and Oceanus, and other issues of this and the following two years make frequent reference to *Victoriae Brittannicae*.[21] Taken with the other evidence, these coins reinforce the idea of a sea-borne expedition, and the bridge coins may have reference to the bridging of the Forth or Tay or both. At Carpow a large enclosure has been found which is probably the bridgehead of the bridge of boats. Severus' first objective may have been Fife, for which the Agricolan road via Stirling lay too far west; and these considerable engineering works would be the context for the confused references to dyke-

SEVERAN CAMPS IN SCOTLAND

Roman Miles

0   10   20   30   40   50

● 63-acre camp
○ 110-acre camp
□ 120-acre camp
■ 165-acre camp
▪ Severan fort

Land over 1000 feet

8   Severan marching camps in Scotland (pp. 131, 200–1)

1 Muiryfold
  (Pass of Grange)
2 Glenmailen
  (Ythan Wells)
3 Kintore
4 Normandykes
5 Raedykes
6 Kair House
7 Balmakewan
8 Keithock
  (Battledykes)

9 Marcus
10 Oathlaw
   (Battledykes)
11 Lunanhead
12 Kinnell
13 Cardean
14 Eassie
15 Kirkbuddo
16 Lintrose
17 Longforgan
18 Grassy Walls

19 Scone
20 Innerpeffray, West
21 Innerpeffray, East
22 Broomhill
23 Carpow
24 Auchtermuchty
25 Ardoch
26 Ardoch
27 Craigarnhall
28 Cramond
29 Inveresk

building and filling up marshes (for the approach-roads) and to
bridge-building, to be found in Herodian and Dio.[22] Beyond Fife the
line of marching camps runs on at least to Aberdeen, reminding us
of Dio's statement that Severus did not desist before approaching
the extremity of the island, where he made accurate observations of
the sun's height in summer and winter respectively.

Dio suggests that after the death of Severus Caracalla immediately
concluded peace, withdrew the garrisons and returned to Rome. But
in fact the arrival of Caracalla and Geta in Rome did not occur till
late in the year, and coin issues of 212 continue to record their victory;[23] we may believe that Dio's hostility has suppressed a further
campaign in 211 which brought the war to a conclusion.[24] Certainly
the picture of expensive failure painted by the historians is belied
by the subsequent history of the frontier. The Imperial expedition
did not conquer Scotland, it is true, but the evidence proves that this
was not the intention. In the event both Caledonians and Maeatae
learnt their lesson and the British frontier remained at peace until
296.

Our view of Severus' Scottish intentions will affect our interpretation of another important and difficult problem. Herodian tells us
that Severus divided Britain into two provinces, and the implication
of his narrative is that this occurred in 197.[25] The two provinces,
Britannia Superior and Britannia Inferior, soon appear on inscriptions,[26] the earliest of which, however, is later than the death of
Severus. Dio implies that Chester and Caerleon were in Superior and
York in Inferior,[27] while the Bordeaux inscription [28] of Lunaris tells
us that in 237 Lincoln as well as York was in Inferior.[29] This distribution of legions implies that the governor of Superior was a consular
and that his colleague in Inferior was of praetorian rank, and this is
the situation which indeed reveals itself on the British inscriptions
from Caracalla onwards. It seems clear that one of the purposes of
the reform was to prevent the concentration of a large army in the
hands of a single governor and thus a repetition of the affair of
Albinus. Severus similarly divided the command in Syria in 194, and
in 212 or 213 Caracalla reorganised Pannonia with the same end in
view. But in the reign of Severus himself we have plenty of evidence

for the activities of consular governors in the Pennines and beyond. Lupus, Pudens and Senecio were all men of the higher rank. Moreover, none of the inscriptions gives any hint that they were operating outside their proper province.

To explain this contradiction some scholars have suggested that in times of war the governor of Superior took command in the north by virtue of his higher rank; but if one governor were under the orders of the other it would vitiate the purpose of the reform. All we can be certain of is that the situation under Severus himself was not the same as that found later under Caracalla and his successors. There are various possibilities. Collingwood suggested that under Severus Britain was first divided between two governors of *consular* rank, and that therefore governors such as Senecio were in their own province, Inferior.[30] This might still be the correct explanation if we were sure that only vexillations of Legions II and XX, and not the entire units, were operating in the northern wars. But it is far more likely that the whole army of Britain was united for the purpose under single command, and this is implied by the inscription on an altar [31] dedicated in person by L. Julius Julianus, legate of II Augusta, in Northumberland, for the legate is unlikely to have commanded a vexillation.

Another suggestion, first put forward by Ritterling and elaborated by Birley,[32] is that Lower Britain was a procuratorial province under Severus. This suggestion is based on the curious fact that on two inscriptions of Senecio the intervention of the procurator Oclatinius Adventus is attested in the restoration of forts.[33] Certain small areas had been administered by procurators since the beginning of the Empire – the best known is Judaea – but the promotion of procurators to the control of more important provinces – *agentes vice praesidis* – is a feature which develops from the time of Severus. The suggestion, however, leads to difficulties. Not only is there no mention of the phrase *agens vice praesidis* or *proc. et praeses* in the inscriptions concerned; but Birley has been driven to admit that all three legions were probably under the governor of Upper Britain and that the procuratorial province of Inferior was centred on Carlisle with only auxiliary forces under command. This arrangement would make the defence of the frontier an impossibility, as well as once more vitiating the purpose of the reform.[34]

One solution is to reject Herodian's evidence – he is often muddled

– and to attribute the division to Caracalla, c. 213. But a reasonable and less drastic alternative may be that when Severus decreed the division of the province in 197 he did not foresee the long struggle ahead. When the recalcitrance of the Brigantes and the difficulties in the north became clear the division must have been suspended for the duration of the war. All forces must surely have been placed unequivocally under the control of the consular commander. The identity of Britannia Inferior may perhaps have been preserved by appointing a procurator to carry out its civilian administration, but there is evidence against the suggestion;[35] and we may conclude that Senecio was merely making use in the emergency of the particular talents of Oclatinius Adventus. For Herodian and Dio both record his unusual military abilities; he was sufficiently distinguished to be promoted praetorian prefect by Caracalla, and to be offered the empire itself in 217.[36] If civilian working-parties from the civitates were assisting in the work this might be an additional reason for the presence of the procurator.

Under Caracalla, once peace was restored, the two provinces resumed their normal administration. Nevertheless, the two commands even then were not entirely distinct. At Corbridge a military arsenal was occupied apparently for most of the third century by vexillations of legionaries from Upper as well as Lower Britain. In other words, troops from Superior were seconded to Inferior, and movement to and from their bases must have taken place from time to time.[37] It seems likely, too, that the governor of Superior had other rights in the Lower province, to judge by two inscriptions from Greta Bridge,[38] and one from Chesterholm mentioning beneficiarii from his staff on duty there. Troops might even be transferred from one province to the other, as must have happened when Cohors I Baetasiorum moved into the new fort at Reculver on the Kent coast (p. 211).

Not many governors of Britannia Superior are known. Geta Caesar had held this office in 208, at least until his elevation to the rank of Augustus in 209. It was quite probably under him that Alban was martyred at Verulamium (p. 371). An inscription recently found at Reculver records a consular governor Rufinus; this may have been A. Triarius Rufinus, consul ordinarius in 210, but Q. Aradius Rufinus, consul some ten or fifteen years later, is another and more likely possibility. The names of two others, C. Junius Faustinus Postumianus, who had previously served on Severus' staff in Britain, and T. Julius Pollienus Auspex, are known, but the dates of their tenures are uncertain. Auspex is thought to be identical with the man who governed Numidia *c*. 217–20, and his tenure of Upper Britain, if so, will have fallen in the period *c*. 223–6.[39]

The early governors of Britannia Inferior are better known. C. Julius Marcus is recorded on a milestone from the Military Way and on building records at Old Carlisle and Netherby: he was here in 213–4. His successor was perhaps the elder Gordian, later emperor; an inscription from Chester-le-Street[40] gives part of his name, . . . *diano*. If this is the same governor as that whose name is erased on a stone from High Rochester[41] he was in Britain in 216. It is noteworthy that the names of both these governors had been erased, suggesting that they had incurred imperial displeasure, for what reason we do not know. In 217 and 218 the province was probably held by Ulpius Marcellus the Younger. Two inscriptions from Chesters mention him in conjunction with the Second Ala of Asturians.[42] This regiment was certainly at Chesters in the third century, as two other inscriptions there,[43] dated to AD 221–2 show; and the late Antonine garrison of the fort was Cohors I Delmatarum. Chesters, like other forts in the north, seems to have experienced a change of garrison under Severus. This Ulpius Marcellus cannot therefore be identified with the governor sent by Commodus, but was possibly his grandson; from the location of his activity he must have been a governor of Lower Britain, and these years seem suitable.[44] Modius Julius was governor in 219 under Elagabalus and has left inscriptions at Birdoswald and Netherby.[45] He was succeeded by Tiberius Claudius Paulinus. This man had been commander of Legio II Augusta, after which he had been appointed to two successive governorships in Gaul before returning to take charge of Lower Britain in 220. A letter of his addressed from Tampium to a Gallic friend, Sennius Sollemnis, offering an appointment with Legio VI, survives on an inscription in Normandy, and his name recurs on a stone at High Rochester.[46] Before the end of 221 he had been succeeded by Marius Valerianus, who left inscriptions at Chesters dated 221, Netherby (222) and South Shields, and who thus overlapped the accession of Severus Alexander in March 222. His successor in 223 was Claudius Xenophon, known from inscriptions from Cawfields and Chesterholm; he was followed by Maximus, who restored a granary at Great Chesters in 225.

The two emperors Caracalla and Geta returned to Rome in 211 after their British victory, but within thirteen months of Severus' death Caracalla encompassed his brother's murder, and thereafter was sole ruler. Geta, however, had been popular with the army, and there were protests from the troops in Italy. It seems that the Army in Britain, too, went through a period of insubordination in 212, for in 213 a number of inscriptions were set up in uniform terms throughout the north under Julius Marcus, declaring the loyalty and devotion of the troops to Caracalla and his mother. Examples have been found at Risingham, High Rochester, Carrawburgh, Chesterholm, Great Chesters, Whitley Castle, Old Carlisle, Old Penrith and perhaps Ambleside and Netherby. They have every appearance of a demonstration officially enjoined, and it was not until after this public penitence that the regiments of the British army were accorded the title *Antoniniana*, or Caracalla's Own.[47]

Caracalla's settlement of the northern frontier was based on renewed treaties with the Caledonians and Maeatae, and though the details are unknown, their general character can be assumed from similar arrangements on the Continent. Subsidies were sometimes paid in return for renunciation of inter-tribal warfare, control of assembly and the provision of troops. We are told that he withdrew garrisons; this perhaps refers to the evacuation of Cramond and Carpow.[48] We know, too, that *Brittones dediticii*, that is tribesmen who have made unconditional surrender, were transferred to the German frontier accompanied in at least one case by a staff of *Brittones gentiles*, or allied tribesmen. Control of assembly may perhaps be deduced from the record of the names of *loca* in the Lowlands, which have been interpreted as legal meeting-places, no doubt under supervision.

This experiment of a treaty relationship had been introduced by Commodus – so it has been argued (p. 188f.) – but this time a better scheme of supervision was organised. The Severan reconstruction of Hadrian's Wall, though sufficient in its reputation for Spartian writing in the fourth century to give Severus the credit for its inception,[49] differed in significant detail from the arrangements of Hadrian. The Vallum was not restored. Some turrets on the central crags were suppressed, the ruined wall being rebuilt across their recesses, and the gateways of the milecastles were narrowed – or in one case walled up altogether.[50] Clearly lateral signalling along the whole wall and the surprise appearance of large forces from concealment behind it were no longer envisaged. Instead the wall was now planned to be the base for support of forces acting well in advance of it. The Hadrianic outpost forts situated at Netherby and Bewcastle were restored, and two further outpost forts were added on Dere Street at Risingham and High Rochester. At least four (the name of the garrison at Birrens is not known) were held by part-mounted milliary cohorts, and the last two by additional units as well. Risingham was the headquarters of a Numerus Exploratorum (scouts) and a vexillation of Raetian Gaesati (javelin-men) in addition to the regular Cohors I Vangionum. High Rochester had a Numerus of scouts as well as Cohors I Vardullorum. To judge by its name – Castra Exploratorum – Netherby, too, was held by scouts as well as by its attested garrison Cohors I Aelia Hispanorum. The accommodation offered by the forts is not large enough to contain all these men, the irregulars being doubtless outposted from headquarters in the forts; in this connection attention has been drawn to two inscriptions from Jedburgh relating to the first cohort of Vardulli and the Raetian Gaesati respectively. These suggest that one such outpost lay at the crossing of the Teviot. Another may have been at Tweedmouth, where a Roman military site has produced a scrap of third-century pottery.

Some forts on the Wall were similarly over-garrisoned. At Housesteads in addition to Cohors I Tungrorum, a milliary unit, inscriptions record also a Cuneus Frisiorum, a small unit of irregular cavalry, and the Numerus Hnaudifridi, a unit of Germans. At Great Chesters some Raetian Gaesati were present in addition to Cohors II Asturum, and at Burgh by Sands a Cuneus Frisiorum and later a Numerus of Moors supplemented the regular milliary cohort. Similarly Castlesteads was the headquarters of a milliary cohort, though it was a fort designed for only 500 men.

North of the Wall, which continued to limit the field of action on the south, there thus existed a heavily defended zone, beyond which the Exploratores surveyed a farther area, basing themselves upon such posts as Jedburgh or Tweedmouth; and the *loca*, which they may be expected to have supervised, extend to the Tay. It is also probable that the Votadini now received as an addition to their tribal territory some of the lands surrendered in central Scotland – they certainly possessed them in the fourth century. The unfortified farms and settlements with circular stone walls carry on in all this area in the third century, and may even extend through Fife. It is clear that the peace was guaranteed by Roman forces throughout the Lowlands, and possibly even throughout the whole area ruled by Rome in the Antonine period. In effect, a protectorate existed over the tribes of southern Scotland, and the frontier of Roman Britain more closely approximated to the true geographical border between England and Scotland. Pottery was being exported from the province, for instance to Traprain Law.

In Wales the situation is not so clear. There are, however, here and there suggestive hints of destruction at the end of the second century comparable to those found in the north. The fort at Forden Gaer seems to have been burnt once more. At Brecon the well in the headquarters was filled with rubbish, and traces of fire were found at the gates. At Caerhun the headquarters' well was similarly filled with broken building-stones. It is possible that reconstruction observed at Gelligaer belongs to this period. Extensive reconstruction was undertaken in Severan times at Caersws, Castell Collen and Caernarvon, where an inscription of 198–209 also records the reconstruction of aqueducts, and perhaps at Brecon too. This suggests that in Wales also rebellion had broken out when Albinus removed the garrisons; and the diversion of troops for its suppression may account for the difficulties of Lupus in the Pennines. But the situation was in hand by 209, since the Severan inscriptions at Caerleon and Caernarvon were erected before that year, and road repair was in progress in Caernarvonshire as indicated by a milestone of 198–209. Reconstruction, however, continued leisurely, for the amphitheatre at Caerleon and certain of the interior buildings contain tile-stamps of Caracalla or Elagabalus. This may have been partly due to the absence of detachments of Legio II Augusta in the north, which themselves reinforce the conclusion that Welsh resistance was not severe. As late as 219 vexillations of Legions II and XX from Upper Britain were assisting the reconstruction of Netherby.

Reconstruction and the provision of amenities proceeded in leisurely fashion also in the north. We have inscriptions of the reign of Caracalla recording building at Old Carlisle (213), Risingham (213 or later), Chester-le-Street (aqueduct and baths, 216(?)) and Whitley

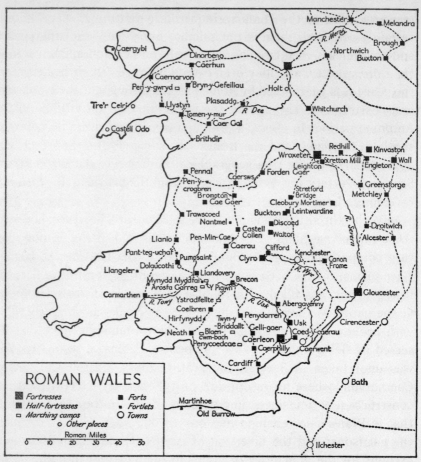

9   Roman Wales

Castle; and at High Rochester ballistaria were under construction in 216. Under Elagabalus work is recorded at Birdoswald (east gate) and Netherby in 219, and at High Rochester (more ballistaria) in 220. Under Severus Alexander principal buildings were being provided at Chesters in 221 and 223–5, a cavalry exercise hall at Netherby in 222 with a temple perhaps in the same year, a gate and towers at Chesterholm in 222–5, an aqueduct at South Shields in 222–3, granaries at Great Chesters in 225, a temple at Ribchester in 225–35 and more ballistaria at High Rochester within the same period. At the legionary fortress of Chester reconstruction of the principia and some barracks was being undertaken about this time. It is noteworthy that some of these records refer to exercise halls, temples, aqueducts or ballistaria (artillery platforms) – buildings, in other words, which are not of primary necessity – for otherwise we might have wondered whether so much reconstruction did not imply hostile activity. But the truth is probably revealed by the Netherby inscription [51] of 222 which records the completion of a cavalry exercise-hall 'whose foundations were laid long ago'. It is also remarkable that the granaries renewed at Great Chesters in 225 and the temple at Netherby were described as old and ruined (vetustate conlabsa), and this serves to remind us that not all buildings were everywhere laid flat in frontier disasters – witness the granary at Haltonchesters which survived from Hadrian till 296 with only minor repairs.

A further problem of defence, destined to become more serious half a century later, was now beginning to arise. Saxon pirates and raiders were making their appearance on the east coast, where two large inlets, the Wash and the Thames estuary, opened invitingly towards the most prosperous parts of the civil zone. Coin hoards in East Anglia, Kent and along the south coast, increasing sharply in numbers in the reigns of Marcus and Commodus, suggest insecurity here before the end of the second century: they do not occur in such numbers again in these parts until the reign of Postumus. The Classis Britannica, based partly on Boulogne and partly on British ports such as Lympne and Dover, where a second-century inscription and a fort respectively attest its presence, was not able to keep the seas clear, for ancient warships had not the range or sailing capabilities for effective permanent patrol. Early in the third century a new fort was built at Reculver on the north coast of Kent, and thither was transferred Cohors I Baetasiorum. The foundation-date is given by an inscription mentioning a consular governor Rufinus: this is probably Q. Aradius Rufinus, consul at some date soon after 225; he will have held Upper Britain a year or two later. The pottery from the primary levels of the fort would suit a date centred on 220. This fort is of a new type, transitional to the fully developed Saxon Shore Forts of the late third century, and in area is almost eight acres. This is much too large for the attested garrison, and we are left to suppose the presence of other forces, no doubt partly naval, in addition. If the Thames estuary was thus protected in the early third century it would be reasonable to expect similar precautions on the Wash, and at Brancaster there is a fort of almost identical type and size. As yet excavation has not been sufficiently extensive to produce firm dating evidence for it, and that it is contemporary with Reculver is at present a matter of inference rather than of proof. A third site which is probably connected with these early measures lies at Caister by Yarmouth at the joint mouth of the Yare and Bure.

The period after 225 becomes increasingly obscure, owing to the lack of historical sources and the growing scarcity of inscriptions. Three further governors of Britannia Inferior are known in the reign of Severus Alexander, but no dates can be assigned to them. Claudius Apellinus restored a ballistarium at High Rochester; Calvisius Rufus was responsible for a building at Old Penrith, and Valerius Crescens Fulvianus restored a temple at Ribchester. Under Gordian III (238–44) the most notable event was the refoundation of the fort at Lanchester after a period of disuse lasting from 196; but the motives behind this reinforcement of the garrison in Durham remains obscure. It was a fort of almost 5½ acres, held in the second century by a milliary part-mounted cohort; but now it was provided with a double garrison similar to the frontier forts – the Cohors I Lingonum, 500 strong, part-mounted, and a vexillatio Sueborum, irregular German cavalry. The fort was large enough to hold both groups without out-posting. Rebuilding at the site is attested under two governors, Maecilius Fuscus and Egnatius Lucilianus. The predecessor of the former had been a certain Tuccianus (the name is not quite certain), who was responsible for a building at Carrawburgh in 237 under Maximin. Lucilianus, who is mentioned also on a dedication at High Rochester, was succeeded by Nonius Philippus, whose name occurs on a dedication dated 242 at Old Carlisle. None of these men is otherwise known. The lack of information about all the governors of Britannia Inferior is no coincidence. The province was becoming a backwater of the *cursus honorum* to which prominent men were no longer sent. This gives us the measure of the success achieved by the new frontier arrangements.

It is possible that the reoccupation of Lanchester was part of a wider military reorganisation by Gordian III. Certainly by the reign of Philip (244–9) the Cuneus of Frisiones, which from the time of Caracalla had been part of the garrison of Burgh by Sands on the Wall, had been moved to Papcastle (taking the title *Aballavensium* from their former station),[52] and by the joint reign of Valerian and Gallienus (253–9) their place at Burgh by Sands is known to have been taken by the Numerus Maurorum Aurelianorum.[53] The reasons behind these troop movements are not clear.

The early third century was a period of social advance in Britain. Pausanias' reference to the deprivation of the Brigantes by Antoninus Pius of most of their territory (p. 173) has sometimes been taken as referring to grants of Brigantian lands to legionary veterans at the foundation of the colony of York at that period. But the first evidence for the colony's existence comes almost a century later, on the Bordeaux inscription of 237 (p. 219, note 28), and it is more probable that the charter was granted by Severus, not to a settlement of veterans but as a promotion of the large civil settlement which had already grown up across the river from the fortress. Grants of higher municipal status to existing towns became more common after the time of Hadrian when the practice of founding military colonies was given up; and such titular grants did not involve a redistribution of land. The Castleford milestone [54] of 251–3 records a distance of twenty-one miles from York, not because the colony possessed a territorium but because it was at that date the provincial capital. York now entered upon a period of wealth and prosperity, and as the administrative centre of the north it exerted a wide Romanising influence.

In 212, or as is now suggested, 214, Caracalla issued his famous edict conferring Roman citizenship on all free subjects of the empire.[55] The effects of this are likely to have been particularly wide in Britain, where in the nature of things Roman citizenship will have been proportionately rare hitherto. It had the effect of levelling privileges but also of increasing them for the majority; in particular, it will have enhanced the position of the towns (p. 353).

Other reforms introduced by Severus and his successors which greatly affected the military zone were the grant of the legal right of marriage to serving legionaries as well as the right to farm, and the grants of land to frontier units which could be divided among the men as allotments. The Sarmatians, originally brought to Britain in 175, were similarly provided as veterans with a block grant of land near Ribchester, and during the period there was a great development of the civil settlements which had always tended to arise round established forts. On Hadrian's Wall they were even allowed to extend into the former controlled zone north of the Vallum, spreading over its filled-in course. From such settlements, to which

213

retired soldiers naturally gravitated, a good flow of new recruits might be expected to present themselves; for local recruitment to auxiliary regiments, whatever their titular origin, was another increasing feature of the times, though, of course, known earlier.[56] Some at least of these settlements were allowed a certain measure of self-government (p. 240), and this developed a corporate feeling.

All this naturally resulted in much greater community of sentiment between the garrisons and the local tribesmen, and in this period the long-lasting hostility of the inhabitants of the Pennines seems finally to disappear. The fact was recognised some time during the third century by the creation of a new *civitas* of the Carvetii in the Eden valley,[57] first attested in the reign of Postumus (259–68). It was perhaps centred on Carlisle, which had by now grown into a sizeable town of seventy acres; the area occupied by the *civitas* may be indicated by the location of the inscriptions mentioning it and by the milestone at Middleton giving a distance of 53 miles from Carlisle.[58] The Ribchester area, however, with its special problems, was separately administered as a regio by a *praepositus* who was also commander of the fort there. The two known holders of the office were seconded legionary centurions.[59]

With the murder of Gordian III in 244 there opened a period of grave trouble for the Roman Empire in general. In the forty years between this date and the accession of Diocletian in 284 at least fifty-five emperors or Caesars were proclaimed, and many were murdered within a short span of days or months. Not only was there a decay of political coherence and of discipline, evidenced by the elevation of so many pretenders by the various armies; there was also a series of damaging invasions across the continental frontiers of the empire in Europe and Asia; and the internal prosperity of the provinces was undermined by rapidly accelerating inflation, accompanied by debasement of the coinage. The population seriously declined, and increasing use was made of barbarian tribesmen to swell the army: an observer might readily be pardoned for supposing that the Roman Empire was nearing its end.

From all these troubles except that of inflation the provinces of Britain remained for a time relatively immune, and their successful weathering of the crisis distinguishes them from most other parts of the empire except Africa. There were two reasons for this. The English Channel placed them beyond the reach of the barbarians who swept across Gaul, and secondly, the reforms of Severus and his successors had placed the British frontier on a secure footing, and by the partition of the original province had reduced the ability of the British army to make emperors. When Postumus rebelled against Gallienus in 259 and established the Imperium Galliarum, Britain and Spain adhered to him, and the former remained part thereof until Aurelian reunited the empire in 274. Thus, for most of this period Britain remained tranquil. Road reconstruction is recorded under several emperors, notably Philip (244–9) and Decius Traianus (249–51), while at Caerleon the barracks of the seventh cohort of Legio II Augusta were completely rebuilt under Desticius Juba, consular governor of Britannia Superior within the period 253–5.[60] It is clear that the cohort had returned to base after prolonged absence probably in the north; its arrival, perhaps, was part of a rearrangement caused by the despatch of legionary vexillations and auxiliaries from Britain to aid the German campaigns of Gallienus in 255. These later accompanied the Emperor to Pannonia in 260.[61] They never returned, for by that date Britain had fallen under the sway of Postumus and remained under separate rule for fourteen years. Repairs were undertaken at the fort of Lancaster by a governor of Lower Britain named Octavius Sabinus who held office under Postumus.

It was very probably in the period 268–82 that the threat of Saxon sea-raiders first became acute. The burial of coin-hoards in unusual numbers is often a good indication of crisis, and there is a sudden steep increase in hoards belonging to these years which is most remarkable.[62] To this period, too, must belong the earth fort at Richborough, which was apparently designed to transform the great monument there into a look-out post. (pl. 16a). The exact date of this fort is uncertain, but its ditches had not been completed, nor had the entrance yet been metalled when the defences were levelled to make way for the large stone fort. The latter can be attributed to Probus (276–82), and it is evident that the earth fort must be attributed to the immediately preceding years. At Burgh Castle in Suffolk, too, a coastal fort seems to have been begun at about the same time (p. 379). Moreover, the account we possess of Carausius' rise to power (p. 376) makes it very clear how serious the danger was; and when we add to this evidence the great programme of Saxon Shore defence which he took over, and the fact that a number of town walls can be accurately dated to the period soon after 270, it cannot be doubted that although Britain was not invaded and ravaged as Gaul had been ravaged (for the sea-raiders lacked the numbers to achieve such success), nevertheless public security was deeply disturbed by what must have been a number of successful descents.[63] The navigable rivers gave daring pirates opportunity for deep penetration and complete surprise, out of all proportion to their numerical strength.

In the reign of Probus (276–82) two attempts were made to re-establish the Gallic empire. The first of these was an unimportant rising led by an Italian named Proculus, who was said to be little better than a brigand. The ringleader of the second was Bonosus, whose father was a British schoolmaster, though he himself had been born in Spain of a Gallic mother. He had been in charge of the Rhine fleet at Cologne when it was burnt by the Germans, and he rebelled to avoid the consequences of his carelessness. Probus, however, soon put him down; but his attempt may have had repercussions in Britain, where about this time an unsuccessful rebellion was raised by a governor whose name has not survived. It was suppressed with the aid of Burgundian and Vandal barbarian forces which had been sent only a year or two previously to Britain after their surrender, which followed the great victory of Probus over the invaders of Gaul in 277. Where these German irregulars were stationed is still a problem to be solved, but their presence is a pointer to the growing barbarisation of the army which is a feature of this and the following century.

One of the causes of growing unrest in Gaul and Britain was the monetary policy of Aurelian and his successors, who attempted to reform the coinage by replacing the disgracefully debased issues of the Gallic empire with heavier, more respectable currency. The old coins, it seems, were to be exchanged for new at a very unfavourable rate, and in Britain the unpopular reform was successfully resisted: the new coins are rarely found. It is perhaps the triple facts of the unpopularity of the legitimate régime, the growing insecurity of the times and the increasing barbarisation of the army which explain the swift success of Carausius, who in 286 established a separate empire in Britain itself (p. 376).

1. At the end of March 193.

2. It is suggested below (p. 285) that the towns of Britain were put in a state of defence at this time.

3. The destruction-deposits at Rudchester, Haltonchesters (unpublished) and Corbridge, mentioned on p. 187, better suit this context because the next period at each site is Severan and a gap in the frontier, unplugged for twenty-five years, is inexplicable as well as stratigraphically undemonstrated. If, on the other hand, it was in the reign of Commodus that the Wall was both damaged and repaired, why are there no building-inscriptions of that emperor? And what would then be the significance of all the Severan inscriptions that we do have? And is it possible to conceive that the Maeatae, after wreaking so much destruction in 180, refrained from damage to the forts when they found them empty of defenders in 196–7?

The large group of pottery yielded by the 'destruction deposit' at Corbridge does contain groups of genuinely late pottery, e.g. from a burnt pottery-shop, but much else of it has been shown to be substantially earlier material. If rubbish was not reimported to level up for rebuilding, as seems unlikely since much of the burnt debris lay *in situ*, there were perhaps two fires, the main one (possibly accidental) occurring in the late sixties. A coin of Severus minted in 198 or later is recorded from the deposit. It is clear from its find-spot that it came from make-up, since appropriate floor-levels had been removed within the east wing of 'Site xi', the big store-building, by terracing the foundations: the coin may therefore have been dropped after the destruction itself. The absence of 'destruction deposits' below the S-E corner of Site xi is due (a) to proximity to the fort rampart and (b) to the fact that make-up deposits had not yet been laid to level the courtyard when construction was abandoned. Attempts to redate the Corbridge destruction on the evidence of coarse pottery are thus subjective, and would in any case leave a typological gap for the period 180–200. But in the later second century the rate of typological change in coarse pottery was slowing down.

4. Milecastle 37 stands on rock, so the damage is not due to subsidence; and if the Romans themselves had desired to demolish it they would have done so methodically and with the proper tools.

5. On the occasion of rebuilding the York wall, necessitated by collapse, see Baatz, *Gnomon*, 36 (i), (1964), 88 ff.; Frere, *Arch Journ.*, cxviii (1963), 257. It should be noted, however, that recent excavations have revealed traces of a fire which severely damaged the *principia* in the late second century.

6. Dio, lxxvi 5, 4: 'Because the Caledonians did not keep their promises but had prepared to assist the Maeatae . . . Lupus was compelled to buy peace from the Maeatae for a large sum, and he received a few prisoners of war in exchange.' This must mean more

than a belated *threat* of war from the Maeatae if we are to account for the prisoners; it implies a hard-pressed governor facing great military obstacles to the recovery of his province.

7. See the important study of these events by A. R. Birley, *AA*,[4] 1 (1972), pp. 179 ff.

8. It is curious that this mention of the penetration of the Maeatae is the only hint we find in Dio of the extent of the disaster to the frontier. Perhaps we have his abbreviators to thank for this, for we only possess a summary of his account. The strong later tradition, however, which originated with the writers of the fourth century, that Severus was the builder of the Wall, bears witness to the scale of restoration which it made necessary.

9. An inscription near Halifax, dated 208, is dedicated to *Victoria Brigantia* (*RIB*, 627); and one from Benwell (*RIB*, 1337) is dedicated to the Victory of the Emperors in the time of Senecio.

10. And perhaps Virius Lupus is even more likely than Ulpius Marcellus to have been accompanied to Britain by a detachment of Legio I Italica (p. 192, note 31); the other inscription, however, is unlikely to be so late.

11. *ILS*, 1151.

12. *ILS*, 5899.

13. *ILS*, 2618; *RIB*, 1234.

14. Dio, lxxvii, 10, 6.

15. *RIB*, 1672–3, 1843–4, 1962 and 2022: see also 1629 and 2053 for work done by individuals.

16. See, however, p. 394.

17. Herodian, iii, 14, 1. But A. R. Birley (*AA*[4], 1 (1972), 186–7), notes that Herodian is here using one of his rhetorical clichés, and that his account is unreliable.

18. *ILS*, 9123. Severus in all his wars relied heavily on what was virtually a standing army largely composed of vexillations of the Rhine and Danube legions.

19. See *RIB*, 1143, for a reference to the officer in charge of these granaries *tempore expeditionis felicissi (mæ) Brittanic(æ)*.

20. *CIL*, vi, 1643: Pflaum, *Les Carrières Procuratoriennes Equestres sous le Haut-empire romain*, (Paris, 1960), No. 259.

21. For the coins see Oman, *Numismatic Chronicle*, 1931, 137–50, and *RIC*, iv (i), pp. 120, No. 225; No. 786 (=*BMC*, Pl. 52 i); 284, No. 441 (bridges); *RIC*, iv (i), p. 120, Nos. 228, 229, and *BMC*, v, p. 357, No. 5 (Sea gods); ibid., *passim* (Victory).

22. Herodian, iii, 14, 5; Dio, lxxvii, 13, 1.

23. *RIC*, iv (i), pp. 85–6.

24. Further evidence is provided by the inscription from Carpow (*JRS*, lv (1965), 223), which was not set up before 212, and proves that evacuation did not immediately follow Caracalla's return to

Rome. It shows the presence of part of Legio II Augusta at the fortress.

25. Herodian, iii, 8, 2.

26. *CIL*, viii, 2080, 2766 (=*ILS*, 2762), 5180.

27. Dio, lv, 23, 3 and 6. He states that legions II Augusta and XX Valeria Victrix lay in the upper and legio VI Victrix in the lower province.

28. *JRS*, xi, 101, *L'Année Epigraphique*, 1922, No. 116: An altar set up by Lunaris 'Sevir Augustalis of the Colonies of York and Lincoln in the province of Lower Britain'.

29. The lead seal of Lower Britain from Felixstowe (*JRS*, xlv (1955), 147), being a portable object, is not relevant to the question. Nevertheless, the province may have extended thus far to the south-east (p. 242).

30. In this case we would have to suppose that Britannia Inferior, though only possessing one legion, would be deemed worthy of a consular command because of the very large force of auxiliaries it contained: for the other explanation, that Severus intended to enlarge Inferior to include Scotland possibly with an additional legion, is ruled out, as we have seen, by the absence of any hint of an intention to occupy the Lowlands.

31. *RIB*, 1138: cf *CIL*, xi, 4182.

32. Ritterling, *RE*, xii, s.v. *Legio*, 1608–9; Birley, *Archaeologia Aeliana*⁴, xi (1934), 131–7, *Trans. Cumberland and Westmorland Ant. & Arch. Soc.*², liii (1953), 58–62.

33. Risingham, *ILS*, 2618=*RIB*, 1234; Chesters, *RIB*, 1462.

34. Another suggestion (by J. C. Mann and M. G. Jarrett, *JRS*, lvii (1967), 61 ff.), that in the first division Lower Britain was consular and Upper Britain praetorian, lacks evidence to recommend it.

35. First Virius Lupus is described in the *Digest* (xxviii, 6, 2, 4) as *praeses Britanniae* – governor, in other words, of an undivided Britain; and Herodian himself (iii, 14, 1), refers to Senecio as 'the governor of Britain'. Next, the career of Varius Marcellus (*ILS*, 478), who, as we have seen, was appointed procurator in 197, and who must have remained in Britain several years, describes him as *procurator Britanniae*, not *Britanniarum*, as would have been the case if the division were effective: the same is true of Crescens Calpurnianus *legatus iuridicus Britanniae*, who might have been expected to specify Britannia Superior.

36. Herodian, iv, 12, 1, and 14, 1; Dio, lxxix, 14.

37. As, for instance, the Vexillations of Legions II and XX, who were building at Netherby in 219. *RIB*, 980, Birley, *Governors*, p. 88.

38. Greta Bridge, *RIB*, 745, 747; Chesterholm, RIB, 1696.

39. Rufinus, *Antiquaries Journal*, xli (1961), 224–8; *JRS*, li (1961), 191; Postumianus, *EE*, v, 270; Auspex, *ILS*, 8841; *JRS*, xl (1950), 63; A. Stein, *Die Legaten von Moesien* (1940), 83.

40. *RIB*, 1049. See A. R. Birley in M. G. Jarrett and B. Dobson, *Britain and Rome* (Kendal, 1966), p. 59.

41. *RIB*, 1279.

42. *RIB*, 1463–4.

43. *RIB*, 1465–6.

44. If we could assume that Ala II Asturum was moved to Chesters by Ulpius Marcellus I about 184–185 and remained there under Severus, the necessity of supposing two governors of this name would disappear. See p. 188 for similar troop movements at Benwell.

45. *RIB*, 1914; Netherby, *RIB*, 980, with A. R. Birley, *Epigraphische Studien*, iv (1967), p. 88.

46. *CIL*, xiii, 3162; *RIB*, 1280.

47. E. Birley (*Epigraphische Studien*, iv, 10 ff.), has drawn attention to a group of inscriptions attesting the presence of troops from both German provinces *c.* 217; they are thought to have provided a loyal stiffening for the British garrison.

48. Yet the gates of Carpow were rebuilt in stone at some date after 211, and pottery suggests continued occupation for some decades. It is possible that Carpow was retained as an outpost supplied by sea.

49. S.H.A., *Vita Severi*, 18: *Britanniam, quod maximum eius imperii decus est, muro per transversam insulam ducto, utrimque ad finem oceani munivit.*

50. *Archaeologia Aeliana*[4], viii, 319: Milecastle 22, perhaps because it lay close to the Dere Street gate.

51. *RIB*, 978.

52. *RIB*, 883.

53. *RIB*, 2042.

54. *RIB*, 2274.

55. For the date see *Journal of Egyptian Archaeology*, xlviii (1962), 124–31.

56. Cf. Nectovelius, *nationis Brigans*, serving in Cohors II Thracum, who died at Mumrills in the second century (*RIB*, 2142).

57. *RIB*, 933 (tombstone of a man of quaestorian rank *in C. Carvetior.*) from Old Penrith, and new inscription (1964) from Brougham mentioning the *R(es) P(ublica) C(ivitatis) Car(vetiorum)*, *JRS*, lv (1965), 224.

58. *RIB*, 2283.

59. *RIB*, 583, 587.

60. The younger Valerian, mentioned on the stone (*ILS*, 537 = *RIB*, 334) died *c.* 255.

61. *CIL*, xiii, 6780 (Legio xx at Mainz in 255: legionary vexillations were always drawn from all legions in a province, so we may be sure that Legio II Augusta was represented). *ILS*, 546 (AD 260).

62. The numbers are as follows: 238–49, 19 hoards (1·7 a year); 253–68, 24 hoards (1·6 a year); 268–70, 23 hoards (11·5 a year); 270–75, 128 hoards (25·6 a year); 275–82, 41 hoards (5·9 a year).

Those closing with coins of the Tetrici (270–3), in particular, are markedly more numerous in eastern England and in the Bristol Channel region than elsewhere.

63. Several sites in Sussex, for instance, seem to have been burnt about this time (e.g. the villas at Fishbourne and Preston and the village at Park Brow).

10

The administration of Roman Britain

When Claudius left Britain he entrusted its government to Aulus Plautius, his legate, and the occupied territory became an imperial province. Under the Roman Republic all provinces had been at the disposition of the Senate; but under the imperial system, though Augustus left to the Senate the control of the more civilised and peaceful districts, where troops were not in general stationed, he himself retained under his personal command the majority of provinces in which permanent garrisons were now being maintained. In this way he was able to remain commander-in-chief of the army without obvious constitutional change. These districts formed parts of his proconsular command, but except when he happened to be present in person, their actual administration was entrusted to deputies, whose title became *Legati Augusti pro praetore*. As an administrative hierarchy evolved, senators who had served the qualifying office of praetor were sent to take charge of provinces containing either no forces at all or no more than one legion; while those with armies of two or more legions were entrusted to senators who had held the consulship. Britain was thus a consular province, but its governor, like other consulars, had the same title of emperor's deputy as his praetorian colleagues in lesser provinces. All ranked as praetors, so that the emperor's proconsular power might remain overriding.

A governor was carefully chosen from the men available for qualities consistent with the policies he was to enforce, as is clear from the careers known to us. Indeed, there is evidence for very careful original selection and subsequent training of all those who were deemed suitable for promotion in the emperor's service. That training was by experience. The Roman empire was sufficiently large to afford its administrators a wide geographical range of opportunity, and the system of promotion normally made sure that a man served in a variety of offices which tested both military and administrative capacity. The direction and level of his abilities would soon be discovered, and his appointments and promotion would be controlled accordingly. Although in theory a man might reach the governorship of Britain with military experience amounting to only a year or two as a legionary tribune at the outset of his career, and a short spell later as a legionary commander, a study of actual careers shows us that, as might be expected, the truth was not so simple or the government so naïve, and that in practice most governors had enjoyed a considerably more protracted experience, especially in the higher ranks.

Vespasian could send three men to Britain direct from their consulships; two of them had had wide previous experience of the province in war as legionary commanders (and Agricola had served his tribunate in Britain as well). This policy bore fruit at the time, but so narrow a specialisation was not usual. By the second century a fairly regular system of promotions had been evolved for those who were being groomed for the command of Britain. After the praetorship the great majority commanded a legion in Upper Pannonia, though a few were given their legion in Lower Moesia or Lower Germany. Pannonia and Moesia formed part of the Danube frontier, where the army was strong and the chances of seeing action high. Thereafter they governed a praetorian province; that selected was often Upper Dacia or else one near the scene of campaigns. After holding the consulship they were almost invariably sent to govern either Lower Moesia or Lower Germany. Then followed the British Command. For almost half of them this was the climax of their career; the others went on either to the seat of a major war or to the crowning glory either of the proconsulship of Africa or some comparable office.

In Britain a governor's duties might be largely military, as was natural to the commander of a powerful army with active frontier commitments; but besides these his responsibilities were manifold. In the first century his work was complicated by the delicate relationships which had to be maintained with client kings, those native rulers who had been left in office under treaty relationship with the

Roman power. At all times his was also the supervision of the civitates, his the responsibility for military recruitment, for road-building and for the functioning of the public courier-system. The governor, too, was the court of appeal in provincial law-suits, and he exercised primary jurisdiction not only in all cases which involved Roman citizens (a growing commitment, this) but in all cases which involved capital punishment or condemnation to the mines or salt-works, and in all civil cases which involved more than a certain sum. When not campaigning, for instance in the winter months, it was his duty to go round on circuit.

In criminal cases a Roman citizen could usually appeal to Caesar, as Paul did, though, where certain crimes and their penalties had been defined by statute, this right may have been curtailed. By the second century most cases which involved the death penalty for citizens were automatically referred to Rome for the emperor's decision, the governor's duty being merely to forward a summary of the facts. For non-citizens, *the peregrini*, the governor's was the final court, and his powers of sentence were limited only by an edict of Hadrian exempting members of the civitas councils from liability to the death penalty. In civil cases of difficulty the governor might seek elucidation from Rome, as we find Virius Lupus doing in an inheritance case quoted in *Digest*, xxviii, 6, 2, 4. By the third century, when citizenship had become universal, a system of regular appeal courts had been evolved for both civil and criminal cases.

The legal aspects of a governor's task were complicated by the variety of codes which might have to be taken into account. Roman law itself was probably binding on Roman citizens and communities, but peregrini still lived under their local Celtic codes of law save in so far as these might conflict with basic Roman principles. To assist the governor in the legal side of his work, and to relieve this heavy burden, Vespasian created a new office, that of *Legatus Iuridicus*. The iuridicus was an officer of praetorian status, responsible to the emperor, but subordinate to the governor; he acted as his deputy in legal matters. The names of five legati iuridici of Britain are known, and at least two were distinguished lawyers. The first recorded holder of the post was C. Salvius Liberalis Nonius Bassus, who was probably appointed as early as 79. He was a member of the younger Pliny's circle and had a reputation for learning. His successor was L. Iavolenus Priscus, another noted legal authority, whose term in

Britain preceded his consulship and the governorship of Upper Germany, and one of whose British cases is cited in the *Digest*.[1]

Iuridici are also found in Spain (as early as *c.* 73), Cappadocia and occasionally elsewhere: so it would be mistaken to seek to account for the creation of the office purely in terms of the needs of Britain.[2] But it is probably no coincidence that the first known holder of the British post was a colleague of Agricola, for it was that governor who doubled the area of Roman Britain, bringing under Roman control for the first time the more primitive peoples of the north, whom Roman army records perhaps distinguish from the Britanni of the lowland zone under the name Brittones. There must have been urgent need of a legal expert on the governor's staff to advise on the frequent problems which might arise over the incorporation of such people within the province, such as how best to adapt the taxation system to cover the semi-nomadic pastoralists who presented a new problem to Roman administration. In an earlier chapter, too, we have noted the achievements of Agricola in extending self-government to new civitates in the south when military government was lifted with the movement of troops to the north. In many cases towns sprang up on the sites of abandoned forts, implying a transfer of Caesar's land to native hands. All this required legal definition – a full-time task. Distinct from such problems, but no less pressing, was the need to relieve a governor so deeply involved in distant campaigns of the routine assize work of the civilian areas. Private litigation was bound to increase with the spread of civilised manners: it is no coincidence that just at this period we begin to find Roman legal terms on tablets excavated in London.

The incorporation of Cogidubnus' dominions after his death may have presented other approximately contemporary problems, but there is no evidence that this in itself had any bearing on the establishment of the post. In the first place we do not know when Cogidubnus died; in the second, such kingdoms had been incorporated before without the intervention of a special officer. The appointment was an administrative convenience which proved of permanent value. In later times we know of C. Sabucius Maior Caecilianus, who became iuridicus of Britain in the last years of Marcus, of M. Vettius Valens, who was so highly regarded that he was appointed Patron of the province, and of M. Antius Crescens

Calpurnianus, who was left as acting governor during his term of office about 202.[3]

Below the governor, and subject to his orders though appointed by the Emperor, were the legionary commanders; they, too, had the title of *Legati Augusti* (though not *pro praetore*) and were of praetorian rank. It is probable that each legion in Britain formed the core of an army district, so that auxiliary regiments would receive their orders from the commanders of the legions to which they were attached. The legates would thus naturally have some responsibility for the administration of districts under direct rule; occasionally they might administer the whole province in the absence of the governor, as happened in 69. From the time of Caracalla the command of Legio VI Victrix at York was combined with the governorship of Britannia Inferior.

Each governor, and legionary legate too, was entitled to bring with him an unofficial staff of friends, his *cohors amicorum*, who would assist him with services and advice. But there was also a regular and permanent staff attached to his *officium* or headquarters, consisting of soldiers seconded from regimental duties. This administrative staff was commanded by a centurion, the *princeps praetorii*, below whom there were three *cornicularii* (adjutants), and three *commentarienses* (registrars), assisted by their *adiutores*. The governor also enjoyed the services of thirty *speculatores*, ten from each legion in the province, The duties of these were largely judicial, including the custody and execution of prisoners; but they also carried despatches, for instance, to Rome. In addition to them, there were a large number of *beneficiarii*, who seem often to have been posted in the frontier regions, or at important points on roads farther south, in a way which suggests that their responsibility included the security of supply-routes.[4] Various other grades, such as *stratores* (equerries), also existed whose precise functions are not always certain. Besides these there was a large clerical staff of slaves or freedmen, including shorthand writers, copyists and secretaries. There survives one letter which emanated from the secretariat of the governor of Lower Britain: the excellence of its drafting, in Latin remarkable for its polished terseness and lucidity[5] suggests the high standard maintained by these staffs. Finally, there was also a governor's bodyguard, the *equites* and *pedites singulares*.

The Colony at Colchester was probably intended as the capital of the province originally, replacing as it did the old capital of Cunobelin. But as early as 60 there is evidence that London was taking over its destined pre-eminence, at least for financial administration. By the beginning of the second century a large fort had been established on the outskirts of this city, probably for the governor's guard; but London has also yielded tombstones of soldiers (one of them a centurion) from Legions II, VI and XX. The presence of men from all three legions suggests attendance at a headquarters. Even more conclusive is the tombstone of a *speculator* from Legio II Augusta named Celsus, erected for him by one of his colleagues: for such men were detached from their legions for service in the governor's officium.

The only field in which the governor's competence was not supreme was the financial, a responsibility which was in the hands of the Procurator Augusti Britanniae. This official was a member of the Equestrian Order of Roman society which ranked next below the Senatorial. Members of this order under the Republic had enjoyed few official responsibilities, and had earned the reputation of an opposition to the Senatorial government. But under Augustus and his successors, especially Claudius, they had been given the opportunity of a larger share in the administration of the provinces; they came to form in effect a sort of Civil Service, as by degrees a regular hierarchy of office (not, however entirely excluding military posts) was evolved for them. The word *procurator* itself meant little more than steward or bailiff: the importance of the individual depended upon his position in the service. In Britain we know little about the junior procurators who must have served here under the procurator of the province; but by analogy with Gaul and elsewhere we may feel confident that there were procurators of imperial estates,[6] of mines and of the main individual taxes such as customs dues, and the death-duties to which Roman citizens were liable. At their head was the Procurator Britanniae, whose responsibility included receiving the revenue, supplying and paying the army and officials, and superintending the emperor's financial interests.

To achieve Equestrian rank it was necessary to possess capital to the value of 400,000 sesterces. Careers in the equestrian cursus were thus open to many provincials of good family as well as to retired centurions from legions or the guard. As a preliminary to administrative office they normally served what were known as the *tres militiae* in the army: these were successively the offices of prefect of an auxiliary infantry regiment 500 strong, then of military tribune, usually in a legion but sometimes as commander of an auxiliary unit 1,000 strong, and finally prefect of a cavalry regiment 500 strong. A few specially selected officers then served a fourth militia as prefect of a milliary ala, and this distinction usually pointed the way to subsequent high promotion.

Each of these commands might last two or three years, if not longer: thereafter promotion led to junior procuratorships. These men also, therefore, like their senatorial colleagues, gained a wide experience in a variety of duties in many provinces.

The provincial procurator was responsible to the emperor alone, and was not the subordinate of the governor, though his duties normally demanded close co-operation with him. But sometimes, as when Classicianus made an adverse report on Suetonius Paullinus, duty demanded otherwise; and even when it did not, there might often arise a conflict of personality. Tacitus praises Agricola for not antagonising the procurators, and in the *Digest* there is a quotation from the early third-century jurist Ulpian advising a governor not to intervene in financial matters.[7] No doubt the emperor was usually glad to receive independent reports from each official on the activities of the other, and the division of function certainly prevented the too-easy organisation of rebellion. Albinus had already been promoted Caesar before he undertook his expedition.

Procurators were graded according to their salary. The Procurator of Britain, like most other provincial procurators, was a *ducenarius*: he received 200,000 sesterces a year.[8] But though he thus ranked high, the position itself was not often held by men destined for further promotion. We know the names of ten holders of the office, and only three of them can be shown to have risen higher. Decianus Catus was presumably disgraced by Nero, and Classicianus died in office. No details are known of the careers of Ti. Claudius Augustanus (a contemporary of Agricola) or of Q. Lusius Sabinianus (a second-century procurator) or of M. Cocceius Nigrinus (who made a dedication to Caracalla), except the bare fact that they held the office. M. Maenius Agrippa had commanded the British fleet before becoming procurator early in the reign of Antoninus Pius, and this was his last post before retirement. Britain was likewise the last appointment of C. Valerius Pansa, who may have succeeded him.

Cn. Pompeius Homullus, on the other hand, who was procurator of Britain about the beginning of Trajan's reign, went on to be procurator of Lugdunensis and Aquitania in Gaul, one of the most senior ducenarial appointments, and was then promoted to the office of *a rationibus*, the emperor's secretary for finance. The remaining two were Sex. Varius Marcellus, a kinsman of Severus, who subsequently rose high in his service, and Oclatinius Adventus, whose career has already been mentioned (p. 204f.). It is interesting to note the difference in calibre required for the two offices of governor and procurator of the British province. No doubt the small size of Britain and the absence there of major financial problems accounts for the relative unimportance of its procurator.

The headquarters of the financial administration were soon established at London, perhaps even before 60. Decianus Catus certainly seems to have been operating from a centre other than *Camulodunum*, and his successor was buried in London. This city, too, has produced the wooden writing tablet stamped *Proc. Aug. Brit. Prov. dederunt* ('issued by the procurators of Britain'). On analogy with his colleagues elsewhere, the procurator will have had a staff of cornicularii and beneficiarii and other assistants seconded from the army, and will have possessed a *tabularium* or record office; but no evidence for these things survives.

Other Equestrian officials in Britain were few. The Classis Britannica was commanded by a prefect of centenarial rank. The headquarters of this fleet lay at Boulogne, but it had bases in Britain, and much of its duty was performed off the British coasts. Four of its prefects are known by name, and a fifth, whose name is lacking, is attested under Severus (p. 200). Q. Baienus Blassianus held the command under Trajan and L. Aufidius Panthera, who left a dedication at Lympne, was promoted to this post in the later years of Hadrian after serving as prefect of a milliary ala in Pannonia. His immediate successor was possibly M. Maenius Agrippa, a man who was closely connected with Britain all his official life. He had started by commanding an auxiliary regiment of Britons in Moesia, and was then appointed by Hadrian to the command of a cohort of Spaniards and sent with them *expeditione Britannica*. As we have seen (p. 161), the arrival of this and other reinforcements is best placed about 130. After further service in Moesia, Agrippa returned to Britain first as admiral of the classis Britannica and then as procurator of the province. About 150 the fleet was commanded by Sextus Flavius Quietus, who had previously been chief centurion of Legio xx and had led an expedition to aid in the suppression of a Moorish revolt in 145–7. The British fleet was his last command.

One other official of sexagenarial status is known. About 205 L. Didius Maxinus held the office of procurator in charge of the gladiators recruited and trained in Gaul, Britain, Spain, Germany and Raetia. The existence of gladiators in Britain is not without interest, and there is a little further evidence bearing on it (pp. 346–7).

Apart from the *annona*, or levy of corn devoted to feeding the army, the chief sources of revenue were the *tributum soli*, a tax based on the productivity of land, and the *tributum capitis*, or poll tax (which included other forms of property). The former was based on a very careful survey of the land in a census, when every detail of its ownership and yield was recorded. From time to time fresh censuses were carried out, and the importance attached to them can be understood from the fact that a census of Gaul occasionally called for the supervision of the Emperor in person; at other times special high-ranking senatorial *legati ad census accipiendos* were appointed. In Britain it is improbable that special legates were required, but a census may be the reason behind the appointment of Neratius Marcellus as governor about 101; for he was not the normal *vir militaris*, but moved in the upper circles of Roman society, a man more at home with administration than campaigning. From the time of Hadrian special procurators of sexagenarial status were also appointed to assist in the census. The names of two are known. T. Statilius Optatus undertook the duty under Hadrian, and followed it with a similar office in Gaul. M. Arruntius Frugi was *procurator ad census* under Antoninus Pius. Before the reign of Hadrian other sorts of *ad hoc* assistant had been employed. We know of a censitor of the Roman citizens at Colchester who held this post just about the time of Marcellus' governorship, and of a *censitor Brittonum Anavion(ensium)* who held office somewhat later in Trajan's reign,[9] perhaps about 112.

The total number of Roman officials, at least in the civil part of the province, was thus not unduly large. This was made possible by the encouragement of local self-government and responsibility among the conquered people. At first this policy was achieved very largely by the device of client kingship, whereby friendly tribes were left under the rule of their own royalty, with whom treaties were made.

Cogidubnus was the most successful of these kings, but two more are known by name, while the existence of still others may be suspected (pp. 84ff.). Cartimandua was in a class by herself, for her Brigantian kingdom lay beyond the frontiers of the province and was not really under Roman control save at the cost of special military effort. Prasutagus was also outside the province but encircled by it, and Ostorius Scapula felt justified in intervening in the affairs of the Iceni to the extent of disarming them in 47. Cogidubnus succeeded to a kingdom re-created by Roman intervention, and he amply justified the experiment. The monuments of Roman Chichester are the most distinguished of their date and kind in the province, and the early development of villas on the Sussex plain is another pointer to this king's effective Romanising influence.

By degrees, however, a more genuine system of local self-government, which had already proved successful in Gaul, was introduced. This was based on *civitates peregrinae* – self-governing communities of non-citizens. In addition, self-governing towns of Roman or Latin citizens were early established, whose buildings and institutions could serve as models for the others. A Roman colony in the first century was usually still a deliberate settlement of Roman veterans, as it was under the Republic. Colchester was founded in 49, and it had both a military and a civilising purpose, as Tacitus makes clear (p. 98). Towards the end of the first century similar coloniae were placed at Lincoln and Gloucester (p. 146f.). The veterans were Roman citizens, and they were placed in self-governing towns surrounded by a *territorium* of countryside administered from them. At Colchester native *incolae* were allowed a share in the enterprise, to judge by the size of the city. *Verulamium*, founded about the same time as Colchester, was very probably a *municipium*. This was a status given normally to pre-existing towns, and it did not involve a settlement of veterans; the inhabitants might rank as Roman or Latin citizens, depending on the type of grant. *Verulamium* itself was a new foundation but close to an important native centre; it was probably of Latin status. A municipium, like a colony, was a self-governing unit, and possessed a territorium which might embrace all or only part of the tribal lands. In the case of *Verulamium* the extent of the territorium is unknown, but it did not embrace the whole of the huge canton of the Catuvellauni, for the civitas of the

IMP·TITO·CAESARI·DIVI·VESPASIANI·F·VESPASIANO·AVG
P·M·TR·P·VIIII·IMP·XV·COS·VII·DESIG·VIII·CENSORI·PATRI·PATRIAE
ET·CAESARI·DIVI·VESPASIANI·F·DOMITIANO·COS·VI·DESIG·VII·PRINCIPI
IVVENTVTIS·ET·OMNIVM·COLLEGIORVM·SACERDOTI
CN·IVLIO·AGRICOLA·LEGATO·AVG·PRO·PR
MVNICIPIVM·VERVLAMIVM·BASILICA·ORNATA

10 A possible reconstruction of the Forum inscription at *Verulamium*. (At full size the inscription measures 13 feet 4 inches by 2 feet 4 inches. Pp. 134, 231.) The pieces actually surviving are stippled. Lines 3 and 4 were subsequently erased, after Domitian's death and *damnatio memoriae*, and they are only faintly legible.

latter is still separately attested at a later date, though it may have been administered from Verulamium.

Below these self-governing Roman or Latin towns ranked the civitates peregrinae. The difference between them was more than a variation in the status of their respective inhabitants: it was a difference in organisation. A Roman or Latin town possessed an independent existence, being itself both the unit of administration and the legal *origo* of its inhabitants (a person's origo was not necessarily his place of birth but the registered place of family origin which each individual legally required). For the civitates peregrinae, on the other hand, the legal unit was the whole tribal area and not the town at its core. The reason for this was perhaps the absence at first of a satisfactory level of urbanisation. Many tribal areas in Gaul and Britain were of very large size, without predominating towns, and the Celtic aristocracy, which would have to take the lead in the new organisation, was by tradition based on its country estates rather than on towns.

The towns were quickly provided, of course, and were the seat of the local administration, but they did not take over the identity of their civitates until the third century in Gaul, and in Britain may never have done so. There exist sufficient inscriptions which show, on the one hand, a tribal origo [10] and, on the other, a difference of organisation between the capital town and its civitas,[11] to make it quite certain that Roman adaptability did not force an urban mould on a society not yet ready for it.

The existence of civitates in Britain is directly attested by five inscriptions which have been found at Wroxeter, Cirencester, Kenchester, Brougham and Caerwent.[12] Moreover, the capitals of the civitates can be recognised by their nomenclature, for the name of the civitas is added in the genitive to that of the town: Cirencester, capital of the Dobunni, was *Corinium Dobunnorum*. In Gaul in the third century the town name begins to be dropped, so that, for instance, *Condate Redonum* (Rennes) became known simply as Redones; but in Britain we have only one example of this.[13]

The difference between the two types of community was, however, merely one of law and organisation. From the first the Romans sought to encourage the growth of towns. City life was the basis of ancient classical civilisation: a civilised life was inconceivable to men of the Mediterranean world without a city as its stage. R. G.

Collingwood once described the philosophy of the city in a classic passage. 'Deep in the mind of every Roman, as in the mind of every Greek, was the unquestioned conviction which Aristotle put into words: that what raised man above the level of barbarism, in which he was merely an economic being, and enabled him to develop the higher faculties which in the barbarian are only latent, to live well instead of merely living, was his membership of an actual, physical city.' [14] Today our cities are too large and we have to look to smaller organisms, the school, the college, the society or small country town, to find the same nursery of community-feeling that in ancient times was embodied in the city. But city-life was something hitherto unknown to the Celts in Britain as it was to the Germans; urbanisation had to start at the beginning, and the process, although eventually successful, never produced towns of fully Mediterranean character.

Towns were needed not only as centres of local government but also to aid the spread of education and Roman civilisation. To this end models were set up at *Camulodunum* and *Verulamium* where the physical buildings as well as the methods of town life and organisation might be observed; and to this end loans were made and practical assistance in their construction given. It must not be forgotten how new all this was to the Britons of the time of Claudius. Even the oppidum of Cunobelin had been no more than an amorphous collection of round huts and unorganised squalor. By contrast, excavation at *Verulamium* has revealed some of the earliest half-timbered buildings of the new town, which bear the unmistakable stamp of imported architecture, with such close parallels both in structure and in plan to the barracks of contemporary Roman forts that we can be sure that military stockpiles of material were also made available in addition to military technicians. Though the magnitude of the task compelled a certain starkness, the essentials of a classical town were there – the straight streets intersecting at right angles' and the colonnaded porticos, albeit of wood.

The organisation of new *civitates peregrinae* followed as opportunity arose and local fitness for the step became apparent. The unit was usually the existing tribal area; but sometimes, as in Kent and Hampshire, new units were created – the Cantiaci and Belgae – where there was no pre-Roman tribe of sufficient size, and in Sussex the civitas of the Regnenses was set up to replace the *regnum* of Cogidubnus. At first large areas had been kept under direct military rule, administered locally by commandants of forts under the supervision of their legionary legates, and in general the development of self-governing civitates will have taken place only when the military moved forward. This will certainly have been true of areas such as Dorset and the South-West which had resisted initial conquest; the Mendips, too, were under military government at first. We have no evidence in Britain for the military *praefecti civitatis*, who in the backward Danubian provinces were charged with the establishment of local self-government and the training of local leaders in its methods; but British tribes were equally backward, and they may have existed;[15] one is known in Holland.

The physical indication of a self-governing community was the possession of a forum with basilica, which housed the meetings of the council and the administration of local justice. The date of the foundation of such fora will give us an indication of the date of the grant of local self-government. Thus, at Chichester and Winchester the fora seem to have been built late in the Flavian period, when Cogidubnus may be expected to have died. The Silchester forum is of about the same date, and all three towns may originally have formed part of his dominion. The fora at Exeter and Cirencester are also Flavian; here this denotes the removal of military control by Frontinus or Agricola. Nowhere indeed is a pre-Flavian forum yet known, except possibly at London, but on other grounds we may expect the Cantiaci, whose capital at Canterbury was first laid out in Claudian times, to have been granted self-government as early. The main development, however, is evidently Flavian.

The erection of a forum with basilica in London in Flavian times shows us that this rapidly expanding town achieved self-government at this time;[16] and as it was never a civitas-capital, we must assume that it became either municipium or colonia. Most probably it was first the one and was later promoted to be the second. Other towns may have risen in rank as time passed, and probably did so, though the fact cannot be demonstrated with certainty in Britain. A Coritanian auxiliary soldier has his origo stated not as *Coritanus* but as *Ratis* on a military citizenship certificate of 106; and, as this class of document is meticulous in its use of terms, it has been suggested that Leicester (*Ratae*) had achieved municipal rank by this date. But the man, M. Ulpius Novantico, was already a Roman citizen as a result of a special grant in the field, and this is plainly the reason why his origo is given in this form, which is normal for Roman citizens; it has no bearing on the status of Leicester. Suggestions of a similar sort for Chester and Silchester are equally poorly authenticated.

Nevertheless, there remains the general probability, based on analogy with the history of other provinces, that some of the more advanced civitas-capitals did achieve higher status during the later second and third centuries. From the middle of the second century new grants of municipal or colonial rank became increasingly common in many parts of the empire, largely as a result of applications arising from local patriotism and rivalry.

There was also a tendency at that time to give self-government to smaller units, so that civitates became subdivided. We have evidence of this latter process in Britain, where the original civitas of the Durotriges, whose capital was doubtless *Durnovaria* (Dorchester), was later split: a new group was created, called the Durotriges Lendinienses, with capital (it has been suggested) at Ilchester. The Carvetii, too, must once have formed part of the Brigantes. But of the promotion of civitas-capitals themselves to *ius Latinum* or colonial status there is no certain evidence. We can only say that it would be surprising if towns in the south, like Cirencester, Leicester or Wroxeter, with their evidence of intense Romanisation, were not rewarded with promotion; or if towns like Carlisle, Catterick or Kirkby Thore in the north, full of retired enfranchised soldiers as they must have been, were not awarded charters. It is, perhaps, worth noting that in the Antonine Itinerary, a road-list attributable to the early third century, it is precisely *Verulamium*, Leicester, Wroxeter and Canterbury which lack their tribal suffixes (as would be the case if they had been promoted to higher status).[17] Cirencester is not mentioned; but it, together with Canterbury, Leicester and Wroxeter, are given their tribal suffixes in the Ravenna List. This, however, since it mentions the forts of the Antonine Wall, is patently based in part on sources no later than the second century, and may possibly thus give us an earlier situation for these towns.

Colonies and municipia had constitutions modelled on that of republican Rome. They were governed by a council or senate known as the Ordo, which was usually about 100 strong and membership of which was limited by a property qualification. The chief executive officers, corresponding to the Roman consuls, were a pair of *Duoviri iuridicundo*, whose title shows them to have been responsible for local justice but who also presided at meetings of the ordo or of the assembly, and bore general responsibility for public shows or religious festivals. They were assisted by two aediles, whose field was the maintenance of public buildings, drains and streets. Often there was a pair of quaestors (whose responsibility was local finance) as well. In some of the older municipia the first two pairs had the title quattuorviri, but under the Empire this had become old-fashioned, and is no longer found, for instance, in Vespasian's Spanish municipal charters. Each member of a pair could veto his colleague's decisions, but the junior magistrates were subject to the authority of the duoviri. Election to these offices was by the assembled citizen body, at least at first; but by the second century such things were left more and more to the ordo itself. Magistrates who were unavoidably absent for more than a day could appoint a prefect to act for them. There were heavy penalties for magistrates acting contrary to decrees of the ordo or failing to consult it on all important matters. Every fifth year the senior pair were chosen from persons of especial standing and enjoyed the title of quinquennales. The functions of these were akin to those of the Roman censors. They had to fill up the membership of the ordo (primarily from ex-magistrates not already enrolled), supervise the letting of public contracts and the registration of such changes of ownership as might affect taxation. The seviri Augustales, the six officials of a college of Augustales, had no administrative responsibilities, but they played an important part in the maintenance of the Imperial cult in colonies and municipia.

The constitution of the civitates peregrinae was almost exactly similar except for the normal absence of quaestors and seviri Augustales: their magistrates did not receive Roman citizenship unless Latin status had been granted to the town. Nevertheless, the prestige of office was sufficient during the first two centuries to call forth candidates despite the heavy expenditure which success involved. Not only did most communities exact a charge for election to office but successful candidates were under heavy moral pressure to pay for games or spectacles, or to donate buildings, an aqueduct, or at the very least a statue, for the public good. With the gradual rise of prices and growth of inflation office became a heavy burden, and compulsion was eventually introduced. This bore all the more heavily when responsibility for collecting taxation and forwarding it to the Procurator, which had always been part of their collective duty, was made a

237

personal liability of decurions, who had to make good any shortage.

The possibilities of acquiring Roman citizenship through service in local government would appear to have been limited in Britain, though lack of evidence may perhaps give an unduly restricted picture. There was, however, another avenue to the citizenship. Enlistment in the auxiliary forces of the empire was regularly rewarded with a grant after twenty-five years' service, and until the reign of Antoninus Pius the grant was extended to children already born to the recipient. In the second century there existed at least nineteen auxiliary regiments recruited in Britain, amounting to 14,000 men. If as the basis of an extremely rough calculation we assume that half these soldiers survived to retirement age and that half of these again settled elsewhere than in Britain we find that 3,500 – or 14,000 a century – may have swelled the ranks of Roman citizens in Britain. The position is complicated by the fact that as time went on local recruitment became a predominant feature, so that regiments of 'Britons' on the Continent contained increasingly few natives of the island. Instead Britons will have enlisted increasingly in the regiments garrisoning Britain. Of the 42,500 auxiliaries who formed the army of Britain one-quarter – 10,625 – might on the same assumption be reckoned as eventual settlers in the province, or 42,500 a century. This, as we shall see, might amount to 2·12 per cent of the total population, a figure which would be augmented by retired legionaries and by the descendants of freedmen, of whom a number are known to have been engaged in trade and industry. How many of these new citizens settled in the civitates of the civil zone rather than in the vicinity of their old forts cannot be reckoned; but some will have done so, and those that did will have found themselves at a social advantage. An example of the process is seen on the inscription at Brough-on-Humber recording the erection of a stage-building by M. Ulpius Ianuarius, aedile of the vicus in the reign of Antoninus Pius. It is obvious from his names that his father or grandfather acquired citizenship by a grant of Trajan, no doubt after auxiliary service.

The government of the civitates was in the hands of the provincial aristocracy, to whose ranks wealth was a necessary passport. The responsibilities of the senates were entirely local, except that they did have the privilege of choosing delegates to the annual meeting of the provincial council. The *concilium provinciae* was the nearest approach we find in the Roman empire to representative government, but in the political sphere its powers were small, being practically limited to passing resolutions in praise or criticism of retiring governors. But it was the only body able to speak in the name of the provincials as a whole, and it could appoint suitably influential persons to act as patrons of the province, whose duty it was to make representations and especially to institute prosecutions on its behalf in Rome. The main purpose of the concilium, however, was to maintain the provincial centre of the Imperial Cult and its annual festival.

We know little of the provincial council of Britain: it must be assumed that the arrangements were parallel with those of Gaul. There the meeting took place annually at the altar of the imperial cult near Lyon and was attended by delegates from all the civitates, which appear to have had some system of proportional representation. A provincial high priest (or *sacerdos*) was chosen each year: he had to reside at the centre and pay for the shows and ceremonies which took place. Tacitus mentions as one of the causes of discontent in Britain, at the time of Boudicca's rebellion, that those who were chosen as sacerdotes had to pour forth all their wealth. From his account it is clear that at any rate at thi. date the British cult centre was at Colchester. But in Britain we lack the large series of inscriptions which was set up in Gaul both at the cult centre and in individual civitates in honour of provincial priests, and which throws so much light on the organisation of the council. There are two inscriptions from London, the first a dedication set up in the name of the Province of Britain to the divinity of the Emperor, the second the tombstone of a *provincialis* (perhaps a servant of the council); but these are no sure grounds for supposing that the cult and council moved with the rest of the administration to London. We possess the names of two *patroni provinciae Britanniae*, proof that the council was continuing to function down to the third century. The first was M. Vettius Valens, who had been Iuridicus of Britain perhaps about 150, and who may have been grandson of the Vettius Valens decorated by Claudius for his part in the invasion of 43. The second was C. Julius Asper, consul in 212. He was also patron of Mauretania Tingitana, but his connections with Britain are unknown.

Within the civitates were subordinate units known as pagi and vici. A vicus was the smallest unit of self-administration in the Roman provinces. The status was granted to certain sizeable villages or small towns, and it is clear from continental inscriptions that the civitas-capitals themselves ranked as either single vici or groups of vici (depending on their size) within the civitas.[18] An aedile of the vicus of Petuaria (Brough on Humber) is known, though Brough itself may have served as the *caput* of the civitas of the Parisi – if this really existed, which is not certain.[19] *Durobrivae* (Water Newton), a small town in Catuvellaunian territory, is also known to have been a vicus.[20] But certain civil settlements in the military districts, where traders and retired soldiers had combined to form sizeable villages outside forts, were also granted restricted self-government as vici. Examples are known from Hadrian's Wall and its vicinity, where at Old Carlisle a third-century inscription was set up by *vik(anorum) mag(istri)* and at Chesterholm and Housesteads inscriptions mentioning vicani have been found. The system even extended to the Antonine Wall where an altar set up by the vicani living at *Veluniate* (Carriden) has recently been found.[21]

Pagi, on the other hand, were country areas originally inhabited by sub-divisions of the Celtic tribes. We know the names of some of these (p. 77, notes 6, 7), but there are no inscriptions from Roman Britain to throw light on their local organisation. Additional hints are provided by the subdivision of the civitas of the Durotriges, which surely suggests the elevation of one of its pagi to independence, and by the nucleation of the Cantiaci, so evident on the map of Roman Britain, round the two centres of Canterbury and Rochester.

In conclusion, something must be said of the reorganisation of Britain in the fourth century. It is well known that Diocletian effected a complete reform of the administrative system of the empire, the finishing touches to which, especially on the military side, were carried through by Constantine. Their general purpose was the creation of smaller provinces to improve administrative efficiency, and the separation of the military from the civil arm (pp. 260, 382). The resulting multiplication of officials introduced the further necessity of elaborating the rather simple chain of command of the early empire.

Under the Diocletianic Tetrarchy the empire was ruled by two Augusti assisted each by a Caesar: Gaul and Britain were controlled by Constantius, Caesar to Maximian. Administrative responsibility was centralised in the hands of the Praetorian Prefects, whose numbers varied during the first half of the fourth century with the number of emperors; but by degrees a territorial prefecture of the

Gauls became permanently established whether or not an emperor was in the region, and to this the provinces of Britain naturally belonged. Within the prefecture the provinces were divided into groups or dioceses, each controlled by a deputy (*vicarius*) of the prefect. The two Severan provinces of Britain now became four, and these constituted the diocese of Britain under the control of the *vicarius Britanniarum*. If we may judge both from probability and also from the fact that the *praepositus* of the diocesan treasury [22] had his seat there, the headquarters of the Vicar lay in London.

The four provinces of Britain are named in the Verona List, a document which can be closely dated to the years 312–14, as Britannia Prima, Britannia Secunda, Maxima Caesariensis and Flavia Caesariensis. The first two are clear enough, but the curious choice of names for the second pair has given rise to speculation. Collingwood held that they were named after the two Caesars, Flavius Constantius and Galerius Maximianus. But it is hard to see why Galerius, the Caesar of the east, should have been commemorated while the two Augusti were not. An alternative view [23] would explain them as two halves of a short-lived third province entitled Caesariensis, so named after its capital, Caesariensis being the adjective of Caesarea. Though we do not know of any Caesarea in Britain, it is possible that London was given this title after its loyal welcome of Constantius in 296; and it is likely enough that one of the first actions of Constantius was to divide the two-legion command of Upper Britain, giving Chester to a new province centred on London and formed from the southern part of Inferior and the eastern part of Superior. At a later date, but before the time of the Verona list, a further reorganisation would have created two provinces out of Caesariensis, the one named Flavia after Constantius and the other Maxima in honour of the western Augustus, M. Aurelius Valerius Maximianus. If this is so, then the redivision will have taken place before the abdication of Maximian in 305. If London was given the title Caesarea in honour of Constantius it may have been changed to Augusta in that year, when Constantius was elevated to the rank of Augustus: as Augusta it was certainly known later in the century.[24]

Under Diocletian's arrangements the British provinces were all governed by *praesides* of equestrian rank;[25] but later in the century the Notitia shows that Maxima had been promoted in status, for its governor had become a senatorial *consularis*. This may have happened under Constantine, who was the first to reintroduce consulares; but there can be no certainty about the date.

It is not possible to show in any detail where the divisions between these provinces lay, but Dr J. C. Mann [26] has been able to demonstrate that Maxima and Prima were formed from the Severan province of Britannia Superior, and that the capital of Maxima was London, while Prima lay in Wales and the west of England, with its capital almost certainly at Cirencester. The remaining two, Secunda and Flavia, were carved from Britannia Inferior. York can be shown to have been the capital of one and Lincoln of the other, and if the theory of a division of Caesariensis is accepted it would follow that York lay in Britannia Secunda; again, since after Constantius' recovery of Britain the military district of the north was still controlled by a *praeses*, and the command not yet separated under the *dux*, it seems probable that the York province comprised the whole of this district. If so, the Lincoln province may have extended far enough south-east to include the civitas of the Iceni.[27]

That the northern command was at first still in the hands of the praeses is shown by an inscription from Birdoswald recording the restoration of fort buildings under his supervision;[28] subsequently, perhaps still under Diocletian, perhaps later under Constantine, a *dux* was appointed to command the garrison, and the civilian administration was separated. It is uncertain when the office of Count of the Saxon Shore was inaugurated, but it cannot have been before the reign of Constantine, who inaugurated the rank of count (*comes*). The office certainly existed in 367, for in his account of the disasters of that year Ammianus [29] refers to a *comes maritimi tractus* (p. 391), an obvious periphrasis. The problems connected with the *comes Britanniarum*, a third commander known to us in the Notitia, are discussed on pp. 261 and 268f.

In 369 a fifth British province, Valentia, was established. It was so named in honour of the reigning emperors Valentinian and Valens, and came into being as part of Count Theodosius' reconstruction of Britain. The Notitia tells us that it had a consularis as governor; its geographical position, however, is still obscure. The distribution of late Roman pottery assures us that it did not, as has sometimes been suggested, embrace the lowlands of Scotland, for nothing can be more certain than that Hadrian's Wall at this time still marked the limit of Roman Britain. Our choice seems confined either to part of northern England or to North Wales. In the latter area the fort of Caernarvon was rebuilt, but the area is hardly of sufficient importance to warrant a consularis as governor. More likely is the suggestion of Dr J. C. Mann that the York province was now subdivided; Carlisle might well have become the capital of Valentia. This idea is supported by the fact that the title of the Duke in the Notitia is. *dux Britanniarum*, for this implies that his command extended over more than one province, though the forts listed as under his control all lie in northern England.

Much of the revenue of the later empire was collected in kind rather than in cash, under a method of requisition which had grown up in the inflation of the third century and was regularised by Diocletian with his system of annual indictions. When the overall requirements of the empire had been calculated tax-payers were assessed according to their individual code or *iugum*, and the duty of collecting the right total in their areas rested personally on the decurions of each city. This taxation in kind was the responsibility of the Praetorian Prefects, working through their Vicars and the governors of the provinces. The independent financial administration of the procurators of the early empire had disappeared with the merging, in the late third century, of the office of procurator with that of equestrian praeses.

There was, however, a second financial ministry controlled by an officer whose title became *comes sacrarum largitionum*. This ministry combined two departments. One was the *res summa*, which was responsible for such revenue as was still collected in gold and silver as well as for the requisition of clothing or its manufacture in state mills; it also controlled the mints and mines. The other was the *res privata*, which supervised imperial property. Both of these departments had their representatives in Britain, the *rationalis rei privatae per Britannias* and the *rationalis summarum Britanniarum*.[30] In addition, the Notitia records among the subordinates of the comes sacrarum largitionum two other British officials, the head of the treasury in London and the controller of the weaving works at Venta.[31] To judge by what is known elsewhere, the diocesan officers of these two departments disposed a numerous assortment of subordinate staff; but even so, the provincial governors were often required to assist the collection of the revenues concerned. The mint which had been established in London by Carausius continued in operation until 325–6; it was later reopened by Magnus Maximus for the production of gold and silver.

With four provincial governors and a vicarius Britain cannot have been under-administered. It was, however, upon the *curiales* – the decurions of the towns – that the imperial government relied for local implementation of central decisions, for it was the city-councils which had to appoint managers of the public post, supervisors of the state granaries and collectors of taxes in money and in kind, as well as recruiting-officers for both army and other branches of public works; and on them fell the organisation of corvées of compulsory labour and the repair of roads. Not only were such services unpaid but they might even at times be financially oppressive or even ruinous. Any shortage in the amount of taxation due could be legally extracted from the decurion responsible for its collection, and if that failed the whole council had an obligation to underwrite the deficit.

Membership of the councils had long been compulsory for suitably qualified persons and in practice became hereditary, since it was illegal to abandon the position for most other professions. Moreover, initiative was blocked by increasing supervision from above. *Curatores civitatis* had occasionally been appointed even in the early empire as special commissioners to supervise where necessary the administration of local finance; by the early fourth century these appointments had become permanent and universal.

The heavy burdens of personal expenditure, and of legal restriction and compulsory service made the position of decurion increasingly unpopular in the later empire. Those who could secured exemption, and occasionally numbers were made up by the enrolment of other persons as a penalty. Exemptions from curial duties could be obtained by promotion to the higher social status which accompanied the superior ranks of the imperial service, and such promotion could often also be secured on an honorary basis and even by bribery. By degrees the wealthier or more ambitious members of the class secured exemption, and among those that were left it was possible for the richer members to allot the heavier burdens to their poorer colleagues.

All this has some bearing on the problems presented by the prosperous villa of fourth-century Britain. Though we have little information specifically related to the curiales of Britain either in the codes or in the literature, or even from inscriptions, it is clear that decurions were compelled by legislation to live in the cities, and were forbidden to migrate to their estates.[32] These would presumably have to be run by bailiffs. In Britain some of the wealthy villas, for instance in the region of Cirencester, are close enough to the towns for it to have been possible for their owners to commute, and thus carry out their obligations. But the largest, and especially those which though more remote are yet of a luxury which proves occupation by owners, must be presumed to have belonged to families which were exempt from curial obligations, the owners having achieved equestrian or even senatorial rank.[33]

Nor must we forget that Britain was frequently used as a place of exile for distinguished and presumably still wealthy persons in the fourth century.[34] It is even possible that the wealth and comparative security of Britain in the fourth century acted as a magnet to wealth from the continental empire, land being considered a prime investment. These are problems on which little work has yet been undertaken.

1. *ILS*, 1011 (Salvius Liberalis); *ILS*, 1015 (Iavolenus Priscus); *Digest*, xxxvi, 1, 48, quoted by Birley, *Roman Britain and the Roman Army*, p. 51.

2. And cf. the situation in Spain under Augustus: Strabo, iii, 4, 20.

3. Caecilianus, *ILS*, 1123; Valens; *CIL*, xi, 383; Calpurnianus, *ILS*, 1151.

4. See also H. von Petrikovits, *Das römische Rheinland* (Köln, 1960), pp. 72–4. Beneficiarii consularis are attested at Dorchester-on-Thames and Winchester in the civil zone and at Wroxeter, Catterick, Lancaster, Binchester, Greta Bridge, Lanchester, Chesterholm, Housesteads and Risingham in the military area. A strator consularis was buried at Irchester.

5. The 'Marble of Thorigny'; *CIL*, xiii, 3162.

6. This is probably the explanation of the *principia* or headquarters restored by 'Naevius imperial freedman and assistant to the procurators' which is recorded on a third-century inscription found at Combe Down near Bath, *RIB*, 179. An imperial freedman of the time of Marcus Aurelius, named M. Aurelius Marcio, held office as procurator in Britain (*ILS*, 1477) and was thought by Mommsen (*Staatsrecht*, iii, 555, note 1) to have had charge of an imperial estate.

7. *Digest*, i, 16, 9.

8. The other grades were *sexagenarii* (60,000), *centenarii* (100,000) and *trecenarii* (300,000), the last reserved for the heads of the profession in Rome.

9. *ILS*, 1338. Pflaum, *Les Carrières Procuratoriennes Equestres sous le Haut-empire romain* (Paris, 1960), No. 95. It is not certain what or where the Britons of Anavio were. The term Brittones implies northern Britain, and they are likely to have belonged to some area under direct rule, named from a fort. *RIB*, 2243, a milestone from Buxton, reads ANAVIONE M P XI meaning eleven miles from the fort of Brough on Noe; but Richmond (*Archaeologia*, xciii, 42), has shown that this stone must read *a Navione*, 'from Navio'. The river Annan in Dumfriesshire was probably named *ANAVA* (ibid., 22), but the region of Anavio cannot have been there, as southern Scotland lay outside the province between *c.* 105 and 140, nor can Annandale be thought of as Brigantian territory. A different Anava must be sought.

10. E.g., *Nectovelius ... nationis Brigans ... RIB*, 2142.

11. In addition to those cited in *Antiquity*, xxxv (1961), 29–36, see *Germania*, 40 (1962), 83. For a contrary view see J. C. Mann in Jarrett and Dobson, *Britain and Roman* (Kendal, 1966), pp. 109 ff.

12. Wroxeter ... *civitas Cornoviorum* (*RIB*, 288); Cirencester ... *et ins(tituit) (R)espub(lica)* (*RIB*, 114); Kenchester a milestone, *r(es)p(ublica) c(ivitatis) D(obunnorum)* (*RIB*, 2250); Brougham ... *r(es)p(ublica) c(ivitatis) Car(vetiorum)* (*JRS*, lv (1965), 224; Caerwent ... *ex decreto ordinis respubl(ica) civit(atis) Silurum* (*RIB*, 311). The last is the most significant, revealing as it does the whole machinery of government. A sixth, from Brough on Humber, may have attested the *civitas Parisorum*: see *RIB*, 707, for the restoration *C(ivitas) [P(arisorum)]*. Note also the further six, from Hadrian's Wall, listed on p. 198 and p. 218, note 15.

13. The Ravenna Cosmography, compiled in the seventh century from much earlier sources, mentions ten civitas capitals in Britain: *Calleva Atrebatum* (Silchester), *Corinium Dobunnorum* (Cirencester), *Durovernum Cantiacorum* (Canterbury), *Isca Dumnoniorum* (Exeter), *Noviomagus Regnensium* (Chichester), *Ratae Coritanorum* (Leicester), *Venta Belgarum* (Winchester), *Venta Icenorum* (Caistor by Norwich), *Venta Silurum* (Caerwent), *Viroconium Cornoviorum* (Wroxeter). Some of these are confirmed by the early third-century Antonine Itinerary, which adds an eleventh, *Isurium Brigantum* (Aldborough). The Antonine Itinerary refers to Caistor by Norwich as *Icenos* (in the third-century Gallic fashion) in one list, though elsewhere it names it *Venta Icinorum*. Cf. also *Notitia Dignitatum Occ.* xi, 60: *Ventensis*, p. 337 below.

14. *Roman Britain and the English Settlements* (1936), 186.

15. For the *territorium* belonging to an auxiliary fort see *RIB*, 1049.

16. If not indeed sooner: for what appears to be an earlier and smaller forum, erected soon after the Boudiccan rebellion, has been found below the Flavian building.

17. *Durnovaria* (Dorchester) does too, but is nowhere definitely attested as a civitas-capital.

18. Constituent vici are attested in the colonia of Lincoln (*RIB*, 270–1).

19. See, however, *RIB*, 707, for the restoration C(*ivitas*)/[P(*arisorum*)].

20. A mortarium-stamp, *Cunoarus Vico Duro(brivae)* is known from examples at Castor and South Shields.

21. Old Carlisle, *RIB*, 899; Chesterholm, *RIB*, 1700; Housesteads, *RIB*, 1616; Carriden, *JRS*, xlvii (1957), 230. See also pl. 6a for Old Carlisle.

22. *Notitia Dignitatum Occ.* xi. 37: *praepositus thesaurorum Augustensium* [*in Britannis*].

23. An idea first put forward by Bury (*Cambridge Historical Journal*, i (1923), 1–9, and developed by Birley (*Acta et Dissertationes Archaeologicae*, iii (1963), 83–8.

24. Ammianus Marcellinus, xxvii, 8, 7; xxviii, 3, 1.

25. *Praeses* had long been an unofficial word for governor; now it became the official title of equestrian governors. Similarly, men of equestrian rank had been increasingly used during the third century, and especially since the reign of Gallienus, to replace senatorial governors: Diocletian merely brought the process to completion.

26. *Antiquity*, xxxv (1961), 316–20.

27. Dr Mann (op. cit.) has pointed out that the title of the Count of the Saxon Shore, *comes litoris Saxonici per Britannias*, shows that his command, which ran from the Wash to the Solent, overlapped more than one province.

28. *RIB*, 1912; see p. 382.

29. *Ammianus Marcellinus*, xxvii, 8, 1.

30. *Notitia Dignitatum Occ.*, xii, 15 and xi, 20.

31. *Praepositus thesaurorum Augustensium* (*Not. Dig. Occ.*, xi, 37) and *procurator gynaecii in Britannis Ventensis* (*ibid.*, xi, 60); see p. 337 for the identity of Venta.

32. The surviving laws on the subject (Cod. Just. viii. 10.6, Cod. Theod. xii, 18.1, Cod. Just. viii, 10.8, and Cod. Theod. xii, 18.2.), mostly apply to the eastern empire, but it cannot be doubted that the principle was general.

33. On the expansion of these orders in the fourth century see A. H. M. Jones, *The Later Roman Empire* (Oxford, 1964), pp. 525–9, 741. The family of Pelagius, one of the few fourth-century British personalities of whom anything is known, was wealthy enough to send him to study law in Rome; the law was one of the avenues of promotion open to curiales.

34. Palladius, the *magister officiorum*, Ammianus Marcellinus, xxii, 3, 3; Valentinus and others, *ibid.*, xxviii, 3, 4; Frontinus, *ibid.*, xxviii, 1, 21. A similar situation might account for the Lullingstone busts at an earlier period (pp. 312 and 319, note 9).

11

The Roman Army in Britain

The part played by the Roman army in the history of the British provinces is fully discussed in other chapters, and an estimate of its strength has been attempted on pp. 182–6. There were, however, many other ways than the application of military policy in which the substantial garrison stationed in this island affected the life of Roman Britain. For instance, in the highland zone the army formed the only contact between the great majority of the native population and Rome. The merchants who served the garrison were not averse to trading also with the natives, and the successful intercourse of all three is seen in the great expansion of civil vici round the forts in the third and fourth centuries. For this reason, and also because the wealth of military antiquities, available for study in Britain, illustrates the archaeology of the Roman army in a way which is unique in the Roman Empire, a brief account must be given of the organisation and character of the provincial army. Finally, it is necessary to consider the bearing of the Notitia Dignitatum upon the fourth-century forces in Britain.

As is well known, the army of the early empire consisted of two distinct categories of troops. In addition to the legions of Roman citizens, the government made use of forces raised among subject peoples. Even under the Republic, Rome had called upon her allies for help in war; the still wider responsibilities of defence under the empire were far too heavy a burden for the manpower of Italy to shoulder unaided. Furthermore, certain specialist forces, such as cavalry, archers and slingers, could not be raised in Italy in the quality or quantity required. Augustus therefore balanced the legionary forces at his disposal with an approximately equal number of *auxilia*, or lighter-armed auxiliary regiments raised among the provincials.

The legions of citizen troops were recruited at first in Italy, but increasingly after the early second century from citizens in the Danube provinces and in Gaul or Spain, and ultimately from less civilised provinces, such as Britain herself. This was a process due primarily to the spread of Roman citizenship in these regions during the first century; but it was accelerated by the twin facts that the conditions of legionary service became increasingly unattractive to the inhabitants of Italy, while a growing reservoir of men eager to enlist grew up in the neighbourhood of the fortresses themselves among the children of serving soldiers.

A legion had a fighting strength of about 5,300 men, of whom 120 were mounted; in addition, a considerable number belonged to administrative grades. It was organised in ten cohorts, each of which consisted of six centuries, except the first cohort, which was formed of five centuries of double strength. The normal strength of a century was eighty men; they were heavily armed infantry whose strength lay in their weapons, their discipline and their training. Against ill-armed and ill-disciplined native levies – which for the most part was all they had to face in the first two centuries AD – they were irresistible.

The legion was commanded by a Roman senator of praetorian rank (pp. 222–4), who was assisted by six military tribunes. One of these was of senatorial family, a young man at the start of his career (the *tribunus laticlavius*); the remaining five were generally not so youthful, being men of equestrian rank (*tribuni angusti-clavii*), serving in the second of their three *militiae* (p. 227f.). Many of them would therefore tend to be in their thirties; but occasionally an older man, promoted from the centurionate, might be found among them. The duties of the tribunes were largely administrative, though the *tribunus laticlavius* ranked second in command of the legion. The real leadership was provided by the centurions who commanded the fifty-nine centuries composing the legion. These were tough experienced soldiers who had normally reached their position either by promotion from the ranks or, in rare cases, by transfer from the praetorian guard; a few were sometimes appointed directly from civilian life. The centurions were graded according to the seniority of the cohort to which they were attached. The most senior of them served in the first cohort and were known as *primi ordines*, a rank to which the leading centurions of the other cohorts also belonged;

the chief centurion (*primus pilus*) commanded the first century of the first cohort, and held a position of considerable influence and power. The second centurion (*princeps*) had charge of the administrative staff. Vegetius remarks upon the very detailed book-keeping which was maintained by the legionary staff.[1]

The auxiliary troops were not normally Roman citizens: they were raised from among the warlike tribes within the empire, whose capacities could thus be utilised for defence, and were rewarded with citizenship, occasionally after valour in battle, but normally on discharge after twenty-five or more years service. The regularisation of this system seems to be due to a reform of Claudius, and the bronze diplomas certifying individual grants throw useful light, as we have seen (p. 182), on the composition of provincial armies.

The auxiliary forces were not formed into units as large as the legions, but into cohorts (for infantry) and alae (for cavalry), both nominally either 500 or 1,000 strong. The alae were almost all of the smaller size (*alae quingenariae*); but by the late first century a few *alae milliariae* had been formed for exceptional duties at critical points, never more than one being assigned to any one province. The subdivisions of an ala were called *turmae* – sixteen of them in a quingenary ala and twenty-four in a milliary – commanded by decurions. The infantry cohorts were likewise normally of the smaller size (*cohortes quingenariae*), and either consisted solely of infantry (*cohortes peditatae*) or else included a mounted contingent of 120 men (*cohortes equitatae*). Milliary cohorts of double strength were, however, quite commonly found from Flavian times onwards, and they, too, could be either *peditatae* or *equitatae*. Their subdivisions were centuries commanded by centurions. The Dura papyri, which give a detailed picture of the internal organisation of a milliary cohort, suggest that by the early third century considerable changes had taken place in the establishment from that described by Hyginus half a century earlier.[2]

Originating as they did as territorial units, auxiliary regiments in the early empire were often commanded by the local chieftains who had raised them, and they not infrequently served in the area of their homeland. But this system broke down notably in 69 under the stress of loyalties divided by the civil war. Thereafter two steps were taken. Units now rarely served in their home areas (a precaution which it was impossible to maintain except nominally, owing to the difficulties of ensuring other than local recruitment); and, more significantly, they were regularly commanded by Roman officers centrally assigned. These commanders were men of equestrian rank serving their *militiae* (p. 227f.), all of whom held the title of prefect, except those commanding milliary cohorts, who ranked as tribunes.

Several cavalry regiments in the British garrison continued to retain in their titles the memory of the man who first raised them, for instance, the Ala Indiana, the Ala Petriana, etc.; the majority, however – and all the infantry – had territorial titles such as Cohors I Hispanorum, II Pannoniorum, etc.

Originally these regiments consisted almost entirely of men from the area named, the exceptions being a few men and N.C.O.s drafted in to stiffen or train them. A good illustration of this process is provided by Tacitus in his account of a terrible little incident which took place in 83. A cohort of Usipi had been raised in Germany and transferred to Britain: they may have been forcibly enlisted during Domitian's campaign that same year. A regular centurion and soldiers were seconded for training purposes, and these they murdered; next they stole three warships and attempted to sail home round the north of Scotland, suffering great privations from shipwreck and starvation, and being reduced to selective cannibalism, on the way. A few survivors reached the coasts of Germany, but were sold into slavery by their captors, and thus arrived eventually at the Roman frontier to make their story known.[3]

Certain regiments, such as the famous Batavi, were raised from tribes who had a treaty-obligation to provide drafts, and whose taxation was remitted in compensation; and some specialised regiments, such as the Hamian archers from Syria who served in northern Britain, probably managed to maintain their ethnic character.[4] But for the rest, the difficulty of maintaining a flow of recruits from distant sources meant that local enlistment in the area of service soon diluted their original character; they came to be manned by local romanised provincials who were attracted by the prospect of steady employment, and who saw in service an avenue to the citizenship. Indeed, it became not unknown for Roman citizens of provincial origin to serve in the auxiliaries. Thus, gradually the original character of the auxiliary forces changed, as in the calibre of their recruitment they drew closer to that of the legions: they had become part of 'the establishment'.

To remedy this state of affairs a third type of force came into existence during the late first century; these were a new type of national or tribal levy known as the *Numeri*. Like the original *auxilia*, these were regiments raised among barbarian tribes on the fringes of the empire, and transferred for service far from their native land. They were barbarian light-armed fighters, whose recruiting problem could be solved – as had been done earlier with the Batavi – by compulsory drafts levied under treaty. British numeri were serving on the Upper German frontier in the reign of Antoninus Pius, and Sarmatians raised in much the same way were sent to Britain itself in 175. Numeri are not otherwise attested in Britain until the third century (pp. 159, 208), at which period they seem to be mainly drafts sent over from Germany. Later in the century, in 277 or 278, defeated Burgundian and Vandal tribesmen were sent across to Britain in some numbers, and these, too, probably served in numeri. By this date on the Continent, it is true, lands which had become deserted after the great raids were beginning to be resettled with barbarians known as *laeti*: the term implies that they were farmers with a hereditary obligation of military service. But in Britain there is no evidence of deserted lands at this time, and little to suggest barbarian peasant settlements. Such tribesmen as were transferred were more probably drafted as regular forces.[5]

The remaining arm of the Roman forces in Britain was the Classis Britannica. Its headquarters lay at Boulogne, where a number of inscriptions testify to trierarchs and *milites* of the fleet; but during the second century it built another headquarters fort at Dover. It was from time to time used in offensive warfare, such as the Claudian invasion itself, Vespasian's campaign in the south-west, that of Frontinus in Wales or those of Agricola and Severus in the north; but its main and more enduring functions were those of transport and supply, and it is worth remembering that it contained craftsmen skilful enough to be sent to help in building the Hadrianic frontier. Down to the third century these routine functions were naturally concentrated in the English Channel, and it is between Dover and Pevensey that the tiles stamped CL BR are found; in addition to naval bases their distribution indicates involvement of naval personnel with the production of iron and timber. From the third century naval defence for the first time became important, and the system of Saxon Shore forts shows the fleet being given more extended bases to cope with a new situation; for only with the opening of the era of Saxon sea-raiding and its extension by the Irish on the western coasts did the more modern naval duty of ceaseless patrolling devolve upon this fleet – a duty well illustrated in the fourth century by Vegetius' description of the camouflaged scouting craft used for advance-warning. 'Lest the scouting craft should give themselves away by their colour, the sails and ropes are dyed blue like the waves . . . and the sailors wear blue uniforms so that they may scout more secretly by day as well as by night.' [6]

The Roman army on the march in hostile territory was accustomed to build entrenchments for the night: it was as if they carried a walled town in their packs, said Vegetius.[7] These earthworks are known as marching camps, and are quite distinct from forts and fortresses. For one thing, they usually relate to the progress of a campaign rather than to the strategic command of a district;[8] for another, they lack permanent buildings, since the army in the field camped in leather tents.[9] This meant that less space was required per man than in permanent works; a legionary fortress takes up about fifty acres, but a legionary camp [10] about twenty. Roman marching camps are an easily recognisable class of earthwork with their straight sides and rounded corners, and with their entrances defended either by *titula* – a detached length of bank and ditch covering the entrance gap to break up a rush (pl. 6b) – or else by *claviculae*, the curved horn-like extensions of the rampart which projected either inside or outside the entrance, so as to compel attackers to expose their unshielded side to the defenders. The clavicula, in every case that can be dated, is a Flavian device. Great numbers of marching camps are known in Britain, ranging in size from less than 1 acre up to 165 acres at St Leonards and other sites in southern Scotland. Often they have been discovered from the air when all surface traces have disappeared; but many notable examples still survive in Wales and the north virtually as their makers left them, and they form a unique and precious contribution to the study of military antiquities available nowhere else in such variety.

The permanent stations of the legions are termed fortresses. The best known and longest occupied are those of York, Chester and Caerleon, but others, occupied for a shorter time (though in no sense temporary in intention), are known at Lincoln, Gloucester, Wroxeter and Inchtuthil. As already mentioned (pp. 87, 94, 200), there is also a class of 20–30-acre fortresses, perhaps designed for legionary vexillations who may or may not have been accompanied by auxiliaries. Examples lie at Longthorpe, Newton on Trent, Kinvaston, Clyro, Carpow and probably Wall and Malton; apart from Carpow, they seem to belong to the early years of conquest. Only Longthorpe has yet been excavated sufficiently to throw light on the buildings, and thus on the type of garrison which they contained; it had a mixed garrison of legionaries and auxiliary cavalry.

The fortress was the legionary base and headquarters, even if for many decades detachments were absent on other duties, as clearly happened in the second and third centuries at Caerleon. Whenever possible, these fortresses were placed close to navigable rivers for ease of supply – we may recall the pilot of Legio VI, who is recorded on an altar at York [11] – and the site chosen commands the approaches to a wide region; near by lies the civil town which normally grew up to house the traders, the cult-centres and the families of the garrison. At Chester and Caerleon amphitheatres are known, the main purpose of which was to provide for arms-drill under instruction; they emphasise the continual training on which success depended. At Chester excavation has brought to light very interesting traces of a wooden amphitheatre built by Legio II Adiutrix, but replaced in stone on a much larger scale when Legio XX took over the fortress. The fullest plan of a fortress is that recovered by excavation at Inchtuthil; on it can be recognised the regular and disciplined organisation which maintained nearly 6,000 men in 50 acres: the headquarters (*principia*) in whose chapel (*aedes*) the standards and the image of the emperor were housed, the hospital covering 1·3 acres and containing wards for every century, the granaries, the workshop (covering 0·9 acre) and the centurial barracks. Only the legate's house had not been installed, though the ground had been levelled for it, when the moment of evacuation came. Here is presented a picture of a first-century timber fortress with a completeness unique in the Roman world. It has much to teach us of the character of the Roman army and the superiority of its techniques. The supply-problem alone gives sufficient food for thought, when we recollect the seven miles of timber walls required for the main frame of the men's barracks, and the eleven tons of unused iron nails which were buried at evacuation to prevent their falling into native hands;

all this and other material had to be brought up from base during active campaigns.

The forts provided for auxiliary regiments resembled legionary fortresses in miniature. Their size, of course, varied with the accommodation required. Quingenary cohorts, whether *peditatae* or *equitatae*, seem normally to have had forts of 3·5 acres, though there is variation above and below this figure; it seems probable that the former could if necessary fit into a fort only 2·8 acres in area.[12] A milliary cohort could fit a fort of only 4·52 acres, as at Fendoch, but the normal size was about 5 acres. Certainly milliary forts are as large as 6 or even 6·5 acres, but some of these may have had to accommodate extra storage space. A quingenary ala normally occupies a fort of 5·5 acres, but Carzield is almost 2 acres larger than this. Finally, the fort at Stanwix which housed the Ala Petriana Milliaria is 9·3 acres.

These figures are interesting not only because they can help to indicate the size of unit in forts where this is not otherwise attested but also because they illustrate the fact that different Roman armies had quite different rules for field-construction. If we compare these fort–garrison ratios with those of Upper Germany and Raetia we find that there the provision of space was notably more lavish: the fort-areas for the different kinds of unit are consistently larger by a factor of 1·6 or 1·7. Of course, many differences in detail also exist, such as in methods of granary-construction, but these are not nearly so striking – or so hard to explain – as this notable difference in fort-sizes.

The earliest forts in Britain go back to the Claudian period, and at both Great Casterton and Hod Hill they can be seen to lack the back gate and street (*porta and via decumana*) of later forts, and to have the *via principalis* in the middle rather than in the forward part of the fort; these characteristics have been found also in the contemporary fort at Valkenburg in Holland. The range of time covered by Romano-British forts enables us to trace the development of castrametation from these beginnings through the more familiar fort-plans of the Flavian period and second century, and on to the new Shore Forts of the third, in which gates become central once more and the bank, the rounded angles and internal towers by degrees give place to square angles and external bastions together with the omission of the earth rampart behind the wall. This corresponds to the change from an offensive to a defensive attitude of mind which characterised the later Roman army. Its forts in the first and second centuries were primarily bases for the offensive; the Saxon Shore forts and the walled towns of the later empire served as defended strongpoints against invasion (p. 291f.). Nevertheless, the conservatism of the British army is very striking. The new architectural ideas were never applied to the great mass of auxiliary forts; new ones built early in the fourth century, such as Piercebridge or Newton Kyme, and even forts rebuilt in 369 still display the castrametation of two centuries earlier. The earliest stone defensive wall in Britain is that added to the rampart surrounding Inchtuthil. More stone walls were appearing under Trajan and Hadrian, but turf forts continued to be constructed down to the Antonine period. Internal buildings were often still built of timber, even in the middle of the second century; usually, however, the principal range was of masonry, while the barracks were of wood, though even in these there is a tendency during the second century for stone footings to be provided.

Turf-work, indeed, might be called the speciality of the Roman army. We can see it under construction on Trajan's column, and we have Hadrian's own praise of its suitability for military work in his address to the army of Africa.[13] In Britain we have linear works in turf, such as the Cleaven Dyke, the mounds of the Vallum and the Turf Walls of Hadrian and Pius; we also possess a remarkable range of information concerning the ramparts and defensive systems of forts in turf and clay. Much of this knowledge is due to the work of Sir Ian Richmond, who established the angle of incline and thus the height of Hadrian's Turf Wall, and whose exacavations at Glenlochar showed that the turf of that fort's rampart had been fetched from a distance owing to the friability of the turf on the spot. The street-metalling in the fort had been obtained at heavy cost in labour by sieving the subsoil, the separated earth being used for the rampart core. Just as small details like these illuminate the hardships of military life, so the pride of a well-drilled unit can be recognised in the 4-inch spread of gravel – if we remember the raking it would require – which covered the berm between the rampart and the ditch at Glenlochar.

The turf-work of the army of Britain is another feature which distinguishes its practice from that of the army of Upper Germany.

In Britain ramparts were formed of earth or rubble held between facing cheeks of piled turf, which sloped upward at about seventy-five degrees, while in Germany fort-ramparts were often provided with a timber front of horizontal boarding held back by posts.[14]

Nowhere is the contrast between science in defence and the lack of it seen to better advantage than at Hod Hill, where the trim economy of the deadly Roman perimeter may be measured against the bulky ineffectiveness of the Celtic oppidum whose corner it occupies. Despite its enormous rampart and ditch, this oppidum appears to have fallen without difficulty to a Roman assault. The ditches of the Roman fort are only seven instead of thirty feet deep, but are planned to entice and then trap the attacker within the field of fire of javelins hurled from the rampart; the causeways leading to the gateways are (but do not appear to be) wedge-shaped, by which design an attacking rush would be cast off in confusion into the accompanying ditches; and the defence of each gate is aided by the fire of ballistae once mounted on turf platforms in the adjoining rampart. In the third-century defences of High Rochester much heavier emplacements mark the positions of stone-throwing machines (onagri); the balls of such machines, bigger than a man's head, have been found also at Risingham.

Skill in field-construction was valued so highly that both legionary and auxiliary troops were given special training in turf-building. This is the purpose of various small and often otherwise pointless earthworks which have come to be recognised as Practice-camps. In north Wales groups of them exist at Dolddinas about two miles from the fort of Tomen-y-Mur as well as at Tomen-y-Mur itself, and at Rhyd Sarn about two-and-a-half miles from the fort at Caer Gai; in south Wales others can be seen near Loughor and on Gelligaer Common; but by far the largest group, some eighteen in all, lies in central Wales on Llandrindod Common, a short distance south of the fort of Castell Collen. Others have been recognised in northern Britain, the best-known group being on Haltwhistle Common near Hadrian's Wall. It seems probable that these earthworks mark the sites of successive field-day operations. In building turf the chief skill is required at the carefully rounded corners, and at the claviculae or titula protecting the entrances: the majority of practice camps are of the smallest possible size consistent with these requirements.

Legionary troops underwent the same kind of training. Two camps survive from a once larger group at Bootham Stray just out-side York, and at Cawthorn in the same county exist the remains of much more elaborate exercises for constructing not camps but forts, to which two successive vexillations of Legio IX were subjected. More realistic battle-practice was also staged from time to time. At Woden Law in Roxburghshire there are lines of siege-works near a hill-fort, which, since the latter was apparently unoccupied at the time, have been thought to relate to manoeuvres rather than to actual warfare. The same conclusion is possible for the famous siege-camps at Birrenswark in Dumfriesshire. Here the hill-fort was certainly under bombardment from spring-guns firing lead bullets from the great ballista-emplacements which are today so notable a feature of the site (pl. 5a).

A final class of military work has still to be mentioned, the signal stations. Britain is rich in well-preserved examples of the early Roman turf signal-post containing a timber look-out tower, from which messages could be transmitted by semaphore or fire signals;[15] both on the Gask ridge between Strageath and Bertha and in the Stainmore pass the remains of connected systems of such posts can be studied. On Hadrian's Wall the turrets represent a similar ar-rangement in stone, and there are also beacon emplacements on the Antonine Wall. The much larger and stronger signalling emplace-ments of the late fourth century on the Yorkshire coast are precious illustrations of a different type provided for a different purpose; these lie on high headlands, and were intended for liaison with the fleet (p. 395f.).

In all these aspects of the subject Britain is richly provided with illustrations. The Roman army, however, fulfilled an economic as well as a politico-military role in the province. Its mastery of build-ing techniques in wood and stone were of the utmost importance to the growing towns, and there is no doubt also of its role in the diffusion of such arts as sculpture. To a limited extent also the army engaged in industry, and where it did so it led the field in technical ability. The legions made their own tiles and, down to about 120, much of their own pottery. At one period Legio IX seems to have worked a factory at Scalesceugh near Carlisle about which little is known, and similar establishments not yet explored existed near the fortresses of Gloucester and Caerleon. The best known of these military factories is that at Holt, Denbighshire, where a pottery and tilery of Legio xx, covering some twenty acres, lies twelve miles south of Chester beside the River Dee. Here a walled enclosure contained barrack accommodation for some two centuries, while outside it lay a bath-building, workshops, a heated drying shed and a battery of kilns of very advanced design. The whole plant seems to have been especially active in the late first and second centuries, but was not abandoned until the middle of the fourth.

It has sometimes been suggested that the metal-working depot at Wilderspool also belonged to Legio xx, but there is in fact no evidence that it was legionary or even a military establishment at all. The only site known to us where military metal-working was carried out on any scale was at Corbridge. There in the third and fourth centuries two walled compounds were established for legionary artificers seconded at various times from all three legions and engaged in large-scale armament manufacture.

Pottery and tile-making, however, are more widely attested because auxiliary forces played a part in them. A tilery is known at Pen-y-Stryd near the fort of Tomen-y-Mur, and others exist at Muncaster near the fort of Ravenglass and at Grimscar near Slack, while extensive pottery and tile works have recently come to light at Brampton near Carlisle. Pottery was made at Quernmore not far from the fort of Lancaster, and even closer associations of kilns with forts have been proved at Gelligaer and at South Shields. All these must either have been worked by soldiers or at least have been supervised by them. The evidence for military supervision of lead-mines in Derbyshire and Northumberland will be mentioned in Chapter 14 (p. 323), and to it could be added a suggestion of the same thing in Cumberland, where a building outside the fort of Caermote yielded lead-ore.

Immense quantities of leather were required by the army not only for footwear but also for items of uniform, shield-coverings and tents. Recently excavations at Catterick, immediately outside the fort, produced evidence for a depot where leather was prepared on a large scale and equipment manufactured from it during the period 80–120. The implication of this discovery is that the army itself undertook the direct supply of at any rate a large part of its own needs in this field instead of relying upon contractors, the raw material being no doubt delivered at Catterick as part of the taxation imposed upon the Brigantes. That it was delivered on the hoof is suggested by the great quantities of bones which accompanied the debris of manufacture.

Timber in bulk was another requirement, and though we have no evidence for army saw-mills, it cannot be doubted that military needs were met at least partly by establishments worked directly by soldiers. It is possible, indeed, that the sites in the Weald which have yielded stamped tiles of the *Classis Britannica* (p. 252) were concerned with timber for shipbuilding in addition to the production of iron.

Thus, the Roman army engaged in productive industry, mainly for its own purposes; it was as a consumer, however, that it made its greatest mark on the economy of Britain. Its food-requirements stimulated cereal production in the south and introduced it for the first time to some northern regions. Its consumption of pottery had to be met by imports on an enormous scale, and gave prosperity also to the numerous British firms who supplied military markets. Finally, its wealth was a standing attraction to merchants. Thus, the existence of the Roman army in northern Britain and in Wales caused a revolution in previously existing patterns of trade and civilised settlement.

In the late third and early fourth centuries the Roman army was largely reformed by Diocletian, and even greater changes in it were made by Constantine. The purpose of the reforms was partly to ensure the growth of a professional class of officers and partly to promote greater mobility by the creation of a central field army distinct from the static troops on the frontier. To achieve this not only were the civil and military branches of provincial administration almost completely separated but the numbers of legions and other formations were greatly increased; a distinction of precedence was made between the *limitanei* on frontier duties and the *comitatus* (later *comitatenses*) who formed the mobile field army. Later in the century a further distinction was recognised between the regional armies of *comitatenses* and the central core of *palatini* who served under immediate imperial control. In Britain the effect of these measures was soon apparent in the organisation, and even in the composition, of the provincial army.

Much of our information about fourth-century forces is derived from the Notitia Dignitatum. This is a collection of lists enumerating the chains of command, the civil and military officials of the empire, and the various staffs and units controlled by each. There is still disagreement between scholars about the status of this document and the exact date at which it was compiled, but there is little doubt that the lists originated in the offices of the Primicerii Notariorum, whose duty it was to keep such lists for the eastern and western parts of the empire, the lists themselves being based upon 'returns' submitted from time to time by the officials concerned. The most recent view is that the document as we have it was compiled about 395 and subsequently corrected during the next twenty-five or thirty years.[16] Yet those who hold that the Notitia was an official working copy in a government office at a date as late as 420–5 have to face two apparently insuperable difficulties. The first is that some of the lists are patently obsolete, and the second is that many others are hopelessly confused as a result of uncorrected cross-postings and promotions. An alternative and perhaps simpler view sees the Notitia as a copy of an official document of about 395, which subsequently was altered and edited to the best of his ability by some private individual, perhaps engaged on military history, who had no access to up-to-date official files. Both theories involve assumptions, but the second 'will allow us to suppose that there were rational men in the Roman Record Offices',[17] for it does not assume that they used the Notitia as it stands.

The forces in Britain are listed under three commands. In chapter xxviii of the Western Section appear the forts and troops controlled by the *comes litoris Saxonici*, while chapter xl catalogues those of the *dux Britanniarum*. The third army was that of the *comes Britanniarum*, whose headquarters staff is listed in chapter·xxix, though we have to turn to chapter vii, a general distribution of palatini and comitatenses in the West, for details of the infantry and cavalry forces under his control.

This arrangement of forces certainly came into existence only by degrees. We have already noted (p. 240) that, though Diocletian first began the separation of the civil and military arms by instituting *duces* as commanders of frontier armies, the system did not become universal until the reign of Constantine, and that it was quite possibly not until the latter reign that the army of Britain was brought into line. The forces of the *dux* in Britain all ranked as limitanei, and this is the status also of the troops on the Saxon Shore; even the legions were thus graded.

Though the *dux* was probably first appointed by Diocletian or Constantine, it does not follow that the list of regiments assigned to him in the Notitia is as early. This list is in two parts. First comes a catalogue of sixteen units and their forts, all of which (in so far as they can be identified) lie in Durham or Yorkshire, except two in eastern Westmorland (Fig. 11, p. 264). Three of the units are vexillations of cavalry, a new type of formation first appearing in the third century and becoming frequent in the fourth. Two of these vexillations [18] were probably raised initially in the third century, though it seems likely that they reached Britain first under Constantine or even later; the third, the *equites Crispiani*, were clearly first raised under Constantine, since they are named after his son. The remaining units in this first part of the Duke's list are infantry, and apart from Legio VI they consist of ten numeri, only three of which show any sign of being old units. [19] The rest have local or fancy names typical of troops raised during, and perhaps late in, the fourth century, though local names are sometimes found earlier.

The second half of the Duke's list is headed *item per lineam valli* and records the garrisons of the forts of Hadrian's Wall in almost perfect geographical order from east to west, including those on the Cumberland coast, and with the insertion or addition of Chesterholm, Ribchester, *Virosidum* (accepted as Bainbridge) and *Olenacum*, which is here taken to be Lancaster. [20]

There are two curious features of this part of the list. The first is that, with two exceptions which themselves clearly go back to the third century, all the regiments are old-style alae or cohorts; these give the list an old-fashioned appearance which sharply contrasts with the other contents of the Notitia and particularly with the units appearing in the first half of the same chapter. The other is that the garrisons attributed to fourteen forts out of the twenty-three in the catalogue can be shown to have been present there during the third century, and this total might be increased by a further five where at present there is no evidence for the identity of the third-century garrisons.

Nevertheless, the catalogue cannot in fact be the third-century list itself, for in the first place the commanding officers of all infantry units, even cohorts 500 strong, are now *tribuni*; and secondly, at four forts a different garrison is listed from that known in the third century; and at one other, Olenacum, the Ala I Herculea, so named in honour of Maximian, is placed. The true explanation must be that casualties in the struggle between Constantius and Allectus were slight, and that most of the regiments returned comparatively intact to their home forts. The list must therefore represent the garrisons of these forts in the period between 296 and 367. If we are to believe that the same units remained on after 367 in the Wall-forts, we must explain how, in the great disturbances of that and the following year, when the frontier region for the first time suffered much damage despite the presence of its garrison, so great a proportion of regiments should have emerged unscathed and allowed to continue unreformed; and why, if the regiments were the same, the details of Count Theodosius' restoration of their forts should have been so radical as to suggest that a very different type of garrison was then installed (pp. 394–5).

To this view of the date two objections can be raised. One is that the list omits mention of the outpost forts beyond the Wall, which were certainly held in the fourth century, in some cases down to 367. The other is that the forts of Haltonchesters (*Onnum*) and Rudchester are listed as occupied, whereas excavations have suggested that they were not in fact occupied in the period 296–367. The first of these difficulties is not cogent, for other forts in north-west Britain which are known to have been occupied in this period are also omitted.[21] The situation at Haltonchester, and Rudchester, however, cannot yet be fully explained. Either the facts ascertained in the areas excavated are not typical of the whole or else the compiler of the list has made a slip. Why the more southerly forts of *Olenacum*, Ribchester and *Virosidum* [22] should be included in a list *per lineam valli*, it is impossible to explain. All three seem without doubt to have been occupied after 369; at Bainbridge excavations have proved this, while at Ribchester the coins go down to Valens and Gratian and at Lancaster to Arcadius and Honorius. Their significance will be considered shortly.

The list *per lineam valli* itself, then, is best taken to reflect the state of affairs in the period 296–367, even if deficiently. But the first part of the Duke's list must give an altogether later picture; and it is noteworthy that the forts in this part of the list are the only ones to figure in the Duke's insignia at the chapter's head. In the third century the forts catalogued in it had quite different garrisons (as far as they are known), which consisted of alae and cohorts. By the

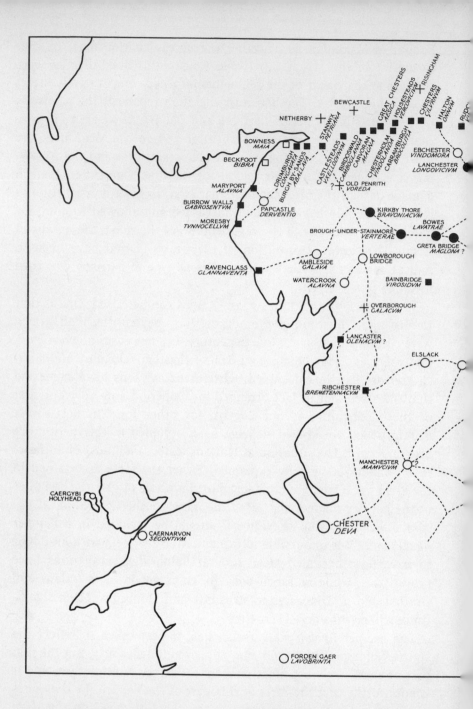

NETHERBY +

BEWCASTLE +

STAINWX
PERIANA +

GREAT CHESTERS
AESICA ✕

HOUSESTEADS
VERCOVICIVM ✕

CHESTERS
CILVRNVM ✕

RISINGHAM ✕

HALTON
ONNVM ✕

RUDC ✕

BOWNESS
MAIA ☐

BECKFOOT
BIBRA ☐

DRUMBURGH
CONGAVATA ■
BURGH BY SANDS
ABALLAVA ■

CASTLESTEADS
VXELODVNVM ■
?

BIRDOSWALD
CAMBOGLANNA ■
CARVORAN
MAGNA ■
CHESTERHOLM
VINDOLANDA ■
CARRAWBURGH
BROCOLITIA ■

EBCHESTER
VINDOMORA ○

LANCHESTER
LONGOVICIVM ○

MARYPORT
ALAVNA ■

BURROW WALLS
GABROSENTVM ■

MORESBY
TVNNOCELLVM ■

PAPCASTLE
DERVENTIO ○

OLD PENRITH
VOREDA +

KIRKBY THORE
BRAVONIACVM ●

BOWES
LAVATRAE ●

BROUGH-UNDER-STAINMORE
VERTERAE ●

GRETA BRIDGE
MAGLONA ? ●

RAVENGLASS
GLANNAVENTA ■

AMBLESIDE
GALAVA ○

LOWBOROUGH
BRIDGE ○

WATERCROOK
ALAVNA ○

BAINBRIDGE
VIROSIDVM ■

OVERBOROUGH
GALACVM +

LANCASTER
OLENACVM ? ■

ELSLACK ○

RIBCHESTER
BREMETENNACVM ■

MANCHESTER
MAMVCIVM ○

CAERGYBI
HOLYHEAD ○

CAERNARVON
SEGONTIVM ○

CHESTER
DEVA ○

FORDEN GAER
LAVOBRINTA ○

11   Map to illustrate the Duke's list in the Notitia Dignitatum
(pp. 261–8, 393–6, 405).

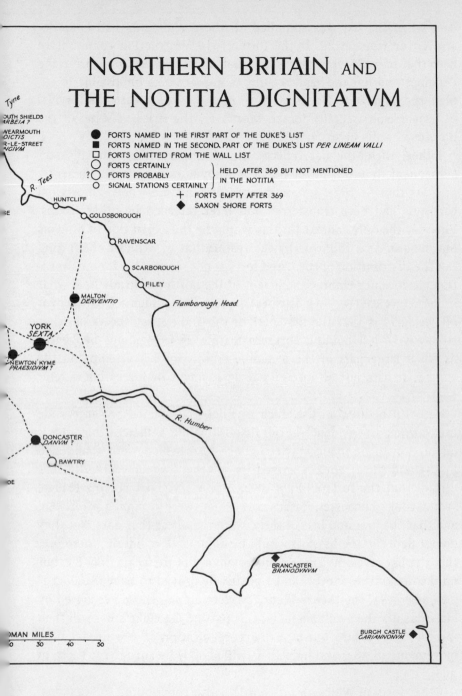

NORTHERN BRITAIN AND
THE NOTITIA DIGNITATVM

● FORTS NAMED IN THE FIRST PART OF THE DUKE'S LIST
■ FORTS NAMED IN THE SECOND PART OF THE DUKE'S LIST *PER LINEAM VALLI*
□ FORTS OMITTED FROM THE WALL LIST
◯ FORTS CERTAINLY
?◯ FORTS PROBABLY — HELD AFTER 369 BUT NOT MENTIONED IN THE NOTITIA
◯ SIGNAL STATIONS CERTAINLY
+ FORTS EMPTY AFTER 369
◆ SAXON SHORE FORTS

Tyne

OUTH SHIELDS
ARBEIA ?

WEARMOUTH
DICTIS

R-LE-STREET
NGIVM

R. Tees

HUNTCLIFF

GE

GOLDSBOROUGH

RAVENSCAR

SCARBOROUGH

FILEY

MALTON
DERVENTIO

Flamborough Head

YORK
SEXTA

NEWTON KYME
PRAESIDIVM ?

R. Humber

DONCASTER
DANVM ?

BAWTRY

OE

BRANCASTER
BRANODVNVM

ROMAN MILES

0   30   40   50

BURGH CASTLE
GARIANNONVM ◆

265

date when the list was compiled all these regiments had been destroyed or transferred. If the former, the destruction cannot have been that of 296; for if we assume that Allectus used troops from the Pennines and left the Wall-regiments in place it is impossible to explain the damage to Hadrian's Wall in 296 coupled with the survival of its garrison virtually intact. Moreover, the titles of some of the units can hardly be so early.

Either, then, the list reflects the situation after some disaster subsequent to 296 (and the only one known to have been sufficiently grave is that of 367–9);[23] or it represents a time when the original garrisons had been transferred and later replaced by other troops. Virtually the only context for this would be the expedition of Magnus Maximus in 383, followed by the restoration by Stilicho about 396. But the distribution of the listed forts is not reasonable for a restoration: it does not embrace sufficient of the north nor firmly hold what it does embrace (Fig. 11). The best explanation, which seems to cover all the facts is that the first part of the Duke's list shows us what troops were left holding northern Britain after Maximus had withdrawn a large part of the available troops for his attempt on the empire. It lists not an intentional deployment of forces but a remnant.[24]

Short of a full coin-list, such as might be yielded by large-scale excavations, the evidence at our disposal is not sufficient to enable a distinction to be made between those forts which were abandoned in 383 and those which survived for another twenty years. But it is certain that the forts of Papcastle, Ambleside, Low Borrow Bridge, Watercrook, Ebchester, Elsack and Ilkley were occupied after 369, and that the first and last of these were rebuilt at that date. Yet they do not figure in the list.[25] It would be difficult to maintain, therefore, that the list gives the Duke's full command in the years 369–83; but until some of these forts can be positively proved to have been occupied after 383, the theory that they were among those evacuated by Maximus fits the available facts; this part of the Duke's list will then merely show us how much of the reorganisation of 369 survived the movements of 383, and indeed, as will shortly be suggested, those of 396.

Other forts in Wales and its borders also contributed to Maximus' expedition. The evacuation of Caernarvon must be attributed to him on the strength of its coin-evidence, and Forden Gaer, which was

266

probably reconstructed in 369, seems to be another, as also do the forts at Brecon and Cardiff. Legio xx from Chester probably formed the nucleus of his force. It is significant that it nowhere appears in the Notitia in either the British or the continental lists, and must have been lost by Maximus, if indeed it had not been previously destroyed in the troubles of 367–9, which seems unlikely. The coin series at Chester diminishes strikingly after Valens (364–78) and Gratian (367–83).

If absence from the Duke's list is accepted as implying evacuation under Magnus Maximus, it seems to follow that the Wall forts cannot have been among those evacuated by him, for they *are* listed, even though the troops shown in them appear to belong to an earlier date. The reason for keeping this list, if it really is out-of-date, is perhaps that it preserves a record of the last regular troops to hold the wall. If Count Theodosius installed *laeti* or *gentiles* (settlements of barbarian irregulars perhaps from abroad) these would not be included in the Duke's command but would be organised in their own tribal groupings under Roman prefects. Chapter xlii of the Notitia, which catalogues the *laeti* and *gentiles* of the western empire, breaks off short before reaching Britain, and thus deprives us of confirmation.

Lancaster, Ribchester and Bainbridge remain to be considered. Though they are wrongly included in the section dealing with the wall, their appearance in the list at all should mean that they were not evacuated by Magnus Maximus. They may therefore be the only three forts held in Valentia after 383. This would account for their appearance in a different section from the rest of the Duke's forces, all of which could well lie in Britannia Secunda. However, the absence of their badges from among the Duke's insignia at the head of chapter xl should mean that their evacuation had occurred before these were compiled. Presumably, then, they were abandoned by Stilicho.

Our conclusion must be that the first part of the Duke's list reflects the position in Britain after 383, though the list as we have it is based on a later 'return'. Indeed, it is unlikely that returns were made to the western primicerius from Britain during Maximus' supremacy; and, as Mommsen first pointed out, the seconding of the chief clerk (*princeps*) of the Duke's staff from that of the Magister Militum is an arrangement which only came about after 395.[26]

From this it is clear that Stilicho's reorganisation of Britain in about 396 did not involve the movement of reinforcements for the *dux* on any scale, for otherwise strategic positions such as Ilkley and Manchester would have figured in the catalogue. Indeed, on the contrary, the evacuation may already have begun.

The list of the Count of the Saxon Shore in chapter xxviii appears to be of the same date (for his princeps, like the Duke's, is appointed from the staff of the Magister Militum), but it too probably reflects an earlier situation, that brought about in 369.[27] The office of Count itself was a development of Constantine, but the appearance of *comites rei militaris*, in charge of regional armies, is first recorded under his sons; and such counts normally commanded comitatenses. It is probable that originally this was true of the Count of the Saxon Shore, whose command, like that of Carausius, may once have covered both sides of the Channel; but by the time of the existing list the comitatenses had been withdrawn, and the continental stations had been re-organised under the *dux tractus Armoricani* and the *dux Belgicae Secundae*.[28] The Count was now in the anomalous position of controlling merely limitanei, and fewer of them than the *dux*. There are other hints, too, that the list is late. One is the presence of Legio II Augusta at Richborough. Under Diocletian the legions were still at full strength, but in later years legionary detachments on permanent posting were upgraded to legions, though they remained at about 1,000 men; the parent formations remained correspondingly reduced in numbers. It is clear that Richborough, a fort of only six acres, could not accommodate more than about 1,000 men; yet the presence there of its *praefectus* (as the commander was now called) shows that it was the headquarters of the legion. Another indication of the lateness of the list is that a former garrison of Pevensey (*Anderita*), the *milites Anderetiani*, is listed in the Notitia under the Duke of Mainz; and the *classis Anderetianorum* lies at Paris.[29] The garrison at Pevensey in chapter xxviii is the *numerus Abulcorum*.

The third commander in Britain, the *comes Britanniarum*,[30] has caused considerable confusion, owing to the belief that his office cannot have been created until after 410.[31] Collingwood was for this reason converted to the view that Britain was re-occupied later in Honorius' reign. 'The last phase of Roman government . . . began in or about 417 and ended some years before 429.' This theory has had considerable influence on subsequent writers,[32] but it has no basis in reality.

There had been at least one *comes Britanniarum* before the middle of the fourth century, when Gratian, father of the emperor Valentinian, commanded the British army in this rank.[33] This was presumably a personal appointment *ad hoc*, perhaps during a crisis which involved the despatch of comitatenses (p. 387f.); for, if there had still been a field army in Britain in 367–9, it is likely that Ammianus' fairly detailed account of the crisis would have mentioned it.

The appointment of permanent *comites* in charge of regional armies of comitatenses belongs to the late fourth or early fifth centuries, but there is no general agreement that the inception of the office dates to a period after 410, as Collingwood held.[34] In the Notitia the Count of Britain commands six cavalry and three infantry regiments, a force of some 6,000 men at the most.[35] Such an army is ludicrously inadequate to the task of recovering Britain after its loss. On the other hand, the list as it stands must date from the reign of Honorius, since one of the cavalry units has the title *equites Honoriani seniores*. Two other of its cavalry units appear to be newly promoted to the comitatenses from the armies of the Duke and the Count of the Saxon Shore;[36] and one of the legions, the Secundani iuniores, may also have been promoted from the limitanei of the latter. The force as a whole must therefore date some years after 396, and it seems reasonable to assign its creation either to Stilicho (as a counter-balance to his withdrawal of large forces of limitanei early in 402 for the defence of Italy – a withdrawal which must have virtually destroyed the commands of both the Duke and the Count of the Saxon Shore) or else to Constantine III when he removed most of the remaining troops in 407 for his invasion of Gaul. But we may bear the possibility in mind that the command was actually established earlier, perhaps by Magnus Maximus, the list as we have it merely reflecting a later situation.

One of the Count's cavalry regiments, the *equites Honoriani seniores*, appear twice in the same chapter of the Notitia, being listed also in Gaul under the *Magister equitum Galliarum*.[37] Time, therefore, has to be allowed for this transfer before the chapter reached its final form about 420. That there were still Roman troops in Britain as late as 409, is apparent from a passage in Zosimus,[38] but their numbers must have been very small. The withdrawals of Stilicho followed by those of Constantine III had left the island virtually denuded of standing forces, and it is easy to understand the necessity for the cities of Britain now to undertake their own defence.

1. Vegetius, ii, 19.

2. Ann Perkins, *The Excavations at Dura-Europos*: Final Report v, part i, *The Parchments and Papyri* (Yale, 1959), p. 28; Hyginus Gromaticus, *de munitione castrorum*, 27.

3. Tacitus, *Agricola*, 28.

4. Good illustrations of Syrian archers in action can be seen on Trajan's column. Cichorius, *Die Reliefs der Traiansäule* (Berlin, 1896–1900), Scene: lxvi, lxx, cviii, cxv; See also I. A. Richmond, *Papers of the British School at Rome*, xiii (1935), 16–17.

5. A settlement of *laeti* may be the explanation of the extremely early commencement-date (perhaps as early as the end of the third century), of the Saxon cemetery outside Caistor by Norwich (J. N. L. Myres and B. Green, *Th Anglo-Saxon Cemeteries of Caistor by Norwich and Markshall, Norfolk*, Oxford, 1973, pp. 43 ff. Otherwise they must be regarded as barbarians who had obtained the *receptio* and had been allowed to settle within the empire in a depopulated region. It has often been suggested that a century later, in 372, a similar transference of Alamannic tribesmen took place under their king Fraomar: this would amount to a settlement of *foederati* in Britain (foederati being free barbarians, under their own rulers, who were allowed to settle under treaty in return for military duties). However, a careful reading of Ammianus Marcellinus, xxix, 4, 7, shows only that after the virtual annihilation of the Bucinobantes (the division of the Alamanni of which he had been made king) Fraomar was transferred to Britain with the rank of tribune to take command of a numerus of Alamanni which was already part of the garrison.

6. Vegetius, iv, 37.

7. *Ibid.*, i, 21.

8. This is well illustrated in parts of Wales, where the camps keep to the high plateaux, where alone large bodies of troops could manoeuvre or encamp, while the permanent forts tend to be sited below, at the junctions of valleys.

9. The Latin equivalent for under canvas was *sub pellibus*; Caesar, *BG*, iii, 29, etc.

10. It is not often possible to be sure for what sized force a camp was prepared; but the problem is settled at Rey Cross, Westmorland, a camp of 20·1 acres, which can be shown by its planning to be intended for a legion (*CW*,² xxxiv (1934), 50).

11. *RIB*, 653.

12. The area is calculated from overall dimensions (rampart-front to rampart-front), even though this means that there will be variations due to differing widths of rampart and intervallum road. Some authorities calculate sizes on internal area, but this method has the great disadvantage that it can only be applied to excavated forts, preventing comparison with unexcavated ones.

13. *ILS*, 2487.

14. At Lincoln the fortress had a rampart of this type.

15. Compare the wooden towers seen on Trajan's Column, Cichorius, op. cit., Scene i; *Papers of t.. British School at Rome*, xiii (1935), 35, fig. 14; Macdonald, *Roman Wall in Scotland* (Oxford, 1934), pl. iv.

16. A. H. M. Jones, *The Later Roman Empir* (Oxford, 1964), iii, Appendix 2.

17. Birley, *Cumberland and Westmorland Antiquarian and Archaeological Society Transactions*,[2] xxxix (1939), 210.

18. The *equites Dalmatae* and the *equites catafractarii*.

19. The numerus barcariorum Tigrisiensium, cf. *RIB*, 601; the numerus Nerviorum, possibly an earlier cohort reformed, according to Birley; and the numerus exploratorum, cf. p. 208.

20. Castlesteads (*Uxellodunum*) and Maryport (*Alauna*, here spelt *Alione*) are out of order, and Bowness (Maia) and Beckfoot (Bibra) are omitted. Alione has been identified with Watercrook, but seems to fit Maryport better. For Lancaster, see note 22 below.

21. Such as Ambleside, Low Borrow Bridge, Watercrook, Overborough and probably Old Penrith. Nor if, in order to explain the absence of the outpost forts, we were to brush aside the difficulty over the survival of the Wall-garrisons and date the list to the period after 369, would the list even then conform to the actual position, since the forts listed on p. 266, equally absent from the list, are known to have been in occupation then.

22. There seems to be no good reason to accept the identification of *Olenacum* with Old Carlisle, th *Olerica* of the Ravenna Cosmography (*Archaeologia*, xciii, 42). In our list it is sandwiched between *Bremetenraco* (Ribchester) and *Virosido* (which is here accepted as Bainbridge on the strength of its garrison). Not only are place-names ending in -*acum* a feature of the west side of the Pennines (*Bremetennacum, Galacum, Bravoniacum*), though not north of the last (Kirkby Thore), but also the list proceeds in geographical order wherever possible. *Olenacum* is a cavalry fort (*Ala I Herculea*); this rules out Ilkley and Low Borrow Bridge, which are too small; but Lancaster would suit very well both in size and in geographical position.

23. D. Hoffmann (*Das Spätrömische Bewegungsheer* (1970), p. 350), well puts the case for a context in 369.

24. J. H. Ward (*Britannia*, iv (1973), 250 ff.), accepts this diffi-

culty but regards the distribution as evidence of a partial reoccupation in the fifth century.

25. The terminal date for Newton Kyme and Manchester within the fourth century is not so certain.

26. The Duke's title of *spectabilis* is another indication of revision no earlier than this date.

27. His command, too, includes units brought over by Count Theodosius (D. Hoffmann, *Das Spätrömische Bewegungsheer* (1970), p. 350).

28. See *Notitia Dignitatum Occ.*, xxxvii, 14, and xxxviii, 7, for two Gallic positions *in litore Saxonico*.

29. Chapters xli, 17, and xlii, 23.

30. His title is described in error as *comes Britanniae* in the heading of chapter xxix, but given correctly in line 4 as well as in chapter vii.

31. Bury in *JRS*, x (1920), 144; Collingwood, *Roman Britain and the English Settlements* (Oxford, 1936), 297–8.

32. E.g., H. M. Chadwick in Norah K. Chadwick, *Studies in Early British History* (Cambridge, 1954), p. 13.

33. Ammianus Marcellinus, xxx, 7, 3.

34. Bury himself, *History of the Later Roman Empire* (London, 1923), i, p. 118, note 3 (three years after his article in *JRS*, x) suggested that the Count of Strasbourg, an officer in every way analogous with the Count of Britain, was appointed as early as 397.

35. A. H. M. Jones, *The Later Roman Empire*, ii, 680–2; iii, 379.

36. The *equites catafractarii iuniores* and the *equites Stablesiani*.

37. Chapter vii, 202 and 172.

38. Zosimus, vi, 1, 2.

12

The towns

Something of the origin and status of the towns of Roman Britain has already been described in Chapter 10. Here their history and character will be discussed, and then an assessment will be made of the part they played in the civilisation of the province.

Urbanisation in any true sense was something new in Britain. Some towns, such as Canterbury, Rochester or Silchester, succeeded pre-Roman oppida on the same spot: others, like Colchester, *Verulamium*, Chichester or Dorchester (Dorset), succeeded their native predecessors on a freshly chosen site near by. In no case did the earlier oppidum possess the true characteristics of a town: its contribution lay in its population or prestige. The choice between building on a new site or retaining the old was decided upon grounds of accessibility and of relationship to the new road-system or to a Roman fort thereon. Dorchester at its river-crossing was a much more suitable site than Maiden Castle, high on its waterless hill-top; but the town may also owe much to an original military establishment on this spot. Colchester was an official foundation for which a new site was needed: that chosen was occupied previously by the legionary fortress, and lay half a mile from the site of Cunobelin's oppidum. Belgic Canterbury already occupied the best local site at the crossing of the Stour, as did Belgic Rochester at the crossing of the Medway: in both these cases it was necessary only to tidy the site by filling in gullies and imposing regular streets. Silchester, though not at a river-crossing, was already an important centre, with no obvious rival in the immediate neighbourhood: it, too, was adapted.

Until recently little was known of the earliest phases of the towns of highest status, the *coloniae*, save that three of them (p. 231) were veteran settlements. Archaeology had revealed only glimpses of these

273

places in their maturity, when their remains differed little from those of other cities. But excavations in Gloucester since 1968 have thrown remarkable light on the earliest period of the *colonia* there: the veterans were accommodated in half-timbered or clay-walled hutments on stone cills, closely following the design and plan of the barracks of the fortress which they succeeded, but built at an even greater density. During subsequent decades these were replaced piecemeal, but only in the middle of the second century did a court-yard house of sophisticated Italianate type first make its appearance. In 1972 excavations in Colchester began to reveal a very similar pattern. There buildings belonging to the fortress, whose defences had been levelled, continued in occupation (with modifications) until destroyed in 60. These discoveries vividly illustrate the role and development of veteran coloniae (p. 98) in a way so far unparalleled in the empire, and emphasise the para-military aspect of their purpose. But colonies could also serve a second intention, as models of urban life: this was the first and most direct way in which the Roman army influenced the civilisation of the province.

The role of the Roman army in the development of towns was two-fold. The first, provision of technical aid, was the fruit of policy. The second, though essentially unintentional, was equally important. Roman forts tended to be placed at strategic points, especially where the new roads crossed rivers. Round them traders' settlements quickly sprang up, for 500 men with money to spend represented a market rarely available elsewhere; but if given time to take root, the settlement remained when the troops moved on. This can be seen to have happened at many sites, such as Chelmsford, Exeter, Cirencester or Water Newton. When the army left, the fort site was conveyed to civilian authority, and the settlement in most cases spread over the site of the demolished military buildings. Even quite small settlements, like Great Casterton, Dorchester on Thames or Brough on Humber, were in this sense official foundations, because army lands were made available to them.

But in another sense we may distinguish between what are sometimes called the large and small towns of Roman Britain, or more accurately (since sizes tend to overlap) between towns which were intended as administrative centres and those which were not. In colonies, municipia and civitas-capitals we can see the hand of the Roman surveyor at work. The streets were laid off on a rectangular grid (pl. 8a), administrative buildings were provided and a distinct effort was sometimes made to provide the colonnaded streets of a classical town. The 'small' towns were not thus treated. They resemble little more than spontaneous village growths and are called towns only because they were walled later in their history. Such small settlements might develop round the stations of the public post, where accommodation and changes of horses were provided at intervals along the principal roads, or they might grow up as local market centres; some, like Bath, owed their prosperity to a thermal establishment of note; others in the north never lost their military connection, but became thriving centres for trade, relaxation and eventual retirement in the immediate vicinity of garrison stations. Such settlements were Carlisle or Corbridge or Kirkby Thore, and the important vici at Housesteads, Chesters or Old Carlisle. Whatever the main reason for their growth, they owed little to official action, save in some cases the original transfer of military land or the occasional presence of government agencies; their prosperity was due to normal economic factors.

With the civitas-capitals it was different. Traders and manufacturers, of course, contributed to their growth, but the government intended also that the ruling classes should play their part in these. Such towns had a social and political as well as an economic role. British society, however, was not by nature town-centred; the tribal aristocrats had their country estates, and needed pressure or encouragement to take up residence in the new towns. Those who had political ambitions would soon conform; in others fashion, the need for education or the requirements of business would gradually induce a willingness to follow. Now that private warfare was no longer possible, wealth could be increased only by investing in new directions, in trade, in urban property or in manufacturing industry. An early example of such investment can be perceived in the Claudian block of shops in insula xɪv at Verulamium, for the individual traders' tenements there form parts of a single larger property of unitary design. Tacitus saw evidence of the success of Agricola's educational policy in the spreading popularity of Roman language and dress, and of porticos, bathing establishments and elegant dinner parties. Nevertheless, conversion to town life was a slow process. At *Verulamium* it may have been exceptionally slow, for there no sizeably luxurious town houses with recognisable dining-rooms are known before the middle of the second century; but even at Canterbury the earliest masonry house dates only from about 100, and at Silchester also those houses which can certainly be recognised as of first-century date are relatively small and simple. Even at its most developed, town life was probably for the landed aristocracy a seasonal activity, as it became again in the sixteenth and later centuries: part of the year will have been spent in the towns on official business, and after the season was over they will have repaired to their estates, where, however, the same slow development of the villa is manifest.

Something of the official nature of the assistance given to the early towns has already been seen in the new forms of building technique and design which were introduced at a very early stage (p. 234). More evidence is provided by the plans of public buildings. In Gaul the forums being built in the Flavian period were often double precincts: an oblong court had two entrances, each set in about the middle of the long sides of the building; one half of the court contained a temple and altar (the *capitolium* of the town); the other half formed the market square backed by the basilica. The forum at *Verulamium* approximates to this type, but it is exceptional in Britain, where the normal forum was not so elaborate. In this the court is much more nearly square, surrounded on three sides by porticos and shops or offices, the fourth being occupied by the basilica. The entrance lies in the centre of the short side facing the basilica, behind which lies a further range of offices. Such a plan bears an obviously close relationship to the principia of a fortress, and is certainly derived from it. This type of building had been developed for administrative convenience, and it served its new purpose well; but the adoption of this rather than the Gallic type shows that architects were not imported from abroad to plan the new cities, and is another indication of the influence of army designers in the government's urbanising programme. The absence of capitolia-precincts shows that resources were not unlimited. Nevertheless, the Romano-British type of forum could be adjusted in size to suit the needs of each city.[1]

The utilisation of building types already introduced by the army can be traced also in the plan of public baths, where the various rooms of graded heat extended in a long line behind a *palaestra* or exercise courtyard, instead of being grouped more compactly alongside it, as for instance at Pompeii. But in the middle of the second century this type of building was already being modified to suit local climate, for at Wroxeter and Caerwent and probably also at Leicester, a large hall was provided to replace the palaestra, so that exercise could be taken under cover. The idea may have been first adopted in the legionary baths at Chester.

Public buildings of this sort, which had prestige value, were, of course, early provided and on a monumental scale, and as their first appearance and later development are important keys to the history of the towns, some details must now be given. Forums and basilicas of the Flavian period have already been discussed (p. 235). Before the end of the first century *Verulamium* had been given a market building in masonry, consisting of a courtyard 136 feet long and 36 feet wide, flanked by two rows of nine shops, and a Romano-Celtic temple also in masonry had been built near by. The Triangular Temple soon followed. The implications of a thriving commerce are striking, for the city already possessed a very large forum. At Silchester the Public Baths are similarly of first-century foundation; there is a possibility that they are earlier than the forum and date from the reign of Cogidubnus (p. 326). At Canterbury a Theatre or Amphitheatre of Romano-Celtic type was provided, perhaps about 90.

The provision and maintenance of public buildings continued unabated for more than a century. At Chichester an amphitheatre was built early in the second century, and at Caistor by Norwich the forum and public baths seem both to have been provided in the reign of Antoninus Pius: the town was then already over fifty years old, and the delay must be attributable to the poverty resulting from the Boudiccan rebellion. At Wroxeter the whole development of the town began later than most, since its site was occupied by the military until about 90. The Forum was built on the site of the unfinished first-century Baths, now demolished to make room for it, perhaps under orders from Hadrian himself.[2] The building bore a dedicatory inscription to him dated 129–30. A previous military occupation of the site is probably also the reason for the Hadrianic date of the forum at Leicester. Certainly this forum and the one at Wroxeter are the only public buildings which can surely be ascribed to his reign, and possibly therefore to the emperor's personal initiative during his British visit. Fresh public baths on a larger scale than those of Silchester were provided at Wroxeter shortly after the middle of the second century on a site immediately opposite the Forum, where they were given a covered exercise hall and a very large open-air swimming bath, and were combined with a shopping precinct and the largest public latrine so far discovered in Britain. The whole insula is a notable example of town-planning. Some time about the year 165 the town-centre and many neighbouring properties were damaged by fire, but the Forum was at once restored, and a new temple of semi-classical design replaced some of the burnt shops farther south.

About ten years earlier a similar disaster had destroyed the Forum at *Verulamium* and all the central part of the town – at least 52 acres; such conflagrations were unavoidable risks when most buildings were half-timbered. But this one proved a blessing in disguise, enabling many improvements to be undertaken. A Theatre was now provided in connection with the Romano-Celtic temple near by, and new temples of classical type were added to the Forum, while the market-hall was remodelled. Somewhat later, perhaps when the town-wall was built in the early third century, two monumental arches were erected across Watling Street to mark the original limits of the town and no doubt to record its status.

At Cirencester the Flavian basilica became badly cracked by settlement of its foundations where they coincided with the buried ditches of the fort below, which had not been noticed by its builders, and was completely reconstructed about the middle of the second century; and perhaps slightly earlier a market square, much larger than the one at *Verulamium*, was added near the forum, possibly in replacement of a first-century timber predecessor.

The reign of Antoninus Pius thus saw great advances in the towns of Britain. Even at Brough on Humber (*Petuaria*), where a small town was developing on or near the site of a fort recently evacuated, a theatre was being built in this reign.[3] At Leicester public Baths, attached to what is probably a covered exercise hall similar to the one at Wroxeter, were begun about 140 and completed some ten years later; and towards the close of the century, the original Forum being found to provide insufficient market space, a big secondary market square and hall were provided north of it on a site where a derelict private house had to be demolished to make space. Thus, all through the second century public buildings were being built or improved, and notable among them are the extra market-places which came to be required. We even find a new town established during the middle of the century at Moridunum, Carmarthen, the capital of the Demetae in west Wales; it was probably based on the military vicus which had grown up there outside the Flavian fort, but now there are signs of a regular system of streets and an amphitheatre was provided. The town was laid out in time to receive the normal provision of earth and then stone defences, at the end of the century (p. 285); they enclosed about 25 acres. Whether a grant of self-government to a new *civitas peregrina* is implied is not yet certain.

As late as about 220 the original earthen theatre at Canterbury was completely remodelled, being transformed into a great masonry building of classical type. But during the third century emphasis shifted to the provision of defensive walls, and no further work is known on public buildings until its close. At that period the forums of both Caistor and Silchester seem to have been reconstructed, the latter certainly after a fire. At *Verulamium* a long porch was provided for the basilica on its Watling Street frontage, the theatre-temple was surrounded by new colonnades and the theatre itself reconstructed and enlarged; the market-hall was also rebuilt at this time, and a third monumental arch was erected, spanning Watling Street between the market and the theatre. At Cirencester the basilica was maintained throughout the fourth century, and alterations were made to the forum as also to the market-square near by; indeed, an additional market-area seems to have been provided behind the basilica by blocking off a street. Only at Wroxeter is a contrary picture given, for there the forum was again destroyed by fire towards the close of the third century and was not rebuilt, and the neighbouring temple seems to have been dismantled; the Baths, however, which may have been involved in the conflagration, continued in use and were again reconstructed.

Public baths seem to call for both aqueducts and drains, two features for which Roman civilisation was famous. In Britain we are less well informed than is appropriate about either. In the case of drains, their materials have often been subsequently robbed away, leaving little evidence of character; moreover, the streets beneath which they lie are less rewarding to the excavator than the buildings each side. Aqueducts, on the other hand, tend to escape identification because of the slight nature of their remains, which are easily destroyed by the plough. At Dorchester, Dorset, and at Wroxeter the water was tapped from streams and then brought into the upper part of the towns along open leets which follow the contours of the neighbouring valleys. For the former the River Frome was tapped more than 9 miles above the town; near Wroxeter the dam which ponded back the Bell Brook at the point of departure is still visible. The Raw Dykes at Leicester have sometimes been taken for an aqueduct, but the shape of the earthwork is that of a navigable canal, leading perhaps to docks.[4] A more remarkable system existed at Lincoln: a spring was tapped about 1¼ miles away, and the water was pumped from this on an uphill course through a pipeline sealed in concrete to withstand pressure; a large reservoir just inside the town wall, and partly supported by it, has recently been identified as the *castellum divisorium*, or distributing tank. Many other towns, such as *Verulamium* or Caerwent, must once have possessed water-supplies by aqueduct, since they show traces of distribution pipes made of hollowed timber jointed together every 4–7 feet by iron collars. At Silchester one of these pipe-lines was traced for about 700 feet across the town and then below the town-wall to a masonry foundation outside. It is possible that a water-tower here fed a gravity distribution system which had been installed before the defences were built.

Surplus water was used to flush the drains. At Wroxeter an overflow duct running along the edge of the main street provided water to flush the house-drains along its course, each of which was provided with a sluice. Analogy suggests that each householder was assigned a particular hour of the day during which he might open his sluice. The fullest evidence, however, for urban drainage comes from Lincoln. Here all the principal streets of the upper town seem to have possessed stone-built sewers big enough for a boy to walk along; into them fed smaller drains from private houses. At intervals man-holes gave access from the streets above when inspection or cleaning became necessary. Sewers of the same sort certainly served at least the larger streets at some other towns, but the system was rarely so complete: sometimes the sewer was originally built to serve some individual building, as at Colchester, or the public baths of Silchester. And at *Verulamium* a large sewer on the Lincoln scale started at the back of the forum and ran down to the river, taking subsidiary drainage from a public latrine and private houses on its way, the latrine itself being permanently flushed by two overflow ducts from elsewhere – perhaps two public fountains near the Theatre. Another sewer ran at right angles to the first along Watling Street, where it was found built into the foundations of a monumental arch; the latter was traversed also by a second channel which probably carried a clean-water supply. Other streets in *Verulamium* had wooden rain-water ducts along their sides which may also have served the houses which they passed; and the same type is known at Canterbury. Even quite small towns sometimes possessed notable drains, as for instance Kenchester.

Much money, it is clear, was spent on the provision and repair of public buildings through the centuries. But the history of a town is more than the history of its public buildings. Private houses and shops in the earliest phases of all the towns were built of cheap materials – usually clay applied to a timber framework, but some-times clay alone – partly because this was a natural architecture in the south-east and one already well proven by the Roman army, and partly because it was less costly than stone and less committing in its finality. In London the debris of a serious fire which devastated at least 65 acres about the year 130 shows that the city even then consisted largely of such buildings, and at *Verulamium* they con-tinued to be built until the fire of *c.* 155. At this city the earliest use of opus signinum for concrete floors does not appear much before 100, and almost no private buildings made use of flint and mortar for a further fifty years. Nor did mosaics make their appearance there much before 150, though at Canterbury slight traces of a destroyed mosaic of the first century have been recorded.[5] The *Verulamium* house-plans of the first and early second centuries are small rect-angular structures some 50–65 feet in length and perhaps half as wide, often set at right angles to the streets and divided into some five or six rooms, of which one or more is floored in rough yellow concrete or opus signinum, the rest in clay.

At Cirencester painted wall plaster has been found in such build-ings as early as Flavian times, and concrete or opus signinum made their appearance as early: here, too, stone began to replace timber-framing for the walls early in the second century if not earlier, doubt-less because of the ready availability of easily worked Cotswold limestone. The earliest houses which can be recognised at Silchester were slightly larger than those of *Verulamium*, being about 80 by

40 feet in dimensions; they sometimes had a corridor or veranda round three if not all four sides, and their timber-framed walls rested on flint footings. A similar style of construction is found later in the second century applied to quite large and luxurious houses at both *Verulamium* and Leicester; in the latter town a wall above its masonry footing was built of unfired clay bricks set in sand,[6] while at *Verulamium* the wall was cast in one piece by tamping the clay between shuttering.

The earliest block of shops at *Verulamium* had been destroyed in the Boudiccan sack. This event was a serious set-back for the town, and there is little indication anywhere of reconstruction for another fifteen years. Eventually, about 75, at roughly the same time as work on the Forum started, the shops in insula xiv were rebuilt on much the same lines as before, and were clearly still in single ownership. The nature of the construction, based on timber sill-beams set beneath the level of the soil, necessitated replacement of timbers every twenty-five years or so. The plans of successive rebuildings, however, show no fundamental change until about 150, by about which date it seems evident that the tenants had been able to acquire their own premises; for the buildings of the fourth reconstruction were much more individualistic, and were set for the first time at right-angles to the street, though still behind a timber colonnade. Shortly after they had been built, the whole street was destroyed by the great fire which has already been mentioned. The clearance which this effected gave opportunity for replanning much of the town, and in the second half of the second century very large private houses, built at least partly in flint and mortar, rendered fire-proof with tile roofs, and richly provided with frescoes, mosaics and tessellated pavements, make their appearance. It is clear that by the Antonine period the wealthy classes at *Verulamium* had been fully converted to town life and now invested large sums in luxurious town mansions. In plan these new houses do not much resemble contemporary villas in the countryside, but nor are they closely planned like the houses in the densely packed towns of the classical south. A Romano-British town-house type had been evolved. Each building seems to have stood in its own grounds, often at the corner of an insula, and was L-shaped, or of courtyard plan, consisting of anything from ten to thirty rooms connected by a corridor. There is little indication of an upper storey.

Verulamium seems to have been slow to grow, for at other towns such developments probably occurred somewhat earlier. At Cirencester parts of quite sizeable masonry houses have been shown to belong to the first half of the second century, and at Canterbury to as early as 100. The earliest buildings in each case, however, are always of clay or half-timber. At Cirencester a block containing timber-framed shops of the Flavian period is known, which is strongly reminiscent of that at *Verulamium* in plan; and here, too, before the middle of the second century it can be suggested that individuals had been able to buy their own premises, since about the time of Hadrian piecemeal conversion into stone was being undertaken in some shops but not in others. Such developments suggest that traders were becoming increasingly prosperous. At Wroxeter wealthy traders, who perhaps had already founded their fortunes in the legionary *canabae*, seem to have been present from the beginning, for detached shops some 70–90 feet long lined the main street of the town, and no multiple blocks have yet been found there.

Not many towns are known to have been provided with defences in the first century. Colchester had no rampart, as Tacitus makes clear, in 60;[7] but the early bank and ditch at *Verulamium*, enclosing about 119 acres, are probably of Claudian date, and Silchester (pl. 7), too, was then defended in similar fashion. There were precedents for the walling of chartered cities, but earth ramparts are difficult to parallel among the towns of the Continent;[8] and in any case it is hard to see why Silchester alone of peregrine towns should have defences at this date, unless this different treatment is due to the town being part of Cogidubnus' realm at th time and not within the province. The late first-century colonies at Lincoln and Gloucester lay inside former legionary fortresses, whose earth ramparts they presumably used; but at Lincoln there is evidence that the rampart, and one of the gates, was later faced with stone some considerable time before the town-wall proper replaced it. This reconstruction may date from the colony's foundation; there are indications of a similar sequence at Gloucester. No defences earlier than its town-wall, apart from the fort, have yet been discovered in London, but a peculiarity of its street-plan may perhaps suggest that they will one day be found.

The other towns of Roman Britain grew up as open settlements, as did the towns of Gaul; but unlike these, they received defences before it was too late. In Gaul, apart from the walled colonies of the Augustan period in Provence, and a few towns dangerously exposed near the frontier which received walls in the later second or early third centuries, the great majority of the towns were still undefended when the barbarian hordes broke over the Rhine in the third quarter of the third century. The walls which were belatedly provided thereafter enclosed only fractions of the areas formerly built-up, and their foundations were largely composed of re-used masonry salvaged from the ruins. In Britain it was different. The town-wall never contain re-used masonry,[9] and the walled areas either comprise the whole town or exclude only outlying parts. It is only rarely, as at Caistor by Norwich (pl. 8a) or Silchester (pl. 7), that a definite shrinkage of the urban area can be attested, and even then the scale of the reductions is not comparable with those across the Channel.

The reason for the contrast is twofold. In the first place, of course, Britain did not suffer such serious inroads as Gaul. But in the second place it is now certain that almost all its towns received a preliminary circumvallation, consisting of an earth rampart and ditch, towards the close of the second century, at the period of their greatest prosperity.[10] When walls were added later it was naturally found easiest to cut back the front of the existing rampart and face it with the wall so that the same ditch could continue in use. In this way the new wall usually enclosed the same area as the rampart which preceded it; but sufficient examples exist where a different line was followed to show that two periods of work are involved and not merely two phases of the same programme,[11] which the dating-evidence in any case shows to be impossible.

Gaul and Britain, therefore, differ in the history of their urban fortifications, and this contrasted picture calls for explanation. Its effect is clear: the town-walls of Britain enclosed living communities, while those of Gaul formed strong-points at the heart of their former selves.

To establish the date of town defences is a task of importance to the historian, partly because once built the walls became a lasting mould, controlling expansion down to Plantagenet times and beyond (pl. 8b); partly because defences themselves are indicative of historical pressures. The *Digest* contains two passages, one of them a rescript of Marcus, which make it clear that towns could not erect defences at pleasure: imperial permission had to be obtained.[12]

284

Their appearance accordingly marks the application of policy, and no doubt anticipates (or follows) unrest. But imperial policy was applied on a wide front. If types of defensive structure can be identified they are more likely to be contemporary than historically haphazard. It follows that the latest date proved among members of a type should guide our dating of the rest.

Various dates in the second half of the second century have been suggested for members of the large group of Romano-British earth ramparts, depending on the evidence which each has produced.[13] The latest suggested dates are *c.* 185 at Dorchester on Thames and 'some years earlier than 200' at Chichester. At Silchester it was *c.* 160–70, and at Exeter *c.* 150. But, as we have seen, a variety of dates for the same phenomenon is very unlikely. Mass provision of earth ramparts for towns is something quite without parallel in the Roman empire, and here they must surely represent the application of a single policy in a single context which demanded the rapid simultaneous fortification of all sizeable settlements. Such a programme could only be carried out at speed in earthwork, on which large corvées could be made to labour. To build walls would be to restrict the work to the availability of skilled workmen, and thus prolong the operation.

Bearing these considerations in mind, and recalling the inherent difficulty of obtaining precisely contemporary dating evidence, we may suggest that the context for all these earthwork defences lies in the unsettled years between the death of Marcus and the recovery of Britain by Severus. Within those years the disturbances of Commodus' reign – the northern invasion and the army unrest – may be thought more remote, less likely, than the attempt of Albinus on the empire and its consequences. Britain was Albinus' base and might become his retreat; and even if a Roman invasion did not materialise, he cannot have failed to foresee the probable results of exposing the province to the barbarians by removing so large a part of the garrison. To give the towns the means of defending themselves would be the corollary, and it is certainly true that no town has yet produced signs of sack at this period. The provision of earth ramparts to protect the towns was a programme which lay within his power, whereas it is doubtful whether masonry walls could have been provided in so many places within the time at his disposal. Such a context would go far to explain the otherwise puzzling incompleteness of the second-century bank and ditch at *Verulamium*. This earthwork had to enclose an exceptionally large area, and if it had not been completed when Severus recovered the province the necessity of doing so would have passed.

At some towns the gates of these defences were probably of wood, as they certainly were at Brough on Humber; but at *Verulamium* and Cirencester monumental gateways of masonry were provided, possibly after the passing of the crisis, incorporating double carriage-ways and projecting drum-towers. These gates are of quite different plan from those later provided for the walls.[14] The only important towns which have so far failed to yield evidence of an earthwork phase in their defences are Colchester, Canterbury, Leicester, and London (p. 283). It is fairly certain that no bank pre-existed on the circuit of the walls in these towns, and if they had earlier banks these must have taken a different line.

The date assigned to the earth ramparts affects the date attributable to the masonry walls which were subsequently added. Until recently these walls themselves were thought to belong to the period of Albinus or Severus, but they must in reality be placed later in the third century. It is certain that the pottery used to date the walls of Silchester, Caerwent and Aldborough[15] has been dated too early, and at other towns, which have been more recently excavated, evidence of a considerably later period has been forthcoming.

At the end of the century a new military architecture was introduced to Britain with the construction of the main series of the Saxon Shore Forts. The walls of these were about twelve feet thick and twenty-five feet high without earth banks behind them, and without internal towers, but possessing projecting towers or bastions in front. The town-walls of Gaul, most of which can be dated within or just before the reign of Diocletian (284–305), were built in the same style. It is noteworthy that with few exceptions the town-walls of Britain belong to an earlier style than these, with internal banks even when, as at Canterbury or Verulamium, the defence was not following an earlier rampart-circuit: if towers were provided they were internal not external.[16] We can be confident that they were built before the reign of Probus (276–82) when the new series of British Shore-forts was begun, but in some cases not long before. Canterbury and Brough on Humber have both yielded coins of about 270 from their ramparts; at Dorchester on Thames pottery indicated a similar date; and the pottery contemporary with the walls of Caerwent and Witherley can hardly be earlier. The walls of Rocester, too, have been dated with fair probability to about this same time.

Some walls were thus certainly being built soon after 270, but it is possible that not all are quite so late. The walls cannot be rigidly divided into types, but it is quite probable that so large a programme of skilled work was spread over a period of thirty years or more, during which time modifications of form were introduced, best recognised in the gates.

The only towns where we have a *terminus ante quem* for the walls are *Verulamium* and London. At *Verulamium* they incorporated the two gates previously built for the earth rampart, but a third gate in contemporary style was provided elsewhere on the circuit where the road to Silchester left the town; this gate had a single carriage-way and two foot-passages, and was flanked by rectangular towers. The date is indicated by a hoard of five coins, ending with one minted in 227–9, which was concealed in the floor of one of the other wall-towers. The hoard is not likely to have been buried later than 240; so the tower – and therefore the wall of which it is a part – was in existence then.[17] The one known gate of Roman London is of very similar design to the new south-west gate of *Verulamium*, and in one of the wall-towers of the circuit were coins and forgers' coin-moulds which indicate a date of *c.* 210–20 for the building. The principal gates of Silchester were also of this design, but the minor north and south gates of the town had only single apertures eleven feet wide set behind deep incurves of the defensive wall and crowned each with a tower above: such was also the type adopted for the south gate of Caistor by Norwich. At Colchester a similar small gate set back behind an incurve has been found, but here the great Balkerne gate with its double carriage-way and two foot-passages facing the road from London belongs to an earlier tradition in which monumental style counted more than defensive capacity. The walls of all these towns have bonding courses of tile or iron-stone.

The walls of Canterbury, Brough and Caerwent have no bonding courses. The known gates at Canterbury are with one exception simple arched openings flush with the walls and only eight feet wide; retaining walls at the rear held up the bank. The gates at Brough on Humber are of almost identical simplicity, though the north gate was slightly set back between rectangular inturns of the wall and carried a tower. The north and south gates at Caerwent closely resemble those of Canterbury, being simple openings just over eight feet wide; but here the east and west gates, bridgin' the main road through the town, may have had double portals like one of the gates of Canterbury, and certainly had two towers.

Though much more evidence is needed, at present it seems possible to suggest that a programme of wall-building was begun in the first half of the third century, perhaps as early as Caracalla, matching the programme of improvement and reconstruction on the military sites of the north, and with the intention of making permanent the earth-work defences already in existence. In this programme London may have received priority of treatment. The *coloniae*, however, stood somewhat apart from it. At Colchester some stretches of the town-wall had been built free-standing at a date thought to be within the period 120–50, and had their rampart added later; but north of the Balkerne Gate the wall and bank are known to be contemporary and datable to the late second century at the earliest: this sounds like an interrupted programme completed only, perhaps, in the crisis of 193–6. Lincoln, on the other hand, and probably Gloucester too, already had narrow stone walls which had been built at or soon after the foundation of these cities as *coloniae*, in order to revet the first-century legionary ramparts which still encircled their sites. At both of them the early narrow wall was later replaced by a wider one; this is probably an early third-century development. At Lincoln there is the additional complication of the so-called 'lower *colonia*', a hitherto suburban area on the steep hillside between the *colonia* and the river Witham, which late in the second century was enclosed with an earth bank topped by a timber palisade, thus doubling the size of the defended area. At a later date, perhaps early in the third century, this bank in turn was cut back to take a stone wall. The latter may be contemporary with the new wide wall round the original *colonia*, but the upper town still retained its southward defences dividing it from the lower enclosure. It will be observed that the lower town at Lincoln exhibits the same defensive history as the general run of Romano-British cities; the existing walls of the *colonia* at the top of the hill were not considered to be sufficient protection. This fact reinforces the view that the earthwork defences of Romano-British cities were provided against a crisis. Lincoln is not alone in presenting a complicated sequence of defences: at Cirencester the late second-century rampart has been found to have been subsequently revetted by a narrow stone wall which was later replaced, though not continuously, by a wider one.

In the early third century, it was still possible to design gateways in monumental style with double carriage-ways and two square towers, or even, though rarely, still to use the plan with drum-towers; later in the century the remaining towns were walled, but now the gate-designs showed an increased concern for security and were made as small as practicable. It is noteworthy that one of the portals of the double west gateway of Silchester was subsequently blocked.

Three towns do not appear to have been walled until the beginning of the fourth century. These are Catterick, Thorpe by Newark and Great Chesterford, and at none of these were banks provided behind. This might be thought to show the influence of the new military architecture, but no external towers seem to have been supplied; the north gate at Great Chesterford was of the Canterbury type.

If the late-third-century walls suggest the growth of danger, this is confirmed by a sudden great and most striking increase in coin hoards buried during the reigns of the two Tetrici, Aurelian, Tacitus and Probus – that is between 270 and 282 – and by the construction of the main series of Saxon Shore forts which soon followed. It is worth recalling also that the forums of Silchester and Wroxeter were burnt down at some point about this period, and that the forum of Caistor by Norwich had to be rebuilt, whatever the cause.

The economic crisis of the late third century was not of sufficient duration to affect the town life of Roman Britain seriously. At *Verulamium* no building activity, apart from two arches and the town wall, can be demonstrated during the first half of the third century, but not much was required now that the half-timbered houses of the early town had been replaced in masonry; for these new buildings could be expected to last at least a century if adequately maintained. The most that can be said is that the crisis may have necessitated the postponement of major reconstruction. About 275, at the height of the crisis, a row of large semi-detached shops of masonry, linked by partial porticoes, were, however, put up along the main street on a site which had remained vacant since the second-century fire. At other towns, such as Cirencester or Caistor by Norwich, both new building and reconstruction seem to have continued perfectly normally throughout the century. The opening decades of the fourth century saw the renewal of a period of structural activity at *Verulamium*. A number of private houses were restored or enlarged at this time, as well as some of the public buildings, and more new large private mansions were built. Here as elsewhere the return of firm government and the restoration of the currency resulted in renewed confidence, while the measures taken by Diocletian and his successors to enforce attention to their duties on the curial class had immediate effects on the residential parts of the towns, whatever their later results might be. There is no doubt that in Britain, whose insularity had preserved it from the worst disasters of the third century, the curial class emerged relatively more prosperous than in many other provinces. Only at Wroxeter does the failure to rebuild the forum, after its late-third-century destruction by fire, suggest a decline of initiative. No doubt the senate house and law courts were transferred to alternative premises. Little is yet known of the structural history of the large private houses which figure prominently on air-photographs of this town, but at least one was rebuilt in the early fourth century. On the site of the forum traces survived of irregular occupation during the fourth century, associated with industrial activities; these show that even if civic magnificence had waned, commercial activity continued unabated. The same phenomenon has been recorded in the lower part of Lincoln; here earlier buildings of some prominence had been dismantled by the fourth century and their place taken by more modest structures which may be shops or workshops. Here again commercial activity continued to flourish, as it did at Cirencester.

Some time after the middle of the fourth century the defences of almost all the towns in Britain were modernised by the addition of projecting towers or bastions to carry defensive artillery. Such towers were closely spaced so that covering fire could be provided along the face of the wall: well-preserved examples can still be seen at many towns in Gaul, with their arched catapult ports at or above the level of the wall-walk. The arrow-firing catapult had an effective range of about 200 yards against concentrations, and could kill individuals at 100 yards. It had long been used by the Roman army in the field and for the defence of forts, but the third century witnessed a change of tactics arising from the greater numbers and stronger organisation of the barbarian enemies who had now to be encountered. The

Roman army was compelled to adopt a defensive role, and the manning of well-defended strong-points became of greater importance than in former times, when forts had been designed as bases for the offensive. This change is well illustrated in the design of the new Saxon Shore forts in Britain (p. 255f.), where the value of artillery for defence had been appreciated from the late third century. Now this defence was applied to the towns; but the addition of bastions normally necessitated filling up the old ditch, which ran too close to the wall to allow room for towers, and a new ditch was dug farther out, often 60 or 100 feet wide, whose purpose was to disrupt and halt the enemy within convenient catapult range. The new towers vary in shape and size from town to town. They may be rectangular, pentagonal, pear-shaped or semicircular, and either solid or hollow; but all are additions to the original wall,[18] and many contain large blocks of stone taken from earlier buildings or tombs.

When did this development occur? It was certainly the result of a single decision (though several years may have elapsed before it was fully implemented), and accordingly, the latest date for any bastion should help to date the rest. A coin of 330–5 was found below a bastion at Caerwent, and at Aldborough the early ditch, obliterated to make way for the bastions, contained pottery down to the middle of the fourth century. Similar evidence has come from Chichester. But it was the excavations at Great Casterton which throw more decisive light on the problem, for here two coins minted between 354 and 358 were found associated with two different bastions. Accordingly, they can hardly have been put up before 360; and, bearing in mind the limitations of archaeological dating-evidence and the scarcity of coins of the House of Valentinian in Britain before 369, we can hardly doubt that this reorganisation of the town-defences of Britain was the work of Count Theodosius. He it was who recovered Britain in that year from the chaos and disorder of the great barbarian invasions of 367, and we have the record of Ammianus that he restored the towns.[19] His other achievements in Britain are discussed on pp. 395 ff; there is some evidence to suggest that garrisons were now provided to man the new urban defences, just as troops were certainly stationed in some of the towns of Gaul.

A noteworthy fact is that even quite small walled towns were included in the programme, and there is no doubt, therefore, of their continued value to the imperial government. Many no doubt contained official store-houses for the collection of military supplies and the posting-stations of the *cursus publicus*; but the proliferation of fortified strong-points scattered generally throughout the province also served a more general purpose. The barbarian forces of this period were formidable enemies in the field, but they lacked the ability and means to take fortified places if these were defended.[20] Moreover, invading barbarians lacked the elaborate supply-system of the Roman army and depended on forage during raids. If supplies of corn and livestock could be denied them by concentration within defended walls they could do nothing but starve or retreat. Strong, up-to-date urban defences thus had a strategic as well as a tactical role in the defence of Britain, and their provision certainly enabled the towns to hold out far into the fifth century, long after the official garrison had been withdrawn (pp. 420–22).

To modern eyes the towns of Roman Britain seem very small. London within its walls had an area of only 330 acres, Cirencester 240, and *Verulamium* and Wroxeter about 200 each. And these towns were twice the size of the remainder. Winchester with 138 acres and Canterbury with 130 were still larger than normal; and a more numerous group – Colchester, Chichester, Leicester, Silchester and Exeter – were about 100 acres (the first a little more, the last a little less). Aldborough with 60 fell considerably short. Two civitas-capitals and two coloniae were smaller still; but there were geographical and historical reasons to account for the small size of Caerwent (44 acres) and Caistor by Norwich (35), while Gloucester (46) and Lincoln (41) originated in veteran settlements tightly packed within the ramparts of former legionary fortresses. It is noteworthy that Lincoln expanded to normal size, for the extended rampart encloses 97 acres. Silchester, however, was unable to make full use of the 230 acres enclosed by the Outer Earthwork, and when the new rampart was built it reduced the town to 100 acres.

The walled areas represent what it was economical to defend in the third century. Many towns must once have been larger: Canterbury possessed a suburb across the River Stour which was excluded, as was ribbon development along the Richborough road. Extramural ribbon-development was excluded at Colchester too, and no doubt at many other towns. Small though they appear by modern standards, however, the majority were not excessively small among contemporary provincial towns. Roman Paris in its heyday occupied about 135 acres and Cologne 240; the walls of Avenches enclosed 375 acres, but the built-up area within occupied much less than half of this. Nor were they unduly small by medieval standards, for in most cases the Roman town walls defined the lines taken by their medieval successors. There is plenty of evidence that the towns fulfilled their purpose as centres of trade and administration as well as could be expected in a province initially quite un-accustomed to town life, and that, at least by the fourth century, developing commercial activity was providing a spontaneous impetus which more than counter-balanced any failure of the aristocracies to identify themselves completely with the town.

The ordo of a civitas normally consisted of 100 decurions, to judge by evidence from other provinces. There is indirect evidence to support this figure in Britain. The central room in the range of offices behind the basilica at Silchester, which is usually identified as the *curia*, was large enough to seat 108; but if, as is more likely, this chamber was really the shrine where the Tutela goddess and imperial images were housed, there is another hall of even larger size close by which would suit the meetings of the ordo even better. At Caerwent the central room, only 30 feet square, is hardly large enough for a full ordo, and like its counterpart at Silchester was open to the basilica; but the next room to the west could hold 110 seats comfortably. At Wroxeter a similar situation is found.

Nothing thus prevents an assumption that the normal ordo was composed of 100 decurions. But no town shows anything approaching 100 contemporary wealthy houses inside its walls. At Silchester and Caerwent, whose plans are most fully known, there are perhaps twenty-five such houses; and this suggests that in these places perhaps only a quarter of the curial class took up urban residence, the others remaining based upon their estates. It is not uncommon to find villas distributed in clear relationship with towns. At Wroxeter the number of wealthy houses may have been higher than at Silchester, and Sir Ian Richmond has suggested that here exceptional conditions obtained, causing the wealthier classes to be concentrated in the town owing to the proximity of the unsettled hill-folk of Wales: there is certainly a scarcity of villas in Cornovian territory. But at *Verulamium* also it is likely that a larger number of wealthy magnates lived in the town, and here, too, there is a dearth of large villas in the neighbourhood. It may be that at Cirencester, when the plan is better known, the same will be found true, though in this case there are some fifteen villas within 10 miles of the city.

The commercial character of the towns is illustrated partly by the shops which lined the forums and main streets, and partly by exceptional discoveries such as were made in the Wroxeter forum. Here the second-century fire overwhelmed the stalls of traders which had set up in the eastern portico, and piles of mortaria and samian vessels, and even a crate of whetstones, were discovered lying where they had fallen. These finds suggest the busy activity of a market day. Some of the chambers round the forum courtyard were evidently used for official purposes, and some perhaps as shrines or meeting-rooms for guilds; but many were undoubtedly let out as shops.

At Silchester the Rev. James Joyce, who excavated the forum in the years following 1866 with a skill greatly in advance of his time, recorded the contents of each: in one a 'singular quantity of coins' and niches in the walls which might have held strong-boxes; in a second a small bar of silver partly used; in three others the remains of numerous steelyards; in yet another the spurs of game-cocks with the skulls of four dogs buried in the floor; and in the shop next door a pottery pan, two feet in diameter, built into the corner. One of the compartments in the forum of Caerwent produced remains suggestive of an oyster-bar.

The shops which lined the main streets were often the quarters of manufacturing craftsmen who made goods to order. At *Verulamium* considerable evidence was found of bronze casting and engraving in some of the shops, where perhaps cooking utensils were turned on the lathe; in others blacksmiths had worked, and in yet another the discovery of crucibles containing a residue of gold pointed to a working jeweller.[21] In two others ovens and a long-handled shovel suggested bakers. Similar evidence comes from Cirencester, while at Caistor by Norwich and Wroxeter there is evidence for glass porduction on a small scale, and at York for the carving of jet ornaments. The craftsman Basilis, whose stamp has been found on three table-knives from London, no doubt had a similar sort of workshop.

Trade in foodstuffs, clothing and other perishables usually leaves less traces in the ground, though documentary evidence of the medieval period shows the large part played by such merchants.[22] At Cirencester part of the market-square was thought to have been occupied by butchers from the number of bones buried, and at Canterbury and London portions of large donkey-mills point to wholesale production of flour. On the Continent traders often formed themselves into Corporations (*collegia*), for example that of the butchers, who set up an inscription to Tiberius at Périgueux. In Britain we can point to only five such guilds, a *collegium peregrinorum* at Silchester, examples at Caerwent, Bath and York of type unspecified, and a *collegium fabrorum* at Chichester. The latter, a guild of artificers with many parallels on the Continent, is remarkable for the date of its appearance: it figures on the temple-inscription erected under Cogidubnus, and is important evidence of that king's early and successful efforts to introduce Roman institutions. We cannot doubt that many more such guilds existed. Their purpose was partly to further the commercial interests of their members (though their political activity was much more circumscribed than that of modern trades unions), and partly to fulfil a philanthropic or social aim. Guild feasts were held, and members' subscriptions entitled them to decent burial at the guild's expense.

At some towns other, larger, industries existed, but little is known of them in detail. Many, perhaps all, of the principal towns possessed considerable tileries and potteries in their immediate vicinity. Examples of these are known at Colchester, Lincoln and Canterbury, while near Gloucester a municipal tilery was responsible for tiles stamped *R(ei) P(ublicae) G(levensium)*, sometimes with the names of the duoviri added. Outside Canterbury a Roman chalk quarry is known, and very large stone quarries must have been in operation in the near neighbourhood of such towns as Bath, Cirencester, Wroxeter or Lincoln: an example is known at Sibson near Water Newton. Timber, too, must have been in great demand. The discovery of large deposits of bones from the heads of cattle at both Silchester and Leicester points to tanning as a local industry, and certainly leather, both for clothing and footwear, will have been in demand almost everywhere. At Silchester, too, the remains of boiling vats in an area near the west gate has been thought to suggest a cloth-dyeing quarter.

The mere existence of such industries must show that a sizeable artisan element should be included in any estimate of the population of a town. Slaves, too, undoubtedly existed in some numbers as the domestic staff of large houses and probably also in certain industries;[23] but there is little evidence for large-scale employment of freedmen in commercial enterprises by British proprietors, such as is well attested abroad. Some, however, appear to have been employed in the pottery industry, as for instance the five Sexti Valerii (with different cognomina) at Colchester, who stamped mortaria (p. 326). At *Verulamium* a large house, built in Antonine times, was clearly divided into domestic quarters at the back and commercial premises along the street-front, somewhat after the Italian manner; and we may suppose that freedmen were set up in business here, just as there is a possibility that the early shops in insula xiv, all of which show signs of single ownership, were thus let out. But such suggestive evidence is rare. The majority of shops were single buildings, most probably owned by their proprietors. The freedmen whose names we do know, for instance in the lead industry, are clearly either imperial freedmen or the representatives of Gaulish or Italian capital. Nothing is known of the status of artisans, but from the fact that many of them were literate, we may suppose them free.

The total population of the towns is hard to estimate owing to deficiency of evidence. Only at Silchester and Caerwent have we anything like a complete town-plan, but at neither is much known about the contemporaneity of buildings owing to the inadequate technique of the early excavators who first revealed them. The population of Silchester was reckoned by Sir Ian Richmond as not less than 2,500 on the showing of the plan, and possibly twice or thrice this figure on the assumption that many wooden buildings were missed by the excavators. Mr George Boon has estimated 4,000. A somewhat similar figure – between 2,000 and 3,000 – has been suggested for Caerwent. A very rough calculation shows that the amphitheatre at Silchester could accommodate something like 2,700 seats: this might approximate to the adult population of the town. The Colonies of Colchester, Lincoln and Gloucester, on the other hand, being official foundations where more purely Roman ideas of town-planning may have been applied, were probably closely built up; comparison with other coloniae of known size and settlement suggests that Colchester may have had an initial population approaching 15,000 and Lincoln and Gloucester perhaps something like 5,000 each, figures which may well have dropped towards the provincial average for towns of their sizes as time went on. Tacitus assesses the total casualties at London, *Verulamium* and Colchester during the

Boudiccan sack at 70,000, and his language suggests use of an official source. Even if exaggerated, this figure supports a population for Colchester and even *Verulamium* of about 15,000 each, and perhaps one as large as 30,000 for London.

Some check can be provided for these estimates from the population figures of those medieval towns which were still surrounded by their Roman walls. In the last quarter of the fourteenth century the estimated population of Canterbury was 3,800, Colchester 4,400, Exeter 2,300, Winchester 2,100 and Chichester 1,300; but at this period numbers had been much reduced by plague.[24] Elizabethan Leicester, it has been said, 'had no obvious means of livelihood'; it was not an industrial town, but throve by providing services to the countryside.[25] In this it invites comparison with Romano-British Ratae. In the sixteenth century its population was about 3,000, and before the Black Death had been over a thousand more. Shrewsbury, in some sense the successor of Wroxeter, had a population of 4,000 in 1545, as did Gloucester: only one provincial town in England at this time contained more than 10,000 people, and not more than fourteen others exceeded 5,000. Professor Hoskins has shown that a considerable number were at the level of 3,000–4,000 each, but that there were also a great number of active market towns with populations of about 1,500. All this by inference throws welcome light on the situation in these towns in Roman times. A few great towns like Cirencester or *Verulamium* or Colchester may have approached 20,000, but estimates of about 5,000 for the larger and 2,000–3,000 for the smaller civitas-capitals will not be wildly wrong, while the other walled centres may have had populations ranging down from 1,500 to as few as 300–500, depending on their size and function.

The larger towns were probably more cosmopolitan than our limited evidence allows us positively to assert. London in particular was the centre of a wide commerce with the continental ports and river systems, and its temples to Mithras and Isis reflect this aspect of its life. Greeks are attested at Lincoln and Carlisle as well as London, and a Caledonian set up an inscription at Colchester. Gauls are known in five towns. At Bath lived a lady from Metz, a stone-mason from Chartres and another man from the Moselle valley near Trier. M. Nonius Romanus at Caerwent also seems to have been a Rhinelander to judge by the deity he worshipped. At York one of the Seviri Augustales, despite his Greek name, was a native of Bourges

(p. 365) and was married to a lady from Sardinia; other Gauls are known at Lincoln and Cirencester. When we remember the scarcity of inscribed evidence at the majority of towns we may well believe that these are a small sample.

Many such men will have been engaged in trade, for instance the import of wine or pottery; but others will certainly have come over as teachers [26] and as purveyors of the arts, whose influence was quickly assimilated by local talent. Sculptors' workshops certainly existed in some towns (p. 358), and both mosaicists and fresco-painters were similarly based. From the towns their products, and the classical influence which they represented, reached out to the wealthy villa-owners in the surrounding districts, while the more humdrum products of trade and industry penetrated through the periodic markets to the poorest peasants of the deepest countryside.

1. The forum of Caerwent, a town of only 44 acres, measures only 251 by 182 feet; that of Silchester 313 by 275 feet; that of Wroxeter 394 by 265 feet; that at Cirencester 550 by 345 feet. The forum of London may have been even bigger.

2. This failure to complete the early baths at Wroxeter is often taken as a mark of civic bankruptcy, and it is difficult to explain it otherwise if the building was civic. But since the impetus to urbanisation in civitas-capitals was government policy, such a failure would be very remarkable, and adds support to the alternative explanation, suggested on p. 140, that the building was military. Public Baths were not normally provided in towns before the Forum: Silchester is an exception, which may be due, as suggested, to its lying in Cogidubnus' realm.

3. This theatre has not yet been found, but is attested on an inscription, *RIB*, 707, see p. 238.

4. Moreover, the level of the water is 20 feet below that of the Public Baths only 1¼ miles away; for an aqueduct this is an incredible error when water was available over 50 feet higher at a hardly greater distance from the town.

5. Other second-century mosaics are known at Silchester and Caerwent (D. J. Smith in A. L. F. Rivet (ed.) *The Roman Villa in* (1969), p. 77).

6. Unfired clay-brick construction over stone footings was found during 1965 in the earliest period at *Camulodunum*, in a building destroyed in the Boudiccan rebellion.

7. The defences of the fortress which previously occupied the site had apparently been levelled when the *colonia* was founded (*Britannia*, iv (1973), p. 302).

8. There seems to have been an earth rampart, of uncertain date, at Cologne; it may be pre-colonial. Aventicum, walled *c.* 74, had no bank.

9. The only exception seems to be the late wall (probably of the late third or fourth century) round the lower colony at Lincoln; re-used stones at Bath and Kenchester almost certainly came from bastions added in the second half of the fourth century.

10. A few had been defended earlier. At *Verulamium* the first-century defence had become obsolete by about the end of Trajan's reign and was filled in. At Silchester two successive circuits of earth-work have been attributed to the reign of Cogidubnus. At Brough on Humber earthwork defences were provided in the Hadrianic period; but it may be that Brough was still an Army supply-depot. The bank at Caerwent has been described as first-century, but it contains pottery down to the end of the second century (*Archaeologia Cambrensis*, ciii (1954), 59, where the section has clearly been misinterpreted).

11. *Verulamium* is the best example, but at Caistor by Norwich an air-photograph shows ditches on a different line, as does one at Mildenhall (Wilts); and at Brough on Humber the first bank en-closed a larger area than the second. At Caerwent the wall was built over the earlier ditch in parts of the circuit.

12. *Digest*, l, x, 6. *De operibus, quae in muris vel portis vel rebus publicis fiunt, aut si muri exstruantur, divus Marcus rescripsit praesi-dem aditum consulere principem debere.* Cf. *ibid.*, 1, viii, 9, 4.

13. In the absence of inscriptions, the date can only be shown to be later than the latest coin or datable sherd contained in the bank or sealed by it; but there can be no guarantee that such objects were not already old when buried.

14. The east gate at Lincoln is of similar pattern, and it, too, shows signs of being earlier than the widened town-wall. Similar gates had been provided a little earlier at the fort of Castell Collen, and a nearly contemporary example exists at Risingham.

15. The foundation-trench at Aldborough yielded a coin fairly certainly attributable to Julia Domna.

16. The style is still that of the second-century fort-defences of the Roman army in Britain.

17. It was certainly in existence before *c.* 275–85, as another coin-hoard shows; for by then this particular tower had collapsed owing to weak foundations and the second coin hoard was buried in the ruins.

18. The only apparent exceptions are those at *Verulamium* and Caistor by Norwich. Re-examination would probably show that these, too, are additions, perhaps being bonded into a wall face already decayed; for the walls at both these towns are of flint and mortar, which is quick to crumble.

19. Ammianus Marcellinus xxviii. 3.2. *in integrum restituit civitates*; *ibid*. 3.7: *instaurabat urbes*.

20. Fritigern leader of the Goths, *c.* 376, is reported to have said: 'For my part I am at peace with walls.' Ammianus Marcellinus, xxxi, 6, 4.

21. Gold-crucibles have also been found at Cirencester and London. We may recall the inscription from Norton: *Feliciter sit genio loci. Servule utere felix tabernam aureficinam* (*RIB*, 712).

22. It is worth noting that a list of the principal traders of Coventry, Northampton and Leicester in the early sixteenth century, as compiled by W. G. Hoskins (*Provincial England* (London, 1964), p. 79), includes the following: Bakers, Builders, Butchers, Drapers, Dyers, Fullers, Mercers, Millers, Shoe-makers, Tanners, Tailors and Weavers. We have no such records for Roman Britain, but the probable importance of these trades should not be forgotten, despite the difficulty of identifying undoubted archaeological traces.

23. See the inscription quoted in note 21 above.

24. See J. C. Russell, *British Medieval Population* (Albuquerque, 1948), especially chapters vi and xi. Even if inaccurate, these figures are useful as a guide.

25. W. G. Hoskins, *Provincial England* (London, 1964), p. 88.

26. *Gallia causidicos docuit facunda Britannos*, Juvenal, xv, 111.

13
The countryside

Cultivation of the soil had been the most prominent feature of the economy of southern Britain during the Iron Age, and towards its close the Belgic kingdoms had even produced an exportable surplus of corn, as we learn from Strabo.[1] Both villages and isolated farms are found in the earlier part of the Iron Age; it is possible that the Belgae made greater use of the isolated farm, to judge by the large numbers of them which Caesar saw in the south-east.[2] After the Roman conquest cultivation was intensified and certain improvements were introduced.

The new colonies at Colchester, Lincoln and Gloucester were designed to give retired veterans a stake in the land; they lived for the most part in the town, but cultivated allotments in the surrounding country. The normal method of land-division in such cases was centuriation, a carefully surveyed partition of the territorium into rectangular plots like a chess-board. No certain traces of this system have survived in the neighbourhood of the British colonies, but Tacitus describes the expropriation of Trivantian natives in the territory of Camulodunum, and we need not doubt that colonial allotments existed round these three towns. In the immediate radius of quite a number of others, too, it has been noted that villas are rare, as for instance Canterbury, Silchester, London or Caistor by Norwich; so perhaps it was normal for the inhabitants of towns to cultivate farms and market-gardens in the neighbourhood, though without centuriation.

Apart from these areas, however, the pattern of agricultural exploitation in Roman Britain as revealed by the archaeological record is on two levels. Peasant settlements, whether villages or single farmsteads, still broadly continue and develop the pre-Roman pattern in all areas, and in some they form the principal or only agricultural manifestation. In addition, and at a higher level of culture and comfort, we find Romanised buildings known as villas. These became more frequent as time went on. They can be seen as a new system growing up beside, and out of, the old. On the one hand, they clearly continue the tradition of the old isolated Celtic-farmstead, but on the other, they exhibit new features in their quick adoption of Roman techniques and in their capacity to exploit new opportunities. They represent the application of capital by individual owners breaking free to some extent from the past, while the peasant settlements show the continuing rule of custom, and the cramped development imposed by traditional land-working and subdivision by inheritance. The villas belonged to men of wealth and enterprise, who could sell the timber from their estates and then cultivate the richer soils exposed; who could appreciate and exploit the superior profitability of sheep and stock-raising over arable farming, when organised on a large scale as only a big landowner could. It must not be forgotten that land was one of the safest and most sought-after investments in the ancient world. Though some of the villa-owners may have been speculators from other provinces or their agents, and others retired centurions from the garrison, the vast majority were the wealthier members of native British civitates. The very simplicity and slow development of the majority of early villas makes this clear. Such people had close political and business connections with the towns, and they needed the new roads to convey their produce thither. As a result, the villas tend to cluster in the vicinity of towns and to lie not too far from roads: they are not as ubiquitous as peasant farmsteads nor so purely rural.

The peasant settlements continued to use the 'Celtic' field system (pl. 10b), and even in some cases grain-storage pits and the ancestral round huts of wood or stone in an irregular layout; the inhabitants naturally used Roman coinage and bought their pottery in Romano-British markets, but their standard of living remained low. The only real signs of improvement are that the use of storage pits gradually disappears and that sometimes rectangular cottages are found instead of round huts, as for instance at Park Brow, Sussex, or at Studland, Dorset. Though these might achieve the comfort of quite recent dwellings of the same sort, with painted walls, glass windows and even wooden floors, they could never be confused with villas.

Before the Little Woodbury excavations of 1938–9, the pits in such settlements were interpreted as dwellings rather than as storage places, and in consequence high estimates of population gained credence and the sites themselves were regarded as villages. But the demonstration at Little Woodbury that many pits could belong to one isolated farm caused a reaction, and for some years many authorities thereafter held that the isolated farm was the sole unit of agricultural settlement in the Iron Age and even in the Roman period in Britain. But this was to go too far. Though isolated farms were certainly an important ingredient of rural settlement in both periods, excellent evidence exists for large nucleated settlements which can be called villages. Massive settlements can be seen on air-photographs of the Fens, and in other areas not only do unified tracts of fields exist which are too large for working by a single farm (as at Figheldean Down), but in parts of Wessex Romano-British settlements covering up to twenty acres, with small rectangular building platforms arranged along a street, have been identified. The agricultural basis of such villages is beyond doubt.

The Romano-British villa has been variously defined. *Sensu stricto* it should be the centre of a farm or agricultural estate, but this has not been demonstrated in every case; and undoubtedly some country houses, indistinguishable architecturally from villas, derived their *raison d'être* from other forms of exploitation, such as potteries or quarries. This is especially notable in the area of the Nene Valley potteries. There is a range of size and wealth within the category of villa, but all, whether built of stone or timber, are Romanised buildings of sufficient size or distinction to lift them out of the cottage class; they are single establishments, not parts of villages, even though many will be found to possess subsidiary outbuildings connected with their function.

This general twofold pattern of rural organisation, however, is certainly oversimplified, since archaeological investigation unaided cannot often throw light on tenure. Some villas are large and wealthy, others simple and furnished only with necessities. The former were clearly the centres of their own estates, but the latter may represent rent-paying units on the estates of others. One may have been farmed by its owner and his family; another by a bailiff and slaves. A hint that even in pre-Roman times slaves were used in agriculture is provided by the iron gang-chain found in the Belgic farmstead at Park Street; and the discovery of the skeletons of ninety-seven new-born babies in the yard of the villa at Hambleden, Buckinghamshire, suggests the exposure of the unwanted female offspring of a slave-run establishment. Different evidence for the same sort of thing has been detected at Llantwit Major, Glamorgan, where early in the fourth century the main residence was demolished but the farm buildings continued in use for another century. Here, it seems clear, an absentee landlord was acting through a bailiff. It is probable, however, that on many of the more sizeable estates the home-farm was run with the assistance of slaves and the rest let out to tenants (*coloni*). Such a relationship would explain the not infrequent areas, like that round Winchester, where villas and native settlements are intermixed. Coloni would normally hold a lease for five years, continuable annually thereafter. But by the early fourth century, their legal position had deteriorated. They had become bound to the soil like medieval serfs under a hereditary tie, paying rent in kind as often as in money, and occasionally, at any rate, having customary obligations of part-time work on what may loosely be described as manorial lands.[3]

Similarly, the peasant farmsteads may represent free owners in one district or free tenants in another; while in a third the inhabitants may have been *coloni Caesaris*, or tenants under the bureaucratic control of officials administering imperial estates. Such relationships are not documented for students of Roman Britain, and they can be established only by inference, and that infrequently.

Beyond the lowland zone where arable cultivation was normal the inhabitants of the highland zone continued to live a more primitive life. Here pastoralism remained predominant despite evidence that cereal cultivation had been introduced and become established. Villas are hardly found in these regions: either wealth did not accumulate sufficiently or the standard of Romanisation remained too low. Successful pastoralists sometimes took to mixed farming but continued to live in traditional mode, as can be seen in the large round house set up in the third century inside the old hill-fort at Dinorben in Denbighshire.

Though the Roman government did not buy corn to feed the army, but obtained the necessary supplies by means of the *annona* or corn tax, the very necessity of paying this tax in kind, as well as finding money for other provincial and local taxes, must have stimulated agricultural production from the first, while the growing demand for meat and leather as well as corn created by the new towns will have enabled farmers to enrich themselves. Increasing prosperity can be recognised at many villas. Near *Verulamium* the well-known examples at Park Street and Lockleys both began as Romanised reconstructions of previous Belgic farms after the Boudiccan rebellion, and successive enlargements in the middle second and early fourth centuries point to continuing accumulation of capital. It is noteworthy that even the earliest Roman building at Park Street occupied more than four times the area of the native structures below, and represents therefore both a material upward step in living-standards as well as a considerable capital outlay. There should be other examples of such early development in the vicinity of the new towns of the south-east. Other villas were later in starting. At Ditchley, Oxfordshire (pl. 9b), a timber house of very simple rectangular type had first been built about 70, but the first stone structure, a villa of winged corridor type, replaced it about the time of Trajan. A similar sequence, this time from a late-first-century circular hut to a later-second-century complex of two rectangular cottages set adjacent to each other in ⌐-fashion, is known at Catsgore near Ilchester, Somerset; at Newport, Isle of Wight, some sort of timber-framed building underlay a villa erected apparently towards the close of the second century, and at Hambleden, Buckinghamshire, a quantity of first-century samian among the published finds suggests the possibility of a similar sequence. At Bignor, Sussex, though pottery of the late first century is known from the site, the earliest structure so far identified was not erected much before 200. It was a timber-framed building apparently of corridor type, which after a fire was succeeded by a simple oblong building of masonry. Such rectangular blocks containing four to six rooms are the simplest form a villa could take, closely resembling the small early private houses found in towns; it is just this form which appears the earliest, in the late Neronian villas at Park Street and Lockleys. Simple though it was, it showed a great advance in comfort and privacy over earlier types of house which, whether round or rectangular, lacked internal subdivisions, and sheltered men and beasts without distinction. The acquisition of wealth, in other words, was introducing a social distinction between the farmer and his labourers. Simplicity of plan, however, as Bignor and the first building at Cox Green near Maidenhead show, is no indicator of absolute date: it points rather to the extent of the owner's resources. A further refinement soon added at all these villas was a corridor, so that rooms did not have to be used as passages. At or soon after this stage, projecting wings were added to each end of the building, linked by the corridor and with the ridge line of their roofs, at right-angles to that of the central block. One of the wings was sometimes used to house a bath-suite, though often these were placed in a separate building to lessen the risk of fire. Both are proofs of growing luxury.

A further indication of increasing culture is the appearance in these larger villas of a central dining-room, larger in size than the other rooms, and a sure sign of the growing Romanisation of manners. The symmetrical façade presented by such a winged corridor house with its central entrance became fashionable and no doubt indicated a certain social status, for we find such façades applied to earlier structures; sometimes, as at Bignor, in such a way as to show that it was appearance rather than purpose which was uppermost in the mind of the designer. There is thus a typological development from the simple rectangular form through to the tripartite winged corridor villa (that is, a villa having a corridor and wings at the back as well as the front), but these developments have no relationship with absolute dating; they could occur at any time according to resources. It remains true, however, that most villas show successive enlargement well down into the fourth century: in other words, agriculture was a continuously thriving industry.

The largest villas were almost all mere elaborations of the basic design already described, with the wings lengthened so as to clasp and even sometimes to enclose a courtyard. Such establishments were big indeed, and were served by a numerous household of domestic slaves and agricultural workers; they were the centres of large estates, the busy life of which is portrayed for us in contemporary fashion only in the funerary reliefs of the Moselle valley and eastern Gaul. At Bignor and at North Leigh in Oxfordshire it can be shown that the courtyard house is the climax of a long history of enlargement. The same is true of the great villa at Woodchester, Gloucestershire. In such houses the farm-buildings, which are normally inseparable even from the most luxurious establishments, are found grouped in and around an outer yard. Only at Fishbourne, Sussex, do we have in Britain an example of a classical luxury-villa apparently unconnected in its original form with estate manage-

306

ment; and, as we have seen, this villa is anomalously early in date, and stands therefore outside the normal development of the British country house. It was the home of some exceptionally wealthy owner, either a high Roman official or more probably the royal family of the Regnenses. Nevertheless, other equally early villas are known on the coastal plain of Sussex, at Angmering in Essex, and in Kent at Eccles, and it is clear that exceptional Romanisation was active in this area. For the majority of early villa-owners, however, it was sufficiently costly to provide a Romanised permanent home of simple form; expansion and the provision of luxuries came later. Fishbourne (pl. 12a), Angmering and Eccles are the only villas so far known to have had mosaics and bath buildings in the first century: [4] at the great majority baths began to be added only in the later second century, and mosaics even later. However, many of the later villas have notably large baths, and some, like the Castle Dykes villa near Ripon in Yorkshire, even possess a separate bath building in addition to a private suite of baths. This suggests that provision was made for estate workers, for whom the baths would also form some sort of social focus. If this is so, it throws a favourable light on the relationship existing between master and man in the countryside. Mosaics, which are today often regarded as the hall-mark of the villa, are rare indeed, even in the second century. At present only seven villas – those at Fishbourne (Sussex), Boxmoor and Park Street (Hertfordshire), High Wycombe and Latimer (Hertfordshire), Well (Yorkshire) and Winterton (Lincolnshire) – are known to possess mosaics laid down in the second century. The vast majority of villa-mosaics, like the wealthy villas which they adorned, are characteristic of the fourth century in Britain.

A rather different class of building, and one of more primitive type, is the aisled house, sometimes known as the barn-dwelling or basilican villa. This is essentially a hall or barn whose roof is carried by two rows of supports dividing the building into nave and two aisles. The form is useful for many purposes. There is often a wide entrance suitable for carts at one end and a smaller doorway in the middle of one of the longer sides. At some farms the principal building recorded is one of this sort, and it can often be shown that subsequent alteration has partitioned off a set of rooms, at one end or other of the hall. In villas of this type it is not always certain that the main residential building has not been missed by the excavators, since it might be some distance away; but if the type can be isolated it seems clear that part of the hall must have housed the family and the remainder served the utilitarian purposes of the farm. At other villas such a building, though displaying evident signs of human occupation, is clearly subordinate to a more conventional residence; and in these cases it has been assumed to house a resident staff of workmen, perhaps slaves. At others again it may have more closely corresponded to a normal barn. At Bignor an example lies in the outer yard, where it certainly belongs to a late stage in the history of the villa, when there was plenty of accommodation elsewhere on the premises for a resident staff; and here it is associated with other buildings for which a connection with stock can be inferred. S. Applebaum has reasonably identified it as a barn whose nave stored fodder for the fifty-five head of cattle which could be accommodated in the aisles;[5] the two small rooms divided off at one end would be for the cowherds. It has also been suggested that some at any rate of these aisled buildings served a social purpose between landlord and tenant like that of the medieval hall which they so closely resemble – perhaps for feasts or even customary courts. This is perhaps to take inference rather far, for if they served a single social purpose of wide application few large villas should lack them, and there should be more uniformity of phenomena.

The aisled house-type, though typologically simple, is not necessarily early, and does not appear to have originated in Britain, though far more plentiful here than in other provinces. Its source is not yet generally agreed, but similar buildings are known in the regions round the mouth of the Rhine. Perhaps the earliest example of the independent aisled house so far known in Britain is that at Exning, Suffolk, where the original building, all in timber, was erected in the early second century and was later partly rebuilt in stone; an earlier aisled hall, but this time incorporated with other rooms and suites in one architectural whole, occurs in the Flavian palace at Fishbourne. The architectural form was the simplest and cheapest large building which could give the appearances of Romanisation to those who were not yet ready to abandon the traditional house-byre way of life. It was thus suitable for adoption in larger establishments to house the workers, when the family itself had moved to a more commodious dwelling, but it could also be entirely devoted to live-stock and their fodder.

A curious feature is the distribution of aisled houses in the narrower sense – that is buildings showing domestic sub-division at one end – for they cluster in Hampshire and in the regions round the Humber and the Fens; elsewhere if they occur at all such buildings are not certainly designed for human occupation, and are always subsidiary to the main house. It is not easy to explain this distribution, which does not appear to correspond to that of known immigrant groups or recognisable economic factors. The distribution of Romano-British barrow-burials, which originated in much the same continental region as that suggested for aisled houses, is quite different.

With the passage of time and improvement of living standards, the 'upper' end of many aisled houses was partitioned off into rooms, and a bath-suite was sometimes inserted in an aisle. It is the problem of lighting these rooms, some of which are out of contact with an exterior wall, which has given rise to the term basilican villa, since clerestory lighting would seem to be necessary. At some sites, such as West Blatchington, Sussex, where the rooms were planned from the beginning and were not added afterwards, this is likely enough; but at others, where they were afterthoughts, dormer-windows may have been inserted.

Occasionally attempts were made to give an aisled house a fashionable façade around the central doorway. At Stroud, Hampshire, two projecting wing-rooms, one at either end of the house, were part of the original design. At others, for instance Winterton, Lincolnshire, elaborate and doubtless expensive mosaics were inserted in an aisled building subsidiary to the main villa, which suggests the provision of a separate establishment for a younger generation of the family rather than accommodation for labourers. But whatever the later developments, parts of the original hall or barn at the 'lower' end always survive, and often a hearth is found at the 'upper' end of the surviving barn. This suggests that the building was still partly devoted to customary activities whatever these may have been; but the wide variety of possibilities illustrate the difficulties of too rigid a classification of such buildings.

Romano-British villas notably tend to exploit the richer soils. The lighter soils – chalk uplands, gravel terraces – though here and there supporting villas, are predominantly the areas where peasant settlements are found, on which they continued to occupy their ancestral sites. In Sussex, for instance, the South Downs were covered with settlements of this sort, some continuously occupied from Iron Age times, some new; all are, or were once, associated with traditional 'Celtic' fields. The villas, on the other hand, are found either on the coastal plain to the south or on the rich soils on the edge of the Weald north of the hills. The reason for this is not certain, because little is known of the occupation of these soils in pre-Roman times; but it is clear that their exploitation by capital would pay richer dividends than the chalk uplands, even if the complications caused by age-old traditional tenures in the latter area did not hamper development. Similar uneven distribution of villas can be seen in many parts of the country, for instance in East Anglia. In Norfolk they are concentrated along the borders of the Wash in the west of the county; much of the rest was occupied by peasant villages. In Essex the villas are in the north and west of the county; the coastal areas and adjoining lands were thickly populated by peasant settlements occupied with herding, fisheries and salt-production.

The methods of cultivation used by the villas is still obscure, but if improvements were introduced (p. 315f.) they could be applied more readily in new areas than in the old upland farms where field banks, accumulated by centuries of ploughing, resisted change of layout and indeed have yielded only in recent years to the bulldozer. Such physical difficulties would not occur, however, in the level gravel lands, and villas do make their appearance on these, for instance in the Oxford region; the tenacity of traditional farming in such areas is no doubt due to shortages of capital characteristic of large populations tied to their customary small-holdings.

The size of villa-estates must have varied considerably, and we have little evidence on which to base a calculation. The comparatively modest villa at Ditchley had a granary in the fourth century whose capacity has been calculated to reflect an estate of about 1,000 acres. At the much larger establishment at Bignor consideration of natural boundaries suggests an arable area of about 2,000 acres with additional strips of forest, downland and alluvial marsh which could be used for grazing.

In the north of England the presence of a large garrison undoubtedly had the effect of introducing arable cultivation at the expense of primitive pastoralism. Large areas of 'Celtic' fields exist in Upper Wharfedale in the neighbourhood of Grassington, and villas, which became plentiful in East Yorkshire during the third and fourth centuries, are found occasionally even in the Pennines (in Upper Airedale) and as far north as Old Durham. We have already noticed the veteran settlement of the early third century round Ribchester in Lancashire (p. 213f.), and there are hints of others in western Yorkshire.[6]

There was an obvious advantage in cereal production near the market, though much of it may have been for purely local use. But the *pax Romana* also meant a rise in native population. Parts of Cumberland and Westmorland are thickly studded with native settlements; these were probably still mainly pastoral, but such of their produce as was not taken by the tax-collector will have found a ready sale in the crowded *vici* of the region. In the limestone hills of the Peak district many peasant cultivators settled in the caves of the region; the finds from these prove that they were not temporary refuges but permanent homes. In North Wales, also, settlements with terraced fields on the hillsides seem to be a new feature of the Roman period; but here again cultivation was probably combined with cattle-keeping. Nevertheless, the discovery of an asymmetrical plough-share, almost certainly from a mould-board plough, in the hill-fort of Dinorben, where a large round house was occupied in the late third and early fourth centuries, should warn us that primitive living conditions do not necessarily imply primitive agricultural techniques.

There are two very large areas of southern Britain where the absence of villas – and even towns – is noticeable. The first of these is Salisbury Plain and Cranborne Chase. Here an area of more than 900 square miles is virtually devoid of villas, but farmsteads and villages of peasant type abound. Important road junctions at Old Sarum and Badbury Rings, which might have been expected to favour the growth of small towns, signally fail to show signs of any such tendency. Yet this area had been highly productive and fully populated in pre-Roman times: the absence of normal development is striking, more especially since villas are found on the chalk in Hampshire, and it has given rise to the suggestion that the whole area at an early date had been converted into an imperial domain, perhaps as a result of confiscation following the bitter resistance hereabouts

311

to the original occupation: the inhabitants would accordingly have been condemned to poverty because of the heavy exactions to which they were subject. Unfortunately no inscription has yet come to light to prove the truth of this theory, but it is perhaps supported by one found at Bath set up by C. Severius Emeritus 'centurion in charge of the region'.[7] It is also supported by the fact that arrangements for local storage of the corn-harvest in pits were greatly reduced after the conquest. Professor Hawkes has brilliantly reinterpreted the results of General Pitt-Rivers' excavation of rural sites in this region, and even if his figures should have to be reduced owing to the uncertainties of exactly dating local pottery from the storage pits, it still remains true that almost a half of the harvest remains to be accounted for, no doubt by requisition; for if it were only better marketing methods, or even the introduction of barns, that were responsible for the reduced number of pits, there should be more signs of prosperity. From the later second century onwards increasing attention seems to have been paid to stock-raising, and by the fourth there may have been a very considerable changeover to ranching. This again, since it involved a transfer of population and the abandonment of farms, suggests implementation of official policy.

Imperial estates certainly existed in Britain. Nero inherited part of the royal lands of the Iceni under Prasutagus' will, and more may well have been confiscated after the rebellion. Other provinces provide better evidence of the way in which imperial possessions grew as the result of inheritance or confiscation. In Britain we may surmise that Severus enlarged the patrimonium at the cost of the supporters of Albinus (p. 195), though there is little to prove it. An inscription from Combe Down, Bath, set up in the reign of Caracalla to record the restoration of a ruined headquarters by Naevius, imperial freedman and assistant to the procurators, may have some relevance here;[8] but since restoration rather than construction *ab initio* is in question, it is perhaps more likely that the stone records an established imperial interest, possibly in the local quarries of Bath stone. Again, the villas of Lullingstone and Ditchley have been thought to have suffered a period of desertion at the beginning of the third century, and this again might imply confiscation.[9] Finally, the inscription from the villa at Clanville, Hants., erected in 282–3 to the Caesar Carinus, probably implies imperial ownership.[10] Land held by the emperor, however, was not inalienable, and could be transferred by gift or by sale; thus, the pattern of imperial ownership was ever liable to change.

The second area noticeably lacking in villas is the silts of the Fen Basin, a vast region almost three times the size of the other. Increased flooding had made virtually the whole of this uninhabitable during the Iron Age, but in the first century AD a slight change in the relative levels of land and sea allowed reoccupation. Drainage was accordingly undertaken on a large scale, and thus fairly certainly by government agency; a single authority is indicated by the single programme of surveying and levelling over the whole wide region at one time. In this the Roman scheme offers a notable contrast to the piecemeal approach which has characterised the later history of Fen-drainage. The best-known work is the Car Dyke, a canal running from the neighbourhood of Cambridge round the periphery of the Fens to Lincoln. This course enabled it to be used to divert surplus water from one river-system to the next, but it was also intended to serve the needs of transport; a further link, the Fossdyke, from Lincoln to the Trent made it possible for barges to travel by inland waterways as far as Brough on Humber or York. Military depots on the Yorkshire Ouse and even on the Tyne could receive the farm-produce of the Fens, and the returning barges sometimes brought a cargo of coal. Subsidiary canals led into the Car Dyke, and roads were also built. But though in outline the orderly appearance of the whole scheme bears an official stamp, the new land thus reclaimed was not centuriated. The settlements therein were entirely native in character and show no signs of central planning or of official land-division, which the myriad small water-courses would have made impracticable. The parallel is with the Agri Decumates of southern Germany rather than with colonial settlement. Nevertheless, it is probable that this virgin territory was public land, peasant settlers receiving farms in return for rent and no doubt being placed under the control of a *procurator saltus*.

Apart from a few exceptionally early sites dating from about 60, the settlement of the Fens seems to have started in the late first century, possibly about 80. In this first stage single scattered settlements, some apparently connected with the salt industry, were normal. But from the time of Hadrian multiple settlements became increasingly common, implying a steady rise of population and even perhaps new drafts of settlers, and it was probably now that the Car

Dyke was constructed. Indeed, it is likely that in this fuller exploitation we should recognise one of the results of Hadrian's visit to Britain, for his interest in the reclamation of waste lands is well known, and is attested on inscriptions from Roman Africa. The exact nature of the nucleated settlements cannot be defined without excavation on a large scale, but they may be loosely described as villages, provided that our picture of a village is not too closely coloured by its Anglo-Saxon form: probably they were mainly groups of farms concentrated together for kinship reasons.

Though grain-cultivation was undoubtedly an important activity in the Fens, air-photographs show large areas between settlements devoid of sub-division into fields but sometimes demarcated by dykes. This suggests that raising sheep and cattle – and perhaps horses too – played a significant part in the economy, a suggestion supported by the numbers of bones found and also by the pottery cheese-strainers which occur with notable frequency. Many sites, too, yield traces of brine-boiling apparatus, showing that salt-production was another important activity; and it was one which started on a large scale in the late first century.

Flooding was an ever-present danger, as the water-courses rose higher on their levees of silt. There seems to have been some desertion of sites already by the end of the second century, and serious flooding occurred in the early third, causing damage which was not put right for fifty years. A renewal of prosperity, however, can be traced at the end of the third century, though with less numerous settlements; it may be due to more lenient terms of tenancy if analogy elsewhere is any guide. After the opening decades of the fifth century, however, occupation of the area could no longer be maintained, for the breakdown of Roman administration in this period was soon followed by adverse changes in the relative levels of land and sea, causing renewed flooding and the end of human settlement in the region for a millennium.

The Fenland was not the only area where land-reclamation was undertaken. Both Lincoln and Gloucester had territoria which must have embraced much marshy land such as would be useless until drained; and it has been thought that this fact may have been one of the considerations determining their foundation as coloniae, since such land was of little value as it stood to its British owners, whereas Colchester had experienced the passions which might be aroused by expropriation of valuable farmlands. Another area which was re-claimed, this time under army supervision, lay in the neighbourhood of Caerleon, where an inscription from the sea-wall or embankment at Goldcliff near the mouth of the Usk shows it to have been built by legionaries.

The plough used in Iron Age Britain was a simple bow-ard whose wooden share was tipped with a short pointed iron sheath. Belgic farmers improved this plough with longer, wider iron shares, and by its means were able to exploit heavier soils than before. But it was not until the Roman period that any markedly more efficient imple-ment was introduced. The bow-ard, especially with the addition of earth-boards or ground-wrests, is perfectly efficient in the lighter soils, and can turn the sod if the plough itself is tilted. In Romano-British times this plough was made more powerful by the addition of a coulter to cut the soil in front of the share, and of a heavy iron bar-share capable of withstanding much strain. There is also sug-gestive evidence in the form of asymmetrical shares that the mould-board (which automatically turns the sod) was known. But the date of these introductions is uncertain. A fragment of coulter was found at Twyford Down, apparently in an early Roman deposit, but all the other examples of bar-shares and coulters come from fourth-century contexts. It is probable that their use spread gradually through the medium of the villas, while peasants continued to use their simpler traditional equipment. Certainly the new ploughs would encourage the use of larger fields in the new villa-estates, but at present there is no secure evidence for the use of strip-fields in Roman Britain. Traces of field-systems definitely associated with villas, lying as they do on soils much cultivated in after-times, are still mainly to seek. Air photographs sometimes show small rectangular closes round the actual villa buildings, as at Ditchley, Oxfordshire (pl. 9b), or Crom-well, Nottinghamshire, but these being of small extent are almost certainly orchards or vegetable gardens or home paddocks rather than evidence for 'Celtic' fields. A firmer hint is provided at Brading (Isle of Wight), where a large area of Celtic fields exists on the Down above the villa, close enough to it to leave little doubt that they formed part of its estate. It is worth noting, too, that this villa has produced an asymmetrical plough-share, such as should belong to a mould-board plough.

Other tools now introduced, probably in the first instance by the army but of great assistance to the farmer, were the iron-tipped spade, the rake and the scythe. The last was of major importance, for it revolutionised ability to winter livestock, and the spade facilitated draining. But the wide range of lesser tools now generally available, such as chisels, draw-knives, spoke-shaves and the carpenter's plane, must have greatly increased ability to make what was necessary on the spot. A reaping-machine named the *Vallus* is mentioned by Pliny as current in Gaul, and is represented on the well-known relief from Buzenol. Though there is no evidence at present that this was used in Britain, the enormous scythe-blades, up to seven feet long (twice the length of modern examples), known from Great Chesterford and the villa at Barnsley Park near Cirencester, suggest that daring experimentation was being carried on.

Another invention whose use became widespread was the corndrying furnace. Corn-drying, of value in times of wet harvest, and the parching of the grain both prevented germination during storage and facilitated milling. It was particularly necessary for the treatment of spelt. The practice had been followed in the Iron Age, but the exact nature of the primitive equipment in use at that time is not known. No doubt the same simple apparatus continued to be used in the first and second centuries, for spelt was a principal crop in Roman Britain. However, in the third and fourth centuries the use of carefully insulated structures with double floors and underground flues became widespread, and marked a great technological advance available alike to villa-owners and peasant farmers. Similarly, Roman technology improved the water supply of farms. A few villas, as at Abinger, Surrey, possessed an aqueduct or leet; but the great majority of farms came to depend on wells – sometimes up to 200 feet deep – the ability to dig which enabled larger flocks and herds to be maintained.

Several new crops were introduced, including rye, oats, vetch and flax, as well as the cabbage, parsnip, turnip, carrot, celery and other vegetables. Here again the winter-feeding of animals received assistance: Columella had already noted the importance of the turnip for this purpose in Gaul. A number of fruit trees are also now attested for the first time, among them being the vine, the plum, the apple, and the mulberry and walnut, and probably the sweet cherry; it is possible that specialised cultivation, following the precepts of classical agricultural treatises, was undertaken here and there. Near

Grimsby in north Lincolnshire an area of over twelves acres was found to be covered with a rectangular grid of closely spaced ditches, which were possibly intended for the planting of fruit trees. Much smaller plots, somewhat similar in appearance and perhaps in function, are characteristic of many of the Fenland settlements. Among flowers the rose, violet, lily, pansy and poppy are thought to be Roman importations. That animal strains were improved is not so easy to demonstrate, but there is suggestive evidence for a larger breed of horse which is likely to have been an introduction; larger cattle, too, appear more frequently than in the Iron Age, and may be due either to the import of fresh varieties or to selective breeding from existing strains. Among other introductions are normally counted the goose and the pheasant. Bee-keeping was widespread, if the large vessels used for hives have been correctly identified.

All this shows that the Romano-British farmer had many advantages over his predecessors. Corn-growing was no doubt always a principal activity owing to government pressure, but for the same reason can never have yielded outstanding wealth. It is noteworthy that the villas of East Anglia and the Midlands, which were probably then as now the main corn-producing areas, are with few exceptions of poor or medium quality. The really large and luxurious villas are clustered in the Cotswold country and in Somerset – lands which have always been best suited to sheep and cattle. But even in predominantly arable estates mixed farming was probably practised. At Bignor, for instance, certain of the outbuildings have been interpreted by Applebaum as a sheep-pen (accommodating 197 sheep), a lambing enclosure and a byre for twelve yoke of plough-oxen, in addition to the cattle-stall for fifty-five cows which has already been mentioned (p. 308); and he has recognised pig-sties at others, for instance, Pitney in Somerset and Woolaston Pill in Gloucestershire.

The climax of villa prosperity was not reached before the beginning of the fourth century. It had, however, no doubt been maturing during the third, for in 301 Diocletian's price-fixing edict could assign the maximum permitted price within their classes to two British woollen products, the Birrus Britannicus (a hooded waterproof cloak somewhat resembling a duffle coat) and the Tapete Britannicum (a woollen rug suitable for saddles or couches); clearly these products had already acquired their empire-wide reputation before this date, and they point to a flourishing woollen industry which must have been based ultimately on the villas [11] (p. 337). Nevertheless, at the beginning of the fourth century many of these establishments were rebuilt or extended, and others were constructed on new sites: to this period also, and to the succeeding century, belong the great majority of the best villa mosaics.[12]

In seeking to explain this prosperity some have suggested a flight of capital to Britain after the late-third-century troubles in Gaul and Germany. There is, however, little evidence for this save likelihood, and the prosperity can be explained in more general terms. In the first place Britain herself had survived the third century with her economy largely undamaged, and now found herself in a unique position in the western empire. Builders were sent from Britain to restore Autun by Constantius Chlorus *c.* 298, and in 359 Julian was able to increase the regular export of corn from Britain to the Rhineland to 600 barge-loads during an emergency. These two passing references which happen to have come down to us are pointers to the truth that, though in earlier centuries the British economy had depended on loans and the activities of continental businessmen, and had relied on imports even for its better table-wares, by the fourth century the loans had been repaid, business was in local hands and the balance of trade was favourable. This self-sufficiency is further discussed in the next chapter.

The prosperity of the countryside in the fourth century has long been recognised, but it used to be contrasted with an apparent decay of the towns: for Collingwood the success of the villas represented a flight from the towns. But, as we have seen, there is no evidence for profound urban decay before the fifth century. Villas had always had a close connection with the towns, and their prosperity in the fourth century is a sign of the continuing and increasing wealth of the British curial class as a whole. This, though characteristic of Britain, is exceptional in the Roman world; it is to be explained partly by the economic considerations already mentioned, and partly by the fact that in these provinces the aristocracy had never lost its close ties with the countryside from which it renewed its vigour and its wealth. It is not without significance that we hear little of peasant revolts in Britain, similar to the serious outbreaks which recurred in Gaul with increasing severity in the third and fourth centuries, before the opening decade of the fifth. This may mean that the peasants of Britain remained more prosperous than

318

their Gallic counterparts, and that, as in later history, there was an absence of sharp cleavage between landlord and tenant in Britain such as gave rise to class-warfare elsewhere.

1. Strabo, iv, 199.
2. Caesar, *BG*, v, 12.
3. For *coloni* in Britain see *Codex Theodos.*, xi, 7, 2. Recent work (*Britannia* v (1974)) now suggests that the fourth-century story at Llantwit Major was different from that suggested in the text; the general point, however, remains valid.
4. First-century mosaics are also known at the incompletely excavated villa at Rivenhall, Essex (*Britannia*, iv (1973), pp. 115 ff.).
5. The width of the aisles, 14 feet 6 inches, in this and other such buildings seems to bear some relationship with the length of a beast plus the width of a feeding stall and gangway.
6. There are two dedications to *dea Brigantia* and one to *deus Bregans*: all three are dedicated by Aurelii, two of them giving their praenomen as Titus. These names suggest descendants of second-century veteran auxiliaries, one of the stones being dated to 208 (*RIB*, 623, 627, 628).
7. *RIB*, 152; *ILS*, 4920. C(*enturio*) reg(*ionarius*). The scope of his office, not being further described, is likely to have been local.
8. *RIB*, 174. The villa at Combe Down also produced a lead seal inscribed P(*rovinciae*) Br(*itanniae*) S(*uperioris*).
9. But the difficulty of distinguishing pottery of the first half of the third century from that of the late second suggests caution on this point. Nevertheless, the Lullingstone villa had belonged to a prominent Roman official in the late second century, as the portrait busts prove.
10. *RIB*, 98; but it may be a milestone reused, cf. recent finds at the Rockbourne villa.
11. As early as *c.* 220 a *tossia Britannica* – thought to be a cloak or tunic – was considered worthy of being sent by a Governor of Inferior as a presentation to a friend in Gaul. *CIL*, xiii, 3162.
12. For a contemporary view of British prosperity at the end of the third century see *Incerti Panegyricus Constantio Caesari dictus* viii (v), 11: *et sane non sicut Britanniae nomen unum, ita mediocris erat iacturae rei publicae terra tanto frugum ubere, tanto laeta numero pastionum, tot metallorum fluens rivis, tot vectigalibus quaestuosa, tot accincta portibus, tanto immensa circuitu . . .*

14
Trade and industry

Britain had enjoyed commercial contacts of one sort or another with the Continent from distant prehistoric times. In the first century BC the tin trade of Cornwall had begun to decline, whether the cause was Caesar's destruction of the Venetic fleet, or, more generally, the availability of richer and nearer supplies elsewhere, and it did not fully recover thereafter; for the Romans made no serious attempt to open up Cornwall before the third century. By the time of Nero, when the peninsula was occupied, sufficient tin was being obtained from Spain; and the limited exploitation of Cornwall, which is all we find in the later first century, shows that the industry could not compete with this nearer source.

Cicero, contradicting what sound like earlier anticipations, wrote to a friend in May 54 BC that it was now known that there was no trace of either gold or silver to be had in Britain.[1] But Caesar himself mentions merchants who knew the coasts, traces of whose trade we can recognise in the early Italian wine-amphorae found here and there near southern ports. The more specific account which later on Strabo gave of the imports and exports of Britain in the time of Augustus has already been quoted (p. 61). The wide market which existed for fine pottery-wares from Italy and the Rhineland, as well as for the amphora-borne products of Campania and Southern Spain, has been revealed by excavation at the principal Belgic oppida such as *Camulodunum* or Bagendon; more valuable imports, such as drinking vessels in precious metal, have come to light from time to time in chieftains' tombs.

One of the results of the Claudian Conquest was the arrival of a mass of fresh merchants, speculators and prospectors in the wake of the armies. 'Britain produces gold and silver and other metals,' writes Tacitus, better informed than Cicero, 'which are the reward of victory; ocean too produces pearls, though of poor quality.

The yield of gold, indeed, was disappointing. In earlier times Ireland had been the chief source of gold in the west, and no doubt much of the gold used in Britain during the Iron Age still came from there. Auriferous rocks certainly occur to a limited extent in Wales and Scotland and also in Cornwall, but the only known Roman workings are at Dolaucothi in Carmarthenshire, where their exploitation had to await the pacification of Wales. Even now the site is not fully explored; both open-cast workings and mining galleries are visible; and recent field work has traced at least two aqueduct systems, one of them just over seven miles long and capable of delivering about three million gallons a day to a series of large reservoirs high on the hill above the workings. The water seems to have been intended partly for breaking down the softer beds of rock, for which purpose a powerful head was necessary, and partly for washing the ore, after it had been crushed in stone mills, thus saving the necessity of carrying it to the river to wash, as had been done earlier. Fire-setting was also used to penetrate the rock. The deeper galleries, some eighty feet below ground, were drained by means of large wooden waterwheels, similar to those known from Roman mines in Spain; a portion of one of these, found in 1935 when the mines were briefly reworked, is in the National Museum of Wales. The Dolaucothi goldfield thus illustrates many of the most impressive aspects of Roman mining technology and deserves further study. It was certainly in imperial ownership and was protected by a fort. But the actual operations may nevertheless have been in the hands of contractors, to judge by the gold jewellery found at the site, which is more appropriate to lessees than to slave labour.

Silver, on the other hand, was readily available by cupellation from some of the lead ores which are easily accessible in various parts of Britain; and lead itself was a valuable by-product, some of which was exported to the Continent and the rest extensively used in bath buildings, water-pipes, lead coffins and the like. The speed with which exploitation followed the over-running of these leadfields is striking testimony to the efficiency and acumen of the prospectors. Our evidence is derived from the inscriptions cast or incised on the ingots (or pigs) – usually about 170–190 lb in weight – into which the lead was run for transport.[3]

The first area to be worked was in the Mendip Hills of Somerset.

It is clear from the distribution of ingots lost in transit that they were being exported to the Continent via Southampton Water, where a port existed at Clausentum. Two carry inscriptions dating them to AD 49, only six years after the conquest, and one found at St-Valery-sur-Somme bears the name of Nero coupled with that of Legio II Augusta. It seems likely from this that in the early years exploitation was begun by this legion, under whose control this area lay at the time. Military government, however, was not intended to be permanent, and as early as 60 we find C. Nipius Ascanius, a civilian prospector, at work: his names imply that he was a freedman; no doubt he was acting for a wealthy Roman patron. The ingot in question was found at Stockbridge, Hampshire, and is therefore probably Mendip lead, as the date and place clearly suggest, but Ascanius' name recurs on a pig from the Flintshire field.[4] The latter can hardly have been worked before Suetonius Paullinus' campaigns had over-run North Wales; the earliest dated ingot from it is one of 74 inscribed *Degeangl(icum)*. Ascanius therefore appears as an interesting example of a prospector working first in Somerset but soon extending his activities to North Wales in the wake of the army. Another slightly later illustration of this sort of 'silver-rush' is provided by three ingots of Vespasianic date found at Wells in Somerset and inscribed with the name of Tiberius Claudius Trifer(na). This man was probably an imperial freedman, and was working the Mendip field in the period 69–79; but soon after this, when Agricola's early campaigns brought the Derbyshire and Yorkshire lead-fields within the reach of prospectors, the same name occurs on a Derbyshire ingot.[5] A pig dated to 91 and bearing the inscription *Brig(anticum)* shows that the Yorkshire field, too, was put into immediate production.

After the initial period of military exploitation, therefore, which itself was due to the military government under which much of south-west Britain was placed in the conquest period, the early working of the lead was in the hands of prospectors or lessees (*conductores*); these were mainly freedmen of the emperor or of wealthy business-men, who worked either singly or in companies. Evidence for companies (*societates*) is found as early as the principate of Vespasian. A *soc(ietas) Novaec.* is mentioned on an ingot of this reign which was found at Clausentum, indicating that this company was working in the Mendips; the productions of the *societas Lutudarensis* of

Derbyshire cannot be precisely dated as yet, but are probably also of about this same period.

To judge by analogy, the mining-rights were an imperial monopoly leased out to contractors by a *procurator metallorum*; and that close supervision was exercised is attested by Pliny the elder.[6] Writing early in the reign of Vespasian he states, 'Lead is made into pipes and thin sheets. It is mined with some difficulty in Spain and Gaul, but in Britain is present in such quantity near the surface that there is a law limiting its exploitation.' Under Hadrian the Derbyshire products now carry the imperial name with the addition *Met(allum) Lut(udarense)*, and none anywhere else mentions lessees. These facts suggest that Hadrian imposed a tightening-up of monopoly and possibly also direct working by prisoners rather than by free lessees; certainly in his reign there must have been exceptional requirements for lead in the new military installations of the frontier. A generation or two later the presence of a quantity of lead ore in pebble form in the Antonine Fort at Brough, Derbyshire, points to collection of material from streams under military supervision here at this period, and in the third century the second cohort of Nervians, stationed at Whitley Castle in Northumberland, appears to have supervised the collection of lead from the Alston field; for lead seals of this cohort, bearing the word *metal(lum)*, have been found at Brough under Stainmore and point to material in transit. Thus, military control of lead-mining was continued in areas under military rule (p. 259).

How long the original system of exploitation remained in operation in the civil zone is uncertain. The latest inscribed ingots are three of Marcus and Verus (164–9) from the Mendip field. Though the lead of this region and probably of Flintshire, too, was sufficiently rich in silver to make its extraction just profitable, analysis has shown that the silver yield in Derbyshire was exceptionally low, as it was in Shropshire and Yorkshire. But the yield of silver even in the Mendips was much lower than that obtainable elsewhere in the empire, and must have disappointed Roman expectations. It seems possible that government interest in direct working of the more southerly fields was relaxed in the second half of the second century, and that the industry was allowed to fall more and more into private hands, which no longer produced large inscribed ingots. Production certainly persisted into later times, since a coin of Gordian III has been found in association with workings in Flintshire, and fourth-century finds

323

are common in the Derbyshire mining district. In the Mendip region, too, the exceptional quantity of silver coins of the late fourth century has been taken, reasonably enough, to suggest a prosperity derived from silver production at this date. The flourishing pewter industry in the same region in the third and fourth centuries points to the same conclusion, since pewter is an alloy of lead and tin.

Imperial interest in British metals was not, of course, abandoned altogether, for private workers are thought to have been compelled to yield half their production to the state, which needed silver for its coinage. The treasury, which is attested in London in the late fourth century, may have had the collection of silver as one of its duties, and there is some evidence to suggest that silver ingots were used at this period for payments of salary instead of coin. Tin, too, was controlled, for an ingot of this metal from Carnanton in Cornwall bears a third- or fourth-century imperial stamp. About the middle of the third century the Roman government began to take a renewed interest in Cornwall, for milestones prove road-building in that period and also in the early fourth century. The purpose of this was certainly to assist the revival of the tin industry, perhaps because of the decline in Spanish production consequent on barbarian invasion, and certainly because of renewed demand for it in Britain from the manufacturers of pewter. This was a new industry which made drinking and dining vessels for the growing number of town and villa dwellers of medium wealth.

The lead–silver industry serves as a convenient illustration of the early penetration and quick exploitation of British resources by Roman enterprise, whether official or mercantile. In other industries we have hints, but no such full information. Copper, which is to be found in Shropshire, North Wales and Anglesey, appears to have been first worked in Roman times and probably by lessees who hired the mineral rights from the procurator; but very little is known of them in detail. It seems that an improved furnace was introduced which was capable of smelting up to 50 lb of copper, the metal being then run off to form a bun-shaped ingot. From stamps on these ingots the name of at least one societas is known, as well as several individual lessees. Copper was hardly ever used in its pure state in Roman Britain; stronger, harder bronze or brass alloys made with zinc, lead and tin were widely produced.[7] It has also been shown that technical knowledge was now sufficient to choose appropriate alloys

324

for the different processes required in manufacturing cast or wrought objects.

The manufacture of bronze objects in Roman Britain was carried on at two distinct levels. On the one hand, we have craftsmen, no doubt mainly based on the towns and on the larger vici of the north, who manufactured objects in classical taste, though in provincial style. At first such people will have been immigrants in the main, but the very large quantity of material, as well as the artistic standards, show that Britons soon learnt the necessary skills. Among their products may be recognised jugs and skillets, fittings for doors and furniture, religious statuettes and personal ornaments. Most of the finer examples of the bronze-smith's art, of course, were imported ready-made from Italy or Gaul; but British craftsmen copied imported models to the best of their ability, and occasionally they achieved distinctive creations of their own, such as the enamelled cups and skillets which were sold as souvenirs of Hadrian's Wall.

Distinct from these, there still existed rural or itinerant craftsmen in the north and west trained in the old traditions of the native bronze industry of Celtic Britain, who sometimes produced minor masterpieces in which the spirit of La Tène art still breathed. Brooches of the elaborate dragonesque, fan-tailed or trumpet types seem to have come from such hands, since their distribution points to an origin in the highland zone; but even when such strongly individual production died out before the spread of more uniform fashions, we still find bronze fittings for wooden tankards or buckets, and bronze cauldrons for brewing or for seething meat. The manufacture of these never died out. They remained in demand among highland-zone households which continued in the Celtic way of life; and after the Roman period was over their continued manufacture did something to compensate for the dearth of pottery.

The timber industry was another which may have early attracted the attention of immigrant *entrepreneurs*; it must have brought great wealth to those who owned or had the control of forests. Apart from the needs of the army, which may have been met by requisition, we have only to remember the immense building programme in the first-century towns, in which almost all private buildings were of half-timber construction. Stone quarries, too, were quickly in operation where suitable rock could be found. The inscription of Cogidubnus at Chichester and that of Agricola at *Verulamium* were both carved on Purbeck Marble quarried in Dorset, and smaller pieces of this stone have been found in pits at Colchester which were filled in before AD 60; the tombstone of Classicianus in London is of Cotswold or Northampton limestone, as are the still earlier tombstones of Facilis and Longinus at Colchester; and the early baths-portico at Silchester, which is certainly of Flavian if not earlier date, is of Bath stone. The early growth of all these industries, for which technical knowledge was necessary, suggests exploitation by newcomers from abroad. The same thing might be said of the early development of the tile-making industry; a tilery in imperial ownership seems to have existed near Silchester, where a stamped tile of Nero has been found.[8] Pottery-making too, though always to some extent in local hands, was certainly stimulated and improved by foreign capital. In the Flavian–Trajanic period there were at least seven Roman citizens who stamped mortaria at Colchester, and six others who were fairly certainly working at an unidentified site in Kent. One, C. Attius Marinus, started his career at Colchester, but later worked for a brief time at Radlett near *Verulamium* before moving on to Hartshill in Warwickshire, where an enormous pottery industry subsequently developed. Most of these men were probably freedmen, notably the Sexti Valerii at Colchester (p. 296). But Q. Valerius Veranius, who came to Kent from the region of Bavai in Belgica, was the son of a citizen, and Q. Rutilius Ripanus, son of Tiberius, who made mortaria in the Radlett region, may also have been a citizen-proprietor. At this early period about a third of the potters stamping mortaria were citizens, while in the second century the proportion is distinctly lower.

The stimulus to Romano-British industries from foreign capital and immigrant speculators was matched by the exploitation of new trading opportunities by numerous continental merchants.[9] Many would come armed with contracts to supply the army with necessities and would remain to make money among the civilians of the province. Such were the importers of samian ware, the red-gloss pottery which hardly any site of the first two centuries AD fails to produce in quantity. The prototype of this class of pottery was Italian: vessels of Arretine ware from Italy reached some wealthy Belgic households before the conquest. By the beginning of the principate of Claudius, however, the Western markets were being captured by the manufacturers of similar pottery in South Gaul (at

Montans and at La Graufesenque near Millau). These continued to ship vast quantities of samian pottery to Britain until the late first century, when they began to lose ground to rival firms more advantageously placed in the Allier valley of central Gaul (at Les Martres de Veyre and Lezoux). Soon after the beginning of the second century the latter had virtually monopolised the market for fine table-ware in Britain, and their successors maintained their hold on the trade, with some rivalry from eastern Gaulish factories, throughout the second century. The well-known Pudding Pan Rock find represents the wreck of a vessel full of a cargo of samian consisting entirely of plain forms, which was lost in the late second century on its way to London. This port must have been one of the principal receiving and distributing centres in Britain for imported pottery.

During the last quarter of the second century another class of continental pottery began to be imported. This was Rhenish ware, a fine pottery with dark lustrous colour-coat, manufactured in the Cologne region, the most popular forms of which were decorated drinking vessels. Vessels of this ware continued to enjoy wide sales in the third century, but local British factories making very similar pottery had already been set up in the Nene valley, at Colchester and elsewhere in East Anglia, and probably also in Kent (p. 329).[10]

Traders in Rhenish and samian pottery were by no means the only people from the Continent who made money in the British market. Much fine glass from Alexandria or Syria was imported in the first century; when factories were established at Cologne and in Normandy during the second, their products, too, found a ready market in Britain, where the industry never seems to have established itself on a wide scale, except for window-glass. The only sites in Britain where Roman glass furnaces have been identified are Wroxeter, Caistor by Norwich, Wilderspool (Lancashire) and Mancetter (Warwickshire). However, many ordinary glass vessels are hard to assign with confidence to any particular source of origin, and the industry itself leaves such insignificant traces that it is quite possible for its place in the British economy to have been underestimated. Bronze jugs, dishes and a few lamps and candelabra from Italy, also, found a ready market among the wealthy, and smaller bronzes, sometimes decorated in enamel, were imported from Northern Gaul. In addition to these, vast quantities of wine, some olive oil (for use in Public Baths and also for lamps) [11] and possibly also fish sauce were marketed here from Spain. This trade had its beginnings before the conquest and greatly expanded thereafter, capturing the British market from Italian exporters. The earliest Spanish amphorae attested in Britain were found in pre-conquest deposits at Colchester: during the second half of the first century Spanish exporters secured a monopoly which continued until the end of the second, when the punitive measures taken by Severus against the supporters of Albinus in Spain disrupted the trade. Only two amphora-stamps from Spanish wine-producing estates after their confiscation have been found in Britain. Another widespread import was domestic hand-mills of Andernach lava from the middle Rhine which are frequently found on military as well as on civilian sites of the first and second centuries; trade in this material had begun as early as the neolithic period, and was to be resumed in the Middle Ages, but in Roman Britain the market was eventually lost to local producers of quern stones.

All these great import businesses necessarily brought over large numbers of provincials from Gaul and Spain, especially in the early days, and most of these will have returned home on retirement with the money they had made. Even more significant is the large and continuous drain of resources in the form of payments to source for the imports themselves.

This draining away of profits to the Continent was part of a process which was augmented both by the interest paid on the large loans which had been necessary to establish the early towns (which are partly attested by Dio) [12] and also by the inevitable drift back to the Continent, at least in the first century, of retired soldiers from the large British garrison whose savings were the product of British taxation. Their numbers were far larger than those of corresponding British veterans returning from abroad (p. 238). From all these causes Britain in the first century, and on a lesser scale throughout the whole of the second, was a province suffering from what nowadays would be called an adverse balance of trade, offset though this was to some extent by rising production and expansion of resources, which were made possible by new techniques and the *pax Romana*. The later prosperity of the province, especially in the fourth century, was in great part due to gradual rectification of the adverse balance, as British products gradually took the place of imports, and profits ceased to drain away overseas. [13]

How this came about may be briefly explained. We have already seen that evidence for the continued exploitation of silver–lead in its old form fails after the later second century, and that this probably means that the industry was reorganised under local enterprise, half the produce perhaps going to the state, but the other half no longer going to speculators from abroad. Such a system would explain inscriptions found on later Roman silver ingots such as that from the Tower of London; this bears the stamp *ex offe Honorini*, 'from the workshop of Honorinus', an inscription which gives no indication of connection with the government.

The import of samian pottery virtually ceased at the end of the second century, partly owing to a decline in the standards of production, but mainly owing to the disruption of the central Gaulish industry in the struggle between Severus and Albinus, from which it never recovered. A little samian from east Gaul reached Britain in the third century, and rather a larger quantity of Rhenish ware. But by this time competition by potters in Britain itself had created an industry capable of producing very tolerable table-ware which satisfied the needs of all who were content to drink from pottery. For those with more ostentatious habits the growing pewter industry in the region round Bath provided locally produced table-wares in metal, though the very rich, at any rate in the fourth century, possessed sets of imported silver, exemplified for us in the Mildenhall treasure.

Fine pottery capable of standing comparison with imported wares was probably first produced in the Nene Valley round *Durobrivae* at a date shortly before 150, and by 200 the industry had developed large-scale production – the so-called Castor ware. Manufacture continued down to the early years of the fifth century, and the sales penetrated almost all Britain. In the Colchester region similar wares were being made in the later second century, and there was even a short-lived attempt to start a samian industry, which failed owing to unsuitable clay and poor production. A similar venture, equally short-lived, attempted samian manufacture in London. The manufacture of a fine red colour-coated ware which recalled the now vanished samian, began to be developed during the later third century by the potters of the Oxford region. Their venture, which included the manufacture of mortaria, achieved a wide success in the fourth century, reaching markets as widely separated as Richborough and Caernarvon. Perhaps in emulation, the potters of the New Forest also began to produce colour-coated wares at the end of the third century, but their products never achieved a more than regional market.

Rather less sophisticated though still handsome wares, usually in grey with a white slip, were made in the Farnham district on the borders of Hampshire and Surrey; these won a regional market for themselves during the third century comparable to that of the New Forest potters farther west.

The more utilitarian domestic vessels were produced in a great number of local potteries, both large and small, all over the lowland zone and even farther north where clay and fuel were available. The wares of those who were fortunate enough to be awarded army contracts – for the army only rarely made its own pottery – achieved a wide distribution in the north; for instance, more than a third of the stamped mortaria from the Antonine Wall were made at Colchester, and many of the rest were products of kilns in the Midlands. The largest and most important of the groups of coarse ware, consisting of cooking vessels and dishes made in two categories of 'black-burnished ware', are now known to have been manufactured at a variety of centres, most of them remote from the military markets they served. Two of the principal areas for vessels of 'category 1' were in Dorset, where pre-Roman industries were expanded, and in Somerset; vessels of 'category 2' appear to have sources in East Anglia and the flanks of the Thames estuary. These factories produced pottery for the Roman army – and also for the civilian market – on a very large scale from the time of Hadrian onwards. Their products are found virtually all over the west and north of Britain; only in the south-east did sales fail to overwhelm local competitors.

Other smaller establishments achieved importance in Derbyshire and Yorkshire from the third century onwards; but in the final period, after many of them had been destroyed in the disturbed conditions of the third quarter of the fourth century, it was the factory at Crambeck which captured the military markets of the north.

If Severus destroyed the prosperity of the samian industry he also disrupted the Spanish wine-trade, and its products were now largely diverted under state control elsewhere. Thereafter the best table wines in Britain came from Bordeaux and the Moselle valley [14] but it is likely enough that local wines of a sort were developed from vines grown in the walled gardens of villas. In the monasteries of the Middle Ages wine was certainly produced as far north as Chester. For Roman Britain we have the edict of Probus of about 277 cancelling previous restrictions on viticulture in Gaul and Britain, and we have the evidence of vine plants found near the villa at Boxmoor, Hertfordshire, and of grape-pips from Silchester, Southwark and Gloucester.[15] We also have a most interesting scene illustrating the vine-harvest in barbotine on one of the Colchester vases.[16] Vines then were certainly grown in Britain, and there is no reason why wine should not have been produced from them. But alternative local intoxicating drinks were available; as well as the mead which Pytheas first recorded, a species of beer was made, the froth of which, according to Pliny, was used by women as a cosmetic.[17] This beer was priced at 4 denarii a pint in Diocletian's price-edict – twice the cost of the Egyptian variety. It is noteworthy that the fine drinking-vessels made by the British potters of the third and fourth centuries are very frequently of quart size or larger, and this reinforces the suggestion that beer largely took the place of wine in Britain after Severus; for such beakers could hardly have been used for the latter.

These changes in the pattern of industry, together with the results of agricultural improvements already described (pp. 315–17), meant that in the third century the economy of Britain became more balanced, as the wealth of the province, after the demands of taxation had been met, came to remain more and more in British hands; and much of the yield of taxation, of course, was expended in Britain on payments to soldiers and officials. Moreover, the increase in local recruitment to the army, and the measures taken by Severus and his successors to give serving soldiers a stake in the soil (p. 213), resulted in a more general settlement in Britain of retired soldiers and their capital. To this we may add the exports of the province, which, though never on a large scale, grew more numerous in the third and fourth centuries. The chief of these, woollen goods and corn, have already been mentioned (p. 317). British pearls were known to Tacitus (p. 321) and were still sold in the fourth century.[18] Another small-scale luxury-trade concerned itself with Whitby jet, which was fashioned into rings, pins, necklaces and even portrait-medallions in York. Jet was a rare substance, which with its electro-static qualities must have been highly prized and correspondingly expensive; it found a market in the Rhineland, where the absence of any trace of manufacturer's waste implies that the objects were sent ready made from York.[19] Another prized product of Britain was its hunting dogs, of which three breeds are known, one being the bulldog; bears, too, were being exported for the Roman arena as early as the time of Agricola.[20] British oysters enjoyed a certain popularity in Rome at least in the first century,[21] and British basket-work was also obtainable there.[22]

Nor was trade exclusively directed towards the continental empire. Slaves were a valuable commodity, the normal supply of which must have tended to dry up with growing frontier stability, and there is little doubt that dealers must have braved the perils of the Irish and northern seas in search of fresh sources, though such a trade leaves little archaeological trace. We may mention the discovery of Roman coins in Iceland and the Roman pot trawled up from the Porcupine Bank, 150 miles from the west coast of Ireland. There are a few finds of coins, bronze trinkets and even of pottery from Ireland itself, mainly near the north and east coasts. Evidence of trade with free Scotland is more considerable. Roman products were widely distributed up the east and west coasts, especially the former, along which commerce continued until the middle of the fourth century, when Irish raids had disrupted the western routes. This trade had its origin in Britain (perhaps in the ports of the Humber and Dee estuaries), but the goods sold were often themselves imports into Britain, such as samian and Rhenish wares or wine in amphorae, and even occasionally rare and costly painted glass vessels from Cologne, some of which reached Orkney. A dedication, apparently of the later second century, at Bowness on Solway was set up by a trader who undertook to gild its letters if sufficient profits were granted to his enterprise;[23] the Solway may have been his last port of call before the risks began.

Other traders reached southern Scotland by land. Commerce was controlled at the exits from Hadrian's Wall; at Housesteads, where the north gate of the fort is on the brink of a steep gradient, a special opening was built through the wall in the valley below at the beginning of the fourth century. Its double system of gates was clearly designed to facilitate the customs examination of travellers, and its provision at this period may point to increased commerce with the protected zone beyond. The exports of Scotland, apart from slaves, are likely to have consisted of hides, furs and wool.

Evidence for weaving, especially in the form of bone combs for packing the threads on the loom, is fairly widespread in Scotland during the Roman Iron Age, while the Roman votive model of a bale of wool from Skye points to the presence of merchants from the province in the western isles. There is evidence also from certain hoards of iron-work concealed in southern Scotland in the second century for the introduction of improved tools, and of new techniques or habits of life implicit in such articles as scythes and farriers' buttresses, cooking gridirons and lampstands, which themselves may be the products of intercourse with traders from the south or with soldiers of the garrison, though they may equally well be attributable to the influence of government policy during the period when this region was occupied.

Nothing has so far been said of the iron industry of Roman Britain, since, with the exception just mentioned, its products were not as far as we know exported; as it already had a respectable antiquity and considerable technical competence, it did not invite the same degree of development from continental newcomers as did the other industries already described. Nevertheless, it is clear that the total consumption of iron in Roman Britain soon greatly exceeded that of the preceding Iron Age; iron tools became much more common, and a greater weight of metal was employed in some of them. This enlarged production was no doubt due to the expanding economy of both town and country made possible by the *pax Romana*.

The chief iron-fields of pre-Roman Britain had been those of the Wealden area of Kent and east Sussex, the Forest of Dean, and the Northampton–Lincolnshire region. Production in each of these was greatly extended, and other less important iron deposits were exploited in Somerset, Warwickshire, west Norfolk, Yorkshire and Northumberland. Indeed, traces of small-scale smelting are even more widely distributed, since ores are entirely absent from very few parts of England. Some of these deposits were wholly or partly exploited by the military. In the Weald tiles stamped by the Classis Britannica are known from four sites, where it seems possible that naval work-shops existed (p. 252); and at Corbridge iron from the deposits near Risingham was worked by legionaries at an army arsenal. But the nature of the remains at the majority of sites suggests that the industry was in the hands of native craftsmen whose production was little interfered with by authority. Iron was not an imperial monopoly; the most that government did was to provide for roads to facilitate marketing the produce. This is especially noticeable in the Weald, though here ridgeway tracks, of pre-Roman character, were also extensively utilised.

The chief technological improvement in the Romano-British industry was the introduction of the shaft-furnace. More primitive iron-smelters had employed the bowl-furnace, which was little more than a shallow hole in the ground into which the draught had to be articially introduced by bellows, and whose capacity was very limited. The shaft-furnace was a structure sufficiently high – about five or six feet – for the required draught to be induced naturally (as in a chimney) once the furnace was alight, and one which could carry a far larger load. Known examples vary from twelve to twenty-eight inches in diameter. Bowl-furnaces, however, continued in use and show a considerable increase in size, suggesting improvements in bellow-design. After the ore had been smelted in these furnaces the resulting blooms had to be reheated in a smithing furnace so that slag still trapped within them could be hammered out. The finished lump seems usually to have weighed about 15 lbs, and could then be worked up by the smith. For large iron objects, such as the substantial six-foot iron bars sometimes used for the support of boilers above the furnaces of baths, several blooms were welded together. Most of the iron objects of the Roman period were of simple wrought iron, often showing very skilful smithing; but there was also some knowledge – though as yet little skill – in the production of harder cutting edges by the processes of carburisation and quenching, and even by pattern-welding.

Coal was much more widely used in Roman Britain than is sometimes appreciated in the south. This is because its outcrops occur only in the west and north, sufficient fuel being so readily available elsewhere as to render coal-carrying unprofitable. It was not mined, so far as is known; but wherever outcrops occurred these were quarried, yielding enough to make mining unnecessary. Its use seems to have been a discovery of the early second century, for its first dated occurrence is at Heronbridge near Chester in a deposit of 90–130; it also appears in some of the forts of the Antonine Wall and in levels of this century at Benwell and Corbridge. Large quantities have been found in forts on Hadrian's Wall and elsewhere, including about a ton in the south guard chamber of the east gate at

Housesteads (which had been converted into a store for it in the early fourth century), and an even larger quantity in the bath-building at Risingham. It is clear that coal was being officially supplied to forts. Elsewhere it was used for industrial purposes as well as for firing hypocausts. Its sulphur-content made it unsuitable for use in smelting iron, but it was used in smithing-furnaces and forges at Corbridge, Wilderspool and elsewhere, and for smelting lead in Flintshire. Many of the villas of Gloucestershire, Somerset and Wiltshire were supplied with coal, evidently from the Somerset outcrops; and this was no doubt the source of that used on the altar of Sulis Minerva at Bath, which was recorded as a curiosity by Solinus in the third century.[24] The occurrence of coal in some of the Fenland sites has already been discussed (p. 313).

The early exploitation of good stone was mentioned earlier in the chapter (p. 325f.) as one of the indications of the activities of prospectors from abroad during the first century. There was increasing production of good building-stone during the second and subsequent centuries as town buildings ceased to be half-timbered, and public and private monuments, town walls and villas all combined to increase demand. Kentish rag from the Maidstone area was used for the town-wall of London, and similar greensand rock was employed both in the town-wall of Chichester and at the villa at Bignor, whose columns, however, were of Bath stone. The limestones of the Cotswolds and of Northamptonshire and Lincolnshire were widely appreciated both for buildings and for funerary monuments and coffins, while farther north the magnesian limestone round York was much in use. In the neighbourhood of Chester the local red sandstone was employed, and it is interesting to find that in the later second century this stone was shipped to Caernarvon for the rebuilding of the earth and timber fort there, though in later reconstructions of this site local stone came to be used. There were few places in the province except part of the south-east where building-stone was not accessible, and except for special work local stone was normally employed. In the south-east flint usually took the place of cut stone, though at Colchester septaria lumps could be obtained from the London Clay. A few large public buildings in towns and some private residences of the wealthiest sort were able to use imported marbles, alabaster or even porphyry from Egypt for detailed decoration, but imports of such material can never have been on a large scale.

Some quarries specialised in the production of domestic millstones such as almost every household needed to buy. In the south many of these were made of greensand rock or of the conglomerate known as Hertfordshire Puddingstone, but the Millstone Grit of the Pennines was also exploited: a workshop for this exists at Wharncliff Rocks near Sheffield. On the whole, however, our knowledge of such undertakings is very deficient. Yet it is clear that corn was rarely converted into flour in Roman Britain before it reached the home. Two towns only have produced fragments of donkey-mills (p. 295), but the larger output which these imply may have been taken up by urban bakeries; we may recall the cake-mould from Silchester apparently figuring members of the Severan dynasty. Watermills, which are so plentiful a feature of the medieval landscape, are very rare in Roman Britain; apart from examples on Hadrian's Wall, they are attested only by the pivots surviving at Silchester and Great Chesterford.

A quarry with a wide market for whetstones probably lay near Stony Stratford on Watling Street; its products have been found as far away as Wroxeter, Richborough, London and Caistor by Norwich, and were clearly distributed by road. Kimmeridge shale, a soft, soapy stone which had been worked for bangles and even lathe-turned drinking vessels in pre-Roman times, was now developed in an ambitious fashion for the manufacture of trays and even couches and three-legged tables of classical design; the table legs were decorated with lion or gryphon heads and claws after the model of the marble and bronze furniture of Italy. One such leg was found at *Verulamium* in a late-second-century context, but the industry maintained itself well into the fourth century.

Salt was a necessity of life, and in pre-Roman times had been obtained by boiling sea-water in vats. This industry continued and underwent considerable development, for its characteristic debris is plentiful in the Fenland and round the coasts of Lincolnshire, Essex, Kent and Sussex. In addition, the place-name *Salinae*, indicating known salt springs, was used for Droitwich and also for somewhere in Cheshire, possibly Middlewich. Ptolemy, indeed, names yet a third *Salinae* in Catuvellaunian territory near the Wash, but this, as Mr A. L. F. Rivet has suggested, may be a mistake for Droitwich.[25]

Leather was another necessity, at least of civilised life; but we know all too little about its production. Indications of tanneries at two towns have already been mentioned (p. 295); there must have been many more, for leather was used not only for footwear but also for workmen's aprons and even for more delicate items of attire, as the famous 'bikini' from London reminds us; and it may well have been used for jugs and buckets, as in more recent times. But in addition to the needs of the civilian population, the enormous requirements of the army had to be provided for. Leather was needed by the military authorities for a wide variety of purposes, including boots, items of uniform and equipment, and also for tents and harness. To a large extent no doubt they undertook their own tanning from hides provided by direct taxation in kind (p. 259), but there will still have remained sufficient demand to make cattle profitable wherever suitable pasturage occurred.

The oyster industry should also be briefly mentioned. This, too, had been exploited in Belgic times, as is indicated both by the reputation of British pearls and also by the discovery of oyster shells in occupation deposits of appropriate date. In Roman Britain oysters were marketed on an immense scale, and were evidently transported alive in tanks, for there is hardly a site which does not yield shells, however distant from the sea. But of the organisation of this industry we know nothing.

Salt, leather and oysters had a continuous even history after the first expansion of production. Woollen goods, on the other hand, though at all times liable to be produced in the home, seem to be a feature primarily of the third and fourth centuries, at least as far as their export is concerned; and it was in 301 that two British items figure in Diocletian's price-edict (p. 317). In the fourth century the government took a hand in the production of cloth for the army and civil service, and weaving mills and dye-works were set up under state control. The Notitia records one such factory in Britain, the *gynaecium*, or weaving works, at Venta.[26] Unfortunately there were at least three Ventas in Britain, and the identity of this one is not certain. It is usually taken, on Haverfield's authority,[27] to be Winchester (*Venta Belgarum*); but this is by no means certain, for both Caistor by Norwich (*Venta Icenorum*) and Caerwent (*Venta Silurum*) lie near good sheep-rearing country; and in East Anglia in particular a number of pieces of large-scale weaving equipment are known. We may refer in particular to the big carding-combs from Caistor by Norwich and in the Worlington (Cambridgeshire) hoard, and to the enormous cropping-shears, 4 feet 4 inches long, from Great Chester-ford, the function of which was to provide a smooth close finish to the surface of woollen cloth. Both of these must have come from wool mills, and the combs suggest some form of machinery.

Apart, then, from the state factory, it is clear that the manufacture of woollen cloth was an important part of the economy of East Anglia in the fourth century, and no doubt also in other parts of south and south-west Britain. Since the demonstration by Sir Ian Richmond that the so-called *fullonica* at the Chedworth villa is really misunderstood parts of the bath-suite, there are no clear instances where fulling can be shown to have been carried on; but the villa at Darenth in Kent, with its large tanks and enormous area of hypocausts, some of which are of unusual construction, can still be said to be probably connected either with fulling or with dyeing, though re-examination of the site is urgently required.

A striking fact about trade and industry in Roman Britain is the ease with which the problems of transport were overcome. Wherever manufactured or produced, goods were easily distributed throughout the province, and the long distances over which exceptionally heavy objects such as stone sarcophagi, large altars and other massive pieces of masonry were moved from their source is most remarkable. These facts point to the skilled development of carts and wagons equal to these demanding purposes, and to the efficient maintenance of the road-system.

The principal roads had been originally laid down for military purposes, as is clear from a detailed study of their alignments, but they also served the increasing purposes of commerce, and their effect was to unify the country as never before. Milestones were usually erected to commemorate the building or repair of roads, and though the survival of these is uneven in different parts of the country, their evidence points to a steady programme of construction and maintenance down to the middle of the fourth century. After this date detailed records cease, but the survival of many of the roads through to the Middle Ages shows that they remained in good working order, at least until the breakdown of provincial organisation.

Subsidiary to the roads in Britain, but not negligible for transport purposes, were her navigable rivers and the canals which in Cambridgeshire and Lincolnshire linked some of the most useful of them.

Finally, there was the coastal shipping, whose influence can be seen in trade with the barbarian North, or in the transport of pottery from the kilns of Colchester to the Antonine Wall, but which was also active between ports in southern Britain, as is suggested, for instance, by the distribution of pewter goods made in the south-west.

All the sea-routes which had linked Britain to the Continent in prehistoric times (p. 15) were still used. Inscriptions from Bordeaux,[28] and the trade in samian pottery, point to direct voyages from the Garonne, Loire and Seine estuaries to Britain, and military inscriptions from the Tyne [29] suggest direct links with the mouth of the Rhine. Undoubtedly for most official purposes the direct cross-channel route from Boulogne had primacy, but it seems likely that after the first century Dover took the lead from Richborough at the British end; this is suggested not only by the imposing Roman light-houses at Dover and the evident decline of Richborough in the second century but also by such details as that the street plan and gates of Roman Canterbury appear to give priority to the Dover road. The port of London, however, soon achieved supremacy in the south-east, and acted like a magnet to conveyers of continental produce. Yet in the end it was the south-western route, linking the Irish Sea and Bristol Channel with Spain and the seas beyond, which survived the downfall of the western empire; for it was by this route that tenuous mercantile connections (p. 424) were maintained between the Dark Age British kingdoms of the west and what remained of the classical Mediterranean world.

1. Cicero, *ad Fam.*, vii, 7, 1.; cf. also *Ad. Att.*, iv, 16. 7.

2. *Agricola*, 12.

3. These usually give the name of the Emperor or of the lessee of the mining rights, and often include the words *ex arg(entariis)*. Analysis has shown that the lead has not always been de-silvered by cupellation, and the term seems to mean simply 'from the lead–silver works'. The weight of the ingots seems to have been intended to render them, while still portable, difficult to steal.

4. On the Stockbridge pig the name is struck cold on the side, the cast panel bearing the name of Nero; on the Flintshire pig *C. Nipi Ascani* is cast on the top. This difference may imply stricter control of lessees in the Mendips in the Julio-Claudian period than

in Flintshire; if so, the position in the Mendips was relaxed in the next reign. It should be noted, however, that the Stockbridge pig has a similar copper-antimony content to that of Flintshire ores (Tylecote, *Metallurgy in Archaeology* (London, 1962), pp. 83–7); but it is difficult to see how the Flintshire field could have been in production as early as 60.

5. *Ti.Cl.Tr.Lut.Br. ex Arg.*, found at Pulborough, Sussex. *Lutudarum* was a lead-mining centre in Derbyshire, probably near Matlock.

6. *N.H.*, xxxiv, 17, 164.

7. At Wilderspool a furnace was found which had been designed to take at least seven crucibles at a time for the production of such alloys.

8. A single stamped tile among the many tiles at Silchester might have been suspected as a plant; but part of a second was later found at the site of a tilery at Pamber, two miles from the town (*Antiquaries Journal*, vi (1926), 75–6).

9. Even in the second century the numbers of private people making the passage to Britain caught the attention of an orator (Aristides, *Orat. Aegyptiaca*, xxxvi, 91).

10. For traders with the Rhineland see *CIL*, xiii, 8164a, a *negotiator Britannicianus* from Cologne; 8793, a *negotiator cretarius Britannicianus* (a pottery-merchant who made a dedication to Nehalennia *ob merces recte conservatas*) from Domburg in Walcheren; and 7300, another merchant, possibly of pottery *ex provincia Britannia*, from Castell by Mainz.

11. Lamps, however, are not common in Britain, even in the towns, and probably the candle remained the chief source of artificial light.

12. lxii, 2, where he records that Seneca had 10,000,000 sesterces on loan in Britain. Seneca cannot have been alone.

13. For a view of the wealth of Britain at the end of the third century see the passage quoted on p. 319, note 12.

14. Cf. M. Aurelius Lunaris, sevir Augustalis of York and Lincoln, who set up an inscription at Bordeaux in 237 (p. 219, note 28), and L. Solimarius Secundinus, *negotiator Britannicianus* also from Bordeaux, though a native of the Rhineland (*CIL*, xiii, 634). The most likely trade with Bordeaux is the wine trade, and it is to some extent confirmed by the wine barrels of silver fir found at Silchester, for this tree is not found nearer than southern France.

15. S.H.A., *Vita Probi*, 18, 8; Silchester, Southwark, *Archaeologia*, lviii (1902–3), 427; Gloucester, *Trans. Bristol and Gloucester Arch. Soc.*, lv (1933), 74. The latter find included grape-skins as well and was thought to be the debris of wine-pressing. The Boxmoor vines seem first recorded by Collingwood in Tenney Frank, *Economic Survey of Ancient Rome* (1937 and 1959), iii, 78, though the excavations were by Sir John Evans in 1851, who does not mention them in his reports; it is probable that Collingwood learnt of the vines orally from Sir Arthur Evans.

16. M. R. Hull, *Roman Potters' Kilns of Colchester* (Oxford, 1963), Fig. 53.13.

17. κοῦρμι or *cervisia*: Dioscorides, *de materia medica*, ii, 88; Pliny, *NH*, xxii, 164.

18. Ammianus Marcellinus, xxiii, 6, 88.

19. The absence of any sign of export of jet objects to free Germany is another indication that they were not made in the Rhineland.

20. Martial, *de spectaculis*, vii, 3.

21. Pliny, *NH*, ix, 169; xxxii, 62; Juvenal, iv, 141.

22. Martial, xiv, 99.

23. *RIB*, 2059.

24. *Collectanea rerum memorabilium* (ed. Mommsen, 1895), 22, 10.

25. A. L. F. Rivet, *Town and Country in Roman Britain* (London, 1958), p. 132.

26. *Notitia Dignitatum Occ.*, xi, 60: *Procurator gynaecii in Britannis Ventensis.*

27. Victoria County History, *Hampshire*, i (1900), p. 292; see now W. H. Manning, *Antiquity*, xl (1966), 60 ff.

28. See p. 340, note 14, cf. *ibid.*, note 10.

29. See pp. 160, 176.

15
The Romanisation of Britain

Romano-British culture arose from the impact of the civilisation of Rome upon the Celtic people of Britain; the result, however, was not a replacement of cultures, but rather what can broadly be described as a synthesis. A convenient illustration of this is provided at the small town of Brough on Humber (*Petuaria*), which may have been the *caput* of the civitas of the Parisi. By the middle of the second century military occupation of the area had ceased, and a civilian town was arising over the site of the fort. It possessed a theatre whose stage-building was presented by a Roman citizen, M. Ulpius Ianuarius, aedile of the vicus of Petuaria, who set up a tablet in honour of the *Domus Divina* of Antoninus Pius and the deified emperors. It would be hard to find a more Roman scene. But about the same time as this dedication was made there was buried in the cemetery just outside the town a local priest. The burial rite was inhumation accompanied by a native iron-bound wooden bucket and two sceptres. This was a native burial-rite; and as if to emphasise the non-Roman character of the ritual the two sceptres had been intentionally bent and broken to devitalise them for the journey to the other world. Nothing could illustrate better the dual character of Romano-British civilisation. Outwardly it was Roman, inwardly it remained Celtic; yet it would be wrong to suppose an inner conflict between the two aspects. The result was a synthesis, intended by Rome, and welcomed by the British people as they came to realise the advantages of peace and wealth conferred by membership of the empire.

At any one time, indeed, there was a wide range of variability within the synthesis, owing to the social stratification of Romano-British society on the one hand, and, on the other, to the widely varying conditions of life and opportunity existing in different regions of the province. At one end of the spectrum lay considerable approximation to the classical way of life and at the other a substantial survival of native characteristics. Moreover, the culture of Roman Britain should not be treated as if it were a static historical phenomenon. Through the four centuries of its existence it had its periods of development and decline, of maturity and decay, despite the comparative slowness of such processes of change in the ancient world when compared with our own. It should be studied, therefore, as far as the evidence allows, against the background not only of historical growth but also of varied social achievement.

We can measure the Romanisation of Britain only with imprecision, for we have to depend so largely upon the evidence of material things – potsherds, iron tools, bronze brooches, house-plans, towns or statues – rather than upon the much more revealing evidence of contemporary testimony. Not that the evidence of material things is of little account. Haverfield long ago made the point that when the provincial adopted the use of Roman things he could be declared civilised enough to realise their value and, further, could be seen to have abandoned any inherited hostility towards them. Nevertheless, the evidence of the written word is invaluable in such an enquiry, and Romano-British writings are denied us until the fifth century.

The Romanising agents responsible for the new culture have been mentioned in earlier chapters: they were the soldiers of the occupying army, service by Britons themselves in the Roman forces, the colonies of Roman citizens, the merchants from the Continent and, at a higher level, the policy of governors like Agricola or of client kings like Cogidubnus. The civilisation thus introduced was not really the metropolitan culture of Rome or even of Italy: it was the provincial version of this, diluted but none the less real, and sufficiently vigorous to unify an empire whose boundaries touched Scotland, the Black Sea, the Euphrates and the Sahara.

In the first century there were two distinct phases of Romanisation, the Claudian and the Flavian, divided by the setback of rebellion and its aftermath. To both of these phases the army made a considerable contribution. We have already examined the influence of its architects upon the growing towns, and it was its sculptors and stone-masons who first introduced the mind of Britain to the arts of sculpture in the round and in relief, and to monumental masonry in general. Moreover, the local garrisons and the military officers who supervised local affairs must have played their part in the spread of the Latin tongue. But even in the reign of Claudius the army alone could not provide all that was required. The temple of the Imperial Cult at Colchester clearly called for outside architectural assistance, as no doubt did the cult itself in the sphere of organisation.

With the withdrawal of the armed forces from most of the lowland zone under the early Flavian governors, further steps of this sort had to be taken to continue the training of the Britons in Roman ways. Tacitus in the *Agricola* specifically alludes to the needs of education, and the presence of Demetrius of Tarsus illustrates the sort of steps that were taken. The success of this programme is suggested by the great increase in literate potters' stamps which is a characteristic of this period, but can best be seen in the inscribed writing tablets which have survived in London. These also illustrate a thriving commerce. Much of this was undoubtedly in the hands of merchants from abroad, but not all. The Rufus son of Callisunus, who wrote to his bailiff about the sale of a slave-girl, seems to represent the first generation of Romanisation in a Celtic family, and can therefore be reasonably claimed as British.

By the end of the first century towns were rapidly developing. In them education was available, public buildings of some splendour were rising, and a Romanised life was led in which the Latin language, Roman dress and continental habits of life such as visiting the baths and giving dinner parties were becoming fashionable.[1] The great variety of plates, dishes, bowls and cooking vessels which were now available, far in excess of anything known in the Iron Age, and many of them of local British manufacture, bears witness to a complete revolution in manners. The widespread use of mortaria for preparing food similarly points to changes of diet, and the vast increase of amphorae shows that wine-drinking was now a luxury not confined to the houses of the aristocracy.

The towns were the vehicle and focus of this progress. In the country things naturally moved at a slower pace, but the owners of estates did begin here and there to Romanise their dwellings. Rectangular houses, internally subdivided into rooms and with at least the lower walls in masonry, began to appear. In this last feature they were in advance of the normal town-house, which was usually constructed of half-timber and clay at this period. But it cannot be said that in either town or country private dwellings of any great size or distinction were erected in the first century. Only in Kent, Essex, and Sussex is it possible at present to identify a few buildings of the greater pretensions suggested by mosaics or bath-blocks, as at Eccles, Rivenhall, or Angmering. Elsewhere expenditure was cautious. Nevertheless, these small villas lay at the head of a long history of development, and their occupants were undergoing the same revolution of manners as has been noted already in the towns. At a lower social level the peasantry were still largely unaffected by innovations in their way of life, though they were using coins and buying the new pottery; the benefits of peace were beginning to be reaped, but increased productivity had to cater for the demands of the tax-collector before it could yield increased prosperity.

By the close of the second century much greater advances had been made. The towns were at the zenith of their early prosperity, and in the countryside quite sizeable villas had appeared. The wealthy classes were wealthier, or at least were making greater permanent parade of their wealth. Industrially the province was, by contemporary standards, fully developed; its natural resources were known and used, and mass-production of pottery had to a great extent broken down the old regionalism of fashion. Even with objects as individual as bronze brooches it is no longer possible to discern local schools of production. In the countryside there is evidence that even the peasants were beginning to construct rectangular cottages roofed with tiles, decorated with painted plaster, provided with glass windows and even sometimes yielding evidence of wooden floors (p. 302); and at some villas baths were being provided for the estate workers, not merely for the owner. Living standards had risen in a spectacular fashion.

Mosaic floors of good workmanship and considerable technical skill were being installed in the towns, and in a few of the villas, by this time. The patterns are simple rosettes enclosed in geometric designs which sometimes give an illusion of perspective; but occasionally more ambitious representational floors, though of comparatively simple design, are found. Examples of these are the Oceanus head or the dolphins-with-cantharus pavements at *Verulamium*, and the boy on a dolphin at Fishbourne. In these scenes no attempt is made to tell a story: the figure is merely a more elaborate variation of the pattern, and where, as in the lion with stag's head floor at *Verulamium*, an attempt is made to portray action it is not particularly successful. Mosaics are rarely signed in Britain, but it is usually held that the artists responsible for them were mainly continental. This conclusion is based partly on the skill which much of this new art displays and partly on the ubiquity of mosaic patterns over the empire. In the fourth century, as we shall see (p. 360), it does become possible to identify various schools of mosaicists in the towns of Britain, but in the second century, apart from one group found at Colchester and *Verulamium*, we have not enough pavements to attempt this. Nor at present does there seem to be any continuity of mosaic production from the second to the fourth century. It is possible, then, that immigrant mosaicists set up business in one or two principal cities during the second century and constructed mosaics throughout the province where demand existed, using local materials in each case for the purpose; and that only in the fourth century did renewed demand on a sufficient scale cause a renaissance of the craft on a more regional basis.[2]

Continental also, no doubt, were the artists who specialised in fresco work for the decoration of walls, though in this craft demand may have been sufficient to support regional schools based on the larger towns. In recent years there has been considerable accumulation of evidence bearing on wall-paintings, and good second-century examples, very diverse in style, are known from *Verulamium*, Leicester and Cirencester. At *Verulamium* the peopled scroll, consisting (pl. 11b) of pheasants and panther-heads emerging from a running spiral acanthus-tendril on a bright yellow background, is the most distinguished piece, but it is entirely two-dimensional. A slightly earlier panel showing a colonnade exhibits some subtle shading to emphasise perspective. At Leicester, however, there are some more ambitious three-dimensional scenes, one showing a figure standing in a coffered niche and another a tragic mask. All these paintings are remarkable for the fully Romanised taste they display, though the general style is rather dated, recalling frescoes current in Pompeii over a century earlier. Nevertheless, it was not until the fourth century that whole scenes with three-dimensional perspective began to be attempted in mosaic.

One of the most extreme manifestations of Roman behaviour was a love of gladiatorial spectacles in the amphitheatre. Not many of the towns of Britain are known to have possessed these structures, but examples survive at Cirencester, Silchester, Dorchester (pl. 9a),

Chichester, Richborough, Caerwent and Carmarthen. As they were cheaply constructed of ramps of earth rather than in the masonry style of the Continent, they are easily destructible, and more must once have existed, for instance at the four *coloniae* and at London. A few smaller examples are known from country areas, as at Charterhouse on Mendip, but it is not certain whether these served the same purpose. Others again are known at the fortresses of Chester and Caerleon and also at least one auxiliary fort; here their main purpose was undoubtedly arms-training, though they may have served for entertainment on occasion.

Gladiatorial shows were very costly, and it is possible that acrobats and wild-beast shows were more commonly exhibited in Britain: certainly such scenes are figured on Castor ware. But we have epigraphic evidence that gladiators were recruited in the province (p. 230), and in 1965 a gladiator's bronze helmet came to light near Bury St Edmunds, Suffolk. Familiarity with the arena, too, is suggested by statuettes of gladiators from South Shields and London, and by one of the more elaborate colour-coated vases made by the Colchester potters, which bears a combat scene in barbotine. The names of the contestants and a reference to Legio xxx (part of the Rhine Army) have been incised after the vessel had been fired, and may have illustrated the owner's rather than the maker's identifications. A similar vessel comes from the Nene Valley potteries. The famous mosaic of cupids dressed and acting as gladiators at the Bignor (Sussex) villa also expects knowledge of the real thing. Probably, then, gladiatorial shows were from time to time exhibited by candidates for office at the more important towns in Britain, as they certainly were in Gaul; and this would account for the allusion at Bignor, which at the date of this late-fourth-century mosaic was one of the largest villas in Britain and clearly the property of a wealthy member of the curial class,[3] if not of someone more important still.

It has sometimes been stated that the towns of Roman Britain were in some sense failures. In part this view rests on faulty deductions about their history and in part on their lack of resemblance to Mediterranean models. It is true that in Britain we do not find the tightly packed insulae and the peristyle houses which appear even in Roman Cologne, nor do more than a few towns possess colonnaded streets such as also Cologne possessed. The Italian town-house with its peristyle is really found in Britain only among the official residences of fort-commanders and once at Gloucester. In the towns the larger houses often have a compact plan of their own, with wings ranging round three or even four sides of a courtyard. It is a different plan from that usually adopted for villas, but is distinct also from the Italian town house: it represents once again a provincial compromise.

It is evident that the Romano-British town is an adaptation rather than an adoption of the classical form of city, but in a sense this points to the vitality of the Romano-British synthesis, once granted that the internal history of the towns was more prosperous than was formerly thought. In size, as we have seen (p. 292), many of them do not fall short of their contemporaries across the Channel, and their public buildings stand comparison. The basilica of London was 500 feet long by about 120 feet wide, which was larger than any known in Gaul, and the forum areas at *Verulamium* and Cirencester are larger than those of Paris, Alesia, St-Bertrand-de-Comminges or Arles, while that at Wroxeter is only 120 square metres smaller than the last. The theatre of Canterbury has a diameter of 80 metres, four-fifths of that of Orange (103 metres), but larger than those of St-Bertrand (70 metres) or Paris (72 metres). When related, therefore, to the wealth of their respective provinces the towns of Roman Britain were not notably inferior to those of Gaul in the scale of their public buildings. In both we find that the classical city has been adapted to the climate and circumstances of northern Europe; in both we find buildings such as Romano-Celtic temples and theatres which are the product of Gallic and British provincial culture; and the same sensible compromise can be recognised in the many frescoes which represent marble veneers in paint, when cold or condensation would have made the veneers themselves an uncomfortable luxury. The latter, however, were used in public buildings.

Something has already been said of the problem of assessing the populations of the towns (p. 296). To number the population of the province as a whole is a task replete with imponderables, but an estimate must now be attempted, taking the end of the second century as the point of reference. If we calculate on the basis suggested we arrive at a figure of 117,000 for the larger towns and civitas-capitals, and some 40,000 for the other large settlements of the civil zone. To this must be added perhaps 40,000 for the inhabitants of vici near forts, though these, of course, reached their greatest numbers in the third century. The army, with three legions in addition to almost 45,000 auxiliaries (p. 184f.), may be reckoned at 63,000 men, and we should add perhaps another 10,000 for dependants not included in the figure for vici. These figures amount to 270,000 people engaged in activities not primarily concerned with food-production; they must be augmented by a further estimate of those engaged in mines, the pottery industry and such activities as charcoal burning, the felling of timber and so on; perhaps 50,000 would not be excessive if we include their dependants. We have thus arrived at a total of 320,000 persons who had to be fed by the labours of the agricultural population. It is much more difficult to arrive at a reasonable estimate of the latter. Somewhat more than 600 villas are known, and the real total may be more like 800; perhaps not more than 500 of them were in occupation at the end of the second century. If purely arbitrarily we follow Collingwood in assigning an average of fifty people to each villa, this would account for 25,000. There remains the peasant class, whose numbers must have been very considerable. Not only do we have here to take account of sizeable villages in addition to isolated farms, but air photography and field-work show that large areas of the midland plain, where suitable soils occur, were thickly populated in antiquity instead of being covered by unbroken uninhabitable forest, as was once imagined. Mr Charles Thomas has recently shown that the native settlements of the Roman period in Cornwall, known as Rounds, imply a population of about 10,000, approaching that recorded in the Domesday survey of 1086. If this is true of such a comparatively undeveloped area as Cornwall it must embolden us when we approach the richer agricultural areas. The population of the Fens cannot have been less than 10,000, to judge by the recorded remains. On this sort of basis, and considering the distribution of finds it is not difficult to conclude that the rural population must have been at least a million; and when we remember the 320,000 unproductive mouths which had to be fed on the agricultural surplus we may feel that the real figure is likely to have been half as much again. Finally, in Wales and the north we have large populations of mainly pastoral folk to take into account. The Brigantes can hardly have been less than 50,000, to judge by the garrisons required to control them, and may have been twice that number; the population of Wales may have been about the same.[4] The conclusion reached, therefore, is that at the end of the second century the total population of Roman Britain may have amounted to rather over two million.[5] This figure is somewhat larger than that estimated for England and Wales at the time of the Domesday Survey in 1086, which can be used as a check on the accuracy of the guess.[6] It is clear that the population must have been considerably reduced during the immediately post-Roman centuries, and it would not be unreasonable to assume that by the time of the Norman conquest the optimum Romano-British level was once again within sight, after which the known figures for medieval England continue to rise.

We have seen that the Latin language began to spread in Britain partly as a result of intercourse with merchants or with the army, and partly as a result of the deliberate policy of governors such as Agricola who set up schools. The Celtic language, of course, survived, and in post-Roman times is found developing in the tongues spoken in Cornwall, Wales and Cumbria. Most educated Romano-Britons were no doubt bilingual, Latin being the language of law, government, business and cultured life, British that of the intimate family circle and of intercourse with the lower orders. Some such theory is necessary to account, not so much for the persistence of British place-names (for place-names are hard to kill), nor for the actual survival of Celtic (for this could have continued as the language of the peasantry), as for the presence in the latter of many loan words derived from Latin. A large proportion of these describe objects and concepts for which there was no British equivalent. Many are words connected with administration, but even more concern education or household goods, daily life, building or the calendar. They not only describe concepts new to the life of Britain but they derive in the main from experience of the middle and upper classes rather than from the agricultural peasantry. Another important factor to be taken into account is the difference between the highland and lowland zones; in the former very little Latin is likely to have been heard away from the vicinity of the forts.

It is not certain how far the art of writing was practised in pre-Roman Britain, but it is unlikely that it was altogether unknown. Caesar mentions that though the Druids did not commit their teaching to writing, the Greek alphabet was used for other purposes in Gaul. When we remember the close connections between Gaul and Britain and that schools existed in Britain at which Druids from the

Continent acquired a higher learning, we may accept the probability that the British language could be, and was, written and read. The probability is perhaps strengthened by knowledge that papyrus was imported in pre-Roman times,[7] and it is certainly supported by the occurrence of Celtic words such as *Rigonus* on Belgic coins. In Gaul, after the conquest, inscriptions in the Celtic tongue are not unknown, though now carved in Roman characters. In Britain, however, no Celtic inscription of the Roman period has been found, whether this is due to the blanketing quality of Roman education in Britain or to a proportionate infrequency of those who had had occasion to write British. What is quite clear is that even artisans could write Latin. This is proved by the many inscriptions written on tiles while they were still unfired, and therefore by the workers in the tileries.[8]

Haverfield took this to mean that 'Latin was employed freely in the towns of Britain not only on serious occasions or by the upper classes, but by servants and work-people for the most accidental purposes. It was also used, at least by the upper classes, in the country.' [9] But Professor Kenneth Jackson has suggested that though this may have been the case, the evidence quoted does not prove that Latin was their normal tongue, since 'the *only* language of writing was Latin; it would not occur to anyone to write in British, nor would they know how to do so'.[10] It is possible that he overstates the case, since as we have seen, pre-Roman British may have been written; but at least the fact remains that artisans knew and could write Latin, with all that this implies for the availability of education in and near the towns. The evidence of graffiti scored by the owners on pottery and other objects is so widespread that we can be certain that at least in the towns the use of Latin, and of Latin names, penetrated very deeply,[11] and this class of evidence extends to villas also.

But Jackson is certainly correct in denying that Latin wholly replaced British. Even in the towns, where it came nearest to doing so, the traders would need British for contact with country-dwellers on market day, and the upper classes for intercourse with the workers on their estates. Graffiti on peasant sites in the country are very rare. Education did not spread thus far, and we need not doubt that the language of the countryside continued to be British.

Thus, the British language survived, the only tongue of the peasant countryside and the bilingual partner of Latin in the towns; Latin words adopted into British were the result of intercourse between those with a cultured background and their servants or estate workers. Moreover, Jackson has been able to show that the spoken Latin of Roman Britain was of a somewhat archaic kind, different in some respects, and of a purer quality, than the so-called 'Vulgar Latin' prevalent in the western provinces as a whole. In part this may well have been the result of insularity, but he has suggested that it was also the result of schooling. Britons, in other words, maintained a purer Latin because they did not learn it in the nursery but acquired it at school. Such a theory is to some extent supported by the apology of St Patrick. He was born of good Romano-British family, but was carried off by Irish raiders in early youth; and in later life he lamented his inability to write good Latin like those who had spoken it from boyhood. Nevertheless, this sort of humility was a fashionable gambit, and should not perhaps be taken too seriously.

It is difficult to believe, with all the evidence we have of the use of Latin in Britain, that it was not spoken in the homes of the upper classes together with British; and it is perhaps better to visualise a British type of Latin, fostered indeed at first by the schools, but kept alive by the insular character of the leading families, and, for all we know, strengthened by whatever institutions Britain possessed for higher education.

The nature of these is quite unknown, but their existence is vouched for by the career of Pelagius, who is generally agreed to have received a first-class education before he left Britain, soon after 380 at the age of nearly thirty, to study law in Rome. They are also adumbrated in the early fifth-century documents usually attributed to Fastidius. Further evidence for an interest in classical Latin and Roman culture is provided by the fourth-century mosaics at the villas of Low Ham, Somerset, and Lullingstone, Kent, and the fresco from the Otford villa in Kent, which illustrate part of the *Aeneid* of Vergil or contain allusions to it. The first of these occupies a whole floor with scenes of Aeneas' arrival at Carthage and reception by Dido (pl. 12 b); the elegiac couplet which accompanies the Europa scene at Lullingstone presupposes knowledge of the epic's first book; while the wall painting from Otford carries a quotation which occurs both in book i and again in book xii. A fourth Vergilian reference is supplied by the undated graffito from Silchester (*conticuere omnes*, the opening line of book ii) which has already been mentioned.[12]

An important part in the Romanisation of Britain was played by Roman Law, which not only enforced the replacement of violence by recourse to the courts, but was also in itself an education in civilised principles. Moreover, having been evolved to meet the requirements of a more advanced civilisation, it facilitated the development of more complex transactions. Rome recognised local legal systems in so far as they did not conflict with her own law, and for the first two centuries local magistrates must have administered whatever traditional laws existed. Roman law itself was fully current only in cities with Roman constitutions or among individuals who held the citizenship. But as time went on the number of the latter increased, and in other fields the court of the governor or the iuridicus established precedents by which Roman legal concepts prevailed. With the growth of commerce and of the habits of peace, the Roman legal system must have played an influential part in the background of provincial life. With Caracalla's grant of Roman citizenship to all free members of the empire a climax in this process was reached, though it was offset to some extent by the fact that the privileges of citizenship were by now unequally applied, *honestiores* enjoying a different set of penalties upon conviction from those applied to *humiliores*. Though the decree made no difference to the constitutional status of former peregrine towns in the provinces – they do not appear to have been regraded as Roman municipia – yet imperceptibly it did affect their position. They became the legal *origo* of the citizens in their territories, and in Gaul at any rate they began to usurp the identity of their civitates. During the third century in Gaul the civitates began to take on the guise of true city-states, and it is possible that the same process went some way in Britain.

Another not insignificant factor of Romanisation was the coinage. Not only did the introduction of a large-scale, regular and consistent monetary system have an enormous influence on the growth of commerce but the propaganda effect of the legends and figure-types of the coins themselves no doubt had a considerable psychological influence. This cannot be immediately measured, but to judge by the wide use made of different contemporary types, the Imperial government had no doubt of their propaganda value. In 139, for instance, over 100 different denarius and 50 sestertius types were minted, not

353

to mention other values. This is a very different policy from that of most other ancient states, whose coin-types were conservative to a degree. In the Roman empire, whose very size made the dissemination of news and views a peculiar problem, the coinage was perhaps the only method of reaching the eyes of every subject; the method was not neglected at least until the third century. Thereafter the types became rather more stereotyped, and no doubt their influence fell with the decay of the monetary system itself. Occasionally issues were made having special reference to Britain: it is possible that some of these were specially directed to the province, for certainly the Britannia issue of 154–5 seems remarkably common as a site find.

The depth and variety of Romanisation in Britain is accurately reflected in the art of the province, particularly its sculpture, ranging as it does from first-class imported pieces in Mediterranean marble through highly competent creations in local stone, down to very simple, and in some cases crude, attempts of no aesthetic worth. Bad though they are, however, these last are not without all value, since they show the atttractive power of classical art, even in a rural *milieu* where the Latin language itself was hardly known.

Roman art was a novelty in Britain, and its adoption was quick and thorough: it is a question whether it amounted to a revolution. In pre-Roman times a very different art had existed here. This was the insular version of the La Tène tradition of the continental Celts, with its passion for non-representational pattern based on curvilinear tendrils, and its ability, if animals or parts of the human frame were to be depicted, to transform their character into something formal, quintessential, no longer real but often horrific.

Collingwood has painted a depressing picture of the psychological difficulties of creative artists reared in this tradition, when they found themselves 'submerged beneath the tide of the dreary mediocrity of Roman provincial art'.[13] It was his view that 'throughout the Roman period British artists were working under what may perhaps be described as a permanent strain'.[14] He evolved the theory that Celtic art was somehow driven underground, to emerge once more in freedom after the collapse of Roman rule in Britain and the disappearence of its art.

Such a picture is quite unreal. In the first place it completely underestimates the achievements of Romano-British art. Secondly, we have no evidence whatever of Celtic artists practising their patterns in secret and handing them on before casting away their tools in despair. These patterns can have reappeared in the sub-Roman period only in one of two ways. Either the tradition was transmitted or it was revived by copying some chance rediscovery or survival. But the revived Celtic art of the later period does not start off where the early Celts left off. Nor was the Roman period bridged by secret strained transmission within the province: the Celtic craftsmen who still worked in the west and north during the third and fourth centuries were tinkers rather than artists and practised a peasant craft. The transmission existed, but it was open, operating in the unconquered quarters of the British Isles.

In considering, and attempting to account for, the sudden interruption of the brilliant art of pre-Roman Britain, we have to remember three of its characteristics. In the first place by the Claudian period it was already showing signs of passing its prime; the processes of degeneration had not proceeded far, but already the simple themes, which were its strength, were beginning to break up in overelaboration and fussy detail. Secondly, it was essentially an aristocratic art, based upon the love of display which found its chief expression in objects of fine metal dedicated to personal adornment and warlike parade. It follows that there were comparatively few workshops and a lack af broad popular foundations. In another sense also it was a narrow art: it was completely divorced from nature and the observation of reality, and the field of its application was circumscribed. It is not difficult, therefore, to account for its collapse. With the Roman conquest the whole basis of society and its aspirations changed very quickly, and they became more civilised. No longer were the nobility in a position to lead their war-bands in their war-chariots, accoutred with gaily decorated panoply. At one blow the major part of the market had disappeared. A whole society had passed together with its ethos. The new society which arose in Roman Britain was able to equip itself with the new necessities of cultured life from the mass of imports which now flooded across the Channel. This process had indeed begun among the rich as early as the reign of Cunobelin, but after 43 all sections of society were able to avail themselves of the novelties of metal and pottery goods imported from the classical world, and to learn appreciation of the skill of the sculptor in stone which was hitherto unknown to them.

For the rest, the advantage of the new 'mass production' outweighed the older virtues of individual craftsmanship. We ourselves live in a comparable age. Only in Wales, Brigantia and the north did the old art linger on in areas still unsubdued, and in these regions it never totally disappeared, though reduced to small-scale activity. In Ireland, of course, and perhaps in parts of northern Scotland, Celtic artists and their patrons remained unaffected by these developments.

The rest of Britain turned eagerly to the manifestations of new techniques. In the Flavian period a great programme of public building was set on foot, with all this involved of new architectural forms and decoration. Little now survives in detail. In Britain we do not have the satisfaction of discovering masses of sculpture built into our Roman town-walls as happens in Gaul, since the British towns escaped the disasters of the third century which were responsible for so much destruction there; the sculpture of Britain has disappeared more finally into the lime-kilns and the buildings of the Middle Ages.

Whether or not the fine contemporary marble head of Germanicus from Bosham (Sussex) once adorned a shrine of the imperial cult, the nearby villa of Fishbourne contained mosaics and works of art, including an almost life-size marble head of a boy. At Bath we have a small fragment of gabled decoration [15] bearing the date 76, and a larger-than-life Bath-stone head wearing the elaborate coiffure affected by fashionable ladies of the Flavian period. And at Colchester there is the fine winged Sphinx, holding a human head between her paws, which once adorned a tomb and probably dates from the late first century.

Nor should we forget the multitude of statues and busts of Titus which, according to Suetonius, were formerly to be seen in Britain. At Richborough the great monument was covered with marble and with bronze statuary, dating from the late Flavian period; only fragments survive. At Silchester there was found in the basilica a fragment of a twice life-size bronze imperial statue wearing a cuirass of pre-Hadrianic style; this is likely to be the portrait of the emperor under whom the civitas was established, perhaps either Titus or Trajan, since Domitian's statues would not have survived his murder.

Most of these would be works of foreign craftsmen in view of their early date and the official character of most of them.[16] But these continental craftsmen had the responsibility of forming taste and setting standards. That they were not unsuccessful is indicated, for instance, by the remarkable limestone portrait head from the Bon Marché site at Gloucester;[17] this is clearly by a British artist who had succeeded in blending classical techniques with Celtic traits in a most striking, almost impressionistic, result. It is clear from this and other works (such as the second-century head of the god Antenociticus from Benwell) that British sculptors soon learnt to love and emphasise the intricate patterns which could be made from locks of hair, and also the ornamental effects to be evoked from folds of drapery (as in the statue of Juno Regina at Chesters and in numerous tombstones and religious relief throughout Britain). The most striking example of this tendency is, of course, the Bath temple-pediment with its Gorgon's locks and the flowing robes of the supporting Victories. This work is justly renowned as the masterpiece of Romano-Celtic sculpture in Britain.

Thus, the inspiration of the new art was not lost on British craftsmen who adopted sculpture as their medium; and the best of them were able to impart something of their Celtic spirit to their creations, which gave them an originality and character which is recognisably a genuine Romano-British synthesis. The same spirit inspired the best of the potters; for though the tendrils and the hunting scenes which are so characteristic of British colour-coated wares in the Nene Valley and at Colchester owe much to continental inspiration, they possess also an originality of their own in which there is a recognisable Celtic element. Indeed, their attempts at more strictly classical scenes, in which human figures take part as gladiators or charioteers, are notably less effective as works of art: they do, however, point the lesson that these potters were Roman as well as British in their outlook. The truth is that the technique of decoration favoured flowing motion rather than stylised scenes.

Thus, by the end of the second century classical art in its many forms had become a commonplace in Roman Britain, and much of it was being produced by native craftsmen. Even sculpture, perhaps the most difficult to assimilate, was being imbued with specifically local traits.

It is never easy to decide whether a particular work with provincial characteristics was made by a Gaulish or a British craftsman, and it is an easy temptation to assign anything good to an immigrant. But where, as at Bath and Cirencester, very large collections

357

of material in local stone exist, it is surely more reasonable to recognise the emergence of a British school. Both Cirencester and Bath were wealthy cultured places with much patronage to offer, the one as the largest and richest city in the province after London, the other as a cult centre and thermal establishment with an extra-provincial reputation which attracted visitors from abroad. Both lay at the heart of good stone country. We cannot doubt that, once local schools of sculpture had been founded by Gaulish masters, the tradition took root in local talent. In fact, we have evidence of both Gaulish and British hands. At Bath there is an inscription to Sulis set up by 'Priscus son of Toutius, a stone-mason, citizen of the Carnutes' (that is, from the Chartres region); but there is also one erected to the Suleviae by 'Sulinus, son of Brucetus, the sculptor'. His name shows him to be of local origin, and another altar to the same goddesses was carved by him at Cirencester, where it was found with two mother-goddess reliefs and so much freshly cut stone-work as to suggest a workshop (or possibly a shrine).

The museum of Cirencester contains a great variety of attractive pieces, such as three well-known groups of Mother-goddesses (pls. 14b, 15b), each as different in design as in skill of execution, heads of Mercury, Minerva and a River God carved with great delicacy of feeling, and a number of fine architectural fragments; among the latter, the most outstanding is the large capital, perhaps from a Jupiter-column, which is adorned on each of its four faces with divine figures of unusual type (pl. 14 a). As far as can be judged by stylistic signs, the dates of these pieces run through the second and third centuries; the first century is represented by two military tombstones (which though not by local hands will have had significant visual influence), and work was still being done in the fourth century, as witnessed by the base of a column inscribed by L. Septimius, governor of Britannia Prima. Bath has an equally distinguished though more diversified collection, as might be expected of a site which drew pilgrims and patients from so wide a field. A number of military tombstones may be by regimental masons, though the men commemorated were away from their units; beside these there is a wide variety of other, principally religious, sculpture, almost all of it in local stone. The date-range here is from the late first through to the third century. Another town in the region, Gloucester, also has some distinguished pieces, though fewer in number.

It is clear that sculptors' workshops enjoyed a very long period of productive life in this region of Britain, and were highly skilled. What is more striking is the discovery that recourse to sculpture for votive purposes was had by persons in the countryside with a much less exacting taste, or at least with less commanding purses. A good illustration is provided by the pieces found in 1957 at Lower Slaughter near Bourton-on-the-Water (Gloucestershire). Here, thrown down a fourth-century well belonging to a typical peasant village in which only one rectangular cottage was found, the remaining dwellings being circular, were a number of reliefs probably of late second- or early third-century date; these had clearly once adorned a rustic shrine. The majority are crude in the extreme, but they afford good evidence of the depth to which Romanised ideals penetrated among the people of the countryside. There are many other examples of such curiously blundered reliefs from rural sites; it will be sufficient to quote that from Rushall Down, Wiltshire, now in the British Museum. Bad though they are in accomplishment, they express an awareness of the fundamentals of Romano-British civilisation.

Another centre of sculptural tradition was Lincoln, where a number of fine works of art have survived, though some are in fragmentary condition. It is likely that here, too, continental craftsmen set the early standards, being summoned to assist the adornment of the new late-first-century colony, and that stone-masons may also have been available from among the legionary veterans. But the relief of a young charioteer shows that it was not long before a distinctively Romano-British style was developed. The influence of this art once again spread far beyond the town itself. Quite competent, and in the case of the Ancaster *matres* delightful, carving is found at various sites in Lincolnshire and surrounding areas, some of them rural shrines. One of the most outstanding is the almost life-sized statue of Minerva from Sibson (Huntingdonshire), possibly in her guise as patroness of potters. No doubt other towns, such as London, exercised a similar influence in their areas; but the evidence has not survived. Most of them lie in areas where stone was not locally available and was therefore eagerly sought out for re-use in medieval times.

With her incorporation in the Roman empire Britain was once more linked to the main streams of European art; and just as society in the empire was to some extent cosmopolitan, so the art to be found in Britain was not entirely provincial (pl. 15a). Works of art in bronze and marble were imported, probably in many cases by wealthy people who themselves had come to Britain from elsewhere; crafts-men from Italy and Gaul were brought in to create works of art *in situ*; but British artists learnt their idiom from these sources, and the best of them gave a fresh interpretation to what they did which can be recognised as specifically Romano-British.

The new art was naturally based primarily on the towns and to a lesser extent on the villas; but nothing is more striking than the extent to which it reached the peasant class. No one can turn the pages of Pitt-Rivers' great reports on his excavations of the native farmsteads of Woodcutts and Rotherley without being impressed by the number of objects in bronze in everyday use (such as dish-handles, box lids or fittings, knife-handles, enamelled brooches or rings with intaglios), and others like bone pins or shale handles, which bear human and animal figures and other patterns of Roman art. The same impression is reinforced at other less fully excavated sites. It is clear that in Roman Britain art was far more pervasive than it had been in the Iron Age, and that all classes according to their means and taste could enjoy its products.

With the renewal of prosperity in Britain at the end of the third century, a new phase of mosaic production opens; artists were greatly in demand, not merely now in the towns but more particularly in the villas, especially the wealthy establishments of Dorset, Gloucester-shire and Somerset, where the great majority of Romano-British mosaics have been found. Most of these seem to have been laid in the first seventy years of the fourth century, though a few can be dated later. The amount of work executed during this period and the many styles involved show clearly that British craftsmen were now at work, however close their initial training by continental masters. Here is perhaps a contrast with the situation in the second century (pp. 345–6).

It is probable that many of the towns now contained firms of mosaicists who served the surrounding districts. A comparison of patterns and styles suggests that there may have been as many as ten different 'schools', three of which have been clearly defined by Dr David Smith. The first of these was centred at Cirencester, and worked both in the town and at villas in the neighbourhood, such as Woodchester, Chedworth, North Leigh and Newton St Loe. Orpheus, surrounded by distinctively drawn birds and beasts, was one of its favourite motifs, but there are many other details of style and pattern which reveal its work. A mosaic in Trier has close stylistic connections with the Cirencester school, but it is not yet clear whether British craftsmen went to Germany (perhaps with Constantius Chlorus) or whether German craftsmen migrated to found the British firm. Another school can be identified in Dorset, perhaps working from Dorchester and serving villas such as Frampton, Hinton St Mary, Low Ham and Lufton. A third operated in the Humber region, centred perhaps at Brough or York and working at Winterton, Brantingham, Horkstow and Rudston. It is often possible to observe in the pavements that the master-craftsman executed the principal figures, leaving routine ornament – or even important detail – to his apprentices. In spite of this, very competent standards were on the whole maintained, the most notable exception being at Rudston. Many of these late mosaics contain good figure work, and the Low Ham example is notably successful as a narrative. Inspiration was no doubt obtained from pattern-books, and regional styles kept alive by the same means: but the initial training must have been supplied by immigrant masters coming from the Continent or even from North Africa.

The last subject remaining to be discussed for the light it throws on the Romanisation of Britain is its Religious Cults, in which once again a wide range of variation may be discerned between the classical and the Celtic. Broadly speaking, the religious observances of the provincials of Roman Britain, and also those of the army, may be divided between those which were officially inspired or enjoined (these being naturally Roman) and those which were more spontaneous. These last varied in their content according to the nationality and Romanisation of the individual worshipper.

The Roman empire was very tolerant of religious variety. The Romans themselves were polytheists, and the official religion of the Roman state was not exclusive. It merely demanded observance, after which the individual was free to worship what he chose. The only cults which were liable to suppression or persecution were those, such as Druidism, which involved practices (like human sacrifice) offensive to civilised thought, or those, such as Judaism or Christianity which by their exclusive claims could be thought of as endangering the safety of the empire. The reason for this attitude lay in the pragmatic character of Roman state religion, which was less a system of faith than one of contract: the gods, it was believed, would protect the state, provided that proper rituals were carried out, any human withdrawal from which – or other deficiency in their fulfilment – being accordingly perilous to the fulfilment of the divine side of the bargain.

The worship of the Capitoline Triad – Jupiter Optimus Maximus, Juno and Minerva, the chief deities of Rome – was accordingly given a high priority both in the army and in towns of official Roman foundation. A *capitolium*, the joint temple of the three, would certainly have existed in each of the four colonies and in the municipia of the province, with statues and altars to the deities concerned. No trace of any of these temples has yet been certainly identified, though it is likely that one of the buildings attached to the forum of *Verulamium* was the capitolium of that town. We have more evidence for the military version of the cult, since altars dedicated to Jupiter Optimus Maximus were renewed each year on 3 January, and the old ones were often ceremonially buried at the edge of the parade-ground.

As a focus of imperial sentiment and loyalty, the cult of the Capitoline Triad lost ground as time passed to a new state religion, the Imperial Cult. Divine honours had long been paid to rulers in the Greek Orient, and it was from Asia Minor early in the reign of Augustus that the practice spread to the west. In 12 BC the cult was formalised with the official dedication of an altar, and later a temple, at Lyon to Rome and Augustus, which were served by Gallic notables organised on a representative basis in the provincial council under an annual president (the *sacerdos Galliarum*). The living emperor was worshipped but in conjunction with the goddess Roma.

This became the pattern for the organisation of the cult in other provinces, though the precise dedication of the altar and temple may have varied according to time and circumstances. Tiberius and most of the Emperors after him refused divine honours during their lifetimes; many of them were deified by senatorial decree after death, and it became normal to offer worship to, and take oaths by, the deified emperors (*divi*) of the past and the *genius*, or more often the *numen*, of the living emperor.

In Britain the cult seems to have been introduced in or soon after

362

49, when a centre was provided for it at the newly founded colony at Colchester, where both an altar and a temple have been found. The precise terms of the dedication are unknown. Tacitus refers to the 'temple of the deified Claudius' and Seneca also uses expressions which suggest that it was a cult personal to Claudius;[18] from this it has usually been concluded that from the outset the British cult was anomalous in omitting Roma and offering worship to Claudius as divine (*divus*) before his death. But this conclusion is very unlikely. Tacitus is writing of the events of 60, six years after the death and official deification of Claudius; he is not describing the original dedication. Nor should the gibes and exaggerations of Seneca be taken to express historical fact. In an extant letter of AD 41 to the Alexandrians, Claudius himself wrote: 'I decline my high priest and temple establishments, for I do not wish to seem vulgar to my contemporaries, and I judge that temples and the like have been defined and set apart by all ages for the gods alone.' This makes his personal policy clear enough, and there is no reason to suppose that he altered it later; it is worth noting, however, that his words were published by the prefect of Egypt as 'the letter of our god, Caesar'.

Recently D. Fishwick had put forward an explanation which easily disperses these difficulties.[19] It is that the altar was the original feature of the cult-centre and that it was dedicated to Roma and Augustus, the living emperor, in the normal way; and that the temple is secondary, being decreed for Claudius after his death and official deification. By 60 work had advanced far enough for the temple's podium to be used in the last stand of the colonists against Boudicca.

We must not forget the reference to the *Domus divina* on the Chichester temple-inscription. This was erected within the lifetime of Cogidubnus, and is therefore hardly likely to date after the death of Vespasian, the next emperor to be deified. Cogidubnus is remarkable for his 'correct' attitude to all things Roman, and the wording accordingly can be taken to imply a wider basis for the provincial cult, now expanded, no doubt, to include the present emperor (and, by extension, the members of his family). The imperial cult achieved a genuine popularity in the province. Dedications to the *Numina Augustorum* are not uncommon, though usually attached in a secondary position to those to other gods. The Domus divina occurs again in a second-century context at Chichester itself, on a stone

363

dedicated to Jupiter Optimus Maximus,[20] and also (among other places) on the early Antonine theatre-tablet at Brough on Humber.[21]

The reconsecration of the temple at Colchester after its destruction by Boudicca, and the maintenance thereafter of its precinct, certainly give no grounds for supposing that the provincial cult and its administration were removed to London. On the contrary, we must assume that it remained at Camulodunum. There would certainly, however, have been other temples and altars of the imperial cult in the chartered towns of the province, and perhaps also in the wealthier civitas-capitals. All, too, are likely to have possessed honorific statues of emperors, so that it is not possible to assert that the few surviving traces of such portraits must necessarily be cult objects. Thus, the bronze head of Claudius from the River Alde, though in all probability removed from *Camulodunum* itself by Boudiccan rebels, is not thought to be a temple-statue. The pre-Hadrianic fragment from Silchester has already been mentioned (p. 356); it came from the tribunal of the town's basilica, and was thus a state rather than a religious effigy. Other fragments, including a larger-than-life bronze head of Hadrian, come from London; and from within the fortress of York comes a fine head of Constantine I in local stone. None of these seems likely to have come from temples. On the other hand, a colossal marble head, perhaps of Trajan, comes from Bosham, Sussex, a parish which has also produced the head of Germanicus already mentioned (p. 356); the possibility of a cult-centre there is stronger. Moreover, three small bronze heads from various sites in the Cambridgeshire Fens, and one from Duston, Northamptonshire, seem to be provincial portraits of some of the emperors of the second century; all are made to be attached to cere-monial sceptres or staffs such as often formed part of the regalia of rural shrines, and they possibly imply that the imperial cult had a share in the observances of the temples concerned. This is, after all, no more than is implied also by such joint dedications as that at Colchester to *Numinib(us) Aug(ustorum) et Mercu(rio) deo*,[22] an example with numerous parallels elsewhere.

A part in the municipal version of the imperial cult was played by members of the corporations known as Seviri Augustales, whose membership was largely drawn from wealthy freedmen. The Bordeaux inscription already cited (p. 203) was set up in 237 by M. Aurelius Lunaris, who described himself as a sevir Augustalis of York and Lincoln. A second member of this body at York was M. Vere-cundius Diogenes, whose coffin-inscription recorded that he came from the civitas of the Bituriges Cubi (whose capital was Bourges). No seviri from other chartered towns are at present attested.

Apart from these cults, which were introduced by government policy, many other cults, both of classical and oriental deities were brought over not only by the army but also by continental merchants or officials. In the civil zone these naturally appear mainly in the towns. The Roman colony of Lincoln possessed organised guilds of worshippers, the Apollinenses and the Mercurienses, and the latter at least was connected with one of the town's constituent vici. London possessed a temple to Isis in addition to its well-known Mithraeum, the marble statuary from which provides such remarkable evidence for the wealth of its congregation. A few other towns, notably Bath and Cirencester, have produced statues or reliefs of Roman deities of completely classical type, and so have a number of the wealthier villas, where the context is more certainly Romano-British; but before these can be assessed, something must be said of Celtic religion and the effect of the *interpretatio Romana* upon it.

The early Celts worshipped the powers of nature; their deities were neither so anthropomorphic nor so departmentalised as the gods of the classical world. The Romans tended to equate Celtic gods with their own, but it is significant that the identifications were not always consistent. The Celtic gods had neither the same attributes nor the same fields of action as their classical counter-parts, and they were harder to apprehend. With the spread of Roman culture in Gaul the Celtic deities began to make their appearance in sculpture, and it is evident from the results that this process greatly assisted the Romanisation of the gods. Yet, even so, many still appear in animal form or with animal attributes such as horns; others are figured with three faces or three heads. Nevertheless, such represen-tations are often accompanied by the cock, which is an attribute of Roman Mercury, or the goose of Mars or the thunderbolt of Jupiter, and these show that an identification had been made. Conversely, a recognisable representation of Jupiter may sometimes hold a wheel, demonstrating that it is Taranis who is thus portrayed, or sometimes the hammer of Sucellus; and a figure clad in Mercury's winged hat and boots may bear the features of an aged man, and be accompanied by Rosmerta, consort of the Gaulish Mercury but without a part in classical mythology.

This clothing of Celtic deities with the attributes, appearance and personality of the Roman gods is called the *interpretatio Romana*. In many instances the synthesis is obvious, as when the physical appearance or attributes are not precisely regular, or when the identification varies, as with the 'horned god of the Brigantes' who is shown sometimes as Mars, sometimes as Mercury, and sometimes perhaps as Silvanus. But even when we are confronted with perfectly classical statues it is still rarely safe, in the absence of inscriptions, to assume that we are in touch with purely classical cults. An inscription will often give us the Celtic equation, as in dedications to Mars Lenus, or Mars Olludius or Apollo Anextiomarus; on the other hand, it may show that a classical deity is intended, as with the statuette of Mars from the Fossdyke at Torksey in Lincolnshire. Here the provincial style of work might have suggested a Celtic deity masquerading as Mars had not the inscribed base carried the legend: 'To the god Mars and the divinity of the emperor; Bruccius and Caratius, both surnamed Colasunus, gave 100 sesterces from their own money; Celatus the coppersmith made the statuette and gave a pound of bronze made at a cost of three denarii.' Here only the title *deus* labels the dedication as provincial.

In Britain we have fuller information about non-Roman deities in the north; the numerous temples in the civil zone of the province have rarely yielded evidence. Even in Gaul, where the names of 400 deities are known, only a quarter of them occur more than once. The Celtic world was full either of very local deities or more probably of many local manifestations of a few transcendent beings. Under Roman influence some of these local gods acquired distinctive character by their recognition as aspects of greater Roman deities, but few enjoyed more than local influence. The dedications mapped on fig. 12 illustrate the range of distribution, which has probably been extended by troop-movement. Many had only a single shrine with no dedications elsewhere; Coventina at Carrawburgh and Antenociticus at Benwell illustrate this. It is interesting also to note that some cults had a distribution limited in time as well as space. Antenociticus was worshipped only in the second century, and the distribution of dedications to the Matres Campestres shows that

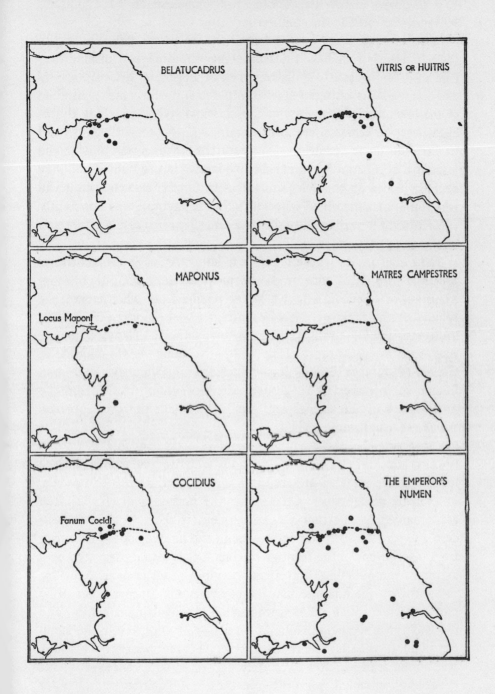

12 Distribution of dedications to some religious cults

they, too, were mainly a second-century phenomenon,[23] for southern Scotland was outside the empire thereafter.

The examples so far quoted have come from the military district of the north; but we have to assume that the same sort of picture is true also of the south. Sulis Minerva at Bath was a Celtic water-goddess who was assimilated with Minerva and who came to own one of the few temples in Britain in the classical style. She is not known elsewhere. Nodens, on the other hand, who possessed a large and wealthy shrine at Lydney in Gloucestershire, which was built in the last third of the fourth century, is also known in Lancashire, and may be identified with the deity known in Irish as Nuada. In Britain he was sometimes identified with Mars, but his temple was apparently the centre of a healing cult; the god himself seems also to have had connections with water.

The other deities whose names are known to us in the south are few, and they occur once or, at the most, twice. Among them Mars Alator is attested on a votive silver plaque from what must be a temple-site at Barkway, Hertfordshire, as well as on an altar from Wallsend, and Mercurius Andescocis once only, at Colchester. Some, like Ancasta at Bitterne, Hampshire, or Cuda at Daglingworth, Gloucestershire, or Viridius at Ancaster, Lincolnshire, have no Roman homonym. We are left to gather our information partly from the architecture of the shrines and partly from cult or votive objects, which are usually uninscribed.

These teach us the great variety of religion available in Roman Britain. Many of the great Celtic gods who are well known on the Continent are attested in Britain either on inscriptions or in reliefs, or even by place-names. Cernunnos, the horned god who is often accompanied by the ram-headed serpent, is represented at Cirencester (with two such serpents). Epona the horse goddess is known from inscriptions in the frontier regions, but is also represented by a figurine from Wiltshire and again possibly at Colchester. Sucellus, the god with the hammer, and Nantosvelta his consort seem to be intended on a rough relief from East Stoke, Nottinghamshire, and the god's own name is inscribed on a ring at York; while the small rural temple at Farley Heath, Surrey, yielded a bronze binding from a ceremonial staff which was crudely decorated with repoussé figures apparently intended not only for these two deities but also for Taranis. *Camulodunum*, the hill of Camulos, and (if Sir Ian Richmond is right) *Aquae Arnemetiae*, are two examples showing how place-names can reveal the presence of Celtic deities; certain river-names may possibly do the same.

The temples themselves are stereotyped in the main. A few wealthy and outstanding cults had temples of classical design, as at Bath, or of even more exotic style, as at Lydney. In the civil zone the majority had much smaller temples of the Romano-Celtic type, where the small square shrine is surrounded by a square ambulatory or portico. The building was sometimes varied by a circular or polygonal plan. Like the classical temple, it was not intended for congregational worship: people made their vows individually, and if crowds assembled on festival days they did so in the open air, or in the theatres which were occasionally provided, as at Gosbecks Farm (near Colchester) and *Verulamium*. Often the temple stands in a walled temenos, and sometimes the planning suggests the former presence of a sacred grove. At Springhead, Kent, a small temple was built over the ritual burial of four infants, interred at each corner of the building, presumably after sacrifice, in the later second century.

The Romano-Celtic temple is common in Roman Germany and in central and northern Gaul; in Britain its distribution lies south of a line connecting Norwich to Caerwent. North of this restricted area, in the civitas of the Coritani, simple round or rectangular shrines lacking the elaboration of a portico are found in the countryside, and even their more ambitious temples were probably not of Romano-Celtic form. At Thistleton Dyer, in Rutland, the temple which in the third century succeeded an earlier circular shrine resembled an aisled basilica with entrance porch, and recalls the analogous Temple B at Pesch in the Rhineland. It is possible that other equally atypical buildings existed elsewhere in Coritanian territory; at both Ancaster and Nettleham recently discovered inscriptions recorded the gift of arches to the deities concerned, but excavation has not revealed the architectural context.

There is no doubt that religious practice tends to be conservative, and in Roman Britain many primitive Celtic cults and customs continued to be observed side by side with the newer modes of worship. Thus, we find votive deposits consigned to the keeping of deities of lakes, rivers or bogs. There are many pre-Roman examples of this custom, one of the richest being the great hoard of objects from Llyn Cerrig Bach in Anglesey (p. 104). Similar deposits have been recognised in the late-first- and second-century hoards of metal-work from Carlingwark Loch and from Eckford and Blackburn Mill in southern Scotland; and even at *Verulamium* the discovery of a large number of coins together with more valuable objects in the former bed of the River Ver has been thought to represent, not casual losses, but intentional offerings to the deity of the stream, made perhaps by travellers crossing a bridge. So, too, with the large collections of fourth-century iron-work found in shafts at Great Chesterford and Silchester; these may quite possibly be due to votive rather than emergency concealment of valuable equipment. Naturally the reason for deposit is not always recoverable, but there are suggestive records of deep shafts whose contents were not the haphazard filling of an abandoned well but appeared purposive, regularly laid and often un-expected. The best known of these was at Jordon Hill near Wey-mouth, Dorset, in which a deposit of iron weapons, all (ritually?) bent, was covered by successive deposits, each containing a coin and the bones of a bird, and each being separated from the next by a layer of stone slabs. Small bronze birds, too, are not infrequent finds on sacred sites, and birds sometimes figure on religious reliefs; they can sometimes be taken to symbolise the souls of the dead, but sometimes they represent the messengers of the gods, or even, if Irish mythology is any guide, the gods themselves.

There are also traces in Roman Britain of the survival of the Celtic cult of the head. In pre-Roman times the Gauls, and the Britons too to judge by a scene on a coin of Cunobelin (Mack 260), collected and preserved the severed heads of their enemies: the head was regarded as the seat of the personality. It is not surprising therefore to find certain divinities represented by a head alone, and this is probably the significance of certain sculptured heads, often of crude workman-ship, which have been found at numerous places in Britain, mainly in Wales and the north. Occasionally, as on the well-known stone from Broadway, Worcestershire, a head or face was added to a phallic carving; this can be taken to represent the fusion of Celtic with Roman ideas. Phallic representations are numerous in Roman Britain, and they signify a Roman contribution. The phallus was re-garded in classical art as a symbol of good luck as well as of fertility: it was a talisman against the Evil Eye, and was sometimes 'demonised' by the addition of limbs, as on a remarkable unpublished stone from the temple at Wroxeter; but the addition of a face or

370

head is probably the result of Celtic influences. Phallic representations themselves are very rare in pre-Roman Celtic art.

There was thus a great diversity of religious experience available in Britain at every level and for all tastes. The native Celtic deities of the land were recognised and propitiated even by strangers. The Roman Gods and the Imperial Cult inspired a loyalty to Rome and imparted a sense of unity within a world-wide empire. Both of these groups of cults, however, despite the round of calendered festivals about which Britain yields very little information, were on the whole impersonal. They all called for observance rather than devotion; the gods answered prayers and vows, but did not call for the soul's allegiance. This last aspect, and the insistence upon codes of conduct, was the contribution of eastern cults; and of these the most important was Christianity, since in due course this became the state religion of the empire.

There is little evidence to suggest that Christianity became widespread in Britain before the closing years of the fourth century. It was introduced, however, perhaps as early as the second, for Tertullian,[24] writing in the early years of the third, asserted that 'parts of the island inaccessible to Rome have been subjected to Christ'; and his evidence is supported a few decades later by Origen.[25] If Christianity, as is likely in Britain at this period, was a minority religion very largely confined to eastern traders, and if Tertullian may be taken literally, it is possible that merchants had made converts on voyages to Ireland or up the Scottish coasts.

That the faith had reached Britain before the time of Severus is suggested by the probability that it was in 208–9 that St Alban became the first British martyr. His death has often been attributed to the persecution of Diocletian, but there is good ancient testimony that no martyrdoms occurred in those parts of the western empire ruled by his colleague Constantius 1,[26] and Britain was part of the dominion of the latter. The text of the earliest manuscript of St Alban's *Passio*, whose detailed knowledge of the topography of *Verulamium* gives it undoubted authority, describes his judge as 'Caesar', who 'without an order from the emperors commanded the persecution to cease, and reported to them that the slaughter of the Saints was stimulating rather than suppressing the spread of Christianity'.[27] This neatly fits the context when Geta Caesar was governor of the civil province during the campaigns of the two Augusti, Severus and Caracalla, in the north.[28]

Christianity, however, was likely to spread fastest in the cosmopolitan society of large ports and cities, and Britain was not at first a favourable environment. One day London may perhaps produce pre-fourth-century evidence; at the present time Cirencester is the only town to have done so, for there the famous word-square, now known to be a Christian cryptogram, is incised on wall-plaster which, to judge by its technical quality, is of second- or third-century date: [29] moreover, such a cryptogram would lose much of its significance after the Freedom of the Church. We can only say that by 314, when the Council of Arles assembled, the urban episcopate of Britain was well established. Three British bishops and a priest and a deacon attended the council;[30] and Dr J. C. Mann has shown that these represented the metropolitical churches of the four British provinces of the day.[31] Even fourth-century relics of urban Christianity, however, are curiously rare. The most substantial is the little church at Silchester, and there are the remains of what may be a cemetery-church at *Verulamium*. A third church, possibly dating to the fifth century, has left even less substantial traces at Richborough. The picture of small numbers and lack of wealth, which these small churches and the paucity of evidence elsewhere suggest, is supported by the record that poverty compelled three of the British bishops attending the Council of Ariminum in 359 to accept Constantius' offer of free transport by the imperial posting service on their journey; though it is fair to add that other British bishops refused this assistance.

Undoubtedly, however, it was through the urban aristocracy that Christianity reached the villas, where wider evidence exists for it. At Lullingstone in Kent we have the remarkable wall-paintings of the mid-fourth century, and at Hinton St Mary in Dorset a mosaic floor containing the portrait of Christ as a centre-piece (pl. 13). Both places were almost certainly chapels for worship. Other villas, such as Frampton and Chedworth, have yielded less spectacular though still authentic traces. But though the most plentiful evidence for Christianity comes from the towns and villas of the south and east, there also exists good evidence for its spread in the north, particularly in the region of Carlisle, where there was probably a bishop.

Despite the edicts of Christian emperors against pagan cults, these still continued to flourish in Britain through the middle of the fourth century, and indeed for a short time between about 360 and 380 received renewed impetus; for excavation has shown that new temples were erected at Lydney in Gloucestershire, and at Maiden Castle in Dorset during the reign of Valentinian, and repairs were carried out at others, for instance at Chew Stoke in Somerset. It is also very probable that the small column re-erected to Jupiter at Cirencester by L. Septimius governor of Britannia Prima [32] is to be dated to this same time. In London much of the fine sculpture which had adorned its Mithraeum was carefully concealed, perhaps some time in the reign of Constantine 1; but if this was due, as is likely, to action by the Christian church of the city suppression was not altogether successful; for after extensive reconstruction the temple continued in use for some time thereafter. It is improbable that this pagan persistence, and even revival, had much to do with the short-lived policy of the emperor Julian; it had already long been a factor of British life, and it outlasted the apostatising movement of Julian by almost a quarter of a century. Rather it was due to the insular character of Britain itself, and to its remoteness from the sources of power which were attempting to supplant paganism by the new official cult.

By the end of the century, however, it is probable that Christianity had made considerable progress. The coin-series at many pagan temples, such as Woodeaton in Oxfordshire, seem to suffer reduction in volume soon after 380. At *Verulamium* the temple-theatre was abandoned about this time or soon after; at Chew Stoke some of the subsidiary buildings went out of use, and at Brean Down the temple itself had been converted to industrial uses as early as about 370. Concomitantly with the decay of paganism, our evidence for Christianity itself becomes richer with the emergence of historical personalities such as Pelagius, Ninian or Patrick, and with the survival of the writings of early fifth-century British Christians such as Patrick or Fastidius; while the suggestive description of the occasion in 429, when St Germanus met the *immensa multitudo* and converted it from Pelagianism to orthodox Catholicism, points to a cult now at last making headway as a popular movement. On the other hand, it is true to add that we are now entering an era when events are recorded from the Christian viewpoint. It would be wrong to regard the conversion of Britain as complete: Vortigern could still find 'magi' to consult. Nevertheless, the British church at this late date began to show a new activity with the missionary movements of Ninian and Patrick outside the old province, and was sufficiently entrenched to survive the Dark Ages. At the moment when Britain, through no wish of her own, ceased to be part of the Roman Empire she was becoming united as never before with the state religion of that empire. Yet the synthesising process was still active: the Christianity of Britain had become Pelagian Christianity, the formulation of a British heresiarch.

1. Tacitus, *Agricola*, 21.

2. Wall mosaics were also made in both periods, c.g. at Wroxeter (*Archaeologia*, lxxxviii (1938), 186) and at East Malling (*Arch. Cant.*, lxxi (1957), 238), but little survives.

3. For illustrations see J. M. C. Toynbee, *Art in Roman Britain* (London, 1962), pl. 56 (South Shields), pl. 176–7 (Colchester), pl. 193 (Nene Valley), p. 225–6 (Bignor). Eadem, *Art in Britain under the Romans* (Oxford, 1964), pl. xxxi a, b (London). For government action to reduce the cost of gladiatorial shows see *ILS*, 5163, and commentary in Pflaum, *Le Marbre de Thorigny* (Paris, 1948), p. 14 and *Hesperia* 24 (1955), p. 320.

4. The Domesday population of Wales is assessed at 100,000 by J. C. Russell, *British Mediaeval Population* (Albuquerque, 1948), p. 54.

5. This is slightly above the figure of one and a half million reached by Sir Mortimer Wheeler in 1930: *Antiquity*, iv, 95.

6. The estimate of J. C. Russell (loc. cit.) for England in 1086 is 1,105,216, to which must be added 100,000 for Wales.

7. Dr. J. P. Wild has shown that scraps of papyrus may have been used in the manufacture of British 'tin' coins (*Antiquity*, xl (1966), 139); the conclusion has been confirmed by later work: D. F. Allen in M. Jesson and D. Hill (ed.) *The Iron Age and Its Hill-Forts* (1971), pp. 127 ff.

8. The best-known examples of these are: (i) *satis*; (ii) *puellam*; (iii) *fecit tubul(um) Clementinus*; (iv) *VI k(alendas) Octo(bres)*; (v) *Pertacus perfidus Campester Lucilianus Campanus conticuere omnes* from Silchester; *Primus fecit X* from Leicester; *Austalis dibus XIII Vagatur sib(i) cotidim* from London.

9. F. Haverfield, *The Romanization of Roman Britain* (Oxford, 1915), p. 34.

10. K. Jackson, *Language and History in Early Britain* (Edinburgh, 1953), p. 99.

11. This is well illustrated by the obscene phrases scored on wall-plaster from Leicester (*JRS*, liv (1964), 182).

12. For further remarkably interesting light thrown by mosaics on classical education in Britain, and in particular on the possible ownership of illustrated manuscripts, see D. J. Smith in A. L. F. Rivet (ed.), *The Roman Villa in Britain* (1969), pp. 90 ff.

13. S. Piggott and G. E. Daniel, *A Picture Book of Ancient British Art* (Cambridge, 1951), p. 11.

14. R. G. Collingwood and J. N. L. Myres, *Roman Britain and the English Settlements* (Oxford, 1936), p. 259.

15. *RIB*, 172.

16. See *RIB*, 149, for a *lapidarius cives Carnutenus*.

17. J. M. C. Toynbee, *Art in Roman Britain* (London, 1962), pl. 8; eadem, *Art in Britain under the Romans* (Oxford, 1964), pl. viii b.

18. Tacitus, *Annals*, xiv, 31: *templum divo Claudio constitutum.* Seneca, *Apocolocyntosis* viii, 3: (Claudius) *deus fieri vult: parum est quod templum in Britannia habet, quod hunc barbari colunt et ut deum orant . . .*

19. *Britannia*, iii (1972), pp. 164 ff.

20. *RIB*, 89; J. M. C. Toynbee, *Art in Britain under the Romans* (Oxford, 1964), p. 164, for dating.

21. *RIB*, 707.

22. *RIB*, 193.

23. Their Benwell dedication (*RIB*, 1334), however, is of third-century date, since it was made by Ala I Asturum *Gordiana*.

24. *adversus Judaeos*, vii.

25. *Homil. iv in Ezekiel interp.*, i.

26. Augustine, Ep., 88, 2.

27. *Tunc impiissimus Caesar exanimis, tanta novitate perculsus, iniussu etiam principum iubet de persecutione cessare, referens gaudere potius religionem caede sanctorum, per quam eandem opinabantur aboleri.* Later MSS change *Caesar* to *iudex*.

28. See Dr J. R. Morris, *Hertfordshire Archaeology*, i (1968), pp. 1 ff.; W. Levison, *Antiquity*, xv (1941), 337–59.

29. *Rotas opera tenet arepo sator: Archaeologia*, lxix, 1917–18 (1920), 197; *JBAA*,[3] xvi (1953), pl. 1.

30. *Eborius Episcopus de civitate Eboracensi provincia Britannia. Restitutus episcopus de civitate Londiniensi provincia suprascripta. Adelphius episcopus de civitate colonia Londiniensium. Exinde Sacerdos presbyter, Arminius diaconus.* Part of the text is corrupt, and presumably *Lindinensi* or *Lindinensium* should be read in one or other place.

31. *Antiquity*, xxxv (1961), 316–20.

32. *ILS*, 5435 = *RIB*, 103.

16

Carausius and the fourth century

The short-lived British empire of Carausius and Allectus was the last of the separatist movements of the third century. Its rise and collapse illustrate the limitations of ancient sea-power. Britain could be held against the empire by one who commanded the Channel, but that command could not be maintained indefinitely because of the inability of oar-powered fleets to remain continuously on patrol. It required the sustaining genius of Carausius to support the experiment, and when this was removed the end came quickly.

M. Aurelius Mausaeus Carausius, like most of the military leaders of the later empire, was a man of humble origin who had risen by ability. By birth a Menapian from the Coast of Belgium, since early youth he had acquired a knowledge of the sea. He had played a distinguished part in Maximian's campaign of 286 against the Gaulish Bagaudae, those bands of deserters, displaced persons and revolted peasantry who were terrorising country and town alike, and later in the same year was given a naval command in the Channel with orders to suppress the raids of Franks and Saxons on the northern coasts of Gaul. Coming under suspicion, however, of diverting rescued treasure from its rightful owners and from the government, and even of postponing attack until the raiders were returning full of booty, he learned, so we are told, that his execution had been ordered by Maximian. Thereupon he lost no time in taking refuge in Britain, where he established himself as emperor.

This occurred probably late in 286, possibly early in the following year. But we know nothing of the reasons why Britain fell so easily into his grasp. The command of the Classis Britannica was not sufficient to outweigh the opposition of three legions: he must have enjoyed a previous popularity which perhaps can be explained by Diocletian's assumption in 285 of the title *Britannicus Maximus*, a style which he soon abandoned during the period of British independence. It was possibly therefore Carausius who had been responsible for the victory which bestowed the title, and if so he would be well known to the British legions. Nothing is recorded of the location or nature of the campaign; it may have been directed against a Saxon or Irish landing. It will be remembered that both Caistor by Norwich and Wroxeter have shown signs of destruction by fire about this time, though these may, of course, have been accidental disasters. For the rest he had sufficient funds to buy the support of the troops, and indeed the timely acquisition of treasure and the lack of opposition to his elevation by the British garrison both suggest that his ambitions were not so suddenly matured as our sources suggest. With the army in his favour, the opinion of the provincials themselves would be of secondary importance; but there is no reason to doubt that for some time they had entertained dissatisfaction with the financial policy of the central government (p. 216). It was to meet such feelings that part of Carausius' propaganda, as put out on his coins, was designed, notably the *Restitutor Britanniae* and *Genius Britanniae* legends. Nevertheless it would be an anachronism to suppose that Carausius led a nationalist movement. He was a would-be emperor of Rome, not a king of Britain.

In the early years of his reign Carausius seems to have been able to retain part of northern Gaul under his control. Maximian had his hands full with wars on the upper Rhine and against the Franks near its mouth. It was not until the autumn of 288 that he started concentrating troops and a fleet against Carausius, and though in the following spring he was able to penetrate to the coast, a naval defeat seems to have followed. The result was an uneasy peace which lasted until 293, a peace which on the Roman side was intended to gain time for further measures, but which to Carausius opened visions of recognition and legitimacy. He now brought the valuation of his coinage into line with the reformed system of the empire, and it may have been now too that he adopted the names M. Aurelius, which were those of Maximian. When it became obvious, perhaps in 292, that despite his overtures war was impending, he began to issue coin-types honouring the other emperors and stressing the triple division of supreme power, with legends such as *Pax Auggg*,[1]

Victoria Auggg, *Providentia Auggg* and the like; some even bore the image of Diocletian or Maximian, and one went as far as to depict the busts of all three Augusti surrounded by the legend *Carausius et Fratres sui*.

No such courtesies issued from the Roman mints, however; Diocletian was disinclined to countenance rebellion. The very existence of Carausius violated the principles of his tetrarchy, which was established early in 293 with the appointment of Constantius and Galerius as Caesars. Constantius at once opened his campaign with a swift attack upon Boulogne, Carausius' main continental base, which he cut off from naval relief with a mole across the harbour-mouth. The town fell with the surrender of its garrison, and Constantius went on to attack the Franks of the Rhine mouth, who seem to have been acting in league with Carausius. From these two blows to his prestige the latter did not recover; shortly afterwards he was murdered by Allectus.

Carausius was an able adventurer and an effective ruler. The only epigraphic evidence to survive is a milestone from the neighbourhood of Carlisle,[2] which shows that his power extended to the northern frontier. It is his coinage which provides the fullest evidence of his appearance, policy and aspirations. At first this coinage was produced with haste and little skill, partly by over-striking previous issues; two coins with the mint-mark BRI may record a temporary mint of this preliminary phase at Wroxeter.[3] Subsequently regular mints were established. In addition to one at London and another whose signature C has been taken to signify *Camulodunum*, *Corinium* or *Clausentum*, Carausius had at least one permanent continental mint, probably at Rouen.

That he was able to maintain his Gallic possessions so long is due no doubt partly to Maximian's preoccupation with barbarian enemies (which made the unofficial recognition of Carausius a temporary convenience provided that he kept his bargain), and partly to the military strength of Carausius himself. As well as the British legions, he controlled at least one on the Continent, for the panegyrist of Constantius mentions a 'Roman legion won over'.[4] This had probably formed part of the force originally assigned to him for the defence of northern Gaul, and it may have been Legio xxx Ulpia Victrix; this legion, normally stationed at Xanten, the nearest fortress to the

Rhine mouth, was the readiest available for transfer to Boulogne, where the walled enclosure is of fortress size.

He may well have controlled vexillations of other legions also, assigned to him for the same original purpose, for among his coins is a legionary series which names six continental legions in addition to xxx Ulpia Victrix and two of the three stationed in Britain.[5] The purpose of this issue is not certain, but it is best explained as intended for donatives to the forces concerned, for its value as propaganda is obviously minimal; and though it is inconceivable that all these legions were themselves under his control, it would be quite in accordance with the military practice of the period for detachments from them to be seconded for special service. If so, Carausius commanded powerful regular forces in Gaul, in addition to the barbarian mercenaries raised among the Franks and new forces conscripted from the ranks of Gallic merchants, which are attested by the panegyrist. But strong though he was, he lacked the power or the initiative to attempt the conquest of the Continent. Indeed, he clearly recognised the collegiate principle of empire.

His originality is clearly seen in his coinage. The legend *Expectate veni* on an early issue is a quotation from Vergil, the only one to appear on a Roman coin. For the first time for more than two generations fine silver was issued as denarii, though these coins quickly disappeared from circulation and were soon discontinued. His normal issues, however, which were minted in great quantity, were radiate *antoniniani* of a much better size and quality than those of the Gallic empire; these must have done much to restore financial confidence.

Carausius has often been credited with building the Saxon Shore forts which were provided late in the third century for the defence of the south-east coasts of Britain. In reality, however, these forts are part of a wider system of security embracing both sides of the Channel; their establishment was probably due to the initiative of the Emperor Probus (276–82). In Britain forts already existed at Brancaster and Reculver, and a small base had recently been fortified at Richborough (p. 215). The fort at Burgh Castle near Yarmouth presents some interesting problems, for it was begun in the old style with rounded corners and internal towers, but with no rampart bank; however, before the defences had been completed drastic alterations were imposed. New external towers or bastions were added to the walls and the internal ones apparently were left unfinished. Large sockets in the summits of the bastions suggest that powerful revolving onagri were mounted; but the tops of the towers are on the small side for this purpose, and perhaps the sockets served some structural purpose. Burgh, then, designed to an earlier specification, was brought into conformity during construction with the new military architecture which was being introduced for new town-walls in Gaul. Its earliest certain appearance on this side of the Channel is at the new stone fort of Richborough, which was already built when Carausius seized power.[6] At Lympne and Portchester the evidence points to the same date of construction, while the dates of Bradwell, Essex, and Walton Castle, Suffolk, are uncertain (pl. 16). Only Pevensey can be shown to belong to a later period.

There is little to recommend the view put forward by D. A. White [7] that these Saxon Shore forts were built as a precaution against Roman rather than Saxon invasion, for they would be of little tactical value against the landing of a Roman army, being too widely scattered and too thinly garrisoned, and in fact they played no part against Constantius in 296. In an earlier period the British bases of the Classis Britannica had been concentrated in Kent and perhaps east Sussex; the effect of the new measures was to create further fleet-bases along the east coast and on the south as far as Portsmouth Harbour; these were linked in each case with a land garrison with the dual function of protecting the base and of rounding up any raiders who penetrated the screen.

Similar late forts are known on the west coast at Cardiff and Lancaster, with smaller enclosures also at Caernarvon and Holyhead. These must be survivors of a once more extensive system which, like the forts on the east coast, was associated with naval activity. Caer Gybi at Holyhead closely resembles the fortified naval bases established on the Rhine and Danube by Valentinian, and the other sites are all on estuaries. But whether these forts were the work of Carausius or of Constantius, or of a later period in the fourth century, is entirely unknown.

Allectus had been the finance minister of Carausius. The words of Aurelius Victor [8] suggest that he was *rationalis summae rei*; a praetorian prefect at this date also had financial responsibilities and would have been better equipped for murder; but would hardly be described in those terms. His reign, which probably began in the autumn of 293, was uninspired and brief. In 296 Constantius was ready, and probably in September an invasion was launched. Preparations had been extensive, for the expedition was in two divisions, one fleet being massed at the Seine mouth under Asclepiodotus, Constantius' praetorian prefect, and the other under Constantius himself at Boulogne. Constantius contented himself with a demonstration in the Channel which was perhaps diversionary in intent, but Asclepiodotus took advantage of low cloud or mist to elude the fleet which was waiting for him near the Isle of Wight and landed somewhere near Southampton Water, where he burnt his boats before marching inland.

Allectus lacked the strategic genius of his predecessor, and gave way to indecision. He made the twin mistakes of leaving the naval initiative to his foes, and of being misled by Constantius' naval activity in the straits into concentrating his forces at the wrong place. These forces consisted partly, as we shall see, of regiments from the north, including the Wall, and partly of Frankish mercenaries. When the news of the landing reached him he had to hurry off to shield London, and only the weather saved him from being caught between two invading armies; for Constantius' transports were unable to make land, and the Caesar himself had to return to Boulogne. Meanwhile a decisive battle was fought somewhere in the region of Silchester, and in it Allectus lost his life. Either because of his haste, or more probably because he could not rely upon his regular troops, he was unable to deploy the whole of his strength, and the casualties were mainly among his barbarian mercenaries.[9] There are signs that Silchester itself was damaged in the resulting tumult.

Some of Constantius' own transports reached London in time to save it from the retreating Franks, and when Constantius himself arrived he was accorded a triumphant welcome. The scene is recorded for us on the great gold medallion found near Arras, which shows the *tutela* of London kneeling to welcome him at her gates, and the legend *Redditor lucis aeternae*. Relief must have been genuine, the danger only just averted. The anonymous panegyrist of Constantius uses almost the same words to describe the scene of thankfulness: *Britanni . . . tandem liberi, tandemque Romani, tandem vera imperii luce recreati.*[10] As we have seen (p. 241), this may

381

have been the occasion for the grant of the title *Caesarea* to London, in honour of Constantius.

Once Allectus was dead, considerable reorganisation and reconstruction had to be undertaken by his conqueror. It seems probable that the two provinces of Britannia Superior and Inferior, into which Roman Britain had been divided since Caracalla, were almost at once reorganised into smaller units; and the question whether there was a preliminary separation into three provinces of Britannia Prima, B. Secunda and B. Caesariensis, before the final creation of the four which are attested in the Verona List of 312–14, has already been discussed (p. 241). These four provinces were Britannia Prima, B. Secunda, Maxima Caesariensis and Flavia Caesariensis.

Diocletian's reforms included the permanent separation of the civil government from the provincial military commands which now began to be organised under *duces*; but the new system was not everywhere applied until the reign of Constantine, and it is not certain when the division of responsibility became effective in Britain. Certainly the Birdoswald inscription shows that under Constantius the *praeses* presumably of Secunda, Aurelius Arpagius, was still in control of troops.[11]

In the north there was much to do on the frontier and in the military areas behind it. It may be that the Picts, as the Caledonians were now described, had seized the opportunity presented by the absence of the Wall-garrison to invade the protected lands north of the frontier and to attack the Wall. This act is nowhere attested by ancient sources, but it is a reasonable inference – both from the campaign, no doubt punitive in character, on which Constantius is recorded to have been engaged in the far north in 306 [12] and also from the observation that some at least of the forts on the wall were damaged by fire at about this time: two have produced building inscriptions of the tetrarchy.[13] The destruction has also been recognised in some of the milecastles and turrets, though in others either the stratification has not survived or else it is not clear how far the observed repairs were necessitated by intentional damage. In addition, destruction has been recognised in some of the vici on or near the Wall.[14]

The garrisons, however, which are named in the second half of chapter xl of the *Notita Dignitatum*, in what is evidently a list of the period 296–367, are in almost every case identical with those attested in the same forts in the third century (p. 262f.). The fact that so many of them survived suggests either that any attack was small-scale or that the troops themselves were elsewhere, having been withdrawn by Allectus for his struggle with Constantius, though in the event they played little part therein. Other troops from northern Britain may have been concentrated by Allectus in addition to those from the Wall, and probably were; but since the first part of chapter xl in the *Notitia*, which contains the relevant forts, is a list of re-placements after the later disaster of 367, it throws no light on the situation now. Whatever troops were used by Allectus, they were clearly absent for so short a time that in any case the opportunity for hostile activity in the north was brief.

The wall-garrison, then, seems to have been sent back to its old stations,[15] and perhaps the only major change made by Constantius was to redeploy elsewhere the additional numeri which had sup-plemented the regular forces there during the third century; at any rate, except for the *numerus Maurorum Aurelianorum* at Burgh-by-Sands, they are no longer heard of on the Wall. The forts on the wall, however, and the milecastles and turrets too, required extensive repair. This, as the inscriptions at Birdoswald and Housesteads sug-gest, was undertaken as soon as possible, as no doubt was the re-establishment of the outpost forts. High Rochester, Risingham and Bewcastle were certainly rebuilt, and so perhaps was Netherby. Wholesale reconstruction extended also to Corbridge and to many of the Pennine forts, such as Bainbridge or Ilkley; and even York and Chester can show extensive renovation of their defences. It is not necessary, however, to imagine that all the restoration south of the Wall was necessitated by enemy action, or that it was undertaken so urgently. At Bainbridge, for instance, the headquarters building sur-vived almost unaltered from the time of Severus until 367, and this is not likely to have happened had the fort been sacked in 296. In general, excavators have not been sufficiently careful to distinguish between demolition and destruction, and the latter can be assumed with any degree of confidence only where the reports speak of wide-spread signs of fire. In the wall region these exist, but there is little certain evidence farther south. Sixty or seventy years had elapsed since the great programme of rebuilding carried out under emperors from Severus to Gordian III, and natural decay may be held responsible for much. This would certainly have caught the attention of Constantius.

At Birdoswald the inscription of the Tetrarchy furnishes support for this conclusion, since it refers to the 'praetorium which had been covered with earth and fallen into ruin'.[16] These words have sometimes been held to illustrate official euphemism intended to conceal the results of enemy action; but as with an earlier example (p. 188), it is better to take it literally. Dr J. Wilkes has shown that in the late third century the supply of equestrian commanders for auxiliary units may have been difficult to maintain in Britain,[17] and the Birdoswald inscription itself shows a centurion in command. In such circumstances the commandant's house, with its provision for the large household of a wealthy official, may well have remained unoccupied and unmaintained.

Neglect, however, extended farther than this. At Birdoswald both the headquarters building and the baths required repair. These, indeed, may have been damaged by enemy action; but elsewhere in the Pennine region forts were completely rebuilt, even though there is no certainty that their predecessors had suffered attack. No doubt the long quiescence of the frontier and the disturbed political conditions of the last thirty years had been responsible between them for much official lethargy. It is extremely unlikely that there had been a large-scale Brigantian rebellion. The Gallic empire may not have had the resources or the interest to maintain the northern frontier at full efficiency; certain regiments may have become gravely under-strength owing to slack recruitment. But there is no evidence that this state of affairs was universal.[18]

Whatever the reasons, there is no doubt that the great majority, if not all, the forts of northern Britain were extensively rebuilt about the beginning of the fourth century.[19] The date suggested for this event by the coins and pottery is necessarily ill-defined, and can sometimes be shown only to be later than about 270. However, the arrival of Constantius and the preparations for his northern campaign provide the required historical context for the initiation of the programme, which is confirmed by building-inscriptions of the Tetrarchy from Birdoswald and Housesteads, dating as they do before 305. Elsewhere in the north new forts were built at Piercebridge, Newton Kyme and perhaps at Elslack, the first, at over eleven acres, being exceptionally large; yet like the others which were now rebuilt, they show little trace of the new military architecture which had already governed the design of the forts on the Saxon Shore. Lancaster alone can be said to belong to the new type; at others the abolition of the earth rampart to make way for extra buildings, so that the fort wall is freestanding inside, is the only sign, and that perhaps coincidental, of its influence.

At Chester the north and west walls of the fortress were rebuilt very largely with material obtained from nearby cemeteries. The date of this work is certainly not earlier than the late third century, since one of the tombstones came from a burial of the time of Caracalla or Elagabalus,[20] but it cannot certainly be ascribed to Constantius. Nevertheless, when we recall the destruction of the Wroxeter forum about this time we may suspect that the damage, whatever its date, was the work of raiders from the Irish Sea. Increased insecurity in this region in the late third century can be suggested as the cause of the reoccupation of the old hill-fort at Dinorben from about 260.

At York a number of buildings previously encroaching on the rampart were demolished and sealed by a new bank, and a new defensive wall was built round the entire circuit except between the north-east and south-east gates,[21] the south-west front being equipped with eight magnificent external multangular towers. The dating-evidence for this reconstruction is meagre, but it can be shown to be later than 270, while the pottery from the accompanying ditch suggests that it began to silt up in the early fourth century. The monumental character of the south-west front, excelling in magnificence the other known fortresses of the empire and built to dominate the river and the colonia beyond it, is best understood in terms of York's position either as an imperial headquarters or more probably (since Constantius remained in Britain less than a year) as the headquarters of the *dux Britanniarum* once that command had been established.

There can be little doubt that the presence of Constantius Caesar in Britain had invigorating results in many directions; but even more important, as its influence became effective, was the return to firm government and a sounder currency. We may be sure that the restoration of the frontier and its outpost system was effected under his own supervision, but the big programme of military reconstruction elsewhere in the north, and perhaps the completion of the system of coastal defence, may have been spread out over more than one subsequent decade. This is probably true too of the revival of building activity which has been recognised at *Verulamium*. Until the middle of the reign of Constantine the influx of new coins from continental mints was very small, and existing coins remained in circulation – a fact which has tended to result in the assignment of too early a date for buildings erected in the early fourth century.

Constantius had returned to Gaul in 297, and it was not until 306 that he crossed once more to Britain.[22] By this time he had become the senior Augustus, for Diocletian and Maximian had abdicated in 305; but his health was already failing. Just as Severus a century before had campaigned far into Scotland after the defences of the province had been rebuilt, so now the time had come to carry the war into enemy territory, so that Roman terms could be imposed.

The emperor was joined at Boulogne by Constantine, his son, before the expedition sailed. The details of the campaign are unknown, but the words of the panegyrist make it plain that the far north of Scotland was reached.[23] It seems probable that Severus' amphibious tactics were employed. Pottery of appropriate date has been discovered at Cramond and Carpow, where contact could be made with the sea; but otherwise there are no known archaeological traces of the expedition. Before midsummer a brilliant victory had been won, and Constantius returned to York, where on 25 July he died. His refined features, as displayed on the Arras medallions, were reflected in the mildness of his rule, and his death was widely lamented. In 297–8 he had sent craftsmen from Britain to assist the restoration of Autun after its devastation by the Bagaudae, and Eumenius, in the speech of thanks which records this, mentions the interest he took in education. The persecution of the Christians which had been ordered by Diocletian in 303 was not strictly applied by him, and within his dominions nothing worse was enforced than the demolition of churches.

As soon as the emperor's death was known, the army at York acclaimed his son Constantine as Augustus in his place. This title, indeed, he had to surrender for a time, but succeeded in obtaining his recognition as Caesar from Galerius. A decisive part was played in his elevation by Crocus, a chieftain of the Alamanni, who had accompanied Constantius to Britain as an ally.[24] His presence illustrates the growing dependence of Roman power upon barbarian allies and the important part their leaders were coming to play in affairs of state; but there is no reason to suppose that he or his men were given land on which to settle in Britain, for there is nothing to show that he had come over for any other purpose than to take part in the campaign. But, as we have seen (p. 270, n. 5) there is evidence for a settlement of Saxons, perhaps as *laeti*, in Norfolk about this time.

Constantine had soon to leave for Gaul, and the following year received the title of Augustus. The short period of his rule as Caesar saw heavy repairs to the roads of Britain – no less than six milestones date from these months – and the programme was maintained for some years to come, as a further thirteen milestones indicate. Thus, his father's policy was maintained, for the care expended on the road-system can be understood as the logical accompaniment of the restoration of the forts, and as illustrating the interest of the government in the renaissance of the British economy.

During most of the first half of the fourth century Britain enjoyed peace and prosperity. At some point, perhaps in the years 315–18, Constantine assumed among other military titles that of Britannicus Maximus; but we know nothing of any campaigning which may have earned it. Both Saxon raiding and Pictish aggression appear to have died down. The edict of Milan in February 313 extended freedom of worship to the Christian Church, and in the following year three British bishops and the representatives of a fourth attended the Council of Arles; though none are known to have been present at those of Nicaea in 325 or Sardica in 343, British Christianity remained firmly in the Catholic fold.

For Haverfield the period was the golden age of Roman Britain, and we may agree that the broader basis of its prosperity surpassed that of the Antonine age. All the instruments of despotism and of soul-destroying officialdom were, it is true, to hand: yet despite them all, Britain entered an era of unexampled well-being, the causes of which have been discussed in Chapters 13 and 14.

The first sign of trouble to come occurred late in 342. The details elude us, owing to the loss of the relevant book of Ammianus' history, but a crisis became sufficiently severe to cause a hurried and apparently unexpected visit by the emperor Constans early the following year, apparently in January or early February.[25] On the death of Constantine and the division of the empire between his sons, Britain had fallen to the rule of Constantine II, the eldest brother; but from 340, after the death of the latter at the hands of his brother's troops, the western part of the empire came under the authority of Constans. It is possible that public opinion in Britain resented the killing of Constantine, and that the mid-winter visit of his brother was designed to forestall rebellion. Whether or not this was so, there were certainly good pretexts for the visit both on the northern frontier and also perhaps on the Saxon Shore; and if, as seems probable, it was on this occasion that the elder Gratian, father of Valentinian and Valens, was posted to Britain with the title of Count and a detachment of the field army, this reinforcement stresses the urgency of the situation.[26]

In the north there seems to have been an attack by the Picts, aided perhaps by the Scots (p. 390), upon the protected lands north of the Wall, for the *areani*, whose duty was to range widely beyond the frontier in search of military intelligence, were somehow involved in action taken by the emperor.[27] Moreover, the outpost forts of High Rochester, Risingham and Bewcastle were all three destroyed or badly damaged by fire at some date intermediate between their restoration by Constantius and the disaster of 367, and only the last two were rebuilt. It is not known whether Netherby, which was also restored at the beginning of the century, suffered the same fate.

Part of Constans' efforts, then, were devoted to reorganisation of arrangements beyond the frontier, where Caracalla's system of a patrolled belt was clearly still in operation: for the *areani*, whatever the significance of their name, exercised the same functions as the *exploratores* of the third century.[28] It cannot be thought that the Roman forces in Britain, especially if reinforced by *comitatenses*, were deterred from restoring High Rochester by superior power, and its evacuation can accordingly be interpreted as based upon a reassessment of policy. This fort, according to Ptolemy, lay in the territory of the Votadini, whose attitude, as far as it can be traced, had always been consistently philo-Roman (pp. 126, 274, 208f.). The act of Constans gave them greater responsibility for defence against the Picts, while still maintaining the nearer fort of Risingham as an outpost on Dere Street.

The visit of Constans can also be connected with developments on the Saxon Shore. The fort of Pevensey was an addition to the series made some time about the middle of the century, as its general coin list and the coin of 334–5 found below a bastion both testify. It could well have been built to the orders of Constans at this time, while at Richborough and Portchester also the coin lists seem to indicate increased activity. Perhaps there were troop tranfers; but it is even likely that this activity marks the establishment of the command of the Count of the Saxon Shore. Territorial counts are not recorded before the death of Constantine I, and, though the forts existed earlier, the command was probably hitherto exercised by the prefect of the Classis Britannica. The Count had certainly been established before 367: if his office originated in 343 the questions arise why it was necessary to make a change and why the new office was given the title of the Saxon Shore. Military reorganisation is usually undertaken for practical reasons, such as a breakdown of the previous system or an impending crisis.

It must be admitted that at present these questions cannot be clearly answered. Owing to the loss of Ammianus' account of these years, we have no knowledge whether Saxon raids were increasing: the distribution of coin-hoards gives little or no indication that this was so. The term *litus Saxonicum* has usually been understood as referring to the shore threatened by the Saxons, but some writers have suggested that it means the shore settled by the Saxons, these being understood as *laeti* in the Roman Service. There is little positive evidence to support this view, since the known garrisons of the Shore forts are regular troops with no Saxon connections; nor does the distribution of so-called Romano-Saxon pottery, which has been regarded (with little justification) as a hybrid fashion designed to appeal to Teutonic settlers, show any recognisable connection with the Saxon Shore. It would go beyond the evidence, then, to suggest that Constans visited Britain to arrange such a settlement; but it is worth recalling that Saxons were to be found on the north-east coast of Gaul, though the date and circumstances of their arrival there are totally unknown.[29]

During the next seven years the quality of Constans' rule degenerated and its popularity declined: early in 350 he succumbed to a conspiracy and his throne was seized by Magnentius. This man was of barbarian descent, and had started his career as a *laetus*; for his family had been settled, it seems, in Gaul, though according to one tradition his father was a Briton. Whether or not he had personal ties with Britain, his rule was welcomed there, as the aftermath made clear.[30] Magnentius' reign was brief, for he was defeated by Constantius II in a great battle at Mursa in Pannonia in 351, where the losses on both sides were very severe. That Britain was drained of troops to support the usurper must be highly probable, and it would account for the inability of the British army to control its foes which is such a feature of the next fifteen years. Magnentius maintained himself in the West for a further two years; but after his death in 353 extensive reprisals, despite the amnesty which Constantius had declared, were taken against his supporters in Britain. The agent employed for this purpose was the imperial notary Paul, whose evil repute as an investigator earned him the nickname of *Catena*, the Chain. The Vicar of Britain himself was forced to suicide after an unsuccessful attempt on his accuser. This Martinus is praised by Ammianus for his just and upright character: the charge, we are told, was brought against him because of his efforts to protect the innocent. Nevertheless, it cannot have been easy for anyone of prominence in Britain to have avoided involvement with the defeated side.[31]

Shortly after this, Constantius elevated Julian to the supervision of the west with the rank of Caesar (355). It was during 359 that, as a preliminary to his campaign along the lower Rhine, Julian caused a large fleet to be built for the transport of grain from Britain; Ammianus refers to a regular movement of corn from this side of the Channel.[32]

Some time between 354 and 358 some curious local coins, copying contemporary issues, made their appearance in Britain: they bear the name of Carausius. Who this 'Carausius II' was is quite unknown, nor is there any other record of a usurper in Britain at this period.[33]

Early in 360 the Scots (who were at this period still based on Ireland) and the Picts of central Scotland broke the terms which had been imposed upon them, presumably by Constans, and began to lay waste the regions near the frontier. Julian hesitated to cross to Britain himself because of his other commitments, especially in midwinter, but he despatched Lupicinus his *magister militum* with four regiments of comitatenses in his stead. Nothing is recorded of his achievements, but he was known for a competent general, and presumably was successful in imposing terms, for he returned to Gaul within a few months. During the interval Julian had been hailed Augustus by his troops, and some anxiety had been felt about the reactions of Lupicinus to the news, if he heard it while still in control

390

of the British garrison as well as of his own force; in the event, however, the precautions taken successfully kept him in ignorance until he set foot once more in Gaul, and could be arrested.[34]

Whatever settlement was reached, it did not last long. The recurrent and successful raids of this decade support the suggestion that the army of Britain was below strength due to the losses suffered by Magnentius at Mursa. In 365 Ammianus records successful attacks by Picts, Saxons, Scots and Attacotti, and late in 367 the position degenerated alarmingly. As the result of a *barbarica conspiratio* a concerted attack was made upon the province. The tribes responsible were once more the Picts, Scots and Attacotti, while the Franks and Saxons descended upon the coasts and frontiers of Gaul. Though it is unlikely that the Saxons altogether neglected opportunities in Britain, the main fury seems to have fallen upon the northern frontier and the western coastlands. The Picts came down from the region north of the Forth, the Scots took boat from Ireland; the Attacotti are of uncertain homeland, either Irish or in the western isles, but their savagery is vividly attested by St Jerome, who in his youth observed their cannibal tastes in Gaul.

United planning had never been suspected of the foes of Roman Britain before, and its success was startling. Hadrian's Wall had always been impregnable when its garrison was there: now it was overrun or by-passed; Nectaridus, count of the Saxon Shore,[35] was killed and the *dux Britanniarum*, Fullofaudes, was besieged or captured. The disaster was the greater because it was unexpected: there was treachery among the areani, who should have sent warning in advance: they had succumbed to bribes not merely to withhold intelligence, but to betray military information to the enemy. The confusion was aggravated by a breakdown of discipline: large numbers of Roman deserters roamed the country, and many others claimed to be on indefinite leave. Almost certainly escaped slaves and coloni also took advantage of the general disorder to flee their masters and enrich themselves with plunder. The gravity of the situation was greatly enhanced by the length of time it took to restore order: almost two years passed before the government regained control. By then Britain might have passed beyond recovery had conquest and settlement been the intention of the invaders; but it was not. Their only aim was the acquisition of slaves, cattle and portable wealth;

and when Theodosius reached London he found the country overrun by small plundering bands rather than by an invading army.

The emperor Valentinian was on the march against the Alamanni when the news reached him. He could not therefore come in person and, as sometimes happens in a crisis, a quick succession of commanders was appointed and recalled before the right man was found. The first was Severus, the emperor's *comes domesticorum*. He was soon succeeded by Jovinus, the *magister equitum*; but in the spring of 368 continuing bad reports and rumours of disaster led to the appointment of the elder Theodosius, a *comes rei militaris* whose son was later to become the emperor Theodosius I, and as a young man accompanied his father to Britain.[36]

With four regiments of the field army, the Batavi, Heruli, Jovii and Victores, he marched from Richborough to London, and from there set about rounding up the scattered bands which were plundering the countryside. Next an amnesty was issued to deserters, and his forces were strengthened with reconstituted elements of the disintegrated provincial garrison. He was now in a position to re-create the diocesan administration with the appointment of Dulcitius as *dux Britanniarum* and Civilis as *Vicarius*, and all was ready for the resumption of initiative the following year. In 369 the remaining parts of Britain were cleared of invaders and a large programme of restoration was begun, which included the establishment of a fifth province, named Valentia (p. 242f.). Indeed, Claudian hints at naval activity in the far north,[37] and victorious terms must have been dictated, for the Notitia subsequently records four regiments of Attacotti in imperial service on the Continent.

A first priority was the reconstruction of the frontier. The treacherous record of the *areani* now resulted in their removal, and this together with the decision not to re-occupy the outpost forts meant that much greater reliance came to be placed upon the federate tribes of the Lowlands; there were now no Roman forces north of the Wall. This change probably marks the inception of a new arrangement under which the Votadini were granted more complete independence with client or federate status, and the assumption of responsibility for frontier protection under their own leaders. The reality of such a change in their status at some moment in the fourth century receives confirmation from the title accorded to one of their chieftains, Paternus by name, who was the grandfather of Cunedda. In the genealogy this man figures as Padarn Pesrut, the second word signifying 'he of the scarlet cloak'; with little doubt this title indicates the award of some form of Roman military authority, and finds parallels in the gift of insignia and even of military rank to chieftains on other frontiers of the empire.[38] The date of Paternus depends upon that assigned to Cunedda, upon which there is not yet general agreement; but it will be shown later on (p. 426) that the most probable period for Cunedda's migration is about 430, which would place 369 comfortably within the *floruit* of his grandfather. A similar arrangement may possibly have been made with the dynasty of Strathclyde, whose kingdom was centred on the tribal territory of the Damnonii. The pedigree of this royal house, too, can be traced back to the fourth century, when the names of two successive rulers are given as Cluim (= Clemens) and Cinhil (= Quintilus): very approximately their *floruits* can be reckoned as *c.* 350–80 and *c.* 380–410. The adoption of Latin names at just this period is suggestive.

Undoubtedly these arrangements reflect the reduced importance of the wall itself as a frontier; its failure as a barrier had been demonstrated by recent events. Against mobile, and amphibious enemies something more was required than a wall which could be so easily turned: this is the context of the increased concern for coastal and urban defences farther south which is one of the features of the Theodosian restoration.

In assessing the amount of damage done by the invaders and the localities where it took place we are hampered once again by the deficiencies of archaeological reports. The tradition of destruction at this time is so strong that any rebuilding is almost automatically assumed to be necessitated by hostile action, and it is difficult to decide how far Theodosian reconstruction was motivated by other causes, such as gradual decay or the needs of military reorganisation.

All the remaining outpost forts now ceased to be held, if indeed they had survived the troubles of 360 and 365. On the wall itself the abandonment of many civil settlements outside forts (in so far as they have been tested by excavation) is convincing evidence of disaster; and it is certainly true that extensive patching and rebuilding was undertaken in the forts themselves, and at some of them gates were walled up.[39]

The programme of restoration has also been recognised at forts farther south, such as Chester-le-Street, Papcastle, Bainbridge and

Ilkley, while the forts at Overborough and perhaps at Brough (Derbyshire) were put out of commission.

This evidence, when combined with the account of Ammianus Marcellinus, leaves little doubt that there had been a grave military disaster. Our assessment of its severity will affect the view we take of the Notitia Dignitatum and the homogeneity of its contents. In this document the garrison of the wall appears as old-style alae and cohorts with few changes from the third-century position (p. 262f.). Is it credible that all these regiments survived the disaster to appear in a list of later date or that, despite the attested activity of their general, Fullofaudes, they remained uninvolved in the struggle?

It is true that Theodosius was able to recall deserters and stragglers to the colours. Did he re-create the cohorts and alae of the wall as if nothing had happened? Two considerations suggest that he did not. The first is the changes which can now be perceived in the planning and character of the wall-forts themselves, suggesting as they do a type of garrison different from its predecessors. The second is the contrast in types of garrison shown by the two halves of chapter xl of the Notitia (p. 262). The wall-forts are garrisoned in the list by alae and cohorts, such as nowhere else in the empire appear in such numbers or uniformity; but the other forts controlled by the Duke, in Yorkshire and Durham, are shown with garrisons of a totally different type. We have seen (pp. 263–6) that this part of the Duke's list is best explained as setting forth part of Theodosius' reconstruction of the latter region. If entirely new regiments had to be formed or brought in to hold the forts of Durham and Yorkshire it is very unlikely that old regiments survived on the wall.[40]

On Hadrian's Wall the fourth period of construction, which has been recognised at a number of forts, milecastles and turrets, is firmly attributable, despite the absence of dated inscriptions, to the historical reconstructions of 369[41] by the discovery of a coin of Valentinian well stratified beneath it at Birdoswald and by the cumulative evidence provided by a careful study of associated pottery. Some of the actual work of rebuilding may have been carried out by corvées provided by the civitates of southern Britain, and even at the expense of private individuals, if the inscriptions noted on p. 198 above may be connected with a tradition preserved by Gildas; this suggestion of Mr C. E. Stevens seems the most likely context for them,[42] and it would account for the differences observed from normal military

394

masonry. Not only is the technique of the rebuilding notably inferior to earlier work, but the regular planning which had always been a feature of Roman forts seems to have been abandoned. At Chester-holm the headquarters building was converted to provide store-chambers and living-quarters, and much the same adaptations are known at South Shields and Housesteads; and at the latter fort pottery found in the granaries suggested that they, too, had been converted to domestic uses. Moreover, some evidence suggests the presence of women and children within the forts: at Housesteads trinkets were found in the barrack-rooms and at Chesters infant-burials came to light in an interval-tower.[43]

Though individually these facts have little weight, cumulatively they do suggest that arrangements for the defence of the wall were changed. The forts now seem to resemble fortified villages, as if the garrisons were no longer regular limitanei but an irregular militia. In North Africa the frontier had long been garrisoned by territorial farmer-soldiers, and in the Notitia we find control of them in the hands of *praepositi limitis* under the command of the *dux*. This cannot have been the system in northern Britain, for there the Duke's list contains no such officers. But if Theodosius transferred *laeti* or *gentiles* to the area from Germany these would be under *praefecti* independent of the Duke's command. Chapter xlii of the *Notitia*, which lists the *laeti* and *gentiles* of the western provinces, breaks off before it reaches Britain, but at Birdoswald it was noted that some of the coarse pottery of this period appeared to be of Rhineland origin, a fact which might support the suggestion of such a transfer. It is known that Alamannic soldiers were serving in Britain at this time, since in 372 Fraomar was sent over to take command of them with the rank of tribune;[44] but as both this rank and their description as a numerus both imply a regular formation, they clearly are not what we are seeking.

Farther south, forts were rebuilt in more regular manner and in a better style, as at Bainbridge and Ilkley. The contrast with the Wall-forts reinforces the deduction that the garrisons were different. A new system of signal stations seems to have been constructed along the road south of Carlisle, where two survive at Wreay Hall and Barrock Fell.

Now, too, the coast of Yorkshire and Durham was provided with a series of signal and look-out towers running from Flamborough Head probably as far as the Tyne mouth. They occupy high headlands, and contained towers which may have risen to 90 or 100 feet, and were clearly intended to co-ordinate naval action by flotillas based on the estuaries of Humber, Tees and Tyne.[45] They probably came under the Count of the Saxon Shore. It is clear that this command was re-organised by Theodosius, for at least one fort, that at Portchester, was abandoned now in favour of a new base at Bitterne near Southampton, and troop movements at other forts best fall into place at this moment.

On the west coasts much evidence is still to seek, but in Wales the fort of Caernarvon was rebuilt and so, probably, was Forden Gaer; coin evidence suggests that other forts also were held, such as Caerhun and Brecon, but whether they were rebuilt and how they were garrisoned are questions impossible to answer owing to the disturbance of the upper levels by ploughing. The fleet-base at Holyhead, with its close resemblance to contemporary naval fortifications on the Rhine, also seems best attributable to Theodosius. There is evidence too for a naval yard in the Bristol Channel at this period, for a *praefectus reliquationis*, T. Flavius Senilis, dedicated a mosaic at the Lydney temple shortly after 367.

In the south of Britain the damage inflicted by the invaders is hard to detect. There seem to be no special concentrations of coin-hoards. None of the towns appears to have been affected, and signs of damage even at villas are rare. Occasionally we may suspect violent destruction, as at Brislington, Somerset, where human skulls and building debris down the well and burnt roofing tiles in the villa itself suggest as much, and the coins go down to Constantius II; but in general it is only possible to say that a number of villas appears to have gone out of occupation about this time, to judge by their coin-lists, though the great majority continued to exist. Raiders frequently achieved their purpose, we may suppose, without setting fire to the house. Indeed, the disappearance of slaves and coloni amid the general confusion may well have been as disastrous to the continued life of a villa as the slaughter of its owner or the sacking of its buildings. Far too little modern work has been devoted to villas, and old accounts are too indefinite for it to be possible to map the passage of the raiders. There is a group of some seven villas in Somerset and five in Hampshire which may have been affected; and scattered examples, such as the Park Street villa, Hertfordshire, or Langton, Yorkshire, have been identified in other areas. On the borders of Dorset the crisis was sufficiently severe to cause the blocking of the main road from Sarum to Dorchester by an extension of the earthwork known as Bokerly Dyke; but the road was shortly afterwards re-opened. The effects of disorder in the countryside are also reflected in the history of the pottery industry. The factories which for so long had produced black-burnished ware (p. 330) seem to have gone out of production, as does the important Hartshill–Mancetter group; after 369 the military markets were supplied very largely by the kilns at Crambeck in Yorkshire. This centre had been of comparative insignificance until the disturbances of 367; but the potters then seized the opportunity presented to them of capturing the waiting market, and their production became so large and so widely distributed in the north that it has become the main means of identifying occupation during the last third of the century; indeed, its distribution has been used to demonstrate conclusively that the Wall remained the frontier of Roman Britain after 369.[46] In general, the effect of the raids appears to have been to leave much of the market in the hands of a few large production-centres, such as the Nene Valley potteries, and those of the Farnham and Oxford districts and the New Forest. Small producers for the most part disappeared, though in the south very crude wares, somewhat home-made in character, began to make their appearance. The results of this centralisation were disastrous later, when in the early fifth century these factories themselves ceased to produce.

The measures taken by Theodosius included assistance to the towns,[47] and it has been suggested on p. 290f. that it was he who ordered the external towers which were added to their walls at about this period. The purpose of these towers was to support ballistae and stone-throwing machines which could give covering fire along the face of the wall and keep attackers at a distance. Such engines would probably call for the services of a small specialist force.

There is no record of town garrisons in Britain in the Notitia, but the presence of troops in some of them seems indicated by the distribution of certain types of military belt-plates and buckles datable to the late fourth century and later. These are often popularly taken to indicate the presence of 'Germanic mercenaries'; but it is a fallacy to suppose that items of military uniform indicate nationality or pay-status. The earliest examples are of continental manufacture,

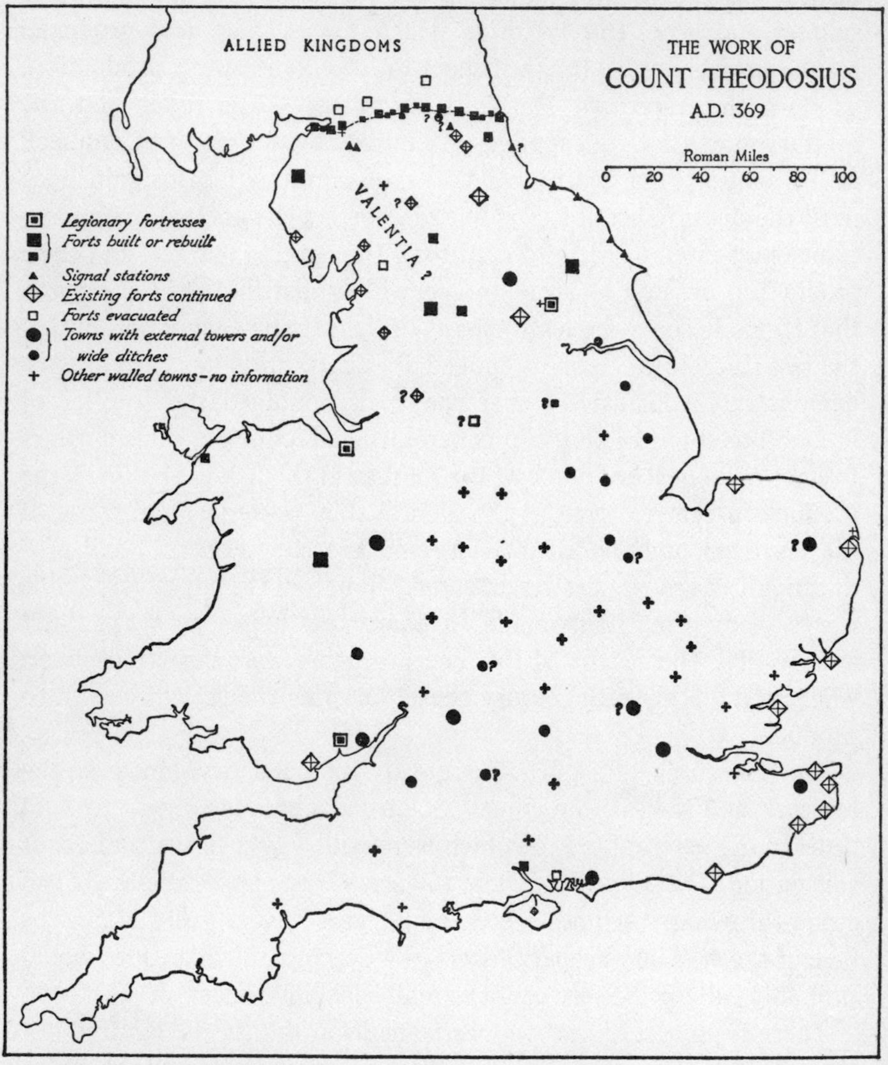
ALLIED KINGDOMS
THE WORK OF
COUNT THEODOSIUS
A.D. 369
Roman Miles
0 20 40 60 80 100
VALENTIA ?
Legionary fortresses
Forts built or rebuilt
Signal stations
Existing forts continued
Forts evacuated
Towns with external towers and/or wide ditches
Other walled towns – no information

13 The work of Count Theodosius in Britain

and appear to have formed part of the uniform of regular troops transferred to Britain under Theodosius. Before long, however, British-made examples of this equipment appear as local workshops went into production. Examples of both types have been found in forts of the Saxon Shore, but they also occur in some numbers elsewhere in southern Britain, particularly in the towns. They must indicate the presence of regular troops, perhaps in small detachments; and the reason why they do not figure in the Duke's list is likely to be that they were not under his command but under that of the *vicarius*. The insignia of the Vicar of Britain at the head of chapter xxiii of the Notitia, alone among *vicarii*, consists of castellated enclosures instead of representative maidens; this must surely indicate that he controlled troops. City garrisons seem the most likely kind.

The wide range and extraordinary thoroughness of the reorganisation carried out by Count Theodosius are now clear (fig. 13) and there can be no doubt of its effectiveness. It was, indeed, the last constructive large-scale intervention of the central government in Romano-British affairs, and though the action of usurpers and the deterioration of Roman military power on the Continent in due course led to the evacuation of almost all the armed forces in Britain, the work of Theodosius in the towns of the island enabled them to hold out far into the following century. Evidence is accruing that in towns as well as villas the last quarter of the fourth century was in general a period of great prosperity.

1. *Pax trium Augustorum*, etc.
2. *RIB*, 2291 = *ILS*, 8928.
3. *Viriconium* = *Briconium*.
4. *Panegyrici Latini*, viii (v), 12, 1.
5. II Augusta and xx Valeria Victrix. Why Legio VI Victrix was omitted is not known. Possibly this legion had opposed his elevation.
6. See J. S. Johnson, *Britannia*, i (1970), pp. 240 ff.
7. *Litus Saxonicum* (1961), 29–30.
8. *de Caesaribus*, xxxix, 41. *Allectus . . . Qui cum eius* (sc. *Carausii*) *permissu summae rei praeesset*. Eutropius (ix, 22) calls him merely *socius eius*.
9. *Panegyrici Latini*, viii (v), 16, 2. Allectus *adeo . . . properavit ad mortem ut nec explicaret aciem nec omnes copias quas trahebat instruxerit, sed cum veteribus illius coniurationis auctoribus et mer-*

cenariis cuneis barbarorum tanti apparatus oblitus inruerit . . . nemo fere Romanus occiderit imperio vincente Romano.

10. *Panegyrici Latini*, viii (v), 19, 1–2.

11. *RIB*, 1912; see pp. 242, 384. The inscription dates to the period 296–305; probability suggests that it was erected before 300.

12. *Panegyrici Latini*, vi (vii), 7, 2: an earlier campaign in 296 or early 297 is perhaps to be deduced from the statement in the Panegyric of 297 (viii (v), 20, 3), that tribes in the far north of the island are now obedient to the emperor's will.

13. Housesteads, *RIB*, 1613, and Birdoswald, *RIB*, 1912.

14. Damage on the Wall includes the forts of Benwell (*AA* [4], xix (1941), 34), Haltonchesters (*JRS*, lii (1962), 164), Great Chesters (*AA* [2], xxiv (1903), 31, 51), Housesteads (*AA* [4], xxxix (1961), 287) and probably Birdoswald (*CW* [2], xxxi (1931), 128); perhaps milecastles 40 and 48 (*CW* [2], xiii (1913), 321) and the following turrets 49b, 50b (*ibid.*) and 44b (*AA* [2], xxiv (1903), 13). The vici at Old Carlisle and perhaps Benwell have to be included (P. Salway, *The Frontier People of Roman Britain* (1965), pp. 76, 118) and probably the villa at Old Durham. There was destruction at Corbridge (*ibid.*, p. 54), where burnt layers have been recorded (*AA* [4], xxxiii (1955), 246), and at Carrawburgh, where the Mithraeum was burnt and pillaged (*AA* [4], xxix (1951), 27). The outpost forts of Bewcastle (*CW* [2], xxxviii (1938), 208), Risingham and High Rochester (*Northumberland County History*, xv (1940), 107), were also affected. At Malton (Yorks) corn from the granaries was taken out and burnt along the rampart; the excavators took this to mark an evacuation (P. Corder, *Defences of the Roman Fort at Malton* (1930), pp. 34, 66–7).

15. At Rudchester and Haltonchesters excavations have shown that parts at any rate of these forts were unoccupied between 296 and 369. It remains to be seen whether they were wholly evacuated, or whether much smaller garrisons, needing less extensive accommodation, were present. The evidence of the *Notitia* (p. 262f.) would suggest (but does not prove) that the latter is the true explanation: if it turns out that two adjacent forts on the Wall were left empty by Constantius I close to the main eastern route southwards from Scotland, it would throw interesting light on the nature of his restoration of the frontier. At present it is difficult to see what alternative arrangements can have been made.

16. *RIB*, 1912; see pp. 242, 382.

17. In M. G. Jarrett and B. Dobson, *Britain and Rome* (1966), pp. 121 ff.

18. No coins later than *c*. 270–4 have been found in third-century deposits on Hadrian's Wall. This fact cannot in itself be taken to indicate the end of Wall-period II at about this date, for coins later than *c*. 270 but earlier than Carausius are everywhere rare in Britain. It would be more indicative of a depleted garrison in the later third century if radiates of *c*. 270 could be shown to be rare on the Wall.

The absence of published information about many excavations both old and new prevents accurate assessment; but the percentages of radiates to other coins in recent excavations at Carrawburgh (43 per cent) and Housesteads (62 per cent) – at Birdoswald in 1929 it was 17 per cent – give little support to such a theory.

19. An alternative view of events in Britain during Constantius' reign is possible. According to this, Allectus used troops from the Pennines, not from the Wall, for his operations in the south; these suffered heavy casualties and had to be replaced by new formations, much as listed in *Notitia Dignitatum Occ.*, xl, though this list as it stands incorporates later information. On his recovery of Britain, Constantius found military installations both on the Wall and in the Pennines in bad shape due to lack of maintenance, and determined on a complete restoration. There was no attack from the north in 196; indeed, the Picts sent complimentary messages (as is implied by the panegyrist of 297, p. 400, note 12 above). The signs of fire and tumbled masonry listed on p. 400, note 14, were due to the demolition of crumbling buildings, which was an essential preliminary to rebuilding. In 306 Constantius attacked the Picts in anticipation of, or retaliation for, a threat to Roman interests. This sequence of events has not been adopted in the text, since the facts on balance favour the traditional interpretation; but more evidence is needed to decide the point.

20. *RIB*, 488.

21. The *portae decumana* and *principalis sinistra*.

22. This may have been the occasion of the grant to London of the title *Augusta*, which it certainly possessed later in the century, Ammianus Marcellinus, xxvii, 8, 7; xxviii, 3, 4; see p. 241 above.

23. *Panegyrici Latini*, vi (vii), 7, 1–2.

24. Aurelius Victor, *de Caesaribus*, xxxix, 41.

25. Libanius, *Oratio*, lix (Teubner), 139–41, who mentions that Constans was accompanied by only 100 men; Firmicus Maternus, *de errore prof. relig.*, xxxviii, 6; *Codex Theodos.*, xi, 16, 5, for an edict issued at Boulogne on 25 January 343.

26. Ammianus Marcellinus, xxx, 7, 3; A. H. M. Jones, *The Later Roman Empire* (1964), p. 124.

27. As a brief reference back by Ammianus (xxviii, 3, 8), to events recorded in his lost books attests.

28. The word *areani* is usually emended to *arcani* in the text of Ammianus, to yield the meaning 'intelligence agents'. *Areani* may mean 'Men of the sheep-folds', which would have reference to the native-style farmsteads in which they now maintained themselves; alternatively, it may be taken as 'Men of the open spaces'. In either case it would be a customary, rather than official, term, derived perhaps from army slang.

29. *Archaeological Journal*, xcvii (1940), 135.

30. Cf. also the Richborough portrait-pendant, J. P. Bushe-Fox, *Richborough*, iv (1949), pl. xlii, 171.

31. Little is known of the vicarii of Britain. In 319 Pacatianus held the office (*Codex Theodosianus*, xi, 7, 2); one of Martinus' immediate successors was Alypius (Ammianus Marcellinus, xxiii, 1, 3). Two late vicars, probably both in the reign of Honorius, were Victorinus (Rutilius Namatianus, *de reditu suo*, 493–510) and Chrysanthus (Socrates, *Eccl. Hist.*, vii, 12 and 17). Still less is known of the governors. Flavius Sanctus, a connection of Ausonius, was one of them about the middle of the fourth century (Ausonius, *Parentalia* (Loeb), xviii, 7–8).

32. Ammianus Marcellinus, xviii, 2, 3; Libanius, *oratio* xviii, 82 (Teubner); Julian, *Letter to the Athenians*, 279–80, says he had 600 ships, 400 of which were built in less than ten months; Zosimus, iii, 5, mentions 800 ships.

33. For the date of Carausius II see J. P. C. Kent, *Numismatic Chronicle*,[6] xvii (1957), 78–83.

34. Ammianus Marcellinus, xx, 1; xx, 9, 9; Julian, *Letter to the Athenians*, 281.

35. Described as *comes maritimi tractus*; see p. 242.

36. *Zosimus*, iv, 35, 5.

37. Claudian, *de quarto consulatu Honorii*, 23–44.

38. A. H. M. Jones, *The Later Roman Empire* (1964), ii, p. 611.

39. There was damage at Corbridge despite its defensive walls, *AA*,[4] xxxiii (1955), 248; xxxviii (1960), 154–7; cf. the coin hoards mentioned in *AA*,[4] xv (1938), 261–2; the *mansio* seems to have been abandoned now. The vici at Benwell, Housesteads and Old Carlisle were deserted; that at Piercebridge farther south may possibly have been rebuilt in 369. The villa at Old Durham seems also to have been destroyed. On these sites see P. Salway, *Frontier People of Roman Britain* (1965). On the Wall itself signs of destruction have been noted at Chesters (*AA*,[2] vii (1876), 211) and considerable alterations after destruction or demolition at Birdoswald (*CW*,[2] xxx (1930), 169–71); at Housesteads considerable alterations took place, but there is no evidence of disaster. Attention may also be drawn here to the arm wrenched from a silver statuette of the Victory of Legio vi (*RIB*, 582), which was found in Lancashire, and to the fine gilt-bronze leg hacked off an over life-sized imperial statue which was found in Roxburghshire. Sir George Macdonald (*JRS*, xvi (1926), 7–16) showed that both represent loot, the second probably, the first certainly, from the fortress of York. They must surely be related either to the events of 196 or those of 367.

40. To avoid the logic of this conclusion it is necessary *either* to assume that, despite the evidence cited, casualties on the wall in 367 were slight, whatever happened farther south – an unreasonable solution – *or* to accept the suggestion put forward on p. 401, note 19, that the first part of chapter xl of the Notitia, listing the Duke's

troops in Yorkshire and Durham, reflects essentially the restoration of Constantius in 296. The weight of the evidence is against this theory too, and it involves rejecting a Pictish invasion in 296. Nevertheless, it would ease the dilemma of 369 by removing the necessity of believing that the list of garrisons on the wall is necessarily of different date from that of the first part of the Duke's list. Both halves of the list, the old-fashioned cohorts and alae on the wall and the new equites and numeri south of it, could now equally be regarded as surviving through the early fourth century right down to the date of the Notitia's first composition (c. 395). But though such a solution simplifies the problem of the Notitia, it overrides the considerable body of evidence that the military disaster of 367–8 was so serious as to make a reorganisation of forces extremely probable.

41. Ammianus Marcellinus, xxviii, 3, 7; *limitesque vigiliis tuebatur et praetenturis.*

42. *English Historical Review,* lvi (1941), 359.

43. For sprawling buildings at Birdoswald see CW², (1931), 129; for additional buildings inserted at Housesteads AA², xxv (1904), 241 ff., AA⁴, ix (1932), 223 ff.; at Chesterholm AA⁴, viii (1931), 195, ix (1932), 217; at Chesters, Bruce, *Handbook to the Roman Wall* (11th edition, 1957), p. 94. For principia at Chesterholm see AA⁴, xiii (1936), 225–9; at Housesteads AA², xxv (1904), 223–5, and trinkets, *ibid.,* 235; at South Shields Richmond, *Guide to Roman Fort* (1953), p. 6; Housesteads granaries AA⁴, ix (1932), 224; for burials Bruce, *op. cit.,* 91. At Malton twenty-nine such burials belong to the period 296–367, P. Corder, *Defences of the Roman Fort at Malton* (1930), p. 67.

44. Ammianus Marcellinus, xxix, 4, 7; see p. 270, note 5.

45. Compare the description given by Vegetius (iv, 37), of the scout-craft and warships in British waters, which are the essential complement of the scheme (p. 253).

46. J. P. Gillam, *Carnuntina: Römische Forschungen in Niederösterréich* (1956), pp. 64–77.

47. Ammianus Marcellinus, xxviii, 3, 2 and 3, 7.

17
The end of Roman Britain

In 370 Britain was once more enjoying firm government and effective defences: forty years later she ceased to be part of the Roman Empire. The civilisation and prosperity of the island during these years had never been higher; but the growing power of external barbarians constituted a danger both to Britain and to the whole western empire which by slow degrees overbore resistance. The plight of a rich people entirely dependent for defence upon a power whose interests in the final analysis were centred elsewhere is not without its interest today.

Not that consciousness of separate interest was felt in Britain. The imperial system was so old and so full of prestige that for generations to come the British continued to regard themselves as in some sense members of it still. But the repeated withdrawal of troops between 383 and 407 meant that all too soon the defence of the island devolved upon local effort. This was a responsibility which by tradition or experience the provincials here as elsewhere were all too unfitted to undertake.

A contributing cause of this situation was that very consciousness of being an integral and significant part of the empire. In 383 and again in 407 usurpers set up by the army in Britain took large forces over the Channel to support their claims to rule. Few if any of these troops returned, any more than did those who were recalled by the central government for the defence of Italy.

The rebellion of 383 was the work of Magnus Maximus. A native of Spain, he had seen service in Britain under Count Theodosius, and at the time of his revolt was probably *dux Britanniarum*. He was a capable commander, but discontented with his slow promotion; the support of his troops was easily gained, since the emperor Gratian had become unpopular with the regular army because of the favouritism he showed to his German levies. Maximus, it seems, was popular in Britain, for he was long remembered as a hero in Celtic folk-memory and tradition, and Gildas preserves a story that he was accompanied to Gaul by many British volunteers. He held the West until his death at the hands of Theodosius I in 388. Orosius judged that his vigorous and upright character would have fitted him to rule had it not been for his illegal seizure of power.[1]

His expedition involved the evacuation of many of the forts still held in Britain; the garrisons concerned were apparently those of the western Pennines and North Wales and included Legio xx from Chester (p. 266, fig. 11). These positions were never re-occupied. He is often credited with the final evacuation of Hadrian's Wall, but this view can no longer be maintained. It was based on the belief that coins later than those of Gratian (367–83) were absent from forts on the Wall, a belief now known to be mistaken. Though few in number such coins exist.[2] Their rarity can be accounted for, partly by the deficiencies of the archaeological record (and the casualness with which finds from excavations have been – and still are – treated), but mainly by the almost universal scarcity of coins of this period as site-finds throughout Roman Britain, and especially in the north. Moreover, the quantity of pottery from the levels of the latest period is normally large, and by comparison with that from earlier deposits is suggestive of a longer occupation than fourteen years.

The troops which Maximus took with him were no doubt rewarded with promotion into the field-army; and, indeed, the Notitia preserves a record of the Seguntienses – apparently the former garrison of *Segontium* (Caernarvon) – among the *auxilia palatina* in Illyricum.[3] If they were thus raised in grade it is unlikely that their return to Britain as limitanei was envisaged; and there arises the question what arrangements were made by Maximus to fill the vacuum caused by their departure. The island was beginning to be denuded of its manpower.

Now that we can believe in the continued occupation of the Wall, the problem is not so grave as it once appeared. Maximus is known to have conducted a campaign against the Picts and Scots in the year before his rebellion.[4] The success of this and the continued existence of the powerful friendly kingdoms of the Votadini and Strathclyde north of the frontier must have seemed to him sufficient security for a reduction of garrisons behind the Wall. Indeed, it is probable that he created a third friendly dynasty in south-west Scotland in the area of the Novantae: at any rate, the dark-age dynasty of Galloway, alone of those in Scotland, counted Maximus as the founder of its line.

In North Wales the situation was more serious, for with the removal of Legio xx from Chester, and the evacuation of Caernarvon, a serious gap in the defences was opened, of which the Irish soon took advantage. It used to be held that the solution to the problem which Maximus adopted was the transplantation of Cunedda and a strong force of Votadini to North Wales to replace the regular forces; but the chronology indicated by Cunedda's pedigree will not fit this supposition (p. 426). Nevertheless, the striking part played by Maximus in Welsh tradition, and the ancestry of several lines of Welsh kings attributed to him, strongly suggest that in this region too allied native kingdoms may have been established. If so, they lacked the requisite strength, for by the end of the century Scots from Ireland were settling in the Lleyn peninsula (Caernarvonshire), while in Pembrokeshire and the Gower peninsula of South Wales another Irish tribe, the Deisi, are recorded. At Wroxeter Irish attackers may have successfully looted the town. This requires confirmation by modern excavation, but Thomas Wright who dug there a century ago records two late-fourth-century coin hoards, one of them accompanying the skeleton of an old man who seems to have hidden himself in the hypocausts of the public baths: Wright considered that the baths themselves had been burnt.

After the death of Maximus the western provinces came under the rule of Valentinian II, who was only a boy. No doubt in Britain the administration carried on, but there are indications that Picts as well as Irish continued to raid, no doubt with relative impunity. Both were sea-borne and could plunder where they willed; the Picts had no need to penetrate the philo-Roman kingdoms of the Lowlands and the unrewarding stretches of northern England, when richer plunder could be won from descents on the south. It was not until the period 396–8 that the central government turned its attention to the military problems of Britain. At that time Stilicho, the Vandal general who was the power behind the throne of the young emperor Honorius, ordered some sort of expedition, whether or not he took personal command. Our only source of information about it is found in various references to the achievements of Stilicho in the poems of

Claudian. These naturally lack precision, but they suggest naval activity against Irish, Picts and Saxons;[5] by 399 security had been achieved.[6]

But though he could mount a punitive expedition, Stilicho lacked the strength to augment the British garrison [7] (p. 267f). Indeed, even the *status quo* was impossible to maintain. Troops were pressingly required for the defence of Italy, and in 401 we find him withdrawing forces from Britain for the war against Alaric.[8] It seems clear that this movement must have deprived the command of the Duke, and probably also that of the Count of the Saxon Shore, of all effectiveness, if indeed they survived at all; and as already explained (p. 269), this is the most likely occasion for the establishment, by way of compensation, of a small field-army in Britain itself under the *comes Britanniarum*. The Notitia records a number of British regiments serving in Europe and even in Egypt and the East; some of them may have been formed from the survivors of Maximus' volunteers, but Stilicho's need was great enough to leave no possible sources of recruitment untapped. Even Attacotti were soon to be found among the auxilia palatina.[9] Thus in the interests of the empire Britain lost not only a large part of its remaining garrison, but also, it seems, many of its own young men, whose services were shortly to be needed at home.

A few years later, in 407, another and final withdrawal took place. This time it was the work of a usurper, the last of three set up, as Maximus had been, by the army in Britain. The soldiers had legitimate grievances against the central government. In the first place they were now too few to fulfil their task successfully, and the burden was considerable: Irish records, for instance, describe a harrying of the southern coasts by Niall of the Nine Hostages, a high king of Ireland, which may have occurred in 405. In the second place a clear division of interest was opening between the government's concentration on the defence of the empire's heart and the local interests of the troops, many of whom had close ties with their garrison stations. Promotion to the ranks of the comitatenses cannot have been regarded as an unqualified benefit, when it involved abandoning their homes. Nevertheless, they still possessed a sense of their ultimate responsibilities.

The chronology of the year 406 is too uncertain to tell us whether Marcus, the first of these short-lived pretenders, was made emperor

407

in Britain as a result of these general grievances, or whether his elevation was related to the serious crisis which developed in the autumn. We know nothing of him save that he was a soldier, and was soon killed because he did not please the army. Perhaps he was the Count of Britain. Late in the year news came of a barbarian invasion of Gaul, which culminated at the end of December in a massive crossing of the frozen Rhine by hordes of Vandals, Alans and Sueves, which the Roman forces on the Rhine were too depleted to resist. The army of Britain – so Zosimus informs us [10] – became alarmed lest the enemy should cross the Channel; but the sequel suggests that he has too narrowly interpreted their feelings. Stilicho was fully engaged in Italy and in the Balkans: it was hopeless to look for timely help from him. If the West was to be saved, intervention from Britain was required. Yet in Britain itself some appear to have taken another view – that Britain held first claim on the forces it contained: it was sufficient to obey orders and defend the island.

After the short-lived Marcus, the next to become emperor was Gratian, a native Briton who was a member of the urban aristocracy.[11] His elevation took place not later than the beginning of November 406, and he reigned four months. By this time the seriousness of affairs in Gaul was becoming obvious, and the army wished to cross there; but Gratian made no move, which when his background is remembered is not surprising, and he was cut down.

Now the choice fell on Constantine III, a common soldier but one of some ability, who ably played upon the British and imperial associations of his own name, and renamed his sons Julian and Constans. There was need for speed if the Channel ports were not to fall, and at once he crossed to Gaul, sending ahead officers to take command of the surviving forces there, and by able soldiering and diplomacy he restored the situation; in the following year (408) he won control of Spain. It seems clear that Constantine represented the view that the defence of the West required an Augustus in the prefecture of the Gauls as in the time of Constans, Julian and Valentinian, and this was a view shared by the majority of the army of Britain; they realised that the defence of Britain was inseparable from that of Gaul. Marcus and Gratian, on the other hand, may have possessed a narrower vision of their responsibility which was unacceptable to the army. By the beginning of 409 Honorius himself was persuaded to see the validity of the former view, and he extended recognition to Constantine. The latter, however, again like Maximus, was led on to intervene unsuccessfully and fatally in Italy itself; his hold on Spain was broken by the rebellion there of his British *magister militum*, Gerontius; the barbarians whom he had settled in Gaul broke out once more, and he himself was compelled to surrender to the forces of Honorius and suffer execution in the summer of 411. Once again a usurper had failed to content himself with the prefecture of the Gauls, and once again he had broken himself as a result. But this time there was a difference. Britain had virtually no forces left, and Gaul itself was in a turmoil of barbarian invasion and peasant revolt. Though Honorius regained nominal control of the Gallic provinces for a short while later in 413, real power there was in the hands of the Visigoths and Burgundians; there were no troops to spare, and it was not until 417–18 that imperial forces were active once more in the north. In the meanwhile Roman control of Britain had lapsed, and in the event was never to be reimposed. How this came about must now be examined.

The separation from Rome in 410 came not as a 'withdrawal of the legions' – almost all effective forces had long ago gone to Italy or Gaul – but as a hiatus in the apparatus of central government. Our principal information about what happened comes from Zosimus, who, though not himself a contemporary, can be shown to derive much of his material from those who were. After describing the difficulties in which Constantine found himself as a result of the rebellion of Gerontius, together with an uprising of the Germans settled in Gaul which he instigated, Zosimus then proceeds:

> 'The barbarians across the Rhine attacked everywhere with all their power, and brought the inhabitants of Britain and some of the nations of Gaul to the point of revolting from Roman rule and living on their own, no longer obedient to Roman laws. The Britons took up arms and, braving danger for their own independence, freed their cities from the barbarians threatening them; and all Armorica and the other provinces of Gaul copied the British example and freed themselves in the same way, expelling their Roman governors and establishing their own administration as best they could.' [12]

A few paragraphs later, after dealing with other matters, Zosimus mentions a letter of Honorius to the cities of Britain in which he told them to undertake their own defence – an instruction which can best be understood as the reply to a previous message to the emperor from Britain itself, reporting the steps which had been taken and asking for help. Further information comes from a mid-fifth-century Gallic chronicle, in which a devastation of Britain by the Saxons is recorded in 410; and Procopius summed up the situation in the following words: 'Constantine was defeated in battle. But in spite of this the Romans were never able to recover Britain, which from that time onward continued to be ruled by usurpers (tyrants)'.[13]

Much has been built upon the slender foundations of this outline. Professor E. A. Thompson, struck by the phrase 'living on their own, no longer obedient to Roman laws', has argued persuasively that what happened was not a rebellion against this or that emperor, but a total rejection of Rome and her empire which culminated in a social revolution on egalitarian lines.[14] On this theory the subsequent appeal to Honorius came from the threatened land-owning class. It is known, of course, that such a peasant pipe-dream was fleetingly successful in Brittany a few years later; but the actions reported in Britain in 410 are not consistent with a peasant revolution. They were taken by the curial class in the interests of the towns, which they freed from danger. If an outbreak of slaves and coloni did take advantage of the Saxon raid of 410 it was soon suppressed and did not play a significant part in events. The truth probably is that expulsions of Roman administrators came to be associated with such outbreaks in the fifth century, and that the motives and perpetrators of this one were not sufficiently distinguished by Zosimus.

Dr J. N. L. Myres has indicated the significance of the Pelagian heresy to the political background of this period.[15] Pelagius himself was a Briton, but there is no evidence that he ever returned home after his departure for Rome as a young man, when about 380 he set out to embark on a legal career. In Rome he came out in opposition to Augustine's view on the part played by divine grace in the Christian life. He could not accept that man's capacity for good is most effective when his will is surrendered as a vehicle for the divine will, or believe that human beings are utterly dependent for salvation on the grace (or *favour*) of God because the frailty of their natures renders them completely unable to achieve it on their own. These ideas were repugnant to him, for he himself took what in reality was the more superficial position: that man is the captain of his soul and by the exercise of unaided human will can be the architect of his own salvation. His heresy, in fact, was a denial of original sin. Dependence upon divine grace was particularly objectionable to him because of the contemporary overtones of the word *gratia* on the human and political plane, where it stood for undue influence and favouritism.

Pelagianism had gained a strong hold on the ruling classes in Britain, as is evident from subsequent events, though there is no evidence that hitherto its ideas had penetrated the lower orders of society. Yet, since it was opposed to the corrupt practices which had long disfigured the administration of law and government, and placed great weight on man's ability to win salvation by his own efforts, it is reasonable to recognise that its influence may have strengthened the will of those who were prepared to assume responsibility for action. But the action taken was not a breach with Rome: the subsequent appeal to Honorius makes this very clear. What occurred was an ejection of Constantine's administrators in an attempt to resume relations with the legitimate emperor.

The party in Britain which four years earlier had eschewed continental adventures had now, in fact, been justified by events. Constantine had proved a total failure: he had removed the garrison of Britain, but could not even hold Gaul. The context of Honorius' letter, addressed to the civitates ($\pi\delta\lambda\epsilon\iota\varsigma$) of Britain, makes it plain that there was no longer a *dux* or *comes Britanniarum* in the island, for otherwise it would have been his duty to organise the defence, and no longer a *vicarius* or governors, to whom otherwise the letter would have gone. The generals had left with their armies, and the administration had been expelled. When the Saxon raids had begun once more early in 410 many influential people had evidently come to the conclusion that resistance would be more effectively organised directly by the people whose lives were at stake than by officials who now lacked any backing. But to expel them, even if it was hoped to obtain subsequent approval or even fresh officials from the legitimate emperor, called for courage; and it exhibited the exercise of a free will which is certainly best understood in terms of Pelagian philosophy.

With the removal of the higher administration, authority must have fallen first into the hands of the provincial or diocesan council, as the only central body representing the civitates. These councils were still active in other provinces, though we know nothing of the British one (p. 238f.). There were probably still small bodies of regular troops garrisoning the walled towns, but to resist the Saxons effectively a wider provincial militia had to be raised. It remained technically illegal for private citizens to take up arms, and C. E. Stevens has suggested that part of the purpose of Honorius' rescript was to authorise the breach of the *lex Julia de vi publica* which had been committed.

For some years to come it is unlikely that there was much political change: as long, indeed, as expectation remained of a resumption of Honorius' authority in Britain. Some scholars still, indeed, believe that official Roman control was re-asserted briefly between 416 and 419, and an army sent over; the theory is based on the conviction that the listing of forces in Britain in the *Notitia Dignitatum*, a document which bears traces of revision down to the 420s, must be taken seriously. This is not the view taken here, for, apart from the manifest confusion of the information contained in the Notitia, it is hard to explain why there is no trace at all in the archaeological record of the money used to pay such troops (p. 416). There were two dangers. One was the outbreak of social revolution, such as actually occurred in Brittany a few years later; the other was the seizure of power by war-leaders who might be tempted to set themselves up as 'tyrants', usurping the functions of government. The first danger was successfully evaded: we have no record of peasant republics in Britain, and much evidence that the land-owning class continued to exist. But the appearance of monarchy could not long be delayed: indeed, the right of military leaders to establish legitimate rule had for centuries been vindicated at Rome itself.

Some of these leaders may have aspired to the title of emperor: Gildas records that the parents of Ambrosius had 'worn the purple'. Such persons will have been leaders of the Romanising party. But the best authenticated British ruler of this period, Vortigern, does not seem to have made this claim. Vortigern, indeed, is a title, not a name; the word means 'high king': Gildas makes the point by referring to him as *superbus tyrannus*. It is significant that Vortigern chose a British, not a Roman, title: the somewhat garbled accounts of his contact with St Germanus show him to be a Pelagian, and we can recognise that by 425, when his rule began, there was a powerful Pelagian party in Britain, anti-Roman in sentiment, but aristocratic

412

in background. The wealth of its members and the strength of their following is graphically described in Constantius' Life of Germanus: when they made their appearance at a large assembly they stood out 'conspicuous for riches, brilliant in dress, and surrounded by a fawning multitude'. They were the successors of what might be called the Little Britain party of 406, and their policies were directed towards maintaining the independence of the island. Vortigern was afraid of Roman intervention,[16] and his settlement of Saxon federates in Kent may have been undertaken with this in mind; indeed, he was prepared to go to dangerous lengths in his use of Saxon assistance.

Powerful though it was, however, this party did not include the majority of Britons. Myres has shown how even families could be divided on the Pelagian issue. But the appeal addressed by the British catholic bishops to the continental church, and ultimately to pope Celestine, for help against the heresy, shows the solid character of the opposition; the readiness of the church to look to Rome, and the success achieved by the mission of St Germanus, must have done much to weaken Vortigern's authority. Again, the appeal for military assistance made to Aetius in or soon after 446 – the so-called Groans of the Britons – has been recognised as originating from this same other side, which had been rightly alarmed by the scale of land-gifts made to the Saxons and was now struggling against their rebellion. Ambrosius succeeded to the leadership of this pro-Roman and catholic party, and it was under him that victory, at least for a time, was won over the German settlers.

The first visit of Germanus, who was at that time bishop of Auxerre, was made in 429, in company with Lupus, bishop of Troyes. Under papal influence they had been chosen by a council of Gallic bishops and sent to Britain to arrest the spread of Pelagianism, and to counter the influence of a certain Agricola, the son of a bishop, who was held to be its leading spirit.

Their preaching was successful, and it culminated in a great assembly at which the Pelagians were routed. Immediately afterwards the bishops visited the shrine of St Alban at *Verulamium*, and the assembly itself was probably therefore held at that town. An incident at it was the healing of the daughter of a 'man of tribunician power', a title which shows that there was still a Roman-type garrison-commander in charge of the city. Shortly after this Germanus, who had once been a general in the Roman army, won the Alleluia

413

Victory over a force of Picts and Saxons; it was fought in a mountainous district which was possibly in North Wales. He began the campaign by baptising the British forces, and taught them to cry 'Alleluia' at the moment of attack; the terror of this sound unnerved their adversaries, who fled. This incident vividly illustrates the plight of Britain, harassed by invaders and lacking experienced leadership, and it shows that though Christianity had made headway in the towns and among the aristocracy, the peasantry were still largely unbaptised.

Germanus retained his interest in British affairs, for some years later, perhaps in 446–7, he made a second visit, accompanied now by Severus, bishop of Trier; it was on this occasion that he encountered Elafius, *regionis illius primus*, a description which anticipates the πρῶτος τῆς πόλεως (*primus civitatis*) recorded in the southwest in the early sixth century.

These visits show the closeness of the contact which still existed between Britain and the church in Gaul. As late as 455, when the arrangements for fixing Easter were modified by Leo I, the change was duly adopted by the Celtic church, though by the time a further alteration was introduced some forty years later, communications had been broken.

Almost the last fixed point in British fifth-century chronology is provided by the unsuccessful appeal to Aetius which was recorded by Gildas. 'To Agitius, thrice consul, the Groans of the Britons . . . the barbarians drive us to the sea, the sea drives us to the barbarians; between these two means of death we are either killed or drowned.' By Agitius he means Aetius, the *magister militum* and leading figure in the western empire from 433 to 454. His third consulship was held in 446 and his fourth in 454; the message, therefore, might date from any time between these two dates, though 446 itself is the most likely year. The appeal for help was unanswered, but the date itself has played an important part in attempts to fix the chronology of the Saxon invasions (p. 424f.).

During the first half of the fifth century the civilisation of Roman Britain was running down with increasing speed. The first slow beginnings of this process are recognisable as early as the time of Magnus Maximus. Between 378 and 388 there was a very marked decline in the amount of new currency in circulation, amounting almost to disappearance. To some extent this was offset by the survival in circulation of earlier issues; but even coins of the House of Valentinian I are less plentiful on the majority of British sites than those of Constantius. Though coins of the period 388–402 appeared in somewhat larger quantity than those of 378–8, there are very few sites where they approach the proportions of previous decades: at these few sites, however, the percentage of Theodosian bronze is very high. This indicates that except at a few apparently exceptional places, where business continued as usual, or where money was changed for the collection of taxation, the use of coinage for everyday transactions decreased very notably during the last twenty years of the fourth century, some time before supplies were interrupted for good. The reason may have been partly the inflation which continued serious at this time, and partly also the intermittent difficulty of obtaining supplies of cash: for both these conditions would favour the revival of barter. Indeed, this tendency can be observed in western Britain as early as the age of Valentinian I. It is worth remembering, too, that there was at least one place in Britain which even in the third century did not use coins at all,[17] the island of Lundy.

But another of the principal factors influencing the decreasing availability of coinage was implicit in the government's own attitude to currency. The foundation of the fourth-century coinage was the gold solidus. These coins were used for the payment of government officials and the army, and it was a main preoccupation of the state to recover the gold thus issued. The bronze currency was used for this purpose; the gold was recovered by taxation (much of which had to be paid in this metal) once it had been exchanged by its recipients for the small bronzes used for everyday transactions. In general, then, the government was concerned to see that sufficient bronze was in circulation to recover the gold. But in Britain from the time of Maximus the number of troops on the pay-roll was greatly reduced, and was shortly to be decreased even more drastically. This must have meant a greatly decreased despatch of gold to Britain, and consequently a greatly reduced despatch of copper too: for the government was less concerned for the general utility of the currency as a means of exchange than as a means of payment and taxation. It did not therefore interest itself unduly in the plight of provincials, who found themselves unable to obtain sufficient currency for everyday purposes.

415

Sites in Britain yield very few copper coins minted after 402. Gold and silver coins are, of course, very rare as site-finds, but finds from hoards make it clear that coins in these metals continued to arrive down to about 406 and, in the case of silver, rather later. It seems probable, then, that payments in gold continued to be received down to this date, but supplies of copper were judged adequate without reinforcement from 402. Silver may have continued to arrive, though in much reduced quantity, after 406 because of the importance of Britain as a source of raw silver.

There had been a re-organisation of the western mints in 395, after which Trier and Arles produced very little bronze; but this reform did not have the catastrophic effect on British supplies of coin which was once imagined, since it has been established that the mint of Rome increased its output to counterbalance the reduction. Issues of the Rome mint in bronze down to 402 are found in some quantity in Britain, but thereafter the supply ceased. Though Constantine III did issue coins, these are very rarely found this side of the Channel, and the later issues of Honorius are virtually absent. From 407 Britain was, in effect, without new coins of any kind. Thereafter the existing coins continued to circulate, getting more and more worn; but increasingly few people found it necessary to use them. They were hoarded instead, and large numbers of these hoards were never recovered, whether because their owners perished in the disturbances of the period or because the hoards themselves became worthless. By 430, as Dr J. P. C. Kent has shown,[18] the use of coinage as a medium of exchange was a thing of the past.

For how long a period the few large potteries which had survived the troubles of 367–8 continued to produce their wares (p. 397) is a question which cannot be answered. They certainly survived down to about 400, for there is no shortage of pottery in association with coins of Honorius. Perhaps the end came about the years 410–20. The life of the factories cannot be unduly prolonged into the fifth century, for no changes of shape or ware have been recognised as succeeding those current in the last quarter of the fourth century; and at *Verulamium* a deposit which could be roughly dated within the period 420–40 contained no recognisably contemporary pottery.

The growing insecurity of transport and the escape of slaves are two factors which might easily have crippled the industry even if no raiders looted the plant. Indeed, since pottery-kilns are relatively simple to construct, it must have been the economic difficulties which were decisive. The disappearance of mass-produced pottery left a void both for the contemporary householder and for the modern archaeologist. The former was sometimes able to eke out his resources with home-made wares, some of which in the south-east bear a curious resemblance to Belgic wares of four centuries earlier. But the majority had to change their habits. Metal-workers still sold bowls and cauldrons; the rich could buy glass and still possessed plate; for most people and for most purposes vessels of wood or leather no doubt came to suffice.

The Yorkshire signal-stations probably ceased to function soon after 400, for none has more than a single structural period, and the latest coins were not numerous. At least two, those at Huntcliff and Goldsborough came to a violent and even dramatic end at the hands of raiders, and thereafter the coastal approaches lay exposed.

It was probably about the same time that effective occupation ceased on Hadrian's Wall. The precise date is a vexed question. The type of garrison present there in the last period may not have been entitled to regular payment in cash; but despite the inadequacy of published records, it is known that coins minted later than 389 have been found at Chesterholm and Birdoswald, and in Coventina's Well at Carrawburgh, while coins at Corbridge and South Shields go down at least as late. Both Birdoswald and Chesterholm seem to have been violently destroyed,[19] and this may have happened in one of the raids at the turn of the century. Other forts, however, may conceivably have remained in occupation longer. If the second generation of occupants were of too little military value to attract the eye of Stilicho or Constantine they may well have remained in their forts until either they were overwhelmed piecemeal or they migrated to less lonely localities.

Many of the villas continued in occupation into the fifth century, and at some of them, for instance Great Casterton in Rutland or Hucclecote in Gloucestershire, new mosaic floors were laid down at the very end of the fourth century or even perhaps later. Their ultimate fate is obscure. Some, no doubt, were sacked, as the villa at North Wraxall in Wiltshire seems to have been. Here the coin-series ends with Gratian, and not only were corpses together with architectural fragments from the villa flung down the well but also two items of late Roman military uniform were unearthed, perhaps be-

longing to troops billeted on the owner, but more probably lost
during a skirmish with the raiders. The villa may have been destroyed
at any time in the early fifth century, for no great reliance can be
placed on the apparent absence of the small coins of the house of
Theodosius, which are in any case normally rare as site-finds. At
Great Casterton, Rutland, part of the villa was burnt down in the
first quarter of the fifth century, but squatter occupation continued
thereafter; at Lullingstone, Kent, also, occupation of the villa ended
in fire, and here also a piece of military equipment has been recorded.

The majority of villas, however, appear to have met no violent end
but to have undergone gradual decay; at Bignor, Sussex, and Whittington Court, Gloucestershire, the roof-tiles were found lying where
they had fallen on the collapse of the decayed rafters. The villa at
Langton, Yorkshire, is one of the few at which a money-economy was
active in the last decade of the fourth century or later; here again
the villa seems to have been abandoned at the end, rather than destroyed.

At many villas coins become very rare from 378. This does not
necessarily mean more than a growing reliance upon barter; but at
King's Weston, Gloucestershire, Atworth, Wiltshire, and Ditchley,
Oxfordshire, there was a perceptible decline in the standards of
living. Part of the bath-wing at Atworth was converted for farm-
purposes as a corn-dryer, while other rooms were crudely paved with
stone. At King's Weston there was a reduction in the number of
rooms in use, and the end of occupation was marked by a skeleton
lying in the collapsed hypocaust; there were the marks of sword-cuts
on the skull. At Ditchley fires were lit on the floor of a living-room.
This sort of decline may be attributed to the growing insecurity of
the times. If some of the villa-owners repaired to the security of their
town-houses the estates might be left in the hands of bailiffs. The
picture that St Patrick gives of his early life, however, shows that
villa proprietors could continue to inhabit their villas as least down
to 430, disturbed from time to time by marauding bands (who might
carry off members of the staff or family into slavery), but otherwise
continuing the cultivation of their estates and the practice of the
Christian faith. When Patrick returned home after his captivity his
father, Calpurnius, a decurion of his civitas and a deacon of the
church, implored him to remain at home and undertake *munera*, or
public office.

Nevertheless, there are few, if any, places where continuity can be suggested between Romano-British estates and Saxon Manors. At Wingham, Kent, very early Germanic pottery has been found in the ruins of a villa; but this does not necessarily indicate continuity, for the Saxons may have been billeted on the villa as part of a federate settlement. This may also have happened at Rivenhall, Essex. At Withington, Gloucestershire, H. P. R. Finberg has shown that the area of a seventh-century Saxon monastic estate very probably reflects that of the earlier villa; but this is evidence for the influence of geographical factors rather than for historical continuity: there is nothing to show that the villa itself survived the early fifth century, if as long.

We can feel sure that though owners might cling to their villas as long as possible, nevertheless conditions eventually became too insecure for personal safety; and that more seriously still, the slaves and coloni, upon whose labours productivity depended, were found increasingly difficult either to retain or to replace. In the majority of cases it was the economic basis rather than the physical buildings of the villas which was the first to disintegrate: when that happened the ruin of the buildings themselves would not be long postponed. It is noteworthy that Gildas, writing about 540, could describe the sack of towns; but he knew nothing whatever of villas. They had passed from the scene so long before his time that not even a tradition was left.

The state of the peasantry is less easy to analyse. As much of eastern Britain came under Saxon occupation, some of the earlier population may well have migrated westwards, and thus have swelled the numbers of those Britons who soon after the middle of the fifth century migrated to Brittany. Others, however, certainly remained; this is suggested partly by the survival of place- and river-names, partly by archaeological evidence, and also by a few historical references, such as the Life of St Guthlac, who encountered Celtic-speaking Britons in the Fens as late as 700. One of the archaeological indications is the pottery, which may genuinely be described as Romano-Saxon, from Anglo-Saxon cemeteries. This pottery, often hand-made, shows by its traditional fabric and superior techniques, often combined with Saxon decoration, that native potters were working for new masters; it must be carefully distinguished from the mass-produced wares of the fourth century which have also – and

419

too readily – been labelled Romano-Saxon from the supposed Germanic inspiration of their decoration. A few rural sites may even point to continuity of occupation, as perhaps at Elmswell, Yorkshire. But British survival is more easily demonstrated from the brooches, buckles, hanging bowls and decorative techniques, which point to the work of British bronze-smiths: some of these smiths may have been itinerant masters of high standing, but the commoner objects are more likely to be the product of local industry. Of course in the south-west, and in northern Wales and the North, beyond the immediate reach of Saxon settlers or war-bands, indications of British survival may take a less elusive form which is beginning to be better understood. For here there is growing evidence from recent excavations for reoccupation – and refortification – of the hill-forts of the Iron Age, and for the establishment of new strongholds in similar positions. The type-sites are South Cadbury and Cadbury Congresbury, both in Somerset, and Dinas Powys in South Wales; and there are others which are likely to reveal relationships with nearby sub-Roman cemeteries. The movement back to the hill-forts may have been much more widespread than at present is certainly attested: investigation of this aspect of the period is still in its infancy.

Much has been discovered in recent years to counteract the older view that the towns of Roman Britain were in complete decay from the middle of the fourth century. Excavations at the civitas capitals of *Verulamium* and Cirencester and the small towns of Catterick and Dorchester on Thames have all revealed the survival of active life well into the fifth century, and, at the two first, large houses adorned with fine mosaics were still being built in the latest decades of the fourth. These were the dwellings of aristocrats like Gratian who could accept a throne, and of the leaders who took the initiative in 410. At *Verulamium* three later phases could be recognised. In the first a large mosaic in such a mansion was sacrificed to utility, when a corn-drying oven was dug through it. This suggests a period when growing insecurity in the countryside made it wise to hurry the newly cut harvest within the safety of town-walls. The oven was in use long enough for repairs to become necessary to its furnace-room, but no contemporary pottery or coins were found in the contents of this. If precise dating was rendered impossible by the lack, at least the absence of pottery and coins suggest a period beginning no earlier than 430 for its use, when such things were no longer obtainable.

Thereafter the house itself was demolished, and its site occupied by a large buttressed hall or barn, whose wall contained a bonding-course of tiles, all of which were broken fragments recovered from earlier structures. Roman building techniques were still practised, but it was impossible to obtain new tiles. When this building in turn had perished, its site was crossed by a pipe-line of wooden tubes jointed with iron collars. Such fresh-water mains had been common in earlier centuries; the interest here is to find the technique still practised at a date which cannot be earlier than 450 and may be considerably later. Evidently the aqueduct and public fountains of the town were still in use, and Romanised life still continuing. We cannot doubt that it was the town-walls, refitted by Count Theodosius and still manned by troops in late Roman uniform, which made this sort of urban survival possible.[20]

But town life depended upon trade and ultimately upon supplies of food. With the decay of the former, decline was inevitable; yet towns would still have a function as strong-points so long as the surrounding region could be cultivated in comparative security. The date when even this ceased to be possible was naturally different in different areas; varying, too, were the destinies of each individual city. In the east Caistor by Norwich may have perished in a massacre and remained empty, while Canterbury or Dorchester on Thames could receive Germanic settlers and continue to be occupied. These lay within the regions settled by the earliest Anglo-Saxons. The Saxon laeti round Caistor, their numbers periodically replenished from their homelands, seem to have remained entirely outside the ambit of Roman civilisation; whereas the later foederati at Canterbury and Dorchester, if not less primitive, were at any rate assigned a different role, which placed them inside the towns. At York, too, there was continuous occupation of some vigour; the legionary principia continued to stand for centuries, and the defences were repaired from time to time. At what stage change from British to English town occurred excavations have not yet clearly revealed. *Verulamium* survived as a Roman city, as we have seen, well into the dark age, but today its site is empty. The date of its evacuation is quite unknown; we can only say that if life there survived until the German tide was halted late in the fifth century by the British recovery signalised for us by the battle of Mt Badon there was nothing to prevent it continuing peacefully until the Saxon victories of 571. Archaeology is

421

silent, partly because of the destruction of the upper levels by cultivation, partly because of the lack of datable material. On the whole our verdict must be against organised survival much later than 500: here and there squatters may still have inhabited the ruins, but the maintenance of buildings first put up even in the late fourth century must by then have become an insuperable difficulty.

At Silchester, too, there is suggestive evidence of continued life in the form of fifth-century metal-work and glass; and the well-known inscription carved on a stone column in the Ogham script points to the presence of an Irishman in the town at a date which can hardly be earlier than the sixth century and may be later. Round this town the late fifth-century territorium seems to be indicated by earthworks which are best understood as boundaries rather than defences as such: they mark a stage of agreement or equilibrium between the invaders and the Britons such as would suit the aftermath of Badon. The final stage of Bokerly Dyke is perhaps a similar phenomenon. It is certainly no earlier than the fifth century, as the coins show; and, now that early Saxon material is known in Hampshire and the Salisbury region, it is easier to place the dyke later in the century than was once thought likely.

Farther west again, some of the towns may have had an even longer reprieve. Unfortunately evidence bearing on the point is scarce. At Cirencester the forum was maintained to a date when coins were no longer used, and the presence of unburied bodies in the side-ditch of a street has been explained in terms of a great plague; but whether the plague of 433 or that of a century later cannot be decided. At Exeter the coin-list ends with Magnus Maximus; but this in itself means only that the supply of coinage was interrupted. The erosion of the upper Roman levels has deprived us of other sorts of archaeological evidence; William of Malmesbury, however, makes it clear that until they were expelled by Athelstan (perhaps in 928), Britons continued to live in Exeter side by side with the Saxons, in an independent community occupying their own particular quarter of the city, which was known as Britayne as late as the thirteenth century.[21] At Caerwent a fire destroyed the basilica and various shops and houses at some date in the fifth century; this town was dangerously exposed to Irish raids in the Bristol Channel, and seems to have become deserted before the revival of western trade, which began to bring in Mediterranean pottery in the later fifth century. The most profitable line of investigation of the problems of British survival in the towns is likely to be the examination of surrounding cemeteries; important evidence has been obtained at Cirencester and still more at Dorchester (Dorset), where Mediterranean pottery has also been found within the town itself.

As the material prosperity which had characterised late Roman Britain waned, so a spiritual revival took place. During the fourth century there had been a flowering of Celtic religion which is witnessed by the many sacred sites built or refurbished during that period; the process reached its climax in the last third of the century and thus may rightly be connected with the decline of civil security at that time. Christianity was not a powerful force in Britain before the last decade or two of the fourth century, but from then onwards it became the leading spiritual influence in the island, and it was Christians who took the lead in the struggle for Celtic independence and survival. Partly, perhaps because of its patriotic associations, together with the undoubted authority it had inherited from the Roman past, and partly because of its superior spiritual qualities and its links with education, Christianity now became the religion of the people, not merely of the aristocracy. It gained ascendancy through monastic foundations which were centres of learning as well as of devotion, and through the missionary activities of influential saints.

The spiritual revival of Britain, however, was not solely a matter of religion, for there was also a revival of art. This had its genesis in the West, where some of the sources of inspiration for decorated metal-work were certainly supplied by Irish settlers, but where native bronze-smiths had also kept alive the techniques of their craft throughout the Roman period, and now found their opportunity.[22] Indeed, western Britain assumed a new significance as slowly the eastern parts of the island were submerged by Germanic immigrants. Vortigern had connections with the later dynasty of Powys, and may himself have sprung from a noble Cornovian family. Much of the military strength of fifth-century Britain must have been supplied by the tribes of Wales, and this strength was sufficient to maintain the independence of the West for many centuries.

The result was a new pride, and the genesis of a new sub-Roman culture, which gave birth to the language and civilisation of early medieval Wales. The Irish Sea became the centre of a Celtic province in which western Britain and Ireland were closely linked. Long after contact with northern Gaul and the Rhineland had been interrupted by Saxon settlements, and cross-Channel trade had fallen into Germanic hands, connections with south Gaul and with the Mediterranean itself were maintained within the fifth to the seventh centuries, tenuously it is true, but sufficiently to be significant, by merchants and travellers using the western sea-ways. Pottery imported by these means has now been recognsed at a number of sites round the Irish Sea and Bristol Channel. Further evidence of contact with the Continent can sometimes be deduced from the fifth- and sixth-century inscribed stones of the Celtic West; these are suggestive of the influence of Christian missionaries from Gaul.

The three chief enemies of Roman Britain at this time were the Irish, the Picts and the Saxons. Of these, the first became a less serious menace during the second quarter of the fifth century; for with the spread of Christianity to Ireland, and the growth of friendly relations which resulted from a dynastic marriage, the raiding ceased. It was the Picts who were regarded by the British as their chief danger, and though raids by Saxons were from time to time recorded, it was to the latter that Vortigern turned when seeking help against them. The earliest permanent Saxon settlements in Britain were the result not of haphazard seizure of lands by raiders or land-hungry settlers but of planned dispositions by British authority in areas thought to stand in special need of protection or to offer outstanding strategic advantages for the defence of Britain.

One of the best-known dates of English history is 449, traditionally the year of the landing of the Saxons. It derives from Bede, and because of his great reputation as a historian the date itself has acquired more authority than perhaps Bede himself intended; for he has left evidence of his uncertainty of the chronology of the period.[23] No historian, however great, can write reliably of events almost two centuries before his own time unless he has access to reliable sources. Bede's main source for fifth-century events in Britain was Gildas, the sixth-century British ecclesiastic, whose historical sections are a subsidiary element in a work of moral exhortation. After the separation from Rome he tells of a long period of great material prosperity in which victory was achieved over Picts and Irish, who were driven home and made to abate the severity of their raiding. This period ended with renewed attacks and the outbreak of a great plague, and was followed by the invitation of the 'proud tyrant' to the Saxons to come to his assistance against the Picts. This arrangement was successful for a time, and the Saxons were kept amiable with subsidies; but at last came a rebellion of the Saxons and great slaughter and destruction of cities, ending in the enslavement of some and the escape overseas of many other Britons.

This narrative of Gildas was derived from oral tradition and not tied to dates; but the truth of its general sequence can be confirmed from other sources. Gildas did, however, quote one document which can be approximately dated, the Groans of the Britons; but there is no reason to suppose either that he himself knew the date of the third consulship of Aetius or that he placed the document in the correct position in his narrative. In fact, he placed it before the period of prosperity, and this is certainly wrong; for if the first arrival of the Saxons followed a plague, which itself followed a period of British prosperity of sufficient duration to witness victory over raiders from across the sea, the rise and fall of kings, and an increasing corruption of the people (all of which are incidents attributed to it by Gildas); and if all this long sequence has to be placed after 446, then the arrival of the Saxons becomes impossibly late, and their eventual rebellion would fall well in the second half of the fifth century. This is quite contrary both to the archaeological evidence and to what little independent historical evidence we possess. It is clear that in following Gildas over-conscientiously Bede has misdated the coming of the Saxons: his dating has no independent validity, and is twenty years too late. And since the *Anglo-Saxon Chronicle* founds its dating system on Bede, the mistake has had far-reaching consequences.

The prosperity-period of Gildas can safely be assigned to the decades following 410, during which, as Myres has pointed out,[24] we have independent evidence for the rise and fall of kings, victory over invaders and corruption (the Pelagian heresy) in church and state. The rebellion of the Saxon federates which Gildas so vividly describes is best equated with the event recorded in the contemporary anonymous *Gallic Chronicle* of 452, which under the year 442 states, 'Britain long troubled by various happenings and disasters passed under the authority of the Saxons'; for it is clear that to the composer of this chronicle what happened in Britain that year appeared as a decisive break with the past: he is not recording the arrival of Saxon allies. The chronicle was published too soon after the event for the success of subsequent British resistance to be appreciated. Finally, the migrations of Britons to Brittany, which Gildas attributes to Saxon pressure after the rebellion, can be shown to have happened by about 460.[25]

If, then, the rebellion occurred in 442 the first arrival of the Saxons, in response to Vortigern's invitation, must have occurred some years before this,[26] perhaps about 430. This is a date which suits the archaeological evidence bearing on their arrival very well and is not unsupported by the documents;[27] it is also the most probable period for another but similar step taken by Vortigern. This was the transfer of Cunedda to North Wales. Cunedda's date can be worked out only very roughly. He was the great grandfather of Mailcun (Maelgwn), who died in 547, a contemporary of Gildas: allowing thirty years to a generation from a *floruit* for Mailcun about 530, the *floruit* of Cunedda would fall about 440; conversely, two generations from Paternus Pesrut (p. 392f.) in 369 would bring us to about 430. Cunedda was the first of his family for four generations to have a British rather than a Roman name, and this reinforces the view that he belonged to the immediately post-Roman period in Britain. His transfer from Manau Goddodin, the kingdom of the Votadini, to North Wales was made in order to drive out or subdue the Irish settlers there. Its result was the foundation of the royal line of Gwynedd, but the move itself was modelled on Roman statecraft, and could have been undertaken only by a strong central government controlling all Roman Britain. A context after the rebellion of the Saxons seems impossible.

The earliest Germanic cemeteries in Britain are found near the estuaries of the east coast, the Humber, the Wash and the Thames. These river-mouths are natural entries for invaders, but the cemeteries themselves, at least in their opening phase, are best interpreted as representing defenders placed in these regions to resist sea-borne Pictish invaders, and even perhaps to meet them on the seas.[28] The conclusion is reinforced by the known history of settlement in Kent, where settlement of federates is attested in history, and by the abandonment of raiding by the Picts, which suggests the successful impact of new measures. Three early cemeteries in Surrey, at Mitcham, Croydon and Beddington, seem to represent communities intentionally placed to guard the southern approaches to London.

Another important and very early group of burials lies in the Oxford region. The identity of their route to the centre of England was always a problem when it was assumed that the burials were those of invaders. But as a federate settlement the group makes much better sense, when we remember that the most prosperous region of late Roman Britain had lain in the Cotswolds just west of this region. Such dispositions in the east of the island were well placed to oppose and counter Pictish raiders penetrating from landfalls on the eastern coasts, and they seem to have been successful; raids from the north are no more heard of. But when the federates themselves rebelled it was all too apparent that they had been given a stranglehold on Britain. This was the context of the appeal to Aetius.

Down, then, to 442 Vortigern successfully maintained the independence of Britain. But the rebellion of his Germanic federates introduced a period of chaos fatal to the villa system, and destructive to Vortigern's own supremacy. In the later fifth century the leadership had passed to Ambrosius Aurelianus and after him to Arthur. Little is known of either. Ambrosius appears in the pages of Gildas, but Arthur does not, and his activities and personality are almost impenetrably overlaid by medieval romance. The evidence is sufficient to allow belief that he had a real existence and that he was probably the victor of Mount Badon. It is likely that he succeeded Ambrosius in the leadership; indeed, he is called *dux bellorum* in the *Historia Brittonum*, which suggests a memory of late Roman military titles, and may indicate some sort of unified command arranged between several petty kingdoms. Using mounted forces, these leaders were able to strike back at the Saxons, who had little body armour and inferior weapons. The use of cavalry enabled unexpected blows to be struck from distant bases, and it was a form of warfare in which small numbers of horsemen could rout many times their number of ill-armed barbarian foot-soldiers. It is perhaps no coincidence that eight out of twelve battles traditionally associated with Arthur were fought at fords, and so were other fifth-century battles; a well-planned charge even by a few horsemen on a force of foot soldiers crossing a stream could be expected to produce maximum confusion.

A long period of fluctuating warfare culminated at some date rather before 500 in a British victory at Mount Badon, an unidentified site perhaps in the south-west; after it there was peace for two generations. Gildas, writing soon after 540, is able to speak of 'our present security' and of a generation which had no experience of the great struggle. Soon after 550, however, the Saxon conquest was renewed. In 571 an area from Buckinghamshire to the upper Thames was overrun, and six years later came the fall of Gloucester, Cirencester and Bath. About 590 the Britons in the north suffered a serious defeat at Catterick, and by 600 most of Britain had fallen to the Saxon kingdoms with the exception of the Dumnonian peninsula, Wales and parts of the Pennines and north-west.

But though the struggle was long drawn out, two facts are clear. The official connection of Britain with the Roman empire ended in 410 and was not renewed; but the Roman framework and civilisation of the province was in some sense maintained until 442. Thereafter it was Celtic rather than Roman Britain which maintained the struggle, and the history of the dark age which followed is to be pieced together by new disciplines.

1. Orosius, vii, 34, 9.
2. CW^2, li (1951), 4–15.
3. *Notitia Dignitatum Occ.*, vii, 49.
4. Prosper Tiro, *Chronicon, Gratiani*, iv (AD 382): *incursantes Pictos et Scotos Maximus strenue superavit.*
5. Claudian, *de consulatu Stilichonis*, ii, 250–5 (written AD 400).

> 'Me quoque vicinis pereuntem gentibus' inquit
> 'munivit Stilicho, totam cum Scotus Iernen
> movit et infesto spumavit remige Tethys.
> illius effectum curis, ne tela timerem
> Scotica, ne Pictum tremerem, ne litore toto
> prospicerem dubiis venturum Saxona ventis.'

6. Claudian, *in Eutropium*, i, 391–3.

> quantum te principe possim
> non longinqua docent, domito quod Saxone Tethys
> mitior aut fracto secura Britannia Picto.

7. The sole archaeological trace of his activities, four titles stamped HON AVG ANDRIA from the fort at Pevensey, have recently been shown to be modern forgeries: D. P. S. Peacock, *Antiquity*, xlvii (1973), 138 ff.

8. Claudian *de bello Gothico* 416–18:

> venit et extremis legio praetenta Britannis
> quae Scoto dat frena truci ferroque notatas
> perlegit exanimes Picto moriente figuras.

9. *Notitia Dignitatum Or.*, ix, 29; *Oc.*, v, 197.

10. Zosimus, vi, 3, 1.

11. Orosius, vii, 40, 4: *municeps tyrannus.*

12. Zosimus, vi, 5.

13. Procopius, *de bello Vandalico*, i, 2, 38. Procopius was writing over a century later, but C. E. Stevens has shown (*Athenaeum* (Pavia) 1957, 340–1), that he is here probably using a contemporary source. This paper is a very valuable discussion of sources and chronology from 406 to 411.

14. *Antiquity*, xxx (1956), 163–7.

15. *JRS*, l (1960), 21–36.

16. Nennius, *Historia Brittonum*, 31 (part of an early strand in this work).

17. Solinus, *Coll. rerum memorabilium* (ed. Mommsen, 1895) 22, 7: *Siluram quoque insulam ab ora quam gens Brittana Dumnonii tenent turbidum fretum distinguit. Cuius homines etiam nunc custodiunt morem vetustum; nummum refutant; dant res et accipiunt, mutationibus necessaria potius quam pretiis parant.*

18. In R. H. M. Dolley, *Anglo-Saxon Coins* (1961), pp. 1–22.

19. Birdoswald, CW^2, xxx (1930), 170: Chesterholm, AA^4, viii, 211.

20. See the study of late Roman and Dark Age military buckles etc., by S. Hawkes and G. C. Dunning in *Medieval Archaeology*, v (1961), 1–70; and *Bericht der Römisch-Germanischen Kommission*, 43–4 (1962–3), 155–231.

21. I owe this information to Professor W. G. Hoskins.

22. See the brilliant study of this industry by C. F. C. Hawkes in W. F. Grimes, *Aspects of Archaeology in Britain and Beyond* (1951), pp. 172–99.

23. In his *Chronicle* of 725 he dates the Saxon landing 449–52; in his *Church History* of 731 he three times dates it 446–7 (*H.E.*, i, 23, ii, 14, v, 23), and twice 449–56 (*H.E.*, i, 15, v, 24).

24. 'Adventus Saxonum', in W. F. Grimes, *Aspects of Archaeology in Britain and beyond* (1951), pp. 221–41.

25. J. Morris, 'Dark Age Dates', in M. G. Jarrett and B. Dobson, *Britain and Rome* (1966), 145 ff.

26. Gildas, *de excidio* 24, uses the phrase *multo tempore* of the interval.

27. Nennius, *Historia Brittonum*, 66.

28. To Gildas (*de excidio* 11) the Picts were *transmarini*: they came across the sea.

Abbreviations

AA², *AA⁴*	*Archaeologia Aeliana*, second, fourth series etc., Society of Antiquaries of Newcastle upon Tyne.
Arch. Camb.	*Archaeologia Cambrensis*, Cambrian Archaeological Association.
Arch. Cant.	*Archaeologia Cantiana*, Kent Archaeological Society.
Antiq. Journ.	*The Antiquaries Journal*, Society of Antiquaries of London.
Arch. Journ.	*The Archaeological Journal*, Royal Archaeological Institute.
BBCS	*Bulletin of the Board of Celtic Studies*, University of Wales, Cardiff.
B.M.	British Museum.
BMC	*Coins of the Roman Empire in the British Museum*, London, 1923 etc.
CIL	*Corpus Inscriptionum Latinarum.*
CW²	*Transactions of the Cumberland and Westmorland Antiquarian and Archaeological Society*, second series.
EE	*Ephemeris Epigraphica.*
ILS	H. Dessau, *Inscriptiones Latinae Selectae.*
JBAA³	*Journal of the British Archaeological Association*, third series.

430

JRS	*Journal of Roman Studies.*
NCH	*Northumberland County History,* Newcastle upon Tyne.
PIR	*Prosopographia Imperii Romani.*
Proc. Camb. Ant. Soc.	*Proceedings of the Cambridge Antiquarian Society.*
P. Hants. F.C.	*Papers and Proceedings of the Hampshire Field Club and Archaeological Society.*
PPS	*Proceedings of the Prehistoric Society.*
PSAS	*Proceedings of the Society of Antiquaries of Scotland.*
PUBSS	*Proceedings, University of Bristol Spelaeological Society.*
R.C.H.M.	Royal Commission on Historical Monuments.
RE	Pauly-Wissowa, *Realencyclopädie d. Class. Altertumswissenschaft.*
RIB	R. G. Collingwood and R. P. Wright, *The Roman Inscriptions of Britain,* i, Oxford, 1965.
RIC	H. Mattingly and E. A. Sydenham, *The Roman Imperial Coinage,* London, 1923 etc.
SHA	Scriptores Historiae Augustae.
Sx.A.C.	*Sussex Archaeological Collections,* Sussex Archaeological Society.
Sy.A.C.	*Surrey Archaeological Collections,* Surrey Archaeological Society.
T. Birmingham A.S.	*Transactions and Proceedings of the Birmingham Archaeological Society.*
T. Dumfries and Gal. Ant. Soc.	*Transactions of the Dumfriesshire and Galloway Antiquarian Society.*
T. Durham and N.A. Soc.	*Transactions of the Architectural and Archaeological Society of Durham and Northumberland.*
VCH	The Victoria County History.

Bibliography

GENERAL

F. Haverfield, *The Romanization of Roman Britain* (Ed. 3), Oxford, 1915.

F. Haverfield and G. Macdonald, *The Roman Occupation of Britain*, Oxford, 1924.

F. Sagot, *La Bretagne Romaine*, Paris, 1911.

I. A. Richmond, *Roman Britain*, London, 1963.

I. A. Richmond (ed.), *Roman and Native in North Britain*, London, 1958.

E. Birley, *Roman Britain and the Roman Army*, Kendal, 1953.

R. G. Collingwood and J. N. L. Myres, *Roman Britain and the English Settlements*, Oxford, 1937.

R. G. Collingwood and R. P. Wright, *The Roman Inscriptions of Britain*, I, Oxford, 1965.

M. P. Charlesworth, *The Lost Province*, Cardiff, 1949.

A. L. F. Rivet, *Town and Country in Roman Britain*, London, 1964.

A. Birley, *Life in Roman Britain*, London, 1964.

H.M. Ordnance Survey, *A Map of Southern Britain in the Iron Age*, Chessington, 1962.

H.M. Ordnance Survey, *A Map of Roman Britain* (Ed. 3), Chessington, 1956.

W. Bonser, *A Romano-British Bibliography*, Oxford, 1964.

Governors of Britain: D. Atkinson, *JRS* XII (1922), 60ff.; E. Birley in G. Askew, *The Coinage of Roman Britain*, London, 1951, 81; A. R. Birley, *Epigraphische Studien* IV (1967), 63.

C. H. V. Sutherland, *Coinage and Currency in Roman Britain*, Oxford, 1937.

K. Jackson, *Language and History in Early Britain*, Edinburgh, 1953.

J. M. C. Toynbee, *Art in Roman Britain*, London, 1962.

J. M. C. Toynbee, *Art in Britain under the Romans*, Oxford, 1964.

P. Salway, *The Frontier People of Roman Britain*, Cambridge, 1965.

C. Thomas (ed.), *Rural Settlement in Roman Britain*, London, 1966.

V. E. Nash-Williams, *The Roman Frontier in Wales* (2nd. ed., by M. G. Jarrett, Cardiff, 1969).

R. M. Butler (ed.), *Soldier and Civilian in Roman Yorkshire*, Leicester, 1971.

CHAPTER 1   The earliest British Iron Age, pp. 14–26

D. W. Harding, *The Iron Age in the Upper Thames Basin*, Oxford, 1972.

M. Jesson and D. Hill (ed.), *The Iron Age and its Hill-forts*, Southampton, 1971.

I. A. Richmond, *Hod Hill*, ii, London, 1968.

Sir Cyril Fox, *The Personality of Britain* (Ed. 4), Cardiff, 1943.

S. Piggott, in I. A. Richmond (ed), *Roman and Native in North Britain*, chapter 1.

S. S. Frere (ed.), *Problems of the Iron Age in Southern Britain*, London, 1961.

C. F. C. Hawkes, 'The A.B.C. of the British Iron Age', *Antiquity*, xxxiii (1959), 170 ff.

A. H. A. Hogg, 'Early Iron Age Wales', in I. Ll. Foster and G. Daniel, *Prehistoric and Early Wales*, London, 1965.

E. M. Jope, 'Daggers of the Early Iron Age in Britain', *PPS*, xxvii (1961), 307.

T. C. M. Brewster, *The Excavation of Staple Howe*, Scarborough, 1963.

R. E. M. Wheeler, 'Prehistoric Scarborough', in A. Rowntree, *The History of Scarborough*, London, 1931.

M. E. Cunnington, *All Cannings Cross*, Devizes, 1923.

C. F. C. Hawkes, 'The Early Iron Age Settlement at Fengate, Peterborough', *Arch. Journ.*, c (1945), 188ff.

H. N. Savory, 'An Early Iron Age site at Long Wittenham, Berks.', *Oxoniensia*, ii (1937), 1 ff.

J. N. L. Myres, 'A Prehistoric . . . Site on Mount Farm, Dorchester', *Oxoniensia*, ii (1937), 12 ff.

K. M. Richardson and A. Young, 'An Iron Age A site in the Chilterns', *Antiq. Journ.*, xxxi (1951), 132 ff.

J. G. D. Clark and C. I. Fell, '. . . Micklemoor Hill, West Harling', *PPS*, xix (1953), 1 ff.

H. C. Bowen, *Ancient Fields*, London, 1961.

G. Webster and B. Hobley, 'Aerial Reconnaisance over the Warwickshire Avon', *Arch. Journ.*, cxxi (1964), 1 ff.

G. Bersu, 'Excavations at Little Woodbury', *PPS*, vi (1940), 30 ff.

A. Fox, 'Celtic Fields and Farms on Dartmoor', *PPS*, xx (1954), 87 ff.

S. Applebaum, 'The Agriculture . . . at Figheldean Down', *PPS*, xx (1954), 103 ff.

H. Helbaek, 'Early crops in Southern Britain', *PPS*, xviii (1952), 194 ff.

C. F. C. Hawkes, 'The Excavations at Quarley Hill', *P. Hants, F.C.*, xiv (2) (1939), 136 ff.

A. Fox, 'Excavations at Kestor', *Transactions of the Devon Association for the Advancement of Science Literature and Art*, lxxxvi (1954), 21 ff.

D. Dudley, 'An Excavation at Bodrifty . . .', *Arch. Journ.*, cxiii (1956), 1 ff.

M. A. Cotton, 'British Camps with Timber-laced Ramparts', *Arch. Journ.*, cxi (1954), 26 ff.

Dinorben: H. N. Savory, *Antiquity* xlv (1971), 251 ff.

Ivinghoe Beacon: M. A. Cotton and S. S. Frere, *Records of Buckinghamshire* xviii (1968), 187 ff.

R. E. M. Wheeler, *Maiden Castle, Dorset*, Oxford, 1943.

R. E. M. Wheeler, 'Bindon Hill, Dorset', *Antiq. Journ.*, xxxiii (1953), 1 ff.

A. Fox, *South West England*, London, 1964.

E. C. Curwen, *The Archaeology of Sussex*, London, 1937.

E. Mackie, 'Radiocarbon dates and the Scottish Iron Age', *Antiquity* xliii (1969), 15 ff.

J. R. C. Hamilton, *Excavations at Jarlshof*, London, 1956.

A. L. F. Rivet, 'The Iron Age in Northern Britain', *Antiquity*, xxxvi (1962), 24 ff.

R. Feachem, *A Guide to Prehistoric Scotland*, London, 1963.

L. Alcock, 'Excavations at Castell Odo', *Arch. Camb.*, cxi (1960), 78 ff.

L. Alcock, *Dinan Powys*, Cardiff, 1963.

CHAPTER 2   Iron B and Iron C in Britain, pp. 27–41

P. Jacobsthal, *Early Celtic Art*, Oxford, 1944.

J. M. de Navarro, 'The Celts in Britain and their Art', in M. D. Knowles (ed.), *The Heritage of Early Britain*, London, 1952.

R. R. Clarke and C. F. C. Hawkes, 'An Iron Anthropoid Sword from Shouldham, Norfolk . . .', PPS, xxi (1955), 198 ff.

S. Piggott, 'Swords and Scabbards of the British Early Iron Age', PPS, xvi (1950), 1 ff.

J. B. Ward Perkins, 'Iron Age Metal Horses' Bits of the British Isles', PPS, v (1939), 173 ff.

E. M. Jope, 'Chariotry and Paired Draught . . .', *Ulster Journal of Archaeology*, xviii (1955), 37 ff.

J. F. Dyer, 'Drays Ditches, Bedfordshire', *Antiq. Journ.*, xli (1961), 32 ff.

Sir Cyril Fox, see p. 40, note 1.

R. J. C. Atkinson and S. Piggott, 'The Torrs Chamfrein', *Archaeologia*, xcvi (1955), 197 ff.

W. F. Grimes, 'Art on British Iron Age Pottery', PPS, xviii (1952), 160 ff.

I. M. Stead, 'A . . . La Tène Barrow in Eastern Yorkshire', *Antiq. Journ.*, xli (1961), 44 ff.

I. M. Stead, *The La Tène Cultures of Eastern Yorkshire*, York, 1965.

F. R. Hodson, 'Cultures of Continental type in Britain', PPS, xxx (1964), 100 ff.

M. A. Cotton, 'Pre-Belgic Iron Age cultures of Gloucestershire', in E. M. Clifford, *Bagendon, a Belgic Oppidum*, Cambridge, 1961.

D. F. Allen, 'The Paul (Penzance) Hoard . . .', *Numismatic Chronicle* [7], i (1961), 91 ff.

C. F. C. Hawkes, 'The Hill-forts of Northern France', *Antiquity*, xxxii (1958), 154 ff.

A. S. R. Gordon, 'The excavations of Gurnards Head', *Arch. Journ.*, xcvii (1940), 96 ff.

C. A. R. Radford, 'Report on the excavations at Castle Dore'; *Journal of the Royal Institution of Cornwall*, i (1951), 1 ff.

L. M. Threipland, 'An excavation at St. Mawgan-in-Pyder', *Arch. Journ.*, cxiii (1956), 33 ff.

D. F. Allen, 'Iron Currency Bars in Britain', PPS, xxxiii (1967), 307 ff.

J. P. Bushe-Fox, *Excavations at Hengistbury Head, Hampshire*, Oxford, 1915.

A. Bulleid and H. St. G. Gray, *The Glastonbury Lake Village*, Glastonbury, 1911, etc.

H. St. G. Gray and A. Bulleid, *The Meare Lake Village*, Taunton, 1948 and 1953.

K. M. Kenyon, 'Excavations at Sutton Walls', *Arch. Journ.*, cx (1953), 1 ff.

J. B. Ward Perkins, 'An Early Iron Age site at Crayford, Kent', *PPS*, iv (1938), 151 ff.

S. S. Frere, 'An Iron Age site at West Clandon . . .', *Arch. Journ.*, ci (1944), 50 ff.

M. A. Cotton, 'A Classification of Hill Forts . . .', in S. S. Frere (ed.), *Problems of the Iron Age in Southern Britain*, London, 1961, 61 ff.

A. Fox, 'South-western Hill-forts', in S. S. Frere, op. cit., pp. 35 ff.

D. F. Allen, 'The Origins of Coinage in Britain', in S. S. Frere, op. cit., pp. 97 ff.

D. F. Allen, 'The Belgic Dynasties of Britain and their Coins', *Archaeologia*, xc (1944), 1 ff.

D. F. Allen, *The Coins of the Coritani*, London, 1963.

D. F. Allen, 'The Chronology of Durotrigan coinage 'in I. A. Richmond, *Hod Hill* ii, London, 1968.

D. F. Allen, 'A study of the Dobunnic coinage' in E. M. Clifford, *Bagendon, a Belgic oppidum*, Cambridge, 1961.

D. F. Allen, 'The coins of the Iceni', *Britannia* i (1970), 1 ff.

I. M. Stead, 'A La Tène III burial at Welwyn Garden City', *Archaeologia* ci (1967), 1 ff.

I. M. Stead, 'A La Tène burial at . . . Baldock, Hertfordshire', *Antiq. Journ.*, xlviii (1968), 306 ff.

D. P. S. Peacock, 'Roman Amphorae in pre-Roman Britain', in M. Jesson and D. Hill, *The Iron Age and its hill-forts*, Southampton, (1971), 171 ff.

A. J. Evans, 'A Late Celtic Urn-field at Aylesford, Kent', *Archaeologia*, lii (1890), 315 ff.

J. P. Bushe-Fox, *Excavation of the Late Celtic Urn-field at Swarling, Kent*, Oxford, 1925.

A. Birchall, 'The Aylesford-Swarling Culture . . .', *PPS*, xxxi (1965), 241 ff.

C. F. C. Hawkes and G. C. Dunning, 'The Belgae of Gaul and Britain', *Arch. Journ.*, lxxxvii (1930), 150 ff.

W. H. Manning, 'The Plough in Roman Britain', *JRS*, liv (1964), 54 ff.

Sir Cyril Fox, *A Find of the Early Iron Age from Llyn Cerrig Bach*, Cardiff, 1946, for currency bars, slave-chain, etc.

J. W. Brailsford, 'A corrected restoration of the Belgic Iron Frame from Welwyn', *Antiq. Journ.*, xxxviii (1958), 89 ff.

R. R. Clarke, 'The Early Iron Age Treasure from Snettisham, Norfolk', *PPS*, xx (1954), 27 ff.

Ipswich Torcs: *Antiquity* xliii (1969), 208 ff.; *PPS* xxxviii (1972), 219 ff.

D. F. Allen, 'Belgic coins as illustrations of Life . . .', *PPS*, xxiv (1958), 43 ff.

CHAPTER 3   Caesar's expeditions, pp. 42–54

C. E. Stevens, '55 B.C. and 54 B.C.', *Antiquity*, xxi (1947), 4 ff.

C. E. Stevens, *Latomus*, xi (1952), 3 ff. and 165 ff.

J.-J. Hatt, *Histoire de la Gaule romaine*, Paris, 1959.

C. Hignett, in *Cambridge Ancient History*, ix (1932), chapter xiii.

T. Rice Holmes, *Ancient Britain and the Invasions of Julius Caesar*, Oxford, 1907.

R. E. M. and T. V. Wheeler, *Verulamium, a Belgic and Two Roman Cities*, Oxford, 1936, for Wheathampstead.

CHAPTER 4   Caesar to Claudius, pp. 55–77

C. E. Stevens, 'Britain between the Invasions', in W. F. Grimes (ed.), *Aspects of Archaeology in Britain and Beyond*, London, 1951, 332 ff.

D. F. Allen, papers cited on p. 436.

R. P. Mack, *The Coinage of Ancient Britain* (2nd ed.), London, 1964.

G. C. Boon, *Roman Silchester*, London, 1957.

G. C. Boon, 'Belgic and Roman Silchester', *Archaeologia* cii (1969), 1 ff.

K. M. E. Murray, 'The Chichester Earthworks', *Sx.A.C.*, xciv (1956), 139 ff.

R. E. M. and T. V. Wheeler, *Verulamium, a Belgic and Two Roman Cities*, Oxford, 1936.

S. S. Frere, 'Verulamium, Three Roman Cities', *Antiquity*, xxxviii (1964), 103 ff.

C. F. C. Hawkes and M. R. Hull, *Camulodunum*, Oxford, 1947.

D. P. S. Peacock, 'Roman amphorae in pre-Roman Britain' in M. Jesson and D. Hill (ed.), *The Iron Age and its Hill-forts*, Southampton, 1971.

S. S. Frere, *Roman Canterbury* (3rd ed.), Canterbury, 1962.

S. S. Frere, 'Canterbury Excavations', *Arch. Cant.*, lxviii (1954), 101 ff.

R. R. Clarke, 'The Iron Age in Norfolk and Suffolk', *Arch. Journ.*, xcvi (1939), 1 ff.

R. R. Clarke, *East Anglia*, London, 1960.

S. S. Frere, 'A Claudian Site at Needham, Norfolk', *Antiq. Journ.*, xxi (1941), 40 ff.

H.M. Ordnance Survey, *Map of Southern Britain in the Iron Age*, introduction.

T. C. Lethbridge, 'Burial of an Iron Age Warrior at Snailwell', *Proceedings of the Cambridge Antiquarian Society*, xlvii (1953), 25 ff.

R. R. Clarke, 'The Early Iron Age Treasure from Snettisham, Norfolk', *PPS*, xx (1954), 27 ff.

F. T. Baker, 'The Iron Age Salt Industry in Lincolnshire', *Lincolnshire Architectural and Archaeological Society, Reports and Papers*, viii (1960), 26 ff.

S. Hawkes, 'Some Belgic Brooches from South Ferriby', *Hull Museum Publications*, No. 214 (1963), 23 ff.

K. M. Kenyon, *The Jewry Wall Site, Leicester*, Oxford, 1948, 124 ff.

G. Webster, *Arch. Journ.*, cxv (1958), p. 53 on Leicester.

E. M. Clifford, *Bagendon, a Belgic Oppidum*, Cambridge, 1961.

C. W. Dymond and H. S. Tomkins, *Worlebury*, 1866.

T. C. Hencken, 'The Excavation of . . . Bredon Hill', *Arch. Journ.*, xcv (1938), 1 ff.

J. W. Brailsford, 'Early Iron Age C in Wessex', *PPS*, xxiv (1958), 101 ff.

S. S. Frere, 'Some Problems of the later Iron Age', in S. S. Frere (ed.), *Problems of the Iron Age in Southern Britain*, London, 1961.

C. F. C. Hawkes, 'Britons, Romans and Saxons . . . in Cranborne Chase', *Arch. Journ.*, civ (1947), 27 ff.

A. L. F. Rivet, *Town and Country in Roman Britain*, London, 1964 chapter vi, 'Historical Geography'.

A. Fox, *South West England*, London, 1964.

D. M. Liddell, 'Excavations at Hembury Fort, Devon', *Proceedings of the Devon Archaeological Exploration Society*, 1 (1930–32), ii (1935).

L. Alcock, 'Celtic Archaeology and Art', in E. Davies (ed.), *Celtic Studies in Wales*, Cardiff, 1963.

W. Gardner and H. N. Savory, *Dinorben*, Cardiff, 1964.

I. A. Richmond, 'The Cornovii', in I. Ll. Foster and L. Alcock (eds.), *Culture and Environment*, London, 1963

W. J. Varley and J. W. Jackson, *Prehistoric Cheshire*, Chester, 1940.

W. J. Varley, 'The Hill-forts of the Welsh Marches', *Arch. Journ.*, cv (1948), 41 ff.

R. E. M. Wheeler, *The Stanwick Fortifications*, Oxford, 1954.

A. Raistrick, *Prehistoric Yorkshire*, Clapham, 1964.

P. Corder, 'Belgic . . . pottery found at North Ferriby, Yorks.', *Antiq. Journ.*, xviii (1938), 262 ff.

I. A. Richmond, 'Queen Cartimandua', *JRS*, xliv (1954), 43 ff.

S. Piggott, in I. A. Richmond (ed.), *Roman and Native in North Britain*, Chapter i.

M. Macgregor, 'The Early Iron Age Metalwork Hoard from Stanwick, Yorks.', *PPS*, xxviii (1962), 17 ff.

G. Jobey, articles on native settlements in Northumberland and Durham, *AA*[4], xxxvii (1959), xxxviii (1960), xl (1962), xlii (1964).

R. C. H. M. (Scotland), Inventory, *The County of Roxburgh*, i, Edinburgh, 1956, 35 ff.

J. R. C. Hamilton, 'Brochs and Broch-builders', in F. T. Wainwright (ed.), *The Northern Isles*, London, 1962.

S. Piggott and K. Henderson, *Scotland before History*, London, 1958.

A. H. A. Hogg, 'The Votadini', in W. F. Grimes (ed.), *Aspects of Archaeology in Britain and Beyond*, London, 1951.

M. A. Cotton, 'British Camps with Timber-laced Ramparts', *Arch. Journ.*, cxi (1954), 26 ff.

I. A. Richmond, 'Ancient Geographical Sources', in I. A. Richmond (ed.), *Roman and Native in North Britain*, London, 1958.

R. Feachem, *A Guide to Prehistoric Scotland*, London, 1963.

S. Piggott, in F. T. Wainwright (ed.), *The Problem of the Picts*, London, 1955.

J. P. V. D. Balsdon, *The Emperor Gaius*, Oxford, 1934, pp. 88–95.

CHAPTER 5   The Claudian Conquest: rebellion of Boudicca, pp. 78–114

J. P. Bushe-Fox, *Excavations at the Roman Fort at Richborough*, iv, Oxford, 1949, 11 ff.

B. W. Cunliffe (ed.), *Excavations at the Roman Fort at Richborough*, v (1968).

Aylesford crossing: A. R. Burn, *History*, 1953, 105.

Bredgar hoard: *Numismatic Chronicle*, 1959, 17 ff.

Lakenheath hoard: *Proc. Camb. Antiq. Soc.*, lvi–lvii (1963–4), 123 f.

S. S. Frere, 'A Claudian site at Needham, Norfolk', *Antiq. Journ.*, xxi (1941), 40 ff.

I. A. Richmond, 'Queen Cartimandua', *JRS*, xliv (1954), 43 ff.

E. M. Clifford, *Bagendon, a Belgic Oppidum*, Cambridge, 1961, for Boduocus.

Chelmsford: V.C.H., Essex, iii, *Roman Essex* (1963), 63 ff; *Britannia* iv (1973), 301 f.

Great Casterton: M. Todd, op. cit. on p. 449.

Longthorpe and Newton: *JRS*, lv (1965), 75 f.; lxiii (1973), 214; *Britannia* v (1974).

G. Webster, 'The Roman Military Advance under Ostorius Scapula', *Arch. Journ.*, cxv (1958), 49 ff.

M. R. Hull, *Roman Colchester*, Oxford, 1958.

B. W. Cunliffe, *Excavations at Fishbourne* i–ii, Leeds, 1971.

D. E. Eichholz, 'How long did Vespasian serve in Britain?', *Britannia* iii (1972), 149 ff.

R. E. M. Wheeler, *Maiden Castle, Dorset*, Oxford, 1943.

L. Alcock, 'Excavations at S. Cadbury Castle, 1970', *Antiq. Journ.*, li (1971), 1 ff.

I. A. Richmond, *Hod Hill* ii, London, 1968.

Waddon Hill: G. Webster, *Proceedings of the Dorset Natural History and Archaeological Society*, lxxxii (1960), 88 ff.; lxxxvi (1965), 135 ff.

A. Fox, *Roman Exeter*, Manchester, 1952; *JRS* lv (1965), 217; *Britannia* iii (1972), 344; iv (1973), 313.

Kinvaston: G. Webster, *T. Birmingham A.S.*, lxxiii (1955), 100 ff. J. K. St. Joseph, *JRS*, xlviii (1958), 94.

Metchley: J. K. St Joseph and F. W. Shotton, *T. Birmingham A.S.*, lviii (1934), 68 ff. G. Webster, ibid., lxxii (1954), 1 ff.

Wall: J. Gould, *Lichfield and South Staffordshire Archaeological and Historical Society*, v (1963–64), 1 ff.

Wroxeter, fort: J. K. St. Joseph, *T. Birmingham A.S.*, lxix (1951), 54; *JRS*, xlviii (1958), 95.

Wroxeter, fortress: *JRS*, xlv (1955), pl. xix; liv (1963), 162–5.

Gloucester: C. Green, *JRS*, xxxii (1942), 39, corrected by I. A. Richmond and H. E. O'Neil, *Transactions of the Bristol and Gloucestershire Archaeological Society*, lxxxi (1962), 14 ff.; lxxxiv (1965), 15 ff. and H. Hurst 'Excavations at Gloucester 1968–71', *Antiq. Journ.*, lii (1972), 24 ff.

Colonia Victricensis: K. S. Painter, *Antiq. Journ.*, xliii (1963), 123 ff.

A. Fox and W. Ravenhill, 'Old Burrow and Martinhoe', *Antiquity*, xxxix (1965), 253 ff.

I. A. Richmond, 'The Four Coloniae of Roman Britain', *Arch. Journ.*, ciii (1946), 57 ff.

Q. Veranius: see A. E. Gordon, *University of California Publications on Classical Archaeology*, ii (1952), 231 ff.; E. Birley, *Roman Britain and the Roman Army*, Kendal, 1953, pp. 1 ff.; C. E. Stevens, *Classical Review*, n.s., i (1961), 4 ff.

Lincoln: G. Webster, *JRS*, xxxix (1949), 57 ff. F. H. Thompson, ibid., xlvi (1956), 22 ff. D. F. Petch, *Arch. Journ.*, lxvii (1960), 40 ff.

Roman Wales: I. A. Richmond, in I. Ll. Foster and G. Daniel, *Prehistoric and Early Wales*, London, 1965, pp. 151 ff. and see Nash-Williams, cited p. 433.

Sir Cyril Fox, *A Find of the Early Iron Age from Llyn Cerrig Bach, Anglesey*, Cardiff, 1946.

D. R. Dudley and G. Webster, *The Rebellion of Boudicca*, London, 1962.

C. E. Stevens, 'Notes on Roman Chester', *Journ. Chester and N. Wales Arch. Soc.*, xxxv (1942), 49 ff.

Colchester. C. F. C. Hawkes and M. R. Hull, *Camulodunum*, Oxford, 1947; M. R. Hull, *Roman Colchester*, Oxford, 1958.

D. Fishwick, 'Templum divo Claudio constitutum', *Britannia* iii (1972), 164 ff.

A. R. Burn, *Agricola and Roman Britain*, London, 1953.

Cirencester fort: J. S. Wacher, *Antiq. Journ.*, xlii (1962), 3 ff.; xliv (1964), 15 ff.

Great Chesterford fort: W. Rodwell, *Britannia* iii (1972), 290 ff.

Classicianus: *RIB* 12, and references cited there.

R. Merrifield, *The Roman City of London*, London, 1965.

S. S. Frere, 'Verulamium, Then and Now', in London University Institute of Archaeology *Bulletin*, iv (1964), 61 ff.; and 'Verulamium, Three Roman Cities', *Antiquity*, xxxviii (1964), 103 ff.

Usk: *Britannia* ii (1971), 246 f.; iii (1972), 302; iv (1973), 272.

CHAPTER 6   The Flavian Period, pp. 115–140

J. Clarke, Chapter ii in I. A. Richmond (ed.), *Roman and Native in North Britain*, London, 1958.

R. E. M. Wheeler, *The Stanwick Fortifications*, Oxford, 1954.

Brough on Humber: J. S. Wacher, *Antiq. Journ.*, xl (1960), 58 ff.

P. Corder, *The Defences of the Roman Fort at Malton*, Leeds, 1930, 55 ff.

R.C.H.M. (England), *Eboracum, Roman York*, London, 1962.

Carlisle: J. P. Bushe-Fox, *Archaeologia*, lxiv (1913), 295 ff.

Rey Cross, etc.: I. A. Richmond, *CW* ^{2}, xxxiv (1934), 50 ff.

Roman Wales: I. A. Richmond, in I. Ll. Foster and G. Daniel (eds.), *Prehistoric and Early Wales*, London, 1965; V. E. Nash-Williams cited on p. 433.

M. G. Jarrett, 'Early Roman Campaigns in Wales', *Arch. Journ.*, cxxi (1964), 23 ff.

Chester: *RIB* 463; R. P. Wright, *Roman inscribed . . . stones from Chester*, Chester, 1955, 48, No. 199; F. H. Thompson, *Roman Cheshire*, Chester, 1965.

I. A. Richmond, 'Gnaeus Julius Agricola', *JRS*, xxxiv (1944), 34 ff.

A. R. Burn, *Agricola and Roman Britain*, London, 1953.

Carrock Fell: R. G. Collingwood, *CW* ^{2}, xxxviii (1938), 32 ff.

Bar Hill, etc.: Sir G. Macdonald, *The Roman Wall in Scotland* (ed. 2), Oxford, 1934.

Loudoun Hill: S. N. Miller (ed.), *The Roman Occupation of South Western Scotland*, Glasgow, 1952, pp. 188 ff.

Dalswinton: *JRS*, xli (1951), 52 ff.; I. A. Richmond and J. K. St. Joseph, *T. Dumfries. and Gal. Ant. Soc.*, xxxiv (1955–6), 9 ff.

Glenlochar: *JRS*, xli (1951), 52 ff. I. A. Richmond and J. K. St. Joseph, *T. Dumfries. and Gal. Ant. Soc.*, xxx (1951–2), 1 ff.

Gatehouse of Fleet: *JRS*, li (1961), 161; lii (1962), 164.

Forth *Limes*: C. E. Stevens, *Antiquity*, xxxiv (1960), 310.

I. A. Richmond, 'The Agricolan Fort at Fendoch', *PSAS*, lxxiii (1938–39), 110 ff.

Inchtuthil: *JRS*, li (1961), 158.

Cleaven Dyke: I. A. Richmond, *PSAS*, lxxiv (1939–40), 45 ff.

Roman Camps: J. K. St. Joseph, *JRS*, xlviii (1958), 86 ff.; li (1961), 123; lix (1969), 105 ff.; lxiii (1973), 216 ff.; I. A. Richmond, *Arch. Journ.*, xciii (1937), 314.

Verulamium inscription: *Antiq. Journ.*, xxxvi (1956), 8 ff.; xxxvii (1957), 216.

Dorchester on Thames: *JRS*, liv (1964), 166.

Fora: Cirencester, *Antiq. Journ.*, xlii (1962), 7; xliv (1964), 11. Winchester, *Antiq. Journ.*, xliv (1964), 204. Silchester, G. C. Boon, *Roman Silchester*, London, 1957, 67, 94. Leicester, *Britannia* iv (1973), 1 ff. Caistor by Norwich, *Britannia* ii (1971), 1 ff. Exeter, *Britannia* iv (1973), 313.

Stracathro: *JRS*, xlviii (1958), 91, 132; li (1961), 123.

Newstead: R.C.H.M. (Scotland), inventory, *The County of Roxburgh*, ii,, Edinburgh, 1956, pp. 312 ff. I. A. Richmond, *PSAS*, lxxxiv (1949–50), 1 ff.

A. S. Robertson, *The Roman Fort at Castledykes*, Edinburgh, 1964; *JRS*, xliv, 87.

Bochastle: *Transactions of the Glasgow Archaeological Society*[2], xiv (1956), 35 ff.

Oakwood: K. A. Steer and R. W. Feachem, *PSAS*, lxxxvi (1951–52), 81 ff.

Milton: *T. Dumfries, and Gal. Ant. Soc.*, xxviii (1949–50), 199 ff.

Chew Green: *AA*[4], xiv (1937), 129 ff.; *NCH*, xv (1940), 70.

Cappuck: I. A. Richmond, *PSAS*, lxxxv (1950–51), 138 ff. R.C.H.M. (Scotland), inventory, *The County of Roxburgh*, ii, Edinburgh, 1956, 354 ff.

443

Oxton: *JRS*, xlviii (1958), 88.

Pen Llystyn: A. H. A. Hogg, *Arch. Journ.*, cxxv (1968), 101 ff.

Wroxeter: *JRS*, liv (1964), 162.

CHAPTER 7   The Retreat from Scotland: Hadrian's frontier, pp. 141–164

J. P. Gillam, Chapter iii in I. A. Richmond (ed.), *Roman and Native in North Britain*, London, 1958.

I. A. Richmond, 'The Roman Frontier Land', *History*, xliv (1959), 1 ff.

High Rochester: I. A. Richmond, *AA* [4], xiii (1936), 171 ff.; *NCH*, xv (1940), 63 ff.

Stanegate frontier: E. Birley, *Research on Hadrian's Wall*, Kendal, 1961, chapter v.

Hardknott: *JRS*, lv (1965), 222.

Wales: I. A. Richmond, in I. Ll. Foster and G. Daniel, *Prehistoric and Early Wales*, London, 1965. G. Simpson, *Britons and the Roman Army*, London, 1964. V. E. Nash-Williams, cited on p. 433.

R. Merrifield, *The Roman City of London*, London, 1965.

I. A. Richmond, 'The Four Coloniae . . .', *Arch. Journ.*, ciii (1946), 57 ff.

Jarrow: *RIB*, 1051; I. A. Richmond and R. P. Wright, *AA* [4], xxi (1943), 93 ff.

J. Collingwood Bruce, *Handbook to the Roman Wall* (12th ed., I. A. Richmond), Newcastle, 1966.

H.M. Ordnance Survey, *Map of Hadrian's Wall*, Chessington, 1964.

I. A. Richmond, 'Hadrian's Wall 1939–49', *JRS*, xl (1950), 43 ff.

E. Birley, as above.

J. Morris, 'The Vallum again', *CW* [2], l (1950), 43 ff.

B. Swinbank and J. E. H. Spaul, 'The spacing of the forts on Hadrian's Wall', *AA* [4], xxix (1951), 221 ff.

Legion IX: J. Bogaers, 'Romeins Nijmegen', *Numaga*, 12 (1965), 10 ff. and in *Studien zu den Militärgrenzen Roms*, Köln/Graz, 1967, 54 ff.

CHAPTER 8   The Antonine Wall: the second-century frontier,
pp. 165–193

J. P. Gillam, in I. A. Richmond (ed.), *Roman and Native in North Britain*, London, 1958, chapter iii.

I. A. Richmond, 'The Roman Frontier Land', *History*, xliv (1959), 1 ff.

Inveresk: *JRS*, xxxvii (1947), 165; xxxviii (1948), 81.

Lanchester: *T. Durham and N.A. Soc.*, ix (1) (1939), 112 ff.; x (4) (1953), 394.

Bothwellhaugh: S. N. Miller (ed.), *The Roman Occupation of South Western Scotland*, Glasgow, 1952, pp. 172 ff.

Carzield: I. A. Richmond, *T. Dumfries, and Gal. Ant. Soc.*, xxii (1938–40), 156 ff.

Lyne fortlet: *PSAS*, xcv (1961–62), 215 ff.

Lyne fort: *PSAS*, xxxv (1900–1), 154 ff.; xcv (1961–62), 208 ff.; *Britannia* iii (1972), 9.

Raeburnfoot: *T. Dumfries. and Gal. Ant. Soc.*, xxxix (1960–61), 24 ff.

Durisdeer, etc.: S. N. Miller (ed.), *The Roman Occupation of South Western Scotland*, Glasgow, 1952, pp. 124 ff.

Sir George Macdonald, *The Roman Wall in Scotland* (2nd ed.), Oxford, 1934.

A. S. Robertson, *The Antonine Wall*, Glasgow, 1968.

K. A. Steer, 'The Antonine Wall 1934–59', *JRS*, l (1960), 84 ff.

R. W. Feachem, 'Six Roman Camps near the Antonine Wall', *PSAS*, lxxxix (1955–56), 329 ff.

K. A. Steer, 'The Nature and Purpose of the Expansions on the Antonine Wall', *PSAS*, xc (1956–57), 161 ff.

A. S. Robertson, *An Antonine Fort, Golden Hill, Duntocher*, Edinburgh, 1957.

Wilderness Plantation: *JRS*, xli (1951), 61.

Glasgow Bridge: *JRS*, xlv (1955), 86.

Carriden inscription: *PSAS*, xc (1956–57), 1 ff.; *JRS*, xlvii (1957), 229–30.

Whitemoss: *PSAS*, lxxxiii (1948–49), 28 ff.

Lurg Moor: *JRS*, xliii (1953), 105.

Cramond: *JRS*, lii (1962), 161; *Britannia* v (1974).

Ardoch: O. G. S. Crawford, *The Topography of Roman Scotland*, Cambridge, 1949, pp. 34 ff.

Bertha: O. G. S. Crawford, op. cit., 59; *PSAS*, liii (1919), 145 ff.; *JRS*, xlix (1959), 136.

E. Birley, *Roman Britain and the Roman Army*, Kendal, 1953, pp. 31 ff.

R. G. Collingwood and J. N. L. Myres, *Roman Britain and the English Settlements*, Oxford, 1936, pp. 149, 171.

K. A. Steer, 'John Horsley and the Antonine Wall', *AA* [4], xlii (1964), 1 ff.

G. Simpson, *Britons and the Roman Army*, London, 1964; 'Caerleon and the Roman Forts in Wales . . .', *Arch. Camb.*, cxi (1962), 103 ff., cxii (1963), 13 ff.

Rome inscription: *American Journal of Archaeology*, lxiv (1960), 274.

Homesteads: G. Jobey in C. Thomas *op. cit.* on p. 433.

Julius Verus: E. Birley, 'Senators in the Emperors' Service', *Proceedings of the British Academy*, xxxix (1954), 197 ff.

F. Haverfield, *PSAS*, xxxviii (1904), 454 ff.; *AA* [2], xxv (1904), 142.

Lancaster: I. A. Richmond, *Transactions of the Historic Society of Lancashire and Cheshire*, cv (1953), 1 ff.; *JRS*, xlix (1949), 106.

Birrenswark: S. N. Miller (ed.), *The Roman Occupation of South Western Scotland*, Glasgow, 1952, p. 97.

Corbridge hoard: *AA* [3], viii (1912), 74 ff.

Newstead: I. A. Richmond, *PSAS*, lxxxiv, (1949–50), 1 ff.

CHAPTER 9   Severus and the third century, pp. 194–221

Sextus Varius Marcellus: H.-G. Pflaum, *Les Carrières Procuratoriennes Equestres sous le Haut-empire romain*, Paris, 1960, No. 237.

I. A. Richmond, 'The Roman Frontier Land', *History*, xliv (1959), 1 ff.

K. A. Steer, in I. A. Richmond (ed.), *Roman and Native in North Britain*, London, 1958, chapter iv.

E. Birley, *Research on Hadrian's Wall*, Kendal, 1961.

C. Valerius Pudens: *JRS*, li (1961), 192.

E. Birley, 'Excavations at Corstopitum, 1906–58', *AA* [4], xxxvii (1959), 12 ff.

Cramond: *JRS*, xlix (1959), 104; *Britannia* v (1974).

Carpow: R. E. Birley, *PSAS*, xcvi (1962–63), 184 ff.; see also *JRS*, xlv (1965), 223; lxiii (1973), 222.

Marching Camps: *JRS*, xlviii (1958), 93; li (1961), 123, and especially lix (1969), 113 ff.; lxiii (1973), 228 ff.

Brittones dediticii: H. T. Rowell, 'The Honesta Missio from the Numeri of the Roman Imperial Army', *Yale Classical Studies*, vi (1939), 73 ff.

Loca: Ravenna Cosmography, v, 31; *Archaeologia*, xciii, 15 and 19; *NCH*, xv (1940), 97.

Wales: I. A. Richmond, in I. Ll. Foster and G. Daniel, *Prehistoric and Early Wales*, London, 1965. G. Simpson, *Britons and the Roman Army*, London, 1964.

Haltonchesters granary: *JRS*, lii (1962), 164.

Dover: *Britannia* ii (1971), 286; iii (1972), 351.

Reculver: *JRS*, l (1960), 236; li (1961), 191. I. A. Richmond, 'A New Building-inscription from ... Reculver', *Antiq. Journ.*, xli (1961), 224 ff. (cf. *JRS*, lv (1965), 220).

J. K. St. Joseph, 'The Roman Fort at Brancaster', *Antiq. Journ.*, xvi (1936), 444 ff.

R. Macmullen, *Soldiers and Civilians in the later Roman Empire*, Cambridge, Massachusetts, 1963, ch. i.

Ribchester: I. A. Richmond, 'The Sarmatae ... and the regio Bremetennacensis', *JRS*, xxxv (1945), 15 ff.

P. Salway, *The Frontier People of Roman Britain*, Cambridge, 1965.

J. P. Bushe Fox, *Excavations of the Roman fort at Richborough, Kent*, iv, Oxford, 1949, 60 ff.

J. S. Johnson, 'The date of the ... Saxon Shore fort at Richborough', *Britannia* i (1970), 240 ff.

B. W. Cunliffe (ed.), *Excavations of the Roman fort at Richborough, Kent*, v, Oxford, 1968.

CHAPTER 10   The administration of Roman Britain, pp. 222–247

E. Birley, 'Senators in the Emperors' Service', *Proceedings of the British Academy*, xxxix (1954), 197 ff.

E. Birley, 'Beförderung und Versetzungen im römischen Heere', *Carnuntum Jahrbuch*, 1957, 3 ff.

J. Fitz, 'Legati Augusti pro praetore Pannoniae Inferioris', *Acta Antiqua*, xi (1963), 245 ff.

A. H. M. Jones, *Studies in Roman Government and Law*, Oxford, 1960.

E. Birley, *Roman Britain and the Roman Army*, Kendal, 1953.

H.-G. Pflaum, *Les Procurateurs Equestres sous le Haut-empire romain*, Paris, 1950.

H.-G. Pflaum, *Les Carrières Procuratoriennes Equestres sous le Haut-empire romain*, Paris, 1960.

D. Atkinson, 'The Classis Britannica', in *Historical Essays in Honour of James Tait*, 1933, pp. 1 ff.

S. S. Frere, 'Civitas – A Myth?', *Antiquity*, xxxv (1961), 29 ff.

Verulamium: see bibliography of chapter 12 below.

London: R. Merrifield, *The Roman City of London*, London, 1965.

C. E. Stevens, 'The Roman Name of Ilchester', *Proceedings of the Somerset Archaeological Society*, xcvi (1951), 188 ff.

P. Guirand, *Les Assemblées provinciales dans l'empire romain*, Paris, 1887.

J. A. O. Larsen, *Representative Government in Greek and Roman History*, Berkeley, 1955.

D. Fishwick, 'The Imperial Cult in Roman Britain', *Phoenix* (Classical Association of Canada), xv (1961), 159, 213.

Verona List: A. H. M. Jones, *JRS*, xliv (1954), 21 ff.

A. H. M. Jones, *The Later Roman Empire*, Oxford, 1964.

CHAPTER 11   The Roman army in Britain, pp. 248–272

Classis Britannica: see D. Atkinson, op. cit., under chapter 10, and B. W. Cunliffe op. cit., under chapter 9.

I. A. Richmond, 'Roman Britain and Roman Military Antiquities', *Proceedings of the British Academy*, xli (1955), 297 ff.

Camps: *NCH*, xv (1940), and references cited under chapter 6 above. O. G. S. Crawford, *'The Topography of Roman Scotland'*, Cambridge, 1949. G. D. B. Jones, *BBCS*, xxi (2) (1965), 174 ff. R. E. M. Wheeler, *Prehistoric and Roman Wales*, Oxford, 1925, 220. R.C.H.M. (Scotland), inventory, *The County of Roxburgh*, ii, Edinburgh, 1956, pp. 316, 375. Rey Cross, *CW* ², xxxiv (1934), 50 ff. *JRS*, xli (1951), pl. vi; xlv (1955), pl. xvi; li (1961), pl. ix. Inchtuthil plan: *JRS*, li (1961), 158.

Kinvaston plan: *JRS*, xlviii (1958), 94. Longthorpe plan: Britannia v (1974).

Chester: F. H. Thompson, *Roman Cheshire*, Chester, 1965.

Caerleon: G. C. Boon, *Isca*, Cardiff, 1972.

V. E. Nash-Williams, *The Roman Frontier in Wales*, 2nd. ed. by M. G. Jarrett, Cardiff, 1969.

R.C.H.M. (England): *Eboracum, Roman York*, London, 1962.

Fendoch: I. A. Richmond, *PSAS*, lxxiii (1938–39), 110 ff.

Carzield: I. A. Richmond, *T. Dumfries, and Gal. Ant. Soc.*, xxii 1938–40), 156 ff.

M. Todd, *The Roman Fort at Great Casterton, Rutland*, Nottingham, 1968.

Cleaven Dyke: I. A. Richmond, *PSAS*, lxxxiv (1939–40), 45 ff.

Glenlochar: *T. Dumfries, and Gal. Ant. Soc.*, xxx (1951–52), 1 ff.

Hod Hill: O. G. S. Crawford and A. Keiller, *Wessex from the Air*, Oxford, 1928, pl. i; *JRS*, xl (1950), pl. viii *a*. I. A. Richmond, *Hod Hill* ii, London, 1968.

High Rochester, Risingham: I. A. Richmond, *AA* [4], xiii (1936), 171 ff.; *NCH*, xv (1940).

Dolddinas: G. D. B. Jones, *BBCS*, xviii (1960), 397 ff,; *JRS*, li (1961), 131.

Rhyd Sarn: G. D. B. Jones, *BBCS*, xix (1960–62), 254.

Loughor: *JRS*, xlviii (1958), 97; *Antiquity*, xxxv (1961), pl. xli.

Llandrindod Common: V. E. Nash Williams, *The Roman Frontier in Wales*, 2nd. ed. by M. G. Jarrett, Cardiff, 1969.

I. A. Richmond, 'The Four Roman Camps at Cawthorn, Yorkshire', *Arch. Journ.*, lxxxix (1932), 17 ff.

Woden Law: R.C.H.M. (Scotland) inventory, *The County of Roxburgh*, i, Edinburgh, 1956, pp. 169 ff.

I. A. Richmond, 'A Roman Arterial Signalling System in the Stainmore Pass', in W. F. Grimes (ed.), *Aspects of Archaeology in Britain and Beyond*, London, 1951, pp. 293 ff.

R. G. Collingwood, *The Archaeology of Roman Britain*, London, 1930; new edition by I. A. Richmond 1969.

Gask Ridge: *PSAS*, xxxv (1901), 15 ff.; cf. ibid., lxxiv (1940), 37 ff. O. G. S. Crawford, *The Topography of Roman Scotland*, Cambridge, 1940, 52 ff.

Scalesceugh: *CW* [2], xvi (1916), 282, 290; ibid., xxii (1922), 456 f.; T. May and L. E. Hope, *Catalogue of Roman Pottery in the Tullie House Museum*, Carlisle, 1917, 85.

W. F. Grimes, *Holt, Denbighshire*, London, 1930 (*y Cymrodor*, xli).

Wilderspool: F. H. Thompson, *Roman Cheshire*, Chester, 1965.

Muncaster: R. L. Bellhouse, CW^2, lx (1960), 1 ff.

Brampton: R. Hogg, CW^2, lxv (1965), 133 ff.

Catterick, *JRS*, l (1960), 217 f.

A. H. M. Jones, *The Later Roman Empire*, Oxford, 1964.

J. P. Gillam, ' "Also, along the line of the Wall" ', CW^2, xlix (1949), 38 ff.

C. E. Stevens, 'The British Sections of the Notitia Dignitatum', *Arch. Journ.*, xcvii (1940), 125 ff.

CHAPTER 12   The towns, pp. 273–300

A. L. F. Rivet, *Town and Country in Roman Britain*, London, 1964.

Dorchester and Maiden Castle: R. E. M. Wheeler, *Maiden Castle, Dorset*, Oxford, 1943, fig 1*b*, p. 15.

Chelmsford: V.C.H. Essex iii, *Roman Essex*, London, 1963; *Britannia* ii (1971), 271; iii (1972), 331 f.; iv (1973), 301.

Exeter: A. Fox, *Roman Exeter*, Manchester, 1952.

Cirencester: J. S. Wacher, *Antiq. Journ.*, xli (1961) – xlv (1965).

Great Casterton: P. Corder, *The Roman Town and Villa at Gt. Casterton, Rutland*, Third Report, Nottingham, 1961.

Dorchester-on-Thames: S. S. Frere, *Arch. Journ.*, cxix (1962), 114 ff.; *JRS*, liv (1964), 166.

J. S. Wacher, *Excavations at Brough on Humber 1958–61* (1969).

P. Salway, *The Frontier People of Roman Britain*, Cambridge, 1965.

Verulamium: S. S. Frere, *Antiquity*, xxxviii (1964), 103 ff.; London University Institute of Archaeology *Bulletin*, iv (1964), 61 ff.; *Antiq. Journ.*, xxxvi (1956) – xlii (1962). *Verulamium Excavations* i Oxford, 1972.

Canterbury: A. Williams and S. S. Frere, *Archaeologia Cantiana*, lxi (1948), 1 ff.

Silchester: A. Fox, *Antiquity*, xxii (1948), 172 ff.; G. C. Boon, *Roman Silchester*, London, 1957.

R. G. Goodchild, 'The origins of the Romano-British Forum', *Antiquity*, xx (1946), 70 ff.

Caerwent, forum and bath: V. E. Nash Williams, *BBCS*, xv (1953), 159 ff.

Wroxeter: K. M. Kenyon, *Archaeologia*, lxxxviii (1938), 175 ff.

Verulamium market: K. M. Richardson, *Archaeologia*, xc (1944), 81 ff.

R. E. M. and T. V. Wheeler, *Verulamium, A Belgic and Two Roman Cities*, Oxford, 1936.

Canterbury: S. S. Frere, *Antiquity*, xxiii (1949), 153 ff.; *Roman Canterbury* (3rd ed.), Canterbury, 1962.

Chichester amphitheatre: G. M. White, *Antiq. Journ.*, xvi (1936), 149 ff.

Caistor by Norwich: C. F. C. Hawkes, *Arch Journ.*, cvi (1949), 62 ff.; S. S. Frere, *Britannia* ii (1971), 1 ff.

D. Atkinson, *Excavations at Wroxeter* 1923–27, Oxford, 1942.

Wroxeter Baths: K. M. Kenyon, *Archaeologia*, lxxxviii (1938), 175 ff.; G. Webster, *Antiq. Journ.*, xlvi (1966).

K. M. Kenyon, *The Jewry Wall site*, Leicester, Oxford, 1948; see also *JRS*, liv (1964), fig. on p. 161; *ibid.* xxxix (1949), 142 ff.

Leicester forum: M. Hebditch and J. Mellor, *Britannia* iv (1973), 1 ff.

Dorchester aqueduct: K. M. Richardson, *Antiq. Journ.*, xx (1940), 435 ff; R.C.H.M., *Dorset* II (iii) (1970), 585 ff.

Wroxeter aqueduct: G. Webster, *Transactions of the Shropshire Archaeological Society*, lvi (2) (1959), 133 ff.

Lincoln aqueduct: F. H. Thompson, *Arch. Journ.*, cxi (1954), 106 ff.

Silchester pipeline: *Archaeologia*, lv (1897), 422 ff.

Wroxeter ducts: J. P. Bushe Fox, *Excavations on the Site of . . . Wroxeter*, iii, (1914), Oxford, 1916.

Lincoln sewers: I. A. Richmond, *Arch. Journ.*, ciii (1946), 26 ff.

Kenchester: G. H. Jack and A. G. K. Hayter, *Excavations on the Site of . . . Magna*, ii, Hereford, 1926.

M. R. Hull, *Roman Colchester*, Oxford, 1958.

R. Merrifield, *The Roman City of London*, London, 1965.

Wroxeter: I. A. Richmond, 'The Cornovii', in I. Ll. Foster and L. Alcock, (eds.) *Culture and Environment*, London, 1963. G. Webster, 'Viroconium, A study of Problems', *Transactions of the Shropshire Archaeological Society*, lvii (2) (1962–63).

Silchester bank: G. C. Boon, *P. Hants. F.C.*, xxi (1) (1958), 9 ff. and *Archaeologia* cii (1969), 1 ff.

Silchester Wall: M. A. Cotton, *Archaeologia*, xcii (1947), 121 ff.

Lincoln defences: D. F. Petch, *Arch. Journ.*, cxvii (1960), 40 ff. F. H.

Thompson and J. B. Whitwell, *Archaeologia* civ (1973), 129 ff.

Caistor by Norwich bank: *JRS*, li (1961), pl. x; see also our pl. 8a.

J. S. Wacher, *The Civitas Capitals of Roman Britain*, Leicester, 1966.

Chichester walls: J. Holmes, *Sx. A.C.*, c (1962), 80 ff.

Caerwent walls: V. E. Nash Williams, *Archaeologia*, lxxx (1930), 229 ff. O. E. Craster, *Arch. Camb.*, ciii, 1954, 54 ff.

Aldborough walls: J. N. L. Myres, K. A. Steer and A. M. H. Chitty, *Yorkshire Archaeological Journal*, 157 (1959), 1 ff.

Gallic walls: R. M. Butler, *Arch. Journ.*, cxvi (1959), 25 ff. J. S. Johnson, *Britannia* iv (1973), 210 ff.

Witherley: A. Oswald and P. W. Gathercole, *Trans. Birmingham A.S.*, lxxiv (1956), 30 ff.

Rocester: G. Webster, *North Staffordshire Journal of Field Studies*, ii (1962), 37 ff.

Gloucester: see the papers by I. A. Richmond, H. E. O'Neil and H. Hurst, cited on p. 441.

Great Chesterford: V.C.H. Essex, iii, *Roman Essex*, London, 1963.

P. Corder, 'The Reorganisation of the Defences of Romano-British Towns in the Fourth Century', *Arch. Journ.*, cxii (1955), 20 ff.

Barbarian warfare: E. A. Thompson, *The Early Germans*, Oxford, 1965, chapter iv (from *Past and Present*, xiv (1958)).

J. Joyce, 'Account of further excavations at Silchester', *Archaeologia*, xlvi (1880), 344 ff.

Industry: I. A. Richmond, in J. S. Wacher, *The Civitas Capitals of Roman Britain*, Leicester, 1966, 76 ff.

CHAPTER 13   The countryside, pp. 301–319

A. L. F. Rivet, *Town and Country in Roman Britain*, London, 1964.

A. L. F. Rivet (ed.), *The Roman Villa in Britain*, London, 1969.

R. G. Collingwood, in Tenney Frank, *An Economic Survey of Ancient Rome*, iii (1937 and 1959).

'Report on Conference on Romano-British Villas', *Archaeological News Letter*, vi (2) (1955), 29 ff.

H. C. Bowen, *Ancient Fields*, London, 1961.

C. F. C. Hawkes, 'Britons, Romans and Saxons . . . in Cranborne Chase', *Arch. Journ.*, civ (1947), 27 ff.

G. R. Wolseley, R. A. Smith and W. Hawley, 'Prehistoric and Roman Settlements on Park Brow', *Archaeologia*, lxxvi (1926–27), 1 ff.

Studland: N. H. Field, *Proc. Dorset Nat. Hist. and Arch. Soc.*, 87 (1966), 142 ff.

S. J. Hallam, 'Villages in Roman Britain', *Antiq. Journ.*, xliv (1964), 19 ff.

Villages: R.C.H.M. (England), inventory, *Dorset*.

S. Applebaum, 'The Agriculture . . . at Figheldean Down, Wiltshire', *PPS*, xx (1954), 103 ff.

W. H. Manning, 'The Villa in Roman Britain', *Antiquity*, xxxvi (1962), 56 ff.

Park Street: H. E. O'Neil, *Arch. Journ.*, cii (1945), 21 ff.

Hambleden: A. H. Cocks, *Archaeologia*, lxxi (1920–21), 141 ff.

Llantwit Major: V. E. Nash Williams, *Arch Camb.*, cii (1953), 89 ff. A. H. A. Hogg, *Britannia* v (1974).

W. Gardner and H. N. Savory, *Dinorben*, Cardiff, 1964.

Lockleys: J. B. Ward Perkins, *Antiq. Journ.*, xviii (1938), 339 ff.; *Antiquity*, xiv (1940), 317 ff.

Ditchley: C. A. R. Radford, *Oxoniensia*, i (1936), 24 ff.

Catsgore: C. A. R. Radford, *Proceedings of the Somerset Archaeological Society*, xcvi (1951), 41 ff.

Newport: P. G. Stone, *Antiq. Journ.*, ix (1929), 141 ff.

Bignor: *JRS*, xlvii (1957), 223; xlix (1959), 131; l (1960), 234; lii (1962), 189; liii (1963), 155, and fig. 34; see also S. E. Winbolt and G. Herbert, *The Roman Villa at Bignor, Sussex* (guide book), Chichester.

Cox Green: C. M. Bennett, *Berkshire Archaeological Journal*, lx (1962), 62 ff.

North Leigh: VCH, *Oxford*, i, 1939, 316 ff.

S. Lysons, *Roman Antiquities at Woodchester*, London, 1797.

B. W. Cunliffe, *Excavations at Fishbourne* i–ii, Leeds, 1971.

Angmering: L. Scott, *Sx.A.C.*, lxxix (1938), 3 ff.; lxxx (1939), 89 ff.

Eccles: A. P. Detsicas, *Arch. Cant.*, lxxviii (1963), 125 ff.; lxxix (1964), 121 ff.; lxxx (1965), 69 ff., and following volumes.

Castle Dykes: O. G. S. Crawford, *British Association* (*Leeds* 1927) *Handbook*, xi, Leeds, 1927.

High Wycombe: B. R. Hartley, *Records of Buckinghamshire*, xvi (4) (1959), 227 ff.

Winterton: I. M. Stead, *Antiq. Journ.*, xlvi (1966), 72 ff.

J. T. Smith, 'Romano-British Aisled Houses', *Arch. Journ.*, cxx (1963), 1 ff.

S. Applebaum, unpublished D.Phil. thesis, Oxford University; see also 'Agriculture in Roman Britain', *Agricultural History Review*, vi (1958), 66 ff.

Exning: *JRS*, l (1960), 228.

Barrow Burials: R. F. Jessup, *Journal of the British Archaeological Association* [3], xxii (1959), 1 ff.

West Blatchington: N. E. S. Norris and G. P. Burstow, *Sx.A.C.*, lxxxix (1950), 1 ff.; xc (1951–52), 221 ff.

Stroud: A. M. Williams, *Arch. Journ.*, lxv (1908), 57 ff.; lxvi (1909), 33 ff.

G. A. Holleyman, 'The Celtic Field-System in South Britain', *Antiquity*, ix (1935), 443 ff.

V.C.H., Essex iii, *Roman Essex*, London, 1963.

R.C.H.M. (England), *A Matter of Time*, London, 1960.

S. Applebaum, 'Distribution of the Romano-British Population in the Basingstoke Area', *P. Hants. F.C.*, xviii (1), (1953), 119 ff.

Grassington: E. Curwen, *Antiquity*, ii (1928), 168 ff.

R.C.H.M. (England), inventory, *Westmorland*, London, 1936.

R. G. Collingwood and J. N. L. Myres, *Roman Britain and the English Settlements*, Oxford, 1936, p. 210, map 2.

J. W. Brailsford, 'Early Iron Age C in Wessex', *PPS*, xxiv (1958), pp. 101 ff.

Fens: S. J. Hallam, op. cit. (p. 453). C. W. Phillips (ed.), *The Fenland in Roman Times*, London, 1970.

J. G. D. Clark, 'Report on excavations on the Cambridgeshire Car Dyke . . .', *Antiq. Journ.*, xxix (1949), 137.

Ploughs: F. G. Payne, *Arch. Journ.*, civ (1947), 82 ff. W. Manning, *JRS*, liv (1964), 54 ff. A. Fenton, *PSAS*, xcvi (1962–63), 264 ff.

Cromwell: *JRS*, li (1961), pl. xi; see also *Britannia* v (1974), pl. 23.

Great Chesterford: *Arch. Journ.*, xiii (1856), 1 ff.

Corn-drying ovens: W. Gowland, *Archaeologia*, lxxi (1920–21), 158 ff. E. C. Curwen, *Antiq. Journ.*, xiii (1933), 109 ff. R. Goodchild, *Antiq. Journ.*, xxiii (1943), 148 ff. P. Corder, *The Roman Town and Villa at Great Casterton, Rutland*, ii, Nottingham, 1954, 19 ff.

Abinger: villa, *The Builder*, xxxvi (1878), 19 f.; *Sy.A.C.*, xxix (1916), 154 f.; leet, *Sy.A.C.*, xliv (1936), 149.

Grimsby: D. F. Petch, *Lincolnshire Architectural and Archaeological Society Reports and Papers*, ix (1961), 15; *Lincolnshire History and Archaeology* I (2), 55.

Bee hives: *Sy.A.C.*, lvii (1960), 57.

Tapete Britannicum: *JRS*, xlv (1955), 114 .

CHAPTER 14   Trade and industry, pp. 320–341

R. G. Collingwood, 'Roman Britain', in Tenney Frank, *An Economic Survey of Ancient Rome*, iii (1937 and 1959).

R. F. *Tylecote, Metallurgy in Archaeology*, London, 1962.

Dolaucothi mines: V. E. Nash Williams, *BBCS*, xiv (1950), 79 ff. G. D. B. Jones and P. R. Lewis, *Bonner Jahrb.* 171 (1971), 288 ff.; *Antiq. Journ.* xlix (1969), 244 ff. Water-wheel: G. Boon, *JRS*, lvi (1966), 122 ff.

Dolaucothi aqueduct: G. D. B. Jones, *BBCS*, xix (1960), 71 ff.

Lead pigs: G. Webster, 'The lead-mining industry in North Wales in Roman times', *Flintshire Historical Society Publications*, xiii (1952–53), 5 ff. R. F. Tylecote, op. cit.; and *JRS*, xlvii (1957), 230 f.

Brough fort: *Journal of the Derbyshire Arch. and Nat. Hist. Society*, lix (1938), 61 ff.

Lead Seals: I. A. Richmond, *CW* [2], xxxvi (1936), 104 ff.; *AA* [4], xi (1934), 101 f.

A. J. Evans, 'Coinage and Currency in Roman Britain', *Numismatic Chronicle* [4], xv (1915), 433 ff.

K. S. Painter, 'A Roman Silver Treasure from Canterbury', *JBAA* [3], xxviii (1965), 1 ff.

Pewter: W. J. Wedlake, *Excavations at Camerton, Somerset*, Bath, 1958, 82 ff.

Tin: F. Haverfield, V.C.H., *Cornwall*, London, 1924.

R. E. M. Wheeler, *Prehistoric and Roman Wales*, Oxford, 1925, 270.

R. G. Collingwood, 'Romano-Celtic Art in Northumbria', *Archaeologia*, lxxx (1930), 37 ff.

C. F. C. Hawkes, 'Bronze-workers, Cauldrons and Bucket

Animals . . .', in W. F. Grimes (ed.), *Aspects of Archaeology in Britain and Beyond*, London, 1951.

G. C. Dunning, 'The Purbeck Marble Industry in Roman Britain', *Archaeological News Letter*, i, 11 (March 1949), 15 ff.

F. Oswald and T. D. Pryce, *An Introduction to the Study of Terra Sigillata*, London, 1920.

Glass, Caistor by Norwich: D. Atkinson, 'Caistor Excavations, 1929', *Papers of the Norfolk and Norwich Archaeological Society*, xxiv (2) (1930), 93 ff. Wilderspool: F. H. Thompson, *Roman Cheshire*, Chester, 1965, Mancetter: recent work.

M. H. Callender, *Roman Amphorae*, Oxford, 1965.

R.C.H.M. (England), *Roman London*, London, 1928.

J. A. Stanfield and G. Simpson, *Central Gaulish Potters*, Oxford, 1958.

B.M., *The Mildenhall Treasure*, London, 1947.

B. R. Hartley, *Notes on the Roman Pottery Industry in the Nene Valley*, Peterborough, 1960.

M. R. Hull, *The Roman Potters' Kilns of Colchester*, Oxford, 1963.

G. Simpson, 'The Aldgate Potter . . .', *JRS*, xlii (1952), 68 ff.

H. Sumner, *Excavations in New Forest Roman Pottery Sites*, London, 1927.

M. Fulford, 'The Distribution and dating of New Forest Pottery', *Britannia* iv (1973), 160 ff.

Surrey Archaeological Society, *A Survey of the . . . Farnham District*, Guildford, 1939.

Council for British Archaeology (Research Report 6), *Romano-British Coarse Pottery: A Student's Guide*, London, 1963. Research Report 10: *Current Research in Romano-British Coarse Pottery*, London, 1973.

J. P. Gillam, 'Types of Roman Coarse Pottery Vessels in Northern Britain', *AA* [4], xxxv (1957), 1 ff.

J. P. Gillam, 'Romano-British Derbyshire ware', *Antiq. Journ.*, xix (1939), 429 ff.

J. P. Gillam, 'Dales Ware', *Antiq. Journ.*, xxxi (1951), 154 ff.

P. Corder, *The Roman Pottery at Crambeck . . .*, York, 1928; see also *Antiq. Journ.*, xvii (1937), 392 ff.

Jet: R.C.H.M. (England), *Eboracum, Roman York*, London, 1962, 141 ff.

Porcupine Bank: *JRS*, xxiv (1934), 220 f.

Roman finds in Ireland: *Proc. Royal Irish Academy* 73, Section C, No. 2 (1973), 21–97.

Skye bale: V. G. Childe, *Scotland before the Scots*, London, 1946, p. 85, fig. 20; see also *PSAS*, lxvi, 289; xlix, 66.

S. Piggott, 'Three metal-work hoards . . .', *PSAS*, lxxxvii (1952–53), 1 ff.

Classis Britannica tiles: Bardown, *JRS*, xlii (1952), 107. Cranbrook, *JRS*, xlix (1959), 137. Bodiam, *JRS*, li (1961), 196.

E. Straker, *Wealden Iron*, London, 1931.

G. Webster, 'A note on the use of Coal in Roman Britain', *Antiq. Journ.*, xxxv (1955), 199 ff.

Cake mould: G. C. Boon, *Antiq. Journ.*, xxxviii (1958), 237 ff.

Whetstones: D. Atkinson, *Excavations at Wroxeter 1923–27*, Oxford, 1942, 129; T. C. Cantrill, *Arch. Camb.*, lxxxvi (1931), 96 ff.

J. Liversidge, *Furniture in Roman Britain*, London, 1955.

Salt: R. G. Collingwood, in Tenney Frank, op. cit., 105 ff. S. J. Hallam, 'Romano-British Salt Industry in South Lincolnshire', *Lincolnshire Architectural and Archaeological Society Reports and Papers*, viii (1960), 35 ff.

Leather: R. Merrifield, *The Roman City of London*, London, 1965 ('bikini' and shoes). J. Curle, *A Roman Frontier Post . . . the fort of Newstead*, Glasgow, 1911.

Tents: I. A. Richmond, *CW*[2], xxxiv (1934), 62 ff.

Carding combs: W. H. Manning, *Antiquity*, xl (1966), 60 ff.

Great Chesterford hoard: *Arch. Journ.*, xiii (1856), 1 ff.

Worlington hoard: J. Liversidge, *Proc. Camb. Antiq. Soc.*, xlix (1955), 89.

Chedworth: I. A. Richmond, *Transactions of the Bristol and Gloucestershire Archaeological Society*, lxxviii (1959), 5 ff. R. Goodburn, *The Roman Villa, Chedworth*, London, 1972.

Darenth: G. Fox, *Archaeologia*, lix (1905), 205 ff. G. Payne, *Arch. Cant.*, xxii (1897), 49 ff.

I. D. Margary, *Roman Roads in Britain*, London, i (1955), ii (1957).

R. E. M. Wheeler, 'The Roman Light-houses at Dover', *Arch. Journ.*, lxxxvi (1930), 22 ff.

CHAPTER 15   The romanisation of Britain, pp. 342–375

J. M. C. Toynbee, *Art in Roman Britain*, London, 1962; *Art in Britain under the Romans*, Oxford, 1964.

Brough on Humber, burial: P. Corder and I. A. Richmond, *Antiq. Journ.*, xviii (1938), 68 ff.; the same, 'Petuaria', *JBAA*³, vii (1942), 1 ff.; cf. *RIB*, 707.

Rufus, son of Callisunus: I. A. Richmond, *Antiq. Journ.*, xxxiii (1953), 206.

Verulamium mosaics: R. E. M. and T. V. Wheeler, *Verulamium, a Belgic and Two Roman Cities*, Oxford, 1936, 142 ff. S. S. Frere, *Antiq. Journ.*, xxxix (1959), 13 ff.; xl (1960), 1 ff.

Colchester mosaics: D. J. Smith, *Arch. Journ.*, cxxiii (1967), 40 ff., and in A. L. F. Rivet (ed.), *The Roman Villa in Britain*, London, 1969, 77 n. 3.

Fishbourne: B. W. Cunliffe, *Excavations at Fishbourne* i–ii, Leeds, 1971.

Mosaics: J. M. C. Toynbee, *Art in Britain under the Romans*, pp. 228 ff. D. J. Smith in A. L. F. Rivet (ed.), *The Roman Villa in Britain*, 71 ff.

Wall-paintings: J. M. C. Toynbee op. cit., pp. 213 ff.; *Art in Roman Britain*, pl. 195 ff. S. S. Frere, *Antiq. Journ.*, xxxvii (1957), 1 ff.; xxxix (1959), 1 ff. J. S. Wacher, *Antiq. Journ.*, xliii (1963), pl. xi. J. Liversidge in A. L. F. Rivet op. cit., 127 ff.

Amphitheatres: Cirencester, J. S. Wacher, *Antiq. Journ.*, xliii (1963), 23 ff.; xliv (1964), 17 ff. Chichester, G. M. White, *Antiq. Journ.*, xvi (1936), 149 ff. Caerleon, R. E. M. and T. V. Wheeler, *Archaeologia*, lxxviii (1928), 111 ff. Chester, F. H. Thompson, *Roman Cheshire*, Chester, 1965; *JRS*, li (1961), 165 ff.; lvi, 201. Carmarthen, *Britannia* ii (1971), 243 f.

Rounds: C. Thomas, *Rural Settlement in Roman Britain*, London, 1966, 87–96.

Low Ham: *JRS*, xxxvi (1946), pl. xi. J. M. C. Toynbee, *Art in Roman Britain*, pl. 235; *Art in Britain under the Romans*, pl. lviii; our plate 12b.

Lullingstone: G. W. Meates, *Lullingstone Roman Villa*, London, 1955. J. M. C. Toynbee, *Art in Roman Britain*, pl. 229; *Art in Britain under the Romans*, pl. lx.

Otford: *JRS*, xvi (1926), 238, 244; V.C.H., *Kent*, iii (1932), 122, pl. 25.

C. F. C. Hawkes, 'Bronze-workers, Cauldrons and Bucket-Animals in Iron Age and Roman Britain', in W. F. Grimes (ed.), *Aspects of Archaeology in Britain and Beyond*, London, 1951.

K. S. Painter, 'A Roman Marble Head from Sussex', *Antiq. Journ.*, xlv (1965), 178.

I. A. Richmond, 'Three fragments of Roman official statues . . .', *Antiq. Journ.*, xxiv (1944), 1 ff.

I. A. Richmond and J. M. C. Toynbee, 'The Temple of Sulis-Minerva at Bath', *JRS*, xlv (1955), 97 ff. B. Cunliffe, *Antiquity*, xl (1966), 199 ff.; *Roman Bath*, Oxford, 1969.

Lower Slaughter: J. M. C. Toynbee, *JRS*, xlviii (1958), 49 ff.

Rushall Down: B.M., *Antiquities of Roman Britain*, London, 1951, p. 53, fig. 25.5.

Lincoln: I. A. Richmond, *Arch. Journ.*, ciii (1946), 26 ff. J. M. C. Toynbee, *Art in Roman Britain*, pl. 88.

Ancaster: S. S. Frere, *Antiq. Journ.*, xli (1961), 229 ff.

Sibson: J. M. C. Toynbee, *Art in Roman Britain*, pl. 26.

Pitt Rivers, *Excavations in Cranborne Chase*, i–iv (1887, 1888, 1892, 1898).

D. J. Smith, 'Three fourth-century Schools of Mosaic in Roman Britain', *La Mosaïque Gréco-Romaine*, C.N.R.S., Paris, 1965, 95 ff., and in A. L. F. Rivet, *The Roman Villa in Britain*, London, 1969, 71 ff.

H. Last, 'Rome and the Druids: a note', *JRS*, xxxix (1949), 1 ff.

Parade ground: L. P. Wenham, *CW* [2], xxxix (1939), 19 ff.

D. Fishwick, 'The Imperial Cult in Roman Britain', *Phoenix* (Classical Association of Canada), xv (1961), 159 ff. and 213 ff., and 'Templum divo Claudio constitutum', *Britannia* iii (1972), 164 ff.

M. R. Hull, *Roman Colchester*, Oxford, 1958.

Bosham: J. M. C. Toynbee, *Art in Roman Britain*, 50; K. S. Painter, see above.

A. Ross, 'The horned god of the Brigantes', *AA* [4], xxxix (1961), 63 ff.

Foss dyke: J. M. C. Toynbee, *Art in Roman Britain*, pl. 19; B.M., *Guide to the Antiquities of Roman Britain*, London, 1951, pl. xiv.

459

Temple of Antenociticus: F. G. Simpson and I. A. Richmond, *AA* [4], xix (1941), 37 ff.

Shrine of Coventina: *AA* [2], viii, 1 ff.

Nodens: R. E. M. and T. V. Wheeler, *Report on the excavation of the ... Roman ... site in Lydney Park, Gloucestershire*, Oxford, 1932; cf. *RIB*, 616, 617.

Mars Alator: J. M. C. Toynbee, *Art in Britain under the Romans*, 328 ff. B.M., *Guide to the Antiquities of Roman Britain*, London, 1951, fig. 31.

Ancasta: *RIB*, 97.

Cuda: *RIB*, 129.

Viridius: *JRS*, lii (1962), 192.

Sucellus: J. M. C. Toynbee, *Art in Roman Britain*, pl. 78.

Farley Heath: R. G. Goodchild, *Antiq. Journ.*, xxvii (1947), 83.

Arnemetia: I. A. Richmond, *Roman Britain*, London, 1963, p. 76.

Temples: R. G. Collingwood, *The Archaeology of Roman Britain*, London, 1930; new edition by I. A. Richmond, 1969. M. J. T. Lewis, *Temples in Roman Britain*, Cambridge, 1966.

Gosbecks Farm: M. R. Hull, *Roman Colchester*, Oxford, 1958, pp. 259 ff. R. Dunnett, 'The excavation of the Roman theatre at Gosbecks', *Britannia* ii (1971), 27 ff.

Springhead: W. S. Penn, *Arch. Cant.*, lxxiv (1960), 113 ff.; cf. ibid., lxxiii (1959), 1 ff.

Thistleton Dyer: *JRS*, lii (1962), 171 f.

Ancaster and Nettleham: *JRS*, lii (1962), 192.

S. Piggott, 'Three metal-work hoards . . .', *PSAS*, lxxxvii (1952–53), 1 ff.

Verulamium, water cult: S. S. Frere, *Antiq. Journ.*, xxxvii (1957), 14 f.

Jordon Hill: C. D. Drew, *Proceedings of the Dorset Natural History and Archaeological Society*, liii (1931), 265 ff.

Broadway: C. F. C. Hawkes, *Antiq. Journ.*, xxviii (1948), 166 ff.

J. M. C. Toynbee, 'Christianity in Roman Britain', *JBAA* [3], xvi (1953), 1 ff.

W. H. C. Frend, 'Religion in Roman Britain in the fourth century', *JBAA* [3], xviii (1955), 1 ff.

M. W. Barley and R. P. C. Hanson (ed.), *Christianity in Britain, 300–700*, Leicester, 1968.

Churches: Silchester, S. S. Frere, *Archaeologia* cv forthcoming. Verulamium, I. E. Anthony, *Hertfordshire Archaeology* i (1968), 9 ff. Richborough, P. D. C. Brown, *Britannia* ii (1971), 225 ff.

Lullingstone: G. W. Meates, *Lullingstone Roman Villa*, London, 1955, pp. 126 ff. idem, *Lullingstone Roman Villa* (Ministry of Works Guide), London, 1962. J. M. C. Toynbee, *Art in Roman Britain*, pl. 204–5; *Art in Britain under the Romans*, pl. liv–lv.

Chew Stoke Temple: P. Rahtz, *Proceedings of the Somerset Archaeological Society*, xcvi (1951), 112 ff.

R. Merrifield, *The Roman City of London*, 1965.

Woodeaton: R. G. Goodchild and J. R. Kirk, *Oxoniensia*, xix (1954), 15 ff.

Bream Down: *JRS*, xlix (1959), 129; *PUBSS*, x (1965), 195 ff.

CHAPTER 16   Carausius and the fourth century, pp. 376–403

D. A. White, *Litus Saxonicum*, Madison, Wisconsin, 1961.

I. A. Richmond, Chapter v in I. A. Richmond (ed.), *Roman and Native in North Britain*, London, 1958.

I. A. Richmond, 'The Roman Frontier Land', *History*, xliv (1959), 1 ff.

R. A. G. Carson, 'The Mints and Coinage of Carausius and Allectus', *Journal of the British Archaeological Association*, xxii (1959), 33 ff.

Briconium: G. F. Hill, *Numismatic Chronicle*, 1925, 336.

P. H. Webb, in Mattingly and Sydenham, *Roman Imperial Coinage*, v (2), London, 1933, pp. 426 ff.

Burgh Castle: A. J. Morris, *Proceedings of the Suffolk Institute of Archaeology*, xxiv (2) (1949), 100 ff. A. J. Morris and C. F. C. Hawkes, *Arch. Journ.*, cvi (1949), 66.

Cardiff: V. E. Nash Williams, *The Roman Frontier in Wales*, 2nd edition by M. G. Jarrett, Cardiff, 1969, 70 ff.

Lancaster: I. A. Richmond, *Transactions of the Historic Society of Lancashire and Cheshire*, cv (1953), 1 ff.

Caernarvon and Holyhead: V. E. Nash Williams, op. cit., pp. 63, 135 ff.

D. E. Eichholz, 'Constantius Chlorus' invasion of Britain', *JRS*, xliii (1953), 41 ff.

Arras medallion: A. J. Evans, *Numismatic Chronicle*, 1930, 221 ff.

High Rochester and Risingham: I. A. Richmond, *AA* [4], xiii (1936), 170 ff.; *NCH*, xv (1940).

Bewcastle: I. A. Richmond *et alii*, *CW* [2], xxxviii (1938), 195 ff.

Bainbridge: B. R. Hartley, *Proceedings of the Leeds Philosophical and Literary Society*, ix (3) (1960), 107 ff.

Ilkley: *JRS*, liii (1963), 129. B. R. Hartley, *loc. cit.* xii (2) (1966), 23 ff.

Piercebridge: G. S. Keeney, *T. Durham and N. A. Soc.*, ix (1939), 43 ff.

Newton Kyme: *JRS*, xlvii (1957), 209.

Elslack: T. May, *Yorkshire Archaeological Journal*, xxi (1911), 113ff.

Chester: F. H. Thompson, *Roman Cheshire*, Chester, 1965.

York: R.C.H.M. (England), *Eboracum, Roman York*, London, 1962.

Pevensey: J. P. Bushe Fox, *JRS*, xxii (1932), 60 ff.

Romano-Saxon Pottery: J. N. L. Myres, in D. B. Harden op. cit. on p. 464.

Chester le Street: *Arch. Journ.*, cxi (1954), 196; *JRS*, xlix (1959), 106; l (1960), 215.

Overborough: O. North and E. J. W. Hildyard, *CW* [2], liv (1954), 66 ff., and J. P. Gillam, ibid., 96.

Signal Stations: F. J. Haverfield, *JRS*, ii (1912), 201 ff. Barrock Fell: R. G. Collingwood, *CW* [2], xxxi (1931), 111; *Antiquity*, iv (1930), 472. Scarborough: R. G. Collingwood, in A. Rowntree, *The History of Scarborough*, London, 1931, pp. 40 ff. Huntcliff: W. Hornsby and R. Stanton, *JRS*, ii (1912), 215 ff. Goldsborough: W. Hornsby and J. D. Laverick, *Arch Journ.*, lxxxix (1932), 203 ff.

Portchester: B. W. Cunliffe, *Antiq. Journ.*, xliii (1963), 218; ibid., xlvi (1966), 39 and following volumes.

Caernarvon: R. E. M. Wheeler, *Segontium and the Roman Occupation of Wales*, London, 1924.

Lydney: R. E. M. and T. V. Wheeler, *Report on the Excavation of the . . . Roman . . . site in Lydney Park, Gloucestershire*, Oxford, 1932.

Villas: F. J. Haverfield, V.C.H., *Somerset*; London, 1906, pp. 298 ff.; V.C.H. *Hampshire*, London, 1900, 293 ff

Park Street: H. E. O'Neil, *Arch Journ.*, cii (1945), 21 ff.

Langton: P. Corder and J. L. Kirk, *A Roman Villa at Langton . . . East Yorkshire*, Leeds, 1932.

Bokerly Dyke: C. F. C. Hawkes, *Arch. Journ.*, civ (1947), 62 ff.; P. A. Rahtz, ibid., cxviii (1961), 65 ff.

J. P. Gillam, 'Roman Pottery in north Britain', *Carnuntina* (Römische Forschungen in Niederösterreich, iii), Graz-Koln, 1956, 64 ff.

S. C. Hawkes and G. C. Dunning, 'Soldiers and Settlers in Britain, fourth to fifth century . . .', *Medieval Archaeology*, v (1961), 1 ff.; *Bericht der Römisch-germanischen Kommission*, xliii–xliv (1962–63), 155 ff.

CHAPTER 17 The end of Roman Britain, pp. 404–429

C.E. Stevens, 'Gildas Sapiens', *English Historical Review*, cvi (1941), 353 ff.

Maximus: see M. P. Charlesworth, *The Lost Province*, Cardiff, 1949, pp. 26 ff.

Wroxeter: T. Wright, *Uriconium*, London, 1872.

Marcus, Gratian, Constantine: see the paper of this title by C. E. Stevens in *Athenaeum – Studi Periodici di Letteratura e Storia dell' Antichità* (Pavia), xxxv (1957), 316 ff.

Pelagianism: J. N. L. Myres, *JRS*, l (1960), 21–36. See also W. Liebeschuetz, *Historia* 12 (1963, 227 ff. and *Latomus* 26 (1967), 436 ff.

J. Morris, 'Dark Age Dates', in M. G. Jarrett and B. Dobson, *Britain and Rome*, Kendal, 1966, 145 ff.

Coinage: A. Ravetz, 'Roman Coinage of the Fourth Century in Britain', unpublished Ph.D. Thesis, University of Leeds, 1963; 'Fourth-century Inflation and R.B. coin-finds', *Numismatic Chronicle*,[7] iv (1964), 201 ff. J. P. C. Kent, 'From Roman Britain to Saxon England', in R. H. M. Dolley (ed.), *Anglo-Saxon Coins*, London (1961), pp. 2 ff.; idem, *CW* [2], li (1951), 4 ff. A. J. Evans, 'Coinage and Currency in Roman Britain', *Numismatic Chronicle* [4], xv (1915), 433 ff. K. S. Painter, 'A Roman Silver Treasure from Canterbury', *JBAA* [3], xxviii (1965), 1 ff.

Villas: Great Casterton, P. Corder, *The Roman Town and Villa at Great Casterton, Rutland*, i–iii, Nottingham, 1951, 1954, 1961. Hucclecote, E. Clifford, *Transactions of the Bristol and Gloucestershire Archaeological Society*, lv (1933), 323 ff. North Wraxall, *Wiltshire Archaeological Magazine*, vii (1862), 59 ff. Lullingstone, G. W. Meates, *The Lullingstone Roman Villa*

(Ministry of Works Guide), London, 1962. Whittington Court, H. E. O'Neil, *Transactions of the Bristol and Gloucestershire Archaeological Society*, lxxi (1952), 13 ff. King's Weston, G. C. Boon, ibid., lxix (1950), 5 ff. Atworth, A. S. Mellor and R. G. Goodchild, *Wiltshire Archaeological Magazine*, xlix (1940), 46 ff. Ditchley, C. A. R. Radford, *Oxoniensia*, i (1936), 24 ff. Wingham, excavation by F. Jenkins, 1965.

H. P. R. Finberg, *Roman and Saxon Withington*, Leicester, 1955.

J. N. L. Myres, 'Romano-Saxon Pottery', in D. B. Harden (ed.), *Dark Age Britain*, London, 1956, pp. 16 ff.

Towns: S. S. Frere, 'The End of Towns in Roman Britain', in J. S. Wacher (ed.), *The Civitas Capitals of Roman Britain*, Leicester, 1966, with references there cited; also for York, H. G. Ramm, 'The end of Roman York' in R. M. Butler (ed.), *Soldier and Civilian in Roman Yorkshire*, Leicester, 1971, 179 ff.; and for Caistor J. N. L. Myres and B. Green, *The Anglo-Saxon Cemeteries of Caistor by Norwich and Markshall, Norfolk*, Oxford, 1973, 31 ff.

Bokerly Dyke: C. F. C. Hawkes, *Arch. Journ.*, civ (1947), 62 ff.; P. A. Rahtz, ibid., cxviii (1961), 65 ff.

W. H. C. Frend, 'Religion in Roman Britain in the fourth century', *JBAA* [3], xviii (1955), 1 ff.

M. W. Barley and R. P. C. Hanson (ed.), *Christianity in Britain 300–700*, Leicester, 1968.

L. Alcock, chapter vii in I. Ll. Foster and G. Daniel, *Prehistoric and Early Wales*, London, 1965.

L. Alcock, 'Pottery and Settlements in Wales and the March, A.D. 400–700', in I. Ll. Foster and L. Alcock, *Culture and Environment*, London, 1963.

L. Alcock, 'Celtic Archaeology and Art', in E. Davies (ed.), *Celtic Studies in Wales*, Cardiff, 1963.

E. K. Chambers, *Arthur of Britain*, London, 1927.

L. Alcock, *Arthur's Britain*, London, 1971.

J. R. Morris, *The Age of Arthur*, London, 1973.

INDEX

aqueducts, 279–80, 316, 321, 421
Aradius Rufinus, Q., 205, 211
arches, monumental, 281, 289
Ardoch, camps and fort, 131, 142, 171, 202
areani, 388, 392, 401
Ariminum, council of, 372
Ariovistus, 42
Arles, council of, 372
Arlingham bend, ford at, 95
Armorica, 31–2, 34, 43–4, 67, 68, 69
Arnemetia, goddess, 369
Arosfa Gareg, camp, 121
Arras gold medallions, 381, 386
Arretine pottery, 64, 143, 326
Arruntius Frugi, M., 230
art: Celtic, Romanised, 343, 354–61, 423; la Tène, 29, 40, 354
Arthur, 427
Artorius Castus, L., 190
Arviragus, 141
Ascelepiodotus, 381
Athelstan, 422
Atilius Bradua, M., 142
Atrebates, 36, 45, 61, 68, 75, 246
Atrius, Q., 48, 49
Attacotti, 391–2, 407
Attius Marinus, C., 326
Atworth, villa, 418
Auchinhove, camp, 130
Aufidius Panthera, L., 229
Augusta *see* London
Augustus, role of, 240, 241
Augustus, 40, 57, 58, 69, 76, 149, 222, 227, 240, 241, 248, 263, 284
Aurelian, 215, 216
Aurelii, T., 319
Aurelius, M., 185, 186
Aurelius Arpagius, 382
Aurelius Lunaris, M., 340, 364
Aurelius Marcio, M., 245
Aurelius Mausaeus Carausius, M. *see* Carausius
Aurelius Valerius Maximianus, M., 241
Aurelius Victor, 380
auxilia, 159, 237–9, 248–51, 255, 257, 407
auxiliary cohorts, division of, 136, 159, 167, 185
Avidius Quietus, T., 141–2
Aylesford: cemetery, 37, 38, 39; crossing, 81

Badbury Rings, 311
Badon, Mt, battle of, 421, 427
bagaudae, 376, 386
Bagendon, 38, 66, 67, 320
Baginton, fort, 107
Baienus Blassianus, Q., 229
Bainbridge, fort, 151, 196, 197, 262, 267, 271, 383, 395
bakers, 294, 336
Balmuildy, fort, 166, 167–71
Barburgh Mill, fortlet, 166, 181
Bar Hill: fort, 167, 179, 180, 192 n. 31; fortlet, 125, 139, 172
Barkway temple (?), 368
barn dwelling *see* house, aisled
barns, 307–9
Barnsley Park, villa, 316
Barrock Fell, signal-tower, 395
barrow burials, R.B., 309
barter, 414–15
basket-work, British, 332
Batavi, 111, 251, 252, 392
Bath, 275; coal at, 335; *collegium*, 295; cults at, 365, 368; fall of, 428; industry, 295, 329; inscription from, 245, 312, 313; population, 297; sculpture, 356, 358; stone, 335; temple, 357
baths: town, 276–7; villa, 306, 307, 345
Battersea shield, 40
bears, British, 332
Bearsden, fort, 167, 185
Beckfoot, fort, 150, 157, 271
Beddington, Saxon cementery, 426
Bede, 54, 154; sources and chronology, 424
Bedriacum, 115
bee-keeping, 317
beer, British, 59, 331
Belgae, 16, 34–40, 48, 57; *civitas* of, 86, 234
Belgic Gaul, 42–3, 44, 56
Belgic mints, 57, 59, 62, 64–7
Bellovaci, 36, 43
belt-buckles, late Roman, 397 f.
beneficiarii consularis, 205, 226, 245
Benwell: coal at, 334; damaged (AD 296), 400; fort, 150, 175, 178; inscription, 188, 198; sculpture, 357; temple, 193, 366; *vicus*, 402
Berikos, 59

Flintshire, 322, 335, 339
Floors, 281; *see also* Mosaics
foederati, 421
Forden Gaer, fort, 146, 186, 209, 266,
  396
Forest of Dean, 18, 33, 39, 66, 333
Forges, 335
Forth-Clyde *limes*, 125–6, 128, 165–75
fortlets, 152
fortresses, 86–91, 109–10, 118, 122,
  143, 146, 253–4
forts: Claudian, 86–7, 88–9, 90, 91, 94,
  95, 100–1, 107, 108, 253, 255;
  Neronian, 107; Flavian, 117, 118,
  120–1, 124–7, 129, 133–7, 142–5;
  Trajanic, 145, 146; Hadrianic,
  149–51, 153–4, 157–9, 256;
  Antonine I, 166, 167, 185; Antonine
  II, 185; Antonine III, 185, 188;
  Saxon Shore, 252; Severan, 195, 201,
  207–11; Fourth-century, 256,
  379–82, 394–6; Fifth-century, 417
forum with basilica, 134, 235, 276–9,
  294, 348
Fossdyke, canal, 313, 366
Fosse way *limes*, 17, 89, 91, 96, 113
Fox, Lady, 114
Fox, Sir Cyril, 28, 104, 113
Frampton, villa, mosaic, 361, 372
Franks, 376–81, 391
Fraomar, king, 270, 395
freedmen, 226, 270, 322, 326, 364;
  see also Naevius
frescoes, 346, 348, 352
Fritigern, 300
Frontinus *see* Julius
Fronto, 161
fulling, 338
Fullofaudes, dux, 391, 394
furniture, shale, 336
furs trade, 332

Gabrantovices, 77
Gaius (Caligula), 74–6, 83
Galacum, 271
Galerius Maximianus, 241
Gallic chronicle, 425
Gallienus, 215, 247
Galloway, dynasty of, 406
Gangani, 77
Gaskridge signal towers, 258
Gatehouse of Fleet, fortlet, 127, 136

Gauls, 18, 30, 36, 42, 43, 47, 49, 53–4,
  76, 98, 296–7, 358, 360
Galligaer: camps, 257; fort, 146, 185,
  186, 209; industry, 259
Genunia, 173
gentiles, 267, 395
Germanicus, 61, 75, 364
Germanus, saint, 373, 412–14
Germany: Lower, 148, 165, 176, 187,
  198, 220 n. 47; Upper, 163 n. 9,
  176, 220 n. 47, 256–7
Gerontius, 409
Gesoriacum, 46
Geta Caesar, 199, 203, 205, 207, 371
Gildas, 394, 405, 412, 414, 419, 424–7
Gillam, J. P., 163, 167, 403
gladiators, 346–7; procurator of, 230
Glamorgan, 19, 20, 69, 120
Glasgow Bridge, fortlet, 167
glass, 294, 327, 332, 345, 417, 421
Glastonbury, 30, 32, 69
Glenlochar, fort, 127, 143, 166, 181,
  256
Gloucester (*Glevum colonia*), 17, 97,
  288, 289; art, 357; fall of, 428; fort,
  87, 91; fortress, 91, 97, 146–7, 288,
  292; *see also* Kingsholm; grapes,
  331; house style, 348; roads, 96;
  status, 358; *territorium*, 314; tile
  factory, 258, 295; town, 114, 146–7,
  231, 274, 283, 296–7, 348;
  town-wall, 288
Gloucestershire, Iron Age, 30, 32, 66,
  85
Gods: emperor as *see* Imperial cult;
  Roman and Celtic, 358–9, 365–71
Godmanchester, fort, 86
gold, 18, 294, 300, 320, 321, 415, 416
Goldcliff inscription, 315
Goldsborough signal tower, 417
Gordian I, 206
Gordian III, 212, 214
Gosbeck's farm theatre, 369
Governor: career, 222–3; duties,
  223–5; in fourth century, 241, 382;
  staff, 226
Government *see* Roman *and* Imperial
  entries
Graecinius Laco, P., 83
Graffiti, 351, 353
Grange, pass of, 202
Grassington field system, 311

Gratian, elder, 269, 388
Gratian, emperor, 404, 405, 417
Gratian, usurper, 408, 420
Great Casterton: fort, 86, 107, 135, 255; defences, 291; town, 274; villa, 417, 418
Great Chesterford: fort, 107; iron hoard, 316, 370; mill, 336; town defences, 289
Great Chesters, 150, 155, 158, 175, 207, 208, 210, 400
Greek coins, 30
Greensforge, fort, 96
Greta Bridge, 139, 151, 195, 205, 245
Grimsby, 317
Grimscar tilery, 259
Groans of the Britons, 413, 425
guilds see collegia
Gurnard's Head cliff, castle, 31
Gussage All Saints, 29
Guthlac, saint, 419

Hadrian, 147–8, 165, 314
Hadrian's Wall, 71, 145, 148–60; breaching of, 175; broad wall, 152–4; coal at, 334; commander, 160; crossed in AD 180, 187; destruction, 196, 383; end of, 165; extension, 153, 157–8; forts, 149–51, 152–5; garrison, 145, 147–53, 163 n. 21, 165, 175, 195, 262–4, 382; in Notitia, 262–4, 382; intermediate wall, 158, 179, 181 f., 192; Maximus and, 267; milecastles, 151–6, 159–60; Military way, 151; narrow wall, 153–4; outposts, 157; patrol track, 156; reconstruction: Constantian, 262, 266, 382–5, 400 n. 18; Severan, 207, 213, 383; Theodosian, 394; reoccupation, 178; turf wall, 152–5, 158, 165, 166, 181, 256; turrets, 151–5, 285; vallum, 151, 154–7, 171
Hallstatt culture, 20–2, 25, 73
Haltonchesters, 24, 27, 33, 150, 155, 175, 187, 211, 217 n. 3, 263, 296, 400 n. 15; plough marks, 163
Haltwhistle Burn, fortlet, 145
Haltwhistle Common, camps, 257
Ham Hill, fort, 90
Hambleden, villa, 68, 304, 305
Hampshire, 31, 35, 86, 234

Hamworthy, military depot (?), 89
Harbledown, 49, 80
Hardknott, fort, 146, 151, 191
Harling, West, 21
Hartley, B. R., 180, 181, 198
Hartshill potteries, 326, 397
Haverfield, F., 177, 312, 337, 343, 351, 374, 387
Hawkes, Prof. C. F. C., 112, 312, 429
head cult, 370
Helvius Pertinax, P., 190
Helvetii, 42
Hembury, 69
Hengistbury Head, 31, 68
Hereford, 96
Herod of Chalcis, 114
Herodian, 218, 219
Heronbridge coal, 334
Heruli comitatenses, 392
Hide trade, 332
High Crosby, fortlet, 145
highland zone, 15–16, 17–18, 304, 310, 325, 349, 350
High Rochester, fort, 143–4, 166, 206, 207, 208, 210, 212, 257, 383, 388, 400
High Wycombe, villa, 307
hill forts, Iron Age, 24–7, 31–4, 38–9, 68–73, 89–90, 119, 176, 257, 420
Hinton St Mary, mosaic, 361, 372
Hoards: coin see coin hoards; offering to deities, 370
Hod Hill, fort, 68, 89, 90, 255, 257
Holmes, Rice, 46
Holt, 258
Holyhead see Caer Gybi
Home, camp, 86
Honorinus, 329
Honorius, 406, 409–10; coins of, 416; rescript of, 408–12
Horace, 58
Horkstow, villa, 361
Hosidius Geta, Cn, 80, 83
Hoskins, Prof. W. G., 297, 300, 429
house plans: Iron Age, 19; R.B., 276, 281–3, 305–9, 344, 347–8
houses, aisled, 307–9, 319; Iron Age, 23–4
Housesteads, fort, 150, 155, 175, 196, 198, 208, 245, 247, 383; coal at, 335; damaged (AD 296), 384, 400; Theodosian reconstruction, 395,

Housesteads – *contd.*
400, 402, 403; trade route through
gate, 332; *vicus*, 240, 275, 402
Hucclecote, villa, 417
Hunsbury, 30
Huntcliff signal tower, 417
Hyginus, 250, 270
Hypocausts, 335, 338

Iceland, trade with, 332
Iceni: *civitas* of, 84, 135, 242;
coinage of, 37, 64–5, 84, 93;
rebellion (AD 47), 93, 99, 312;
rebellion (AD 60), 103–7
Icknield Way, 16
Ilchester, 236
Ilkley, fort, 151, 196, 197, 266, 268,
271; fourth-century reconstruction,
383, 395
Illyricum, 405
immigrants, 297, 320, 326, 328, 340,
346
Imperial cult, 98, 105, 239–40, 293,
344, 356, 362–4, 371
Imperial estates, 312–13, 321, 323
Imperial statues, 94, 356
Imperial tilery, 259
Imperial weaving works, 337
imperium Galliarum, 215
imports: Iron Age, 38, 40, 63; R.B.,
320, 326–8, 340, 355
Inchtuthil, fortress, 87, 129, 137, 142,
162, 253, 254, 256
incolae, 231
industry *see* bronze, leather, pottery,
etc.
infantry organisation, 250, 251, 261,
262
Ingleborough, 72, 125
interpretatio Romana, 366
Inveresk, fort, 126, 166, 167
Ipswich, torcs, 40
Irchester, 245
Ireland, 15, 127–8, 139, 332, 423–4
Irish god, 368
Irish raiders, 253, 332, 401, 406–7,
423, 424, 427
Irish settlers, 406–7, 426
Iron Age classification, 19–20; Iron
A, 20–6, 69; Iron B, 27–35, 65–7, 68,
69, 72, 73; Iron C, 34–40, 64, 70, 73

iron industry, 17, 18, 20, 39, 252,
333–4
Isis, temple of, 297, 365
Isle of Wight, 89
Itius, portus, 46
iuridicus, 135, 198, 224–5
ius Latinum see Latin right
Ivinghoe Beacon, 24
Ixworth *see* Pakenham

Jackson, Prof. K. H., 77, 351–2, 374
Jarlshof, 25
Jarrow inscriptions, 148
Javolenus Priscus, L., 224
Jedburgh inscription, 208
jet, 294, 330–1
Jordon Hill cult, 370
Jovii, comitatenses, 392
Jovinus, 392
Joyce, Rev. J., 294
Judea, rebellion in, 148, 162
Julia Domna, 199
Julia Pacata, 108
Julian, emperor, 318, 390
Julius Agricola, Cn., 109, 115, 118,
120, 122–38, 139, 140, 141, 143,
147, 184, 223, 225, 235, 252
Julius Alpinus Classicianus, C., 108–9,
110, 228, 326
Julius Asper, C., 239
Julius Caesar, C., 17, 36, 42–55, 56,
71, 228, 320
Julius Frontinus, Sex., 36, 56, 102,
115, 120–3, 133, 134, 135, 235, 252
Julius Indus, 108
Julius Julianus, L., 204
Julius Karus, C., 145, 146
Julius Marcus, C., 205, 207
Julius Pollienus, T., 205
Julius Severus, Sex., 148, 158, 161,
252
Julius Verus, Cn., 158, 176–7, 179, 191
Junius Dubitates, 164
Junius Faustinus, C., 205
Junius Silanus Torquatus, L., 83
Juno, 362
Jupiter, 191, 362, 364, 365, 373
Jurassic route, 16, 28, 32
Jurisdiction, 224–6, 236–7
Justius Superus, 113
Juvenal, 141, 191

476

477

478

Marlborough bucket, 39
Mars, 365, 366, 368
Martinhoe, fortlet, 109
Martinus, *vicarius*, 390
Maryport, fort, 150, 151, 193, 271
Matlock, 340
Matres campestres, 366
Maxima Caesariensis, 241, 382
Maximian, 240, 241, 263, 376–8, 386
Maximus, governor, 207
Mead, 331
Meare, 32, 69
Medway, river, 79–81, 83
Melandra, fort, 151, 191
Menapii, 44
Mendips, 32, 99, 103, 235, 321–4, 339, 340, 381
Mercury, 365, 366, 368
Metchley, fortress, 94, 96
Middleton milestone, 214
Middlewich, salt at, 336
Mildenhall (Suffolk), treasure, 329
Mildenhall (Wilts), 299
milecastles *see* Hadrian's Wall
milecastle 37, 196, 217
milestones, 213, 324, 338
military policy in Britain: Antoninus Pius, 165, 173, 187; Caracalla, 189, 214; Carausius, 379; Claudius, 78–84; Commodus, 189; Constans, 387; Constantius I, 381; count Theodosius, 393; Domitian, 128; Hadrian, 147–50; Magnus Maximus, 404–6; Nero, 101, 108; Severus, 201; Stilicho, 268, 406; Titus, 123, 126; Trajan, 145–7; Vespasian, 123
Military Way, 151, 170
milites Anderetiani, 268
militiae, 227–8, 249, 251
Milking Gap settlement, 163
milling, 295, 336
Milton, fort, 136, 143, 368
Minerva, 359, 362, 368
mining, 259, 321
mints: Iron Age, 57–9, 62, 65–6, 84–5; R.B., 243–4, 378; Rome, 416
Mitcham, Saxon cemetery, 426
Mithraeum, 297, 365, 375
Modius Julius, 206
Moesia, 83, 136, 137, 148; Lower, 148, 223, 229; Upper, 178
Mommsen, Th., 267

monarchy, post Roman, 412
money lenders, Roman, 105, 328, 340
monetary policy of Aurelian, 216
Mons Graupius, battle, 131–2, 133
Moresby, fort, 150, 157–8
Morini, 44
mortaria, 264, 294, 296, 326, 329, 330, 340
mosaics: town, 298 n. 5, 345–6; villa, 307, 309, 318, 319, 345–7, 352, 360–1, 372, 374, 417, 420; and education, 375 n. 12
Mummius Sisenna, P., 148, 158, 161, 163
Mumrills, 126, 167, 172, 193
Muncaster tilery, 259
municipia, 99, 231, 236, 274
Mursa, battle of, 389
Myres, Dr J. N. L., 410, 413, 425

Naevius, freedman, 245, 312
Nanstallon, fort, 90, 114
Nantmel, fort, 102
Nantosvelta, goddess, 368
Narcissus, 78
naval activity, 211, 252–3, 333, 392
Neath, camp and fort, 121
Nectaridus, count, 391
Nectovelius, soldier, 220
Needham, 84
Nene valley potteries, 329, 347, 357, 397
Nepos P. Metilius, 141
Nepos, Platorius *see* Platorius
Neratius Marcellus, L., 142, 230
Nero, 101–2, 108, 228, 312, 313, 339
Nerva, 120, 142, 147
Netherby, 157, 206, 208, 383, 388
Nether Denton, fort, 145
Nettleham inscription, 369
Newbrough, fort, 145
Newcastle: bridge at, 153, 155, 160; fort, 150, 152; inscription, 160, 176
New Forest potteries, 330, 397
Newport, Isle of Wight, villa, 305
Newstead, fort, 126, 136, 142–3, 144, 166, 175, 179, 181, 188, 198, 200
Newton Kyme, fort, 151, 256, 384
Newton St Loe, villa, 361
Newton upon Trent, fortress, 87, 97, 254
Niall of the Nine Hostages, 407

Pelagius, 247, 352, 373, 410
Penkridge see Stretton Mill
Pen Llystyn, fort, 136
Pennines: Antonine reoccupation, 177; celtic fields, 311; evacuation, 405; stone, 336
Penydarren, fort, 185
Pen-y-Stryd tilery, 259
peregrini, 99, 224, 231
Perennis, 190
Pertinax see Helvius
Petillius Cerialis, Q., 106, 109, 112, 115, 117–20, 121, 122, 123, 125, 132, 133, 138
Petronius Turpilianus, P., 108–9
Pevensey: fort, 252, 268, 379, 388; tile stamps, 428 n. 7
pewter, 324, 329, 339
Pflaum, H. G., 190, 193, 200
phallic cult, 370–1
Philip II of Macedon, 35
Philip, emperor, 215
Picts, 72, 382, 387, 388, 390, 391, 400, 405–7, 414, 424
Piercebridge, 256, 384, 402
Piggott, S., 275
Pike Hill signal tower, 145
Pilgrims' Way, 16, 80
Pins, ring-headed, 73
Pitney, villa, 317
pits, storage see storage pits
Pitt-Rivers, General A., 312, 360
plague, 297, 422
Platorius Nepos, A., 148, 158
Plautius, A., 48, 50, 78, 83, 91–2, 222
Plautius Silvanus Aelianus, Ti., 83
Pliny, elder, 331
Pliny, younger, 141, 142, 224
plough-marks, 163 n. 23
ploughs: Iron Age, 22; R.B., 311, 315
Plumpton Head, camp, 120
Plutarch, 128, 139, 141
Poenius Postumus, 106–7
Polyclitus, 108
Pompeius Falco, Q., 148
Pompeius Homullus, Cn., 229
Pompeius Magnus, Cn., 83
Pomponius Mamilianus, T., 142
Pontypridd, camp, 121
Poole harbour, 67
population: provincial, 348–50; town, 296–7

Porcupine Bank, pot from, 332
porphyry, 335
Portchester, fort, 380, 389, 396
Postumus, emperor, 214, 215
potters, art of, 357
pottery: Arretine, 64, 143, 326; black-burnished, 330; Castor ware, 347; coarse ware, 330; Dark Age, 242, 423 f.; Gallo-Belgic, 64, 119, 424; hand-made, 397; industry, end of, 397, 416–17; Iron Age A., 22, 24; Iron Age B., 27, 29–32, 41; Iron Age C., 38; made by army, 89, 259; Mediterranean, 422–3; Rhenish, 327, 329, 332; Romano-Saxon, 389, 419–20; Samian, 180, 326–7, 329, 332, 339; stamps, 134, 329; supply to army, 330
potteries, 89, 258–9, 295–6, 326–7, 329, 357, 397
Powys, dynasty of, 423
practice camps, 257
praefectus civitatis, 235, 251, 268
praefectus reliquationis, 396
praepositus, 214, 247
praepositi limitis, 395
praesides, equestrian, 241–2, 247
Praetorian guard, 82, 112
Praetorian prefect, 240, 243
Prasutagus, 84–6, 93, 104, 231, 312
Preston villa burnt, 221
Primus civitatis, 414
princeps praetorii, 225
Priscus, pretender, 190
Priscus Touti f., 358
Probus, emperor, 215, 216, 286, 331, 379
Procopius, 410, 429
procurator ad census, 230
procurator, provincial, 83, 105, 108, 204, 227
Proculus, rebel, 216
prospectors, continental, 320–4
provincial council, 105, 238–9, 411–12
provincial organisation, 203–6, 222–5, 238–40
provincialis, 239
Pudens see Valerius Pudens, C.
Pudding Pan Rock, 327
Pulborough, 340
Pytheas, 30, 331

St Mawgan in Pyder, 31
salaries, payment of, 324, 417
Salinae, 336
Salisbury Plain, 68, 311
Sallustius Lucullus, 141
salt production, 310, 313–14, 336, 337
Salvius Liberalis, C., 224
Samian ware, 180, 326–7, 329, 332, 339
Sarmatians, 186, 213, 252
Saturninus, revolt of, 141
Saxon federates, 427
Saxon raiders, 211, 215–16, 387, 389, 391, 407, 410, 411, 413, 414, 419–24
Saxon settlers, 389, 419, 421, 422–4
Saxon Shore, 252; Count of, 242, 247, 261, 268, 269, 388, 391, 396, 407; forts, 211, 226, 252, 255, 256, 289, 291, 379–80, 385, 399
Scalesceugh, 258
Scilly Isles, 41
Scole, fort (?), 107
Scotland: Celtic culture, 356, 365, 367; Constans in, 387; Constantius I in, 385–6; Flavian evacuation of, 137, 139–40, 142–4, 146; Iron Age in, 25–6, 29, 72–4; marching camps, 202–3; metal work hoards, 370; Severus in, 199–204; Theodosian arrangements in, 393–4; trade with province, 332–3; *see also* Antonine Wall *and* Hadrian's Wall
Scots, 388, 390–1, 405–6
sculpture and sculptors, 343, 356–60, 364
Sea Mills, 103, 113
sea power, 120, 129, 132–3, 170, 201, 252–3, 258, 393, 406
Secundani iuniores, 269
Segontiaci, 52
Seguntienses, *palatini*, 405
self government, local, 99, 230, 231, 233, 234–8
Selgovae, 72, 74, 123, 126–7, 143, 144, 147–8, 149, 174, 176, 188
Selsey, *oppidum*, 38
Seneca *see* Annaeus
Senecio *see* Alfenus
Sennen cliff castle, 31
Sennius Sollemnis, T., 206
Sentius Saturninus, Cn., 83
Septimius, L., governor, 358, 373

Septimius Severus, L., 194–6; army reforms, 213, 215; campaigns in Scotland, 199–204, 372; divisions in Britain, 203–5; effects on trade, 329–31; frontier under, 195–8, 207–9; inscription, 188; martyrdom of St Alban under, 205, 371; visits Britain, 199
Setantii, 77
Severius Emeritus, C., 313
Severn: river *limes*, 17, 92, 97, 122; valley, 32
Severus, bishop, 414
Severus, count, 392
Severus, emperor *see* Septimius
Severi Augustales, 297, 364–5
shale, 336, 360
Sheepen dyke, 63
shipping, trade by, 339
shops, 282–3, 293
Shrewsbury, 17, 297
Sibson, 295, 359
siege-camps, 258
signal-beacons, 170
signal towers, 131, 151, 152, 160, 258, 396–7
Silchester (*Calleva Atrebatum*), 58, 59, 61, 62, 103, 273; amphitheatre, 296, 346; baths, 277, 298, 326; battle near, 381; church, 372; *collegium*, 295; commerce, 294; *curia*, 293; defences, 283, 285, 287–9, 299; fifth-century, 422; fire, 279; forum, 135, 236, 277, 279, 293, 298; graffiti, 353; grapes, 331; houses, 276, 281–2; industry, 295, 326; inscription, 422; metal hoard, 370; mill, 336; mosaics, 298 n. 5; population, 296; sculpture, 356, 364; size, 292; status, 235–6, 246; tilery, 326, 340; villas, 293; water supply, 280
Silures, 69–70, 92, 94–6, 97–103, 109, 120–2; *civitas* of, 233
Silvanus, god, 366
silver, 18, 320, 321–4, 329, 416
Simpson, Dr G., 175, 192
Slack, fort, 151, 191, 259
slang, army, 401
slaves, 25, 295, 303–4, 332, 396, 416
Smith, Dr D. J., 360, 375
smiths: Iron Age, 20, 29, 40; R.B.,

1a Hod Hill, Dorset from the west. Iron Age hut-sites and streets can be seen in the ploughed south-eastern corner of the hill-fort. The Roman fort lies at the north-eastern corner

1b Roman forts, Dalswinton and Dumfriesshire.
An Agricolan fort of 8.59 acres, with its annexe, has been replaced by a late Domitianic fort of 10.29 acres with annexe

2 The Roman road running from Wroxeter through the Church Stretton gap and southwards towards Leintwardine

3 Hadrian's Wall near Milecastle 24 looking east. The Wall lies under the
road; the ditch to its north and vallum to the south show clearly

4 The fort of Housesteads, Hadrian's Wall. Milecastle 37, and the Military Way looking west. The vallum is filled-in in this area

5a The south Roman siege-camp and Roman fortlet at Birrenswark, Dumfriesshire, looking west

5b The defence-systems of successive Roman forts at Ardoch, Perthshire

6a Roman *ala*-fort and civil settlement at Old Carlisle, Cumberland

6b Roman marching camps at Pennymuir, Roxburgh, with *tutuli* at the gates

7 The Roman town and cantonal capital of the Atrebates tribe at Silchester, Hants

8a The site of *Venta Icenorum* (Caistor by Norwich) from the south-west showing the town wall and ditch on the south side cutting through the earlier street system which appears to be bounded by two ditches further south

8b The site of *Noviomagus Regnensium* (Chichester) from the south-west. The town wall and bastions (of mediaeval date on Roman foundations) can be seen near the bottom and following the curving road round the north-west side, returning beyond the open space, centre top

9a The amphitheatre at *Durnovaria* (Dorchester, Dorset). This earthwork
overlies a Henge-monument

9b Roman villa at Watts Wells, Ditchley

10a The Roman Road from *Cunetio* (Mildenhall) to *Venta Belgarum* (Winchester) looking south-east near Andover

10b 'Celtic' field systems at Burderop Down

11a Bronze horse-brooch and bone dolphin from *Verulamium*; the length of the dolphin is 1.75 inches

11b 'Peopled Scroll' in painted wall plaster of Antonine date, from *Verulamium*; length 12 feet

12a First-century mosaic from Fishbourne, Sussex. At a subsequent period the room was divided by a partition across the middle

12b Fourth-century Vergilian mosaic from the villa at Low Ham, Somerset, showing Aeneas, Dido and Venus; 13 feet square

13 Christian Mosaic from Hinton St Mary, Dorset

14a Large stone capital decorated with Native Gods from *Corinium Dobunnorum* (Cirencester)

14b Relief of three *Matres* (mother goddesses) bearing loaves and cakes or fruits; height 2 feet 7 inches

15a Bronze statuette of Venus from *Verulamium*; height 8 inches

15b Relief of *Matres* in a classical style from Cirencester; height 16 inches

16a The site of Richborough from the north, showing the foundation of the Tetrapylon, the earth fort of the third century, the Saxon shore fort and a short length of the Claudian ditches

16b The Saxon shore fort of Portchester Castle standing at the head of Portsmouth Harbour

17a Dane's Camp, Bredon Hill, Glos., showing traces of a field system below the fort

17b Badbury Rings, Dorset, multivallate hill-fort. The Roman road to Dorchester passes in front of the fort, and another, whose ditches show in the ploughed field in the left foreground, runs south to Hamworthy almost at right-angles to it

18a Roman marching camp (33 acres), annexe and pit-rows at Glenlochar, Kirkcudbrightshire

18b Roman marching camp east of Balmuildy, Lanark, perhaps connected with the construction of the Antonine Wall

19a Roman fort and annexe at Greensforge, Staffs

19b The Romano-British villa at Cromwell, Nottinghamshire

20a Streets and buildings at *Viroconium Cornoviorum* (Wroxeter). The town baths are under excavation at the top left corner

20b Soil marks showing a typical Fenland settlement at Pinchbeck Common, Lincs.

21 Iron Age Hill-fort, Herefordshire Beacon, Malvern hills, showing hut platforms (and a Norman motte) in the interior.

22a Hill-fort, Quarley Hill, Hants; univallate type

22b Hill-fort, Yarnbury Castle, Wilts., showing traces of an earlier demolished fortification within

23a Wroxeter, buildings excavated 1912-14 in the foreground, with the forum and early baths in the centre background, and later baths background right

23b Roman pottery from Verulamium. The three scrolls, etc., are Nene Valley ware, and the colour-coated beaker on the right is Rhenish. In the front is a 'black samian' vessel with appliqué masks (Lezoux ware), and the rest are locally made

24a Verulamium excavations. A mid-second-century mosaic overlies the remains of a small early second-century timber-framed house in *insula* 28. The post-holes in the foreground belong to the later building

24b Antonine mosaic at Verulamium, *insula* 21. The walls of the room have masonry footings but were carried up in clay. The section-face shows clay and much fallen wall-plaster

25a View, looking west, of the Roman road running through Kenchester (*Magna*); the town-walls enclose the field in the centre, west of the farm

25b Kenchester, looking north. A typically irregular lay-out of a small town

26a and b First-century black and white geometric mosaics from Fishbourne, Sussex

27a Three *Matres* (mother goddesses) seated on a couch, from Ancaster, Lincs; height 16.5 inches

27b Relief showing *genii Cucullati* in crude though effective 'shorthand'. Cirencester (height 11.25 inches)

28 The pre-Roman Coinage:

1 Gallo-Belgic A (*gold*) 2 Gallo-Belgic C (*gold*) 3 Gallo-Belgic E (*gold*) 4
British A (*gold*) 5 British B (*gold*) 6 Durotriges class A (*silver*) 7 Durotriges
Class C (*bronze*) 8 British Q (*gold*) 9 Commius (*gold*) 10 Tincommius
(*gold*) 11 British R (Dobunni) (*gold*) 12 Dobunni, Anted-rig (*gold*) 13
Dobunni, Catti (*gold*) 14 Dobunni, Bodvoc (*gold*)

29 The pre-Roman Coinage:

1 British H (*gold*) 2 British I (*gold*) 3 Coritani, Esup-Asu (*gold*) 4 Coritani, Volisios Dumnocoveros (*gold*) 5-7 Varieties of British L (*gold*) 8 British N (Iceni) (*gold*) 9 Tin or Speculum coinage, class 1 10 Tincommius (*gold*) 11 Verica (*gold*) 12 Verica (*gold*) 13 Tasciovanus (*gold*): VER mint mark in pattern on obverse 14 Tasciovanus (*gold*): CAM mint mark on reverse 15 Tasciovanus *Rigonus* (*gold*)

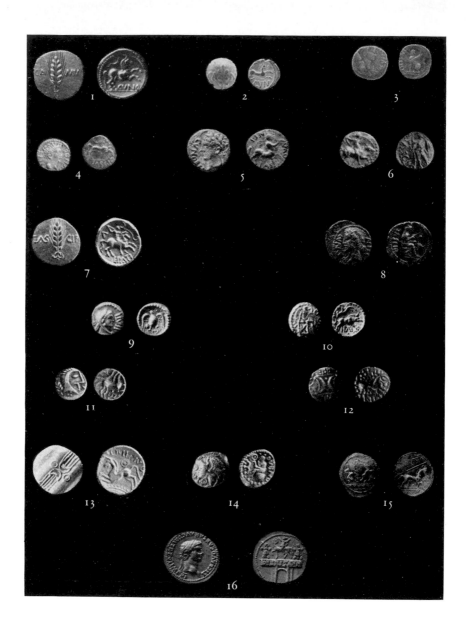

30 Belgic and Roman coins:

1 Cunobelin (*gold stater*) 2 Cunobelin (*gold 1/4-stater*) 3 Cunobelin (*silver:* Mack 237) 4 Cunobelin (*silver:* Mack 236) 5 Cunobelin (*bronze:* Mack 242) 6 Cunobelin (*bronze:* Mack 244) 7 Epaticcus (*gold*) 8 Cunobelin (*bronze:* Mack 248) 9 Epaticcus (*silver*) 10 Epaticcus (*silver*) 11 Iceni (*silver*) 12 Iceni, Anted (*silver*) 13 Dubnovellaunus (*gold:* Essex type) 14 Dubnovellaunus (*silver:* Kent type) 14 Vodenos (*silver:* Kent type) 16 Claudius (*aureus: de Britann.* on arch, *RIC* 8)

31 Roman coins relating to Britain:

1 Hadrian (*sestertius* A.D. 134-8: *Britannia* seated, foot on pile of rocks, *RIC*845) 2 Hadrian (*sestertius* A.D. 134-8: *exer(citus) Britannicus, RIC* 912) 3 Antoninus Pius (*sesterius* A.D. 143-4: *Britannia* seated on globe *RIC* 744) 4 Antoninus Pius (*as*, A.D. 154-5, *RIC*934) 5 Commodus (bronze medallion, A.D. 185: Grueber No. 12) 6 Clodius Albinus (*denarius*, A.D. 194-5, *RIC* 23) 7 Septimus Severus (*aureus* A.D. 210-11, *RIC* 334) 8 Septimus Severus (*as*, A.D. 208, *RIC* 786) 9 Caracalla (*as*, A.D. 208, *RIC*, 441) (No. 9 by courtesy of the *Royal Numismatic Society*)

32 Roman coins relating to Britain:

1 Carausius, 286-93 (*bronze, RIC* 883) 2 Carausius (*denarius:* Expectate veni, *RIC* 555) 3 Carausius (*antoninianus, Carausius et frates sui: moneta Auggg,* British Musuem) 4 Allectus, 293-6 (*quinarius,* galley type, *RIC* 128) 5 Constantius I Caesar, Arras gold-medallion *(redditor lucis aeternae, Londinium)* 6 Maximian I (*bronze,* mint of London, 296-305: *RIC* 1 and 2) 7 Magnus Maximus 383-8 (*gold* solidus, mint of London (*Augusta*), *RIC* 2(b))